CRITICAL DIALOGUES IN LATINX STUDIES

D1523175

Critical Dialogues in Latinx Studies

A Reader

Edited by
Ana Y. Ramos-Zayas and Mérida M. Rúa

NEW YORK UNIVERSITY PRESS
New York

NEW YORK UNIVERSITY PRESS
New York
www.nyupress.org

References to internet websites (URLs) were accurate at the time of writing. Neither the author nor New York University Press is responsible for URLs that may have expired or changed since the manuscript was prepared.

Library of Congress Cataloging-in-Publication Data
Names: Ramos-Zayas, Ana Y., editor. | Rúa, Mérida M., editor.
Title: Critical dialogues in Latinx studies : a reader /
edited by Ana Ramos-Zayas and Mérida Rúa.
Description: New York : New York University Press, [2021] |
Includes bibliographical references and index.
Identifiers: LCCN 2020048481 | ISBN 9781479805198 (hardback) |
ISBN 9781479805211 (paperback) | ISBN 9781479805181 (ebook) |
ISBN 9781479805235 (ebook)
Subjects: LCSH: Hispanic Americans. | Latin Americans—United States. | United States—Relations—Latin America. | Latin America—Relations—United States.
Classification: LCC E184.S75 C74 2021 | DDC 305.868/073—dc23
LC record available at https://lccn.loc.gov/2020048481

New York University Press books are printed on acid-free paper, and their binding materials are chosen for strength and durability. We strive to use environmentally responsible suppliers and materials to the greatest extent possible in publishing our books.

Manufactured in the United States of America

10 9 8 7 6 5 4 3 2 1

Also available as an ebook

CONTENTS

Introduction

MÉRIDA M. RÚA AND ANA Y. RAMOS-ZAYAS

There is no inkling of our international outlook, our solidarity with struggles of other peoples, especially our sense of identity with the peoples of Latin America. There is no hint of the deep traditions of striving for freedom and progress that pervade our daily life.
—Jesús Colón, *A Puerto Rican in New York*

Jesús Colón somberly penned these words in the 1961 preface of *A Puerto Rican in New York and Other Sketches*. The book is one of the first (if not the first) literary works written in English that captures the particularities of Puerto Ricans' adjustments to US urban life. In doing so, it also attends to the ways in which those experiences are inextricably tied to other ethnoracial communities, the colonial context of the island, and US interventionist projects in the rest of Latin America and the Caribbean.

A member of the first considerable migration from the island, Colón lived among his people as a worker, activist, socialist, writer, and public intellectual, authoring articles and news commentaries, composing and translating poetry, and writing short stories and sketches, more than four hundred pieces written in his lifetime (Acosta-Belén and Sánchez-Korrol 1993, 20). He arrived in New York City as a sixteen-year-old stowaway aboard the SS Carolina in 1917, the same year the US Congress passed the Jones–Shafroth Act, which collectively naturalized residents of Puerto Rico as US citizens. Jesús Colón remained in his adopted city until his death almost six decades later.

In the intervening years, he relied on his standpoint as "a Puerto Rican in New York" to critically meditate on the history and social experiences of his people from the period between the two world wars through the cold war era (Acosta-Belén and Sánchez-Korrol 1993; Delgado 2005; Flores 1981).[1] Colón's people, of course, were Puerto Ricans, but they did not exist in isolation. *A Puerto Rican in New York and Other Sketches* is also filled with impressions and accounts of Latinas and Latinos and Latin Americans. Everyday women and men like "the [older Puerto Rican] lady who lived near the statue of a man on horse" (111–114) and "Mr. Clark," a New York–New Jersey waterfront dock foreman "born in Panama of Jamaican parents" (31), as well as Simón Bolivar, "the liberator of Latin America" (59), Rafael Leonidas Trujillo y Molina, "the dictator and virtual owner of all property, all life and liberty in the Republic of Santo Domingo since 1930" (73), and Ana Roque de Duprey "the founder of the first Puerto Rican feminist society" (63), populate Colón's sketches, illustrating the ample and linked world of diasporic Puerto Ricans and Latinas and Latinos in the United States.

His moving depictions and potent critiques of economic exploitation and racism recognize the far-reaching tentacles of US imperialism: from unpleasant casual happenings on New York City subways to the detention of labor leaders, workers, and intellectuals in Pisagua, "a concentration camp in one of the most inhospitable places in Chile" (66). Repressive governments in Venezuela, Nicaragua, Guatemala, Cuba, Chile, the Dominican Republic, and Puerto Rico were (and continue to be) "coddled and protected" by the US government and serve the interests of Wall Street, "in which these dictators are like junior partners" (73). Preoccupied not only with the workings of power from above but also from below, Colón's sketches feature the growth and development of political consciousness, solidarity and mutual aid among community members, and the celebration of the ingenuity and creativity of the poor and working classes. Although he contributed to several papers in New York and Puerto Rico and maintained a regular column in organs of the Communist Party USA, the *Daily Worker* (1955 to 1957) and the *Worker* (1958 to 1968), Jesús Colón never earned a living as a journalist or writer (Acosta-Belén 1993, 185). His efforts to develop a professional career as a writer were often thwarted due to racism. The sketch "Hiawatha into Spanish," as an example, reflected on the rescission of a job offer at a film agency office because Colón was Black.

While some scholars have written about the historical, political, and literary significance of Colón's writings as chronicles, journalistic essays, and *testimonios* (Acosta-Belén and Sánchez-Korrol 1993; Flores 1981; García 2008; Kanellos 1993; Vázquez 2009), few have pointedly considered the author's preference for the *sketch* as a style, a method, and a pedagogical practice (García 2008). Colón, after all, titled the book *A Puerto Rican in New York and Other Sketches*, not other chronicles, other essays, or other *testimonios*. The sketch is a short hybrid form of stand-alone storytelling that conveys detailed impressions of places and people in the day-to-day. Still, these distinct, self-contained compositions can form a collective panorama of everyday life. Given the format, and much like its analog in the art of drawing, sketches may appear as incomplete or works in progress to some observers (García 2008; Outes-León 2017).[2] Colón infers as much in contemplating on his own writing in the sketch "A Puerto Rican in New York":

That, as everything else, the reasons have a beginning, a process of development and an end that has not been reached yet. So, without trying to answer the question directly I will try to give you something of the background and a few observations that I made in my childhood and my youth. Observations—deeper and broader—that I am still making. (197)

Some may find it unorthodox to begin a volume that is explicitly concerned with the role of the social sciences in Latina/o/x Studies by citing from an author who has been studied for his literary and historical value. However, this is precisely one of the key contributions of Latinx Studies: the field builds upon the tradition noted in the anthropology and sociology of thinkers like Roberto Alvarez, Ruth Behar, Norma Cantú, Virginia Domínguez, W. E. B. Du Bois, Rod Ferguson, Jovita González, Avery Gordon, Zora Neal Huston, Renato Rosaldo, and others of blurring conventional distinctions between the humanities and the social sciences. Cuban-Jewish anthropologist Ruth Behar, for instance, encourages us to read ethnography with an eye toward learning how they were written, how they became literary feats, as well as sociological contributions. What she terms "blurred genres," the vanishing line between fiction and nonfiction where ethnography is often positioned, dovetails with Jesús Colon's epistemological project and with our own goals in this anthology.

By opening this anthology with Jesús Colón we aim to highlight the role that history, memoir, and even autobiographical fiction invariably play in most empirically sound and theoretically sophisticated Latinx humanistic social sciences. As significantly, it is precisely the open-endedness of Jesús Colón's "sketches"—their critical pedagogical aspect and how they lend themselves to pointed yet fluid discussions—that inspires us to approach the humanistic social sciences in Latinx Studies in the form of critical diálogos. Notably, Jesús Colón's sketches lend themselves to critical diálogos. For Colón, sketches were intended to bequeath a historical record and tradition and to provide a tool for critical consciousness raising (Acosta-Belén and Sánchez-Korrol 1993, 24). For us, the editors, Jesús Colón's deployment of the sketch serves as a template for how to approach our proposition of critical diálogos in this anthology.

Critical Dialogues in Latinx Studies integrates and analyzes the social histories and contemporary lives of a diverse range of Latina and Latino populations, including immigrants, exiles, refugees, and US-born groups from across the Americas. The anthology introduces scholars to new approaches, theoretical trends, and understudied topics in Latina/o/x Studies, while also fostering rigorous classroom discussion and scholarly research in a variety of disciplinary and interdisciplinary research areas. Our central concern in *Critical Dialogues* is not simply to document or do a genealogy of Latina/o/x Studies as an academic field, but to stretch its points of reference and contributions: we want to continue Jesús Colón's tradition of studying Latinx/a/o populations beyond an exclusive US framework and at the intersection of a Latin American, Caribbean, global, international, and transnational optics. What we articulate in this volume is an approach to Latina/o/x Studies that actively and continuously works toward a dialogue-based, multidirectional analysis; we view such analysis as inherently comparative, not because it compares "national groups" or discrete "cultures," but because it organizes research questions and pedagogical projects around a range of equivalent social frameworks, cultural patterns, geographies, and histories.

In this volume, we demonstrate what this dialogue-based, multidirectional analysis might look like through a series of nine "critical diálogos" that become the volume's cornerstones and organizational framework.[3] In this framework, each individual essay is not exclusively a stand-alone piece, but becomes a crucial fragment of a larger disciplinary debate and interdisciplinary conversation in the humanistic social sciences. The critical diálogos question the rigid categories to which the social sciences have grown accustomed (e.g., a section on "gender," "race," "sexuality," "youth"), in favor of weaving salient Latina/o/x themes into broader scholarly discussions (e.g., a section on kinship and forms of relatedness or the world of work). Disrupting predictable discussions and predetermined categories, we incite readers to remain attentive to the nuance, richness, intersectionality, and complexity that characterize the everyday lives, affects, and aspirations of Latinx populations, the political economic structures that shape enduring racialization and marginality, and the continuing efforts to carve out new lives as diasporic, transnational, global, and colonial subjects of US empire.

A brief preface anchors each of the anthology's nine critical diálogos, providing conceptual direction and thematic suggestions for the scholarly conversation that organically emerge from the essays in the section. We view these prefaces as important for several reasons. First, they allow us to show instructors and students a less prescriptive approach to a section topic. It may be that a section on "kinship/family" will, in fact, be discussed in terms of how LGBTQ+ subjectivities reconfigure affective relationships, for instance. Second, beginning with a brief framing preface that slightly unsettles what is expected of a section allows for greater openness in pedagogical discussions and possible classroom activities. The prefaces allow us to introduce more imaginative approaches to each debate as well as enabling us to explain our rationale for what may perhaps seem as an unorthodox combination of essays. Different ways of combining the essays could certainly yield different interpretations and debates. We encourage readers to look for those as they envision other ways of connecting or arranging the essays or ways of putting them in dialogue with each other. We encourage readers not only to engage actively with each individual essay but to get involved in actively configuring the debates. Ultimately, *Critical Dialogues* is as much about epistemological concerns and how we ask the questions as it is about the pedagogical potentials that this recrafting of Latina/x/o Studies might offer. Rather than holding on to the categories and concerns of mainstream social science disciplines, we demonstrate what our research, teaching, and practice gain by actively refusing to view populations, histories, and experiences circumscribed by nationality or rigid national boundaries.

We situate *Critical Dialogues* not only in a humanistic social science tradition but in a tradition of collectivity, egalitarian aspirations, and social justice typical of the social movements on which Latina/o/x Studies are built. We bring together a remarkable group of scholars from an array of fields, life stages, professional trajectories, and institutional affiliations; our contributors include established and "up-and-coming" scholars, full professors and graduate students, and individuals in universities and community colleges. Who is included as a contributor becomes fundamental to how we understand radical inclusion and challenge the neoliberalization of US academia. A combination of abridged "canonical" essays and never-published works, the essays in the anthology demonstrate the contribution of Latina/o/x Studies to humanistic social sciences. They bring attention to methodological traditions and innovations to uncover untold aspects of Latinx social history and lived experiences. By no means are we claiming that this is a comprehensive group of Latinx scholars or themes; many excellent, influential authors, some who have perhaps greater name recognition, are not here. This is largely because of space constraints, but also because of a deliberate effort to broaden who sits at the academic table. This volume does not propose to serve as a definitive treatment of the field, but rather as an invitation to expand critical conversations, enhance intellectual discussions, and encourage future research on the prevailing and emerging themes, concepts, and methodologies integral to the interdisciplinary field of Latinx Studies.

Like most diálogos, the ones here were never linear or seamless; they involved us, not only as co-editors, but also as moderators and interlocutors. While we tried to facilitate conversation among the contributors in each section, we also offered suggestions and possibly privileged specific themes and approaches. At times, the diálogos were harmonious and resonated among all participants and us as interlocutors; other times, they were grounded on disagreements about terminology, approach, literature cited (or not), or even more granular aspects of the writing process, like narrative choice, structure, and organization. As interlocutors, we were the first ones to read all the essays and give detailed feedback to the authors; thereafter, we got input from external reviewers and engaged the contributors in more direct conversation with each other, particularly as they worked toward the final versions in this volume. It is telling, and important to highlight that, while the interactions among collaborators were primarily virtual, most of these individuals had met each other in person at some point in their careers or, at the very least, knew of one another and the others' work. This is important to mention, because we align our scholarship with the ethnographic convention of reflexivity,[4] from an anticolonial/decolonial and antiracist stance grounded in history and political economy. We draw on "rigorous reflexivity" to rupture prevailing categories and modes of analysis. We critically engage issues of power bound up in what we as scholars are able to behold, who we engage, and how we choose to structure and write about our insights and collaborations (Jackson 2005, 162–65). Our biographies and the social webs and political contexts through which we navigate invariably shape the epistemological, thematic, and theoretical approaches to our research projects.

As a Puerto Rican from Chicago and a Puerto Rican from Puerto Rico, and as co-editors, our personal biographies, professional experiences, and community connections shape the very impetus to organize this project as collaborative, critical dialogues rather than as a more conventional thematic anthology. Both of our academic works have largely centered on the experience of Puerto Ricans, whether in the United States (Ramos-Zayas 2003, 2012; Rúa 2012) or in Puerto Rico (Ramos-Zayas 2020). Yet, rather than viewing Puerto Ricans as a liminal population frequently invisible in both traditional American Studies and Latin American Studies, we insert Puerto Ricans as critical to fostering a hemispheric shift in what we consider US-centered Ethnic or Latinx Studies (De Genova and Ramos-Zayas 2003; Rúa 2012). Moreover, our academic training and epistemological approach were specially influenced by trailblazing and contemporary Chicana feminists, including Gloria Anzaldúa, Sandra Cisneros, Cherríe Moraga, Mary Romero, Vicki Ruiz, and Patricia Zavella.

Likewise, the essays in these critical diálogos, while attentive to local and regional idiosyncrasies, aim toward a hemispheric, internationalist recasting of Latinx Studies that decenters the US nation-state as a primary unit of reference as well as acknowledging frameworks of US imperialism, colonialism, and white supremacy on a global scale.

Despite these important similarities, we arrived at Latinx Studies through different trajectories. Rúa holds a PhD in American Cultures from the University of Michigan, where she trained as an interdisciplinary scholar specializing in Latina and Latino Studies. She entered the field at a moment when American Studies was not only critically examining its relationship to Ethnic Studies but also turning its attention to the hemispheric and transnational with a renewed interest in US empire post-9/11. Yet and still, Latinx Studies, especially Caribbean-based and Central American–based Latinx Studies, remained at the edges of the field. Ramos-Zayas was formally trained in a very traditional anthropology department at Columbia and was only able to situate her work in Latinx Studies by reaching out to more senior colleagues, attending interdisciplinary conferences, and being affiliated to interdisciplinary academic units throughout her professional life. Our respective years of teaching in a Latino and Caribbean Studies Department at a large state university and Latina and Latino Studies Program at a small liberal arts college, and classroom discussions and experiences with students of various Latinx backgrounds, among others, guided our decision to invite scholars from across the country and across the Latinx Studies spectrum. But it was also a much early connection in our careers, teaching at an alternative high school serving predominately low-income and poor Puerto Rican and Latinx students in Chicago, where in fact we first met, that motivated this organization of diálogos among a diverse group of contributors with different institutional affiliations and ranks.

In *Critical Dialogues in Latinx Studies*, we propose a Latino Studies humanistic social science approach that brings together social history and contemporary lives through an interweaving of current and canonical scholarship covering a wide range of nationalities, social classes, and legal experiences. Central to this endeavor is fostering academic dialogue between Latino Studies and related ethnic and racial studies fields, including African American Studies, Native American Studies, Asian American and Pacific Islander Studies, and even Latin American and Caribbean Studies and drawing upon these connections without conflating these groups' unique histories and experiences. Each section carries readers chronologically, thematically, and introduces them to one of nine key "critical diálogos" or disciplinary and interdisciplinary debate.

The nine critical diálogos on which this anthology is built are not intended to constitute a comprehensive approach to the humanistic social sciences in Latinx Studies. However, this volume is one of very few Latinx Studies anthologies that includes foundational and innovative work on Central American and Caribbean populations. We encourage further comparative and relational work, not only across Latinx nationality groups or regions but work that also considers other interdisciplinary ethnic studies fields like African American Studies, Native American Studies, Middle Eastern Studies, and Pacific Islander and Asian American Studies. We also highlight the relevance of nontraditional destinations and areas of community formation as well as South-South migrations and research that situates Latinx Studies in the Global South. Although some progress has been made in the fields of Afro-Latinidades and Indigeneity, and some important work in this area has been included here, we still feel there is a great opportunity for further research, including examinations of Latinxs and whiteness. We feel that demographic changes in most US cities have not always led to an increase in the ethnographic, demographic, or historical research in those areas. The increase in populations of Ecuadorians, Colombians, and Peruvians in NYC; of Venezuelans, Puerto Ricans, Dominicans, and Brazilians in Florida; of Central Americans in Chicago, DC, and LA; and of Mexicans and Central Americans in the "New South" are some examples of the demographic patterns that we are hoping encourages scholars to undertake research. Likewise, we feel Latinx Studies needs to develop stronger connections to critical public health, disability studies, and environmental justice fields.

Organic and public intellectuals of color had historically formulated and frequently applied knowledge produced from everyday life and communal enlightenment. While institutions of higher learning would later come to appropriate, tame, and undermine many of these initiatives and forms of knowledge, as American Studies scholar Rod Ferguson has eloquently documented (Ferguson 2012, 2017), we hope to reanimate them here. Our goal is to reinvigorate intersectional, international, critical, and comparative dimensions of Latinx Studies by providing alternative terms, frameworks, and paradigms for the debate. We shift the questions but also the very sites of inquiry. *Critical Dialogues* foregrounds "the deep traditions of striving for freedom and progress that pervade our daily life," as Jesús Colón urges us to do (1961, p. 10).

NOTES

1 Colón's extensive personal archive of photos, books, pamphlets, newsletters, leaflets, periodicals, correspondence, and his own writings documenting Puerto Rican daily life in New York City and other parts of the country is a centerpiece of the Center for Puerto Rican Studies Archive of the Puerto Rican Diaspora (Acosta-Belén and Sánchez Korrol 1993; Rúa and Torres 2010).

2 *A Puerto Rican in New York* contains both types of sketches with illustrations by Ernesto Ramos Nieves. Thanks to Molly Murphy for bringing attention to the uses of the sketch in art history.

3 A handful of recent anthologies exist in the growing field of Latinx Studies. The more wide-ranging volumes tend to highlight scholarship in either the social sciences or humanities or offer a singular theoretical orientation, and they usually feature contributions by prominent senior scholars. *The New Latino Studies Reader* (edited by Ramón A. Gutiérrez and Tomás Almaguer, University of California Press, 2016), for example, offers previously published chapter contributions from the last decade by established scholars mainly organized around social science themes that unpack various facets of Latinidad. Anthologies that put forward a field-specific or lone theoretical approach include *A Companion to Latina/o Studies* (edited by Juan Flores and Renato Rosaldo, Blackwell, 2011), comprised of forty original cultural studies essays written by well-known scholars, and *Critical Latin American and Latino Studies* (edited by Juan Poblete, University of Minnesota, 2003), which foregrounds a postcolonial and poststructural, linguistic-centered concern in Poblete's scholarship. Other edited collections frequently adopt a narrower, region-specific focus, such as *The Latina/o Midwest Reader* (edited by Omar Valerio-Jiménez, Santiago Vaquera-Vásquez, and Claire F. Fox, University of Illinois Press, 2017) and *U.S. Central Americans: Reconstructing Memories, Struggles, and Communities of Resistance* (edited by Karina Alvarado, Alicia Ivonne Estrada, and Ester Hernández, University of Arizona Press, 2017). Likewise, such recent Latinx Studies anthologies consist of "encyclopedia-style" short essays around key concepts in the discipline, as is the case of *Keywords for Latina/o Studies* (edited by Deborah Vargas, Nancy Raquel Mirabal, and Lawrence LaFountain-Stokes, NYU Press, 2017). Without taking away from the merits of these preceding anthologies, the

proposed edited volume aims to address what we view as thematic, scholarly, and structural limitations.

4 See, for instance, Ruth Behar and Bruce Mannheim, "The Couple in the Cage: A Guatinaui Odyssey," *Visual Anthropology Review* 11, no. 1 (1995): 118–27; Sarah E. Turner, "'Spider Woman's Granddaughter': Autobiographical Writings by Native American Women," *Melus* 22, no. 4 (1997): 109–32; and Kate Lenzo, "Reinventing Ethos: Validity, Authority, and the Transgressive Self," (1994), among others.

REFERENCES

Acosta-Belén, Edna. "The Building of a Community: Puerto Rican Writers and Activists in New York City, 1890s–1960s." In *Recovering the U.S. Hispanic Literary Heritage, Volume 1*, edited by Ramón Gutiérrez and Genaro Padilla, 179–95. Houston: Arte Público Press, 1993.

Acosta-Belén, Edna and Virginia Sánchez-Korrol. "The World of Jesús Colón." In *The Way It Was and Other Writings* by Jesús Colón, 13–32. Houston: Arte Público Press, 1993.

Colón, Jesús. 1961. *A Puerto Rican in New York and Other Sketches*. New York: Mainstream Publishers.

———. 1982. *A Puerto Rican in New York and Other Sketches*. New York: International Publishers.

De Genova, Nicholas and Ana Y. Ramos-Zayas. 2003. *Latino Crossings: Mexicans, Puerto Ricans, and the Politics of Race and Citizenship*. New York: Routledge.

Delgado, Linda C. "Jesús Colón and the Making of a New York City Community, 1917–1974." In *The Puerto Rican Diaspora: Historical Perspectives*, edited by Carmen T. Whalen and Victor Vásquez-Hernández, 68–87. Philadelphia: Temple University Press, 2005.

Ferguson, Roderick A. 2012. *The Reorder of Things: The University and Its Pedagogies of Minority Difference*. Minneapolis: University of Minnesota Press.

———. 2017. *We Demand: The University and Student Protests*. Berkeley: University of California Press.

Flores, Juan. "Forward." In *A Puerto Rican in New York and Other Sketches*, ix–xvii. New York: International Publishers, 1982.

García, David A. "A Master of the Rosary: Apology and Confession in Selected Writings of Jesús Colón's *A Puerto Rican in New York and Other Sketches*." *Afro-Hispanic Review* 27, no. 2 (Fall 2008): 45–70.

Jackson, John, L. 2005. *Real Black: Adventures in Racial Sincerity*. Chicago: University of Chicago Press.

Kanellos, Nicolás. "A Socio-Historic Study of Hispanic Newspapers in the United States." In *Recovering the U.S. Hispanic Literary Heritage, Volume 1*, edited by Ramón A. Gutiérrez and Genaro Padilla, 107–28. Houston: Arte Público Press, 1993.

Outes-León, Brais D. "The Aesthetics of the Sketch: Incompletion and the Boundaries of Art Theory in Joaquín Torres-García's La ciudad sin nombre (1941)." *MLN*, 132, no. 2 (March 2017): 329–53.

Ramos-Zayas, Ana Y. 2003. *National Performances: The Politics of Class, Race, and Space in Puerto Rican Chicago*. Chicago: University of Chicago Press.

———. 2012. *Street Therapists: Race, Affect, and Neoliberal Personhood in Latino Newark*. Chicago: University of Chicago Press.

———. 2020. *Parenting Empires: Class, Whiteness, and the Moral Economy of Privilege in Latin America*. Durham: Duke University Press.

Rúa, Mérida M. 2012. *A Grounded Identidad: Making New Lives in Chicago's Puerto Rican Neighborhoods*. New York: Oxford University Press.

Rúa, Mérida M., and Arlene Torres. "Introduction: At the Crossroads of Urban Ethnography and Puerto Rican Latinidad." In *Latino Urban Ethnography and the Work of Elena Padilla*, edited by Mérida M. Rúa, 1–22. Urbana: University of Illinois Press, 2010.

Vázquez, David J. "Jesús Colón and the Development of Insurgent Consciousness." *Centro Journal* 21, no. 1 (Spring 2009): 79–99.

US Imperialism and Colonial Legacies of Latinx Migrations

The first critical diálogo sets the tone for the explicit comparative and relational dimensions of the anthology. This critical diálogo focuses on US settler colonialism westward and empire building in the Atlantic, the US racialization of colonial subjects and spaces of "model" subjectivities, and the affective and emotive outcomes of land appropriation and boundary policing. There would be no discussion of "Latino" or "Latino Studies" as a field had it not been for the migrations and exile conditions caused by US interventions in Central America, the Caribbean, and South America as well as what became the US Southwest. These conditions are as evident in the current historical moment as they were throughout the twentieth century. Beginning with the historical contexts, rather than, say, a focus on "Latinx/a/o" as a series of cultural identity practices, allows us to provide the framing for identities as social constructs rather than cultural references. Moreover, given the contemporary condition of fascist and white supremacist tendencies, both in the United States and in the Americas more broadly, we believe it is important to remind readers that there are parallels to be drawn between various old-school modalities of US support of South American dictatorships, North American and Central American land grabbing, and the militarization of the Caribbean, and more contemporary neoliberal and financial involvement in the Americas. An opening diálogo on US Imperialism and Colonial Legacies of Latinx Migrations, to us, provides the best explanation to why Latin Americans "migrate" to the United States. It is not only in pursuit of some mythical "American dream" but because they have been, quite literally, uprooted by US policies in their respective countries. The critical diálogo in this section revolves around the question: *What can the histories of specific national, regional, and temporal communities tell us about the shifts and modifications of US colonial and imperial nation-state projects?*

Pedro Cabán's discussion of Puerto Rico under US empire and Laura Pulido's study of settler colonialism and nonnative people of color approach this question by highlighting the geopolitical and historical manipulations of US empire building, both within the US nation-state and at its edges. Significantly, these processes of empire have to be situated in US interventionism and regimes of representation as suggested by Susan Coutin's focus on accompaniment and sanctuary practices at various border crossings and Maria Elena Cepeda's examination of transnational scripts and gendered formations of Colombianidad.

1

Puerto Rico

The Ascent and Decline of an American Colony

PEDRO CABÁN

Puerto Rico has been a territorial possession of the United States for over 120 years. During this period, the United States has imposed a colonial state that has governed Puerto Rico and managed its political economy. The colonial state has taken numerous forms, beginning in 1898 as a military regime, and currently as a titular democratic government that is subservient to a financial control board that the US Congress imposed in 2016. In the following pages I compare two transformative periods in Puerto Rican history: 1898 to 1900 and 2016 to 2019. These junctures bookend the history of US colonial rule, which is marked by Puerto Rico's early conversion into a lucrative commercial and strategically significant asset of the evolving American empire and its subsequent descent into a debt-ridden, poverty-stricken, ecologically damaged territorial possession of questionable value to the United States. These two periods are marked by the imposition of two very different colonial state forms.

After wresting control of Puerto Rico from Spain in 1898, the United States installed a military regime that ruled by decree for two years. On April 12, 1900, almost nine months after Hurricane San Ciriaco devastated the archipelago, President McKinley signed into law the Foraker Act, which would "temporarily provide revenues and a civil government for Porto Rico, and for other purposes."[1] The law forced Puerto Ricans to bear the expenses of their own colonial subordination. The Foraker Act created a colonial state with virtually absolute power over the lives of Puerto Ricans. But it also was a sweeping policy to rapidly promote American capitalist development. All key officials were appointed by the president. But in order to gain the acquiescence of Puerto Rico's political leaders, the Foraker Act set up a popularly elected lower house.

On July 1, 2016, the United States enacted the Puerto Rican Oversight, Management, and Economic Stability Act (PROMESA). The law rescinded the colonial state's budgetary authority that US Congress had granted in 1952 when it approved the establishment of the Commonwealth of Puerto Rico (or the Estado Libre Asociado in Spanish). PROMESA created a Financial Oversight and Management Board (FOMB), which effectively displaced the colonial state in managing the island's political economy. Today Puerto Rico is under the technocratic rule of an externally imposed financial control board whose primary function is to extract value from an impoverished island nation for the benefit of financial capital.

During each of the two periods (1898 to 1900 and 2016 to 2019), Puerto Rico was devastated by hurricanes. On August 19, 1899, barely a year after General Nelson Miles's troops invaded Puerto Rico, the island was struck by Hurricane San Ciriaco. San Ciriaco was described as one of the most destructive hurricanes to ever strike the island. The governor-general accurately predicted that the hurricane "will be long remembered in the history of Porto Rico."[2] On September 17, 2017, fourteen months after PROMESA was signed into law, Hurricane María devastated Puerto Rico. No other hurricane caused as much loss of life and destruction of property as did María. Its effects on a traumatized but resilient society have lingered. Both hurricanes transformed the economic landscape, profoundly disrupted the lives of millions of Puerto Ricans, and tested the capability of the federal government and colonial state to manage relief and rehabilitation operations. The hurricanes also created an array of challenges to colonial rule and contributed to changes in colonial policy.

By comparing two distinct and brief moments that are approximately 120 years apart, this essay highlights the persistent fault lines in US colonial rule. The exigencies of American imperialism are translated into particular colonial state forms and policies that are intended to advance the strategic and material interests of the empire. But the state form is always provisional since it creates conditions for its own dissolution. This is simply because the colonial state is never intended to be a democratic institution that is responsive to the people of Puerto Rico. Its primary function is to maintain political stability in an environment that is continually under assault, either from hurricanes or economic policies that push ever more Puerto Ricans into precarity. The resulting inequities are the source of labor conflict, strikes, multiple forms of resistance and noncompliance, and as the summer of 2019 showed, massive public uprisings. Another fault line is the failure of colonialism to socialize Puerto Ricans into believing that their political subordination is a consequence of the inferiority of their culture. The uprising revealed in uniquely Puerto Rican fashion their refusal to submit to the dictates of Americanization. Rather than embrace American exceptionalism, the Puerto Ricans create and nurture its antithesis: a vibrantly expressive national cultural identity that draws on and reinterprets the iconography of a century of resistance to colonialism.

Political and National Disasters under Colonialism

After ejecting Spain from the Caribbean, US capital flowed into Puerto Rico and Cuba to finance the development of the sugar industry. Puerto Rico was soon converted into a vital source of sugar for the US market. But Puerto Rico also figured prominently in the strategic calculations of American expansionists. The island nation was designated as a forward defense station for the soon to be built Panama Canal. Famed naval strategist Alfred Thayer Mahan observed that the canal "can affect the rapid peopling of the American Pacific coasts" and this would be an "inestimable contribution toward overcoming the problem of distribution and that of labor." The canal would also "disperse the threatening question of Asiatic immigration to the Pacific coasts by filling up the ground" and allow for the "indefinite strengthening of Anglo-Saxon institutions upon the northwest shores of the Pacific."[3] It is ironic that Puerto Rico was implicated in a strategy to spread Anglo Saxon institutions and values in order to block Asian immigration.

The governor-generals who ruled Puerto Rico (1898 to 1900) promoted Puerto Rico's transition to a sugar-based economy under the control of absentee monopoly corporations. The military regime enacted an array of monetary, fiscal, tariff measures that, in combination with the abundance of cheap rural labor, virtually guaranteed the sugar corporations obscene profits. Investments flowed into Puerto Rico, and the economy was restructured to satisfy the burgeoning American market for sugar. The coffee industry was especially hurt by these policies. Deprived of credit and once vibrant export markets, the coffee industry would never regain its dominant position. Moreover, the coffee plantations were particularly vulnerable to hurricane damage, as San Ciriaco would prove. The change in sovereignty and the hurricane initiated a far-reaching and long-lasting transformation of Puerto Rican economy and society.

Hurricane San Ciriaco (August 8, 1899)

Puerto Rico has been victimized by many hurricanes, but until María struck in 2017, San Ciriaco was singular for the loss of life and property it inflicted on the island. The Category 5 hurricane was a catastrophic event that killed more than four thousand people, most of whom drowned. The loss of lives exceeded threefold the total lives lost in all "previously recorded hurricanes."[4] "Property loss was calculated as $20 million [$6 billion in 2019]."[5] Puerto Rico was ill prepared for the hurricane. Overnight the hurricane exposed Puerto Rico's vulnerabilities by creating a humanitarian disaster of unprecedented proportions. Four months after the hurricane, 221,087 people—almost a quarter of the population of 918,926—were indigent, and death rates increased from 26 to 35 per 1000 inhabitants.[6] General Davis, the governor-general, reported, "The people were without available resources and without the means of getting any, food was destroyed, business paralyzed."[7]

San Ciriaco devastated the coffee plantations. Coffee was the country's primary export crop and comprised the largest percentage of export earnings in 1899. Over 250,000 of Puerto Rico's 800,000 peones depended on the coffee industry for their livelihood.[8] San Ciriaco left in its wake an economy in shambles, a huge unemployed rural labor force, and thousands of impoverished Puerto Ricans who faced imminent starvation. Resolution of the crisis was a national security issue. The United States was a late imperialist power without any experience in the management of overseas territories. If colonial officials failed to prevent a humanitarian catastrophe in a small tropical island, European imperialist powers would view the United States as an ineffectual, possibly bumbling nascent colonizer. The United States feared that failure in Puerto Rico would embolden its European rivals to challenge America's growing hegemony in Latin America and the Caribbean. Moreover, failure to resolve the crisis would humiliate Elihu Root, who as secretary of war was America's foremost prominent of imperialism. He famously declared that "we of America . . . possess the supreme capacity not merely to govern ourselves at home . . . but the capacity to govern men wherever they were found."[9]

The United States War Department, which had jurisdiction over the newly acquired overseas territories, acted quickly to stave off a humanitarian crisis. The department allocated $400,000 ($11.3 million in 2017) for emergency relief. Congress authorized a miserly $200,000 for individual emergency relief but was willing to provide $950,000 for road construction to provide employment for "people who are suffering from starvation and sickness."[10] The Central Porto Rico Relief Committee, headed by New York governor Theodore Roosevelt, collected private donations and shipped 32,445,000 pounds of food to Puerto Rico, in addition to clothing and medicine.[11] General Davis reported that "supplies of all sorts were being rapidly forwarded to the island, and at one time during the month of September it looked as if we would be swamped with the large amount of these supplies."[12]

Notwithstanding the War Department's energetic relief efforts, conditions in the mountainous regions were alarming. A War Department official estimated that two hundred thousand people were on the verge of starvation and warned that "if not fed at home they will migrate to the cities, leaving the weak to die."[13] Colonial officials faced two critical situations in the aftermath of San Ciriaco. They had to avert an impending humanitarian crisis of a scale that possibly was unmatched in the United States. They also had to create jobs for uncounted thousands of rural workers who lost their livelihood after the farms and plantations were destroyed. General Davis warned that the "most important problem . . . was not economic, but humanitarian. It was a question of saving human lives, not for a day or a week, but for many weeks."[14] Colonial officials feared that the collapse of the coffee industry would create uncontrolled internal migration. Lacking any means of subsistence, thousands of desperate, landless rural workers from the mountainous cordillera would be forced to migrate to the overpopulated coastal areas and create an unimaginable labor surplus. Restoration of the coffee industry was an urgent priority.

The colonial authorities were beseeched by the planters, who faced financial ruin if they did not receive support. The planters bristled at the discriminatory fiscal and monetary measures adopted by the military, "which greatly dimin-ished our wealth . . . has resulted in the present ruinous condition of the coffee industry."[15] The planters warned that without federal assistance, the industry would be destroyed. Elihu Root pleaded with the US Congress to protect the industry because "the importance of this crop is so great, and its success or fail-ure so far reaching and widespread."[16] The irony in all this was that Root himself bore responsibility for the policies that undermined the coffee industry. General Davis acknowledged that those policies "resulted in incalculable harm to the entire population," and that "trade and agriculture languished."[17] San Ciriaco marked the beginning of the end for the coffee industry in Puerto Rico and accelerated the colony's conversion into a labor surplus economy. San Ciriaco was a wake-up call that a wage-based economy, especially one dominated by the sugar industry, was incapable of creating sufficient employment for the island's growing population. Colonial officials, concerned that the growing legions of impoverished and unemployed rural workers would threaten the colonial enter-prise, began to promote emigration in 1900 to reduce the surplus population.

Henry Allen, appointed civilian governor in 1900, introduced two themes that for decades would shape the official discourse about labor migration under capitalism in Puerto Rico. He observed that Puerto Rico "has plenty of laborers and poor people generally." What Puerto Rico needed, Allen said, "were men," presumably white Americans, "with capital, energy and enterprise to develop its latent industries and reclaim its sugar estates."[18] Hurricane San Ciriaco disrupted labor markets and increased the ranks of the impoverished unemployed peones. The hurricane created the perfect opportunity for Allen to put his ideas into effect. In 1900, after hurricane San Ciriaco had devastated the fields and farms, labor recruiters for the Hawaiian Sugar Planters Association, the Cotton Grow-ers Association, and other producer associations descended on Puerto Rico hop-ing to hire workers from the vast pool of surplus labor. More than six thousand Puerto Ricans signed labor contracts and were shipped to Hawaii between 1900 and 1901. Puerto Ricans were also recruited for work in Arizona and a host of other countries. Allen's proposition that the abundance of labor and the scarcity of foreign capital are inimical to Puerto Rico's development has endured to the present.[19] According to this perverse Malthusian reasoning, overpopulation is the major culprit for the unemployment and poverty that afflicts Puerto Rico. This logic absolves the colonial state from ever questioning a growth strategy based on maximizing the profitability of foreign corporations at the expense of the residents.

Hurricane María (September 20, 2017)

María was the most destructive hurricane to strike Puerto Rico in modern his-tory. The most recent study by Harvard University researchers estimates that

4,645 people died between September 20 and December 31, 2017.[20] According to Moody's Investors Service, Puerto Rico sustained $95 billion in property damage and lost production.[21] The catastrophe traumatized the population and created a humanitarian crisis beyond the capability of US mainland or Puerto Rican authorities to resolve. Hurricane María also triggered massive emigration. The United States has been a safety valve through which Puerto Rico's surplus population has flowed since 1900. Prior to the 2006 economic depression, the colonial state planned and participated in the removal of surplus labor. Emigration increased significantly after the 2006 economic depression. The migration of Puerto Ricans between 1950 and 1960 "was one of the greatest peacetime population movements recorded in contemporary history."[22] The exodus of Puerto Ricans to the United States after Hurricane María is without parallel and has ominous implications for Puerto Rico's future economic well-being.

Few would have envisioned that the outmigration of Puerto Ricans since 2005 would surpass the totals recorded during the post–World War II period. Puerto Rico's population stood at 3.19 million in 2019, about the same size as the population four decades ago. Puerto Rico reached its peak population in 2004 and has dropped by 632,000 since then. In 2018, a year after María, the population had declined by 3.9 percent, the largest year-to-year drop in seventy years.[23] The Center for Puerto Rican Studies estimated that in the twelve months following María, over two hundred thousand Puerto Ricans had migrated to the United States.[24] The initial emigration after María was made up of vulnerable and traumatized hurricane survivors. Subsequent emigration was comprised of those who envisioned a dire economic future: low wages, closed schools, shrunken university, understaffed and under-resourced public health facilities, which will only worsen if the junta succeeds in inflicting even more severe austerity.

For over a century, migration was regulated by two factors: (1) labor demand in the mainland and high unemployment in Puerto Rico and (2) government policy to remove surplus population. But after María, Puerto Rico experienced for the first time in its history systemic depopulation. María intensified the pressures for Puerto Ricans to leave their devastated homeland. Puerto Ricans were abandoning their homeland out of a sense of despair and the painful realization that a dire economic future may await those who stay.

Virtually every facet of the physical and human infrastructure collapsed: roads, bridges, dams and water, communications, and electrical stopped functioning for lengthy periods. Hospitals and other public health care facilities systems, already battered by inhumane budget cuts, could simply not cope with the enormity of the human tragedy. But the enormity of the devastation and death is also attributable to the colonial state's decision to disinvest in the infrastructure and permit its gradual erosion. Government austerity measures predating the installation of the junta undermined Puerto Rico's resilience and ability to recover from a natural disaster. Both the pro-statehood New Progressive Party

(PNP) and commonwealth Partido Popular Democratico (PPD) slashed the government work force by tens of thousands and reduced public services.[25] The government drastically reduced expenditures for roads, water treatment facilities, schools, and other critical elements of the physical and human infrastructure from $2.4 billion in 2012 to $906 million in 2017. The University of Puerto Rico budget was slashed by 20 percent.[26] The decisions invariably revealed the colonial state's determination to protect the interests of capital and the expense of the of the population. Yet investors believed that homegrown austerity by the PPD and PNP was not sufficiently harsh to halt the descent to bankruptcy.

The federal government quickly established the Financial Oversight and Management Board (FOMB) after Governor Alejandro Garcia's dramatic announcement that Puerto Rico's $74 billion debt was not payable. The federal government lacked confidence in the colonial state's ability to protect the interests of American institutions or investors and hedge funds that had amassed the vast majority of Puerto Rican municipal bonds. The FOMB is an autonomous entity that serves as a collection agency for high-risk speculators and hedge funds. "La Junta," as the board is commonly known, is laser focused on slashing government expenditures, reducing costs, and increasing tax revenues to amass savings that will be used to pay the bondholders.[27] The magnitude of the reduction in government expenditures prompted large protests, disruptions of board meetings, strikes by university students, angry letters from US legislators, lawsuits, and even denunciations by then-governor Ricardo Rosselló. The impact of pre-María cuts to Puerto Rico's infrastructure magnified the damage caused by the hurricane. The FOMB's latest fiscal plan further weakened the infrastructure and increased Puerto Rico's vulnerability to future hurricanes by slashing government spending by $629 million in 2019 and imposing total reductions of $1.6 billion by 2020.[28]

Most of the cuts will be for education, health care, and public pensions, a direct attack on Puerto Rico's human infrastructure and human capital. In a letter to the junta, senator Elizabeth Warren, representative Nydia Velázquez, and others express "grave concern" that the junta was siphoning off federal funds "intended to benefit the people of Puerto Rico to creditors" and that this was unacceptable.[29] To add insult to injury, Puerto Rico is required to provide the board with a "dedicated source of funding, not subject to further legislative action, to cover its expenses."[30] PROMESA requires Puerto Rico to pay for all the costs the junta will incur, including salaries for board members, staff, and consultants. The Congressional Budget Office estimates that the costs are conservatively expected to reach $370 million for the decade starting 2016.[31] The fiscal crisis that consumed Puerto Rico's political class and caused anxiety among investors further impoverished a vulnerable population. Deploying the colonial state so openly in the interests of capital helps us comprehend why Hurricane María was such an epoch-making catastrophe whose impact reverberated in massive protests that brought down a government in the summer of 2019.

The Trump administration's emergency response after Hurricane María devastated Puerto Rico may well stand out as one of the most ineffectual and incompetently managed episodes in Puerto Rico's history as a colony of the United States. The Federal Emergency Management Administration (FEMA) and the US Department of Defense were the lead agencies tasked with disaster relief and recovery. FEMA's inadequate and disorganized response to the humanitarian crisis was evident from the outset. FEMA was absent during the initial days after the hurricane laid waste to Puerto Rico. Subsequently, FEMA failed to coordinate the relief efforts among the dozens of different nonprofit organizations and government officials involved in the response.[32] Puerto Rican and other Latinx members of the US Congress repeatedly demanded that the Trump administration act decisively, and they warned of a mounting death toll. Representative Luis Gutierrez, for instance, noted that, "We know the U.S. is capable. We can invade foreign countries with hundreds of thousands of troops, flawless communications, food, and security."[33] According to Irwin Redlener, director of National Center for Disaster Preparedness, the US Pentagon knew that Puerto Rico was on the verge of a humanitarian crisis but failed to act because "President Donald Trump did not think it was necessary."[34] Refugees International reported that the federal and Puerto Rican governments' response "was still largely uncoordinated and poorly implemented and that was prolonging the humanitarian emergency on the ground."[35]

Indeed, the General Accountability Office and FEMA itself concluded in separate reports, released in the summer of 2018, that FEMA was unprepared for the scale of relief and recovery effort, was slow to respond, and that it deployed personnel who lacked the required training and expertise, including even rudimentary knowledge of Spanish.[36] FEMA responded quickly and decisively to the victims of Hurricane Harvey, but in contrast it could only manage a flawed response to the victims of María. FEMA approved $141.8 million in individual assistance to Harvey victims nine days after the hurricane struck but only $6.2 million for María victims during the same period. Nine days after Harvey, the federal government had deployed thirty thousand personnel in the Houston region but only ten thousand at the same point for María.[37]

As criticism of the federal disaster relief effort mounted, President Trump publicly dismissed the seriousness of the crisis and launched deceptive and derogatory tweets about Puerto Ricans and their political leadership. In contrast to the federal government's indecisiveness, Puerto Ricans in the United States organized scores of local and national committees and associations to collect donations for survivors of Hurricane María and arranged the required transportation. In Puerto Rico, hurricane survivors organized dozens of autonomous *centros de apoyo mutuo* ("grassroots centers for mutual aid") and solidarity networks, and they provided support to ravished communities as the "negligence of the governments continues to make the people suffer."[38] Without the efforts of these associations, the death count would have undoubtedly been greater.

Hurricanes, Crisis, and the Colonial State

Hurricanes San Ciriaco and María are gateways to interrogate multiple dimensions of US colonialism in Puerto Rico. The two periods–1898 to 1900 and 2016 to 2019—were transformative moments in Puerto Rico's modern history. Both periods start with a transformation in the colonial state form imposed by the federal government. In 1899, the United States disbanded Puerto Rico's parliamentary government, imposed a military government an transitioned to a civilian administered colonial state. In 2016 the federal government imposed a financial control board which usurped the colonial states' fiscal and budgetary authority. In both instances the federal government effected a transition to alternate colonial state forms more capable of advancing US interests.

Hurricanes have compromised the colonial state's ability to effectively manage the island's political economy. The US federal government had to adjust its colonial policy, and even transition to a new colonial state form after San Ciriaco. It did so again in 1932 after Hurricanes Felipe and Ciprian devastated Puerto Rico.[39] The downfall of Ricardo Rosselló's administration in the summer of 2019 is the result of widespread revulsion with his administration's corruption and for its mismanagement of the hurricane relief and recovery program. The release of 889 pages of private chats between the governor and his inner circle in which they mock the dead of Hurricane Maria and freely engaged in misogynistic and homophobic banter was the necessary spark that unleashed the people's repressed anger. Moreover, the chats revealed that Rosselló and his claque held the Puerto Rican population in the same contempt as did Trump and other racists that populate his administration.

The extraordinary events between 2016 and 2019 gave rise to a new political consciousness and the proliferation of activist and solidary networks, feminist collectives and community-based *centros de apoyos mutuo*.[40] These organizations were in the vanguard of the nation-wide summer uprising of 2019 that forced the resignation of Rosselló. They provoked the crisis of legitimacy that may make the archipelago ungovernable. The 2019 summer uprising dramatically recast a long-standing portrayal of Puerto Rico as a hapless colony whose people either fatalistically accepted their plight or lamentably were forced to emigrate to the United States. The historically unprecedented uprising was a collective repudiation of the corrupt, incompetent and morally bankrupt political class that nourishes itself on the colonial state's resources and power. The political class was astonished that a determined cross-generational movement inexplicably rose to renounce the instrumentalities and agents of colonial oppression.

The current crisis of governability raises provocative possibilities about altering colonial policy, and suggests the possibility of a new state form in the coming years. At this point, in the aftermath of the largest public uprising in Puerto Rico's history it is premature to suppose that a new state form will be imposed. But the

Washington Post, the Wall Street Journal some congressional Republicans, and even the FOMB have called for amending PROMESA to give la junta greater powers in determining how Puerto Rico is governed. But Puerto Ricans angrily reject this plan to consolidate further power in the unelected board. In Washington Raúl Grijalva Chairman House Natural Resources Committee was warned that the junta "should not view this as an opportunity to amass more unelected power over the lives of the residents of Puerto Rico."[41] The *consejos de apoyo mutuo* that helped organize the massive protest have been the moving force behind the creation of assembleas de pueblo. These are informal associations comprised of the residents of *municipios* (municipalities) throughout Puerto Rico. The *assembleas* are practicing and promoting a new form of participatory and inclusive democracy. Their efforts have been supported by the Puerto Rican Independence Party, that has proposed major changes to Puerto Rico's constitution to make the insular government more accountable to the people. The conditions are emerging for the possibility of a new state form. What that will be is unknown. But it is clear that PROMESA was the empire's way of saying that the Estado Libre Asociado had outlived its usefulness. Puerto Ricans know that the colonial state is in crisis and vulnerable to change. Protestors cleverly called attention to this by loudly chanting "si, si el ELA se murió, y el pueblo lo interró."[42]

Nowhere is the contradistinction between the two historical moments outlined in this essay more stark than in the federal government's disaster relief responses to hurricanes San Ciriaco and María. In the wake of San Ciriaco, the War Department took exclusive command of the emergency relief and recovery campaign. The official records depict a competent military government that responded with efficiency and alacrity to the immediacy of the humanitarian crisis. In contrast, the Trump administration and the Rosselló administration demonstrated staggering ineptitude in the aftermath of Hurricane María. Barely two weeks after the hurricane President Trump recklessly tweeted that Puerto Ricans "want everything to be done for them."[43] And after learning of the initial estimate of 3,000 Hurricane María related deaths, Trump ridiculed the number and absolved his administration of culpability for loss of life. He fumed that "The people of Puerto Rico have one of the most corrupt governments in our country,"[44] an ironic if not disingenuous claim given his own ethically compromised and scandal prone administration.[45] No US president has so wantonly defamed Puerto Ricans as incompetent, venal, and indolent. Trump's boastful claims that FEMA and he had done an extraordinary job in responding to the emergency, despite the mounting evidence to the contrary, is an iconic instance of imperial hubris. His aggressive dismissals of calls for aid to Puerto Rico is as much a measure of his disdain for black and brown people as it is an indictment of Puerto Rico's marginality to the American empire. Trump's outrageous outburst is merely another instance of a US official denigrating the people of Puerto Rico.[46] After all, racism is constitutive of colonialism.

Admittedly, no recent US president has so deliberately and openly sought to diminish Puerto Ricans as has Trump. Yet Presidents Clinton, Bush, and Obama each made fateful decisions that set Puerto Rico on a trajectory that has resulted in today's crisis. President Clinton rescinded Section 936 which precipitated Puerto Rico's deindustrialization and is the starting point of the crisis.[47] President Bush demilitarized Puerto Rico, resulting in a loss of hundreds of millions that flowed into the local economy and by failing to provide assistance during the wrenching transition. President Obama approved PROMESA. Each bears a measure of culpability for the crisis that has befallen Puerto Rico.

Puerto Rico reached its apogee as a strategic asset and profitable investment site for US capital between the end of World War II through the Reagan administration. Operation Bootstrap and the establishment of the Estado Libre Asociado were achievements unimaginable in 1898. Puerto Rico's current financial crisis, the erosion of its strategic relevance and the stripping of its limited powers of self-government were unimaginable in 1952. Hurricane María was a dramatically poignant revelation that commonwealth is no longer viable. Puerto Rico has become an anachronistic millstone of a now defunct imperialist logic. It is a territorial possession with no function in the current iteration of the American empire.

Conclusion

The brief period from 2016 to 2019 was as transformative for Puerto Rico as was the 1898/1900 period. On the eve of the 20th century the blunt exercise of United States power and the destructive wrath of nature dragooned Puerto Rico into the American imperial project. For nearly a century Puerto Rico held a privileged status in the American empire. But this ended over two decades ago with the closing of US military bases and after American multinational capital abandoned Puerto Rico. The United States has demonstrated a determination through PROMESA and the courts to compel Puerto Rico's subservience. It has also permitted the social desolation and health crisis caused by Hurricane María to fester.

Ultimately the key difference between the metaphorical bookends is that in 1898/1900 the United States constructed a colony in the service of an expanding empire, whereas in 2016/2019 it is forced to deal with an impoverished colony that is irrelevant to American global aspirations. Hurricane María inflicted such overwhelming human and physical devastation that the junta may have erroneously assumed Puerto Ricans would be inured to the suffering its austerity measures have caused. But the people of Puerto Rico, on the island nation and in the diaspora, are waging a vigorous resistance campaign, are demanding the social justice and equity that they rightly claim is their due as citizens of the United States. The 2019 summer uprising suggest that young people will resist austerity rather than emigrate to the increasingly racially and politically polarized

United States. Older Puerto Ricans marched alongside the intrepid young and demanded with equal vigor that Rosselló resign. Puerto Ricans of all generations have come to the realization that Trump' America is deadly hostile toward Latinos. And Puerto Ricans, despite being US citizens do not think of themselves as Americanos nor are they perceived as such.

The events of 2016–2019 may well mark the death knell of a colonial project nurtured by the myth of US beneficence and enlightened administration. The extraordinary events between 2016 and 2019 gave rise to a new political consciousness and the proliferation of activist and solidary networks, feminist collectives and community-based *centros de apoyos mutuo*. These organizations were in the vanguard of the nation-wide summer uprising of 2019 that forced the resignation of Governor Ricardo Rosselló and has thrown the colonial state into crisis. The massive and sustained popular protests dramatically recast a long-standing portrayal of Puerto Rico as a hapless colony whose people either fatalistically accepted their plight or lamentably were forced to emigrate to the United States. The historically unprecedented uprising was a collective repudiation of the corrupt and incompetent political class that nourishes itself on the resources of the colonial state. The government was astonished that a determined cross-generational movement inexplicably rose to renounce the instrumentalities and agents of colonial oppression.

NOTES

1 Division of War Department. *Report of the Military Governor of Porto Rico on Civil Affairs* (Washington, DC: Government Printing Office,1900), 154. https://archive.org/stream/reportofmilitaryoopuer/reportofmilitaryoopuer_djvu.txt.

2 Puerto Rico. Governor, 1901. Military Government of Porto Rico from October 18, 1898, to April 30, 1900—appendices to the Report of the Military Governor: Epitome of Reports Of: I. The Superior Board of Health. II. The Board of Charities. Washington. 139.

3 Alfred T. Mahan, "The Panama Canal and Sea Power in the Pacific," *The Century Magazine*, 82, no. 2 (June 2, 1911): 243.

4 Stuart B. Schwartz, "The Hurricane of San Ciriaco: Disaster, Politics, and Society in Puerto Rico, 1899–1901," *The Hispanic American Historical Review*, 72, no. 3 (August 1992): 304.

5 I. Ray Tannehill, *Hurricanes: Their Nature and History, Particularly those of the West Indies and the Southern Coasts of the United States* (Princeton: Princeton University Press, 1943), 62.

6 "Hunger in Puerto Rico," *New York Times*, December 26, 1899.

7 Puerto Rico. Governor, *Military government of Porto Rico* (1901), 204.

8 Ibid., 200.

9 Pedro Cabán, *Constructing a Colonial People: Puerto Rico and the United States, 1898–1932*, (Boulder: Westview, 1999), 105.

10 United States. War Department. *Annual Report of the Secretary of War* (Washington: 1900), 5449.

11 Edward J. Berbusse, SJ, (Chapel Hill: University of North Carolina Press, 1966), 104.

12 Puerto Rico. Governor, *Military Government of Porto Rico*, 240.

13 "Hunger in Puerto Rico," *New York Times*, December 26, 1899.

14 Puerto Rico. Governor, *Military Government of Porto Rico*.

15 United States. President. *Message from the President of the United States relative to his recent visit to the island of Porto Rico* (Washington: G.P.O., 1906), 7.

16 Ibid.

17 Puerto Rico. Governor, *Military Government of Porto Rico* (1901), 20.

18 Ibid., 75.

19 See History Task Force, Centro de Estudios Puertorriqueños, *Labor Migration Under Capitalism: The Puerto Rican Experience* (Monthly Review: New York, 1979), especially Chapters 4 and 5.

20 Nishant Kishor, Domingo Marqués, et al., "Mortality in Puerto Rico after Hurricane Maria," *The New England Journal of Medicine* 379 (July 12, 2018): 162–70.

21 Jill Diss, "Hurricane Maria could be a $95 billion storm for Puerto Rico," *CNN Money*. 2017. https://money.cnn.com.

22 Puerto Rican Research and Resources Center, *Puerto Rican Migration: A Preliminary Report* (New York: U.S. Civil Rights Commission, 1971), 15.

23 Antonio Flores and Jens Manuel Krogstad, "Puerto Rico's Population Declined Sharply after Hurricanes Maria and Irma," *Pew Research Center,* July 26, 2019.

24 Edwin Meléndez and Jennifer Hinojosa, "Estimates of Post-Hurricane Maria Exodus from Puerto Rico," *Center for Puerto Rican Studies,* September 20, 2018.

25 Javier Balmaceda, "Puerto Rico Oversight Board Appears Doomed to Recycle Failed Austerity Schemes," *Forbes*, March 22, 2017.

26 William Selway, Ezra Fieser, Jonathan Levin, and Laura Blewitt. "Puerto Rico's $74 Billion Burden Left It Helpless When Maria Hit," 2017, www.bloomberg.com.

27 Sergio M. Marxuach, "El Costo Social del Plan Fiscal," *NOTICEL,* 2018. www.noticel.com.

28 Financial Oversight and Management Board for Puerto Rico, *New Fiscal Plan for Puerto Rico: Restoring Growth and Prosperity,* October 23, 2018.

29 Nydia Velásquez, Elizabeth Warren, et. al, Letter to Mr. José B. Carrión, Chairman, Financial Oversight and Management Board. Puerto Rico Report. October 30, 2018.

30 Pedro Cabán, "Puerto Rico and PROMESA: Reaffirming Colonialism," *New Politics* 16, no. 3 (Summer 2017): 120–25.

31 D. Andrew Austin, "The Puerto Rico Oversight, Management, and Economic Stability Act (Promesa; H.R. 5278 S. 2328)," *Congressional Research Service* (2016): 2.

32 Laura Sullivan, "FEMA Report Acknowledges Failures in Puerto Rico Disaster Response." *NPR*, July 13, 2018.

33 *Congressional Record*, 163, no. 154 (Tuesday, September 26, 2017), H7491-H7492.

34 José Delgado Robles, "Expert Says US Military Could Have Done More in Maria's Response," *El Nuevo Dia*, September 21, 2018.

35 Alice Thomas, "Keeping Faith with Our Fellow Americans: Meeting the Urgent Needs of Hurricane Maria Survivors in Puerto Rico," *Refugees International Field Report*. 2017.

36 United States Department of Homeland Security. Federal Emergency Management Association, 2018. *2017 Hurricane Season FEMA after Action Report*. United States. Government Accountability Office, 2018. *2017 Hurricanes and Wildfires Initial Observations on the Federal Response and Key Recovery Challenges*.

37 Danny Vinik, "How Trump Favored Texas over Puerto Rico," *Politico*, March 27, 2018.

38 Red Apoyo Mutuo de Puerto Rico. RAMPR Network of Support. 2018. https://redapoyomutuo.org/english-1/.

39 See Thomas Mathews, *Puerto Rican Politics and the New Deal* (Gainsville: University of Florida Press, 1960); Geoff G. Burrows, "The New Deal in Puerto Rico: Public Works, Public. Health, and The Puerto Rico Reconstruction Administration, 1935–1955." PhD, History, The Graduate Center of the City University of New York, 2014, 35.

40 Molly Crabapple, Puerto Rico's DYI Disaster Relief, *New York Review of Books Daily*.

41 Kate Aronoff, "As Puerto Rico Erupts in Protests and Governor Resigns, 'La Junta' Eyes More Power." *The Intercept*, July 24, 2019.

42 See José Garriga Picó, "El final del ELA, Promesa y el futuro del estatus," January 7, 2019, *ElVocero.com*.

43 Brandon Carter, "Trump Slams Puerto Rico: 'They Want Everything to Be Done for Them,'" *The Hill*, September 9, 2017.

44 Carla Herreria, "Trump Fumes over Puerto Rico Toll as Death Count Rises for Hurricane Florence," *Huffington Post*, September 15, 2018.

45 See Eileen V. Segarra and María E. Enchautegui Román, *Patrones y Tendencias en el Mal Uso de Fondos Públicos en PR*. (Oficina del Contralor de Puerto Rico, 2010). I would like to thank José Caraballo-Cueto for bringing this study to my attention.

46 Brandon Carter, "Trump Slams Puerto Rico: 'They Want Everything to Be Done for Them,'" *The Hill*, September 9, 2017.

47 José Caraballo-Cueto and Juan Lara. "Deindustrialization and Unsustainable Debt in Middle-Income Countries: The Case of Puerto Rico." *Journal of Globalization and Development* 8, no. 2 (2017).

2

Borders and Crossings

Lessons of the 1980s Central American Solidarity Movement

for 2010s Sanctuary Practices

SUSAN COUTIN

Since the 2016 election of President Trump, who vowed to prioritize removing undocumented immigrants from the United States (Hirschfeld and Preston 2016), "sanctuary" has become a key term both for immigrant rights advocates who seek to protect and empower immigrants regardless of their legal status and for restrictionists who condemn policies that treat the undocumented as members of US communities (Daniels 2018). While these debates focus on student tuition, access to driver's licenses, and police collaboration with Immigration and Customs Enforcement (ICE), the term *sanctuary* dates back to the medieval custom of granting church refuge to fugitives and more recently to the 1980s practice of US congregations declaring themselves sanctuaries for Salvadorans and Guatemalans who were fleeing death squads and civil war in Central America (Bau 1985). Sanctuary practices of the 1980s engaged and sought to counter US imperialism and intervention in Central American countries. By engaging directly with Central Americans who had been forced to migrate and by drawing attention to human rights abuses being perpetrated by governments that the United States supported, sanctuary activists challenged these histories of exclusion.

Drawing on ethnographic engagement with the 1980s movement as well as over three decades of engaged research within Central American immigrant communities in the United States, my contribution describes the conditions that led Central Americans to seek asylum in the United States during the 1980s, the sanctuary practices developed at the time, and the connections between those events and current Central American migration and advocacy.[1] Solidary activists accompanied Central American communities at risk of political violence, pursued changes in refugee and immigration law and policy, and opposed interventionist foreign policies. The 1980s movement laid the groundwork for today's struggles, such as the effort to secure residency for Temporary Protected Status (TPS) recipients, support the Deferred Action for Childhood Arrivals (DACA), aid refugees, and prevent deportations. Yet some sectors of the 1980s movement engaged in paternalistic practices, while the movement's focus on refugee rights fueled hierarchies of deservingness by distinguishing political refugees from economic immigrants. Current solidarity work can avoid these pitfalls by transcending borders, creating alternatives to state-based categories of membership, and building communities of practice. Importantly, transnational activism can counter the histories of exclusion that underlie racialized divisions between citizens and noncitizens.

Political Violence and US Foreign Policy

In the United States, sanctuary practices emerged during the 1980s in response to political violence and civil war that uprooted millions of Central Americans. Central American civil wars were fought over access to land, a more equitable distribution of resources, and political repression. In Guatemala, a US-backed coup in 1954 deposed democratically elected president Jacobo Arbenz Guzmán, and room for political opposition shrank. Repression and entrenched social inequality gave rise to armed insurgency, launching a civil war that lasted until peace accords were signed in 1996. During this period, Guatemalan military and paramilitary groups perpetrated human rights abuses against civilians, especially Indigenous groups, who faced massacres and were forcibly displaced from their villages (Nelson 1999). In El Salvador, right-wing governments opposed reforms and persecuted opponents, including the Catholic Church, which sought to defend the poor. In 1980, Salvadoran Archbishop Oscar Romero was gunned down, a killing that has been attributed to Roberto D'Aubuisson, a Salvadoran military leader who organized death squads and founded the political party ARENA (Alianza Republicana Nacionalista, Nationalist Republican Alliance). Guerrilla groups banded together as the Frente Farabundo Martí para la Liberación Nacional (FMLN, Farabundo Martí National Liberation Front) and fought a twelve-year struggle, from 1980 to 1992, against the Salvadoran Armed Forces. During these years, roadblocks, battles, and massacres were widespread throughout El Salvador, and to prevent civilians from supporting the guerrillas, the Salvadoran Armed Forces strafed the countryside (Byrne 1996). Following peace accords in 1992, the FMLN became a political party and has won the Salvadoran presidency twice. In Nicaragua, the Sandinista National Liberation Front overthrew the dictator Anastasio Somoza in 1979, but the United States supported right-wing insurgents, the Contras, throughout the 1980s.

Adopting a cold war lens, the United States considered Salvadoran and Guatemalan governments to be fighting against communism. Despite widespread human rights abuses, the United States provided extensive military and economic assistance to El Salvador and Guatemala during the 1980s. Because the United States supported repressive governments in El Salvador and Guatemala, accepting refugees from those countries threatened to undermine US foreign policy. In 1984, less than 3 percent of the asylum claims filed by Salvadorans and Guatemalans were granted, in contrast to approval rates in the range of 32 to 60 percent for applicants from Poland, Afghanistan, and Iran (Gzesh 2006). Nicaraguans who came to the United States when the left-leaning Sandinistas were in power were given temporary protection through the Nicaraguan Review Program, which was initiated in 1987 and largely prevented Nicaraguans from being deported (Congressional Research Service 1998).

Consistent with the US government's view that Salvadorans and Guatemalans were undeserving of asylum, US detention centers used coercive practices to pressure Central Americans to leave voluntarily instead of filing asylum claims. Detainees were not informed of their right to apply for asylum, were threatened with lengthy detention, and were prevented from meeting with attorneys. A class action suit, *Orantes Hernández v. Meese*, resulted in a permanent injunction preventing these tactics (Gzesh 2006).

[handwritten margin note: super sketchy]

To counter this discriminatory treatment, advocates pursued redress in the courts while also trying to sway public opinion. During the 1980s, congregations declared themselves "sanctuaries" for Salvadoran and Guatemalan refugees in order to advocate for asylum while also challenging US aid to Salvadoran and Guatemalan governments.

Sanctuary Practices and Legacies

The term "sanctuary" has been used to refer to a place of safety, a sacred space governed by "higher" law and open to the most deeply stigmatized (Bau 1985). Sanctuary designations infuse spaces with contested legal, religious, moral, or ethical meanings, differentiating them from surrounding areas (see also Mountz 2013). Today, cities, states, and campuses have adopted the term "sanctuary" for policies that make particular jurisdictions, spaces, and institutions places of safety for noncitizens. Sanctuary policies may prohibit local police from enforcing federal immigration law, protect individuals' records from disclosure, and extend rights to individuals regardless of immigration status (Bauder 2017; Ridgley 2008). California, for example, has enabled undocumented students at public universities to pay in-state tuition rates, granted driver's licenses to the undocumented, and shortened criminal sentences to prevent noncitizens from incurring immigration consequences for certain criminal convictions (Ramakrishnan and Colbern 2015). Current sanctuary measures thus range from noncooperation with enforcement initiatives to active inclusion of noncitizens.

[handwritten margin note: Specifically noncitizens]

[handwritten margin note: sanctuary policies]

Sanctuary activists of the 1980s deployed "sanctuary" in a somewhat different fashion (Coutin 1993). Invoking the medieval tradition of church refuge for fugitives, they defined sanctuary both more narrowly—in most instances limiting sanctuary to Central American refugees rather than to all undocumented immigrants—and more broadly, in that many activists sought not only to provide food, shelter, transportation, medical care, and legal assistance to refugees

[handwritten margin note: in 80's only. to central American refugees]

but also to impact conditions in refugees' homelands. The 1980s sanctuary movement was therefore deeply transnational, responding as much to human rights violations in Central America and US support for authoritarian governments as to denying refuge to Central Americans. Sanctuary activists of the 1980s therefore not only supported Central Americans who had come to the United States but also sent delegations to threatened communities in Central America, reasoning that having an international presence in threatened communities could provide a measure of safety. Sanctuary workers referred to such work as *accompaniment*, seeking to extend sanctuary to those who had not yet fled. Accompaniment required a deep commitment in that it exposed sanctuary workers, to a limited degree, to spaces of illegality and persecution where refugees were located. Thus, activists who brought Central Americans across the United States–Mexico border, housed them, and transported them to places of safety risked becoming "illegal" or "criminal" themselves, though clearly the consequences of criminalization were not as severe for US workers as for Central American asylum seekers. Likewise, sanctuary activists who traveled to Central America felt that they were putting their bodies on the line, though Central American activists ran higher risks and often paid higher prices (Coutin 1993). In addition, movement members helped Central Americans navigate the US detention system. Some participants took out mortgages on their homes to raise money to bond Central Americans out of detention, while others served as guardians so that detained children could be released.

The dilemmas experienced by 1980s sanctuary activists may be instructive to immigrant rights advocates today. One key area of disagreement was whether to form a national structure in order to better coordinate sanctuary work or to remain a loosely knit coalition of diverse congregations, each of which was free to develop its own approach. Similar debates have arisen today among student activists who are sometimes suspicious of hierarchical organizational structures or the limitations of being a nonprofit (Nicholls 2013). Sanctuary activists of the 1980s also generally distinguished Central American refugees from what movement participants considered to be economic immigrants from other countries. They therefore argued that under both US and international law, those fleeing persecution had legal rights to asylum that other immigrants did not enjoy. Activists debated whether Central Americans who were fleeing the guerrilla forces were as deserving of sanctuary as those fleeing death squads and the military. From a humanitarian standpoint, each might be at risk, but some argued that helping the former undercut the movement's political goals. Some congregations limited sanctuary offers to refugees who were willing to give public testimonies, arguing that such talks publicized stories that the US government sought to hide. If sanctuary were not public, they reasoned, then it would only be a Band-Aid on the wounds of war and would not address root causes. Other congregations, in contrast, contended that it was unethical to require persecution victims to speak publicly and that assistance should be driven by need rather than politics. Finally, Central American organizers played key roles in mobilizing US religious activists, but US activists often had greater resources than their Central American counterparts. Some Central Americans resented the pejorative connotations of the term "refugee." One Salvadoran participant recalled, "I used to go around and they would look at me, the exotic refugee, and say, 'Wow! You have two legs just like white people and you walk just like white people!'" (Coutin 1993, 120).

Despite these dilemmas, 1980s work has had important legacies. The 1990 Immigration Act created Temporary Protected Status (TPS) and designated Salvadorans as the first recipients. Since that time, TPS has been an important temporary immigration remedy for individuals whose countries have suffered a civil conflict or natural disaster. As of April 2018, more than three hundred thousand individuals from ten different countries held this status, though the Trump administration has been rescinding countries' TPS designations (National Immigration Forum 2018). Also, after sanctuary activists were put on trial for conspiracy and alien smuggling in 1986, movement members sued the federal government for discriminating against Central Americans in the asylum process. This case, known as "American Baptist Churches v. Thornburgh," or "ABC," was settled out of court in 1991, creating special rules for these asylum applicants. Then, after 1996 legal reforms threatened Central Americans' abilities to remain in the United States, Congress passed the Nicaraguan Adjustment and Central American Relief Act (NACARA), which created a process for ABC class members to become lawful permanent residents. Later, in 2012, when student activists successfully pressured President Obama to create DACA, TPS served as a template for establishing this new program. Solidarity workers who were involved in 1980s sanctuary work went on to other organizations and initiatives, such as providing water or medical assistance to border crossers. Some 1980s sanctuary congregations are once again opening their doors to individuals at risk of deportation (Southside Presbyterian Church n.d.)

Post-War Migration and Continued Exclusion

In 2018, US Attorney General Jeff Sessions announced that all unauthorized border crossers would be federally prosecuted and that domestic violence and gang violence generally would no longer be considered grounds for awarding asylum. These sound like reversals of US policy, but in fact, for those who have been analyzing asylum since the 1980s, there is significant continuity between these policies and decades of excluding Central American asylum seekers from the human rights protections afforded by US and international law. While on its surface asylum law is politically neutral, in reality, concerns about admitting asylees from nearby countries and from regimes that the United States supports have led to disparate outcomes for citizens of these nations.

During the post-war years, violence in Central American countries shifted from war to gangs and crime. Continued violence is due to multiple factors: impunity granted to perpetrators of abuses, an abundance of weapons, corruption, income inequality, the trauma of the war years, the rise of drug cartels, and US. deportation policies, which sent US-based gang members to Central American countries (Beltrán 2017). Central American families—particularly in the Northern triangle of Guatemala, Honduras, and El Salvador—experienced extreme insecurity including forcible recruitment, extortion, sexual violence, assault, and murder. Yet, just as during the war years, the US government has argued that the violence experienced by Central Americans is generally not grounds for political asylum. For example, in a 2008 Board of Immigration Appeals decision, three Salvadoran youths who had been beaten, harassed, and threatened with death and rape for refusing to join the MS-13 gang were denied asylum, even though another youth in their neighborhood who had also refused to join was shot and killed, and despite evidence of similar practices throughout the country (*Matter of S-E-G-* 2008).

As asylum continued to be restrictive, immigrants in the United States underwent criminalization that increased their risk of deportation. Immigration reforms adopted in 1996 expanded the range of criminal convictions that brought immigration consequences, restricted avenues for legalization, and made detention mandatory for many (Morawetz 2000). Secure Communities and related programs increased collaboration between police, prisons, and immigration authorities, with the result that, for noncitizens, coming in contact with the criminal justice system could result in removal (Chacón 2012). Prosecution of immigration violations escalated to the point that these now comprise a significant portion of the federal docket (Gramlich and Bialik 2017). Individuals who were basically from the United States and who may even have acquired lawful permanent residency were being removed permanently, resulting in devastating family separations.

Current policies toward Central Americans continue this history of criminalization and asylum denials by defining the violence that is part of everyday lives as outside the boundaries of protection. President Trump has repeatedly associated Central Americans with crime and gangs, for example, referring to their homelands as "shithole countries" (Bonner 2018) and associating MS-13 with all who enter the country without authorization, even though criminologists have consistently found that the foreign born commit fewer crimes on average than do those born in the United States (Ousey and Kubrin 2009). Advocates successfully made the legal case for domestic violence and gang violence as a basis for asylum, but even before Sessions overruled these rationales, such cases were very difficult to win, with 75 to 80 percent of such claims being denied (Morrissey 2018). A key impact of Sessions's opinion rejecting domestic and gang violence as grounds for asylum is that asylum seekers will not pass credible fear interviews and therefore will be unable to submit their claims. Furthermore, the TPS that had been issued to Salvadorans and Hondurans in the wake of natural disasters has been rescinded despite ongoing violence in Honduras and El Salvador.

Likewise, the family separations that have garnered attention since the Trump administration adopted a zero tolerance policy on unauthorized border crossings are not new. Central American and other immigrant families have been undergoing separations due to restricted legalization opportunities, inability to travel legally, deportation, and prosecution. Current separations of parents and children are a particularly cruel manifestation of the lack of respect for the principle of family unity.

1980s Sanctuary Practices and Solidarity Work Today

The 1980s sanctuary movement declined during the 1990s as peace accords were signed in El Salvador and Guatemala, but the US government's continued failure to observe the rights of immigrants, asylum seekers, and travelers has given rise to new challenges and new forms of activism. A key challenge is that the securitization of immigration law has vilified immigrants, depicting them as potential terrorists, criminals, and security risks (Menjívar 2014). The administration of US immigration policy moved from the Department of Labor, where it was originally housed, to the Department of Justice and now to the Department of Homeland Security. Immigration reforms that were adopted in 1996 broadened the range of criminal convictions that have immigration consequences, restricted opportunities for legalization, and expanded funding for enforcement (Morawetz 2000; Kanstroom 2007). The federal government has promoted partnerships with prison officials and local police agencies in order to detain noncitizens who come into contact with law enforcement, even for minor infractions such as traffic tickets. Immigration forms now have pages of security-related questions, such as "Have you EVER advocated (either directly or indirectly) the overthrow of any government by force or violence?" (US Citizenship and Immigration Services, 12); "Did you EVER recruit(ask), enlist (sign up), conscript (require), or use any person under 15 years of age to serve in or help an armed force or group?" (14); and "Have you EVER . . . Been a habitual drunkard?" (15). The overpolicing of communities of color has exacerbated the criminalization of immigrants.

Immigrant rights activists have sought to counter this sort of vilification through narratives of deservingness. For instance, Pedro, an LA-based student activist whom I interviewed in 2010, argued that sharing personal narrative was a way to overcome the divisiveness of immigration debates and the limitations of categories such as "illegal alien." When asked for an example of such a narrative, Pedro replied:

> I would say something like, "My name is Pedro, my family came here in search of a better life because we had a dream and our dream was for us to—for me to have a better education. And right now I'm going to college, and I work hard, and my family has sacrificed so much, and we're just as American as anybody else. And so we want an opportunity to be successful so that—I want an opportunity to be successful so I can give back. And maybe I didn't come here with the right documents, but I have the right values. Ah, my mom has taught me the value of hard-work. She works at a hotel, um, every day. And so she's given back to this country. She's paying taxes. And so I think you ought just—I just want an opportunity to succeed and also give back to my community that I love, and give back to this country that I love and that has given me so much."

Pedro's narrative defines belonging as a matter of exhibiting "American values"— sacrifice, love of country, contributing to the common good, hard work, seeking opportunity—rather than having the right papers. He thus articulates the "Dreamer" narrative that has fueled the immigrant youth movement and that President Obama also indirectly invoked by referring to "felons, not families" as the group that should be deported. Such narratives of student success can also draw an implied contrast with youths who drop out of high school, join gangs, or acquire criminal records, suggesting that the latter are undeserving. As a gang violence prevention worker complained to me during a 2007 interview, "Like in these recent marches, the immigrant campaign for legalization was divided. 'Do we stand up for the clean-cut immigrant? Or also for the criminal who is part of our community?' And they largely decided to stand up for the clean-cut immigrant."

Some student activists have rejected narratives that distinguish between deserving and undeserving immigrants. For example, Carla, a student leader interviewed in 2016, referred to this distinction as an example of "respectability politics,"[2] noting that the "good immigrant" narrative bases deservingness in characteristics associated with white, heterosexual, middle-class society (see Keyes 2011; Vargas 1997). She explained,

> 'Respectability politics' is wanting everyone in your group to be good so that those outside can say, 'Oh, they are so good that I am going to give them this, because they are so similar to us'—and blah, blah, blah. While more radical activism says, 'Yes, we are different. We have different ideals. That doesn't matter. We have these ideals and we are going to follow what we want and you have to give us our rights even though we are anti-patriotic, though we are LGBT, though we are single

mothers. That is, we don't have to be . . . the perfect people in a white family. We are different and just the same, we deserve our rights.

Likewise, another student activist, Reese, argued "What I would like to see is mainly just like move away from the Dream Act narrative. And instead talk a lot more about undocumented workers, undocumented parents, LGBTQ immigrants, um, even like undocumented Black immigrants because nobody ever, ever talks about them, and they do exist." Through these comments, Carla and Reese reject what they see as exclusionary definitions of deservingness and instead embrace groups, such as single mothers or LGBTQ immigrants, that deviate from white, patriarchal, heterosexual norms. Reese extended inclusion to criminals.

Ending the repeated exclusion of Central American asylum seekers would require bringing asylum policies into alignment with the forms of violence that actually occur on a regular basis in the communities that these individuals are fleeing and then zealously enforcing these protections. Doing so would promote family integrity, support human rights, and alter the dynamics of the historic relationship between the United States and Central American nations.

Conclusion

This short discussion of 1980s sanctuary practices raises several questions for further reflection. First, to what degree can current sanctuary and solidarity work transcend borders? It is important to reconnect migrants and deportees to their families, communities, and histories, and to challenge transborder enforcement initiatives and neocolonial relationships by creating ties with affected communities. Second, can activists devise alternatives to state-based categories of membership? Reese, one of the student activists quoted above, argued that the immigrant rights movement should not only focus on securing a pathway to citizenship for the undocumented but also on attaining social equity so that all would enjoy rights. She explained, "This isn't just for immigrants, you know. It's for . . . all communities of color, that everybody has . . . fair access to education, housing, employment." Reese saw true inclusion as overcoming not only the boundaries between citizens and the undocumented but also between dominant society and other historically marginalized groups. Third, what would it mean for allies and institutions to adopt the principle of accompaniment today? In current activist circles, expressions of solidarity sometimes take the form of transcending difference by claiming, for example, "We are all _____," and then listing the name or location of the victim of a tragedy. Also, at immigrant rights rallies and marches, participants have expressed solidarity with each other, regardless of legal status (see figure 2.1). Applying a principle of accompaniment

Figure 2.1. "Protect each other: unafraid" sign at September 2017 rally in Santa Ana, California, protesting President Trump's rescission of the Deferred Actions for Childhood Arrivals (DACA) program. Photo by Susan Coutin.

in a university setting could mean enabling everyone to attend college regardless of legal status and financial resources as well as taking on something of the condition of illegality experienced by those who are undocumented.

Exploring the contemporary implications of 1980s sanctuary practices reveals the historical embeddedness of forms of resistance as well as the hidden legacies of earlier historical moments. Current activism deploys previously devised tactics in innovative ways (Tilly 2006), such as adapting the notion of "sanctuary" to policies governing interaction between local police and federal authorities (Ridgley 2008). In so doing, earlier forms of resistance are brought forward in time (Coutin 2011) in ways that challenge political violence, complicity, and the denial of rights and humanity. Also, current policy achievements may bear traces of earlier moments of resistance. Uncovering these legacies is a means of revealing hidden, long-term contributions of earlier struggles as well as the circuitous paths that successes sometimes take. Knowledge of such histories reveals that activism can bear fruit in unforeseen ways and suggests alternatives to current political realities. In particular, it helps to create spaces and temporalities in which membership is already achieved and divisions based on nationality, immigration status, or geographic location have the potential to be transcended. These alternate spaces and temporalities are key to acknowledging US colonial and imperial relationships and to imagining another, more just, world.

NOTES

1 My analysis of sanctuary practices derives from my experience doing research about and volunteering with sanctuary- and community-based immigrant rights groups over more than three decades. As a doctoral student in the 1980s, I began my research career writing about the US sanctuary movement. From 1986 to 1988, I participated in sanctuary activities in Tucson, Arizona, and in the San Francisco East Bay. I attended church services, meetings, and rallies, helped to document asylum claims, translated at public events, did volunteer tasks, collected news articles about the movement, studied the transcripts of the 1986 Tucson sanctuary trial, and interviewed more than one hundred movement participants. During the 1990s, I continued to study political and legal advocacy regarding Central American immigrants, this time by working with Central American community groups in Los Angeles. In the 2000s, I built on this earlier work through a study of the significance of the Salvadoran immigrant population for both El Salvador and the United States, and I also carried out research regarding the experiences of 1.5 generation immigrants who were born in El Salvador and raised in the United States. My current research, in the 2010s, has focused on the roles that documents of various sorts play in immigrants' legal cases and also on the forms of executive relief—such as DACA—created by the Obama administration. Throughout all of these projects, I've straddled the line between being a researcher who produces academic work and an activist/volunteer who is affiliated with movements and organizations.

2 Carla may be drawing on the work of Evelyn Brooks Higginbotham (1993).

REFERENCES

Bau, Ignatius. *This Ground Is Holy: Church Sanctuary and Central American Refugees.* New York: Paulist, 1985.

Bauder, Harald. "Sanctuary Cities: Policies and Practices in International Perspective." *International Migration*, 55, no. 2 (2017): 174–87.

Beltrán, Adriana. "Children and Families Fleeing Violence in Central America." *Washington Office on Latin America (WOLA)*. February 21, 2017. www.wola.org.

Bonner, Raymond. "America's Role in El Salvador's Deterioration." *Atlantic,* Jan 20, 2018. www.theatlantic.com.

Byrne, Hugh. 1996 *El Salvador's Civil War: A Study of Revolution.* Boulder: Lynne Riebber.

Chacón, Jennifer M. "Overcriminalizing Immigration." *Journal of Criminal Law and Criminology* 102 (2012): 613–52.

Congressional Research Service. "The Nicaraguan Adjustment and Central American Relief Act: Hardship Relief and Long-term Illegal Aliens." July 15, 1998. www.everycrsreport.com.

Coutin, Susan Bibler. 1993. *The Culture of Protest: Religious Activism and the U.S. Sanctuary Movement.* Boulder: Westview Press.

Coutin, Susan Bibler. "Falling Outside: Excavating the History of Central American Asylum Seekers." *Law & Social Inquiry* 36, no. 3: 569–96.

Daniels, Jeff. "Trump Throws His Support Behind Orange County in its War Against the California Sanctuary State." CNBC, March 28, 2018, www.cnbc.com.

Gramlich, John, and Kristen Bialik. "Immigration Offenses Make Up a Growing Share of Federal Arrests." *Pew Research Center*, April 10, 2017. www.pewresearch.org.

Gzesh, Susan. "Central Americans and Asylum Policy in the Reagan Era." *Migration Policy Institute,* April 1, 2006. www.migrationpolicy.org.

Harris, Lindsay M., and Morgan M. Weibel. "*Matter of S-E-G-:* The Final Nail in the Coffin for Gang-Related Asylum Claims." *La Raza Law Journal* 20 (2015): 5–30.

Higginbotham, Evelyn Brooks. 1993. *Righteous Discontent: The Women's Movement in the Black Baptist church, 1880–1920.* Cambridge: Harvard University Press.

Hirschfeld, Julie, and Julia Preston. "What Donald Trump's Vow to Deport up to 3 Million Immigrants Would Mean." *New York Times,* November 14, 2016. www.nytimes.com.

Kanstroom, Daniel. 2007. *Deportation Nation: Outsiders in American History.* Harvard University Press.

Keyes, Elizabeth. "Beyond Saints and Sinners: Discretion and the Need for New Narratives in the US Immigration System." *Georgetown Immigration Law Journal* 26 (2011): 207–56.

Matter of S-E-G-. 24 I&N Dec. 579 (BIA 2008).

Menjívar, Cecilia. "Immigration Law Beyond Borders: Externalizing and Internalizing Border Controls in an Era of Securitization." *Annual Review of Law and Social Science* 10 (2014): 353–69.

Morawetz, Nancy. "Understanding the Impact of the 1996 Deportation Laws and the Limited Scope of Proposed Reforms." *Harvard Law Review* 113, no. 8 (2000): 1936–62.

Morrissey, Kate. "How Likely Are Asylum-Seekers from Central American Caravans to Win their Cases?" *Los Angeles Times,* May 6, 2018. www.latimes.com.

Mountz, Alison. "Political Geography I: Reconfiguring Geographies of Sovereignty." *Progress in Human Geography* 37, no. 6 (2013): 829–41.

National Immigration Forum. "Fact Sheet: Temporary Protected Status (TPS)." Accessed February 2020. https://immigrationforum.org.

Nelson, Diane M. 1999. *A Finger in the Wound: Body Politics in Quincentennial Guatemala.* Berkeley: University of California Press.

Nicholls, Walter J. 2013. *The DREAMers: How the Undocumented Youth Movement Transformed the Immigrant Rights Debate.* Palo Alto: Stanford University Press.

Ousey, Graham C., and Charis E. Kubrin. "Exploring the Connection between Immigration and Violent Crime Rates in US cities, 1980–2000." *Social Problems* 56, no. 3 (2009): 447–73.

Ramakrishnan, K., & Colbern, A. "The 'California Package' of Immigrant Integration and the Evolving Nature of State Citizenship." UCLA Institute for Research on Labor and Employment. Accessed May 3, 2018. http://irle.ucla.edu.

Ridgley, Jennifer. "Cities of Refuge: Immigration Enforcement, Police, and the Insurgent Genealogies of Citizenship in US Sanctuary Cities." *Urban Geography* 29, no. 1 (2008): 53–77.

Southside Presbyterian Church. "Sanctuary: An Ancient Tradition of Faith Communities." Accessed February 9, 2020. www.southsidepresbyterian.org.

Tilly, Charles. 2006. *Regimes and Repertoires.* Chicago: University of Chicago Press.

US Citizenship and Immigration Services. N-400, Application for Naturalization. September 17, 2019 (revised November 13, 2020). www.uscis.gov/n-400.

Vargas, Sylvia R. Lazos. "Deconstructing Homo[geneous] Americanus: The White Ethnic Immigrant Narrative and its Exclusionary Effect." *Tulsa Law Review* 72 (1997): 1493–596.

3

"A Cartel Built for Love"

"Medellín," Pablo Escobar, and the Scripts of Global Colombianidad

MARÍA ELENA CEPEDA

"Please give me all of your books on the life of Pablo Escobar and the history of that time period in Medellín." My request to the book clerk at the Libreria Nacional in Medellín's upscale Poblado district was simple, yet I was quite torn about it. My accent betrayed the fact that I am not *paisa*,[1] or a native of the Antioquia department where Medellín, Colombia's second-largest city, is located. I wondered if the store clerk thought of me as yet another troublesome rubbernecker, an outsider fascinated by the city's violent recent past and its most famous local son, the alternatively adored and reviled Pablo Escobar, dead since 1993 yet still alive in the global and local popular imaginations. Unfailingly polite, the tall, well-postured Afro-Colombian man in his late thirties released a low sigh and dutifully headed off to the back of the store. I felt rather guilty; it is, after all, quite taxing to be endlessly connected to a virulent set of stereotypes regarding masculinist violence, drug trafficking, corruption, intergenerational trauma, and forced displacement.

This chapter frames these stereotypes—or ideas about Colombia, Medellín, and Pablo Escobar—as cultural narratives that, along with US interventionism and Colombia's potent regionalism, inform the performances of current Colombian stars such as Maluma and broader social scripts about global Colombianidad. In this context, "global Colombianidad" references the regimes of representation that encompass Colombian subjects, including those in the diaspora. The essay discusses the ongoing effects of Colombia's more than fifty-year civil conflict[2] on the development of Medellín, focusing on the narratives around Pablo Escobar and their impact on local and global understandings of the city. It also underscores the centrality of Colombian regionalism and racialized spaces on popular scripts of Colombian identities. Finally, in order to illustrate the centrality of these imposed and organic metanarratives on external conceptualizations of global Colombianidad, I conduct a textual analysis of the 2019 music video "Medellín," a recent collaboration between US performer Madonna and Medellín native and reggaetón superstar Maluma. By deconstructing "Medellín," I demonstrate the ways in which popular cultural scripts about regional identities reverberate globally. More specifically, I argue that we must read global

Colombianidad through the lenses of racialized regionalism and heteropatriarchy, frameworks that deeply inform the ways in which all Colombians are represented, from both within the community as well as from without. The salience of Maluma's localized paisa identity and its impacts on our understanding of Colombian identities reminds us that within the nation and among its diaspora, Colombianidad remains hotly contested. As such, "the concept of one Colombian nation or a national Colombian identity remains, for most, elusive," and as the example of "Medellín" highlights, is most often presented in global media from the perspective of those on the outside looking in (Fanta Castro, Herrero-Olaizola, and Rutter-Jensen, 2017, 2).

US Interventionism in Colombia: Localized Impacts

For over fifty years, Colombia has been engaged in a protracted civil war, the longest of any nation in the Western hemisphere. Since the 1990s, Colombia has also held the dubious distinction of being the most violent country in the region, with the worst human rights record, the highest number of murdered trade unionists, and the world's largest population of internal refugees. On November 24, 2016, the country signed an official peace agreement.[3] While generalized violence has abated since its signing, targeted assassinations—specifically of social leaders and human rights activists—have increased, rendering it impossible to speak yet of a "post-conflict" Colombia. Both of the two most prominent warring factions in Colombia's dirty war, the various guerrilla groups and paramilitary forces, have committed grave human rights violations. Yet notably, since their emergence as US-trained counterinsurgency forces in the 1960s, solely the paramilitary forces have enjoyed intimate ties to the Colombian ruling establishment and are responsible for approximately 80 percent of all human rights violations.[4] This is particularly true in the case of Antioquia and Medellín (Baca and Jiménez 2018; Dyer 2019; Hristov 2009), where the more generalized violence of recent years continues to reverberate in ways that reflect the profound influence of US interventionism. One prominent example is Plan Colombia (2000–2015), a US-backed, ten-billion-dollar counternarcotics initiative first championed by the governments of Andrés Pastrana (1998–2002) and Bill Clinton (1993–2001). Under Plan Colombia, US taxpayers funded the mass aerial fumigation of coca crops in Colombia, a strategy that was ultimately halted due to widespread reports of communal displacement, serious health concerns, and the damage of food crops. Plan Colombia also enabled the Colombian government to siphon money to paramilitary death squads responsible for many of the era's most egregious human rights violations under the guise of counterinsurgency efforts. President Juan Manuel Santos (2010–2018) ended the program in 2015 due to its devastating health and environmental effects. However, under pressure of decertification by the Trump government,[5] by October 2018 the Iván Duque administration (2018–) had initiated a pilot program of aerial fumigation in Antioquia, a long-standing seat of paramilitary power (King and Wherry 2018).

By fall 2019, resistance against the Duque administration and its policies reached an apex. Following mass protests in other parts of South America, a diverse array of Colombians took to the streets on November 21, 2019, for the first in a series of national strikes that quickly became violent. Protesters contested Duque's refusal to implement the 2016 peace accords, potential new austerity measures, and the ongoing violence perpetuated by the armed forces, among other issues. The protests resulted in four deaths, including that of eighteen-year-old Dilan Cruz at the hands of ESMAD riot police, a tragedy that became a rallying point for protestors. Protests quickly spread across the country, including to major industrial centers such as Medellín.

Since Pablo Escobar's spectacular 1993 death on a Medellín rooftop, the city has witnessed not the end of its narco-capital status but a "fusion of politics, property and organized crime, reflected in the paramilitary grip over security for capital investment [that] links the city's bad old days to its good new ones, and largely determines the present and future shape of the built environment" (Hylton 2008, 83, 85). Under Escobar, Medellín emerged as the homicide capital of the world; between 1982 and 2002, more than seventy thousand were murdered in the city, mostly young men. Tied to the presence of paramilitary groups in the region, Medellín's violence was indelibly marked by Cold War counterinsurgency tactics designed to "clean up" the city (Hylton 2008, 38). Medellín's current housing and construction boom—indeed, its self-styled rebirth as the "best corner of the Americas" (Hylton 2008, 41)—would not be possible without the massive influx of cocaine capital. Currently awash in conspicuous consumption, Medellín has not left behind the cutting inequality of its past, yet it has still undergone a major makeover not unnoticed by the world press or the Latin music industry. Medellín's series of "cosmetic operations" enabled the traditionally conservative city to emerge by 2007 as more of a boomtown than Los Angeles and New York combined. Remarkably, by 2008 the murder rate in the city had decreased sixfold, lower than the homicide rates of Detroit, Washington, DC, and Baltimore (Hylton 2008, 71–72).

Tracing the Pablo Escobar Narrative: Local and Global Readings

The memory of Medellín native Pablo Emilio Escobar Gaviria (1949–1993) constitutes "a painful wound in the Colombian psyche," given its intimate association with violence, corruption, and terrorism (Pobutsky 2017, 282). His myth is also a source of considerable dispute, or a "living construct, a crossroad of ideologies navigated and fueled by conflicting interests" (Pobutsky 2017, 287). Much like the civil war that officially raged in Colombia for more than half a century, Escobar's myth is mired in discord. Alternatively cast as a social bandit or as a criminal,

Escobar is also read by some as a visionary master of global economics or as a scapegoat unjustly castigated in what essentially amounted to a "national orgy of greed and power" (Pobutsky 2017, 283–84).

Nearly thirty years after his death at the hands of Colombian federal agents, the tension surrounding Escobar's life testifies to the enduring power of regimes of representation. In what she refers to as Escobar's "cultural renaissance," Aldona Bialowas Pobutsky demonstrates how Escobar looms large in popular outlaw folklore, a genre defined by tabloid-style writing and characterized above all by sensational anecdotes. Fans of popular outlaw folklore, hungry for an unvarnished glimpse of the "authentic" Pablo, eagerly consume the products detailing his every habit and idiosyncrasy, humanizing him in the process. Rather than examining Escobar's societal impact, his drug empire and actions, such outlaw folklore aims to recast the past from a "personal" angle steeped in equal parts fiction and personalization. In this regard, the specter of Pablo Escobar as past and present media spectacle haunts the Colombian popular imagination as much as it shapes global conceptualizations of Colombianidad (Pobutsky 2013, 684–685). The hypermasculine, regionally inflected musical production of local artists such as Maluma reanimates the Escobar narrative for the global reggaetón stage and beyond.

The Paisa Reggaetón Machine: Interrogating the Myth of Regionalized Whiteness

Not even born until the year after Escobar's death, Maluma is still inextricably tied to the ever-present Pablo Escobar national narrative of the 1980s and 1990s. Informed by the discursive stylings of a heavily commodified magical realism as well as a "dirty realism" (Herrero-Olaizola 2007, 43–44), the culture industry built around the Escobar narrative constitutes a source of distress and resentment for many Colombians. Simultaneously, the endless accumulation of tell-all books, films, games, and television series simultaneously provide a significant source of capital for many. These are mediated reiterations of the masculinist violence that has defined contemporary Colombian history (Anderson 2018; Cepeda 2010; Cepeda 2018; Herrero-Olaizola 2007; Ochoa Camacho 2016; Pobutsky 2013; Pobutsky 2017). Escobar's hometown of Medellín has emerged as a protagonist in and of itself in a transnational culture industry that monetizes the pain and marginalization of an entire nation and its diaspora. Maluma's performances of Colombianidad not only reference the Escobar narrative in a manner that benefits him monetarily; they also reinscribe the heteropatriarchal underpinnings and ethnoracial dynamics of much of the contemporary reggaetón scene.

Among the ongoing developments within the global reggaetón industry, including its emergent Medellín-based branch, figures the widely critiqued "whitening" of the genre, a move that goes hand in hand with the music's globalization.[6] This whitening expresses itself most notably in the ethnoracial makeup of the reggaetón's most visible performers as well as in the language favored by those same individuals. Significantly, Rivera-Rideau reminds us that despite its firm grounding in Puerto Rico and more recently in Medellín, we must understand reggaetón as simultaneously local *and* global. As she maintains, it has been "routed" through specific geographic locales that are in turn "rooted" in local communities possessing their own singular understandings of race, class, gender, and national identity (Rivera-Rideau 2015, 16). Some of these specific local articulations are voiced in the Medellín context by recent noteworthy migrants to the Medellín music scene such as Puerto Rican reggaetón star Nicky Jam, who moved to the city in 2007 to reignite his career. As he has stated in interviews, Nicky Jam ties Colombian reggaetón's success (versus that of Puerto Rico) to its greater reliance on "everyday" lyrics (Katz 2017; Moreno 2016) or the ostensibly less localized (and differentially racialized) speech of the Hispanic Caribbean. I would affirm that this linguistic shift in reggaetón's specific racialization, which features a subjectively more "global" variety of Spanish—or the hegemonic accent and lexicon of the South American Andes—rests on the logic that certain varieties of Spanish are inherently superior and more "neutral," "international," (Uribe Yepes 2018; Caramanica 2017) and unmarked than others, an assessment that can also be applied by extension to the speakers of those particular types of Spanish. This example of the neutralization or much-critiqued whitening of reggaetón portends an aesthetic deracination of the music and its performers, one that is pointedly rooted in the erasure of Blackness and that can be traced in large part to dominant US readings of Latina/o/x racial identity as well as localized understandings of race.[7] This is significant, as since its origins, the Afro-Caribbean genre has been noted for its critique of racism and more specifically anti-Blackness (Rivera-Rideau and Torres-Leschnik 2019, 89). I would argue, moreover, that the intensified movement away from Blackness under the hegemony of the Medellín reggaetón industry is no accident, given the long-standing discourse around whiteness in Antioquia.

As in much of the Americas, regionalist discourse in Colombia has historically been framed in oppositional terms (Appelbaum 2003, 39). For example, natives of the Caribbean coast are stereotypically less inclined toward hard work, whereas inhabitants of the nation's highlands are "naturally" industrious. These epistemological frameworks span time and space, informing intergenerational and diasporic understandings of Colombianidad. Shaping not only local but ultimately also global constructs of race, gender, nation, and desire, "[i]n Colombia, history gave race a regional structure such that race cannot be simply understood as a social construction around phenotype, but must also be seen as a social construction around region" (Wade 1991, 46). Within this context, the identity of Antioquia highlands natives, such as Maluma, has long been closely associated with civilization, capitalism, labor, and ultimately whiteness (Tubb

2013, 627), a discursive correlation notably present in local narratives about the late Pablo Escobar. Within Colombia, the *raza antioqueña* (or the "Antioquian race" of the Antioquia department) has long been considered superior, premised on a supposed mixture of Jew, Creole, and Spaniard and corresponding stereotypes of hardworking, astute, and entrepreneurial populations (Rojas 2002, 30). "The white legend" or the myth of paisa whiteness thus boasts an extensive history born of racialized regionalism, and it is rooted in the profound sense of regional exceptionalism undergirding Antioquia's racial claims (Appelbaum 2003, 12; Tubb 2013, 633).

Medellín native Maluma references narco-trafficking and Escobar in his music as part of a performance of street credibility and authenticity, two hallmarks of a successful reggaetón persona. While performing a hegemonic Colombianidad through an exaggerated articulation of heterosexual, cisgendered, Andean, urban, affluent masculinity, Maluma embodies the "neutral," "global" (read: white) face that has increasingly come to characterize contemporary reggaetón. This is part of the driving logic of ethnoracial identity, gender, sexuality, and nation that undergirds collaborations such as that of Madonna and Maluma.

Madonna, Maluma, and the Disparate Performances of Global Colombianidad

Released globally on April 24, 2019, the music video for "Medellín"[8] represents a move toward a generically pop sound for Maluma, and a key step in his efforts—as well as those of Madonna—toward securing a broader global audience. In the press, Maluma has been open about the impacts of his collaboration with Madonna, describing it as "a huge step for my culture, for Latin culture, it's very, very big" (Nolfi 2019). His remarks index both local ("my [Colombian/paisa] culture") and global ("Latin culture") reverberations of "Medellín," based not only on album sales but also with respect to an enhanced visibility for Latina/x/o artists on the international stage.[9] Leah Perry (2016) traces Madonna's entanglement with Latinidad back to her 1984 video for the hit single "Borderline." In both "Medellín" and "Borderline," Madonna styles herself "both as an alluring sex object and as a transgressor of established boundaries" (Kellner, qtd. in Perry, 2016, 2). Her seemingly subversive tactics in "Medellín" constitute a "commodity of diversity as subversion—turning it, and herself, into a product" that has ultimately benefitted Madonna (and, in the case of "Medellín," Maluma) economically (Perry 2016, 21).

"Medellín" is best read through a polysemic lens or an interpretive approach that foregrounds the potential for multiple, and at times contradictory, readings. Here I am most interested in its performative polysemy, or the manner in which artists produce work that inspires various interpretations on the part of audiences.

In this regard, we might recognize Madonna's work as a key site of strategic ambiguity[10] or a type of carefully orchestrated polysemy that may result in one audience understanding "Medellín" as a liberatory text grounded in female sexual liberation and antiageism, while another audience might well read it as a flawed script for Latina/o/x–Anglo unification. Here the power resides primarily with the performer, and it is primarily wielded in the service of economic gain for the artist(s).

"Medellín" is rooted in the premise that both Madonna and Maluma have, as the lyrics note, "[taken] a pill and had a dream"—the dream being their May–December romance, as Madonna was sixty years old and Maluma twenty-five at the time of the video's release. When a similarly clad Maluma joins the dance class and begins consistently interjecting phrases in Spanish, Madonna croons in a smooth Auto-Tuned voice and wakes up in Medellín leading a dance class. A red-light dance sequence marks Maluma and Madonna's illicit affair, as the pair appears to pursue one another, with Maluma as the teasing masculine aggressor.

The clip's visuals consistently frame the performers in ethnoracial contradistinction to one another. Madonna's overexposed, radiant white skin visually accentuates her whiteness vis à vis Maluma's racialized Brown (mestizo) Colombianidad. The ethnoracial visual register in which Maluma may be read confers a Brownness upon him that not only diverges from historic representations of paisa identity within Colombia and among its diaspora but that also departs from the (relative) whiteness conferred upon him in the reggaetón sphere. Maluma capitalizes upon this racial fluidity. As Priscilla Peña Ovalle explains, "Oscillating between the normalcy of whiteness and the exoticism of Blackness, Latinas [and some Latinos/xs] function as in-between bodies to mediate and maintain the status quo. Some . . . can channel this liminality into stardom by maneuvering their in-betweenness toward the more desired racial representation of the period . . . thus maximizing their careers in visual culture" (Ovalle 2011, 7–8). It is through the prism of relative racial fluidity in "Medellín" that Maluma simultaneously signs in for a generic Latinidad, global Colombianidad, and a regionally specific paisa whiteness.

Reclining in an elaborate bed wearing a brilliant blue ball gown, Madonna sips champagne with Maluma in one of the most static scenes of the performance. These moments of relative stillness are juxtaposed against several grainy, less composed shots of the pair sitting on the dance floor in seemingly candid outtakes. Attributing Madonna's mental "viaje" ("trip") to an excess of aguardiente or Colombian cane sugar liquor, Maluma declares: "Que estamos en Colombia / Aquí hay rumba en cada esquina."[11] The song's principal rumba soon materializes, in the form of a carnivalesque outdoor wedding for the unlikely couple. Donning an elaborate white wedding dress reminiscent of the iconic gown she donned for her groundbreaking 1984 "Like a Virgin" video (Camp 2019), a now golden-blonde Madonna deliberately parades her way down the length of the wedding banquet table, framed on both sides by enthusiastic revelers.

The bridge that follows constitutes the musical apex of the video, as the tempo increases and the track's volume swells. Maluma and Madonna trade lines against rhythmic claps, while onscreen Madonna continues to sidle down the wedding banquet table, moving toward Maluma at the table's head. Madonna is the prize to be conquered, as Maluma sings: "Si te enamoro . . . En menos de un año, no no / No' vamo', no' vamo' no vamo' pa' Medallo / (Ay qué rico) . . ."[12] ("Medallo" being the popular local nickname for "Medellín," a lexical choice that confers upon Maluma the status of authentic native son). The married couple blissfully kiss as the colorful partygoers look on, and immediately the scene shifts to grainy black-and-white footage of a satin-robe-clad Madonna fleeing on foot by night as the sound of beating horse hooves fills the air. The tempo of "Medellín" slows once more, as Madonna finally references the industry for which the city is most famous: "We built a cartel just for love / Venus was hovering above us / I took a trip, it set me free / Forgave myself for being me." The equine theme continues as the video's action draws to a close with an overhead shot of Madonna and her young Colombian stallion (the obliging Maluma) on horseback, racing their way across a lush rural landscape at dawn. As we notice throughout this sequence, it is Madonna, and not Maluma, who possesses the power to discursively define their relationship as a "cartel just for love"; Maluma remains mute, an act that references the colonial power to name and ultimately define the racialized Other.

Aside from the presence of Maluma and the inclusion of untranslated Spanish, the video's disparate cultural references—aguardiente, the accordion, local slang, carnival, and general revelry—paint a picture of Colombianidad that would likely pass unrecognized by most non-Colombians, thereby augmenting the text's polysemic character. The "cartel of love" lyric was easily the most widely quoted lyrical element of the single in the weeks immediately following its release, evidence of the Escobar narrative's stubborn legibility in the global popular imagination. The magical, exceptional paisa space to which Maluma pledges to transport Madonna proves an unfulfilled promise to those familiar with the city; for others, the vibrant (if in some ways still deeply troubled) post-Escobar city remains unknown, and in the process "Medellín"'s transgressive potential remains blunted. We are presented with no substantial alternative vision of Medellín or the people who occupy that space. The actual Medellín proves a hollow reference, as the action on display could have taken place in virtually any nameless Latin(a/o/x) American locale. Indeed, the decontextualized nature of the video's imagery and lyrical content permits most non-Colombian viewers the luxury of ignorance regarding the impacts of US interventionism on Medellín, much less on Colombia as a whole. In a globalized media climate, "Medellín" thus highlights the manner in which foundational national narratives such as the contemporary Escobar narrative are scripted from within but also often from without. As the music video for

"Medellín" and Maluma's participation in it evince, such potent discourses profoundly shape Colombian cultural production and its global reception.

Conclusion: Reading the Scripts of Global Colombianidad

As Lily Cho maintains, "[D]iasporas are not just there. They are not simply collections of people, communities of scattered individuals bound by some shared history, race or religion. Rather, they emerge in relation to power, in the turn to and away from power" (Cho, 2007, 11). We must therefore read Colombianidad through the triumvirate lenses of racialized regionalism, heteropatriarchy, and US interventionism, or the powers that inform Colombian identities in their diasporic iterations as well as within Colombia's borders.[13] As we witness in "Medellín," Madonna serves as a proxy for an unexamined historic US interventionism whose impacts are felt at multiple levels of Colombian society, among its diaspora, and in its global representations. Located at the center of a vibrant Medellín reggaetón industry that may also be interpreted in analogous terms, in "Medellín" Maluma proves a secondary figure who nonetheless embodies the privileges attached to the interlocking forces of heteropatriarchy and racialized Colombian regionalism in particular. When assessed superficially, the burgeoning Medellín reggaetón industry and the global success of performers such as Maluma appear to offer a positive counterdiscourse to the Pablo Escobar narrative and the long-term impacts of US interventionism on the city and Colombia as a whole. Yet on second glance, neither Medellín as a space nor its emergent music industry provide a meaningful departure from the masculinist violence that has permeated the country prior to and after the 2016 peace accords. Rather, Madonna and Maluma's "Medellín" offers yet one more potent example of how media discourses such as the Escobar narrative act not only as marketing forces in and of themselves but also as epistemological disciplinary mechanisms that regulate the seemingly immutable scripts of contemporary global Colombianidad.

Acknowledgments

Mil gracias to the students of my Spring 2019 course "Latina/o/x Musical Cultures: Sounding Out Race, Gender, and Sexuality" for our initial discussion of the "Medellín" video. I am also grateful to Ana Yolanda Ramos-Zayas, Mérida Rúa, and Dolores Inés Casillas for their insightful editorial comments and suggestions.

NOTES

1 I distinguish here between the Colombian understanding of the "paisa" label from its usage in the Mexican context, in which it denotes a Northern Mexican regional identity. Moreover, for many Mexicans "paisa" is also a class-based term that negatively marks individuals

as working class. For an excellent analysis of the role of paisa identity, diasporic feminisms, and popular music, see Yessica Garcia-Hernández (2016).

2 For further information on the history of Colombia and its long-standing internal conflict, see Ann Farnsworth-Alvear, Marco Palacios, and Ana María Gómez López (2017); LaRosa and Mejía (2017); and Palacios (2006).

3 A history of the Colombian peace process and its potential outcomes can be found in LaRosa and Mejía (2017).

4 This translates into nearly fifteen thousand civilian deaths at the hands of paramilitary groups at the height of the violence between 1988 and 2003. By 2009, the number of political murders in Colombia has exceeded those of any overt Latin American dictatorship (Hristov 2009).

5 In 2017, the Trump government threatened to decertify Colombia, effectively placing the country on a blacklist of nations not deemed to be combatting the global drug trade effectively enough. Under decertification, a country forfeits all US foreign aid not directly tied to antinarcotics measures. In the case of Colombia, this would entail ceasing all aid related to the 2016 peace accords. The Trump administration has also supported a return to aerial fumigation and forced eradication such as deployed under Plan Colombia, despite their well-documented negative impacts.

6 Concurrent with this trajectory is reggaetón's increasing stress on more overtly misogynist, heteronormative lyrical and visual content. Notably, it was the genre's "obscene" material that threatened its commercial viability and circulation during its early years in Puerto Rico. Yet this tendency to rely on markedly heteronormative, masculinist content has only grown with the genre's global commercialization, a fact that Marshall sharply notes as "consistent with mainstream American culture" in its reliance on "macho fantasies about sex" that leaned toward the pornographic and that ultimately reinforced well-worn stereotypes about "hot" Latinas/os/xs (Marshall 2009, 49).

7 For a cogent analysis of the impact of Latina/o/x localized readings of race on musical production and reception, see Michelle M. Rivera (2017).

8 "Medellín" was written by Maluma and Madonna and produced by Frenchman Mirwais Ahmadzaï, a previous Madonna collaborator. Shot on location in Portugal, the video was directed by Spaniards Diana Kunst and multidisciplinary artist Mau Morgó.

9 According to this logic, regardless of a Latina/o/x/ artists' success in Spanish, the opportunity to record in English confers greater prestige (Cepeda 2010).

10 For a nuanced analysis of the dynamics of gender, race, and strategic ambiguity in contemporary media, see Ralina L. Joseph (2018).

11 "We're in Colombia / Here there's a party on every corner."

12 "If I make you fall in love with me . . . / In less than one year / We're goin', we're goin', we're goin' to Medallo / (Oh how delicious) . . ."

13 For a discussion of Maluma and the dynamics of heteropatriarchy in the current global reggaetón industry, see Cepeda (2019).

WORKS CITED

Anderson, Jon Lee. "Letter from Medellín: The Afterlife of Pablo Escobar." *New Yorker* 94, no. 3 (March 5, 2018): 50–59.

Appelbaum, Nancy P. 2003. *Muddied Waters: Race, Region, and Local History in Colombia, 1846–1948.* Durham: Duke University Press.

Baca, Lucía, and Alejandro Jiménez. "In Colombia, Will Peace Continue Costing Lives?" *NACLA Report on the Americas*, August 9, 2018. https://nacla.org.

Camp, Alexa. "Madonna Unveils Carnivalesque 'Medellín' Music Video Featuring Maluma." *Slant Magazine*, April 24, 2019. www.slantmagazine.com.

Caramanica, Jon. "For Nicky Jam a Second Chance as Reggaetón Surges Again." *New York Times*, January 18, 2017. www.nytimes.com.

Ceccarelli, Leah. "Polysemy: Multiple Meanings in Rhetorical Criticism." *Quarterly Journal of Speech*, 84, no. 4 (1998): 395–415.

Cepeda, María Elena. 2010. *Musical ImagiNation: U.S.-Colombian Identity and the Latin Music Boom.* New York: New York University Press.

———. "Putting a 'Good Face on the Nation': Beauty, Memes and the Gendered Rebranding of Global Colombianidad" *WSQ: Women's Studies Quarterly*, 46, nos. 1–2 (2018): 121–38.

———. "Competing Tensions: Maluma, Feminist Memes, and the Specter of Pablo Escobar." Presentation at the Pop Museum Conference, Seattle, April 13, 2019.

Cho, Lily. "The Turn to Diaspora." *TOPIA: Canadian Journal of Cultural Studies*, 17 (2007): 11–30.

Cinquemani, Sal. "Review: Madonna and Maluma Drop New Single 'Medellín' from *Madame X*." *Slant Magazine*, April 17, 2019. www.slantmagazine.com.

Dyer, Chelsey. "Colombia's War of Neoliberal Economics." *NACLA Report on the Americas*, March 7, 2019. https://nacla.org.

Fanta Castro, Andrea, Alejandro Herrero-Olaizola, and Chloe Rutter-Jensen. "Introduction: Territories of Conflict Through Colombian Cultural Studies." In *Territories of Conflict: Traversing Colombia Through Cultural Studies*, edited by Andrea Fanta Castro, Alejandro Herrero-Olaizola, and Chloe Rutter-Jensen, 1–20. Rochester: University of Rochester Press, 2017.

Farnsworth-Alvear, Ann, Marco Palacios, and Ana María Gómez López, eds. 2017. *The Colombia Reader: History, Culture, Politics.* Durham: Duke University Press.

Garcia-Hernández, Yessica. "Sonic Pedagogies: Latina Girls, Mother-Daughter Relationships, and Learning Feminisms through the Consumption of Jenni Rivera." *Journal of Popular Music Studies* 28 (2016): 427–42.

Herrero-Olaizola, Alejandro. "'Se Vende Colombia, Un País de Delirio': El Mercado Literario Global y la Narrativa Colombiana Reciente." *Symposium: A Quarterly Journal in Modern Literatures* 61, no. 1 (2007): 43–56.

Hristov, Jasmin. "Legalizing the Illegal: Paramilitarism in Colombia's 'Post-Paramilitary' Era." *NACLA Report on the Americas* 42, no. 4 (2009): 12–19.

Hylton, Forrest. "Medellín's Makeover." *New Left Review* 44 (March–April 2007): 71–89.

———. "Medellín: The Peace of the Pacifiers." *NACLA Report on the Americas* 41, no. 1 (2008): 35–42.

Joseph, Ralina L. 2018. *Postracial Resistance: Black Women, Media, and the Uses of Strategic Ambiguity.* New York: New York University Press.

King, Evan, and Samantha Wherry. "Eradicating Peace in Colombia." *NACLA Report on the Americas*, December 6, 2018. https://nacla.org.

Katz, Jesse. "24 Hours with Nicky Jam in Medellín: How the City Helped Him Quit Drugs and Get Back on Top." *Billboard*, February 16, 2017. www.billboard.com.

Kulkani, Vishwas. "Why Madonna's 'Medellín' Is a Ray of Light in a Time of Darkness." *National*, April 28, 2019. www.thenational.ae.

LaRosa, Michael J., and Germán R. Mejía. 2017. *Colombia: A Concise Contemporary History.* 2nd ed. Lanham, MD: Rowman & Littlefield.

Marshall, Wayne. "From Música Negra to Reggaetón Latino." In *Reggaetón*, edited by Raquel Z. Rivera, Wayne Marshall, and Deborah Pacini Hernández, 19–76. Durham: Duke University Press, 2009.

Moreno, Catalina. "Nicky Jam Breaks Down What Makes Colombian Reggaeton Unique." *Huffington Post*, September 19, 2016. www.huffingtonpost.com.

Nolfi, Joey. "Madonna Drops Breezy Summer Anthem "Medellín" Featuring Maluma." *ew.com*, April 17, 2019. https://ew.com.

Ochoa Camacho, Ariana. "Living with Drug Lords and Mules in New York: Contrasting Colombian Criminality and Transnational Belonging." In *The Immigrant Other: Lived Experiences in a Transnational World*, edited by Rich Furman, Greg Lamphear, and Douglas Epps, 166–79. New York: Columbia University Press, 2016.

Ovalle, Priscilla Peña. *Dance and the Hollywood Latina: Race, Sex, and Stardom*. Rutgers University Press, 2011.

Palacios, Marco. 2006. *Between Legitimacy and Violence: A History of Colombia, 1975–2002*. Durham: Duke University Press.

Perry, Leah. 2016. *The Cultural Politics of U.S. Immigration: Gender, Race and Media*. New York: New York University Press.

Pobutsky, Aldona Bialowas. "Peddling Pablo: Escobar's Cultural Renaissance." *Hispania* 96, no. 4 (2013): 684–99.

———. "Going Down Narco Memory Lane: Pablo Escobar in the Visual Media." In *Territories of Conflict: Traversing Colombia Through Cultural Studies*, edited by Andrea Fanta Castro, Alejandro Herrero-Olaizola, and Chloe Rutter-Jensen, 282–93. Rochester: University of Rochester Press, 2017.

Rivera, Michelle M. "Crossover Fail: 'Nigga'/Flex's 'Romantic Style in Da World.'" In *The Routledge Companion to Latina/o Media*, edited by María Elena Cepeda and Dolores Inés Casillas, 402–18. New York: Routledge, 2017.

Rivera-Rideau, Petra. 2015. *Remixing Reggaetón: The Cultural Politics of Race in Puerto Rico*. Durham: Duke University Press.

Rivera-Rideau, Petra, and Jericko Torres-Leschnik. "'The Colors and Flavors of My Puerto Rico': Mapping 'Despacito''s Crossovers." *Journal of Popular Music Studies* 31, no. 1 (2019): 87–108.

Rojas, Cristina. 2002. *Civilization and Violence: Regimes of Representation in Nineteenth-Century Colombia*. Minneapolis: University of Minnesota Press.

Tubb, Daniel. "Narratives of Citizenship in Medellín, Colombia." *Citizenship Studies* 17, no. 5 (2013): 627–40.

Uribe Yepes, Andrea. "La máquina paisa de hacer reguetón." *Revista Don Juan*, September 6, 2018. www.revistadonjuan.com.

Wade, Peter. "The Language of Race, Place, and Nation in Colombia." *América Negra* 2 (1991): 41–66.

4

Geographies of Race and Ethnicity III

Settler Colonialism and Nonnative People of Color

LAURA PULIDO

This is an edited version of a "Progress Report" on Race and Ethnicity published in *Progress in Human Geography*. I conceived of it in 2015 in order to better understand Chicanx's complex subjectivity as immigrants, settlers, and colonized people within the context of Spanish and U.S. imperialism. The literature has since developed significantly and the essay should be read as an early contribution. I have also maintained the term, "Chicana/o," which was customary at the time.

Introduction

In this progress report I consider the politics of settler colonialism in relation to nonnative people of color. Over the past decade the concept of settler colonialism, a distinct form of colonization, has become increasingly prominent (Trask, 2000; Wolfe, 2006). Rather than seeking to control land, resources, and labor, settler colonization eliminated native peoples in order to appropriate their land. The United States, Canada, Israel, and Australia are all examples of settler states. Early theorizations focused on white settlers, but questions soon arose from ethnic studies scholars regarding the role of nonwhite peoples. Though global conversations (Lawrence and Dua, 2005; Sharma and Wright, 2008/9), I focus on U.S. ethnic and native studies debates (Byrd, 2011; Tuck and Yang, 2012), as I am concerned with Chicana/o studies' response. While both Asian American and Black studies scholars have contributed to this discussion, Chicana/o studies has been relatively silent. And, for very different reasons, so has geography.

Chicana/o studies' ambivalence, I argue, is due to settler colonialism's potential to disrupt core elements of Chicana/o political subjectivity. Specifically, it unsettles Chicanas/os' conception of themselves as colonized people by highlighting their role as colonizers. Acknowledging such a role is difficult not only because it challenges key dimensions of Chicana/o identity, as seen in Aztlán,

argument

Reprinted from *Progress in Human Geography* 42 (2): 309–18.

Chicanas/os' mythical homeland, but also because of the precarious nature of Chicana/o Indigeneity.

Geography, with a few exceptions (Kobayashi and De Leeuw, 2010; Bauder, 2011), has only considered whites in relation to settler colonialism (Bonds and Inwood, 2015; Radcliffe, 2015). This reflects geography's larger anti-racist scholarship—anchored in a white/nonwhite binary. This, in turn, reflects the overwhelming whiteness of the discipline. Geography simply lacks the racial diversity, scholarly expertise, and comfort to explore such questions.

Despite their differences, I wish to place these two disciplines in conversation. Besides being my intellectual homes, geography must learn to wrestle with the complexities of racial and (de)colonial dynamics. Its contributions to the study of racism will always be limited if the fullness of the racial landscape is overlooked. Chicana/o studies' avoidance of settler colonialism illustrates how racial and political subjectivity is structured by colonization, nation-states, white supremacy, anti-racist struggle, and decolonial projects. Deciphering the historical reasons why Chicana/o studies has failed to grapple with settler colonialism illuminates the deeply geographical nature of racial and political subjectivity. Ethnic-Mexicans, like all people of color, are diverse and multifaceted (contrary to the tidiness implied by "Latina/o"), and it is only through exploring the spatialities of their historical experiences that we can understand this avoidance.

In this report I first introduce settler colonialism and ethnic studies' response to it. Then, drawing primarily on cultural studies scholarship, I explore the precarious nature of Chicana/o Indigeneity and the significance of Aztlán, both of which are deeply geographic. Chicana/o Indigeneity is embedded in questions of scale, territory, boundaries, and empire, while Aztlán is an imagined place. Although I focus on U.S. ethnic studies, these issues should resonate in all settler societies.

Settler Colonialism, Native Peoples, and Nonwhite Others

What makes settler societies unique is their desire to *replace* Indigenous peoples in order to take their land, rather than simply control resources and labor.[1] While the U.S. acknowledges it is a settler society, it does so by evacuating the violence associated with this process. Political scientist Samuel Huntington, a foe of Latina/o immigration, distinguishes settlers from immigrants. He states that settlers came to *build* a country, while immigrants come to *join* it (2004). While settlers are routinely admired in U.S. culture, their celebration requires imagining the process as nonviolent or, at best, involving justifiable violence (Blackhawk, 2006). Key to erasing this violence are transition narratives—discourses that serve to make the past more palatable. Foregrounding settler colonialism, however, highlights the whitewashing associated with hegemonic representations of colonization (Dunbar-Ortiz, 2014) and re-centers native peoples.

Settler colonialism demands that the experience of Indigenous peoples be taken seriously, which has profound implications for white settlers, immigrants, and various minoritized populations, which in the United States includes African Americans, Asian Americans, Latinas/os, Muslims, and other racially subordinated groups. As Indigenous studies scholar Aileen Moreton-Robinson notes, "the question of how anyone came to be white or Black in the United States is inextricably tied to the dispossession of the original owners" (2008: 84).

While many routinely collapse native and ethnic studies, there are important distinctions. First, many in native studies reject the category "minority" and the larger politics of multiculturalism (Byrd, 2011; Kobayashi and De Leeuw, 2010). This is because U.S. minority status usually results from racism, but Indigenous peoples have been colonized. And while the United States has been somewhat willing to acknowledge a racist past, it has refused to grapple with the violence of settler colonialism. Though settler colonization is a racial project (Wolfe, 2016), it cannot be reduced to racism. Indeed, the solution to racism is inclusion, but this does not address colonization (Coulthard, 2014). "When the remediation of the colonization of American Indians is framed through discourses of racialization that can be redressed by further inclusion into the nation-state, there is a significant failure to grapple with the fact that such discourses further reinscribe the original colonial injury" (Byrd, 2011: xxiii).

Theorizing how minoritized groups participate in settler colonialism is challenging (Trask, 2000; Kobayashi and De Leeuw, 2010; Tuck and Yang, 2012; Byrd, 2011; Saranillo, 2013; Sharma and Wright, 2008/9). Though some conceptualize all nonnatives as settlers (Lawrence and Dua, 2005), ethnic studies generally rejects such simple framings. Terms like "arrivant" and "subordinate settler" describe various minoritized positions. Theorizing the roles of Black slaves, Asian immigrants, and Mexican settlers can be discomfiting, which, Eve Tuck and K. Wayne Yang, critical education writers, maintain, is entirely appropriate (2012). They argue that since the United States is both a settler colonial nation-state *and* an empire, it displaces native peoples and compels others onto indigenous lands through slavery, war, and economic dislocation (2012: 7). In an effort to overcome the seeming binary between colonization and racism, feminist scholars Nandita Sharma and Cynthia Wright (2008/9) interpret colonization as the commons, which foregrounds capitalism rather than nationalism, and offers one way forward. Feminist and native studies scholar Andrea Smith has sought to unify these processes under white supremacy, arguing that it is underlain by three logics: slaveability, genocide, and orientalism. Each logic in turn enables a particular social relation: capitalism, colonization, and war, respectively. These logics preclude easy solidarity. Smith writes:

> [A]ll non-Native peoples are promised the ability to . . . settl[e] indigenous lands. All non-Black peoples are promised that . . . they will not be at the bottom of the

racial hierarchy. And Black and Native peoples are promised that they will advance economically and politically if they join U.S. wars (Smith, 2012: 70).

Black studies scholars have responded in diverse ways to these debates. Historian Tiya Miles (2005) explored how Black and Indigenous peoples intersected through white supremacy, slavery, and settler colonization, while challenging conventional ideas of temporality. Instead of assuming slavery followed native dispossession, she shows how they informed each other simultaneously. Other African American studies scholars, often associated with "Afro-pessimism," have rejected relational interpretations and their concomitant politics, as they see global anti-Blackness as immutable (Wilderson, 2010; see also Kauanui, 2017).

Asian American studies has focused on immigrants' role in colonizing Hawai'i, especially how Asian "success" promotes multicultural harmony. "In their focus on racism, discrimination, and the exclusion of Asians . . . such studies tell the story of Asians' civil rights as one of nation building in order to legitimate Asians' claims to a place for themselves in Hawai'i" (Fujikane and Okamura, 2008: 2). While some have argued that settler colonialism works *through* immigrants (Saranillo, 2013), others have explored how narratives of Asian labor's hyper-efficiency have become associated with a negative form of capital (Day, 2016). While this review is hardly comprehensive, it should be apparent that vibrant debates exist in which scholars are struggling to understand how white supremacy and colonization intersect.

In contrast, Chicana/o studies has been peripheral to such discussions. Certainly Chicana/o studies is no stranger to colonization, given U.S. conquest of Mexico (Acuña, 1972; Barrera, 1979; Almaguer, 1994; Rivera, 2006). Chicana studies scholars have challenged conventional historiography (Pérez, 1999), often including native women in their analyses (Castañeda, 1993; Chávez-Garcia, 2004). Scholars have interrogated Chicana/o Indigeneity (Saldaña-Portillo, 2001, 2016; Contreras, 2008; Hartley, 2012), and more recently Indigenous Latina/o migration (Bianet Castellanos et al., 2012; Fox and Rivera-Salgado, 2004). Researchers have considered Chinese immigrants as settlers in the U.S. southwest (Luna-Peña, 2015). Some have compared Chicanas/os and Palestinians in terms of settler-colonialism (Lloyd and Pulido, 2010), while others have complicated such claims (Sánchez and Pita, 2014; Cotera and Saldaña-Portillo 2015). In short, the discipline is dancing around settler colonization and its implications, but has not taken the plunge. Instead, Chicanas/os are still largely scripted as the colonized. Literary scholar Nicole Guidotti-Hernández (2011) suggests that because Chicana/o studies is fixated on the U.S. conquest of Mexico, it has major blind spots. Consequently, the larger historiography of the U.S. West is replete with Mexican violence toward Indigenous peoples that is overlooked (Reséndez, 2016; Smith, 2013; González, 2005; Guidotti-Hernández, 2011).

Along with Guidotti-Hernández, historian Michael González is one of the few to document Mexican dispossession of native peoples. His analysis centers on an 1846 letter written by Mexicans in Los Angeles to the Governor in which they complained about native people and requested that "the Indians be placed under strict police surveillance or the persons for whom the Indians work give [them] quarter at the employer's rancho" (2005: 19). González argues that Mexican Angelenos embraced hegemonic Mexican culture, including eliminating *el indio barbaro* (the savage Indian) (see also Saldaña-Portillo, 2016).

There is also evidence of Mexican complicity in U.S. settler colonialism. Guidotti-Hernández's (2011) study of Euro-American violence toward Mexicans and Mexico's genocide toward *indios barbaros* includes the Camp Grant Indian massacre of 1871. Both Mexico and the United States fought the Apaches because they raided and refused a sedentary lifestyle. In 1871 the United States promised a group of Apaches safety at Camp Grant, Arizona, but locals, including Mexican leadership, massacred 144, mostly women and children. In short, we have clear evidence of Mexicans and Chicanas/os participating in settler colonialism, but we are unable to frankly discuss it and consider its meanings.

Chicana/o Studies' Ambivalence toward Settler Colonialism

An inability to acknowledge such violence and its corresponding subjectivities suggests deep anxieties. Indeed, there are parallels between the United States' refusal to acknowledge settler colonialism (Dunbar-Ortiz, 2014) and that of Chicana/o studies. Recognizing ethnic-Mexicans' role in settler colonization is threatening because it would force Chicana/o studies to recognize multiple subjectivities, which in turn, would require rethinking the dominant narrative. This is similar to American Indian studies acknowledging, for example, that Cherokees owned slaves. But it's not just a desire to avoid uncomfortable work. There is significant confusion regarding Chicana/o Indigeneity, which has been made almost illegible by colonization. Though both Indian and Indigenous are constructed categories. Native studies scholar Brian Klopotek (2016) has argued that Indian functions as a racial term, while Indigenous is a cultural and political one. While ethnic-Mexicans are overwhelmingly Indian, indigeneity is different. Exactly what are Chicanas/os indigenous to? When, if at all, does indigeneity cease? How does Indigeneity function within multiple national formations? Not only do Mexico and the United States have radically different conceptions of and approaches to Indigeneity (Contreras, 2008), but Chicanas/os, as transnational people, exist in the interstices of multiple national and regional racial formations (Saldaña-Portillo, 2016).

Chicanas/os: Indians or Indigenous?

Before examining Chicana/o Indigeneity more closely, I must distinguish between two distinct threads. One thread stems from the centuries-long history of the peoples and lands of North America. A second strand has recently emerged through Indigenous immigration from Latin America to the United States (Bianet Castellanos, 2017; Bianet Castellanos et al., 2012; Fox and Rivera-Salgado, 2004). While Chicana/o studies includes both, they embody different temporalities. Specifically, the second is usually *recognized* as indigenous, while the first is more contentious. I focus on the first, which is foundational to Chicana/o studies.

Chicana/o studies exists as both a scholarly enterprise and a nation-building project. And like any nation, it had to forge a new identity. Previous to "Chicana/o," which became widespread in the 1960s, ethnic-Mexicans living in the United States identified as Mexican American. "Chicana/o" is an explicitly oppositional term that drew upon counter-hegemonic histories, meanings, and experiences. Central to this was reclaiming an Indigenous heritage, which had been undermined by Mexico's ideology of mestizaje as well as U.S. racism. Mestizaje, the idea of cultural and biological mixing, was a nation-building strategy that both assimilated and erased *lo indio* (Cotera and Saldaña-Portillo, 2015). Within Chicana/o studies, the idea of decolonial mestizaje has emerged (Anzaldúa, 1987), as an attempt to overcome the racism of mestizaje (Hartley, 2012; Morgensen, 2011: 183–7; Saldaña-Portillo, 2001).

Debates around Chicana/o Indigeneity must be located in larger discussions of Indigeneity itself (Teves et al., 2015; Bianet Castellanos et al., 2012). According to one definition, the communities, clans, nations, and tribes we call "indigenous peoples" are just that:

> Indigenous to the lands they inhabit, in contrast to and in contention with colonial societies that have spread out from Europe and other centers of empire. It is this oppositional and place-based existence, along with the consciousness of being in struggle against . . . colonization by foreign peoples, that fundamentally distinguishes Indigenous peoples (Alfred and Corntassel, 2005: 597).

While seemingly straightforward, this definition hints at underlying complexities. For instance, locating Indigeneity in relation to a specific place overlooks Indigenous peoples' contemporary and historic mobility (Díaz, 2015). When does tenure begin? Despite having lived in a place for hundreds, perhaps thousands of years, we know that native peoples were on the move. Moreover, U.S. dispossession and the reservation system challenge any simple associations to land, boundary, or place.

An oppositional subjectivity is also central to this definition. While the Indigenous experience has been shaped by struggle, how salient and ubiquitous is it? Consider an urban apolitical Indian with no ties to a homeland—are they still indigenous? Not surprisingly, an oppositional stance conflicts with U.S. definitions, which mark indigeneity by blood (see Simpson, 2014). Still others emphasize cultural practices and connections, including those who are part of native communities, but not blood members (Simpson, 2014). While American Indians have long debated these issues, they have been amplified by native studies, which has highlighted how Indigeneity is rooted in colonization and nation-state processes.

Chicana/o Indigeneity, like all other forms, must be grounded in the state (Hartley, 2012). As noted earlier, Chicana/o subjectivities and identities have been forged in and through overlapping Mexican and U.S. racial formations and nation-building projects (Saldaña-Portillo, 2016). These formations are both sequential and spatially and temporally overlapping. Here, we must draw on our most sophisticated understandings of place—how to understand a region as a palimpsest, a border zone, and a boundary simultaneously? While Mexico incorporated Indigeneity into its nation-building efforts, mestizaje has been highly contradictory. In contrast, the United States sought to obliterate native people physically and forged a white racial and national identity *exclusive* of them. Consequently, in the United States, native peoples are seen as distinct from the larger nation and insist they are sovereign. Though Indigenous Mexicans may oppose the state, like the Zapatistas, they do not necessarily see themselves as distinct nations (Saldaña-Portillo, 2001).

Chicana/o Indigeneity is based on several claims (see Cotera and Saldaña-Portillo, 2015). First, it is based on Mexicans' long tenure in North America. This, however, raises the question of scale: Does North American Indigenous count as U.S. Indigenous? Some American Indians say "no." In response, Chicanas/os charge that American Indians are reifying the colonizers' borders. A second pillar of Chicana/o Indigeneity is the belief that their ancestors originated in what is now the U.S. southwest and migrated south. This supposed homeland, Aztlán, actually appears on several maps.[2] As Chicana/o activists began reclaiming their Indigeneity, they drew heavily on an Aztec heritage: Nahuatl, Aztec art, dancing, and Day of the Dead celebrations. *Aztlán* is even the name of Chicana/o studies' foremost journal. Ironically, activists were actually celebrating an imperial power, since the Aztecs conquered many nations (Contreras, 2008; Urrieta, 2012).

A third claim to Chicana/o Indigeneity is colonization by Spain and U.S. colonization of Mexico. Mexicans lost land, power, status, and rights through the Mexican–American War. The parallels between Indian and Mexican dispossession have long been noted (Horsman, 1981). "That the Indian race of Mexico must recede before us, is quite as certain as . . . the destiny of our own Indians" (Thompson in Dunbar-Ortiz, 2014: 117). Mexico, as an indigenous and colonized country, continues to be subject to U.S. domination.

A fourth and final pillar of Chicana/o Indigeneity is mixing between American Indians and Mexicans, which has occurred for centuries under diverse circumstances, including pre-Columbian migrations, conquest, slavery, refuge, adoption, and everything in-between. There are more than a few Chicanas/os who claim, for example, Pueblo heritage. And though many Southwest tribes, understandably, may not wish to claim Mexican ancestry, it is apparent in their names, language, religious practices, and such. Despite this reality, the United States insists on neat boundaries, however fictitious. Indeed, the Choctaw-Apache Tribe of Louisiana was initially denied federal recognition because they speak Spanish (Klopotek, 2016).

While Chicanas/os identify as Indigenous, they are not considered as such by the U.S. state and society, including many Americans Indians. This is because the United States emphasizes blood, a specific relationship to land (Contreras, 2008: 6), and continuous existence as a polity (Klopotek, 2016). Moreover, native studies scholar Deborah Miranda has noted that some American Indians refuse to recognize Chicana/o Indigeneity because legitimating "mestizos" could diminish their own status (in Hartley, 2012: 61). Others see Chicanas/os as simply another ethnic group desiring Indigeneity (Cotera and Saldaña-Portillo, 2015). These denials of recognition make Chicana/o Indigeneity precarious.

Complicating claims of Indigeneity is the fact that Chicanas/os are categorized as white, although they have never been treated as such (Haney-López, 2003; Menchaca, 2001). White status is the result of the Treaty of Guadalupe Hidalgo. Mexico insisted on classifying its people as white to shield them from U.S. racism. The United States conceded because of its unwillingness to tolerate racial ambiguity, which Mexicans epitomized, and because it sought to categorize all Indians in the newly acquired territory as "savage," in order to justify continued dispossession and war, particularly against the Apache and Comanche (Saldaña-Portillo, 2016: 179).[3] Chicanas/os' legal whiteness and the various attempts to erase their Indigeneity illustrate the power of the state in shaping racial and political subjectivity (Haney-López 2003; Gómez 2007; Gross 2008).

It is because of such a tangled history that Chicanas/os desire to reclaim their past. Chicana/o Indigeneity is rooted in a "longing for a pre-colonial past that can never be known. The allure of Indigenous myth is strong as it may seem to provide a new grammar with which to challenge European and Euro-American domination of Native America" (Contreras, 2008: 165). But this reclaiming is not just about identity, it is also about grieving (Cotera and Saldaña-Portillo, 2015; Saldaña-Portillo, 2016; Contreras, 2008). Much has been lost through colonizations and conquest, and Aztlán addresses that grief.

Aztlán: Colonization and Decolonization

Aztlán, as Chicanas/os' mythical homeland, embodies a binational spatiality (Saldaña-Portillo, 2016). As a diasporic and transnational population, Chicanas/os must reconcile their relationship to two places. Their connection to Mexico (and Indigeneity) is apparent in the Aztecs, while the need to fit somehow in the United States is expressed through Aztlán.

As the ancient homeland of the Mexica, Aztlán is located in the U.S. south-west. Chicana/o activists reappropriated the territory Mexico lost to the United States and called it Aztlán. This was very strategic. First, activists were fashioning a homeland for themselves. For Chicanas/os the concept of Aztlán signaled a unifying point of cohesion through which they could define the foundations of an identity. Aztlán brought together a culture that had been somewhat disjointed and dispersed, allowing it, for the first time, a framework within which to under-stand itself (Anaya and Lomelí, 1989: ii). Aztlán not only performed internal work, but it also did important external work. Essentially, activists claimed land that had been "stolen" from Mexico through the war, as their ancient home-land. This not only foregrounded an imperialist war fueled by manifest destiny (Horsman, 1981), but challenged their perceived status as foreigners and "illegal immigrants." Activists routinely reject imperialist boundaries with the refrain, "We didn't cross the border, the border crossed us."

While Aztlán is clearly a decolonial act, it is also true that other peoples were living on the territory when Chicanas/os claimed it—including the Navajo, Apache, Comanche, Pueblo, Tohono O'odham, Mojave, Paiute, the many native peoples of California, and binational tribes, such as the Yaqui. While many American Indians have engaged in political alliances with Chicanas/os, I see Aztlán as problematic. For over 45 years Chicana/o activists have imagined their homeland on the territories of dispossessed people. Certainly it is understand-able why Chicanas/os would want to claim these lands, but at the very least such a decision must be handled with respect, honesty, and in a spirit of solidarity. As far as I know, Chicanas/os never collaborated or consulted with American Indians on Aztlán. As such, Aztlán is simultaneously a decolonial and coloniz-ing gesture.

American Indians are cognizant of this. While there have been moments of solidarity, and Chicanas/os have been granted membership in such orga-nizations as the International Indian Treaty Council, some reject Chicanas/os as indigenous, as noted earlier (Cotera and Saldaña-Portillo, 2015: 552). These tensions are readily apparent in New Mexico, which has the largest land-based Mexican population in the United States. The land grant struggles of the 1960s were one of the rallying points of the Chicana/o movement and were emblematic of a colonized status. Hispanos have historically celebrated their long history in the region, but American Indian activists have begun challenging dominant narratives of Spanish colonization. The Red Nation recently protested the re-enactment of La Entrada, which marks Spain's reconquest of Santa Fe in 1692. It was not well received by Hispanos. One local responded, "This is our town. You had your chance and you lost" (Chacón, 2016). Such sentiments cannot be dismissed. While it is understandable why Chicana/o studies is reluctant to acknowledge settler colonialism, both intellectual integrity and political com-mitment require recognizing Chicanas/os' multiple subjectivities.

Conclusion

By analyzing Chicana/o studies' muted response to settler colonialism I hope to encourage the discipline to acknowledge the multiple subjectivities of Chicanas/os and other Latinas/os, while also showing geographers the importance of relations between minoritized populations. Clearly, studying the political and racial subjectivity of any group is a deeply spatial exercise. Increasingly, scholars of Indigeneity are drawing on geography, both theoretically (Saldaña-Portillo, 2016; Goeman, 2013) and through popular education, such as Mapping Indigenous LA (https://mila.ss.ucla.edu/). The question of Indigeneity raises issues of land, place, borders, migrations, human-environment relations, and empire—questions that are central to geography. But it also raises questions that geography is less steeped in. I tread carefully here. I refuse to issue the typical call, "geographers should be studying this." I do not think white geographers should rush to study the dynamics I have outlined. White people studying conflict between racially subordinated groups is ethically and politically fraught. This does not preclude them from doing so, but it requires a particular set of experiences and commitments to do so in a way that does not cause further harm. Rather, let us acknowledge how much geography is missing given its demographics and dominant approaches to studying race. Hopefully, one day when the discipline is more diverse, such a call could be made. Addressing settler colonialism is a long, painful, and difficult process, yet grasping its many manifestations is essential.

NOTES

1   This view is increasingly problematized by Latin Americanists, as seen in *American Quarterly*'s special issue on settler colonialism in Latin America (Bianet Castellanos, 2017). For instance, Shannon Speed (2017) argues that native peoples were dispossessed of their land and then forced to work it. Elsewhere, geographer Sofia Zaragocin has highlighted the gendered nature of contemporary elimination (2019).

2   The Gemelli map of 1704 traces this migration, and Aztlán appears on the Disturnell Map of 1847.

3   The Pueblo were the exception because they were sedentary.

REFERENCES

Acuña R (1972) *Occupied America*. New York: Harper Collins.

Alfred T and Corntassel J (2005) Being Indigenous: Resurgences against contemporary colonialism. *Government and Opposition* 40 (4): 597–614.

Almaguer T (1994) *Racial Faultlines*. Berkeley: University of California Press.

Anaya R and Lomelí F (1989) *Aztlán: Essays on the Chicano Homeland*. Albuquerque: Academia/El Norte Publications.

Anzaldúa G (1987) *Borderlands/La Frontera: The New Mestiza*. San Francisco: Aunt Lute Books.

Barrera M (1979) *Race and Class in the Southwest*. Notre Dame: University of Notre Dame Press.

Bauder H (2011) Closing the immigration-Aboriginal parallax gap. *Geoforum* 42 (5): 517–519.

Bianet Castellanos M (2017) Introduction: Settler Colonialism in Latin America. *American Quarterly* 69 (4): 777–781.

Bianet Castellanos M (2017b) Rewriting the Mexican Immigrant Narratives: Situating Indigeneity in Maya Women's Stories. *Latino Studies* 15 (2): 219–241.

Bianet Castellanos M, Najera LG and Aldama A (2012) *Comparative Indigeneities of the Americas.* Tucson: University of Arizona Press.

Blackhawk N (2006) *Violence over the Land: Indians and Empires in the Early American West.* Cambridge: Harvard University Press.

Bonds A and Inwood J (2015) Beyond white privilege: Geographies of white supremacy and settler colonialism. *Progress in Human Geography.* DOI: 0309132515613166.

Byrd J (2011) *Transit of Empire: Indigenous Critiques of Colonization.* Minneapolis: University of Minnesota Press.

Castañeda A (1993) Sexual violence in the politics and policies of conquest. In: De la Torre A and Pesquera B (eds) *Building with Our Hands.* Berkeley: University of California Press, 15–33.

Chacón D (2016) Protestors turn up volume at Entrada. *Santa Fe New Mexican,* 9 September. Available at: www.santafenewmexican.com/news/local_news/protesters-turn-up-volume-at-entrada/article_571ce07b-2a80-59eb-8590-23129975921b.html (accessed 10 November 2016).

Chávez-García M (2004) *Negotiating Conquest: Gender and Power in California, 1770s–1880s.* Tucson: University of Arizona Press.

Coulthard G (2014) *Red Skin, White Masks.* Minneapolis: University of Minnesota Press.

Contreras S (2008) *Blood Lines.* Austin: University of Texas Press.

Cotera M and Saldaña-Portillo J (2015) Indigenous but not Indian? Chicana/os and the politics of indigeneity. In: Warrior R (ed.) *The World of Indigenous North America.* New York: Routledge, 549–567.

Day I (2016) *Alien Capital: Asian Racialization and the Logic of Settler Colonial Capitalism.* Durham: Duke University Press.

Díaz V (2015). No island is an island. In: Teves SN, Smith A and Raheja M (eds) *Native Studies Keywords.* Tucson: University of Arizona Press, 90–108.

Dunbar-Ortiz R (2014) *An Indigenous Peoples' History of the United States.* New York: Basic Books.

Fox J and Rivera-Salgado G (2004) *Indigenous Mexican Migrants in the United States.* La Jolla: Center for U.S.-Mexican Studies, University of California, San Diego.

Fujikane C and Okamura J (2008) *Asian Settler Colonialism.* Honolulu: University of Hawai'i Press.

Goeman M (2013) *Mark My Words.* Minneapolis: University of Minnesota Press.

Gómez L (2007) *Manifest Destinies: The Making of the Mexican American Race.* New York: New York University.

González M (2005) *This Small City Will Be a Mexican Paradise: Exploring the Origins of Mexican Culture in Los Angeles, 1821–1846.* Albuquerque: University of New Mexico Press.

Gross A (2008) *What Blood Won't Tell: A History of Race on Trial in America.* Cambridge: Harvard University.

Guidotti-Hernández N (2011) *Unspeakable Violence: Remapping U.S. and Mexican National Imaginaries.* Durham: Duke University Press.

Haney-López I (2003) *Racism on Trial: The Chicano Fight for Justice.* Cambridge, MA: Harvard University Press.

Hartley G (2012) Chican@ indigeneity, the nation-state, and colonialist identity formations. In: Castellanos MB, Najera LG and Aldama A (eds) *Comparative Indigeneities of the Americas.* Tucson: University of Arizona, 53–66.

Horsman R (1981) *Race and Manifest Destiny.* Cambridge, MA: Harvard University Press.

Huntington S (2004) *Who Are We? The Challenges to America's National Identity.* New York: Simon & Schuster.

Kauanui KJ (2017) Tracing Historical Specificity: Race and Colonial Politics of (In)Capacity. *American Quarterly* 69 (2): 257–265.

Klopotek B (2016) *Indian on both sides: Indigenous identities, race, and national borders.* Unpublished manuscript, Ethnic Studies, University of Oregon.

Kobayashi A and De Leeuw S (2010) Colonialism and the tensioned landscapes of indigeneity. In: Smith S, Pain R, Marston S and Jones J (eds) *SAGE Handbook of Social Geographies.* London: SAGE, 118–138.

Lawrence B and Dua E (2005) Decolonizing antiracism. *Social Justice* 32(4): 120–143.

Lloyd D and Pulido L (2010) In the long shadow of the settler: On Israeli and US colonialisms. *American Quarterly* 62(4): 795–809.

Luna-Peña G (2015) Little more than desert wasteland: Race, development and settler colonialism in the Mexicali Valley. *Critical Ethnic Studies* 1(2): 81–101.

Márquez J (2013) *Black-Brown Solidarity.* Austin: University of Texas Press.

Menchaca M (2001) *Recovering History, Constructing Race: The Indian, Black, and White Roots of Mexican Americans.* Austin: University of Texas Press.

Miles T (2005) *Ties That Bind: The Story of an Afro-Cherokee Family in Slavery and Freedom.* Berkeley: University of California Press.

Moreton-Robinson A, Casey M and Nicoll F (2008) *Transnational Whiteness Matters.* Lanham, MD: Lexington Books.

Morgensen SL (2011) *Spaces Between Us: Queer Settler Colonialism and Indigenous Decolonization.* Minneapolis: University of Minnesota Press.

Nájera LG (2012) Challenges to Zapotec indigenous autonomy in an era of global migration. In: Castellanos MB, Nájera LG and Aldama A (eds) *Comparative Indigeneities of the Americas.* Tucson: University of Arizona Press, 227–241.

Pérez E (1999) *The Decolonial Imaginary: Writing Chicanas into History.* Indianapolis: Indiana University Press.

Radcliffe S (2015) Geography and indigeneity I: Indigeneity, coloniality and knowledge. *Progress in Human Geography.* DOI: 0309132515612952.

Reséndez A (2016) *The Other Slavery.* New York: Houghton Mifflin Harcourt.

Rivera JM (2006) *The Emergence of Mexican America.* New York: New York University Press.

Saldaña-Portillo J (2001) Who's the Indian in Aztlán? Rewriting mestizaje, Indianism, and Chicanismo from the Lacandon. In: Rodriguez I (ed) *The Latin American Subaltern Studies Reader.* Durham: Duke University Press, 402–423.

Saldaña-Portillo J (2016) *Indian Given: Racial Geographies across Mexico and the United States.* Durham: Duke University Press.

Sánchez R and Pita B (2014) Rethinking settler colonialism. *American Quarterly* 66(4): 1039–1055.

Saranillo D (2013) Why Asian settler colonialism matters. *Settler Colonial Studies* 3(3–4): 280–294.

Simpson A (2014) *Mohawk Interruptus: Political Life Across the Borders of Settler States.* Durham: Duke University Press.

Smith A (2012) Indigeneity, settler colonialism, white supremacy. In: HoSang D, LaBennett O and Pulido L (eds) *Racial Formation in the Twenty-First Century.* Berkeley: University of California, 66–90.

Smith S (2013) *Freedom's Frontier.* Chapel Hill: University of North Carolina Press.

Speed S (2017) Structures of Settler Capitalism in Abya Yala. *American Quarterly* 69 (4): 783–790.

Teves SN, Smith A and Rajeha M (2015) *Native Studies Keywords.* Tucson: University of Arizona Press.

Trask HK (2000) Settlers of color and 'immigrant' hegemony: 'Locals' in Hawaii. *Amerasia Journal* 26(2): 1–24.

Tuck E and Yang W (2012) Decolonization is not a metaphor. *Decolonization: Indigeneity, Education & Society* 1(1): 1–40.

Urrieta L (2012) Las identidades tambien lloran. In: Castellanos MB, Najera LG and Aldama A (eds) *Comparative Indigeneities of the Americas*. Tucson: University of Arizona Press, 321–335.

Wilderson F (2010) *Red, White & Black: Cinema and the Structure of U.S. Antagonisms*. Durham: Duke University Press.

Wolfe P (2006) Settler colonialism and the elimination of the native. *Journal of Genocide Research* 8(4): 387–409.

Wolfe P (2016) *Traces of History: Elementary Structures of Race*. New York: Verso.

Wright C and Sharma N (2008/9) Decolonizing resistance, challenging colonial states. *Social Justice* 35(3): 120–138.

Zaragocin S (2019) "Gendered Geographies of Elimination: Decolonial Feminist Geographies in Latin American Settler Contexts" *Antipode* 51 (1): 373–392.

The Politics of Labeling Latinidades and Social Movements

The second critical diálogo considers the politics of strategic essentialism and the intimate relations suggested by conventional pan-ethnic labels. Beyond the militant origins or neoliberal iterations of "Hispanic" and "Latina/o," we consider ethnic labels intersectionally and across generations. We consider the increasing diversification of Latinx communities in terms of class, race, indigeneity, region of settlement, and home countries as well as the current politics of homogenization. We are especially concerned with including not only national populations more directly associated with the "Hispanic" or "Latino" label, as are the cases of Puerto Ricans and Mexicans, but also with the growing number of South American and Central American populations as they shape their own sense of belonging into predetermined and new racialized categories. The main question framing the critical diálogo in this section is: *How do we examine Latina/o or Latinx labeling in ways that complicate identity politics, account for demographic and experiential diversity, and provide effective insights into the relational and aspirational qualities of the lives these labels signify?*

Revisiting her seminal work on ethnic labels, Suzanne Oboler examines the changing meaning and social value of "Hispanic/Latino" in light of the current racialized homogenization of Latinxs as "Mexican." Centered on the expressive cultural practices of US Central Americans, Maritza Cardenas foregrounds queering Latinx positionalities that rearticulate and reimagine diasporic cultural identities. Michelle Maldonado's contribution raises questions about how we identify scholarship as Latinx Studies and the place of previously overlooked fields of study in examinations of Latinidades. Finally, Nelly Rosario critically tracks the role of DNA in the social construction of Hispanic labels as well as its potential for furthering knowledge on Latinx lives.

5

Disposable Strangers

Mexican Americans, Latinxs, and the Ethnic Label "Hispanic"
in the Twenty-First Century

SUZANNE OBOLER

1st Man: Oh, why don't you just go back to Puerto Rico!
2nd Man: I'm not Puerto Rican; I'm Ecuadorian!
1st Man: I don't care what kind of Mexican you are!
—altercation overheard on a crowded New York City subway (April 25, 2014)[1]

Trump cuts aid to three Mexican countries.
—television news banner (*Fox & Friends*, April 1, 2019)

And we're not being mean . . . We're just saying it takes more than walking
across the border to become an American citizen. It's what's in our souls.
—US Congressman Duncan Hunter (Lacey 2011)

My research has long focused on ethnic labels. Through their changing meanings
and social value, I aim to understand the changing meanings of race and of citizenship both as theoretical concepts and as lived experiences. My key questions
are: *What does it really mean in people's daily lives to feel that they belong in and
to this society? How do different individuals and groups define and experience their
belonging to the United States?* It could be argued that in some ways, the lived
experience of citizenship is really nothing other than the political expression
of that national belonging. By exploring how individuals or specific groups of
people *live* their belonging, we may be able to get some insight into the meaning
of citizenship in their lives.

In this essay, I trace the ways that the changing meanings and social value
attributed to the label "Hispanic" have impacted Latinxs' experiences of belonging and its political expression in citizenship.

In its current usage, the term "Hispanic" was created in 1977 by Directive 15
of the United States Office of Budget and Management (OMB) (Hattam 2007;
Mora 2014; Oboler 1995). Directive 15 created five official racial/ethnic categories: American Indian or Alaskan Native, Asian or Pacific Islander, Black, White,
and Hispanic. "Hispanic" was defined as "a person of Mexican, Puerto Rican,

Cuban, Central or South American or other Spanish culture or origin, regardless of race" (Forbes 1992; US Bureau of the Census 1988, 51). By 1991, largely due to grassroots mobilizations, the term was officially changed to "Hispanic or Latino" (Federal Register 1997). One of the main purposes of these categories was "civil rights compliance"—i.e., they were created to measure how well the nation was doing in the aftermath of the 1960s civil rights movements, in the fight against the racism and social exclusion that had led racial minorities to organize for justice and equality. For example, how many Latinx students were actually graduating from high school? How many were applying and/or getting into colleges? How many African Americans were being denied loans or mortgages? One way to track society's progress in ensuring racial minorities' full and equal integration was to use the racial and ethnic labels and start counting.

But, like any other names, these labels acquired a life of their own beyond their initial intent. Inevitably, their meanings and social value changed over time. Moreover, no name could fully capture an entire group's diverse experiences. In fact, from early on, many deemed all five ethnic labels to be "masterpieces of ambiguity" (Matute Bianchi 1979).

By the end of the 1980s—and particularly during the 1990s—the terms of the debates on the key gains of the civil rights movements for all the groups had been set, and a backlash began to be felt. For Latinxs, what had changed was *not* their own longtime sense of themselves as communities bound by language, by the acknowledgment of their culture or Latin American heritage, by their common goal of expanding and protecting Latinxs' rights, or of improving their lives and communities' living standards. Instead, at issue was a second round of Latinx identity creation: the construction of a homogeneous "Hispanic" group by US society and state institutions.

In hindsight, the term "Hispanic" undermined the main focus of the 1960s Chicanx and Puerto Rican movements, i.e., the affirmation of individual and group histories, cultures, identities. Furthermore, this ethnic label has had at least three other lasting effects. First, it forcibly reduced societal awareness and visibility of Mexican Americans and Puerto Ricans as longtime US citizens, effectively erasing their presence and respective civil rights movements' demands as conquered and colonized historical minorities. It also forced both groups to redefine themselves and their demands through a "made in the USA" label, "Hispanic"—imposed through bureaucratic fiat. This redefinition ultimately contributed to "sanitize" their respective histories of struggle against conquest and colonization. Finally, by reducing both groups to a label that also included all people in the US of Latin American descent and from Spain, the term "Hispanic" effectively racialized all immigrants, exiles, refugees, and US citizens from sovereign Latin American nations and from Spain, and it homogenized them into a faceless statistical category (Oboler 1995). By the 1990s, all people of Latin American descent were routinely redefined both as members of an amorphous

⌐> Hispanic erases gains of Chicano & PRicuo movements

"Hispanic group" and as "instant" US racial minorities once they crossed the US border. This included political refugees fleeing Central America's wars and an unprecedented number of "economic refugees" (Hass 2008) from Mexico as a result of the 1994 implementation of NAFTA. ← *neoliberal policy*

In this essay I explore the idea that roughly forty years after the ethnic label "Hispanic" was coined, it is being replaced by the use of a new label, "Mexican." This trend, I argue, represents a new, paradoxical, racializing homogenization—a new "linguistic formation" that defines all Latinx people, regardless of citizenship status, as foreign and "illegal" at the societal and official levels, marking them primarily as *strangers* in the United States. More specifically, I argue that today the use of the term "Mexican" expresses the extent to which Mexican Americans' historical experience now also frames the perception, reception, and experiences of non-Mexican Latinxs today (Oboler 2014).[2] — *main point*

In the context of the political and cultural instabilities created by globalization's ongoing relentless destruction of both national communities and of citizenship, this essay is motivated by the Trump administration's cruel and vicious attacks against "Mexicans"—again, a proxy term for all Latinxs. The legal and societal efforts to erase 150 years of Mexican Americans' history and citizenship through the label Hispanic were not new. Long perceived as a "race" of laborers, Mexican Americans have been historically subjected to a racial dynamic that categorizes "Mexicans" as a transnational—and disposable—workforce, rather than rights-bearing citizens. Their belonging thus denied, the label Hispanic served to continue to make them "invisible" as citizens among the citizenry and to render them perpetually foreign to the image of "real Americans," transforming them instead into "disposable strangers" in their own land.

What *is* new today is that the erasure of their belonging is both overt and very public. Moreover, the history and current social location of Mexican Americans—particularly the meaning(s) and social value attributed to the label "Mexican"—has increasingly become a barometer of the contemporary experience of all people of Latin American descent. In this era of societal ambivalence toward all Latinxs, it is an important reminder of the significance and growing hostility toward the "stranger" in modern social dynamics—as one who is needed yet unwanted, present yet unfamiliar—society's "undecidable," in Zygmunt Bauman's (1993) evocative use of Derrida's term.

From Conquered Historical Minorities to Disposable Citizens

Mexican Americans' belonging in this country should never have been in question. After all, the Treaty of Guadalupe Hidalgo that finalized the conquest of the Southwest in 1848 had actually "collectively granted naturalization to [the] former Mexican citizens" (Gómez 2009, 91) and protection of their land, rights, and belonging. Yet by the 1920s, the full import of their conquered status had become *crazy*

so clear that US Congressman James Slayden could glibly explain that, "In Texas, the word Mexican is used to indicate the race, not the citizen or subject of the country. There are probably 250,000 Mexicans in Texas who were born in the state but they are Mexicans, just as all blacks are Negroes, though they may have five generations of American ancestors." Moreover, regardless of citizenship status, their wages were so much lower than those of whites that they were known as "Mexican wages" (Montejano 1987, in Dietrich 2012). As Laura Gómez (2009, 92) suggests, "this history of entering the nation as a colonized people rather than as immigrants—and the history of the vast majority of the first Mexican Americans as second-class citizens living in a contiguous colony—have shaped the racialization of Mexican Americans in ways that have yet to be fully understood by scholars."

Mexicans were essential to the 1920s industrial expansion of the United States, and although still unacknowledged, also in union and social movements to improve labor conditions (Weber 2012, 218–19). In fact, the United States has long welcomed Mexican migration, primarily due to the economic benefits it reaps from the cheap labor its proximity to Mexico guarantees. Responding to US labor needs, over one and a half million immigrants crossed the border between the 1880s and 1930s. They gradually spread from the southwestern agricultural regions into the steel industry and automobile factories of Detroit and the meatpacking plants of Chicago (De Genova 2004; Vargas 2007).

Immigration restrictionists, including nativists and labor leaders, and labor-hungry antirestrictionists, alike, cited Mexican docility, "indolence," and "backwardness" as threats to the nation's founding values. Both sides repeatedly described Mexicans as "mongrels" and "Indians." Restrictionists argued that despite the low cost of Mexican labor to "greedy employers . . . the cost to American society was immeasurable" because it was forced to host "cheap peon labor" and put up with the "un-American living conditions" that "stupid and ignorant" Mexicans would accept. Employers' arguments and supporters of Mexican labor retorted saying, "there never was a more docile animal in the world than the Mexican." Like today, industrialists and growers both noted that Mexicans did work that no American was willing or able to do, arguing their labor was essential to the economy (Reisler 1996, 35). Significantly, both restrictionists and antirestrictionists agreed it was "impossible to affirm that the United States could mold the 'peon' into a worthwhile citizen" (38); or, as congressman Slayden had made clear, "these people" could never be—or become—"real citizens" (Montejano 1987). Hence, "Mexicans" were scapegoated during the 1930s Depression era, and subsequent "repatriation" programs illegally expelled over a million people of Mexican descent, at least 60 percent of whom are believed to have been lawful US citizens (Balderrama and Rodriguez 2006). By the 1940s, Mexican Americans' inferiorization was visible throughout society—even in the treatment of war veterans. As workers and potential citizens, their disposability was exemplified through the egregious exploitation and abuse of Mexican guest workers brought through the WWII Bracero Program and their subsequent repatriation in 1964. In fact, given how public officials "imagined" the national community (Anderson 1983) by the 1960s, Mexican Americans were summarily assumed to be foreigners in US society (Steiner 1972, 130) Less than a decade later, the idea of people of Mexican descent as foreign was officially reinforced by the Supreme Court's *Brignoni-Ponce* decision of 1975, which ruled that "the likelihood that any given person of Mexican ancestry is an alien is high enough to make Mexican appearance a relevant factor" (in Johnson 2009–2010, 1022). In other words, although Brignoni-Ponce was driving the car and was a US citizen of Puerto Rican descent, he could be arbitrarily stopped and questioned on a US highway because the potential "illegality" of his passengers (only one of whom was actually Mexican) was more important than protecting Brignoni-Ponce's citizenship rights under the Fourth Amendment. Moreover, as Johnson observes, the term "Mexican" became synonymous with an "illegality" that specifies their foreignness and has been expanded to include all "Hispanics" or Latinxs in the United States.

Mexican Americans' struggle against the racialization that challenges their belonging has partially involved addressing their own ambivalent attitudes toward Mexican immigrants (Gutiérrez 1991; 1995). Like other prorestriction citizens, they argued that immigrants took jobs away, depressed wages, or undermined unionization efforts (Gutiérrez 1995, 2). This anti-immigrant stance changed significantly due to young Chicanx militants of the 1960s and 1970s who affirmed a new Mexican ethnic identity, acknowledging the territorial conquest of their homeland, "Aztlán."

From "Disposable Citizens" to "Invisible Hispanics"

The shift in the relationship between Mexican Americans and Mexican immigration was one of the least anticipated effects of the civil rights movements' affirmation of Chicanx belonging. Ethnic nationalism had led them to explore their belonging and hence to redefine the boundaries of the United States as a nation and the meaning of citizenship itself. By the 1970s, Mexican Americans increasingly perceived restricting immigrants' access and civil rights as undermining the rights of those who were "Chicanxs in the making" (Gutiérrez 1991) and as further undercutting their own status.

This newfound awareness was to be short lived. The civil rights struggles for inclusion ultimately ended up extending political, legal, and social citizenship both to US citizens—and to legal residents. In fact, by the 1990s, "there was little besides the right to vote to distinguish holders of US passports from those who held a green card" (Schneider 2001, 66–67). In response, in 1996 the Clinton administration established what Menjívar and Abrego (2012, 1383) called a "new axis of stratification." The state created immigration laws designed "to make national citizenship status either harder to obtain, more socially significant, or both." New boundaries of belonging were instituted using legislation to affirm immigrants' legality or illegality. These legislative practices have in turn since contributed to "establish a social hierarchy anchored in legality as a social position" (Menjívar and Abrego 2012, 1383).

By the end of the 1990s, the distinction between US citizens and immigrants, regardless of status, was firmly entrenched. The state used citizenship to legally define and delimit the meaning of belonging—clearly locating citizens in opposition to undocumented Latinxs. For Mexican Americans, the results were contradictory. As citizens, Mexican Americans' belonging was reinforced—and defined in hierarchical relation to Mexican nationals. But at the same time, racial homogenization was by now entrenched through the label Hispanic. Widely disseminated since 1980, the label was effectively blurring legal distinctions among all Latinxs, regardless of national origin, status, or time of arrival. In so doing, it undermined Mexican Americans' legal status and reinforced the invisibility of their historical presence as US citizens.

With the numbers of Latin American immigrants on the rise, the press openly began to spread fears of what *Time* magazine dubbed as "the browning of America" (Henry III 1990). As the label "Hispanic" effectively homogenized people of Latin American descent as immigrants and laborers, the Latinx population as a whole came to be perceived as foreigners and recent arrivals. This undercut the perception of any and all Latinxs as actual citizens or long-term legal residents—including Mexican Americans who were transformed into "Mexican" members of the Latinx "ethnic group." The historical markers that had defined Mexican Americans as historical minorities were increasingly abandoned. Societal pressures came to perceive all "Mexicans" as "foreigners" and eventually, as "illegals"—turning Mexican Americans into permanent strangers in their own land.[3]

The erasure of Mexican American citizenship is exemplified in the impact of Arizona's HB 2281—despite this bill's ultimate defeat in 2017. HB 2281 prohibited "schools from offering courses at any grade level that advocate ethnic solidarity, promote overthrow of the US government, or cater to specific ethnic groups" (Calefati 2010). Noting that the Mexican American studies curriculum adopted by the Tucson Unified School District (TUSD) was promoting "treason," teaching racial thinking, and undermining the core values of the United States, the key proponent of HB 2281, State Superintendent of Public Instruction Tom Horne, explained: "Traditionally, the American public school system has brought together students from different backgrounds and taught them to be Americans . . ." (*Tucson Sentinel* 2011).

What do these teachings include? Few Americans today, for example, have been taught what happened to the over one hundred thousand Mexican people living on conquered lands in the aftermath of the US–Mexico war of 1846 to 1848.

That war transferred 1.3 million square miles, roughly half of Mexico's northern lands, to the United States (Gómez 2009, 89). The issue of the US conquest of Mexico is itself complex, particularly once both Mexico's settler colonialism and Mexican Americans' own indigenous roots are also included in the discussion (Pulido 2018).

Even fewer Americans know that article VIII of the treaty that ended the war officially ensured citizenship for those who chose to remain on this side of the newly established border, or that many who owned properties lost them to the arbitrary expropriations and corruption of the US courts. In addition, most Americans today are not aware of the history of Mexican American contributions, whether in building the country's infrastructure, in the struggle to guarantee equal rights to all workers, or in shaping the debates and outcomes in law, science, economics, education, culture, or politics. In hindsight, then, the Chicanxs' civil rights movements to establish Chicanx Studies represented a response to the long history of official and societal negation of Mexican American contributions to the United States (Rochin and Sosa-Riddell 1992).

Against this background, the passage of Arizona's anti-ethnic studies law, HB 2281, in April of 2010 was a clear reaction against efforts both to educate Arizona's school-aged population about Mexican Americans' history, participation, and culture and to affirm their citizenship and belonging. Horne, for example, defined HB 2281 as "consistent with the fundamental American value that we are all individuals, not exemplars of whatever ethnic groups we were born into" (Calefati 2010).

The neoliberal effort to emphasize individualism has been key to undermining community in the United States and around the world, destroying support systems that long ensured minimal dignity for much of the world's population. In the case of Mexican Americans, the effort goes one step further, for HB 2281 openly and officially denied recognition of Mexican Americans' continuous presence on the American continent, even prior to the US conquest of the settled territories.

Eradicating their historical and geographical roots sets the stage for effectively removing Mexican Americans' belonging and its political expression in citizenship. Overtly racializing Supreme Court rulings such as *Brignoni-Ponce*, state policies like Arizona's HB 2281 and SB 1070 (Arizona's "papers please" racial profiling law), and President Trump's egregious attacks on Mexican American professionals such as Judge Gonzalo Curiel (the presiding judge in the Trump University corruption case) all officially sanction the racializing discrimination against Mexican Americans and, by extension, all Latinxs. According to this implied logic, as anonymous, ahistorical "Mexican" individuals, they can be socially relocated and perceived as "illegal" and "foreign" strangers. It is as if today, to be "Mexican" resembles what it might have been like to be designated a "Jew" in twentieth-century Europe. "Mexican" has become a designation not of a concrete people, nor of a "race," ethnicity, or religion, but rather of the unwanted stranger, whose "foreignness," regardless of his/her real national origin, is marked by racial and social unassimilable difference—and hence viewed as "un-American."

Thus, reduced to invisibility as "Hispanics" and stripped of their identity as American citizens, the history of Mexican Americans has long been in the process of being officially erased—even as their status as "disposable strangers"—is increasingly and publicly consolidated.

From "Invisibility" to "Disposable Strangers"

While there is general recognition that the United States is a country that has been built by immigrant-citizens-in-the-making, in the case of people of Mexican descent, their racialized status instead has meant widespread and overt acknowledgment that, "We don't want them to be associated with us, we want them for labor" (Montejano 1987, 187, in Dietrich 2012).

Nowhere is the notion of "Mexicans," and by extension, Latinxs, as "disposable," more apparent than in today's global labor and employment context, particularly in "new immigrant destinations" like the US south (Odem and Lacy 2009; Zúñiga and Hernández-León 2005). When Katrina struck New Orleans, contractors quickly submitted the federal government forms allowing them to bring in Latin American guest workers. Their efforts were often at the expense of African Americans, who were openly bypassed by the contractors, and of the immigrants themselves, who were brought under false premises and exploitative conditions (Soni 2012), leaving no doubt as to the uses and abuses of immigration in this era of globalization. According to an ACLU report: "The H-2 guest-worker system also can be viewed as a modern-day system of indentured servitude. But unlike European indentured servants of old, today's guest-workers have no prospect of becoming U.S. citizens. . . . They are, in effect, the disposable workers of the U.S. economy."

Once again, race frames the context. As labor organizer Saket Soni (2012) explains, African Americans had been racially "locked out" of the reconstruction of New Orleans, even as Latinx guest workers were racially "locked in" to exploitative labor conditions created by contractors and developers rebuilding the region. Describing "the spaces in which human beings are most stripped of dignity," in New Orleans and across the South, Soni detailed atrocious living and working conditions as well as the outrageous exploitation and humiliation suffered by Latinx immigrant workers. The unfettered ravages of globalization, of displacement, and of disposability of human beings are apparent in the responses by Latinx immigrant workers and organizers alike, as they fight to secure the necessary policies to ensure that they, like African American and other workers, can achieve a life grounded in rights and dignity.

Their struggles bring to light the extent to which the racializing ethnic labels continue to further a divisive fragmentation among those living and working in a region that remains, as Soni aptly reminds us, "in the shadow of slavery."

In the context of labor competition and animosities, race structures Latinxs' and African Americans' expectations of survival and the strategies they adopt. In the case of African Americans, in spite of the racism that has always denied them recognition of full citizenship, they are, today, "at home." Yet, in a highly racialized and exploitative context, now exacerbated by rampant neoliberalism and the consequent insecurities defining people's lives, legal status and belonging are not necessarily any consolation. As one African American activist in New Orleans emphasized, in response to a Latinx worker's frustration about immigrants' lack of legal status in the aftermath of Katrina: "We got citizenship . . . They gave us legal status. And look at what happened to us" (Soni 2012). Thus, although African Americans may no longer be perceived as "strangers" to the "American way of life," they are members of a society that no longer expects citizenship either to guarantee their rights or to ensure the community's security. In contrast, the mobility and displacement forced by globalization has instead led Latinxs to fix their eyes and hopes on the future. It is a pact that emphasizes their "work ethic" and other similar values as contributing to their worth as workers (Nuñez 2012) in an exploitative and highly racializing context that reinforces their status as disposable strangers, permanently excluded from the national community.

Defining "the Stranger" in the Twenty-First Century

So, who are strangers? They may be citizens, or foreigners, or residents who have lived in the United States for years, with or without papers; they may be our neighbors who share our urban apartment building or live down the block but rarely cross our paths. But they're strangers—a term that is neither legally conceptualized nor implied, but one that, as opposed to foreigners, immigrants, or citizens, nonetheless connotes otherness in society. The term "stranger" also suggests that even if they do have a right to be here legally, as strangers, they are excluded from the community, denied belonging or home. That is, "In the native world-view, the essence of the stranger is homelessness. Unlike an alien or a foreigner, the stranger is not simply a newcomer, a person temporarily out of place. He is an eternal wanderer, homeless always and everywhere, without hope of ever 'arriving'" (Bauman 1993, 79).

Strangers, then, "threaten the insider/host's identity"; they disturb "the pre-existing social and cultural boundaries which the host takes for granted" (Petsich and Marrota 2009, 198). This idea is most evident in the aftermath of the 2012 election, when pundits openly proclaimed that the impact of the "Latino vote" had exposed the need to enforce the boundaries of the national community's "American" identity. As conservative mainstream opinion makers explained:

"We are losing the American way of life" (Limbaugh, in Media Matters 2012); "We're Outnumbered, We've lost the country" (Limbaugh, in Edsall 2012); "The white establishment is now the minority" (O'Reilly, in Weinger 2012).

Their statements clearly evoked the divisive "us versus them" binary that in 2016 contributed to Trump's victory and that today shapes the social and cultural boundaries of the national community. Sounding the alarm about the existence of an enemy within—an "other" perceived to be destroying "our country," targeting "our American way of life"—the pundits openly claimed whiteness as the identity of the nation and clamored for its protection. The definition of Latinxs as the enemy was never in question, nor was the nature of their fear, despite the fact that the Latinx voters were part of the same original coalition of African Americans, women, and youth that had elected Barack Obama to the Presidency in 2008.

Indeed, the postelection statements echoed earlier fears voiced in 2005 by political scientist Samuel Huntington. In a highly controversial chapter of his book, *Who Are We?* Huntington posited that "profound cultural differences clearly separate Mexicans and Americans and the high level of immigration from Mexico sustains and reinforces the prevalence of Mexican values among Mexican Americans." Arguing that "Americans" have "overlooked the unique characteristics and problems posed by contemporary Hispanic immigration," Huntington warned that as a result, the United States would lose its identity as a nation. Thus, he clearly excludes Mexican Americans and other long-term Latinx citizens from the nation's citizenry.[4]

Thus, Mexican Americans are recast as the "enemy within" (Chávez 2008)—or, in Bauman's (2001) terms, as the "deviant other," and they are redefined by the state's created illegality (De Genova 2004) regardless of status. The 1977 ethnic labels have today contributed to ensure that the "axis of stratification" that racializes and locates all Latinxs as "Mexicans" has been increasingly reinforced—together with the concomitant wall of fear and distrust between citizens and noncitizens. Moreover, since 2015, "Mexicans" redefined as "illegals," in US society, have now been declared "rapists," criminals, murderers, and "Mexico's worst!" by the president of the United States.

Rodolfo Acuña (2013) observes, "Since the Alien and Sedition Acts of 1798, there has been a pattern of irrational Euro-American angst fed by the notion that someone was taking America away from them." It is in this sense that the renowned African American author James Baldwin's words are prescient:

> The question of identity, [he wrote] is a question involving the most profound panic . . . An identity is questioned only when it is menaced, or when the mighty begin to fall, or when the wretched begin to rise, or when the stranger enters the gates, never thereafter to be a stranger, the stranger's presence making you the stranger, less to the stranger than to yourself. (Baldwin 1976, 79–80, cited in Lipsitz 1991, 70).

The postelection fears of 2012 expressed by the conservative white establishment help both to understand Trump's election and to corroborate the ambiguous position of Latinxs in US society today. On the one hand, the general consensus and elections statistics emphasized that Latinxs are not primarily foreigners but instead US citizens who, as the postelection mainstream media constantly repeated, contributed to Obama's 2012 victory. On the other, despite the fact by 2015, 65.6 percent of Latinxs were US-born citizens (Flores 2017), the immigration debates partially reinforced by the media to this day continue to foster the 1990s prejudice that the majority of Latinxs are "illegals"—strangers who simply do not belong here.

As historian Mae Ngai (2003) observed, "The illegal immigrant cannot be constituted without deportation—the possibility or threat of deportation, if not the fact." Certainly, the ultimate example of the systematic disposability of "Mexicans," regardless of actual legal status, continues to be the arbitrary use of undocumented laborers' deportation, now increasingly also invoked as a deliberate scare tactic to keep in check both the US Latinx community as well as Latin American immigrants and refugees. In the context of the twenty-first century's "axis of stratification," what is perhaps new today is that Mexican Americans' nonbelonging is reinforced by what Stevens has shown to be a "senseless and cruel practice of profiling U.S. citizens for deportation because of their skin color, foreign birth, or Hispanic last names." Writing in 2011, Stevens noted, "Recent data suggests that in 2010 well over 4,000 US citizens were detained or deported as aliens, raising the total since 2003 to more than 20,000, a figure that may strike some as so high as to lack credibility" (2011, 608).

Again, the paradoxical way in which ethnic communities are being positioned in US society through the 1977 ethnic labels is paradigmatic of the instabilities created by neoliberal globalization. In the specific case of the label "Hispanic," the consequent trend in the new forms of racism appears to be to extend the disposability, particularly of people of Mexican decent, regardless of citizenship status, to all Latinxs. Nevertheless, it is also important to recognize that the one certainty in politics and in US history is that processes can be reversed. As Bauman (2009, 2) notes, "No verdict of nature is final, no resistance of reality is unbreakable." Or as Latinxs themselves have affirmed again and again, despite the changing meanings and social value of the labels since their creation in the 1970s: "*Aquí estamos y no nos vamos . . .*"

NOTES

1   Thanks to Kimberly del Busto Ramirez for this NY subway anecdote.
2   This essay reframes and updates a paper presented at the Inaugural Conference of the Red de Investigación Interdisciplinaria y Difusión sobre Identidades, Racismo y Xenofobia en América Latin (INTEGRA). See also Oboler (2014, 75–96).

3 On the concept of the stranger in Mexican American scholarship, see also Suro (1999); Candelaria (1985); Prago (1973).

4 For a brilliant study responding to these claims, see also Chávez (2008).

BIBLIOGRAPHY

Acuña, Rodolfo. "No Dreams: The Case of Ruben Navarette." Law Professors. January 4, 2013. http://lawprofessors.typepad.com.

Anderson, Benedict. 1983. *Imagined Communities: Reflections on the Origin and Spread of Nationalism*. New York: Verso.

American Civil Liberties Union. "ACLU to File Lawsuit Challenging Alabama's New Anti-Immigrant Law." ACLU. June 9, 2011. www.aclu.org.

Balderrama, Francisco and Raymond Rodriguez. 2006. *Decade of Betrayal: Mexican Repatriation in the 1930s*. Albuquerque: University of New Mexico Press.

Bauman, Zygmunt. 1993. *Modernity and Ambivalence*. London: Polity Press.

Bauman Zygmunt. 2001. *Community: Seeking Safety in an Insecure World*. London: Polity Press.

Bauman, Zygmunt. "Identity in the Globalizing World." In *Identity in Question*, edited by Anthony Elliot and Paul du Gay, 1–12. New York: Sage Publications, 2009.

Calefati, Jessica. "Arizona Bans Ethnic Studies." *Mother Jones*. May 12, 2010. www.motherjones.com.

Candelaria, Nash. 1985. *Inheritance of Strangers*. Bilingual Press.

Chávez, Leo. 2008. *The Latino Threat: Constructing Immigrants, Citizens, and the Nation*. Stanford: Stanford University Press.

De Genova, Nicholas. "The legal production of Mexican/migrant 'illegality.'" *Latino studies* 2, no. 2 (2004): 160–85.

Dietrich, David R. 2012. "The Specter of Racism in the 2005–6 Immigration Debate: Preserving Racial Group Position." *Critical Sociology* 38: 723.

Edsall, Thomas B. "Is Rush Limbaugh's Country Gone?" *New York Times*, November 18, 2012. https://campaignstops.blogs.nytimes.com.

Federal Register. Discover US Government Information. 62, no. 210. Oct. 30, 1997. www.govinfo.gov.

Flores, Antonio. "How the U.S. Hispanic Population is Changing." Pew Foundations. FactTank Pew Research Foundation. September 2017.www.pewresearch.org.

Forbes, Jack. 1992. "The Hispanic Spin. Party Politics and Governmental Manipulation of Ethnic Identity." *Latin American Perspectives* 19, no. 4 (1992): 59–78.

Gómez, Laura E. 2009. *Manifest Destinies: The Making of the Mexican American Race*. New York: New York University Press.

Gutiérrez, David G. "Sin Fronteras?: Chicanos, Mexican Americans, and the Emergence of the contemporary Mexican Immigration Debate, 1968–1978." *Journal of American Ethnic History* 10, no. 4 (1991): 5–37.

Gutiérrez, David G. 1995. *Walls and Mirrors. Mexican Americans, Mexican Immigrants, and the Politics of Ethnicity*. Berkeley: University of California Press.

Hass, Erik. To Respect and Protect: Expanding Our Discourse on Immigration. *A Rockridge Institute Report,* April 14, 2008: 1–24.

Huntington, Samuel. 2005. *Who Are We?: The Challenges to America's National Identity*. New York: Simon & Schuster.

Hattam, Victoria. 2007. *In the Shadow of Race: Jews, Latinos, and Immigrant Politics in the United States*. Chicago: University of Chicago Press.

Henry III, William A. "Beyond the Melting Pot," *Time Magazine*, April 9, 1990. U.S. edition.

Johnson, Kevin. "How Racial Profiling in America Became the Law of the Land: *United States v. Brignoni-Ponce*, and *Whren v. United States* and the Need for Truly Rebellious Lawyering." *Georgetown Law Journal* 98 (2009–2010): 1006–78.

Lacey, Marc. "Birthright Citizenship Looms as Next Immigration Battle." *New York Times*, Jan 4, 2011. www.nytimes.com.

Lipsitz, George. 1991. *The Possessive Investment in Whiteness: How White People Profit from Identity Politics*. PA: Temple University Press.

Matute-Bianchi, Maria Eugenia. "The Federal Mandate for Bilingual Education." In *Ethnoperspectives in Bilingual Education Research: Bilingual Education and Public Policy in the United States*, edited by Raymond V. Padilla, 18–38; Michigan: Eastern Michigan University Bilingual Bicultural Education Programs, 1979.

Media Matters. "Limbaugh: 'We're Outnumbered. . . . We've Lost the Country.'" November 7, 2012. www.mediamatters.org.

Menjivar, Cecilia and Leisy Abrego. "Legal Violence: Immigration Law and the Lives of Central Amcrican Immigrants." *American Journal of Sociology* 117, no. 5 (2012): 1380–421.

Mora, G. Cristina. 2014. *Making Hispanics: How Activists, Bureaucrats, and Media Constructed a New American*. Chicago: University of Chicago Press.

Ngai, Mae M. "The Strange Career of the Illegal Alien: Immigration Restriction and Deportation Policy in the United States, 1921–1965." *Law and History Review* 21, no.1 (2003): 69–107.

Nuñez, Gabriela. "The Latino Pastoral Narrative: Backstretch workers in Kentucky." *Latino Studies* 10, nos. 1–2 (2012): 107–27.

Oboler, Suzanne. 1995. *Ethnic Labels, Latino Lives: Identity and the Politics of (Re)Presentation in the United States*. Minneapolis: University of Minnesota Press.

Oboler, Suzanne. "Extraños Desechables: raza e inmigración en la era de la globalización." UNAM, Mexico: *InterDisciplina* 2, no. 4 (2014): 75–96.

Odem, Mary E. Odem, and Elaine Lacy (eds) 2009. *Latino Immigrants and the Transformation of the U.S. South*. Georgia: University of Georgia Press.

Petsich, Juliet, and Vince Marrota. "Bauman, Strangerhood and Attitudes Towards Immigrants Among the Australian Population." *Journal of Sociology* 45 (2009): 187–200.

Prago, Albert. 1973. *Strangers in Their Own Land*. Four Winds Press.

Pulido, Laura. "Geographies of Race and Ethnicity III: Settler Colonialism and Nonnative People of Color." *Progress in Human Geography* 42, no. 2 (2018): 309–18.

Reisler, Mark. "Always the Laborer, Never the Citizen: Anglo Perceptions of the Mexican Immigrant." In *Between Two Worlds: Mexican Immigrants in the United States*, edited by David G. Gutiérrez, 23–43. Rowman and Littlefield, 1996.

Rochin, Refugio I. and Adaljiza Sosa-Riddell. "Chicano Studies in a Pluralistic Society: Contributing to Multiculturalism." *Bilingual Review/La Revista Bilingue* 12 (1992): 132–42.

Rosenberg, Eli. "The Judge Trump Disparaged as 'Mexican' Will Preside over an Important Border Wall Case." *Washington Post*, February 5, 2018. www.washingtonpost.com.

Schneider, Dorothee. "Naturalization and United States: Citizenship in Two Periods of Mass Migration: 1894–1930, 1965-2000." *Journal of American Ethnic History* (2001): 50–82.

Soni, Saket. "Transforming democracy: African Americans and Latinos' Fight for First-Class Citizenship in the South." In Latino/as in the South: Immigration, Integration and Identity: A Special Issue. *Latino Studies* 10, nos. 1–2 (2012): 11–17.

Stevens, Jacqueline. "U.S. Government Unlawfully Detaining and Deporting U.S. Citizens as Aliens." *Virginia Journal of Social Policy and the Law*, 18, no. 3 (July 2011): 606. http://ssrn.com/abstract=1931703.

Steiner, Stan. "Chicano Power: Militance Among the Mexican-Americans." In *Pain and Promise: The Chicano Today*, edited by Edward R. Simmen, 122–40. New York: Mentor Books, 1972.

Suro, Roberto. 1999. *Strangers Among Us: Latino Lives in a Changing America*. Penguin Random House.

Todorov, Tzvetan. 1983. *The Conquest of America: The Question of the Other*. New York: Harper and Row.

Tucson Sentinel. "Horne's Finding on TUSD Ethnic Studies." Jan 3, 2011. www.tucsonsentinel.com.

US Bureau of the Census. Population Division. 1988. *Development of the Race and Ethnic Items for the 1990 Census*. New Orleans, LA: The Population Association of America.

Vargas, Zaragoza. 2007. *Labor Rights Are Civil Rights: Mexican American Workers in Twentieth-Century America*. Princeton, NJ: Princeton University Press.

Weber, Devra. "Keeping Community, Challenging Boundaries: Indigenous Migrants, Internationalist Workers and Mexican Revolutionaries 1900–1920." In *Mexico and Mexicans in the Making of the United States*, edited by John Tutino, 208–35. Austin: University of Texas Press, 2012.

Weinger, Mackenzie. "Bill O'Reilly: 'The White Establishment is Now the Minority.'" *Politico.com*. November 6, 2012. www.politico.com.

Zúñiga, V., and Rubén Hernández-León, eds. 2005. *New Destinations: Mexican Immigration in the United States*. New York: Russell Sage Foundation.

6

Querying Central America(n) from the US Diaspora

MARITZA CÁRDENAS

Central Americans in the United States actively engage the construction of
their own identities and communities, even if in contestation.
—Alvarado et al. 2017

In an interview for the website *Voyage LA*, Zaira Miluska Funes narrates her
experiences of growing up as an Afro-Salvadoran American as well as her reasons for creating the Twitter account @*CentAm_Beauty* and Facebook page
Central American Art and Beauty. Funes, who was born and raised in Los Angeles, explains that she created these social media texts due to her frustration of the
delimited ways "[US] American and Latinx media spotlighted Central America"
("Meet Zaira" 2019). As a response, she created these online spaces to "celebrate
all things Central American related and to provide a positive outlet to my community that our cultures are so much more than what the media and people try
to tell us" ("Meet Zaira" 2019). By referring to Central Americans as "my community" and to Central America as the space housing "our cultures," we see that
Funes conceives of Central America as more than just a geographical unit; viewing it instead as an imaginary space that cultivates community and identification
among peoples from the isthmus. In doing so, her statements index a larger cultural practice in the United States by subjects of Central American descent who
adopt multiscalar forms of identification, fluidly seeing their particular national
identities as coterminous with a broader transregional mode of identification:
Central American.[1]

Funes's words and the creation of these digital spaces illustrate what I have
elsewhere termed Centralaméricanismo—the sociodiscursive processes that
allow some subjects in the US diaspora to become interpellated as Central
American, often (though not exclusively) by promoting the belief that subjects
from the isthmus share a common history and social (dis)location within United
States and Latino/a/x imaginaries[2] (Cardenas 2018, 84). We see some of these
features in Funes's response, when she links the creation of these digital texts
as an effect of Central America(ns) being marginalized and (mis)represented in
US American and Latinx media. This alienation within the category of Latinidad speaks to the ways subjects from the isthmus are simultaneously expanding
and critiquing "Latinx" as an identity label, as they forge alternative panethnic

modes of identification (e.g., "Central American"). Though initially conceived as a site for the resignification of Central America(ns), Funes's Twitter and Facebook have become an important arena for community-making.[3] The Twitter account has yielded one of the more popular hashtags #CentralAmericanTwitter, #GrowingupCentralAmerican, and #IamCentAm, which as Melissa Vida posits, are more than hashtags but spaces that allow Central Americans to step "out of the shadows" and "assert their identities online and form a community" (Vida 2017). As such, this online medium not only forges an autonomous space for Central Americans but is also integral in fostering a diasporic Central American identity.

But before the use of social media spaces to contemplate the needs and limits of identity labels and politics, diasporic subjects would enlist other mediums to articulate a particular US Central American identity. Perhaps no other cultural movement crystallized the emergence of a Central American-American identity like the poetry collective EpiCentroAmerica. At the heart of the Epi-Centros' literary project is transcending nation-based identities by exploring the question "What does it mean to be Central American?" (*EpiCentroAmerica* 2001, 3). Arturo Arias has illuminated the importance of EpiCentroAmerica as a cultural formation stating that they were the "first" to consciously define itself as "Central American-American" (2012, 301). As speaking subjects of an alternative identity paradigm, this essay revisits the important theoretical work of the Epicentros by resituating their cultural forms within a broader queer diasporic practice in order to underscore how their artistic productions challenge epistemological categories regarding the nature of spaces, places, identity, and subjectivity. I frame EpiCentroAmerica as a "queer diaspora" not only because it was largely comprised by queer diasporic subjects in the United States, but more importantly because of the ways in which their artistic expressions *queer* the category of Central America(n) itself. Donald Hall explains that queering as a verb entails destabilizing "systems of classification that assert their timeliness and fixity" and troubles "simplistic notions of identity" (2003, 14). Within a queer diaspora studies framework, "queering" is seen as an "interpretive strategy that produces a disorientation of dominant notions of home, nation and belonging" (Gopinath 2011, 636; Parker 2011, 639). Via critical readings of the poems "Central American-American" by Maya Chinchilla and "Centroamérica is" by Marlon Morales, I illustrate how both contain this queering/querying impetus as they deconstruct ontological notions of Central America and undermine the presume stability of the identity category Central American. This interrogation of the Central American imaginary and identity by the diaspora is one fraught with tension; as the poems as well as their interlocutors reveal the ambivalent positionality of an EpiCentro and US Central American identity, which underscores both the need and limits of using Central America(n) as a unifying term. Ultimately, this tension proves productive as EpiCentros provide alternative ways of thinking about diasporic identities.

EpiCentroAmerica

EpiCentroAmerica, a literary collective and artistic movement comprised of spoken word performers and activists, was formed in the year 2000 in Los Angeles, California. The location of Los Angeles is more than an incidental backdrop, for the transnational networks in the city is what enabled this transregional group to develop. Los Angeles has the distinction of hosting the largest numbers of Central Americans outside of Central America; currently one in five Central American immigrants reside in this urban locale (Terrazas 2011). In Los Angeles the transborder flows of cultural and capital intersect in such a way as to blur the lines between the United States and Central America. Central Americans in Los Angeles can partake in similar cultural practices and have access to consumer products they had in the isthmus.[4] The circuitry of exchange between peoples, commodities, and finances from the isthmus and the United States has completely altered the way immigrant communities relate to their homelands. The fact that Los Angeles plays host to such a deterioration of economic and sociocultural borders is critical in the development of the construction of a US Central American identity.[5] Arjun Appadurai contends that geopolitical spaces can provide the "staging ground for identity," especially those that are "spread over vast and irregular spaces as groups move, yet stay linked to one another through sophisticated media capabilities" (1994, 332). Consequently, for the offspring of Central Americans living in Los Angeles, Central America no longer inhabits America's "backyard" but lives very much within their own physical and cultural limits. Enabled by such processes as imperialism, globalization, and neoliberalism, this deconstruction between such binaries of US America/Central America, and native/foreign, needs to "be seen as a complex, overlapping disjunctive order, which cannot any longer be understood in terms of existing center-periphery models" (Appardurai 1994, 328).

Given the interstitial space the city of Los Angeles occupies, it is no surprise that it is the location that has given birth to a group of poets who choose to imagine themselves in a transregional fashion—EpiCentroAmerica—rather than simply nationalist terms like Salvadoran or larger hemispheric terms like Latina/o/x. EpiCentroAmerica as a signifier is marked by some of the cultural spaces that form the Central American diaspora, as it contains spellings of Central America in both English and in Spanish. That said, it is important to note that Central America is comprised of heterogeneous ethnoracial linguistic communities who often do not utilize Spanish as their primary language. In English the term is comprised of two words (Central America), while in Spanish, the term is constructed as one word (Centroamérica). In their choice of name, the group identifies with both and neither. Capitalizing the letters *C* and *A* visually invokes the English spelling of the term, while the lack of physical space between both words mimics the Spanish use of the term. This consolidation of two poles into one, as well the impetus to remove the distance between the Central and America is a thematic concern for this group, who, because of their current location (Los Angeles), feel apart and a part of Central America. The "Epi" before the neologism CentroAmerica adds another layer of complexity, as it plays on the notion, both visually and phonetically, of viewing EpiCentroAmerica as an epicenter, understood geologically as a physical place of origin. However, by calling themselves EpiCentros (multiple focal points) as opposed to a traditional singular epicenter, it dismantles the belief of an originary starting point. For this US Central American community home is diasporic; it transcends geopolitical borders as it lives in the epicenters where Epicentros are cultivating a new culture. Therefore, their very name rejects a single unifying vision of home.

This desire to contemplate what it means to be Central American, in all of these various textual spaces has involved an intense meditation of the idea of home by the Epicentro members as outlined in their chapbook's introduction:

> I don't recall where, some time in some class, I read a line that said, "writing is my home" and that summed it up for me. This country is not my home, not in the idealistic, sweet narrative, warm and fuzzy way that white authors in all the novels assigned in English classes described as home. Central America is not my home either. (*EpiCentroAmerica* 2001, 3)

Eschewing a conversation typically associated between home country (typically a nation-state) and host country, for EpiCentros, home is elusive as both the United States and Central America are sites of nonbelonging. Unlike some of their white counterparts, there are no "warm and fuzzy" feelings toward the United States, due to the processes of racialization Central American subjects undergo. Indeed, throughout the anthology the Epicentros bring to the fore the material consequences of white supremacy, racial capitalism, imperialism, migration, misogyny, and homophobia.[6] Central America, however, is also not invested with any affective connotations or nostalgic allusions to "homeland" but instead is framed as the imaginary site from which to create an alternative collectivity that enables community-making via "each other's words and worlds" (*EpiCentroAmerica* 3). This form of cultural alienation from multiple national/regional imaginaries, however, is profoundly productive, as Carol Boyce Davies notes, "migration creates the desire for home which in turn produces the rewriting of home" (1994, 84). Similarly, Dorinne Kondo argues that the desire for an identity based on a stable notion of home creates performative acts that attempt to construct a home. These textual performances of "community" problematize that construction by "interrogating its suppression of differences within [and by] highlighting its always provisional nature" (1996, 97).

Yet, as critical as the Epicentros are of a romanticized rooted notion of Central America, or an originary Central American homeland, there is still a gesture of seeing themselves as part of a "transisthmian imaginary" (Rodríguez 2009, 2, 222). The name EpiCentroAmerica, after all, seems to subscribe to the notion that the volcanic and seismic activity that has defined the geographic landscape of the isthmus is also embedded in the US diaspora, particularly in Los Angeles, which is viewed as being connected to the isthmus by the same tectonic plates, and through shared experiences of geological activity. While EpiCentros effectively reroute Central America from its geophysical location, this decentering should not be seen as a complete rejection of this category, and indeed it can be read as a form of diasporic disidentification (Muñoz 1999, 6).

Thus, the meditations on home become textual spaces for this group to rewrite Central America as their choice of identity marker expands the geosocial borders of this imaginary. Displacements and the creations of diasporas in the migrant landscape of contemporary metropolitan cultures have the potential to deterritorialize and decolonize as they decompose and recompose history "interlacing between what we have inherited and where we are" (Chambers 1994, 15). As such, the emphasis on the relationship between writing and the articulation of home from these EpiCentros, as well as the connection between words and worlds, suggests that one's idea of home cannot be simply inherited, but needs to be constructed, and as seen by the following texts, constantly interrogated.

Queering Central America(n)

In the poem "Central American-American" by Maya Chinchilla, the speaker begins by asking whether this neologism comes "with a hyphen?/ a space?" (2014, 22). In posing this question the speaker calls attention to the delimiting ways in which discussions of identity formation and ethnicities function within US cultural politics and Latinidad. Within Latina/o/x studies, scholars have utilized the hyphen as a means to denote their own relationality within the United States with some claiming to live "appositionally" on the hyphen, while others reject the assimilationist history associated with ethnic-American identities by living "off" the hyphen (Allatson 2007, 127). Still other Latina/o/x scholars view the hyphen as a metaphor for hybridity of "inhabiting in between identity spaces" (Aldama 2017, 89) and therefore see Latina/o/x communities as either hyphenated or "silently hyphenated" (Aldama 2017, 90). Yet in the poem there is no resolution to this question, as the sign at times appears with a hyphen (in the title) and without it (in the content of poem).[7] Therefore, the use of both (hyphen and space) not only rejects this binary option but also foregrounds the essentialist features of the hyphen, which is always already imposed on subjects of Latin American descent, while at the same time, as Claudia Milian notes, "the representational hyphen extends only to groups that have been 'seen' historically, 'here'" (2013, 143). Constantly framed as "newly arrived immigrants" Central Americans are imposed hyphenation without having the dialectical options presented to other ethnic groups of either living life on or off the hyphen. Therefore, both the title "Central American-American" (which visually mimics a US ethnic identity) and the question presented at the beginning of the poem index a "critical queerness" in regard to identity politics. According to Judith Butler, being critically queer entails an acknowledgment that identity terms are needed while at the same time they must "become subject to a critique of the exclusionary operations of their own production" (1993, 19). Chinchilla's poem encapsulates this impetus as it simultaneously yields and questions a new identity paradigm.

In this sense, Central American-American subjectivity as it appears in the poem is an "identity in the making" (Milian 2013, 139), or perhaps unmaking. The poem is not about a Central American-American becoming an ethnoracial US subject, a hyphenated subject, nor is it about being Central American, as it ends with the speaker asking if they are indeed Central American:

> Where is the center of America, anyway?
> Are there flowers on a volcano?
>
> You can find the center in my heart
> Where I imagine the flowers never die.
>
> [...]
>
> When can we rest from running?
> When will the explosions in my heart stop
> And show me where my home is?
>
> Are there flowers on a volcano?
> Am I a Central
> American?
> Where is the center of America? (2014, 22)

In Chinchilla's poem the speaker's self-reflexivity about their identity within US categories migrates spatially outward and extends to asking questions about the stability of other categories like Central America(n). The speaker's concluding question of whether they are "Central American" not only serves to further unsettle the fixity of the identity paradigm Central American-American (e.g., can you be a Central American-American without being Central American?) but also links this question of identity formation with discourses that view Central America as an ontologically stable geophysical space by asking, "Where is the center of America?" (2014, 22).

But this disorientation we witness in the speaker is vital to the project of resignifying Central America(n). As Gayatri Gopinath reminds us, queerness is a "form of disorientation," a generative strategy that allows for the remaking of spaces and entities (2011, 636). In this text we see how the speakers' disorientation leads them to ponder "where is the Center of America anyway" in order to question dominant articulations that view Central America as a geophysical space with concrete borders. Within these poetic lines an epistemic shift occurs from conceiving Central America as exterior to the United States, to one that imagines it as embodied within the Central American diaspora. This is achieved through Chinchilla's use of the image of the volcano—a governing trope within Central American discourse—which becomes uprooted as it moves from being external to internal to the speaker's body via the image of the constantly changing exploding heart that is now at the center of America.[8] As opposed to conventional representations of Central America, which position it as an isthmus located outside of that other geocultural entity America,[9] in this poem Central America is no longer perceived as grounded in one locale. It is now deterritorialized by its diaspora carrying the center in their hearts. Central America is not static—like its people, it is a migratory subject redefined by the metaphoric explosions from its diaspora. Migration, Iain Chambers contends, has the ability to destabilize the territories of both the Third and First Worlds (1994, 2). This blurring of hemispheric and cultural division transpires in the poem as America/ Central America are not positioned as distinct categories. Instead, Chinchilla provides a remapping of conventional cartographic bodies by playing with the structure in the phrase "center of America," which syntactically links America/ Central America together. As such, in this text rewriting these geopolitical spaces operates in tandem with a broader line of epistemological questions— what, where, and who is Central America(n)? Such questions are posed not in an attempt to provide definitive answers but as a means to resist foreclosing the possibilities of those terms and to create an imaginary space of belonging for subjects in the diaspora.

Likewise, Marlon Morales's poem also queers Central America(n) as it engages in what José Esteban Muñoz has labeled as "world-making"—texts that function to critique "regimes of truth" by providing alternate views of the world (1999, 195). In it, he presents us with a disorienting notion of Central America:

> Centroamérica is
> Fiction
> Fabricated in the mind of money hungry promoters
> of consumer propaganda
> and the self-hating national pretense they invented
>
> Pieced together like a quilt in thought
> Cut up in deed
> It's an autopsy

Rotting flesh sewn back together
with sutures that will never heal
like barbed wire that keeps us apart. (2001, 35 original emphasis)

Noteworthy, the poem lacks any punctuation, suggesting that its totality needs to be read as the definition of what constitutes Central America, while simultaneously alluding to the fact that perhaps readers may not know what it is. Morales employs both concrete and abstract language as Central America is conceived as a creative discursive act, a quilt, and a grotesque body. By juxtaposing such varying images and metaphors, Morales avoids giving readers a stable classification. This is reinforced by the fact that there is no period in the poem, implying that this characterization, like its object of study, is not complete or set in stone, nor will it be the only version of Central America to be produced from the speaker—possibly a US diasporic subject. By labeling the object of discussion as Centroamérica—the signifier deployed in Spanish articulations of the isthmus— followed by the verb "is" written in English, the speaker is presenting this vision of Central America to Spanish and English-speaking audiences, or perhaps those who are immersed in both cultural terrains.

Like Chinchilla's text, one of Morales's most compelling interventions is the way his poem seemingly dislocates Central America from its dominant cartographic image of a landmass. By having "Fiction" as the first word after the title, Morales criticizes the notion of viewing Central America as an autonomous ontological entity. Central America is conceived as an abstraction—as a process rather than a real physical space. It is viewed as a discursive construction, a figment of creative imagination, one deployed at times as a commodity, as a means to consolidate heterogeneous cultures for the distribution of capital, or in the case of US articulations of Central America like the Central American Federal Trade Agreement (CAFTA) or "banana republics," for the accumulation of capital. This notion of Central America as a process is echoed in the image of the quilt, which serves as a reminder of the lack of organic unity present in Central America and calls attention to the labor and work involved to produce Central Americans. The quilt, which is an entity defined by its stitching of different fabrics and colors, is a metaphor that highlights how heterogeneous peoples from the isthmus are forcefully sutured in the production of its configuration and in the use of umbrella terms like "Central American." Though initially, such panethnic terms might be comforting—an emotion connoted by the image of the quilt—in the second stanza the image of Central America rapidly descends from an object of comfort to a frightening image of a Frankenstein type of body, which like the quilt is also created through a forced and unnatural re-membering of fragments. The text implies that a Central American imagined community and identity provides a sense of belonging in abstraction. However, the minute this ideology becomes institutionalized to impose a forced unity, there is a disjuncture as it becomes "cut up in deed"—splintered in the very acts that attempt unification (Morales 2001, 35). The item of comfort, therefore, turns into the monster, as the needle that was once used to suture a quilt becomes the same tool that forcefully reassembles a dead body.

The image of a fragmented corpse is significant as it reiterates a theme of fragmentation as well as evokes the idea of diaspora, which like the quilt is constructed in and held together by the concept of Central America(n). But the image of a splintered cadaver is also a type of political commentary and critique since images of fractured bodies, autopsies, and wounds allude to the violence in that region. During the civil wars of the 1970s and 1980s it was commonplace for civilians to encounter fragmented, mostly decapitated bodies in the streets. This imagery brings a materiality to the poem as well as illuminates how the Central American civil wars have been a defining feature of collective memory and source of trauma for the US diaspora. In this aspect, the poem highlights the complex relationship US Central Americans have with their current setting, as the United States was largely involved and continues to enable this regional violence via imperialism and neoliberal policies, which in turn becomes one of the pivotal forces that creates a Central American diaspora.[10]

In addition, by (re)presenting Central America as a body—a metaphor for the nation—Morales's text is explicitly rejecting ideologies that view Central America as a national formation or *patria grande*.[11] According to literary critics John Beverly and Marc Zimmerman, in Central America, poetry has been the key medium for the expression of "nationalist discourses" (1990, x). But Morales uses poetry, the vehicle that once promoted a type of nationalism, as a means to undermine it through the depiction of Central America as a particular type of body politic—a soulless fragmented corpse; one that is composed through labor and violence. Lacking any autonomy or totality, it is a disjointed body that can only attain wholeness through the constitutive process of stitching its parts back together. By presenting Central America in this fashion, the poem asserts that nationalism is not an act of volition but an act of imposition. The "sutures that never heal" are scars and reminders of the ways in which totalitarian projects like nationalism and histories engender physical and epistemic violence by imposing a sense of unity on diverse cultures and peoples. In this work, Central America as a totality is both fictional and ephemeral since the very stitches that hold the body of it together are precisely what prevent it from "healing" and "keeps it apart." This textualization of Central America sees it as a specific ideological construct, a form of nationalist "propaganda" that is able to create a totality via "barbed wires that keep us apart" (Morales 2001, 35). The image of "barbed wire," a material associated with fences and borders, is a deliberate figurative device that emphasizes that a concept like Central America(n) is bound by what it excises.[12] Through this corporeal representation Morales argues that Central America cannot and should not be defined exclusively as a type of nation/

nationalism or geophysical space. His poem reveals the dangers linked with concepts of nation/nationalism and serves as a reminder of how these unifying gestures and "homelands" can produce more moments of exclusion. As a potential voice for the diaspora, Morales's poem provides an alternative compass that can help navigate and remap current problematic constructions of Central America(n) that have been deployed by the United States and the isthmus (e.g., seeing it synonymous with mestiza/o), which often marginalize Indigenous and Black subjectivities.

And yet, despite the poem's scathing critique of Central America, calling it a "national pretense of consumer propaganda," there is still an implicit desire to be a part of this isthmus imaginary (2001, 35). This tension is visually represented in the structure of the poem, for although the words attempt to dislocate the dominant trope of the isthmus, the form of the poem manifests an image of a bridge connecting two poles. The use of bold font in the title, punctuated by the bold letters of the last verse, reproduces an isthmus as it mimics a landmass that links two distinct elements. Furthermore, the fact that there are only two stanzas highlights the center of the page whose blank white canvas becomes the remarked space of the isthmus. The figure of the isthmus thus haunts this work as a palimpsest whose ghostly trace ironically surfaces precisely in those moments that seek to erase it. Like the content of the poem that suggests that Central America itself is a problematic fiction, the production of this type of poem also elucidates its necessity in the terrain of constructing new panethnic identities.

An Identity Based on Faults

This tension, this simultaneous affirmation and disavowal of Central America, enables the creation of a transnational (US Central American identity) and translocal identity (EpiCentro)—an identity that aims to find new linkages that forge the histories of the isthmus with the space of Los Angeles. The choice of name (EpiCentros) becomes even more relevant as epicenters and fault lines become new chronotropes added to discourses about isthmian identities. Geologists conceive earthquakes as transformative, as they remap and alter familiar territory and provide new cracks and fissures. These ruptures emerge from the collision of opposing cartographic bodies that generate new contours to our inhabited world. As a metaphor for a US Central American identity, this diasporic subjectivity is framed as transregional and contentious but generative. Tectonic plates and fault lines spatially and temporally exceed borders and physical parameters. The fact that despite apparent stillness tectonic plates are always moving invokes Stuart Hall's notion of cultural identities as a process never completed but always undergoing constant transformation (1994, 394). Producing new "explosions," the fault lines reveal the need of finding organic creation of collectivities, ones that occur within situational politics rather than "barbed wire fences," which are traditional borders used in identity politics. A US Central American identity will still nonetheless have to find arbitrary moments of closure, but like epicenters, these forms of mapping will be shaped by common yet unpredictable disturbances. Tectonic plates, after all, are volatile and rhizomatic. Each moment of tension and earthquake creates new fault lines and new sites of continuities and discontinuities. Epicenters and fault lines are constantly reproduced, each different from the rest, but with a connection to previous ones—a powerful metaphor for the ways multiple migratory movements from the isthmus will shape, alter, and contest (US) Central American identity. Thus, the poem, as a metonymical device for this form of US diasporic identity, operates as its own earthquake—a discursive fault line that decenters through multiplication, as it adds multiple cracks into the Central American imaginary, while still forging alternative transregional connections.

NOTES

1 Throughout this essay I use the terms "Central American" to denote a diasporic subjectivity, "US Central American" to refer to subjects born and/or raised in the United States, and "Central American-American" to explain a particular critical identity paradigm within US Central Americans.

2 I use the term Latina/o/x to connote the historical trajectory of the Latino sign, which began with "Latino" but now has been replaced by "Latinx."

3 Funes is not the only prominent social media blogger who fosters Centralaméricansimo. Others include Victor Interiano, creator of the popular Facebook and Twitter account known as "Dichos de un Bicho."

4 As a brief example, in Los Angeles, the stores La Curacao contain fast food restaurant Pollo Campero, which has most of its franchises in Central American countries.

5 For a more detailed explanation of how the setting of Los Angeles has been pivotal in the articulation of a US Central American identity, see *Seeking Community in a Global City* by Hamilton and Stoltz Chinchilla (2001) and *U.S. Central Americans* by Alvarado et al. (2017).

6 Some of the Epicentro poets that discuss these issues include Maya Chinchilla, Leyda García, Jessica Grande, Raquel Gutiérrez, Marlon Morales, and Rossana Pérez.

7 Though the lack of resolution regarding the use of the hyphen in Chinchilla's poem might be interpreted as indicative that a Central American–American subjectivity parallels other Latinx subjectivities like Gloria Anzaldúa's description of a border subject, it is worth noting that Central American scholars have not read the use of the hyphen as exclusively referencing a hybrid subject. For instance, Arturo Arias states that Central American–American subjectivity is unhyphenated not because of "a hybridity so advanced" but due to "a population that has not yet earned the hyphen to mark its recognition" (171). The hyphen here does not connote in-betweenness and instead indexes subalternity. For more on this discussion about the hyphen in Central American–American vis-à-vis Latinx subjectivity also see Claudia Milian's *Latining America* (2013, 141–43) and Maritza Cardenas's *Constituting Central American–Americans* (2018, 10–12).

8 The coat of arms of the now defunct nation-state known as the United Provinces of Central America featured an image of five volcanoes surrounded by water. The five volcanoes were meant to represent the five former provinces: Guatemala, El Salvador, Nicaragua, Honduras, and Costa Rica.

9 Although the term America is the name given to the New World, it has become synonymous with the United States of America. The use of America as interchangeable with the United States acknowledges this problematic imperial/colonial gesture that sees the United States as the most defining feature of this hemispheric entity.

10 Some examples include: Guatemala coup d'état (1954); military aid to Guatemala, El Salvador, Panama invasion (1989); Central American Federal Trade Agreement (2004); El Salvador Partnership for Growth (2011).

11 Central America as a *patria grande* assumes that certain peoples from the isthmus are inheritors of a broader common history and culture. For a more detailed discussion of this ideology see chapters 1 & 2 in *Constituting Central American–Americans* (Cardenas 2018).

12 The invocation of "barbed wire" in Morales's poem intertextually references Gloria Anzaldúa's seminal work of *Borderlands/La Frontera*, where she describes the "barbed wire" of the United States/Mexico border fence as "my home/this thin edge of/barbwire" (1999, 25). Despite the similarities in their poems, Morales, however, does not frame Central America as a homeland or imbue its qualities with emotive attachments. Instead, his depiction reemphasizes the words of the Epicentros, which state that "Central America is not my home either" (2001, 3).

REFERENCES

Aldama, Frederick Luis. "Hyphenation." In *Keywords for Latina/o Studies*, edited by Deborah Vargas, Nancy Raquel Mirabal, and Lawrence La Fountain-Stokes, 89–92. New York: NYU Press, 2017.

Allatson, Paul. 2007. *Key Terms in Latino/a Cultural and Literary Studies*. Oxford: Blackwell Publishing.

Alvarado, Karina O., et al. 2017. *U.S. Central Americans: Reconstructing Memories, Struggles, and Communities of Resistance*. Tucson: University of Arizona Press.

Alvarado, Karina Oliva, and Maya Chinchilla. "Welcome to EpiCentroAmerica: An Anthology." *Welcome to EpiCentroAmerica*, January 4, 2011. http://epicentroamerica.blogspot.com/.

Anzaldúa, Gloria. 1999. *Borderlands/La Frontera: The New Mestiza*. San Francisco: Aunt Lute.

Appadurai, Arjun. "Disjuncture Difference in the Global Cultural Economy." In *Colonial Discourse and Postcolonial Theory: A Reader*, edited by Patrick Williams and Laura Chrisman, 324–39. New York: Columbia UP, 1994.

Arturo Arias. "Central American-Americans: Invisibility, Power and Representation in the US Latino World." *Latino Studies* 1 (2003): 168–87.

———. "EpiCentro: The Emergence of a New Central American-American Literature." *Comparative Literature* 64, no. 3 (2012): 300–15.

Beverley, John, and Marc Zimmerman. 1990. *Literature and Politics in the Central American Revolutions*. Austin: UT Press.

Boyce Davies, Carole. 1994. *Black Women, Writing, and Identity: Migrations of the Subject*. New York: Routledge.

Butler, Judith. "Critically Queer." *GLQ: A Journal of Lesbian and Gay Studies* 1, no. 1 (1993):17–32.

Cardenas, Maritza E. 2018. *Constituting Central American-Americans: Transnational Identities and the Politics of Dislocation*. New Jersey: Rutgers University Press.

Chambers, Iain. 1994. *Migrancy, Culture, Identity*. New York: Routledge.

Chinchilla, Maya. "Central American-American." In *The Cha Cha Files: A Chapina Poética*, 21–22. San Francisco: Kórima Press, 2014.

EpiCentroAmerica. 2001. Gucamaya.

Gopinath, Gayatri. 2005. *Impossible Desires: Queer Diasporas and South Asian Public Cultures*. Durham: Duke UP.

———. "Foreword: Queer Diasporic Interventions." *Textual Practice* 25, no. 4 (2011): 635–38.

Hall, Donald E. 2003. *Queer Theories*. New York: Palgrave.

Hall, Stuart. "Cultural Identity and Diaspora." In *Colonial Discourse and Post-Colonial Theory: A Reader*, edited by Patrick Williams and Laura Chrisman, 392–403. New York: Columbia UP, 1994.

Hamilton, Nora, and Norma Stoltz Chinchilla. 2001. *Seeking Community in a Global City: Guatemalans and Salvadorans in Los Angeles*. Philadelphia: Temple UP.

Kondo, Dorinne. "The Narrative Production of 'Home,' Community, and Political Identity in Asian American Theater." In *Displacement, Diaspora and Geographies of Identity*, edited by Smadar Lavie and Ted Swedenburg, 97–118. Durham: Duke UP, 1996.

"Meet Zaira Miluska of Central American Art & Beauty in San Pedro." *Voyage LA Magazine LA City Guide*, May 14, 2019. http://voyagela.com.

Milian, Claudia. 2013. *Latining America: Black-Brown Passages and the Coloring of Latino/a Studies*. Athens: University of Georgia Press.

Morales, Marlon. 2001. "Centroamérica is." *EpiCentroAmerica* 35. Gucamaya.

Muñoz, José Esteban. 1999. *Disidentifications: Queers of Color and the Performance of Politics*. Minneapolis: University of Minnesota Press.

Parker, Emma. "Introduction: Queer, There and Everywhere." *Textual Practice* 25, no. 4 (2011): 639–47.

Rodríguez, Ana Patricia. 2009. *Dividing the Isthmus: Central American Transnational Histories, Literatures, and Cultures*. Austin: UT Press.

Terrazas, Aaron. "Central American Immigrants in the United States." *Migrationpolicy.org*, Jan. 10, 2011. www.migrationpolicy.org.

Vida, Melissa. "How #CentralAmericanTwitter Evolved Beyond a Hashtag into a Much Needed Community." *Remezcla*, Nov. 21, 2017. https://remezcla.com.

7

More than Christian and Mestizo

Race, Culture, and Identity within Latino/a Theology and Religious Studies

MICHELLE A. GONZÁLEZ

Still Talking about *Mestizaje*

Latino/a theologians love to write about *mestizaje*. I do not say this dismissively, as I myself have written on the topic in my own work.[1] This emphasis on racial/cultural/biological mixture and hybridity of Spanish and Indigenous has been a clear marker of theological debates since the earliest work of Virgilio Elizondo, a Roman Catholic priest who was one of the first Latino theologians.[2] While many theologians have highlighted the problematic nature of the term *mestizaje* and the manners in which it eclipses the racial diversity, racism, and pigmentocracy within the Latino/a community, *mestizaje*, and conversations about it, continue to have currency among Latino/a theologians, in huge part due to the manner in which race becomes a primary marker for theological discussions of minoritized populations.[3] And while some theologians have incorporated the term *mulatez* as a way of debunking the privileging of Indigenous cultures in Latino/a identity constructions, they do not escape critique. As noted by Cuban American ethicist Miguel de la Torre, "In an attempt to create a counterbalance to what Latino/a scholars of Indigenous roots have termed *mestizaje*, predominantly white scholars from the Caribbean have named their culture *mulatez*, and in so doing, have masked their own complicity with internal Hispanic racism."[4] As de la Torre highlights, both *mestizaje* and *mulatez* are problematic, for they "whiten" Latino/a racial identity by privileging mixture in relation to whiteness and eclipsing Indigenous and Afro-Latino/as.

The marginalization of Black and Indigenous Latino/as is also mirrored in the privileging of Christianity within Latino/a theologies. To be fair, theology as an academic discipline emerged from a Western Christian context. Theology, traditionally defined as "faith seeking understanding" and literally translated as "God-Talk," developed exclusively in light of the study of Christianity, and the first theologians were male religious clergy.[5] Today, however, while recognizing its Christian roots, scholars utilize the term theology to categorize the study of religious beliefs and their manifestations. Theology is one of many approaches to the study of religion, which are all often placed under the broader category of Religious Studies. Within Latino/a theology there is a heavy emphasis on the ecclesial context of Latino/a faith and pastoral concerns (in light of church ministry and outreach). While not all Latino/a theologians are wedded to these ecclesial concerns, Latino/a theology has historically been in dialogue and engaged with Christian churches.

This chapter is a constructive response to scholarship on *mestizaje* and *mulatez* in Latino/a theology and the ways in which Latino/a theologians have created an overwhelmingly racialized (defined in racial categories) and Christian construction of Latino/a identity. The first section briefly introduces the field of theology broadly and the particularity of Latino/a theology in light of liberation theologies. The second section addresses the construction of Latino/a identity within Latino/s theology. The final section proposes interdisciplinary dialogue with Religious Studies and Latino/a Studies as a means of interrogating the more essentialized elements of Latino/a identity within theological discourse.

Setting the Stage: Latino/a Theology

Theologians trace their academic heritage to the founding of the University of Paris in the Middle Ages and the study of theology within an academic setting. Prior to this, theology existed exclusively within the realm of the church and was overwhelmingly written by ecclesial leaders. Traditionally, theology has been mischaracterized as fideistic claims about God that emerge from within a religious tradition. Religious studies, on the other hand, is associated with the detached and therefore objective and more scientific study of religion. It is seen as the more "academic" approach to religion, with more affinity to and relevance within the broader secular academy.[6] Scholars in religious studies tend to avoid theologians because religious studies research contextualizes the study of religion within an interdisciplinary framework that engages the social, political, and cultural context of religion. Although theology in the United States exists in a milieu in which, due to the First Amendment (separation of church and state), religion is privatized, theologians themselves contribute to their own isolation and often engage in incestuous debates, for example, about the nature of God, that have little relevance and make little sense outside of a small circle of academics.

Latino/a theologians endeavor in intellectual isolation that limits the nature and scope of their writings and interlocutors. As noted by R. J. Hernández-Díaz, "Hispanic theologians, who have been by and large too fixated on disciplinary boundaries, have emphasized cultural and social context to such an extent that it reduces the applicability of their work to broader discussions."[7] Liberation theologies provide a primary conversational partner for Latino/a theologians. The late 1960s saw the explosion of liberation theologies among white feminists,

African Americans, and Latin Americans.[8] Often considered the younger sibling of Latin American liberation theology, Latino/a theology remains critically engaged and informed by the struggles, commitments, and concerns of the US Latino population. From its inception, Latino/a theology has sought to speak both for and from the history, spirituality, and contemporary situation of US Latino/a communities.

Latino/a theologians entered the academy at a time when a line had been drawn by Black liberation theologians who made race the primary lens through which to understand oppression and liberation here in the United States. A similar line was drawn by liberation theologians in Latin America, where poverty and class became the epistemic framework through which to understand oppression and liberation. Both Latin American and Black liberation theologies trace their origins to works published in 1968 by James H. Cone and Gustavo Gutiérrez. While Cone articulated his Black liberation theology in the United States, Roman Catholic priest Gustavo Gutiérrez wrote his liberation theology from a Latin American perspective. The former privileged race as an analytic category, the latter economic class. These thinkers came into dialogue beginning in the 1970s through the Ecumenical Association of Third World Theologians (EATWOT).[9] United States–based Latino/a theologians, rightfully wanting to distinguish themselves from and avoid being eclipsed by their Latin American counterparts, did not engage in class analysis, proclaiming that they were not Latin Americans and that their theological voice could not be subsumed into a one-site-fits-all category rooted in the Spanish language. Latino/a theologians turned to their other minority counterparts, Asian Americans and African Americans, and privileged the category of culture and ethnicity through a language centered on race.[10]

Racialized Theological Subjects

Monographs and essays by Latino/a theologians frequently begin with a section or chapter naming the sociocultural situation of historical and contemporary Latino/a peoples as historically marginalized and silenced. Therefore, to name and describe one's culture has been considered a subversive act of empowerment for Latino/as. Elizondo asserts that a *mestizo* reality, located at the borders between cultures, must be seen as the privileged place of God's revelation and is seen as a theological category as well as a biological and cultural one. Accordingly, *mestizaje/mulatez* becomes an affirmation of diversity, as difference is recast as an asset, and new understandings of plurality, diversity, and difference are cherished. Latino/a theology emerges from this racial and cultural mixture and from the sense of people living between two worlds.

Cuban American theologian Jorge Aquino explores "the racialized condition of Latin@ religious identity" by tracing the development of *mestizaje* in Latino/a theology. Aquino highlights the distinctive ways in which Mesoamerican- and Caribbean-descent Latinos use *mestizaje* in their early work: "The former (Elizondo, Bañuelas) tend to use *mestizaje* as both an analytic term and a term of self-identification. While Caribbean-descended scholars (Solivan, Segovia, and Espín) likewise use *mestizaje* as an analytic, they do not give themselves out as *mestizos* by descent or cultural identification."[11] In other words, Latino/a scholars of Central American and Mexican descent deployed *mestizaje* as both an analytic category and a descriptor of the Latino/a community. Scholars of Caribbean heritage used the hybridity and mixture introduced by *mestizaje* as an analytic category without defining themselves, or all Latino/as, as *mestizo* peoples.

From its inceptions, Latina/o theology situated Latino/a racial and ethnic identity in a rigid Black/white racial framework most common in the United States. Moving Latina/o identity away from whiteness, a category associated with oppression in Black theologians' typography became of utmost importance for Latino/a theologians. Latino/as, as a whole, become "people of color," a move that eclipses Latina/o racial diversity and white-skin privilege within Latino/a communities. Discussions of *mestizaje, mulatez,* Latinidad, culture, and ethnicity are just different ways of claiming a nonwhite identity as people of color, even when a significant portion of US Latino/as self-identify as white.[12] Unlike their colleagues in other areas of Latino/a Studies, I argue that Latino/a theologians have yet to explicitly interrogate the racialization of Latino/a people in their work and the ways in which this problematizes, limits, and essentializes Latino/a identity.

In the US theological landscape of the 1970s, 1980s, and 1990s, Black liberation theology foregrounded race as the leading cause of oppression and therefore also where the possibility of liberation needed to be cultivated. According to this perspective, all minority populations were defined as people of color and contrasted against dominant, white European and Euroamerican theologies. What sociologist Salvador Vidal-Ortiz writes about Puerto Ricans can be said of Latino/as as a whole in Latino/a theology: "The sense of otherness is always there, regardless of how much Spanish or European blood one possesses because it is based on how *Americans* in the U.S. see Puerto Ricans. Light-skinned Puerto Ricans become 'people of color' in the U.S. because the term means more than 'race'; it now incorporates racialization and displacement as Puerto Ricans."[13] Latino/a theologians entered this conversation vehemently proclaiming the nonwhite (enter *mestizaje*) nature of Latino/a peoples, even though many of these theologians were themselves racially white or light-skinned Latino/as.

Like most Latinx academics in the United States, Latino/a theologians are overwhelmingly racially white. They still claim an identity as "people of color" and insist in cultural authenticity as a leading criterion for who can study Latina/o theology. These Latina/o theologians center on topics like popular religion, everyday faith life, and the particularity of the Latino/a hermeneutic in the study and practice of religion. An organizing question in their research is whether the author or the subject make a theological study "Latina/o." It is frequently the author, not the subject, of the theology that determines the value and authenticity of the work. Importantly, this is in contradistinction to scholars who work on Latino/a religion through the methodology of Religious Studies, who are all not necessarily Latino/a. Theologians connect the Latino/a of Latino/a theology to its author.

Latino/a theologians often begin their work by situating themselves as racial-ethnic theologians and as spokespeople for the communities they claim to represent. The titles of their work are particularly telling: *Caminemos con Jesús: A Latino/a Theology of Accompaniment* (1995), *Mañana: Christian Theology from a Hispanic Perspective* (1990), *Hispanic Women: Prophetic Voice in the Church* (1992), and *On Being Human: U.S. Hispanic and Rahnerian Perspectives* (2001).[14] Within the writings of many Latino/a theologians, the use of broad terms to describe Latino/a theology, Latino/a culture, Latino/a popular religion, and Latino/a experiences undermines class, racial, nationality, and other differences that better reflect everyday experiences of Latinidad. Latino/a theologians must find a way to honor the distinctiveness and complexity of how race and white privilege function in Latin America, Caribbean, and Latino/a contexts while at the same time saying something meaningful about Latino/as as a whole. Latino/a theologians today face a multidisciplinary context where theology is not the only methodology to study Latino/a religion. A growing scholarship of Latina/o religions by anthropologists, historians, and sociologists challenge the primacy of theology and offer excellent opportunities for collaborative work across disciplinary boundaries.[15] Such scholarship recognizes the complexity, heterogeneity, and nuance of Latino/a religious life. Critical here is to recognize these distinctions while acknowledging forms of unity and solidarity. As Miguel de la Torre and Gastón Espinosa write: "We still have a strong sense for a common *Latinidad* that, regardless of all our different ethnic, theological, generational, sexual, and disciplinary identities, still anchors our scholarship and our psyches in our respective Latino/a communities, countries or origin, religious traditions, and subcultures."[16]

By nature, theology as a discipline operates as an internal conversation with limited interdisciplinary engagements. Historically, theologians have dialogued almost exclusively with philosophy, in large part because the two fields were united until the Protestant Reformation and the modern era. When liberation theologians introduced the centrality of oppression and liberation into the discourse of theology, they also introduced new conversation partners such as literature, sociology, critical theory, and history. However, these new dialogue partners also led to the question of whether these voices embodied authentic theology. Because of this, Latino/a theologians consistently engage conversation partners within academic theology in order to demonstrate the manner in which their work fits into the larger intellectual genealogy of traditional theology. This is in large part due to the nature of the field of theology. The emphasis on Latino/a communities is already seen as a distinguishing marker of Latino/a theology, which if often reduced to a contextual or advocacy discourse based on its privileging of social location. Traditional theological categories and vocabulary such as ecclesiology and Christology tend to dominate Latina/o theology, with attempts to season them with the language and flavor of Latino/a culture. The 1999 volume *From the Heart of Our People* begins with the question, "What would catholic systematics look like if it were done *latinamente*?"[17] We must be wary of theologians' ability to represent any marginalized population and how such constructs can create a homogeneous "ontological Latinidad" within Latino/a theology.[18]

A substantial amount of attention has been given by Latino/a theologians to that which unites Latino/as. As noted by Orlando O. Espín, "Despite the evident diversity, Latino/a communities still have much in common. The extended family and a popular religious cosmovision are the two strongest pillars of Latino/a cultures across all differences, serving as the interpretive, organizing 'grids for most people's daily reality and understanding.'"[19] This is also seen in how Latino/a theologians frequently speak for all Latino/as regardless of gender, race, class, birthplace, generation, and sexual identity. For example, in *Latino/a Social Ethics* (2010), Miguel de la Torre introduces an "attempt to create new skins for our liberative wine by using the tools and materials indigenous to our 'Latinoness.'"[20] Later he states that Latino/as as a whole "tend to be suspicious" of "universal claims," describing the Latino/a community as a homogeneous whole without substantiating his claims.[21] Latino/a theologians have too often enthusiastically and naively accepted the categories of Hispanic and Latino/a, a self-effacing gesture that defines *latinidad* purely in contrast to a default, white Anglo culture.

Latino/a theologians would strongly benefit from engaging in interdisciplinary conversations regarding Latino/a identity, particularly within the broader field of Latinx Studies on the question of the relationship between ethnicity, culture, and race. Latino/as do not enter into discussions of the Black–white binary here in the United States without their own constructions of race from their Latin American backgrounds. I now turn to the study of Afro-Cuban religions to demonstrate a fluid understanding of race, ethnicity, and identity that not only challenges racial categories but also Latino/a constructions of religious identity and belonging.

What Is Afro-Cuban?

The term Afro-Cuban is often used to refer to those religious practices that were brought to the island of Cuba during the transatlantic slave trade. These religious beliefs and practices were contrasted to the Catholicism of the Spanish colonizers. The term later refers to the survival of these religions that were practiced exclusively by Afro-Cuban peoples. Today, however, practitioners of Afro-Cuban religions are not limited by race or Cuban nationality. Scholarship on Afro-Cuban religions pays critical attention to the manner in which academics have constructed the category of Afro-Cuban religious identity and thus serves as a helpful dialogue partner for Latino/a theologians.[22] There are two main entry points to this conversation. The first is how scholars of Afro-Cuban religions interrogate the construction of Afro-Cuban religious identity in their work. The second is that Afro-Cuban religious practices are part of the Latino/a religious world, and these beliefs and practices have been overwhelmingly ignored by Latino/a theologians.

Here my thoughts are heavily informed by *The Cooking of History: How Not to Study Afro-Cuban Religion* (2013), in which Stephan Palmié assesses the nomenclature and approach to the study of Afro-Cuban religions. Building on the work of Susan Leigh Star and James R. Griesemer, Palmié defines Afro-Cuban religion as a "'boundary object' that partially and ambiguously bridges the interests and concerns of differently constituted communities of practice and so allows for a certain degree of collaboration."[23] Referring to the library classification of books on Afro-Cuban religions, Palmié notes: "The steady growth of BL 2532.S3 is not merely a metric for, but a part and parcel of, the process by which the object now known as 'Afro-Cuban religion' is constantly being made and remade."[24] Ultimately at play here is the question of where do religions such as the popularly known Santería begin and other religions end? How do scholars address the question of adherence to multiple religious systems?

For Palmié, Afro-Cuban does not just refer to people and practices that can be traced back to Africa, but becomes a willed designation through religious initiation. Many practitioners of Afro-Cuban religions are not Black. Are these religions still Afro-Cuban? The categorization of a religion as Black is also a factor when one considers how its originating nation serves in defining it. When it comes to Afro-Cuban religions, as Palmié rightfully points out, "'Africa' turns out not to be a continent, but a chronotype—and one that shifts around in space and time, according to the narrative constellation it is supposed to anchor."[25] Africa is whatever the scholar or religion wants it to be.

Palmié's findings about Afro-Cuban religions have strong resonance with the construction of Latino/a faith life by Latino/a theologians. The category of Latino/a religion is overwhelmingly defined by Latino/a theologians as Christian, albeit with sporadic considerations of Indigenous and African religious practices associated with *mestizo/a* and *mulato/a* identity. In other words, Latino/a theologians will argue that African and Indigenous religious worldviews and practices have shaped Latino/a Christianity while keeping the Christian core and focus in intact. Latino/a theologians speak of *flor y canto*, Yoruba religion, yet frame non-Christian sources in a dominant paradigm, usually in the realm of popular religion. Linked to this is the notion of *mestizaje* and *mulatez* as a manner of diluting Indigenous and African histories and cultures, as well as a neglect of the function of power within Latino/a identity making, where the Spanish is always dominant. Justo González, in his now classic volume *Mañana: Christian Theology from a Hispanic Perspective*, coined the phrase "reading the bible in Spanish." This term became canonized into the rhetoric and ideology of Latino/a theologians. However, what about reading the bible in Yoruba, or in Kaqchikel? This is often seen in the study of popular religion. Popular religious practices are defined as those practices that are "of the people" and are often contrasted with official, institutional religion. They are also those practices that are often labeled as mestizo in Latino/a theology. The pervasiveness of popular Catholicism is what in part allowed Afro-Cuban religions to survive, for Catholic imagery and rituals were used as a way to mask African religious worldviews and practices.

Latino/a theologians would benefit from a more precise approach about who is the Latino/a of Latino/a theology and what do they believe and from broadening conversations to engage other academic disciplines. Scholars of religion have demonstrated that among Latino/a populations religion is the one area where we find enduring Indigenous and African beliefs and practices. Latino/a theologians would benefit from collaborative work with Latinx Studies. Similarly, Latino/a Studies as a whole would benefit from a more serious engagement of religion and the ways in which it has created a space for the survival of Blackness and Indigeneity.

NOTES

1 Michelle A. González, *Afro-Cuban Theology: Religion, Race, Culture, and Identity* (Gainesville, FL: University Press of Florida, 2006).

2 See Virgilio Elizondo, *The Future is Mestixo: Life Where Cultures Meet* (Bloomington, IN: Meyer-Stone, 1988); "Mestizaje as a Locus for Theological Reflection," in *Mestizo Christianity: Theology from the Latino Perspective*, ed. Arturo Bañuelas (Maryknoll, NY: Orbis Books, 1992), 7–27.

3 These theologians will be cited throughout this chapter.

4 Miguel de la Torre, "Rethinking Mulatez," in *Rethinking Latino(a) Religion and Identity*, ed. Miguel de la Torre and Gastón Espinosa (Cleveland, OH: The Pilgrim Press, 2006), 159.

5 Anselm of Canterbury, *Proslogium*, trans. M. J. Charlesworth in *The Major Works*, ed. Brian Davies and G. R. Evans (NY: Oxford University Press, 1998).

6 See Margaret R. Miles, "Becoming Answerable for What We See," *Journal of the American Academy of Religion* 68, no. 3 (2000): 472–85; Ann Taves, "2010 Presidential Address: 'Religion' in the Humanities and Humanities in the University," *JAAR* 79, no. 2 (2011): 287–314.

7 R. J. Hernández-Díaz, "Hispanic Liberative Theologies," in *Introducing Liberative Theologies*, ed. Miguel de la Torre (Maryknoll, NY: Orbis Books, 2015), 101.

8 María Pilar Aquino, *Our Cry for Life: Feminist Theology from Latin America* (New York: Orbis, 1993); Leonardo Boff and Clodovis Boff, *Introducing Liberation Theology* (Maryknoll, NY: Orbis Books, 2001); J. Kameron Carter, *Race: A Theological Account* (New York: Oxford University Press, 2008); James H. Cone, *God of the Oppressed* (San Francisco: Harper San

Francisco, 1975); Ignacio Ellacuría, S. J. and Jon Sobrino, S. J., eds. *Mysterium Liberationis: Fundamental Concepts of Liberation Theology* (Maryknoll, NY: Orbis Books, 1993); Elizabeth A. Johnson, *The Quest for the Living God: Mapping Frontiers in the Theology of God* (New York: Continuum, 2007); Fernando F. Segovia and Eleazar S. Fernandez, eds., *A Dream Unfinished: Theological Reflections on America from the Margins* (Maryknoll, NY: Orbis Books, 2001).

9   The Ecumenical Association of Third World Theologians (EATWOT) was founded in 1976 to continue the development of Third World theologies. The first meeting was held when twenty-one theologians gathered in Dar es Salaam in August 1976 for an ecumenical dialogue. EATWOT is committed to fostering new theological models and emphasizes the irrelevance of Western European theology in their contexts. The Third World, in EATWOT, is understood not as a geographical reality but instead as a quality of life or social condition; thus US minorities are included in EATWOT, though this was not always the case. EATWOT theologians do theology from the vantage point of the poor and oppressed.

10 Some suggested readings include: Brian Bantum, *Redeeming Mulatto: A Theology of Race and Christian Hybridity* (Waco, TX: Baylor University Press, 2010); José Comblin, *Called for Freedom: The Changing Context of Liberation Theology* (Maryknoll, NY: Orbis Books, 1998). Miguel de la Torre and Edwin David Aponte, *Introducing Latino/a Theologies* (Maryknoll, NY: Orbis Books, 2001); Orlando O. Espín and Miguel H. Díaz, eds. *From the Heart of Our People: Latino/a Explorations in Systematic Theology* (Maryknoll, NY: Orbis Books, 1999); Gustavo Gutiérrez, *A Theology of Liberation*, 15th anniv. ed. (Maryknoll, NY: Orbis Books, 1988); Ada María Isasi-Díaz, *En la Lucha / In the Struggle: Elaborating a Mujerista Theology* (Minneapolis: Fortress Press, 1993); Nancy Pineda-Madrid, "Latina Feminist Theology," in *New Feminist Christianity: Many Voices, Many Views*, ed. Mary E. Hunt and Diann L. Neu (Woodstock, VT: Skylight Paths Publishing, 2010), 21–29; Ruben Rosario Rodríguez, *Racism and God-Talk: A Latino/a Perspective* (New York: New York University Press, 2008).

11 Jorge A. Aquino, "Mestizaje: The Latinoa/o Religious Imaginary in the North American Racial Crucible," in *The Wiley Blackwell Companion to Latino/a Theology*, ed. Orlando O. Espín (Chichester, England: Wiley Blackwell, 2015), 290.

12 That self-identification must be nuanced, however, for as Edward Telles argues, "Ethnoracial self-identification is clearly endogenous as it may involve a calculus based not only on appearance but also on variables such as culture, personal trajectory, and social status. . . . Race and ethnicity are not simply a matter of identity or consciousness. They also involve the gaze of the other." Edward Telles, *Pigmentocracies: Ethnicity, Race, and Color in Latin America* (University of North Carolina Press, 2014), 10.

13 Salvador Vidal-Ortiz, "On Being a White Person of Color: Using Autoethnography to Understand Puerto Rican's Racialization," *Qualitative Sociology* 27, no. 2 (Summer 2004): 190.

14 Andrés Guerrero's *A Chicano Theology* stands out as a notable exception, as do several of Virgilio Elizondo's writings.

15 See the work of David Badillo, Luís León, Kristy Nabhan-Warren, Timothy Matovina, and Jennifer Scheper Hughes.

16 Miguel de la Torre and Gastón Espinosa, "Introduction," in *Rethinking Latino(a) Religion and Identity*, 5.

17 Orlando O. Espín and Miguel H. Díaz, "Introduction," in *From the Heart of Our People: Latino/a Explorations in Systematic Theology*, ed. Espín and Díaz (Maryknoll, NY: Orbis Books, 1999), 1.

18 See Victor Anderson's Critique of Ontological Blackness in Anderson, *Beyond Ontological Blackness: An Essay on African American Religious and Cultural Criticism* (New York, NY: Continuum, 1995). Also see Michelle A. González, *A Critical Introduction to Religion in the*

Americas: Bridging the Liberation Theology and Religious Studies Divide (New York, NY: NYU Press, 2014).

19 Espín, "Introduction," in *The Wiley Blackwell Companion to Latino/a Theology*, 2.

20 de la Torre, *Latina/o Social Ethics: Moving Beyond Eurocentric Moral Thinking* (Waco, TX: Baylor University Press, 2010), xi.

21 Ibid., 83.

22 See Stephan Palmié, *The Cooking of History: How Not to Study Afro-Cuban Religion* (Chicago: The University of Chicago Press, 2013); Aisha M. Beliso-De Jesús, *Electric Santería: Racial and Sexual Assemblages of Transnational Religion* (New York: Columbia University Press, 2015); Kristina Wirtz, *Ritual, Discourse, and Community in Cuban Santería: Speaking a Sacred World* (Gainesville, FL: University Press of Florida, 2001).

23 Palmié, 11.

24 Ibid., 12.

25 Ibid., 29.

BIBLIOGRAPHY

de la Torre, Miguel, and Gastón Espinosa, eds. 2006. *Rethinking Latino(a) Religion and Identity*. Cleveland, OH: The Pilgrim Press.

Elizondo, Virgilio. "*Mestizaje* as a Locus for Theological Reflection." In *Mestizo Christianity: Theology from the Latino Perspective*, edited by Arturo Bañuelas, 7–27. Maryknoll, NY: Orbis Books, 1992.

Espín, Orlando O., ed. 2015. *The Wiley Blackwell Companion to Latino/a Theology*. Chichester, England: Wiley Blackwell.

Floyd Thomas, Stacey M. and Anthony B. Pinn, eds. 2010. *Liberation Theologies in the United States*. New York: NYU Press.

González, Michelle A. 2006. *Afro-Cuban Theology: Religion, Race, Culture, and Identity*. Gainesville, FL: University Press of Florida.

Isasi-Díaz, Ada María. 1993. *En la Lucha / In the Struggle: Elaborating a Mujerista Theology*. Minneapolis: Fortress Press.

Isasi-Díaz, Ada María, and Eduardo Mendieta, eds. 2012. *Decolonizing Epistemologies: Latino/a Theology and Philosophy*. New York: Fordham University Press.

Medina, Néstor. 2009. *Mestizaje: Remapping Race, Culture, and Faith in Latino/a Catholicism*. Maryknoll, NY: Orbis Books.

Palmié, Stephan. 2013. *The Cooking of History: How Not to Study Afro-Cuban Religion*. Chicago: The University of Chicago Press.

Rosario Rodríguez, Rubén. 2008. *Racism and God-Talk: A Latino/a Perspective*. New York: New York University Press.

8

DNA+Latinx

Complicando the Double Helix

NELLY ROSARIO

Sequencing Gold

The image of the explorer looking through a periscope on a New World needs an upgrade. Today's explorer is still looking at the Americas as *terra incognita*, but this time through the lens of a microscope and at a very different landscape: the genomes of Latinx populations.

In 2013, researchers at the Harvard Medical School and the Broad Institute reported the discovery of a new gold mine (Genovese, Handsaker, Li, Kenny, and McCarroll 2013). Using the genomes of Latinx individuals, they found 10 percent of the DNA thought to be missing from the map of the human genome.

(The research team included mathematician and computational biologist in genetics Giulio Genovese. A different DNA test would determine whether this Giulio Genovese is related to that other Genovese explorer, Christopher Columbus.)

"Latino populations have a relatively distinctive gift to give," said Steven McCarroll, geneticist and co-author of the study (Miller 2013). "Having some recent African ancestry, but just a little, can yield especially powerful information about what the structure of the human genome is in all populations."

Mexican writer, philosopher, and politician José Vasconcelos must be muttering from his grave: *¡Ajá, se los dije!* The Mexican Revolution's "cultural caudillo" exalts the mixing of races in his 1925 essay "La raza cósmica" (Vasconcelos 1925). The "distinctive gift" today's children of the Americas can offer science, as McCarroll suggests, also falls within the many superpowers Vasconcelos believes are inherent to admixed peoples. "A mixture of races," he writes, "accomplished according to the laws of social well-being, sympathy, and beauty will lead to the creation of a type infinitely superior to all that have previously existed."

Paradoxically, Vasconcelos's notion of a "cosmic race" sounds no less eugenic than the purely Nordic or Aryan "master race" promoted by Nazi ideology. Even today, many scientists, in one way or another, promote some version of racialized ideals.

In the Cosmic Race corner is computational biologist Lior Pachter of UC Berkeley, whose computer simulations of common genetic variations yielded "[t]he nearest neighbor to the 'perfect human.'" Result: a Puerto Rican female otherwise known as HG00737 (Borreli 2014). In theory, her genetic diversity protects her from parasites and infectious diseases, and it helps her better cope with stress than most people.

In the Master Race corner is James D. Watson, codiscoverer of the structure of DNA and among the Human Genome Project initiators. Believing in a biochemical correlation between sunlight and sex drive, he told a UC Berkeley audience in 2000: "That's why you have Latin lovers. You've never heard of an English lover. Only an English patient" (Abate 2020). Speaking of passions, the self-proclaimed eugenicist published a book that year entitled *A Passion for DNA*, in which he claims that "[b]ecause of Hitler's use of the term Master Race, we should not feel the need to say that we never want to use genetics to make humans more capable than they are today" (Watson 2000: 208).

In 2014, a broke and ostracized Watson sold the 1962 Nobel Prize medal he won alongside Maurice Wilkins and Francis Crick. The buyer was Alisher Usmanov, the former Soviet Union's richest man. After dropping $4.8 million for the 23K-solid-gold medal, he immediately returned it to Watson in tribute. "Dr. Watson's work contributed to cancer research," said Usmanov, "the illness from which my father died" (Perry 2014).

Eugenics aside, article after article on DNA research similarly points to human-disease eradication as the real holy grail, remaining poker-faced about the potentially adverse uses of scientific findings. History suggests otherwise. So does the hero image used for Harvard Medical School's "Latino Genomes Reveal Hidden DNA" news article: a compass over an ancient map of Haiti, a royalty-free stock image drawn from a 1678 book featuring famous pirates (Pshenichnaya 2020).

For pirates surveying the horizons of science, the double helix holds promise as a modern-day El Dorado, the place of infinite gold that sixteenth- and seventeenth-century Europeans scrambled to find throughout the New World. How scientists, too, love gold, let us count the ways.

GOLD, acronym of Genomes Online Database, the catalog of global genome-sequencing projects out of UC Berkeley Lab. The same lab made a ruler out of gold nanoparticles and DNA to measure how life processes genetic information (Lawrence Berkeley National Laboratory 2006). Another study found that cancer DNA binds to gold (Rettner 2018). Researchers in Canada are using DNA processes to assemble gold nanoparticles—which, with a slight positive charge, can unravel DNA (Chipello-McGill 2016).

So when the New World explorer holds up a map of the human genome and asks you to point the way, shrug and eat a banana.

Extracting Gold from Chiquita Banana

The ideal material for this experiment is the first "First Lady of Fruit" Elsa Miranda, the popular face and voice of Miss Chiquita Banana during the 1940s.

Born in Ponce, Puerto Rico, Miranda rivals female HG00737 as the perfect human for DNA extraction. Unfortunately, Miranda died in 2007, so we will have to extract DNA from an actual Chiquita banana.

Materials (Josephs 2011)

- Sun-ripened Chiquita banana
- Half cup Caribbean seawater
- Resealable zip-top bag
- Arm & Hammer or Purex detergent
- Adolph's Original Meat Tenderizer
- Captain Morgan rum
- Coffee filter
- Glass cup
- Wooden stirrer

Preparation

Place Captain Morgan rum in the freezer.
Let the Welsh pirate, slaveholder, and one-time Lieutenant Governor of Jamaica chill in the ice box. While you wait, travel to the warm, lowland areas of Latin America in search of a sun-ripened Chiquita banana.

Ideal location: Honduras, original "banana republic." The phrase was coined by American writer William Sydney Porter to describe the region's politically unstable countries under economic exploitation by US corporations and its puppet dictatorships. Among the three main corporations was United Fruit Company, called El Pulpo by Latin American journalists. This octopus held a grip on the region throughout the early twentieth century, from the banana and transport economies to infrastructure and politics. In *One Hundred Years of Solitude*, Nobel laureate Gabriel García Márquez describes the 1929 Banana Massacre, in which United Fruit suppressed striking plantation workers and killed over two thousand people, some said to be thrown into the sea.

After World War II, United Fruit genetically modified itself into Chiquita Banana. The jingles and Miss Chiquita Banana character were part of an aggressive marketing campaign to veil its involvement in environmental destruction, human rights violations, and corrupt practices. Chiquita hired researchers like food scientist and microbiologist Samuel Cate Prescott of MIT to publish bogus research promoting the banana's nutritional value over other fruits (Allison 2017). Chiquita claimed to be "the first company to brand a banana," whose "seal outside means the best inside" (Chiquita 2020).

Graciously accept a ripe banana from a Chiquita employee. Ask whether what the website claims is true, that her salary is on average 50 percent above legal minimum wage. She might smile and stare at her rubber boots. When you suddenly wince and ask for directions to the restroom, she might remind you that bananas can replenish nutrients drained from the body by Montezuma's Revenge, a.k.a. the Aztec Two-Step.

Before flying back home with your Chiquita banana, don't forget to stop by Reserva Biológica Río Plátano on the Honduran coast to collect a sample of Caribbean seawater.

On your flight home, resist drinking the seawater or eating the banana. Rehydrate, instead, with applesauce served by the stewardess. Don't compare apples and bananas, though both belong to the kingdom of Plantae.

Praise the banana for its resistance to the tyranny of taxonomy. Such a strange, confusing fruit! Generally yellow on the outside and white on the inside, "banana" is used as a pejorative term for white-identifying Asians. Genetically, it is not ideal, neither as human nor as fruit. Botanically, it is not a fruit at all but a long-ass berry. The tree it grows on is not a tree but a big-ass herb with a pseudo-ostem. Forget Watson's talk of the tropics and Latin lovers: the banana originated in Southeast Asia, its name passed to English from West African Wolof. And according to British journalist Peter Chapman, the banana "does not come to us by the process of botanical intercourse" (Chapman 2008: 22).

Wonder why the starchier bananas used for cooking are called "plantains," though not all are necessarily "true plantains," because true plantains may also be plants cultivated from the genus Musa, scientifically classified under the family of Musaceae, under the kingdom of Plantae. Moreover, you, too, are categorized under this kingdom—in fact, humans share about 60 percent of their DNA with banana plants.

Rub the dark birthmark on your forehead, the one caused by the sticky plantain sap in your Dominican genes and nearly impossible to remove. Ignore claims that bleach, white vinegar, or Sammy Sosa cream will do the trick. Folks in Puerto Rico and the Dominican Republic take pride in the stubbornness of chlorophyll.

At Customs and Border Protection, let this stamp be the only thing you declare.

Procedure

Peel bright blue Chiquita seal off now over-ripened banana.

Put naked banana in zip-top bag and seal.

Mash bag until banana has the consistency of pudding and all lumps are gone. Do not slap bag or mash banana too close to zip seal. (This could cause banana to squirt out, making a huge political mess.)

Subject Caribbean seawater you collected to global warming.

Pour half a cup of heated Caribbean seawater into mashed-banana bag and seal. Gently mix and slosh mixture for 30–45 seconds. Add half-teaspoon of Arm & Hammer or Purex brand detergent into bag and mix. Whether by force or eugenics, the detergent will break up the cell membrane and nucleus surrounding the banana's DNA.

Place coffee filter in glass cup. Pour bag contents through filter, then chuck filter, along with any critical thinking. The filtered liquid containing the DNA is called supernatant.

Add a pinch of Adolph's Original Meat Tenderizer to supernatant. Stir gently. Do not invoke a certain surname. Trust that the meat tenderizer will act like an enzyme, cutting away the proteins surrounding the DNA.

Release Captain Morgan from the freezer. Slowly pour rum down the cup side until the amount of alcohol equals that of supernatant. Being less dense than water, alcohol will float to the top. Try keeping alcohol and supernatant as separate as possible. Segregation increases the yield of DNA.

Let this two-layered mixture sit for a century. Watch the layer where supernatant and alcohol meet until a stringy white substance forms. This precipitation is a result of salty DNA undissolving when coming into contact with alcohol. As it clumps together and rises into the alcohol, the DNA pulls more strands along. It may look cloudy, with tiny bubbles.

Dip wooden stirrer into cup. Spool the DNA around the wooden stirrer.

Speak softly as you hold the stick of Chiquita banana gold up to the light.

Observations and Results

DNA extracted from Chiquita banana may be preserved in alcohol for an indefinite period of time. According to the Centers for Disease Control and Prevention, Latinx people in the United States have a life expectancy of eighty-two, an average of three years longer than that of Caucasians. Healthy Latinx adults face a 30 percent lower risk of death than other racial groups, despite experiencing higher rates of diabetes and other diseases (Breene 2016).

"Scientists refer to this as the 'Hispanic paradox,'" says Steve Horvath, a professor of human genetics of UCLA who researches the "phenomenon." Still alive and well are the culturalist perspectives found in social scientific research on US Latinx populations of the 1960s and 1970s.

In 2019, Miss Chiquita Banana celebrated her seventy-fifth birthday. Investment in her DNA is good as gold for at least another seven years and counting.

Noble Strains

Three national heroes stand on pedestals at the entrance to El Museo del Hombre Dominicano, currently ranked by Lonely Planet as #22 of 120 things to do in Santo Domingo, Dominican Republic.

To most Dominican kids on summer vacation from New York City in 1982, the Museum of the Dominican Man ranks low on their list of things to do. But a ten-year-old who wonders where she fits in the plant and animal kingdoms accepts her uncle's invitation to El Museo.

She stands in the shadow of the copper statues, scratching her head at the Mongoloid, Caucasoid, and Negroid bloodlines represented: Is her DNA a triple helix?

No—and not quite—says Venezuelan-born population geneticist Carlos D. Bustamante of Stanford University:

> In a global context there is no model of three, or five, or even 10 human races. There is a broad continuum of genetic variation that is structured, and there are pockets of isolated populations. Three, five, or 10 human races is just not an accurate model; it is far more of a continuum model. (Rottman 2018)

Her uncle holds up the camera. "Stand straight beside our national heroes," which he names Sebastián Lemba, Bartolomé de las Casas, and Enriquillo.

But where should she stand? Between the runaway slave and the benevolent missionary, or between the benevolent missionary and the noble savage?

Two shots should do.

The photos turn out overexposed.

At right: Guarocuya, a.k.a. Enriquillo. Loin cloth, bare feet, spear in right hand—pure aboriginal glory. Though taken to Spain and christened Enriquillo at an early age, Guarocuya led Taíno natives against the Spanish on Hispaniola from 1519 to 1533. These rebellions forced the Spanish to sign a treaty that granted freedom to surviving Taínos. Named after Enriquillo today are: a rock formation, a lake and its emergent fault zone, and the highest rank in the Association of Dominican Scouts.

At left: Lemba Calembo, a.k.a. Sebastián Lemba. Loin cloth, bare feet, arms breaking free of chains—pure maroon glory. Sold into slavery in Central Africa, then taken to France, Spain, and finally to Hispaniola around 1525. Lemba escaped slavery after seven years and spent the next fifteen leading fellow *cimarrones* on guerilla plantation raids. Known on the island as Captain Lemba, history cast him as both African pirate and first Black antislavery resistance leader of the Americas. Named after him today is Puerta de Lemba, door to the fort where executioners displayed his head.

At center: Bartolomé de las Casas, a.k.a. The Right Reverend Friar and Servant of God Bartolomé de las Casas. Berobed, cross in right hand, bible in left, he is the cleric ostensibly guiding to civilization the two "savages" who flank him. History has it that the Spanish Dominican friar was Enriquillo's mentor. While de la Casas initially participated in atrocities against the natives, he later became a social reformer, the first official "Protector of the Indians." His *A Short Account of the Destruction of the Indies* survives as Latin American Studies de facto reading.

This work likely influenced James Cameron's *Avatar* (2009). The film stars Dominican actress Zoe Saldaña as Neytiri and is set in the year 2154—anagram of 1542, the very year de las Casas penned *Destruction of the Indies*. And just as de las Casas stands heroically in the center of the Dominican triptych, Cameron's white protagonist Jake Sully champions the liberation struggle of planet Pandora's Na'vi population; both offer the image of invader as savior rather than as agent of the oppressor.

Our Saviour, the name of the Catholic school the girl attends in New York. School, her natural habitat, where her mind can expand to four cardinal points. Well behaved and top performing, she is adored by Irish and Italian nuns who struggle to educate the restless natives of a Latinx community living through a crack epidemic. The girl overdoses on assignments: her Thanksgiving diorama features three paper boats sailing across a mirror shard, from a linoleum square to a mound of clay sprouting leafy toothpicks. But like her Taíno predecessor Guarocuya, who was educated and baptized Enriquillo at a Franciscan convent, the girl wants to rebel against her saviours.

The three weathered statues in the photos have a verdigris patina, bioluminescent as Na'vi beings. The national heroes have since been restored to their original copper surface, brown as the girl herself. She is now middle-aged, with little interest in decoding her DNA. All that matters is that the blood of her people insists on flowing 477 years after the destruction of the Indies and 135 years before the destruction of the fictional planet Pandora.

Pandora's Box

Pandora, Greek for "the one who bears all gifts." By thus naming the Na'vi planet in *Avatar*, Cameron points to the myth of Prometheus and Pandora, metaphorically positioning the Americas—and its original peoples—as forbidden container of both gifts and curses.

This ancient Greek myth appears in *Works and Days*, the instructional epic poem written by the poet Hesiod around 700 BC. Scholars contextualize it within the agrarian crisis in mainland Greece that partly motivated city-states to explore more lands and establish new colonies. Think Manifest Destiny, the expansionist, pro-agrarian doctrine that shaped US westward growth.

Pandora's Box is a cautionary tale for the Catholic-school girl, who rereads the illustrated book, grafting the stories of deities onto her very mortal one.

She is Zeus, king-god of sky and thunder with the gift of mimicking the voices of her teachers and her bullies.

Because she loves to make paper dolls and tattoo stories on their bodies, she is Prometheus, charged by Zeus with creating Earth's first creatures. Her guilty pleasure: setting her paper-doll stories on fire over the kitchen stove while her mother is out of sight. After Prometheus steals fire from the gods and gives it to humans, Zeus punishes him for disobedience.

The girl is not chained to a cliff for eagles to daily eat her liver—but she isn't spared from punishment, either. Zeus also punishes humans for accepting stolen fire. Hers is the burning desire to unlock the deepest secrets of human procreation. She checks out Judy Blume's *Wifey* from the library and reads x-rated passages aloud to her friends at recess. Appetite for books is a blessing and a curse for which the nuns give the girl her first ever detention. The girl's insatiable curiosity concerns her family, too. She is *una averiguá, una sabelotodo, una metida.*

She is Pandora, Earth's first woman, the "punishment" Zeus cunningly sends to humans. He endows her with gifts irresistible even to Prometheus's brother Epimetheus: wisdom, beauty, kindness, peace, generosity, and health. Zeus also gives Pandora a container, warning her not to open it—or her sister's diary, or the unlabeled bottle under the bathroom sink. Pandora, of course, opens the container, releasing every plague and evil known to mankind, including her sister's rage and the brain-busting reek of ammonia. In a desperate effort to undo the calamity she unleashed onto the world, Pandora reopens the container. This time, the gift of hope is released, giving humans the strength to recover their losses.

Eff You

The story haunts the girl into her college engineering studies. Later, when she learns about science's interest in mining her genetic container for DNA, a single phrase pops into her Pandora mind: *Fukú americanus.*

Junot Díaz names this generational curse in his novel *The Brief Wondrous Life of Oscar Wao*:

> They say it came from Africa, carried in the screams of the enslaved; that it was the death bane of the Tainos, uttered just as one world perished and another began; that it was a demon drawn into Creation through the nightmare door that was cracked open in the Antilles. Fukú americanus, or more colloquially, fukú— generally a curse or doom of some kind; specifically the Curse and the Doom of the New World. . . . No matter what its name or provenance, it is believed that the arrival of Europeans on Hispaniola unleashed fukú on the world, and we've all been in the shit ever since. (Diaz 2007: 1)

The countershit unleashed worldwide has been humorized in tourism culture through gastrointestinal imagery like Montezuma's Revenge, Bali Belly, Mummy's Tummy, and the Rangoon Runs. Such imagery remaps the site of suffering onto the traveler's body, thereby mocking *fukú's* evisceration of the colonized throughout the globe and across time. But if bananas and antidiarrheals can slow down the Gringo Gallop, there's also a counterspell to *fukú*. As *Oscar Wao*'s narrator assures us, *fukú americanus* can be undone by "a simple word (followed usually by a vigorous crossing of index fingers)" and by the story being narrated itself: *zafa*.

Bless You

Dominican author Naima Coster reminds us in her "manifesta of a zafatista" that the verb *zafar* means to loosen/untie/come undone/loosen up/free oneself of/get free of (Coster 2009). The verb, she writes, "is the perfect description of what good writing can do. It can loosen our bonds, help us find the strength and consciousness we need to untie one another and ourselves, and overturn the original curse of fukú." And just as "Diaz offers his first novel, *Oscar Wao*, as a *zafa*—a counterspell to all the hardships and distortions of history," Coster wants her own "stories to be the uttered words and crossed fingers that help my people be *free*."

Díaz and Coster identify storytelling as a kind of hope unleashed by Pandora's Box alongside the curse. By reclaiming hope through the power of narrative encoded in our double helix, writers can offer a counterforce against the potential scientific conquest of our DNA. As translators/transcribers of the human experience, the writer essentially operates as ribonucleic acid (RNA), the molecule responsible for coding, decoding, regulating, and expressing genes. Writers are the ones who dare venture to that sublime place where, as fellow Dominican writer Raquel Cepeda puts it, "logos and mythos exist in tandem" (Cepeda 2013: xvii).

Find You

Cepeda deploys her work as a *zafa* against the race and identity *fukú* that so embittered her relationship with her father. His near death to heart disease led Cepeda to dig into her genetic history through DNA testing of herself, her father, a paternal uncle, and a maternal cousin. She vividly captures the experience in her memoir *Bird of Paradise: How I Became Latina*.

Born in Harlem and raised in Santo Domingo's Paraíso (Paradise) district, Cepeda writes, "I've been mistaken for being everything except what I am: Dominican" (Cepeda 2013: xiv). From jump, the book title speaks to the nature of her ancestral search. Besides shouting out her childhood in Paraíso, the title *Bird of Paradise* invokes, well, the bird-of-paradise, which, like the banana, kicks Linnaean classification in the ass: DNA studies reveal that this twenty-four-million-year-old family has fourteen genera made up of forty-one species—not counting twenty-four known hybrids. The provocative subtitle *How I Became Latina* (tacked on by publishers as a marketing tactic, according to Cepeda) calls out race and ethnicity as social constructs (Interview by author May 2, 2019).[1]

Cepeda constructs her own identity in the first part of the memoir, taking us through her early years in the Dominican Republic and later in the United States via the prism of hip-hop, then devotes the second part to her DNA-testing experience. In this way, Cepeda positions her lived identity ahead of the empirical one provided by scientific analysis. While this structure reflects the age-old bifurcated discourse around what scientist/writer C.P. Snow called the "two cultures" (Snow 1959) of humanities and science, Cepeda aims her binoculars at the horizon line to guide her "from one place to another with purpose":

> [M]y spiritual self still identifies with the *mythos*, the transcendent qualities found in Jewish Kabbalah, Sufi Islam, Indigenous and West African mysticism and religion. My rational self is drawn by the potential of ancestral DNA testing—the *logos*—to work in tandem with the incorporeal to help us make sense of our whole selves. (Cepeda 2013: 156)

Cepeda's fact-finding mission ultimately brings her to "some sort of understanding and peace with Dad, something that never would have happened" had she not invited him on the journey. She later extends a similar invitation to a group of teenage girls in a Bronx-based suicide prevention program. Her documentary *SOME GIRLS* (2017) captures their transformation after DNA analysis and "a trip to the seat of the Americas": "On that journey to modern-day Dominican Republic, the white supremacist narratives about American history they've been taught are challenged, leaving them free to re-construct their own respective identities" (Some Girls, film 2020).

The release of *SOME GIRLS* coincided with that of another DNA-inspired documentary (under production company Paraiso Pictures, no less) by Cepeda's contemporary in the Latinx/hip-hop community. Puerto Rican music artist Residente (René Juan Pérez Joglar), cofounder of the former group Calle 13, released the self-titled documentary with a companion debut solo album composed of music inspired by his DNA test results. For a sample listen, tune in to Residente Radio on, well, Pandora, the music-streaming service powered by, well, the Music Genome Project.

The album opens with "Intro ADN / DNA." The song was written by Residente, Jeffrey "Trooko" Peralva (Honduran Grammy Award–winning producer), and Lin-Manuel Miranda ("Puerto Rican/American" creator of the hit 2015 musical *Hamilton*):

> Residente, the first time we met was in Puerto Rico
> Your mother was in the room, she took one look at me
> And said "Tu tienes que ser nieto de Wisin Miranda"
> I said "That's right, how did you know that?"
> She said "¡Pero nene, tienes la misma cara!

> Mira, tu abuelo Wisin y mi mamá eran primos hermamos, you two are
>   cousins
> Primo, tú y yo descendimos de Gilberto Concepción de Gracia
> Fundador del partido independentista de Puerto Rico
> Abogado de Pedro Albizu Campos en Nueva York
> Nacimos con revolución en las venas"
>
> . . .
>
> A little blood, a sample of saliva
> Send it to the lab and get it back and see them try to declassify
> A deoxyribonucleic gas just from one fiber
> Scientists can separate a strand
> Tell you in percentages descendancies you long to understand
> Send you to lands of ice dirt and sand
> A map of the world in the lines of your hand
> And you'll find what you planned isn't quite what you get
> You will cry in the rubble with children you've met
> To remind you to struggle and strive through the trouble with life
> Is that life isn't done with you yet
>
> . . .
>
> Then your dreams are lucid, when you spit
> Keep the horizon siempre pa'l frente
>
> . . .
>
> Cambia este mundo profundamente
> As our global artist in residence (Residente 2017)

In the first stanza, Miranda narrates a surprising discovery: he and Residente are third cousins and descendants of Gilberto Concepción de Gracia, founder of the Puerto Rican Independence Party. This is revealed not through DNA analysis but by instant facial recognition. The story goes that, at a Calle 13 concert on the island, Residente's mother recognized in Miranda the face of her son's grandfather. Like Cepeda, Residente first establishes the value of family-attested identity before taking the listener on a journey of genetic discovery.

The companion documentary follows Residente on an ancestral search throughout Asia, Europe, Africa, and his native Puerto Rico, "discovering sounds and uncovering stories" (Residente 2017). From Burkina Faso and China to Tuva and Ossetia, Residente records music with local artists who "make music without expecting something in return," as he said upon the album's release, "artists whom I share DNA with, just how they shared their stories with me" (Residente 2017).

The *Residente* project demonstrates how a progeny of the Americas can mine results of DNA analysis for one story and through it encode transformative narratives. Residente embarked on this project in response to his disillusionment with a music industry driven more by production and profit than by process and creativity.

"When you're making art, you have to be . . . honest and real," he told NPR, "and [bring] back that connection with human beings. I think it's missing in music" (Cala and Tyler-Ameen 2017). If human connection is missing in music, the most universal of arts, then what of science and its own paradox? As scientists mine our genomes for gold, we can only replay the history of medical trials inflicted on the Global South.

It doesn't take DNA analysis, either, for Residente to validate the genetic imprint made on his social consciousness by his actress mother and labor lawyer father. "I grew up going to strikes, knowing that my dad was traveling to Central America or to Cuba . . . He was very into social movements, so I got that from him," says Residente (Cala and Tyler-Ameen 2017). In this vein, the project also works to promote community-development projects, such as SOL(idaridad) es VIDA and The Integrated Community Board of the Morales Neighborhood in Puerto Rico.

The genetic quests of Cepeda and Residente in their art and in their communities exemplify the *social power* and the *social life* of DNA discussed by Alondra Nelson in *The Social Life of DNA*. Nelson expands on ways in which African Americans and Latin Americans have engaged science as a *zafa* to their collective *fukús*. She asserts that "[g]enetic ancestry testing is about more than the unearthing of facts" for inheritors of slavery's generational curse and for those whose intergenerational ties have been severed by conquest fallout. Unlike scientists, this population holds "more intangible aspirations for DNA" (Nelson 2016: 158).

Among such aspirations, Nelson highlights reconciliation projects in places like post-Apartheid South Africa and post-Dirty War Argentina. In Argentina, DNA analysis has helped reunite Las Abuelas de Plaza de Mayo with their biological grandchildren, who, along with their parents, were "disappeared" during the country's military dictatorship from 1976 to 1983. Under the civilian government that followed, this association of activist grandmothers continued their struggle. They turned to American geneticist Mary-Claire King for help in identifying the remains that were found. King is renowned for uncovering the "breast-cancer gene" and for her pioneering efforts as a philanthropic scientist. Her work with Las Abuelas was as poetic as it was scientific: King repurposed the findings of a 1987 study confirming the existence of the genetic mother of all humanity (Earth's first woman Pandora, to the Greeks) to advance the grandmothers' cause. By using the mitochondrial sequence common to all maternal relatives, King was able to match Las Abuelas de Plaza de Mayo with their grandchildren, despite the parents' missing remains.

This is DNA repair writ large. This is the retying of a seemingly hopeless generational severing via *logos* and *mythos*. This is where science decodes the white "diaper" handkerchiefs worn by Las Abuelas not as a flag of surrender but as a call to preserve and honor the memory of the disappeared children of the Americas.

NOTE

1. ———. Interview by Nelly Rosario. Class discussion, Williams College. Williamstown, MA, May 2, 2019.

REFERENCES

Abate, Tom. "Nobel Winner's Theories Raise Uproar in Berkeley / Geneticist's Views Strike Many as Racist, Sexist," *SFGate*, November 13, 2000, www.sfgate.com.

Borreli, Lizette. "Biologist Says Puerto Rican Women Possess Ideal Genotype of the 'Perfect' Human Via DNA Ancestry," *Medical Daily: Under the Hood*, December 11, 2014, www.medi caldaily.com.

Breene, Keeth. "The Hispanic Paradox: Scientists Finally Find out Why Latinos Age More Slowly," *World Economic Forum*, November 24, 2016, www.weforum.org.

Cala, Christina, and Daoud Tyler-Ameen. "Alt.Latino: Latinx Arts and Culture," *Alt.Latino: Latinx Arts and Culture* (podcast). NPR, March 23, 2017, www.npr.org.

Cepeda, Raquel. *Bird of Paradise: How I Became Latina* (New York: Atria Books, 2013), xvii.

Chapman, Peter. *Bananas: How the United Fruit Company Shaped the World* (New York: Canongate US, 2008), 22.

Chipello-McGill, Chris. "Sticky Strands of DNA Assemble Gold Nanoparticles," *Futurity*, January 11, 2016, www.futurity.org.

Chiquita. "Build and Win." "Our Blue Sticker." "Chiquita's History." *Chiquita*, accessed February 1, 2020, www.chiquita.com.

Coster, Naima. "Manifesta of a Zafatista," *ZAFATISTA: A Blog About Literature, Art, Music, and Culture*, Blogspot.com, August 25, 2009, http://zafatista.blogspot.com.

Díaz, Junot. *The Brief Wondrous Life of Oscar Wao* (New York: Riverhead Books, 2007), 1.

Genovese, Giulio, Robert E. Handsaker, Heng Li, Eimear E. Kenny, and Steven A. McCarroll. "Mapping the Human Reference Genome's Missing Sequence by Three-Way Admixture in Latino Genomes," *American Journal of Human Genetics* 93, no. 3 (2013): 411–21. https://do i.org/10.1016/j.ajhg.2013.07.002.

Josephs, Molly. "Find the DNA in a Banana," *Scientific American*, May 12, 2011, www.scientificam erican.com.

Lawrence Berkeley National Laboratory. "A Ruler of Gold and DNA: New Tool Could Expedite Scientists' Push to Learn How Genetic Information Is Processed." *ScienceDaily*, October 15, 2006.

Miller, Jake. "Latino Genomes Reveal Hidden DNA," *Harvard Medical School News & Research*, August 8, 2013, https://hms.harvard.edu/.

Nelson, Alondra. *The Social Life of DNA: Race, Reparations, and Reconciliation after the Genome* (Boston: Beacon Press, 2016).

Perry, Keith. "James Watson Selling Nobel Prize 'Because No-One Wants to Admit I Exist,'" *The Telegraph*, November 28, 2014, www.telegraph.co.uk/.

Piper, Allison. "The Creation of a Banana Empire: An Investigation into Chiquita Brand," *Harvard Political Review*, June 10, 2017, http://harvardpolitics.com.

Pshenichnaya, Olga. "Old map" [ID 6144472]; "Compass on old map" [ID 8648206]; and "Pirate" [ID 6185017], *Dreamstime*, accessed February 1, 2020, www.dreamstime.com/.

Residente (René Pérez Joglar). "Intro ADN / DNA" (Ft. Lin-Manuel Miranda), track 1 on *Residente*, FMG/UCI, 2017.

_____. "Intro [English]." Residente, 2017. Accessed February 1, 2020, http://residente.com/en/.

Rettner, Rachael. "Cancer DNA Binds to Gold. That Could Lead to New Cancer Blood Test," *LiveScience*, December 4, 2018, www.livescience.com/.

Rotman, David. "DNA Databases Are Too White. This Man Aims to Fix That," *MIT Technology Review*, October 24, 2018, www.technologyreview.com/.

Some Girls. Film. Accessed February 1, 2020. https://somegirlsdoc.com/.

Snow, C. P. *The Two Cultures and the Scientific Revolution* (Cambridge: Cambridge University Press, 1959).

Vasconcelos, José. *La Raza Cósmica: Misión De La Raza Iberoamericana, Notas De Viajes a La América Del Sur* (Madrid: Agencia Mundial de Librería, 1925).

Watson, James D. *A Passion for DNA: Genes, Genomes, and Society* (Cold Spring Harbor: Cold Spring Harbor Laboratory Press, 2000), 208.

CRITICAL DIÁLOGO 3

Recasting Spaces, Embodying Community

This critical diálogo draws from an understanding of space as inherently productive of and produced through social, psychological, and historical experiences that make up Latinx local worlds. Building upon the claim that "reading the word [is] reading the world" (Freire 1985), the essays in this critical diáologo examine a variety of Latinx spaces in relationship to language and collective meaning making to highlight the connections between how reading the built and social environment is often inseparable from reading text and words. A question framing the critical diálogo in this section is: *What do we gain, as humanistic social scientists, from reading contexts and texts or language as mutually constitutive forms of vernacular space-making and psychological facets of place in the community-building struggles of Latin American and Caribbean populations in the United States?*

The essays in this critical diálogo approach this question from a variety of perspectives. Cecilia Menjívar examines the transnational experiences of Guatemalan-origin children in the United States. From an environmental psychology perspective, Rebio Díaz considers the vernacular insertion of ambient text—street signs, advertisement—as *testimonio* in Harlem's El Barrio. As modes of inscribing public spaces through the smells, sounds, and visual Mayan cultural markers, Alicia Ivonne Estrada analyzes Los Angeles food markets. Anahí Viladrich studies the connection between social capital and public mental health practices of Argentine immigrants in NYC. "Recasting Spaces, Embodying Community" considers texts and contexts in relation to transnational commitments, the urban environment, and the body and wellness to offer more complex, rigorous, and multidimensional understandings of Latinx communities.

9

Guatemalan-Origin Children's Transnational Ties

CECILIA MENJÍVAR

Can one speak of second-generation transnationalism? The concept of transnationalism links two important aspects of immigrants' experiences—the formation of families and immigrant communities in the host country on the one hand and, on the other, the continued orientation of these groups to their homeland (Glick Schiller et al. 1992, 1). I examine whether attachments to the parental homeland persist among immigrant children and children of immigrants, and what factors might foster or hinder such ties in the long run.

An inquiry into transnationalism among immigrant children may provide evidence to evaluate what transnationalism means beyond the immigrant generation, while assessing whether those transnational spaces (created by the first generation) will be sustained in the long run. Since notions of transnationalism, and perhaps the concept itself, have been largely based on the experiences of the parent generation and perhaps constructed through their vantage point, it will be fruitful to assess the long-term relevance of those experiences as the next generation reaches adulthood in the host country.

There are two caveats I need to make before engaging in this discussion. First, this chapter is based on the experiences of Guatemalan immigrants who arrived in Los Angeles in the 1990s. Since large-scale emigration from Guatemala is relatively recent, it may be too early to speak of a fully developed second generation. Thus, the experiences of the "1.5" generation may shed light on the children's experiences and may be a good gauge of what lies ahead for the second generation. Caution, however, is needed, as the children born in the United States (the second generation) and those born in Guatemala (the "1.5" generation) differ in important aspects (particularly legal status, language, and identity) that may affect their views and orientations to home.

Second, Guatemalan migration to the United States exemplifies key aspects of how transnational ties develop and are maintained. Transnational ties are produced within specific historical contexts, at the intersection of macrostructural (e.g., economy, polity, military, colonial ties between sending and receiving points) and micro processes (e.g., affective ties, memory, feelings of belonging or exclusion, love, laughter). These links are deeply woven, as in the case of

Abridged version from *Journal of Ethnic and Migration Studies* 28, no. 3 (2002): 531–52.

Guatemalan migrants in the United States, whose migration has roots in political decisions, military interventions, and economic policies in which the United States has played a central role historically. As such, origin and destination are intimately connected historically. Guatemalan migration has continued and even increased, especially in the 2010s as violence has persisted (being transformed from political/state violence to everyday violence in the form of crimes) and expanded through militarized border policies that stretch all the way through Mexico. Violence—political in the past, everyday and interpersonal in the present, has shaped Guatemalan migration past and present. Young Guatemalans' transnational ties should be viewed through this lens.

Background

Most Guatemalans with whom I spoke commented on the perils of the trip, the abuses from immigration officials in Mexico, as well as from the *coyotes* (smugglers) whom they hired to bring them into the United States. Children, whether alone or accompanied by adults, also faced robberies, extortion, beatings, and in many instances—particularly the girls—rape. For many, traumatic episodes have not ended upon arrival in the United States; they are arrested and detained by US immigration enforcement. And even when they go straight to their families, they face the hardships of life as undocumented or semi-documented immigrants.

A few observations on transnationalism as it relates to the state and to the immigrants' socio-economic background helps to contextualize the discussion. First, the role of both the sending and receiving states in fostering or hindering social spaces where immigrants can orchestrate their transnational activities is crucial. Scholars have noted the sending state's presence in organizing, fostering, or even co-opting transnational alliances (see Kearney 1995; FitzGerald 2008). As the "guardian of national borders" (Kearney 1995, 548), the state creates legal (and physical) borders that can weaken the maintenance of immigrants' ties to their place of origin. It is within these constraints—often in response to them—that immigrants fashion their own transnational activities. In the Guatemalan case discussed here, both the receiving and the sending states have placed institutional obstacles that may prevent the children's continuation of sustained ties with their origin country. The United States in particular has never formally recognized that U.S.-bound Guatemalan migration has been the result of a long history of US military intervention, economic policies, and neoliberal reforms that disadvantage the majority of Guatemalans. As such, the U.S. government bears responsibility for the lives of Guatemalans who today must make a harrowing journey north to escape the consequences of U.S. interventions, including the generalized violence that decades of military interventions (and direct training) have made possible (Menjívar 2009).

Although people may act transnationally (e.g., remitting gifts and money, staying connected through social media and telephone, coordinating birthday celebrations) despite the receiving state's entry restrictions—as it has been argued that travel is not required for active transnational participation (Portes, Guarnizo, and Landolt 1999)—these conditions may reflect the parent generation's experiences, on whose experiences the concept of transnationalism is based. When children do not remember or might not have ever seen their parents' homeland, and when they cannot travel there easily, and are unable to communicate—culturally and linguistically—with families and other individuals back home, their potential for being interested in maintaining ties with their home country may be curtailed. Many of the Guatemalans I met were undocumented. Of my 26 study participants, eleven had undocumented children (three of whom were in the process of legalizing their status), and ten had children with some form of documentation, often U.S. citizenship. U.S. immigration policies hinder a freer movement for these Guatemalans—adults and children alike. Two Guatemalan consuls I interviewed emphasized that without Guatemalan children having regular physical contact—through travel—with their communities of origin, there would be very little, if any, potential for the children to establish or continue ties with these communities back in Guatemala. Both consuls noted that, even with frequent travel, Guatemalan parents would have to "fight" the forces of assimilation in the United States to make their children even partially interested in the home communities in Guatemala.

Another point relates to ethnicity, as the Guatemalan group in this study comprises two ethnically different groups. This ethnic difference has important, complex consequences for the views and orientations of the children toward their communities of origin. Even though Indigenous Guatemalan children have suffered social and cultural dislocation arising from their migration that is similar to that of their *ladino* counterparts,[1] their orientation toward home is shaped by a linguistic and cultural legacy intimately linked to their place of origin. This cultural heritage does not remain static, but this legacy may nourish transnational ties among Indigenous Guatemalan youth. Although both *ladino* and Indigenous children's perceptions of home have been molded by their experiences in Guatemala, during their journey, and as they arrive in the United States, their contrasting legacies have fashioned their views of "home" dissimilarly. For instance, one of the Guatemalan consuls I interviewed commented on the Indigenous Guatemalans' somewhat greater propensity to register their children as Guatemalans. He linked it to the Indigenous Guatemalans' ownership of plots of land in Guatemala that they want their children to inherit. These parents made efforts to preserve their plots of land, however small, as land is not simply a landholding for them; it is community and where many still have extended family. At the same time, however, Indigenous parents spoke of their children's advantages—as Indigenous people—of living in the United States.

I focus on two spheres in the everyday lives of Guatemalan children to illustrate if and in what ways attachments to their communities of origin were sustained. One area represented an institutional arena—the church—which provided ample opportunities for the parent generation to remain connected to their homeland. The other area is a practice—language—which, if maintained, could greatly enhance the children's ties to the home country. In each area, I examine ethnic differences—how *ladinos* and Indigenous Guatemalans differ in their views and manifestations of links to their homeland.[2] While a thorough analysis by social class is beyond the scope of this discussion and my informants had largely homogeneous class origins and insertion, it is helpful to keep in mind this important social position as well.

Church and Religious Participation

Most of the Guatemalan parents in this study indicated a religious affiliation, which can be roughly categorized as either Catholic or evangelical.[3] About one third were active members of their church, sometimes attending as often as four times per week, particularly among the evangelicals. Among the evangelical churchgoers, some attended the same church as they did in Guatemala, thanks to the presence of the same congregation in both places. In fact, there was substantial communication and exchange between some evangelical church branches in Guatemala and in the United States, making it almost a single religious entity. I once attended an evangelical church service in Guatemala when a Puerto Rican pastor from the sister church in Los Angeles was preaching.[4] This pastor travelled to Guatemala regularly and felt "at home here and there." He, along with other members of the congregation, served as an important link between the two congregations.

Evangelicals

The evangelical church congregations I observed in Los Angeles seemed active in maintaining close institutional ties with sister churches in Guatemala. One of them was predominantly Indigenous, while the other was mostly *ladina*. These churches did not seek to forge links with one specific place of origin, but instead tried to create ties to the members' homelands more generally, in efforts to spread the Word. Every Sunday after the main service, they would sell Guatemalan food and meet and talk with fellow compatriots, and the conversations usually focused on events back home. But whereas the parents in evangelical churches were quite involved in church activities—including those oriented to Guatemala—these churches did not provide spaces for the children's direct participation. The young members participated in the adults' activities, but it was the parents' efforts that kept them active in the church. The children's participation was limited to attending services like everyone else and, occasionally, a talk on the dangers of drugs and early pregnancies.[5]

Though not as enthusiastic as their parents, Indigenous children appeared slightly more engaged than their *ladino* counterparts. This was probably due to the Indigenous parents' concerted efforts to keep these children active in the church. For example, María explained that:

> we [indigenous] have to get into these kids' heads [that they have to have] respect for who we are, that they don't forget where they come from. They can get ahead (economically) here, but they can't forget that they are . . . you know, that they are indigenous, that they have a homeland in Guatemala. . . . Otherwise, they'll never understand who they are . . . If we don't remind them of that, if I don't explain that they have ancestors in Guatemala, they'll never know.

María even sent her youngest daughter—the only one of her children who was born in the United States—to visit her town in Guatemala. While there, the girl attended evangelical services with relatives, which was important for María. It seemed that going to an evangelical church while visiting Guatemala had provided the girl with a sense of continuity between her life in Los Angeles and Guatemala; in that church in Guatemala, they often prayed for the "absent in the families" (the migrants). When the girl came back to the United States, she brought a complete *traje* (indigenous outfit) to wear on special occasions. According to María, however, the girl refuses to wear it because she is still unclear why she needs to be reminded (by wearing a traditional outfit) of a place she hardly knows.

María's oldest daughter, on the other hand, has never been back to Guatemala. She left when she was nine years old, but because she is still undocumented, she cannot leave the United States for it would be too difficult to make it back. She appeared to miss what she vaguely remembered from living in Guatemala yet said that, while she would like to visit her town someday, her "home" is now in the United States. At church she is actively involved in the choir but seemed indifferent to the church's efforts to maintain ties with her hometown. She explained that she knew about her origins, understood her Mayan roots and the importance of her homeland—which her mother always instilled in her—but did not think an allegiance to Guatemala or to her hometown was relevant for her life in the United States. In my conversation with her, she was evidently more interested in obtaining information about educational opportunities in the United States and what life as a college student was like, than in discussing the limited contact she has with her family and hometown. She mentioned that if the church wanted to involve the youngsters, it should set up a program to provide information about opportunities in the United States; she simply did not think activities oriented to their homeland would be attractive to her age group. The girl's perception of ties to home was also shaped by her own ethnicity. She mentioned that, as an Indigenous person, she was more inclined to focus on her life in the United States, as the frame of reference many Indigenous Guatemalans have—their experiences of racism in Guatemala—can lead them to see "less racism" in the United States.[6] In her words, "My mother says that here we [indigenous] have more opportunities than in Guatemala. Here I can be a doctor if I want to, there I can't do it because they don't like us . . . they don't like Mayans . . . or something like that . . . that's what my mother says, I don't know. So it's better that I live here, right?"

Like Indigenous parents, *ladinos* also encouraged their children to participate in church activities. The *ladino* parents also inculcated in their children respect for the brothers and sisters in the church, for the church itself, and for the parents and the elderly. But they did not appear to instill in their children the loyalty to home that the Indigenous parents tried to infuse in their offspring. Ties with the communities of origin did not figure prominently among the *ladino* parents, and the *ladino* children were not exposed to the traditions such as language, dress, and celebrations that signaled an Indigenous identity and home for the Maya children that allowed them to "remember home." Thus, the *ladino* children's orientation to home (if at all present) seemed even more tenuous than that of Indigenous children.

Catholic

The Catholic churches organized groups or "ministries," each with its own "mission." These ministries include dissemination of the Word, choral singing, Bible reading, a meeting for the young, and a group that visited the sick in the congregation. These groups are important arenas where transnational activities are manifested institutionally because they often are composed of people from the same town in Guatemala. In contrast to the evangelical churches, the Catholic churches had created spaces to integrate young members and included youth concerns and activities within the church. The Catholic youth groups were mostly concerned with preventing drug use and teenage pregnancies, which are immediate concerns among parents. While some teenagers with whom I spoke mentioned the importance of such efforts, they did not seem convinced that attending talks on drug prevention at church was preferable to spending a weekend evening in the company of their peers.

Meanwhile, adult members of the Catholic church were engaged in maintaining ties with their churches in Guatemala.[7] Whereas youth had specific arenas of participation in the Catholic church, they did not seem to be any more engaged in transnational activities than their evangelical counterparts. Like the case of the evangelical churches, Catholic Indigenous parents seemed to be slightly more successful in their attempts to orient their children to their communities of origin, mostly because in their case, church activities were usually accompanied by traditions rooted in Indigenous culture.

Rosa, a Kaqchikel woman and a devout Catholic, was excited that her nine-year-old daughter was finally going to receive first communion. The daughter normally would have had this sacrament around age seven, but it had been delayed because of transnational arrangements had to be made. The *traje* that the girl wore for this special day was being woven in Guatemala and had taken longer than expected. Rosa could not conceive the idea that her daughter could wear something else, or that the celebration could be done differently because, according to her, "We respect the tradition, and we have to do what our parents want us to do . . . as if they were here. When I received my communion, I also wore a new *traje*, so it's only natural that my mother [the girl's grandmother] wants my girl to do the same." Rosa made sure they took good pictures of the girl in her *traje*—holding a candle and a rosary and wearing a brand-new pair of tennis shoes—to send back home, so that "everyone is satisfied."

When her older daughter reached her fifteenth birthday and had a "*quinceañera*" celebration in Guatemala, Rosa sent her clothes, money, and pink decorations for the celebration that followed a Catholic mass in the daughter's honor. Later, Rosa received a nice portrait of her daughter in the traditional *traje*, wearing some of the gifts her mother had sent, including a digital watch and a plastic purse fashionable among US teenagers. The first communion and the "*quinceañera*" celebration involved significant coordination between Los Angeles and Guatemala, including collaboration by the priests in both churches. I should note the gender inflected nature of these practices, as women figure prominently in maintaining these traditions and also as those who practice them.

The *ladino* children in the Catholic churches also celebrated the sacraments with reminders from home, but I did not notice among them the same fervor that the Indigenous parents showed in recreating traditional ceremonies and celebrations in the United States. The *ladino* children in Los Angeles seemed largely indifferent to any input from Guatemala. Like the Indigenous children, the *ladino* youth also felt that these traditions were "too Guatemalan." For instance, at a dance celebrating the beginning of the Christmas season, several people initially spoke of the importance of this season in Guatemala and of the special closeness they felt to their hometown at this time of the year. After a period of marimba music (typical in Guatemalan celebrations), a young man announced that he was going to change the music because "we're in the United States, not in Guatemala." Although I expected rock or American music, he decided to play Tex-Mex tunes (by US-based Latino groups), which are very popular in Guatemala as well, but decidedly "less Guatemalan" than marimba. This is perhaps due to the significant influence of Mexican and Tex-Mex cultural production (e.g., music, television programming, etc.) both in Central America and among Central Americans in the United States.

Language

Guatemalan Indigenous and *ladino* children demonstrated an unambiguous preference for English, even as the parents maintain their maternal language and push their children to also speak it. The environment in which the children lived, saturated with English-language television, media, advertisements, and school peers, was not conducive to maintaining Spanish-language skills. The parents, on the other hand, lived in a different linguistic world; their lives were mostly surrounded by Spanish-language media, and Spanish-speaking co-workers, neighbors, etc. Parents of both Indigenous and *ladino* children often complained that even among siblings, the children would prefer speaking in English, and pretend not to understand Spanish when the parents spoke to them. This was a problem the parents felt as they tried communicating with their children; they complained that their children do not want to speak to them, knowing that the parents are not fluent in English and prefer to communicate in Spanish or in their Mayan languages.[8] Generally, thus, the parent generation tends to live in a world dominated by the Spanish language, even when they are native speakers of Maya languages, while the children's world is dominated by the English language.

Several parents (both Indigenous and *ladinos*) told me that whenever they call Guatemala and ask the children to speak to a grandparent or a relative, the children often cannot utter more than a simple salutation. Or the children introduce words in English and use verbatim translations from English that do not make any sense in Spanish. The parents believed that the children boast of their ability to speak English when they pretended that they could no longer communicate in Spanish. When I spoke to some youngsters about the importance of retaining their maternal language, they did not understand its relevance for their present lives and said that they are teased at school, even by other Latino children, for speaking Spanish. In these children's environment, the advantages of retaining the parental language and culture seem irrelevant, as their prospects for a future as professionals who could benefit from such language skills and cultural repertoire do not feel immediate.

The children's limited Spanish and Maya languages speaking abilities can undermine their transnational relationships. Erlinda's son, an Indigenous teenage boy, was sent back to Guatemala to live with his maternal grandmother, a Quiché-speaking woman with limited knowledge of Spanish. The boy had been exposed to Spanish at school in Los Angeles because a teacher, in efforts to make him feel at home, put him to work in groups with other Central American children. He was fluent in English and managed to get by in Spanish, but to communicate with his older relatives in Guatemala he needed knowledge of Quiché. Almost as soon as he got to Guatemala, he started begging his mother to bring him back to Los Angeles. Eventually, Erlinda brought him back and explained that this boy had been lucky because he is a U.S. citizen and could go back and forth, unlike his undocumented siblings.

Going back to Guatemala was sometimes meant as a disciplinary measure for children who conceived of Los Angeles as their "home." The great physical distance was largely irrelevant for the parents, who saw sending the children to Guatemala as a benefit for the children, a situation that has radically changed today. The children who grew up in the United States, on the other hand, saw their travel to Guatemala as "punishment." In more recent years, with increasing trends of violence in Guatemala, parents no longer send their children back as a means to deal with disciplinary issues in the United States. Today, parents in the United States are more inclined to send *for* their children who are still living in Guatemala, especially as children approach teenage years and risk being forced to join gangs, and parents in Guatemala send the children to the United States to protect them from everyday violence.

The language skills of the Guatemalan children placed these children in a sort of suspended space, with tenuous ties both to their communities back home and to those they entered in the United States. And the circulation of people, goods, and money between Los Angeles and the Guatemalan towns from which these immigrants came may create spaces where place-specific language skills lose relevance, at least in everyday life. Since the children tend not to retain their Spanish (or Mayan) language, this linguistic switch to predominantly English has important consequences for their interactions with others, particularly with loved ones who are still in Guatemala.

Transnationalism among Guatemalan Children

Guatemalan immigrants in the United States have actively engaged in different forms of transnational activities. Guatemalan children in this study did not seem as oriented toward their homeland as many of the parents were, or as their parents would have liked the children to be. The children's activities in the social and religious lives of their parents' hometown communities are, if present, only marginal at best, and sometimes seemingly forced. These youngsters, most of whom belong to the 1.5 generation, appear more concerned with their lives and prospects in the United States. Both culturally and socially, they identified with and were interested in the social milieu in which they presently live. The case discussed here sounds a cautionary note to conceptualizations of transnationalism that tend to ignore the forces of immigrant settlement (including everyday exposure to lifestyles, friendships, peers, etc.) and of the nation-state (through immigration policies that make back-and-forth travel extremely difficult, border policies that restrict travel, and family reunification almost impossible). This caution is particularly important for considerations of transnationalism among youth who spend a significant proportion of their formative years in destination societies and who may only access the transnational spaces created by the parent generation.

The inability of many youngsters to travel—due to their vulnerable legal status—has made their parents' transnational projects difficult to implement. When these children no longer remember where they—or their parents—came from, physical contact with the origin communities becomes central for the continuation of transnational links. And if the children cannot communicate—written or orally—with families or other individuals back home, cannot visit (due to legal entanglements and financial impediments), and are not encouraged (or refuse outright) to maintain a sense of obligation to the parental homeland, it is difficult to imagine how they will remain connected to origin communities as intensely as their parents are. This does not imply that the children's lives are played out independently of their communities of origin; important decisions—what school to attend, which friendships are good, or what religious practices children should observe—in their lives often involve families in both places. The children's ties with the parental homeland, however, depend on the parents' activities and interests in keeping them oriented to home.

Indigenous Guatemalan parents seemed more concerned with orienting their children to their homeland than did their *ladino* counterparts. This may be due to the Indigenous Guatemalans' legacy of identity preservation that has equipped them historically to resist encroachment from other groups. It may also be that for Indigenous parents the linguistic tension they may experience in the U.S. communities where they live—between indigenous languages and the Spanish-language-dominated and where Latinidad is often equated with Spanish language—may prompt them to look to their home communities as the only way to maintain their ethnic, cultural, and linguistic identity. Thus, for these parents, to ensure cultural survival, it is vital to expose the children to their homeland.

Although children do not always respond as the parents wish, their parents insist on encouraging the children to remain connected with families and communities back home. Thus, there remains the important question of whether the second generation will carry on its Mayan legacy; and if it is carried on, will an orientation to home be part of its expression? Will they retain, or perhaps reacquire, later in their lives, their linguistic skills? Will they identify with movements that advocate for Indigenous rights? And will any or all these expressions form the bases for transnational connections between these young Guatemalans and their (or their parents') homeland?

Based on this research, there are a few questions to consider in future research, which emerged in my work but were not developed or addressed in depth. A gender angle is significant; as youth with different gender identities experience life differently we may surmise that they will also engage in transnational activities dissimilarly (see Erel and Lutz 2012; Yeoh and Ramdas 2014). The point here was to identify a set of preconditions that may influence the emergence of transnational activities, and to assess the potential long-term sustainability of such activities in the children's generation. Future research can build on by adding the critical importance of race and ethnicity (as demonstrated in this work), gender and sexual identity, religion, and other forms of difference and of social stratification.

Epilogue

The possibilities for Guatemalan youth's transnational connections are being transformed as I write this epilogue. A complex, expanding, and multi-level context of violence has propelled larger migration flows from Guatemala to the United States. Even though youth have migrated on their own in the past (Chávez and Menjívar 2010), migration flows today include larger numbers of children; in 2016 alone almost 20,000 so-called "unaccompanied"[9] Guatemalan minors arrived at the U.S.-Mexico border (Menjívar and Perreira 2019). Given the prevailing violence in Guatemala, itself a sequela of U.S.-supported military campaigns during the Guatemalan civil war, parents—whether in Guatemala or in the United States—make every effort to ensure their children's safety. This may mean that parents will be more likely to have children migrate *to* the United States and less likely to send U.S.-born children to visit Guatemala, as used to be the case when I conducted this research. These transformations do not mean that transnational links will cease to exist. New conditions will create new spaces, practices, and avenues for enacting transnational connections and identities. It is difficult to estimate the extent of the change and what transnational spaces will be created, but no doubt increasing trends in family separation will generate new modalities of family ties across borders and large geographical distances.

NOTES

1   The term *ladino* is complex, and it refers to Guatemalans who do not identify as Indigenous, are largely monolingual Spanish speakers, and do not adopt cultural practices associated with Indigenous groups. In the Guatemalan racial hierarchy, they occupy a position between whites and Indigenous and Afro descendants.

2   Guatemalans in the United States include various groups of Indigenous, *ladinos*, and others (Xinca and Garifuna). Reflecting social hierarchies in Guatemala, in the United States Indigenous and *ladino* Guatemalans (the larger groups) tend to live separately—in different neighborhoods, activating different networks, attending different congregations, and thus it is not surprising that they also congregate apart religiously. I have documented this elsewhere (Menjívar 2002).

3   The expansion of evangelical churches in Latin America has been extensively documented (Stoll 1991). This conversion from Catholicism to evangelicalism was particularly widespread in Guatemala, in connection to counterinsurgency strategies there (Scott 2011).

4   I document at length this case elsewhere (see Menjívar 2011).

5   Churches often are one of the few welcoming institutions to immigrants, and immigrants are familiar with this institution pre-arrival. The internal organization of the churches that immigrants attend varies significantly. For instance, evangelical churches demand quite a significant time commitment from their members, with two or more services per week. I document this elsewhere (Menjívar 1999; 2003).

6   I do not imply that there is no racism in the United States, only that *relatively* speaking, these Indigenous parents perceive more rights—however limited—in the United States as compared to the almost apartheid-like conditions that they are subjected to in Guatemala.

7   Immigrants organize to try to forge such links (see Popkin 1999; Wellmeier 1998). However, the Catholic church does not always provide the institutional space for immigrants to maintain ties with specific communities of origin (Menjívar 1999).

8   A television commercial on a Spanish station that advertises English-language courses on tape uses the situation of a father not understanding his own son (and his grades in school) as an incentive to get parents to learn English (and thus to purchase the language course) to better communicate with their children.

9   Whereas many of these youth are categorized as migrating unaccompanied because they migrate without a biological parent, in most cases these minors migrate in the company of others, such as siblings, cousins, grandparents, aunts, etc. (Menjívar and Perreira 2019).

REFERENCES

Chávez, Lilian, and Cecilia Menjívar. 2010. "Children Without Borders: A Mapping of the Literature on Unaccompanied Migrant Children to the United States." *Migraciones Internacionales* 5 (3): 71–111.

Erel, Umut, and Helma Lutz. 2012. "Gender and Transnationalism." *European Journal of Women's Studies* 19 (4): 409–412.

FitzGerald, David Scott. 2008. *A Nation of Emigrants: How Mexico Manages Its Migration.* Berkeley, CA: University of California Press.

Freire, Paulo. "Reading the World and Reading the Word." Language Arts 62, no. 1 (1985): 15–21.

Glick Schiller, Nina, Linda Basch, and Cristina Blanc-Szanton. 1992. *Towards a Transnational Perspective on Migration: Race, Class, Ethnicity, and Nationalism Reconsidered.* New York: Annals of the New York Academy of Sciences.

Kearney, Michael. 1995. "The Local and the Global: The Anthropology of Globalization and Transnationalism." *Annual Review of Anthropology* 24: 547–65.

Menjívar, Cecilia. 1999. "Religious Institutions and Transnationalism: A Case Study of Catholic and Evangelical Salvadoran Immigrants." *International Journal of Politics, Culture and Society* 12 (4): 589–612.

Menjívar, Cecilia. 2002. "The Ties that Heal: Guatemalan Immigrant Women's Networks and Medical Treatment." *International Migration Review* 36 (2): 437–466.

Menjívar, Cecilia. 2003. "Religion and Immigration in Comparative Perspective: Salvadorans in Catholic and Evangelical Communities in San Francisco, Phoenix, and Washington D.C." *Sociology of Religion* 64 (1): 21–45.

Menjívar, Cecilia. 2009. "Who Belongs and Why." Response to "Which American Dream Do You Mean?", by David Stoll. *Society* 46 (5): 416–418.

Menjívar, Cecilia. 2011. *Enduring Violence: Ladina Women's Lives in Guatemala.* Berkeley, CA: University of California Press.

Menjívar, Cecilia, and Krista M. Perreira. 2019. "Undocumented and Unaccompanied: Children of Migration in the European Union and the United States." *Journal of Ethnic and Migration Studies* 45 (2): 197–217.

Popkin, Eric. 1999. "Guatemalan Mayan Migration to Los Angeles: Constructing Transnational Linkages in the Context of the Resettlement Process." *Ethnic and Racial Studies* 22 (2): 267–89.

Portes, Alejandro, Luis E. Guarnizo, and Patricia Landolt. 1999. "The Study of Transnationalism: Pitfalls and Promise of an Emergent Research Field." *Ethnic and Racial Studies* 22 (2): 217–237.

Scott, Blake C. 2011. *The Crossroads of Religion and Development: Guatemala's Ixil Region, Evangelical Religion, and General Ríos Montt*. LAP Lambert Academic Publishing.

Stoll, David. 1991. *Is Latin America Turning Protestant? The Politics of Evangelical Growth*. Berkeley, CA: University of California Press.

Wellmeier, Nancy J. 1998. "Santa Eulalia's People in Exile: Maya Religion, Culture, and Identity in Los Angeles." In *Gatherings in Diaspora: Religious Communities and the New Immigration*, edited by R. Stephen Warner and Judith G. Wittner, 97–122. Philadelphia: Temple University Press.

Yeoh, Brenda S.A., and Kamalini Ramdas. 2014. "Gender, Migration, Mobility and Transnationalism." *Gender, Place & Culture* 21 (10): 1197–1213.

10

Placing Text

Culture, Place, and the Affective Dimension of Vernacular Ambient Text

REBIO DÍAZ-CARDONA

This chapter looks at the place of written language in the urban context through an exploration of the ambient text (roughly, the written texts that surround us) encountered in the NYC neighborhood of East Harlem/El Barrio. The exercise is informed by the perspective of environmental psychology, a subfield of psychology that is unique within the discipline in its focus on the physical environment (natural or built). Environmental psychology seeks to explore person–environment relations broadly defined and starts from the premise that people and environments mutually constitute each other. I draw specifically from the study of environmental perception, which poses that the perception of the surrounding environment is selective (we do not see everything out there), transactional (both the perceiver and the perceived are partly constituted by each other), and multimodal (environments appeal to all our senses). Environments also have a surrounding or "ambient" quality and must be perceived over time (as they cannot be captured in a single shot) (Heft 2007; Ittelson 1973).

I explore the potential usefulness of the notions of vernacular signage and vernacular ambient text as conceptual tools for exploring the relationships between language, place, and culture in the urban context. The status of urban signage (and its active ingredient, displayed written language) as part of the physical environment tend to be rather ambiguous in environmental psychology as in other disciplines interested in urban settings. Occasionally taken as directly revealing of neighborhood character and/or conflicts, sometimes summarily dismissed as too superficial and inconsequential (even a distraction concealing real social processes obscured by the signs), most of the time it is assumed to serve a neutral function, that of indicating what things are or where they are. I explore the possibility that a potentially crucial contribution of signage is missed when we assume that their role ends once what something is or where it is has been communicated. I focus here on vernacular signage, by which I mean public signs written in languages other than the dominant language in a particular place (English in NYC, for example). Traditional "way-finding" research (Gibson 2009) typically looks at signage as a source of information, casting its use as an information-processing, cognitive endeavor: I read

134

a sign in order to find out what something is or where it is. By contrast in this chapter I explore the affective dimension that vernacular signage may hold, insofar as their surrounding quality have an aggregated effect, helping foster feelings of familiarity, psychological ownership, and inclusion for those who "identify" with the signage.

The material presented here is part of a broader project that seeks to explore the roles of writing in contemporary urban space, considering written language as part of the physical environment.[1] I focus here on a more specific hypothesis, namely, that the language in which a displayed text is written is not psychologically inconsequential, as it may deeply color people's relationship with their surroundings in ways that foster a sense of place and place attachment. I explore this theoretically by proposing to extend the anthropological and linguistic concept of the *phatic* function of language to the analysis of displayed written language. In Roman Jakobson's classic model of communication (1960), the phatic function of language is associated with tests and reassurances that a channel of communication is still open and that if needed, a message can still be carried through. The phatic function, typically associated with orality, then, is being recast here as also applicable to the pieces of written language that surround us in the urban environment.

Vernacular Signage and Ambient Text

To highlight the intrinsic spatiality of written language and their perceivable presence in the surrounding urban environment, I have introduced the term ambient text (Diaz Cardona 2016). It emerged from observational research on the presence of text that I carried out in the NYC neighborhood of East Harlem/ El Barrio between 2007 and 2009. As I walked around its busy streets, I felt immersed in an atmosphere where pieces of text written in various languages (primarily Spanish and English) constituted a salient part of the physical environment as I encountered it.[2]

A basic working definition of ambient text is simply *the texts that surround us in our daily activities*. Empirically, the term ambient text is meant to include any text we come in contact with, regardless of its material support, visual characteristics, length, author, intended audience, genre, language, or meaning. A piece of text is ambient if it takes part (or is just one step away from taking part) in the increasingly general circumstance where texts surround humans and humans surround texts, and if it stands in a viable relation to human perception, in particular, perception by one or more members of its relevant audience, preliminarily defined as those who can read the language in which the text is written. In a multilingual context like NYC, however, typically some of the text that one encounters is written in languages that one does not understand. This, we can assume, becomes more common worldwide as a result of increased global migration and international travel. A reasonable assumption, then, is that not all pieces of ambient text will be understandable to everyone at every point every time.

As I geographically narrowed my observations to focus on the displayed written language on East 116th Street, I initially took a *direct observational stance* with regard to the ambient text found, trying to audit the existing mass of written language available in the street, counting it and categorizing it based on style, size, length, surface type, from the more fixed pieces to the most fleeting. I later switched to a more *phenomenological stance*, broadly inspired on anthropologist Tim Ingold's dwelling perspective (2000), from which I looked at the pieces of ambient text in terms of their being part of my lived experience of the place. The ambient text revealed itself as rich evidence of how the community makes the place its own through its "inscriptive practices" (Ingold 2007). This phenomenological stance gave way in turn to a more *ecological stance*, from which I considered the surrounding texts not primarily in terms of what the environment afforded me as someone experiencing it, but in terms of the work that writing was doing, so to speak, *for the environment itself*, making it viable, stable, durable, usable. Taking inspiration from Latour's call to "making objects participants in the course of action" (2005, 71), I focused on how texts, as a specific type of "nonhuman actor" contributed to create "the stages of interaction" (Latour 1996) that most of us take for granted as we inhabit places and move through our day.

By looking at the environment successively from these various methodological stances, it became clear that the surrounding pieces of written language were doing at least four things beyond informing people of what things were or where they were: 1) they facilitated navigation and helped organize mobility; 2) they helped to connect the place to other places and wider contexts of reference; 3) they contributed to create a sense of place for people whose languages were represented in the environment; and 4) they opened up the place to change and contestation.

In the description of ambient text above, however, no distinction is made between texts written in different languages. And in principle, it would be possible to assume that the way signage works transcends language differences and that therefore such differences are secondary or unimportant. From a strictly functional point of view, if signage is defined by its role in disseminating information in the environment, there is nothing particularly interesting about *vernacular* signage: it is simply a compensatory tool to ensure that those who do not speak the dominant language also get access to the information. From such perspective, there would be nothing particularly interesting about urban signage in general either, vis-à-vis other sources of information available in the surrounding environment: it would simply make information more readily available for those who know how to read in the language in which the signs are written. Still, in terms of their possible impact on the way city dwellers experience the urban environment, the sheer presence and variety of vernacular ambient text in the urban midst deserves at least a second look.

What's in a Surname? Delgado Travel, Calderon Accounting, Agapito's Bar

A common type of store sign in 116th Street combines a Spanish surname with an English word describing the line of business. Some of these bilingual signs have historical resonance. The street itself, 116th Street, is also identified as Luis Muñoz Marín Boulevard, named after the first elected governor of Puerto Rico (from 1948 to 1966). Under Muñoz Marín's watch, the current political relationship between Puerto Rico and the United States was forged, with the island considered a commonwealth, nonincorporated territory of the United States. This political relationship, articulated after more than fifty years of American occupation (starting in 1898), became official with the drafting of the island's constitution of 1952. One of the ways in which Puerto Rico's government sought to deal with the problem of the island's extreme poverty in those years was via a state-sponsored, airborne migration of tens of thousands of Puerto Ricans to the US mainland, primarily to cities in the Northeast. Over a period of some twenty years, starting from the 1930s, tens of thousands of Puerto Ricans flew one-way to the continental United States every year, thus becoming, along with blacks from the South, the first massive "new world" migration in the United States after the tightening of regulations for migration from European countries through the Migration Act of 1924.

The issue of the identity of those who moved to the United States, and the question of whether they would remain Puerto Rican despite the distance, was addressed by Governor Muñoz Marín in a famous speech from 1953. In it, Muñoz speculated that Puerto Ricans relocating to the US mainland would become American and speak English. Puerto Ricans remaining in the island would remain Puerto Rican (in spite of their American citizenship), preserving their identity primarily by virtue of their use of the Spanish language.[3] In the speech, he made fun of a store sign he had seen in a remote village in the mountains of Puerto Rico. The sign, announcing the place's name, read "Agapito's Bar," thus linking an old-fashioned male name from the island's Spanish colonial times with an English word, syntax, and punctuation. "Why did you do that, Agapito, if there is not even one American coming down that little street, not even once a year?" (quoted and translated in Kerkhof 2001).

I think of Agapito's Bar every time I see the Delgado Travel, Calderon Accounting, and similar signs in 116th Street. But these signs are not a joke today and probably never were. Suspended in time in the streets of El Barrio, they may have helped foster a sense of place and belongingness for scores of Puerto Rican and other Latino migrants over many decades. Coming across a big sign that proudly features a Spanish surname coexisting harmoniously with an English word indicating type of business, must have been seen by many newly arrived migrants, as a model and a "good sign" that one could perhaps preserve one's name and make it fit the new landscape, and perhaps carve out a place for oneself in it.

Some of those who came from Puerto Rico to New York around the time of Muñoz's Agapito joke were still around when I lived in the neighborhood (many still are). One such case is that of the older woman in a wheelchair, adorned in clothing and accessories featuring the Puerto Rican flag. In her sixty-plus years living in NY, she tells me, she has lived in many different locations within the neighborhood. But even during those rare periods when she moved out to other places in the city, she would often come back to El Barrio because "this is where I feel at home." Very similar sentiments were expressed by a man in his early forties who had first migrated from Mexico seventeen years before and who had lived in El Barrio almost the entirety of that time. He told me he had gone back to Mexico several times, sometimes for months at a time, but always came back to this neighborhood, even when he had chances to move with friends to bigger, more comfortable, similarly priced apartments in other areas of the city. He also calls El Barrio home and speaks fondly about being able to get everything he needs and about how the neighborhood has improved since he first moved.

Strong positive feelings toward a neighborhood, such as those expressed by these two residents, emerge over time and as a result of enduring contact. In environmental psychological terms, both of these residents express feelings that suggest a high sense of place-identity (Proshansky et al. 1983), the part of one's identity that is intimately linked to a place one identifies with. For some, place-identity figures prominently in their sense of self, while for others not so much. But how to establish whether the presence of vernacular ambient text and vernacular signage in the area contribute to foster a strong sense of place-identity, or the feelings of belongingness and homeliness expressed above? It is hard to tell, but it is reasonable to think that the process is not the same for these two residents. The man tells me about his dreading of having to speak English, and how given that he doesn't read the language, he uses other elements when looking at the cover of a magazine or the newspaper front page to figure out what they say. By contrast the older woman proudly tells me she could answer my questions either in Spanish or English, but jokingly protests, "You lost me already!" as soon as I start asking her my questions in Spanish. She later tells me regretfully that she wished she could speak Spanish better. "It's a shame that I don't, because I'm Puerto Rican and that's my language." This sentiment is not unique to her. What I want to suggest, however, is that in an important social and psychological sense, she (or any specific individual) does not need to speak the language all on her own to be able to claim with some legitimacy that she does, because, in a particular theoretical sense, the place speaks it for her.

Testing, Testing . . . Tú Me Entiendes? An Ambient Phatic Function

In linguist Roman Jakobson's classic model of communication (1960), six different components are considered: sender, receiver, context, message, channel, and code. Each of these becomes the anchor of a specific function of communication: expressive, conative, referential, poetic, phatic, and metalinguistic. The phatic function concerns the channel of communication and is associated with tests and reassurances that a channel of communication is still open and that, if needed, a message can still be carried through. Jakobson takes this notion from anthropologist Bronislaw Malinowski, who identified in the utterances of the groups he studied, instances of language use that did not serve a strictly "linguistic" function but a "social" one. In the typical example, when someone hears "How are you?" they generally understand it to be a greeting and not in any way a request for a detailed account of one's affairs. This kind of communication in any case seemed more about promoting the maintenance of relationships, social cohesion, and so on. From a strictly informational standpoint, however, this kind of communication would be considered "redundant," because it does not transmit new information. Still, this sort of utterances—"testing, testing," "are you still there?," "can you hear me?"—plays a fundamental role in maintaining the conditions of communication.

From the point of view of the environment then, a key question would be, is it only other humans that "confirm" that we are still here and that we are on speaking terms, or are nonhuman components of the environment also capable of instantiating such socially and psychologically consequential reassurances? In line with actor network theory, then, I propose to consider extending the phatic function beyond human actors. By extending this function beyond human actors, it becomes possible to think of signage and of ambient text more broadly as serving a similar confirming function, perhaps a confirmation that "this place still is your place" or that "I'm on speaking terms with you." Other than its function as a source of information for those seeking directions or making decisions about where to shop, the rest of what publicly displayed ambient text does can be conveniently described by reference to such phatic function.

Ambient text, then, may play a psychologically protective confirmatory role: such confirmations may have important securing, stabilizing roles, securing and stabilizing encounters between people, places, and things.

Much of the text displayed on 116th Street would seem to simply play a basic identification or "label" function: "this is street X," "this is a panadería," "this is a cuchifrito place," "this is a record store." This label function would seem, at least for those who are already familiar with such labeled things and places, again, redundant. But such redundancy is relative: in a changing environment, where new people visit every day and new shops open often, it is not useless for the place to *repeat itself* a bit. Furthermore, in sociocultural and political contexts in which language is seen as a marker of a distinct cultural identity, it may be that sometimes the main "content" or message of a sign is simply the language in which it is written, by itself an assertion of that language's relation to place and claims to place. In a bilingual or polyglot context, such as El Barrio or NYC more broadly, a posting in one language becomes a metonymical representation of the whole of that language and its community of users in relation to others. It can be argued, then, that in the multilingual global city, written text can play the phatic function simply by "speaking your language." In this sense, every sign written in Spanish in NYC automatically also reads "*se habla español.*" Such "*se habla español*" subtexts may provide reassurances that change the felt quality of the environment, making it more positive and welcoming for people whose preferred language is Spanish or who have positive associations with that language or see it as part of their heritage. Importantly, this may be the case even for individuals who do not comfortably speak the language themselves but culturally identify with it. That is, I believe, partly what the interaction with the Puerto Rican woman described above revealed; she confidently asserted her competence in Spanish (by offering to answer my questions in that language) because she assumes, rightfully, that she is part of the ambient language and culture that surrounds her. In a deeper sense, again, the place speaks it for her.

One must not fall, however, for the temptation to romanticize a language simply for being subaltern or for being one's own. Injurious things can be stated and even aimed at you *in your own language.* It would also be an error to attribute more unity to the language than it may actually have. Still, while it can be argued that there are as many Spanish languages as there are speakers and speech situations, in this chapter I am not calling into question the existence of the social construct called "the Spanish language." "Spanish" has a considerable level of recognizability and familiarity among New Yorkers, Spanish-speaking and not. At least anecdotally, presumably because of frequency of exposure, it does not seem so hard for non-Spanish-speaking folks to guess correctly when others are speaking Spanish (I venture to say more so than with other languages). Beyond such broad recognizability, however, it is not necessary to attribute unity and integrity to the language. In her classic book, *Growing up Bilingual* (1997), linguist Ana Celia Zentella distinguishes several different types in the speech of Puerto Ricans in East Harlem/El Barrio. The fact that language competence and use are deeply shaped by context is well established. In the case of Spanish in NYC, this is further complicated by deeper historical contexts of power, class, and racialization that shape how the use of Spanish is viewed in different contexts (Urciuoli 1996). When I refer to Spanish, then, I am not assuming unity or any predetermined level of competence among the speakers. I am instead referring to a highly recognizable subset of the linguistic environment and the ambient text of NYC. It might make more sense, in fact, to think of the ambient text in Spanish not as an altogether separate set but rather as a contributor to a larger set, that of *Spanglish* ambient text. Visibly and audibly, the identity of East Harlem/El Barrio, as far as language is concerned, is characteristically Spanglish. Spanglish (rather than Spanish) Harlem would have been a more suitable name.

Ambient Text and Community: Latino Ambient Material Culture

Vernacular signage, and vernacular ambient text more broadly, may help us revisit some of the multiple and contradictory ways in which place, culture, and language tend to be conflated in understandings about Latino identity. The focus on vernacular signage is in line with a shift in discussions about Latino culture and identity from a roots-based or origin-based, time-based mode of understanding identity to a more place-making-based, present-oriented, day-to-day, nonessentializing view.[4] One advantage of adopting a more *ecological* approach to defining identity and identification processes, as advocated here, is to promote a view of culture that is more grounded in actually existing urban contexts, focusing on the lived environment and what it affords to people. In this way we understand Latino culture as a collective, spatially distributed activity system, instead of assuming Latinidad as an individual attribute that a person either possesses or not.

From this perspective we can pose a sort of *sociospatial division of cultural labor*, in particular of language production and use, a division that (in keeping with the actor-network approach) involves not only people but also *things* (non-human actors). In terms of language, while not all Latinos speak Spanish, or speak Spanish the same way or with the same level of comfort, as an attribute of the environment (perhaps as spatialized cultural capital), Spanish can be understood as playing an important role in distributing and approximating peoples, things, places, and activities in and across settings. The collective performance of Spanish is then a subset of Latino culture grounded in specific places and activities. My focus here, again, is not on the individual speaker/reader but on the fact that Spanish is a language spoken, used, and available in the environment, with different speakers and different environmental components setting it in motion in different ways. In this sense, vernacular ambient text (ambient language more broadly) not only "mediates" belongingness and place attachment but vicariously embodies them as well. Urban signage, and ambient text more generally, constitute part of the material culture of an urban environment. Vernacular signage in Spanish is a highly (although unequally) visible subset of Latino material culture in NYC, and in some neighborhoods it is a defining component of the sociospatial tissue where collective life occurs and is socially reproduced.

But what about all the *corporate* material culture surrounding us, too, like that oversized "Heineken" sign in the corner of 116th and Second Avenue, with a few words in Spanish? Can we isolate the fact that the sign is in Spanish from the fact that it is a sign for Heineken or McDonald's? Furthermore, as shown by Dávila (2004), culture and language often end up being co-opted by the gentrification process (not discussed directly in this chapter) that renders them as attractive features that make the neighborhood "exotic" and palatable for tourists and new residents. Clearly, language use in general, and the circulation of ambient text specifically, do not happen in a sociopolitical vacuum.

Just off 116th Street, at the corner of 117th and Second Avenue, there was a mural featuring a quote from Subcomandante Marcos, leader of the Zapatista movement in Chiapas, Mexico. It read: "*Un mundo donde quepan muchos mundos*" ("A world where many worlds can fit"). I used to think of it as probably the most generous piece of ambient text in the neighborhood (in the city?). It seemed to say: I can live right next to you if we can share at least one world. I used to read the slogan to my then-two-year-old daughter every time we passed the mural on our way to a nearby park. "*What a great idea! Can you imagine that?*" I would tell her, hoping some of the deep sense of inspiration the mural provided me with would somehow reach her, too. Shortly before we moved from the neighborhood in the summer of 2008, two spray-painted inscriptions appeared on the pavement of 116th Street. The first one, "*Black and Brown Unity*," was written on the sidewalk of the southeast corner of 116th Street and Lexington. The second one appeared a few days later and read: "*Take back East Harlem*" on the asphalt at the crossing of 116th Street and Third Avenue. *How to explain those two to my daughter?* I would ask myself, linking the two inscriptions in my mind to the Marcos's slogan with its proposed mix of diversity and unity.

The latter inscriptions spoke to a less harmonious reality, but the sentiments they expressed were probably not so different from the ones that inspired the Zapatistas to begin with, who united in order to take back their lives and their land. In this sense, the fact that the inscriptions were in English spoke to a broader alliance, in a context in which the threat of displacement was perceived as deeply entangled with race. In any case, a survey of some of the neighborhood's ambient text helps bring the story of the neighborhood, punctuated by some sharp contrasts, into greater focus.

Ambient Text and Global Cities

In "New Globalism, New Urbanism: Gentrification as a Global Strategy," Neil Smith (2002) suggests that the list of global cities (New York, London, and Tokyo, in Saskia Sassen's original formulation) does not cease to expand, and not primarily to include the capital cities of other developed countries but Third World cities in peripheral countries all over the world, which were a testament to more decentered patterns of migration. Smith makes a strong case that the real globalization takes place in cities of the periphery, often in brutal ways. Based on this idea of an extending list of global cities, it is reasonable to assume that such new peripheral global cities, each one becoming a magnet for regional migration, are likely becoming polyglot cities as a result, if they weren't already.

Following this logic, the increase in mobility of the workforce at a global scale creates a scenario where polyglot cities become the rule rather than the exception. Consequently, ethnoculturally marked practices and products must circulate to ever-new places to help create what we could call the *ambient* conditions of production and reproduction of translocal livelihood wherever migrants go and stay. These amalgams or networks or assemblages of mobile people, products, and practices create worlds that support and are supported by emergent patterns of culture, communication, shared cognition, and affect that cut across sending and receiving contexts. In order for such worlds to hold together and stay meaningfully connected, much has to happen in the way of phatic function. Much, that is, should repeat itself and, in this way, repeat the world that is being intentionally produced, reproduced, and maintained. If social reproduction in the diaspora (and social production of a diaspora) does succeed, it is because of the combination of what humans do and what they do it *with*, a materially hybrid "social glue," distributed across human and nonhuman agents in the environment, in fields that require much phatic work in order to hook up and hold together. "Places gather," according to philosopher Edward Casey (1996). Vernacular signage and ambient text contribute to provide material and symbolic support to the place-making and place-gathering strategies of translocally constituted communities in cities around the world.

By contrast to the traditional, assimilationist model of migration, in contemporary global cities, at least in principle, the *language keeping* becomes easier and more desirable, partly via access to friends and loved ones in sending contexts through cheap and widely available digital communication technology. The persistence of vernacular signage is testimony to the constantly renewed newness of the urban environment in conditions of increased mobility and connectivity: new arrivals could always put the old ambient Spanish to good use, perhaps experiencing, as I did when I moved into the neighborhood, some indescribable comfort in being greeted by the Cuchifrito or the Calderon Accounting sign the first time I saw it. Thus, in NYC at least, vernacular signage does not feel like a transitional, temporary phenomenon, lasting only until migrants' assimilation into English is complete. It rather feels like a defining feature of the city. Whether in Chinatown or Brighton Beach, Greenpoint or Arthur Avenue, Jackson Heights or Washington Heights, West 116th Street or East 116th Street, the specific language, content, and style of the signage may vary, but the fact of language difference, retained, reiterated, renewed in the signage, does not feel redundant at all.

NOTES

1 In a broader theoretical context, I see this as an example of the nondeclining centrality of written language for a variety of societal processes, despite forecasts to the contrary (Coulmas 2013).

2 Other terms that have been proposed to describe publicly displayed written language include linguistic landscape in the field of sociolinguistics (Shohamy et al. 2009) and environmental print in educational psychology (Kuby 2004).

3 For critical analyses of the Puerto Rican experience in the island and in the United States and the ways the island's colonial relationship with the United States mediates the experiences of migration and place-making on both sides: Juan Flores (1993, 2000, 2009); Jorge Duany (2002); G. Haslip-Viera, A. Falcón, and F. Matos Rodríguez, eds. (2004); Ramón Grosfoguel (2003).

4 In *The Diaspora Strikes Back* (2009), Juan Flores explores what happens when migrants move back to their home countries in the Caribbean after many years. The hybridity of the culture that returning migrants, or "remigrants" bring is received with a mix of rejection and attraction that challenges rigid notions of identity, culture, and race.

REFERENCES

Casey, Edward. "How to Get to Space from Place in a Fairly Short Stretch of Time: Phenomenological Prolegomena." In *Senses of Place*, edited by S. Feld and K. H. Basso, 13–52. Santa Fe, NM: School of American Research Press, 1996.

Coulmas, Florian. 2013. *Writing and Society: An Introduction*. Cambridge, UK: Cambridge University Press.

Dávila, Arlene. 2004. *Barrio Dreams: Puerto Ricans, Latinos, and the Neoliberal City*. Berkeley and Los Angeles: University of California Press.

Díaz Cardona, Rebio. "Ambient Text and the Becoming Space of Writing." *Environment and Planning D: Society and Space* 34, no. 4 (2016): 637–54.

Flores, Juan. 2009. *The Diaspora Strikes Back: Caribeño Tales of Learning and Turning*. New York: Taylor & Francis.

Gibson, David. 2009. *The Wayfinding Handbook: Information Design for Public Places*. Princeton: Princeton Architectural Press.

Heft, Harry. "The Social Constitution of Perceiver-Environment Reciprocity." *Ecological Psychology*, 19, no. 2 (2007): 85–105.

Ingold, Tim. 2000. *The Perception of the Environment: Essays on Livelihood, Dwelling and Skill*. London: Routledge.

———. 2007. *Lines: A Brief History*. Oxon and New York: Taylor & Francis.

Ittelson, William. "Environmental Perception and Contemporary Perceptual Theory." In *Environment and Cognition*, edited by W. I. Ittelson, 141–54. New York: Seminar, 1978.

Jakobson, Roman. "Linguistics and poetics." In *Style in Language*, edited by Thomas Sebeok, 350–77. Cambridge, MA: MIT Press, 1960.

Kerkhof, Ema. "The Myth of the Dumb Puerto Rican: Circular Migration and Language Struggle in Puerto Rico." *New West Indian Guide*, 75, nos. 3–4 (2001): 257–88.

Kuby, Patricia., and Jerry. Aldridge. "The Impact of Environmental Print Instruction on Early Reading Ability." *Journal of Instructional Psychology* 31, no. 2 (2004): 106–14.

Latour, Bruno. 2007. *Reassembling the Social: An Introduction to Actor-Network-Theory*. Oxford and New York: Oxford University Press.

Massey, Doreen. "A Global Sense of Place." *Reading Human Geography* 35, no. 6 (1991): 315–23.

Malinowski, Bronislav. "The Problem of Meaning in Primitive Languages," In *The Meaning of Meaning–A Study of the Influence of Language Upon Thought and of the Science of Symbolism* by CK Ogden & JA Richards with supplementary essays by B. Malinowski & F. G. Crookshank. San Diego: A Harvest Book, 1923.

Proshansky, Harold. M., Abbe K. Fabian, and Robert Kaminoff. "Place Identity: Physical World Socialization of the Self." *Journal of Environmental Psychology* 3 (1983): 57–83.

Scannell, Leila, and Robert. Gifford. "Defining Place Attachment: A Tripartite Organizing Framework." *Journal of Environmental Psychology* 30 (2010): 1–10. doi:10.1016/j.jenvp.2009.09.006.

Shohamy, Elana, and Durk Gorter. 2009. *Linguistic Landscape: Expanding the Scenery*. Oxon and New York: Routledge.

Smith, Neil. "New Globalism, New Urbanism: Gentrification as Global Urban Strategy." *Antipode* 34, no. 3 (2002): 427–50.

Urciuoli, Bonnie. 1996. *Exposing Prejudice: Puerto Rican Experiences of Language, Race, and Class*. Boulder, CO: Westview Press.

Zentella, Ana Celia. 1997. *Growing up Bilingual: Puerto Rican Children in New York*. Malden, MA, Oxford, UK, and Victoria, AU: Wiley-Blackwell.

11

(Re)Claiming Public Space and Place

Maya Community Formation in Westlake/MacArthur Park

ALICIA IVONNE ESTRADA

According to the Pew Research Center's section on "Hispanic Trends" in 2017 there were approximately 1.4 million Guatemalans living in the United States, with the largest community residing in Los Angeles. Analyzing the U.S. Census Bureau's American Community Survey, the Pew also represented Guatemalans as a homogeneous national group erasing the existence, experiences, and contributions of Mayas in the United States. In the framework of official counting, and miscounting, the Maya diaspora is marked as illegible and consequently, invisible. The Pew and census's erasure of Maya communities is also reproduced by Los Angeles city officials, English/Spanish media outlets, as well as many Immigrant rights organizations that incorporate indigenous immigrants within a Latinidad that is Spanish speaking and racially mixed.

These official discourses and practices of legibility signal the varied forms of marginalization that Maya immigrants encounter in the United States. In particular, Mayas tend to have less access to legal representation and social assistance, because the services are provided in English/Spanish. This linguistic dichotomy erases the specific needs of indigenous immigrants and privileges European ethno-cultural identities. The violent systemic marginalization experienced by Mayas is further evident in the ways that deportations have disproportionally impacted them.[1] It is in this context of sociopolitical invisibility that Maya immigrants affirm their culture and knowledge as they navigate within a hostile national environment that needs their labor but rejects their presence. In this chapter, I examine the ways Mayas create a sense of community and place through the construction of a weekend *mercado* on the public sidewalks of the Westlake/MacArthur Park neighborhood where many reside.[2] The informal Maya market in this part of Los Angeles serves as an important survival strategy in a racialized city with growing social inequalities. It is in their performance of market relations that vendors and customers transmit the embodied cultural memory and practices of Mesoamerican mercados.[3] Collectively, vendors as well as their customers and members of the community visually reproduce social

Abridged reprint from *US Central Americans: Reconstructing memories, struggles, and communities of resistance* (2017): 166–87.

mercado relations and networks customary in Guatemala. The public performativity and reproduction of mercado dynamics in this Westlake/MacArthur Park community function as an important survival strategy as well as "means of remembering and transmitting [embodied] social [and cultural] memory" (Taylor 2003, 209).

Following cultural theorist Stuart Hall's scholarship on diaspora, I situate Maya immigrants in Westlake/MacArthur Park in a continuous process of change and transformation (Hall 1997, 209). I argue that Maya diasporic identity should be understood as constructed, reconstructed, performed, and articulated through various cultural, economic, and symbolic exchanges and movements that occur between the immigrants' place of origin (Guatemala) and their new residence, one of which is Los Angeles. Many of these exchanges and movements often take place within unequal power relations. In her work on social space and power relations, geographer Doreen Massey suggests that we think of these relations as "power-geometry." In other words, that we consider the connections between power relations and the construction of diasporic communities. Further highlighting that diasporic communities are not only shaped by "who moves and who does not although that is an important element of it; it is also about power in relation to the flows and movements" (1993b, 61). She stresses that because of these unequal power relations "space is by its very nature full of power and symbolism, a complex web of relations of domination and subordination of solidarity and co-operation" (Massey 1993a, 156). I employ Massey's framework to suggest that the mercado created by Mayas in Los Angeles is an essential space for this community since it produces the possibilities for solidarity and what Massey calls "co-operations." Similarly, the recreation of this informal mercado must be understood as existing within violent forms of marginalization and erasure espoused by city officials and non-Indigenous Latina/o community members. Moreover, it is important to recognize that often Latina/os replicate in their relations with Indigenous immigrants national imaginaries that maintain racist ideologies. Consequently, Maya immigrants experience multiple forms of violence from within dominant U.S. society as well as non-Indigenous Latina/os that reside in the area.

In addition to Hall and Massey's scholarship, I engage and expand work on the Maya diaspora (Hamilton and Stoltz Chinchilla 2001; LeBaron 2012; Loucky and Moors 2000; Popkin 1999, 2005) and street vendors in Los Angeles (Hamilton and Stoltz Chinchilla 1996; Bhimji 2010; Rosales 2013). Most of the studies on the Maya diaspora in Los Angeles have concentrated on the reasons for migration as well as the creation of hometown associations, patron saint festivities, and religious organizations. Less scholarship has focused on community formation through the creation of a historical memory (Estrada 2013) as well as the experiences of the 1.5 and second generation (Batz 2014; Boj López 2017). Additionally, studies on street vendors in the city have mainly emphasized the gendering of this labor practice, its conditions, and the strategies employed by the mostly Central American and Mexican workers. I expand on both areas of study by examining the ways the Maya mercado in Los Angeles becomes an essential cultural and economic survival strategy for that neighborhood. Furthermore, noting that the mercado serves to create a sense of community through the public affirmation of shared cultural practices and memories. In doing so, the weekend public market emphasizes community relations between generations as well as across Maya linguistic groups, including K'iche', Kaqchikel, and Q'anjob'al speakers. Thus, the Westlake/MacArthur Park mercado, like many others in multiethnic Latin American cities, becomes a space of contact for diverse Maya linguistic communities and generations. The data used for this chapter are based on ongoing participant observations in Maya organizations as well as research in the community that started in the early 1990s. These ongoing observations and participations stem from my own personal connection to the area. I grew up and lived on Westlake and Sixth Street between 1981 and 1994. Though I no longer reside in the neighborhood I regularly participate in Maya organizations and events.[4]

I begin by briefly contextualizing and examining Westlake/MacArthur Park, which has been the initial site of residence for many Central American immigrants starting in the late 1970s, and is often referred to as "Little Central America." Secondly, I note that while some of the Central American community dynamics still remain today, during the past two decades Maya immigrants have altered or Mayanized the space. I argue that this is particularly visible through the affirmation of specific Maya cultural and linguistic practices that challenge the national identities articulated by non-Indigenous immigrants in the neighborhood. The reproduction of these Maya cultural practices via the weekend mercado as well as the businesses owned and operated by Mayas not only serve as an essential survival strategy but also create a sense of community and place. Lastly, I argue that unequal power relations between the Maya vendors, residents, and city officials also mark the space reproduced on the streets of Westlake/MacArthur Park. The mercado, therefore, must be understood as taking place within a racialized city, where public areas are envisioned in a particular order that emphasizes and legitimizes national (racialized) conceptualizations of space. Often these community-building efforts by Mayas in Los Angeles take place under and within varied forms of inhumane conditions—like substandard housing, exploitation, exclusion, and criminalization—experienced daily by undocumented Indigenous immigrants.

Central Americanizing Los Angeles

Westlake/MacArthur Park is a residential and commercial area approximately two miles west of downtown Los Angeles. Sociologists Nora Hamilton and Norma Stoltz Chinchilla note that by the late 1970s the area was transformed by

Central Americans through the establishment of Guatemalan, Salvadoran, and Honduran restaurants, markets, and bakeries[5] (Hamilton and Stoltz Chinchilla 2001, 59). These spaces provided recently arrived Central American immigrants familiar foods and needed resources like express couriers and newspapers that maintained connections to their homeland. During this time MacArthur Park served as an important meeting space for rallies against human right abuses and a call to end U.S. military aid in Guatemala, El Salvador, and Honduras. At the same time, Hamilton and Stoltz Chinchilla note that by the early 1970s the area had become a transient neighborhood, initially for Mexican and later Central American immigrants, since the living conditions were substandard and consequently, rent was cheaper (2001, 59). This is because many of the apartment buildings were built in the early 1900s in an era when the neighborhood was conceived as one of the most desirable residential areas in the city. By the mid-1950s when the predominately white middle-class residents left the neighborhood, the abandoned apartment buildings were occupied by Mexican immigrants.

While some Maya migrated in the late 1970s, many more arrived in Westlake/MacArthur Park in the 1990s and occupied the same buildings with little to no renovations.[6] Between 1990 and 2000, a series of fires engulfed several apartment buildings in the area because the owners did not meet required fire safety codes and the city failed to enforce these regulations. These fires exposed the substandard and hazardous housing conditions in which many undocumented Mayas, Central American and Mexican immigrants are forced to live. During the 1990s there were several legal cases convicting landlords in the Westlake district for the slum conditions of the apartments they own. By 2010 the U.S. census estimated that the neighborhood continued to be densely populated. It is the second densest neighborhood in Los Angeles. This area of the city is made up of 94.9 percent renters and only 5.1 percent homeowners. The median age of residents is twenty-seven years and the median annual household income is $26,757, which is one of the lowest in the city.[7] These statics show that the Westlake district continues to be one of the most disenfranchised communities in Los Angeles. They reaffirm American Studies scholar Laura Barraclough's claim that "racialized economic divisions are literally mapped onto social space in Los Angeles, which was more segregated between whites and non-whites in 2000 than 1940" (2008, 172).

The dilapidated buildings in the Westlake district continue to visually mark the substandard living conditions of young Maya immigrants, families, and children. Their living spaces tend to be crammed since it is not unusual for several people to share a one-bedroom apartment in an effort to reduce living expenses. The Maya immigrants' living conditions demonstrate that their precarious economic situation restricts their movement and contact with other parts of the city. The limited mobility experienced by undocumented Maya immigrants in Los Angeles highlights the ways in which anti-immigration laws, labor exploitation, and historical racial segregation have carved substandard living spaces in the city for poor undocumented immigrants and Indigenous communities. It also illustrates how sociopolitical ideas that maintain racial, gender, and class hierarchies have historically been encoded in the city's topography.

Confronted with a precarious social position in a racially segregated city and country, Maya immigrants employ varied forms of cultural and economic survival strategies. Through my engagement in collaborative work with Maya immigrants in the area, as well as accounts by residents in the community, I have observed that there are several apartment buildings housing members of specific Maya hometowns and linguistic regions. For example, one of the buildings mainly houses Maya-Q'anjob'al speakers from Huehuetenango, while in another building the majority of the tenants are K'iche' speakers from Totonicapán.[8] The makeup of these apartment buildings illustrates the multifaceted aspects of transnational community networks that include employment opportunities as well as housing and social relations (Menjívar 2002). On several occasions, I have observed Maya residents in the mentioned apartment buildings gather to raise funds for funerals. And while these types of collaborative dynamics take place in some apartment buildings and not others, the sounds of marimba music, the national instrument of Guatemala, and Maya languages are audible in several of the buildings housing Mayas and non-Indigenous immigrants in the area.

The Mayanization of Westlake/MacArthur Park

While street vending exists throughout several immigrant and working-class ethnic communities in Los Angeles, what makes the public vending on Sixth Street a form of Maya mercado is the spatial (re)organization as well as the participation of numerous Maya vendors in that particular place and on those specific days and time. Anthropologist Walter Little's analysis of Guatemalan street vendors in Antigua is useful since he highlights that "interaction of people and place allows not only for the social construction of place, but also for the social construction of identity" (2004, 6). Likewise, the Sixth Street Maya mercado aids in constructing a sense of community in Los Angeles through the recreation of an essential site for social interaction, which fortifies informal social networks. Moreover, the public space where the mercado is located allows for visual forms of cultural affirmation to take place. Particularly illustrated through the regional textiles worn by women and girls, the various Maya languages spoken in public, and the food cooked and consumed on the neighborhood's public sidewalks. These Maya cultural practices simultaneously engage and are in tune with a variety of sensory elements like sound, smell, and vision, which enable a re-inscription of that public space's symbolic meaning.

And though the majority of street vendors on these four city blocks are Mayas, there are also non-Guatemalan and other Latina/o vendors who started to participate in that space. The heterogeneity of the mercado "provides a context in which interethnic relationships can take place" (Little 2004, 101). These forms of interethnic connections are essential tools of survival, because they aid in finding employment and housing as well as addressing other immediate needs like health care. In her work on undocumented Guatemalan immigrants in Los Angeles sociologist Cecilia Menjívar notes that because many immigrants lack formal health care they must "assemble something akin to a 'package' of biomedical treatments and 'traditional' medicines" (2002, 441). As I have observed the Maya mercado constructs a physical space from which to access the forms of healing practices depicted by Menjívar, which as mentioned are necessary to survive in a country that has severely "constrained legal and financial opportunities" for undocumented immigrants (441). In this way, the mercado not only provides access to familiar biomedical treatments, but also traditional herbs used for healing ailments ranging from the common cold to ulcers. Furthermore, it offers Mayas a space to connect with each other, which aids in easing the loneliness often experienced by recently arrived immigrants.

Since most of the Maya residents in this neighborhood are undocumented, their mobility and participation in the U.S. formal economy is limited. Some of the vendors work as day laborers, others as domestic workers, and more often vending becomes a primary form of income particularly for Maya women. One vendor, who sells a variety of *tamales* and *atoles* told me that she had worked at a sweatshop for many years, but that the cost of childcare was too high.[9] Additionally, she was unable to fully attend to her children's needs and consequently, they were falling behind in their academics. She decided to quit her job and started to sell food at the mercado. When she's not selling at the mercado she sells lunch meals to mostly young Maya day laborers. As explained by another vendor many use the money from their sales to provide basic necessities such as food, housing, and education for their families in the United States as well as Guatemala. In this way, the Sixth Street mercado is also economically important because the vendors contribute to both local and transnational (in)formal economies.

The space recreated on Sixth Street reproduces visual and audible characteristics of mercados in Central America. In his scholarship on marketplaces in Costa Rica, Miles Richardson notes that public Mesoamerican markets tend to be vibrant, bustling, and loud (1982, 425). For Walter Little, mercados in Guatemala produce "a neutral locale where families can meet and exchange news" (100). Similarly, the frequent interactions in the mercado on Sixth Street between vendors, customers, and members of the community allows for the reproduction of these types of relations to take place in Los Angeles. For instance, vendors socialize with regulars that stand around the site to eat tamales or drink *atoles*. It is in these frequent interactions that many create friendships, or make new connections with others from the community.

On Sixth Street, or *la sexta* as Mayas in Los Angeles refer to the street, there are specific spaces on the sidewalk and side streets allocated for the products sold.[10] Food is often on the side streets. In the spaces of food and produce the majority of those selling are women, who more frequently wear regional Maya textiles. The type of food sold by Maya women blurs the lines between private and public spaces since the food is often cooked in the private home space of the vendor. The food vended as well as the ways in which it is prepared and presented maintains a sense of "home cooking" from the "homeland" that is sold and consumed in the neighborhood's public city streets. The participation of men is also visible in the food sites of female vendors. In these spaces, where food and produce are sold and consumed, men regularly perform supportive roles. Many of the men are also responsible for carrying *bultos* (containers) of food, produce, and products sold on the mercado days. They often assist in setting up and taking down the crates used at the vending site. Maya women vendors in Los Angeles are usually in charge of deciding what meals will be cooked and sold. Unlike Guatemala, in some food-vending sites in Los Angeles both men and women serve the food.

In addition to cooked meals, fresh produce native to the Mesoamerican region like *chipilín, yerba mora, loroco,* and *chilacayote* are sold.[11] Most of these items are not readily available or more expensive in Latino markets. While selling and consuming native Mesoamerican produce has taken place in the area since the 1980s, the sale and consumption of these products has changed in the past three decades. In the 80s, non-Indigenous Central American vendors sold exported items already packaged, like frozen green mangos and *loroco*, but today the Maya vendors sell them fresh. When asked where they find the produce, women vendors said they grow them in rented lots around Los Angeles or in Maya homes around the city with backyards. Sociologist Pierrette Hondagneu-Sotelo notes that these urban community gardens are "a pocket-sized oasis of trees, flowers, and Mesoamerican vegetables and herbs growing in an otherwise very cemented part of inner-city Los Angeles" (2014, 88). Moreover, the act planting as well as harvesting Mesoamerican produce literary nourishes Maya immigrants through familiar practices (farming/gardening) and community relations.

This physical reformulation of public space illustrates a reproduction of Maya social and cultural dynamics, where the mercado serves not only for economic exchanges but also social connections. Yet, in Los Angeles these social dynamics and informal economic activities take place within a racialized, segregated city that criminalizes these informal labor and social practices. Los Angeles has maintained strict street vending regulations often ticketing vendors with heavy fines, disposing them of their merchandise and at times even jailing vendors for continuing to sell on the streets. In 2018, the Los Angeles city council approved the legalization of street vending. Though initially vendors celebrated the news, once information about the new regulations was provided it created another layer of fear and uncertainty. Many Maya vendors on Sixth Street have noted that the new regulations further criminalize them because they limit where and when they can sell their products. They also note that the cost of the license is too high, and many can't afford it. Thus, the mercado highlights not only the visual presence of Maya vendors and residents in the city landscape but also the marginality of their existence. Their precarious position is often further reinforced by local gangs that harass and demand payment for protection and/or permission to sell in the neighborhood's public sidewalks.

In addition to the mercado, in the past decade approximately six new restaurants offering variations of Guatemalan regional food have opened in those four city blocks, replacing Mexican, Chinese, and Salvadoran restaurants, or at times adding regional Guatemalan food to those existing places. The restaurant Punto Chapin (the name already suggests a space of contact for Guatemalans) replaced a former Chinese eatery.[12] Next to this restaurant is Mazat Express, which delivers packages to small communities in the highlands. The name of the business uses the K'iche' word *mazat* (deer). In doing so, the sign, like the residents of Westlake/MacArthur Park that use Maya languages in their public social interactions with others in the community firmly assert their identity and cultural practices.

Other businesses operated by Mayas are located in three indoor swap meets in the area. One of these businesses is Tienda Tipica, which sells a variety of items, from textiles and shoes used in the highlands to snacks packaged in Guatemala and music DVDs in Maya languages. In this typical store folks stop to buy Maya Guatemalan products, chat with the owners as well as exchange a variety of information that includes educational programs in local schools as a flyer posted on a makeshift bulletin board suggests. At Tienda Tipica a young customer told me, "When ladinos [non-Indigenous immigrants] walk by and see the *cortes*, they make negative comments. You know, like they don't understand why we continue to wear *corte* in Los Angeles." Her statement illustrates the daily forms of racism that Mayas, and particularly women, confront not only within the larger U.S. society, but also within Latina/o immigrant communities. Yet, her affirmation and sense of pride in wearing Maya regional textiles simultaneously challenges U.S. and Latina/o assimilation processes. For Maya scholar Irma Otzoy, the public use of Maya regional clothing functions as active form of cultural resistance that speak "of the Maya as a people, of their roots, of their lives, and their causes" (Otzoy 1996, 149). In this way, shops like Tienda Tipica as well as their customers continuously participate in an active act of cultural resistance. And though Tienda Tipica was the first store in this indoor swap meet to sell Maya *cortes* and *huipiles*, in the past decade several other stores have opened in the vicinity.[13] These new businesses not only illustrate that there is a market for Maya women's textiles in the area but also visibly transpose Maya cultural texts, through selling and wearing textiles, onto the city's public space.

The three indoor swap meets also provide other services: money transfers, calling cards, barbershops, salons and tailors. Additionally, one business functions as a photo and print shop where images of Maya women and children wearing regional clothing are often superimposed onto a background of the Los Angeles skyline. These images literally carve a space in the city for the Maya community. They symbolically illustrate the efforts by members of the Maya diaspora to affirm their culture even as state-sponsored policies attempt to erase their presence. The photos with the city skyline also express a defiance to the continuous erasures of Maya immigrants from dominant U.S. and Latina/o discourses.

In this way, the mercado dynamics demonstrate varied forms of Maya cultural embodied knowledge, which serves as an important element in community survival and construction. These embodied cultural practices illustrate immediate modes of daily survival that become particularly pressing given that Mayas in the United States continue to be denied what philosopher Hannah Arendt calls their "rights to have rights" (1973, 296). This is evident in the literal and metaphorical disposability of Mayas, who have been largely impacted by forced displacement, mass deportations, and detentions.[14] In this way, the mercado on Sixth Street demonstrates an informal response to ongoing structural violence.

Mapping New Routes

The diverse forms of social, economic, and cultural exchanges that take place in the weekend mercado illustrate the multiple ways in which Mayas in this part of Los Angeles transmit, learn, and affirm their embodied cultural knowledge. These efforts to (re)claim the public city sidewalks on Sixth Street need to be understood as taking place within a contested space where Maya vendors redefine the public streets and attempt to defy city cultural and legal regulations. In doing so, Maya vendors not only risk getting a ticket and having their merchandise and work tools confiscated but also experiencing jail time or deportation. Yet, the weekend mercado, coupled with the Maya residents in the surrounding apartment buildings, indoor swap-meet shops, and restaurants on Sixth Street, shows the ways Mayas attempt to survive in a city that severely marginalizes them. The reconceptualization of those four city blocks provides a public space for multiple generations, Maya linguistic communities, religious denominations, and hometowns to meet and (re)connect within familiar cultural contexts and dynamics. Just as it is now customary to publicly hear Maya languages spoken, it is also more common to see Maya women and girls wear their regional textiles as they walk in the community and through the mercado. These practices are often not possible for many Mayas living in other communities across the state and nation.

Thus, the remapping of this public space opens possibilities for informal and formal collaborations between members of the community and creates the potential for constructing cross-ethnic solidarities as exemplified by rallies organized after the shooting of the Maya-K'iche' day laborer Manuel Jaminez Xum. Killed by LAPD officer Frank Hernández on the corner of Sixth Street and Union Avenue, a central section of the Maya mercado, Manuel Jaminez Xum's life and death illustrated the varied forms of violence that Mayas experience from Anglos and Latina/os in the United States. While former Los Angeles Mayor Antonio Villaraigosa (2005–2013), who became the city's first Latino mayor since 1872, hailed Hernández as a "hero," after the shooting Maya community members denounced the violent tactics the officer often used particularly with street vendors, who he frequently ticketed and threw away their merchandise. On 15 March 2011, six months after the killing of Manuel Jaminez Xum, the Los Angeles Police Department cleared Officer Frank Hernández of "any wrongdoing," because he "acted within the law." The LAPD maintained that "the suspect did not follow the officer's orders," which they noted were in English and Spanish (www.lapdonline.org).

Manuel Jaminez Xum's family as well as Maya and non-Maya community members continued rallies that brought local media attention. Their demands included the removal of Officer Hernández and an end to excessive police violence. They also recognized that the community where Jaminez Xum was killed and the mercado is located is predominately Maya. Hence, English/Spanish were not languages accessible to Jaminez Xum and continue to be inaccessible to many other Maya residents. In doing so, they publicly deconstructed hegemonic framings of immigrant communities in Los Angeles as Latina/o and Spanish speaking. Thus, the Maya residents' construction of alternative social spaces like the informal mercado on Sixth Street aid in community-building efforts that can potentially rally people together to demand their "rights to have rights." At the same time, these varied spatial practices by Maya immigrants collectively affirm their place in a city and nation that attempts to erase their existence.

NOTES

1 Two of the largest immigration raids in U.S. history mainly impacted undocumented Maya workers: New Bedford, Massachusetts, raid on March 6, 2007, at the Michael Bianco Inc. and the Postville, Iowa, raid on May 12, 2008, at Agriprocessors Inc.

2 In Guatemala and in the diaspora, those who identify as Maya assert a politicized identity by taking part in a historically grounded and socially constructed collectivity that is tied to common Indigenous ancestors, history, and culture (Bastos and Camus 2003).

3 Daily, open, and public mercados date back to the pre-Hispanic period in countries with large Indigenous populations (Dahlin et al. 2007; Chase and Chase 2014). These mercados are built and dismantled on the same day in a similar way to what archaeologists suggest took place during the pre-Hispanic period.

4 There are numerous Maya hometown associations in the area. I've attended other informal community events as well as gatherings that address a variety of pressing issues like the death of community members as a result of illness, work injuries, suicide, and drug abuse.

5 *Pupusas* are handmade corn tortillas that are filled with any, or a blend, of the following: cheese, refried beans, pork meat, and other types of native produce from Mesoamerica. Often loroco, a Mesoamerican vine with edible buds and flowers, is used in pupusas.

6 James Loucky and Marilyn Moors (2000) remind us that by the late 1970s there were Maya residents living in the Westlake/MacArthur Park neighborhood.

7 See http://maps.latimes.com/neighborhoods/neighborhood/westlake/.

8 Huehuetenango and Totonicapán are departments in the Guatemalan highlands.

9 Mesoamerican drink that is traditionally corn or masa-based.

10 Sixth Avenue, or *la sexta*, in Guatemala City is located at the heart of the Centro Histórico (Historical Center). The area is full of commercial activity that includes a variety of shops and restaurants. In the Guatemalan *sexta*, street vendors are also present selling food and a variety of products that range from clothing items and toys to herbal medicines.

11 The vegetables listed are native to the Central American region and Southern Mexico. *Chipilín* is a leafy vegetable. In Guatemala it is often used in tamales and soups. Like *chipilín*, *yerba mora* is a leafy vegetable but usually eaten in soups or sautéed. *Loroco* is a vine with edible flowers. In Guatemala and El Salvador, it is often used as filling for *pupusas*. Guatemalans also use *loroco* in scrambled eggs. *Chilacayote* is a type of squash. Guatemalans use *chilacayote* as a sweet dessert and to make *aguas frescas* (non-alcoholic sweet beverages).

12 *Punto* means contact in Spanish. *Chapin* is a reference to Guatemalans.

13 Maya woven skirts and blouses.

14 From January through August 2019 the highest number of apprehensions at the U.S./Mexican border were Guatemalans, many of them Mayas. During the same time period, the majority of children who died at ICE detention centers were Mayas: Jakelin Caal Maquin, Felipe Gómez Alonzo, Wilmer Josúe Ramírez, Carlos Gregorio Hernández, and Juan de León Gutiérrez.

12

Health Brokers, Shrinks, and Urban Shamans Revisited

Networks of Care among Argentine Immigrants in New York City

ANAHÍ VILADRICH

> You must use whatever resources you can find . . . Life is hard here [in New York City] and with *tantos quilombos* (so many problems) to resolve you have to ask around . . . There is no other way: health care is so expensive and doctors [referring to U.S. medical practitioners] don't care about us. So you must try this and that [health resources] and when someone doesn't work, you go out and look for something else.

The excerpt above is from Carlos, an uninsured immigrant in his 50s who, in the early 2000s, was working in the construction field in New York City (NYC) despite suffering from several health conditions—including sciatica and arthritis. Carlos regularly stopped by an Argentine barbershop in "Little Argentina," Queens, to chat with his pals and play dominos. While hanging out there, he often got free prescription drugs (mostly anti-inflammatory medications and pain killers) from Dr. Kant, a certified medical practitioner from Argentina. By watching the interactions between Carlos, Dr. Kant and other Argentines who regularly met up in the area, I soon became interested in the role of social capital as the basis for understanding immigrants' reciprocal exchanges within diverse networks of care.

The literature on social capital and health has blossomed in recent decades, particularly regarding the connection between trust-based social relationships and access to valuable resources (Folland & Nauenberg, 2018; Thompson & Moret, 2019). This body of work has allowed for a deeper understanding of how social ties based on interpersonal exchanges, trust, and reciprocity give rise to informal access to valuable material and symbolic resources (Bourdieu, 1985; Portes, 1998). Ethnographic research has further examined the means through which interpersonal webs and community resources enable access to varied social assets (Goetz, 2003; Flores & Rello, 2003; Small, 2004). The importance of social networks is even more pronounced among the foreign-born, particularly given the obstacles that many immigrants encounter when accessing formal

---

This chapter is a modified, updated and shortened version of a previously published article (Viladrich, 2007).

health services—due to their undocumented status, limited English skills, and lack of health insurance, among other barriers (Chávez, 1992; Menjívar, 2002 & 2000; Pitkin, 2000).

As of yet, little is known about the overlapping nature of individual social webs and formal and informal health systems, as in the case of "immigrants treating other immigrants" (Messias, 2002; Viladrich, 2013). Some of the questions that still puzzle theorists and policy analysts alike pertain to immigrants' ability to mobilize both domestic and transnational resources to satisfy their most immediate health needs. What is the role of informal social networks in connecting immigrants to diverse health resources? To what extent is immigrants' reciprocal aid rooted in shared ethnic and community interests? Is the help immigrants provide each other based on belonging to the same ethnic or national group? This chapter attempts to answer these questions by building upon previous research on medical pluralism and the wide range of health care options available to those in need (Chávez, 1984; Freidson, 1970; Kleinman, 1980; Young, 1981 & 1980).

The findings presented here come from the first ethnographic study on Argentines living in NYC (1999–2002), that combined in-depth interviews with participant observation and field notes (Viladrich, 2013). The author's active involvement with Argentines' social networks allowed her to participate in a variety of venues involving numerous Latino community groups in NYC. By observing Argentines' interactions in different social settings—from tango parlors to religious ceremonies—this study assessed the way information on health issues circulates, what type of material help social networks provide, and who the donors and recipients of such assistance are.[1]

A majority of Argentines in the United States (U.S.) come from urban areas, where access to advanced biomedicine has been supported by the popularity of Western psychotherapeutic treatments (Lloyd-Sherlock, 2005). As Kaja Finkler (2001) observed in her research on health services delivery in Medico, biomedicine remains the prevailing mode of delivery both in the private and the public sector in Argentina, with state-of-the-art technologies that mirror the U.S. and Europe. These features distinguish Argentines from other Latin American immigrants, particularly those from rural milieus that are less familiar with Western models of healing.

Inspired by Arthur Kleinman's (1980) seminal work on the intersection of disparate health sectors (i.e., professional, folk, and popular), this chapter analyzes the links among networks of care and, in particular, the ability of Argentine immigrants to procure referrals to diverse types of health providers. In accordance with Kleinman's framework, medical pluralism among Argentine immigrants is here conceptualized in dialogue with complementary explanatory models of health and disease. This chapter particularly describes Argentine immigrants' reliance on diverse health resources, ranging from health brokers

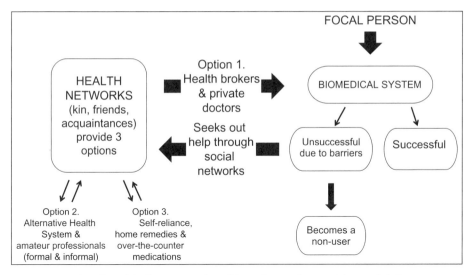

Figure 12.1. Cultural Model of Immigrants' Health-Seeking Behaviors. This model illustrates a conceptual framework based on the role of social networks in providing resources to Argentine immigrants, which allow them to access biomedical, alternative, and ethnomedical health systems.

(i.e., doctors known personally) to psychotherapists and urban shamans—the latter including folk healers and fortune-tellers. Particular attention is paid to the overlapping nature of immigrants' social webs with biomedical services on the one hand and alternative healing practitioners on the other (see Figure 12.1).

Contrary to the intuitive belief that dense and homogeneous networks are more beneficial to their members, this research piece underscores the advantages of heterogeneous and fluid social webs. This notion, earlier developed by Mark Granovetter—who coined the expression "the strength of weak ties" (1973, 1360)—argues that loose interpersonal connections, rather than dense and tight ones, may be more effective in facilitating access to a variety of resources, including referrals to various types of health practitioners. This paper particularly shows how health capital is mobilized on the basis of cooperation, reciprocity, and trust between parties (Bourdieu, 1985; Coleman, 1988; Portes, 1998). In the conclusions, this chapter critically reviews this study's findings and highlights the limits of informal networks of care in providing effective, long-term solutions to the multiple health care needs experienced by vulnerable immigrants in the U.S.

An Innovative Model of Health Brokerage: Doctors and Patients Sharing Fields

The literature has systematically reported the crucial role of community members acting as bridges between vulnerable individuals and health care and social services organizations (Campbell-Montalvo & Castañeda, 2019; Kirmayer et al., 2003; Torres et al., 2014). These community personnel—interchangeably called liaisons, brokers, navigators, lay workers, or peer supporters—play a pivotal role as interpreters and advocates of minority groups, particularly by linking vulnerable and sick individuals with health services and informal webs of care.

This study assessed an alternative model of health brokerage that differs from those community health paradigms. Within this model, services are mostly provided in non-medical settings in which medical doctors and community members share the same lay-ethnic world. Health brokers are defined here as biomedical professionals of Argentine or Latino origin who have made a career via U.S. accreditation and practice. They are members of Argentine social webs, sharing ethnic and social interests that extend beyond the biomedical field. These professionals render accessible, affordable or even free access to health care, however limited it may be, usually by bypassing some of the cumbersome protocols of the U.S. health care delivery system. Interpersonal relationships are then supported by extra-clinical features that somehow circumvent the inequalities of the conventional medical encounter. Ultimately, the health broker model entails a parallel biomedical system that grants informal health care access to those who would otherwise encounter a number of barriers to treating their most urgent health care needs.

During fieldwork, I had several opportunities to witness informal exchanges between Argentine immigrants and medical doctors, who were either from Argentina or other Latin American countries, that involved the provision of health resources within extra-clinical settings. This was epitomized by Dr. Kant, the Argentine physician introduced at the beginning of this chapter. Although living in Long Island, he would regularly visit the well-known Argentine barbershop in Queens—where a large number of Argentines, including the ethnographer, would gather on regular basis. During these visits, Dr. Kant would mingle with his compatriots and participate in heated discussions about Argentine soccer, national politics, and the latest gossip on Argentines in NYC. He would also treat his comrades for minor ailments (anything from bacterial infections to muscle spasms) and distribute samples of prescription drugs on demand. In return, he would be invited to soccer games and treated to dinners or drinks at the social club across the street.

Health brokers' motivation to help others is partially rooted in "bounded solidarity" that implies the provision of social capital on the basis of belonging to the same community of interests (Fernández Kelly, 1994; Portes, 1998). In ethnic social settings, doctors and their friends engage in a *quid pro quo* bartering of services and symbolic goods. Additionally, by sharing social fields with their compatriots, such as tango dancing or soccer playing, not only do doctor-brokers nurture interpersonal relationships but they also solidify their professional reputation and increase their opportunities for client recruitment and referrals.

Argentine immigrants' search for caring practitioners often leads them to networks of acquaintances and friends in order to find professionals who will ascribe to the "old model" of medical practice. Within this model, physicians are supposed to spend quality time with their patients while encouraging them to ask questions and talk about their health concerns at length. In almost all Argentine narratives, the idealized figure of the doctor-broker is opposed to either the image of the HMO doctor-employee or the private doctor motivated exclusively by pecuniary interests. Being treated by familiar doctors, who are considered close acquaintances or even friends, guarantees that one is *en buenas manos* (in good hands). These findings reveal a dual relationship between Argentine immigrants and U.S. health services: on the one hand, study participants believed in the efficacy of Western medicine as well as in the excellence of its technology; on the other hand, many doubted the quality of U.S. health service delivery. They also lamented the pervasive aspects of a globalized culture of medicine—which most perceived as distant from a patient-centered paradigm (DelVecchio Good & Good, 2000).

In most cases, Argentine immigrants did not consult with their health brokers for routine screening tests or checkups. However, they often did do so in emergencies—in many cases, this was due to their inability to perform their everyday chores. Rather than mimicking the clinical encounter in which doctor-patient relationships develop their own interpersonal drama (Finkler 2001), the health broker model contests the usual expectations of the doctor-patient role—although, quite often not without costs. In the words of one study participant "nothing comes without a price," as informal arrangements almost always require payment of some sort. The health broker model presents disadvantages, especially related to its informality: these include lack of supervision, absence of contractual terms, superficial assessment of underlying health conditions, and lack of follow-up. In addition, the importance of interpersonal relationships (e.g., good communication, fair treatment, and the sharing of common extra-clinical interests) often takes the place of accuracy and effectiveness in health care provision.

Finding the right health broker was not an easy task for most of my respondents. It usually meant investing considerable time and social resources, and was often subject to unexpected outcomes. Counting on these professionals was more common for long-term NYC residents, many of whom had long-standing relationships with Argentine and Latino health professionals, as in the case of senior immigrants and members of the tango world (Viladrich, 2013). However, some Argentines reported feeling disenchanted with their health brokers' performance, based on either an inconsistent response to their urgent medical needs or their doctors' dismissive behavior. Some participants even stopped seeing their health brokers when they changed occupations or moved to other neighborhoods. As illustrated in figure 12.1, Argentine immigrants often returned to their social networks to evaluate the results (particularly when their conditions did not improve) and explore next steps. They also consulted with other providers when their health problems continued. Despite these limitations, health brokers in this study symbolize the circulation of health-related capital, as they are generally found by word of mouth and chosen on the basis of informal agreements of mutual trust and reciprocal liaisons.

Psychotherapy for All: Finding and Sharing the Right "Shrink"

The literature has reported the singularity of the Argentine case when it comes to the wide-ranging acceptance of psychotherapeutic practices both at home and abroad (Fierro et al., 2018; Plotkin, 2012; Vezzetti, 1996). The widespread use of "verbal therapies" in Argentina could be traced to the rise of psychoanalysis that began in the 1950s and was rooted in the work of Sigmund Freud and French intellectuals such as Jacques Lacan (Dagfal, 2018; Klappenbach, 2013). In her ethnography on Brazilians and Puerto Ricans in New Jersey, Ana Y. Ramos-Zayas (2012) describes the pivotal role of affect as a symbolic conduit for her study participants' expression of daily racial tensions. This author vividly points out how her respondents relied on psychosocial terms in order to make sense of, and interpret, the complex emotions pervading their interracial relationships. In a related vein, psychoanalytic lingo is an integral part of most Argentines' everyday life and has influenced the lexicon of other therapies—including new age practices (Plotkin, 2012 & 2001).

In contrast to the stigma of mental health disorders found among several Latino groups in the U.S. (Chen et al., 2005; Yeung and Chang, 2000), being *en terapia* (in psychological treatment) is a widespread feature among Argentines, particularly those from middle class origin. This is largely due to a well-established psychoanalytical tradition in Argentina that has continued to blossom along with several schools of cognitive, systemic, and transpersonal therapies (Viladrich, 2013).

If trust is the currency for interpersonal exchanges, the value of dependable relationships becomes even more conspicuous when seeking mental health providers able to treat uninsured patients. Given the fact that standard psychological treatment in the U.S. is usually expensive, and often not covered by health insurance plans, most Argentines would confide in their informal networks of care in order to find well trained, culturally sound, trustworthy, and affordable psychologists.[2] Argentine and Latino venues (e.g., storefronts or community media such as radio shows and magazines) were usually a good starting point for those, among my respondents, looking for such professionals. During fieldwork, I met at least ten Argentine psychotherapists who shared my respondents' informal social webs and attended seminars and events organized by Argentine organizations, including the Argentine Consulate in NYC.

Cristal, a 30-year-old undocumented tango practitioner, narrated how she had met her psychotherapist at the time:

> I found this guy in this magazine [an Argentine publication], and I called him up to ask where I could get a cheap consultation because I couldn't pay, and the guy did not let me go . . . He kept me talking and talking, and he saw me for free. You see NYC is a city where you feel alone . . . Okay, the city welcomes you but you are still alone. I had friends at that time who were telling me that I should see somebody who could help me, so I saw this guy. Then I went back to Argentina for a while and I quit. But some months ago I got very depressed and I started again with the same guy . . . Everything got together: being illegal, not doing what I wanted, and on top my partner was also depressed, so he could not help me either. . . .

Eventually, Crystal's therapist became a health resource for some of her friends for whom this provider would charge lower fees. For my Argentine respondents, counting on a "good" Spanish-speaking psychologist meant finding someone who would speak their same language and share familiar slang and cultural codes. It also stood for finding a mental health professional with whom they would be able to negotiate lower fees and flexible schedules.

Urban Shamans and the Gendered Construction of Hope

Shamanism, as a term constructed in the West, has become one of the most used and abused notions in the social sciences. Associated with heterogeneous faiths and religious practices, a lack of consensus exists regarding its origins and shared properties (Wallis, 1999; Price-Williams & Hughes, 1994). The term "urban shaman" has been utilized by a variety of practitioners and genres: from fictional avant-garde women with supernatural powers (Murphy, 2005) to traditional folk healers practicing in a context of recent urbanization, family changes, and migration (Dobkin de Rios, 1992). Terms such as neoshamans or new age shamanism have also been deployed to name spiritual and holistic healers who rely on meditation, spiritual cleansing, and the search for self-knowledge, and harmony with the self and others (Jakobsen, 1999; King, 1990; Sutcliffe & Gilhus, 2014).

In this chapter, the term urban shaman is used to refer to a cosmopolitan mélange of practitioners—mostly folk healers and psychics of Latino origin—who combine the features of neoshamanism described above with religious-healing practices rooted in folk-belief systems from the Americas (mostly Santería and Spiritism; Viladrich, 2018). It is important to note that despite the fact that practitioners of Santería often perform as "urban shamans" in global milieus, the meanings of Santería's theory and practice amply exceed the conceptualization of urban shamanism. As one of the main religious systems embraced by the Afro-Caribbean diaspora, Santería encompasses a complex hermeneutic system and philosophical doctrine that transcend its curative properties (Viladrich, 2019).

Based on his long-term research with traditional healers in China, Arthur Kleinman (1980, 34) observed that although folk medicine is "the most popular subject for cross-cultural research," studies have failed to report patients' motivations to consult with them. To account for this omission, this section explores the perceptions of Argentine immigrants concerning urban shamans' roles in resolving a myriad of health and emotional issues.

Most study participants referred to urban shamans as *brujos* (i.e., witches, fortune-tellers or psychics) and considered them to be multi-varied practitioners in the sense of being able to deal with different therapeutic domains: interpersonal issues (e.g., marital problems), physical conditions (e.g., gastritis or stomachaches), as well as mental health ailments like anxiety and depression. Unlike classic verbal therapies in which subjects are asked to do self-exploration or make behavioral changes, these providers tend to place the origin and responsibility of the individual suffering in external causes—typically epitomized by either magical or social agents (Viladrich, 2018; Wedel, 2004). By relying on explanatory models rooted in supernatural forces, everything from spirit possession to spells cast by a witch on behalf of an envious relative, Argentines' visits to urban shamans had one common denominator: the concretion of *trabajos* (roughly translated as works or spells, Browner and Preloran, 2000) aimed at counteracting *envidia* (envy), *venganza* (vengeance) or *karma* (old lingering souls from previous lives).

Women in this study were more likely than men to acknowledge consulting with urban shamans, whether sporadically or on a regular basis. Not only were these practitioners recommended by word of mouth but they often belonged to immigrants' interpersonal networks and, in some cases, they did not charge for the session. Contrary to schools of thought in which clients are enrolled in faith-belief systems upon consultation (Garrison, 1977), participants in this study did not join their practitioners' religious or spiritual practice. In most cases, their return to the consultation was triggered by critical circumstances particularly when conventional resources seemed not to work. The typical encounter between urban shamans and their clients would begin with an appraisal of their main problems—normally assessed through divination via tarot cards or cowry shells—and was followed by an explanation of the source (e.g., the lingering of an old soul or the spell of an envious relative). It typically ended with a healing plan that usually consisted of several steps.

Serena, a psychologist who worked at a mental health clinic, had become a regular patron of one of these practitioners. Afflicted by several physical and emotional ailments, ranging from overweight to loneliness and physical extenuation, she had begun to visit various folk healers over the past few years.

Although Serena was seeing an Argentine psychologist in NYC at the time—one who did not have a U.S. license and therefore charged her a very moderate fee—she justified her visits to her *bruja* (witch), a Colombian woman in this case, on the basis of her desperate need for feeling better while coping with her everyday stressors. The belief in *trabajos* (spells) implies that the sufferer has become, intentional or otherwise, the victim of witchcraft and/or negative vibrations—typically from a jealous family member or coworker. In Serena's case, the *bruja* determined that she had been the victim of very harmful *trabajos* (from her jealous coworkers) that had weakened her. The treatment consisted of, first, a *limpieza* (cleansing) and second, a series of procedures including the systematic use of bath oils and spiritual offerings to the guardian angels in her *cuadro* (spiritual realm). At the time of the interview, Serena and some of her female coworkers were spending Saturday afternoons waiting at the urban shaman's office. Before and after each healing session, Serena would sit with others to discuss *los aciertos de la bruja* ("the witch's previous correct assessments") and the potential effect that a follow-up session would have on her prognosis.

Some study participants doubted the veracity of their urban shamans' diagnosis and therapies; however, this apprehension would not stop them from either continuing to seek their services or look for similar practitioners. Through trial and error with different healing practices, participants like Serena were committed to finding what could work best to resolve their critical issues. In fact, most participants did not expect their healers to be right on all occasions and even anticipated a certain degree of ambiguity, even mistakes, in their predictions. Even when my respondents doubted the effectiveness of their urban shamans' diagnosis, they would not question their overall ability to deal with unrestrained metaphysical powers that allegedly transcended the mind-body Cartesian distinction typical of Western therapies. In their view, urban shamans were able to tap into areas that others could not have access to, even if they occasionally missed the mark. Some Argentine women even acknowledged visiting several urban shamans (either simultaneously or one at a time) in order to compare predictions and reach a consensus on challenging issues—such as moving to a different city, seeking new career opportunities or dealing with conflictual relationships.

Furthermore, as in the case of Serena above, study participants would consult with *brujos* and *curanderas* (literally "women who heal") to find solutions to problems that could not be solved by other therapies. In agreement with these findings, Kaja Finkler (2001) has observed that individuals tend to find in witchcraft the source of their problems when other treatments have been unsuccessful. As noted by Arthur Kleinman in his work with traditional healers in China (1980) even when bad news is delivered, sufferers are promised that their fate will improve in the long run—as long as they keep following their healers' prescriptions.[3] Furthermore, despite urban shamans' often imprecise and even inaccurate guesses, Argentine immigrants valued having a place where somebody would listen to their personal worries and help them cope with the anxiety of their everyday struggles.

As first-generation immigrants, most female participants in this study experienced many of the everyday struggles shared by other Latin American groups, including dealing with English as a second language, encountering endless difficulties to find a stable job and affordable housing, as well as the challenges of seeking (and securing) permanent legal status. From a gender perspective, this study shows how Argentine women attempted to cope with their everyday stressors by making informed healing choices that contested dominant medical and therapeutic models of care. By relying on urban shamans, they sought empowering treatment alternatives that relied on a socialization process in which the supernatural was inscribed in the ordinary uncertainties of life. Furthermore, urban shamans provided a safe and rewarding channel for the activation of Argentine women's networks of care for which sharing personal worries continued even after the session was over. Finally, the verdict of an urban shaman often gave my respondents hope as it anticipated a better future with promising life trajectories and upward career paths.

Conclusions: Therapeutic Eclecticism as a Piecemeal Solution to Unmet Health Needs

This essay has illustrated the creative ways through which Argentine immigrants in NYC seek, circulate and obtain much-needed health resources by relying on their networks of care. These results reveal diverse patterns of health-seeking practices, beginning with immigrants' reliance on health brokers—Argentine and Latino doctors who provide informal health assistance in informal settings. Furthermore, while mental health providers comprised a health resource shared by Argentine immigrants' social webs, urban shamans represented a trigger for the activation of women's emotional support systems. These findings speak to a unique case of medical pluralism that is termed here "therapeutic eclecticism," as not only do Argentines rely on a wide range of healing disciplines—from psychoanalysis to tarot—but they also engage in fluid social webs in order to find suitable healers coming from distinct fields. Despite mainstream biomedical models that consider social network resources as separate from the U.S. health system, one of the most salient findings of this study was their ability to overlap with formal organizations, including the U.S. health system.

It is because of their sharing of informal networks of care that Argentines in this study were able to find reliable practitioners—both within and outside the biomedical profession. As discussed above, Argentine immigrants acknowledge the role of health brokers as friendly medical providers who spontaneously switch from the clinical codes of "doing medicine," to the terrain of interpersonal liaisons in which explanatory models of illness are fundamentally shared. By participating in informal Argentine and Latino social fields, health brokers challenge the clinical realm of ritualized power hierarchies in favor of one that allegedly equalizes social differences. Health brokers also embody the human face of healing based on personalized approaches—as opposed to the complex and bureaucratized routines characterizing mainstream U.S. services.

Rather than relying on dense and closed networks, the likelihood of Argentines to find reliable health resources largely depends on their fluid, diverse, and heterogeneous social webs (Viladrich, 2013). In this study, person-to-person referrals to both formal and folk-health providers and therapists was a common marketing strategy. While mental health providers epitomized a shared health resource in Argentine enclaves such as the tango world, urban shamans represented a sort of catalyst for Argentine women's emotional support systems. These findings point to a two-fold meaning of trust: dependable relationships with peers who would refer Argentine immigrants to diverse health resources; and Argentines' reliable relationships with the health providers who would treat them.

Although the healing systems examined here differ in theories and methods, they do share some main similarities: all providers speak Spanish, are readily available, offer flexible contractual routines and fees, and provide personalized responses to immigrants' health needs without requiring additional procedures (i.e., screening tests). These practitioners are also more affordable and less threatening than mainstream biomedical systems. As opposed to the complex and bureaucratized routines characterizing U.S. health services, they embody the human face of healing based on individualized and personalized approaches.

A note of caution is in order here, as we should not overlook the fact that none of the health options analyzed in this paper represent an effective long-term substitute for comprehensive medical care. Argentines' therapeutic eclecticism—characterized by their use of whatever seems to work best—is the tip of the iceberg of their unmet needs and not a rationale for replacing safe, effective, and affordable health services. If, as this study suggests, health brokers are playing the role of informal primary care practitioners, efforts should be made to provide adequate health care access to uninsured populations. To a certain extent, counting exclusively on a health broker for the resolution of one's health problems is a symptom of the failure of the U.S. medical system to provide comprehensive health care to vulnerable immigrant groups.

These study results will hopefully open new research avenues regarding the wide array of healing beliefs and practices among diverse Latino populations in the U.S. Future research could test the existence of the health broker model among other immigrant populations, including assessing health providers' similarities and differences, as well as immigrants' reliance on diverse folk and alternative health care systems.

NOTES

1 As in the case of other South Americans (e.g., Brazilians, see Margolis 2013) Argentines have been largely invisible in the U.S.

2 Psychologists' rates vary depending on training, certification, years of experience, and reputation. While mental health providers in many U.S. cities charge roughly $75 to $150 per session, in New York City prices can be up to $250–300 for a forty-five-minute consultation.

3 Kleinman (1980) also noted that fortune telling and other psychic practices provide similar benefits as psychotherapy and supportive care. They contribute to decreasing anxiety by providing advice and practical solutions.

REFERENCES

Bourdieu, Pierre. The Forms of Capital. In J. G. Richardson, ed. *Handbook of Theory and Research for the Sociology of Education.* (241–58). New York: Greenwood, 1985.

Campbell-Montalvo, Rebecca, and Heide Castañeda. School Employees as Health Care Brokers for Multiply-Marginalized Migrant Families. *Medical Anthropology*, 1–14, 2019.

Chávez, Leo. *Shadowed Lives: Undocumented Immigrants in American Society.* New York: Harcourt Brace Jovanovich, 1992.

Chávez, Leo. Doctors, Curanderos, and Brujas: Health Care Delivery and Mexican Immigrants in San Diego. *Medical Anthropology Quarterly*, 15(2), 31–37, 1984.

Chen, Hongtu, Elizabeth J. Kramer, Teddy Chen, and Henry Chung. Engaging Asian Americans for Mental Health Research: Challenges and Solutions. *Journal of Immigrant Health*, 7(2), 109–116, 2005.

Coleman, James S. Social Capital in the Creation of Human Capital. *American Journal of Sociology*, 94, S95–S120, 1988.

Dagfal, Alejandro A. Psychology and Psychoanalysis in Argentina: Politics, French Thought, and the University Connection, 1955–1976. *History of Psychology*, 21(3), 254–272, 2018.

DelVecchio Good, Mary-Jo, and Byron. J. Good. Clinical Narratives and the Study of Contemporary Doctor-Patient Relationships. In G. L. Albrecht, R. Fitzpatrick, and S.C. Scrimshaw, eds. *Handbook of Social Studies in Health and Medicine.* 243–258. Thousand Oaks: Sage, 2000.

Dobkin de Ríos, Marlene. *Amazon Healer: The Life and Times of an Urban Shaman.* U.K.: Prism Press, 1992.

Fernández-Kelly, Patricia M. Towanda's triumph: Social and cultural capital in the Transition to adulthood in the Urban Ghetto. *International Journal of Urban and Regional* Research, 18(1), 88–111, 1994.

Fierro, Catriel, Javier Fernández Álvarez, and Gustavo Adrián Manzo. Un Siglo de Psicoterapia en Argentina: Psicología Clínica, Psicoanálisis y Desarrollos, Recientes, *Revista de Psicología*, 27(2), 1–27, 2018.

Finkler, Kaja. *Physicians at Work, Patients in Pain. Biomedical Practice and Patient Response in Mexico.* Durham, NC: Carolina Academic Press (2nd Edition), 2001.

Flores, Margarita, and Fernando Rello. Social Capital and Poverty: Lessons from Case Studies in Mexico and Central America. *Culture and Agriculture*, 25(1), 1–10, 2002.

Folland, Sherman, and Eric Nauenberg, eds. *Elgar Companion to Social Capital and Health.* Edward Elgar Publishing, 2018.

Freidson, Eliot. *Profession of Medicine: A Study in the Sociology of Applied Knowledge.* New York: Dodd, Mead, 1970.

Garrison Vivian. The "Puerto Rican Syndrome." In Crapanzano, Vincent, and Vivian Garrison, eds. *Psychiatry and Espiritismo. Case Studies in Spirit Possession.* 383–448. John Wiley, 1977.

Granovetter, Mark S. The Strength of Weak Ties. *American Journal of Sociology*, 78(6), 1360–1380, 1973.

Jakobsen, Merete Demant. *Shamanism: Traditional and Contemporary Approaches to the Mastery of Spirits and Healing.* New York: Berghahn Books, 1999.

King, Serge Kahili. *Urban Shaman. A Handbook for Personal and Transformation based on the Hawaiian Way of the Adventurer.* New York: Simon and Schuster, 1990.

Kirmayer, Laurence, Cori Simpson, and Margaret Cargo. Healing Traditions: Culture, Community and Mental Health Promotion with Canadian Aboriginal Peoples. *Australasian Psychiatry*, 11(1), S15–S23, 2003.

Klappenbach, Hugo. French Ideas in the Beginnings of Psychology in Argentina. *Estudos e Pesquisas em Psicologia*, 13(3), 1204–1219, 2013.

Kleinman, Arthur. *Patients and Healers in the Context of Culture: an Exploration of the Borderland Between Anthropology, Medicine, and Psychiatry.* Berkeley: University of California Press, 1980.

Lloyd-Sherlock, Peter. Health Sector Reform in Argentina: a Cautionary Tale. *Social Science and Medicine*, 60, 1893–1903, 2005.

Margolis, Maxine L. *Goodbye, Brazil: Émigrés from the Land of Soccer and Samba.* University of Wisconsin Press, 2013.

Menjívar, Cecilia. The Ties that Heal: Guatemalan Immigrant Women's Networks and Medical Treatment. *International Migration Review*, 36(2), 437–466, 2002.

———. *Fragmented Ties. Salvadoran Immigrant Networks in America.* Berkeley, Los Angeles, London: University of California Press, 2000.

Messias, DeAnne & K. Hilfinger. Transnational Health Resources, Practices, and Perspectives: Brazilian Immigrant Women's Narratives. *Journal of Immigrant Health.* 4(4), 183–200, 2002.

Murphy, C.E. *Urban Shaman Miniseries. The Walker Papers.* New York: Luna, 2005.

Pitkin, Kathryn Derose. Networks of Care: How Latina Immigrants Find Their Way to and through a County Hospital. *Journal of Immigrant Health*, 2(2), 79–87, 1999.

Plotkin, Mariano B. *The Diffusion of Psychoanalysis Under Conditions of Political Authoritarianism: The Case of Argentina, 1960s and 1970s.* Oxford University Press, 2012.

———. *Freud in the Pampas. The Emergence and Development of a Psychoanalytic Culture in Argentina.* Stanford: Stanford University Press, 2001.

Portes, Alejandro. Social Capital: Its Origins and Applications in Modern Sociology. *Annual Review of Sociology*, 24, 1–24, 1998.

Price-Williams Douglass, and Dureen J. Hughes. Shamanism and Altered States of Consciousness. *Anthropology of Consciousness*, 5(2), 1–15, 1994.

Ramos-Zayas, Ana Y. *Street Therapists: Race, Affect, and Neoliberal Personhood in Latino Newark.* Chicago & London: University of Chicago Press, 2012.

Small, Mario L. *Villa Victoria. The Transformation of Social Capital in a Boston Barrio.* Chicago & London: The University of Chicago Press, 2004.

Sutcliffe, Steven J. & Ingvild Saelid Gilhus. *New Age Spirituality: Rethinking Religion.* Routledge.

Thompson, Gretchen H., and Whitney Moret. Building a Theory of Change for Community Development and HIV Programming: The Impact of Social Capital, Stigma Reduction and Community-level Changes on HIV-related Health Outcomes for Orphans and Vulnerable Households in Mozambique. *Community Development*, 1–20, 2019.

Torres, Sara, Ronald Labonté, Denise L. Spitzer, Caroline Andrew, and Carol Amaratunga. Improving Health Equity: The Promising Role of Community Health Workers in Canada. *Healthcare Policy*, 10(1), 73–85, 2014.

Vezzetti, Hugo. *Aventuras de Freud en el País de los Argentinos: De José Ingenieros a Enrique Pichon Rivière.* Buenos Aires: Paidós, 1996.

Viladrich, Anahí. Botánicas as "Invisible Pharmacies": Afro-Caribbean Religions and their Role among the Latino Population in New York City (Las Botánicas como "Farmacias invisibles": Religiones Afro-Caribeñas y su Rol en la Población Latina de la Ciudad de Nueva York), *Latin American Research Review*, 54(4):893–908, 2019.

Viladrich, Anahí. Botánicas Unplugged: Latinos' Religious Healing and the Impact of the Immigrant Continuum. *African Journal of Traditional, Complementary and Alternative Medicines*, 15(1), 188–198, 2018.

———. *More than Two to Tango: Argentine Tango Immigrants in New York City*, Tucson: The University of Arizona Press, 2013.

———. From Shrinks to Urban Shamans: Argentine Immigrants' Therapeutic Eclecticism in New York City. *Culture, Medicine and Psychiatry*, 31, 307–328, 2007.

Wallis, Robert J. Altered States, Conflicting Cultures: Shamans, Neo-Shamans and Academics. *Anthropology of Consciousness*, 10(2), 41–49, 1999.

Wedel, Johan. *Santeria Healing. A Journey into the Afro-Cuban World of Divinities, Spirits, and Sorcery*. Gainesville, FL: University Press of Florida, 2004.

Yeung, Albert S., and Doris F. Chang. Adjustment Disorder: Intergenerational Conflict in a Chinese Immigrant Family. *Culture, Medicine and Psychiatry*, 26, 509–525, 2000.

Young, James C. *Medical Choice in a Medical Village*. New Brunswick: Rutgers University Press, 1981.

Young, James C. A Model of Illness Treatment Decisions in a Tarascan Town. *American Ethnologist 7*, (1), 106–131, 1980.

CRITICAL DIÁLOGO 4

Surveillance and Policing in Everyday Life

The fourth critical diálogo builds upon a seminal literature on borders and the carceral state to situate "the Mexico/US border" in relation to everyday familial experiences with state-sanctioned violence. We examine the political weight of global parallels, particularly in light of social justice initiatives to abolish repressive and white supremacist border-maintaining institutions, like ICE. The framing question for the critical diálogo in this section is: *What can we uncover from placing the Mexico–US border, as a material manifestation of US nativism and imperialism in Latinx Studies, that extends to education, housing, and other institutions in everyday life?*

Leisy Abrego and Esther Hernández approach this question by challenging the assumption that only in recent times have immigrant families endured separation and confinement at the various borders in the Central/North America isthmus. Vanessa Rosa further considers other forms of boundary policing through an analysis of policy makers rationales for and restrictions placed on Puerto Ricans in New York City public housing. Regarding Palestinians and Puerto Rican solidarity work, Sara Awartani documents the administrative manipulation of college student activism, while Lorena Garcia centers on the disciplining of Latina adolescent sexuality in public schools. Finally, turning to transnational Garifuna populations not easily contained by nation-state borders, Paul Joseph López Oro discusses the articulation and monitoring of Afro-Indigenous Latinidades in Central America and the diaspora.

13

#FamiliesBelongTogether

Central American Family Separations from the 1980s to 2019

LEISY J. ABREGO AND ESTER HERNÁNDEZ

Central Americans from El Salvador, Guatemala, and Honduras have come to be associated with the US–Mexico border in powerful ways in the twenty-first century. In 2014, with a notable spike in the number of minors apprehended at the border, images of young children detained in deplorable conditions dominated representation of this group.[1] In June 2018, a two-year-old girl became the viral symbol of Trump's Zero Tolerance Border Policy.[2] The award-winning photograph portraying Honduran asylum seeker, Yanela, captured the toddler's horror as the Border Patrol agent searched her mother, Sandra Sanchez, next to her. The gripping image, when used as the cover for a Facebook fundraising campaign by the San Antonio, Texas-based organization, RAICES, helped raise the astonishing sum of more than $20 million.[3]

By 2019, these Central American children's pain and suffering at the US–Mexico border had understandably garnered much attention. In the midst of great national distress about the undeniably vile, discriminatory policies and practices of the Trump administration, the images of Central American child victims have come to represent all that is wrong in this historical moment. In one widespread response, the hashtag #FamiliesBelongTogether is used to express solidarity and demand an end to family separation at the border. While well intentioned, this approach overlooks various other forms of US state-sanctioned violence against Central Americans across several decades.[4] To understand these experiences of family separation more holistically, this chapter expands the notion of border beyond the line that divides the United States from Mexico to also include the entire Mexican territory. It centers multiple types of family separation while highlighting the United States' role in creating the conditions that often force families to separate. We understand "family separation" as any moment in which families are forcibly separated—whether through murder as committed during war; across borders, as is the case for transnational families created through migration or deportation; or through government institutionalization, through the use of detention centers and the foster care system.

We focus on children's experiences in Central America, en route through Mexico, and in the United States to make evident the cumulative forms of state violence that target them from a spatial and geopolitical perspective, thereby also calling for a reconceptualization and expansion of the meaning and intention of the #FamiliesBelongTogether campaign. While childhood generally engenders calls for protection and assistance, childhood in Central America has not always automatically been protected (Read 2002). Today, in Mexico, Central American children in transit are detained and deported at higher rates than in the United States. The US response to the arrival of Central American children likewise reveals that some children are not deemed worthy of protection. None of these patterns are entirely new. In many ways, the sending countries remain as economically and socially compromised today as they were in the 1980s during the civil wars.[5]

Family Separations beyond the Present Moment at the US–Mexico Border

The long history of US intervention throughout Central America has produced racialized subjectivities and creative family practices for survival (Abrego and Villalpando forthcoming). Deep inequalities correspond with geopolitical power dynamics, as local Central American elites collaborate and conspire with the interests of US capital, foreign investments, development, and extractive economies (Abrego and Villalpando forthcoming). Throughout the twentieth century, the US government has intervened in the region to protect US companies, even when this meant terrorizing and murdering Central American citizens (Abrego 2017, 2018; Oliva Alvarado et al. 2017; Portillo Villeda 2011). Such harsh realities have been at the root of family separation throughout Central American history.

Family separation can take many forms, only some of which involve crossing national borders. For example, the inconsistency of work required agricultural workers to cyclically leave their families in search of jobs, sometimes not returning to their families (Menjívar 2000, 40). These family separations, propelled by the poverty resulting from US economic interventions, also explain high rates of single motherhood. Often, women are required to work outside the home to provide for their children; many find employment as domestic workers in large cities, far away from their children.[6] Likewise, when the Reagan administration spent billions to prolong the Guatemalan and Salvadoran civil wars in the 1980s, the hundreds of thousands of murders and tens of thousands of forced disappearances left widows, grieving parents, and orphaned children.[7] Like today's family separations at the border, these kinds of separations were also politically motivated, painful, and unjust—leading to intergenerational trauma for family members (Abrego 2014).

Family separation, in its various forms in Central America, often results from US imperialist practices. For example, when the only locally available jobs in a free-trade context pay *sueldos de hambre* (poverty wages), many families make the heart-wrenching decision to seek opportunities farther away, mostly in the United States (Schmalzbauer 2005). Created when core members of family units reside separately in two or more nation-states, transnational families are common in Central America. While they may not be neatly captured in a single iconic photograph, such family separation can be as painful as the family separations taking place under the Trump's Zero Tolerance Border Policy. Indeed, the audio of crying children held in detention apart from their parents[8] was eerily reminiscent of interviews with children in transnational families shared in El Salvador (Abrego 2014).

We certainly do not claim that being placed in cages with unfamiliar people in a strange environment far from home is physically or emotionally the same as being left with relatives at home. However, we argue that there is a spectrum of trauma brought upon Central American children and families, all arising from a related set of US imperialist practices. The suffering being photographed and recorded today, therefore, did not originate unexpectedly in 2018; nor is it an anomaly.

Central American Child Migration

While adults initiate most Central American family separations, children have also migrated, accompanied and unaccompanied, since at least the 1980s (Jonas and Rodríguez 2015). Notably horrific incidents in recent history reveal the depth of each Central American country's inability to procure children's well-being. Indeed, with such a long history of US-funded destabilizations, the region lacks the necessary social, legal, and economic infrastructure to protect most citizens, especially their most vulnerable. On March 8, 2017, for example, a fire in a state-run home for minors in Guatemala killed forty-one girls.[9] The girls, who were protesting against ongoing abuse at the home, set fire in their room. Instead of helping them escape, the government employees in charge of their care purposely locked them in with the flames. This abhorrent incident is symptomatic of a larger trend of violence against children in the region.

After many years of war and widespread state terror, the free-trade agreements that followed leave children more vulnerable to daily unmet basic needs. By welcoming mining, hydroelectric energy projects, and other extractive ventures, Central American governments further impoverish communities (Loperena 2017). In 2017, 74 percent of children in Honduras, 68 percent in Guatemala, and 44 percent in El Salvador lived in households classified as poor.[10] To make matters worse, government spending on social services to protect children in the region is also shamefully low (Menkos Zeissig 2016, 51–52).

Economic inequalities are exacerbated by the consequences of widespread unresolved war trauma.[11] In the absence of opportunities for healing, war trauma leads to the enactment of unspeakable types of violence (Abrego 2017), including against children. For example, in El Salvador, between January and May 2018, of the 2,060 reported cases of rape and sexual assault, 1,331 (65 percent) of survivors were girls between the ages of twelve and seventeen.[12] These conservative statistics suggest young girls are victims of rampant violence throughout the isthmus (Menjívar and Walsh 2016; Walsh and Menjívar 2016, 2017). High homicide rates and their apparent impunity further complement this somber reality.[13]

Poor children in northern Central America face the choice between emigrating/being displaced or being forced to join violent gangs to access resources for survival. As a seventeen-year-old Salvadoran boy named Alfonso explains, multiple sources of violence target children even in their neighborhoods and schools, forcing many to leave:

> [Gang members] had killed the two police officers who protected our school. They waited for me outside the school. . . . The gang told me that if I returned to school, I wouldn't make it home alive. The gang had killed two kids I went to school with, and I thought I might be the next one. After that, I couldn't even leave my neighborhood. They prohibited me. I know someone whom the gangs threatened this way. He didn't take their threats seriously. They killed him in the park. He was wearing his school uniform. If I hadn't had these problems, I wouldn't have come here. (UNHCR 2014, 8)

Since 2009, the United Nations High Commissioner on Refugees has been tracking a steady rise in the number of asylum-seeking children from El Salvador, Guatemala, and Honduras to the United States, documenting the perils and explaining the immediate reasons propelling increased migration (UNHCR 2014). In-depth interviews with over four hundred children conducted in 2013 revealed that most minors were fleeing violence from organized criminal actors—including cartels, gangs, and police—as well as violence within their homes. Understanding these high levels of insecurity, many families also encourage children to leave to give them a chance at a stable life.

The Trump administration has made it more difficult for migrant children to access asylum and refugee protections; clear evidence of this is the elimination of the Central American Minors (CAM) program that between 2014 and 2017 allowed migrant children to apply from within their home country for reunification with their documented parents in the United States. The program processed a minimal number of applications (fifteen hundred applications from Central America and the Caribbean in FY2018) before it was terminated.[14]

After decades of warfare, the three countries in northern Central America have been ravaged by rampant structural and interpersonal violence. There is an urgent need to view the plight of the region's children comparatively, not simply from the lens of poverty, but from a Critical Refugee/Latina/o/x studies lens.[15] This requires us, on the one hand, to identify and name the practices of US imperialism in the Americas, including the widespread displacement of families and parts of families. On the other hand, it entails the recognition of migration policies as settler-colonial practices that stand in the way of survival for refugees in the United States (Speed 2019).

Central American Children Crossing Borders

Lacking any legal recourse, Central American children cross international borders without authorization. The journey by land from the isthmus to the United States is long and dangerous, especially for those relying on smuggling networks. In Latina/o/x Studies, research on borders has largely focused on the line between and geopolitical spaces shared by the United States and Mexico. This is understandable given the long history between these neighboring countries and their peoples. To best capture Central American children's experiences, however, it is important to expand the notion of "the border" to also include the militarization of Mexico. Over the past decade, the southern Mexican border has become increasingly militarized and operates as an extension of the northern border with the United States. In the case of long-term family separation, the militarization at the US–Mexico border is certainly one of the notable barriers preventing loved ones from being together, but Central American migrants are also traumatized and killed throughout the entire length of the Mexican territory (Brigden 2018; Vogt 2018), thereby keeping loved ones apart.

Funded since 2007 through the US security cooperation program known as Plan Mérida (The Mérida Initiative) and since 2014 through its Plan Frontera Sur (Southern Border Plan), and Frontera Sur Segura (Secure Southern Border), Mexico now detains and deports more Central Americans than the United States, effectively serving as a continuation of the US border. In 2014, Mexico detained over 24,500 Central Americans going north, including 1,748 unaccompanied minors.[16] Official government statistics show that Mexico deported over 65,000 Central Americans—among them, 17,093 minors—between 2014 and 2017.[17] In just three years, there was a tenfold increase in deportations of children.

Whether detained or deported, Central Americans report abuses—often severe (Izcara Palacios 2016)—at the hands of gangs, drug cartels, and other organized crime groups in Mexico (Ramos Tovar 2016). Most extortions and thefts are carried out by the Mexican Federal Police.[18] Like adults, children, who constitute a sizeable portion of the victims, cannot request assistance from Mexican authorities when they are victimized—whether by smugglers or by state agents; any contact, even if only to denounce abuses, is likely to lead to detention and deportation. Egregious examples abound in which even children who are raped and file a complaint against detention facilities in Mexico are deported back to Central America before a police investigation begins.[19]

Central Americans experience legal and extralegal violence as a naturalized continuum of their irregular status. In the eyes of Mexican authorities, their unauthorized status trumps their human rights and it is acceptable to subject them to violence as they move through Mexican territory. The Mexican state sees Central Americans as targets of enforcement. Crossing the border into Mexico, therefore, means facing various forms of violence all along its arterial border that extends from south to north (Vogt 2018). Between 2005 and 2012, 84 percent of the cases reported to Mexico's National Commission of Human Rights involved minors abused by state-based National Migration Institute or Mexican migration authorities (Silva Quiroz 2016).

The case of Josseline Quinteros, a Salvadoran child who died at the US–Mexico border in 2008, offers a cautionary example where even the border asserts itself in death to separate families. Josseline's parents could not grieve her at the place where she died in the Sonoran Desert because they lacked legal status to travel to the memorial site. Josseline was able to bring her younger brother to safety but she became sick. Unable to keep up with the group in the journey through the desert, Josseline was abandoned by the coyote, who falsely assured her that rescuers would be coming soon. She died as the temperatures dropped and she was wearing only two layers of clothing.[20] With the expanding militarization of borders, migrant children like Josseline have faced such dangerous extended borders through several presidential administrations in both Mexico and the United States.

Central American Children Who Reach the United States

In May 2014, over sixty-eight thousand unaccompanied minors were detained at the US–Mexico border. That summer, mainstream media showed US audiences the deplorable conditions in which children were detained. The US government has continued to mistreat children—most of whom are Central American—under its custody. While the number of apprehensions at the border has decreased, about thirty thousand children continue to be detained per month, with as many as fifty-eight thousand in May 2018. These children face US immigration policies that fail to recognize them as refugees and block them from attaining asylum, despite clear evidence that they should qualify for protection under international law (UNHCR 2014).

In 2014, then-President Barack Obama used the heightened numbers of child migrants at the border to call for "humanitarian standards for detention of adults with children."[21] His administration took advantage of that political moment to vastly expand family detention, an institutionally violent practice that had become rather limited due to excessive abuses in years prior (Schriro 2017). In less than six months, the Obama administration had increased the family detention capacity thirty-five times over (Hernández 2015, 14), incarcerating these minors and causing deep trauma and despair among children (Abrego 2018). In an open letter to President Obama in August 2016, detained mothers expressed that conditions in detention were so unbearable that "children have considered committing suicide, made desperate from confinement."[22] The US public, not as vigilant of its government's state-sanctioned atrocities then as they have become under Trump, did not denounce such violence. After all, most families were being caged together in immigrant detention centers hypocritically called "family residential centers."

While children and parents generally remained together, US immigration authorities were still found to be abusive to children in multiple ways. A May 2018 report published by the American Civil Liberties Union and the University of Chicago Law School (2018) revealed that Customs and Border Protection, a subagency of the Department of Homeland Security, had systematically abused children physically, sexually, verbally, and psychologically at every stage of interacting with the children since 2015. A Freedom of Information Act (FOIA) request had produced thirty thousand pages detailing the various forms of abuse.[23]

Family separation under the Trump administration, administered through the Zero Tolerance Border Policy, is intricately tied to historical examples of state violence, such as the funding of death squads in Central America, and development programs promoted by the United States and favored by the World Bank and International Monetary Fund (IMF), including the Central American Free Trade Agreement. Each of these violently and over prolonged periods of time displaced people from their lands in northern Central America. In the face of military and economic terror, people fled the devastation only to be met with further militarized violence and carceral immigration policies in the United States. Between May and July 2018, Border Patrol agents were instructed through Trump's Zero Tolerance Border Policy to separate children traveling with their parents. They prosecuted every adult apprehended at the border, even asylum applicants, and processed children through a separate agency. In response to uproar against this policy, the Trump administration claims to have suspended this practice, but only after separating thousands of children from their parents.

Without a plan to reunite families, many parents and children were separated for months and even years without knowledge of the others' whereabouts. Untrained staff at detention centers forced children to take psychotropic drugs to keep them from crying uncontrollably.[24] As evidence continues to emerge and we learn of the thousands of children separated from their parents,[25] we can imagine the long-lasting trauma of such practices on Central American children. As of April 2019, close to two thousand children remained separated from their families, with no clear plan for reunification and the possibility that reconnecting parents and children could take years.[26]

Cumulative Violence beyond the Border, beyond Family Separation

Central Americans face various forms of violence from multiple governments. State-sanctioned violence that favors privatization, incarcerates, criminalizes, and neglects the needs of the population (including basic housing, education, decent wages, and health care) shapes the everyday lives of most people in Honduras, Guatemala, and El Salvador. When people flee from their neighborhoods of origin, however, they tend to locate the source of their problems only in their interactions with gang members. Gang violence, however, must be put in the context of state policies of "mano dura," or a zero-tolerance approach to policing that produces repression and high incarceration rates for impoverished youth. At the same time, low prosecution of all other forms of crime contributes to a generalized perception of impunity. The US government also inflicts its own violence through foreign policies and immigration laws; for instance, in the 1990s the mass deportation of criminalized youth exacerbated conditions of insecurity in the region (Osuna 2015).

There is a hardship and stigma among migrants from impoverished regions and neighborhoods that follows them in their migration journey. Central Americans transiting through Mexico confront similar militarized dangers with state police, immigration officials, smugglers, and drug cartels in what is effectively a long continuous border. Trump's discourse about the "criminal element" among these youth adds uncertainty and danger to these young people's journeys. Such rhetoric of hate and xenophobia travels across borders.

Latina/o/x studies would benefit from comparative analysis of migration across nationalities and border contexts. The experience of Central American children today or in the 1980s, for example, is unlike that of Operation Pedro Pan when Cuban parents and Catholic charities orchestrated the transport of fourteen thousand children to the United States (Casavantes Bradford 2014; Chavez and Menjívar 2010). These were primarily middle-class minors whose caretakers sought protection from communism (Torres 2003). Children fleeing non-communist Central American countries receive ambivalent sympathy and outright denial of asylum protections. Such comparisons reveal the gross political bias in the US government's treatment of refugee children and the lack of acknowledgment of its responsibility in producing refugees in Central America (Abrego 2018).

Central American migration must also be placed in the context of specific development models tied to the Washington Consensus, which emphasized neoliberal policies such as financial reform, dollarization, and structural adjustment (Williamson 1993). These create and sustain the conditions of poverty and violence expelling Central Americans from their homes (Hernández and Coutin 2006)—as is also true in other world regions. Indeed, it is urgent that scholars engage in comparative work across historical periods and regions, including in the Caribbean, to best address the complex structural context of migration.

Today, in a moment of political resistance to the Trump administration, a larger slice of the US polity is paying attention to its government's state-sanctioned violence against marginalized groups. Yes, we should be angry that children and parents are being separated at the border. That is an egregious, easily recognizable form of violence. But is poverty not also a form of violence? Central American children endure conditions that attack their dignity, endanger their lives, and deny them full personhood on a daily basis. In these conditions—many of which are the result of longstanding US practices of political, military, and economic intervention in the region—children are forced to act as grown-ups and denied protections (Read 2002). Yes, families belong together, but not in a family detention center; not under state surveillance; not with insufficient food; not with constant fear of violence or of deportation. Even after all the children and parents who were separated under Trump's Zero Tolerance Border Policy are reunited, we should fight for regional refugee policies and practices of protection that improve conditions and lessen children's suffering in their home countries, while in transit, and in the United States.

NOTES

1　Burnett, John. "From a Stream to a Flood: Migrant Kids Overwhelm U.S. Border Agents." NPR-WNYC, June 20, 2014. Accessed May 24, 2019. www.npr.org.

2　Kirby, Jen. "Time's Crying Girl Photo Controversy, Explained." Vox. June 22, 2018. Accessed May 24, 2019. www.vox.com.

3　Jacobs, Julia. "They Wanted to Raise $1,500 for Immigrant Families at the Border. They Got Over $20 Million." *New York Times*, June 19, 2018. Accessed May 24, 2019. www.nytimes.com.

4　To explore ways that humanitarian forms of solidarity have produced new forms of subjectification, see the work of Fassin (2008).

5　In this podcast segment, journalist Jeremy Scahill interviews historian and professor Suyapa Portillo to discuss the United States' role in producing corruption and violence that fuel the exodus from Honduras. Scahill, Jeremy. "Killing Asylum: How Decades of U.S. Policy Ravaged Central America." *The Intercept*, November 18, 2018. Accessed July 25, 2019. https://theintercept.com.

6　In the case of El Salvador, see Abrego (2014). In the case of transnational family separation from Honduras, see Schmalzbauer (2005); for Mexico, see Dreby (2010).

7　To learn more about the civil wars in Guatemala and El Salvador, see Barry (1987); Booth et al. (2015); García (2006); Hamilton and Chinchilla (2001); Pérez and Ramos (2007).

8　Associated Press/ProPublica. "Children Separated from Parents Cry at Detention Centre-Audio." *The Guardian*. June 19, 2018. Accessed May 24, 2019. www.theguardian.com.

9　Goldman, Francisco. "The Story Behind the Fire That Killed Forty Teen-Age Girls in a Guatemalan Children's Home." New Yorker, March 19, 2017. Accessed May 24, 2019. www.newyorker.com. And Ahmed, Azam. "A Locked Door, a Fire and 41 Girls Killed as Police Stood By," *New York Times*, February 14, 2019. Accessed May 24, 2019. www.nytimes.com.

10　UNICEF Child Alert. "Uprooted in Central America and Mexico." UNICEF-For Every Child, August 2018. Accessed May 24, 2019. www.unicef.org. Orozco, Manuel. "Central American Migration: Current Changes and Development Implications." The Dialogue: Leadership for the Americas, November 2018. Accessed May 24, 2019. www.thedialogue.org.

11 Here, I. Martin Baró is useful (1989). He noted that during the war, sexual violence was widespread in conflict zones, perpetrated primarily by government military forces. After almost nine years of war, he posited that: "Finally, the militarization of social life can create a progressive militarization of the mind. Again, this does not involve a simple or mechanical effect. But there is little doubt that the almost compulsive violence which can dominate interpersonal relations, including the most intimate, and the sociopathic destructiveness manifested by some members or former members of the military forces are intrinsically related to the growing preponderance of military forms of thinking, feeling and acting in social life."

12 Observatorio de Violencia contra las Mujeres. Presentación. Bulletin, June-September 2020. San Salvador, El Salvador. Accessed May 24, 2019. http://observatoriodeviolencia.ormusa.org.

13 Donovan, Louise, and Christina Asquith. "El Salvador Kills Women as the U.S. Shrugs." Foreign Policy, March 7, 2019. Accessed May 24, 2019. https://foreignpolicy.com.

14 United States Citizenship and Immigration Services. In-Country Refugee/Parole Processing for Minors in Honduras, El Salvador and Guatemala (Central American Minors – CAM). Official Website of the Department of Homeland Security. Accessed July 25, 2019. www .uscis.gov/CAM.

15 See Grandin (2006) for a political science perspective and Rodriguez (2009) for a cultural studies isthmian perspective; Oliva Alvarado, et al. (2017) for a diasporic perspective; Menjívar and Rodriguez (2005) for a hemispheric view of state violence; and for a global capitalism lens see Robinson (2018).

16 Tourlier, Matthieu. Policía Federal, la Institutición que Más Roba y Extorciona a Inmigran- tes, Redodem. Movimiento Ciudadano. Accessed May 24, 2019. https:// movimientociudadano.mx.

17 Gobierno de Mexico. Mapa de Estaísticas. Secretaria de Gobierno. Accessed May 24, 2019. www.politicamigratoria.gob.mx.

18 Tourlier, Matthieu. Policía Federal, la Institutición que Más Roba y Extorciona a Inmigran- tes, Redodem. Movimiento Ciudadano. Accessed May 24, 2019. https:// movimientociudadano.mx.

19 Timmons, Patrick. "On other side of border, Mexico detaining thousands of migrant children." United Press International, September 27, 2018. Accessed May 24, 2019. www .upi.com.

20 Regan, Margaret. "The Death of Josseline, An excerpt from 'Weekly' scribe Margaret Regan's new book featuring dispatches from the Arizona-Mexico border." *Tuscon Weekly*, February 18, 2010. Accessed May 24, 2019, www.tucsonweekly.com.

21 Obama, Barack. Letter from the President—Efforts to Address the Humanitarian Situation in the Rio Grande Valley Areas of Our Nation's Southwest Border. White House Office of the Press Secretary, June 30, 2014. Accessed September 15, 2017. https://obamawhitehouse. archives.gov.

22 Madres de Berk. "Mothers to Homeland Security: We Won't Eat Until We Are Released." *New York Times*, Opinion Pages, August 12, 2016. Accessed September 15, 2017. https:// kristof.blogs.nytimes.com.

23 Anyone can file a FOIA request to any US government agency to request information that is not already publicly available. See Freedom of Information Act. How to Make a Request. Office of Information Policy, n.d. www.foia.gov.

24 Daley, Beth. Drugging Detained Children is Like Using a Chemical Straitjacket. The Conversation, July 14, 2018. Accessed May 24, 2019. https://theconversation.com.

25 Jordan, Miriam. "Family Separation May Have Hit Thousands More Migrant Children Than Reported." *New York Times*, January 17, 2019. Accessed May 24, 2019. www.nytimes.com.

26   Jacobs, Julia. "U.S. Says It Could Take 2 Years to Identify Up to Thousands of Separated
     Immigrant Families." *New York Times*, April 6, 2019. Accessed May 24, 2019. www.nytimes.com.

REFERENCES

Abrego, Leisy J. 2014. *Sacrificing Families: Navigating Laws, Labor, and Love Across Borders*. Stan-
     ford, CA: Stanford University Press.
———. "On Silences: Salvadoran Refugees Then and Now." *Latino Studies* 15, no. 1 (2017): 73–85.
     doi: 10.1057/s41276-017-0044-4.
———. 2018. "Central American Refugees Reveal the Crisis of the State." In *The Handbook of
     Migration Crises*, edited by Cecilia Menjívar, Marie Ruiz, and Immanuel Ness, 213–28. Oxford:
     Oxford University Press.
Abrego, Leisy, and Alejandro Villalpando. Forthcoming. "Racialization of Central Americans in
     the United States." In *Precarity and Belonging: Labor, Migration, and Noncitizenship*, edited
     by Sylvanna Falcón, Steve McKay, Juan Poblete, Catherine S. Ramírez, and Felicity Amaya
     Schaeffer: Rutgers University Press.
American Civil Liberties Union, and International Human Rights Clinic at The University of
     Chicago Law School. 2018. "Neglect and Abuse of Unaccompanied Immigrant Children by
     U.S. Customs and Border Protection." Report published by International Human Rights Clinic,
     The University of Chicago Law School. Accessed on May 23, 2018. www.law.uchicago.edu/news
     /international-human-rights-clinic-aclu-report-reveals-frequent-abuse-migrant-children-us.
Barry, Tom. 1987. *Roots of Rebellion: Land and Hunger in Central America*. Boston: South End
     Press.
Booth, John A., Christine J. Wade, and Thomas W. Walker. 2015. *Understanding Central America:
     Global Forces, Rebellion, and Change*. Boulder, CO: Westview Press.
Brigden, Noelle Kateri. 2018. *The Migrant Passage: Clandestine Journeys from Central America*.
     Ithaca and London: Cornell University Press.
Casavantes Bradford, Anita. 2014. *The Revolution Is for the Children: The Politics of Childhood in
     Havana and Miami, 1969–1962*. Chapel Hill, NC: University of North Carolina Press.
Chavez, Lilian, and Cecilia Menjívar. 2010. "Children without Borders: A Mapping of the Litera-
     ture on Unaccompanied Migrant Children to the United States." *Migraciones Internacionales*
     5, no. 3: 71–111.
Dreby, Joanna. 2010. *Divided by Borders: Mexican Migrants and their Children*. Berkeley: Univer-
     sity of California Press.
Fassin, Didier. 2008. "The Humanitarian Politics of Testimony: Subjectification through Trauma
     in the Israeli-Palestinian Conflict." *Cultural Anthropology* 23, no. 3: 531–58. doi: 10.1525/
     can.2008.23.3.531.
García, María Cristina. 2006. *Seeking Refuge: Central American Migration to Mexico, The United
     States, and Canada*. Berkeley: University of California Press.
Gaspar Olvera, Selene, and Mónica Guadalupe Chávez Elorza. 2016. "Menores migrantes en
     tránsito por México: flujos, violaciones de derechos humanos y mejores prácticas." Report
     published by IMDOSOC. Accessed on August 25, 2017. www.researchgate.net.
Grandin, Greg. 2006. *Empire's Workshop: Latin America, the United States, and the Rise of the
     New Imperialism*. New York: Metropolitan Books.
Hamilton, Nora, and Norma Stoltz Chinchilla. 2001. *Seeking Community in a Global City: Guate-
     malans and Salvadorans in Los Angeles*. Philadelphia: Temple University Press.
Hernández, Ester, and Susan Coutin. "Remitting Subjects: Migrants, Money and States." *Economy
     and Society* 35, no. 2 (2006): 185–208.
Hernández, David Manuel. "Unaccompanied Child Migrants in 'Crisis': New Surge or Case of
     Arrested Development?" *Harvard Journal of Hispanic Policy* 27 (2015): 11–17.

Izcara Palacios, Simón Pedro. "Violencia postestructural: migrantes centroamericanos y cárteles de la droga en México." *Revista de Estudios Sociales* 56 (abril-junio, 2016): 12–25. doi: 10.7440/res56.2016.01.

Jonas, Susanne, and Néstor Rodríguez. 2015. *Guatemala-U.S. Migration: Transforming Regions.* Austin: University of Texas Press.

Loperena, Christopher A. "Honduras Is Open for Business: Extractivist Tourism as Sustainable Development in the Wake of Disaster?" *Journal of Sustainable Tourism* 25, no. 5 (2017): 618–33. doi: 10.1080/09669582.2016.1231808.

Martín-Baró, Ignacio. "Political Violence and War as Causes of Psychosocial Trauma in El Salvador." *International Journal of Mental Health* 18, no. 1 (1989): 3–20. doi: 10.1080/00207411.1989.11449115.

Menjívar, Cecilia. 2000. *Fragmented Ties: Salvadoran Immigrant Networks in America.* Berkeley: University of California Press.

Menjívar, Cecilia, and Néstor Rodríguez, eds. 2005. *When States Kill: Latin America, the U.S., and Technologies of Terror.* Austin: University of Texas Press.

Menjívar, Cecilia, and Shannon Drysdale Walsh. "Subverting Justice: Socio-Legal Determinants of Impunity for Violence against Women in Guatemala." *Laws* 5, no. 31 (2016):1–20. doi: 10.3390/laws5030031.

Menkos Zeissig, Jonathan. "La indignación: Oportunidad para reivindicar el rol del Estado." In *Cifras y voces: Perspectivas de cambio en la sociedad guatemalteca*, edited by Instituto Nacional Demócrata para Asuntos Internacionales (NDI), 49–52. Guatemala: Editorial Serviprensa, 2016.

Oliva Alvarado, Karina, Ester E. Hernández, and Alicia Ivonne Estrada, eds. 2017. *U.S. Central Americans: Reconstructing Memories, Struggles, and Communities of Resistance.* Tucson: University of Arizona Press.

Osuna, Steven. 2015. "Policing the Wretched: Transnational Apparatuses of Social Control in the Early 21st Century." PhD diss. Sociology. University of California, Santa Barbara.

Pérez, Rossana, and Henry A. J. Ramos, eds. 2007. *Flight to Freedom: The Story of Central American Refugees in California.* Houston: Arte Público Press.

Portillo Villeda, Suyapa. "Honduran Immigrants." In *An Encyclopedia of the Newest Americans*, edited by Ronald H. Bayor, 933–68. Santa Barbara: Greenwood Press, 2011.

Ramos Tovar, María Elena, ed. 2016. *Reconocimiento, derechos humanos e intervención social: Migrantes en el noreste de México.* Monterrey: Universidad Autónoma de Nuevo León.

Read, Kay. "When Is a Kid a Kid? Negotiating Children's Rights in El Salvador's Civil War." *History of Religions* 41, no. 4 (2002): 391–409.

Robinson, William I. 2018. *Into the Tempest: Essays on the New Global Capitalism.* Chicago: Haymarket Books.

Rodríguez, Ana Patricia. 2009. *Dividing the Isthmus: Central American Transnational Histories, Literature, and Cultures.* Austin: University of Texas Press.

Schmalzbauer, Leah. 2005. *Striving and Surviving: A Daily Life Analysis of Honduran Transnational Families.* New York and London: Routledge.

Schriro, Dora. "Weeping in the Playtime of Others: The Obama Administration's Failed Reform of ICE Family Detention Practices." *Journal on Migration and Human Security* 5, no. 2 (2017): 452–80.

Silva Quiroz, Yolanda. "Violaciones a derechos humanos de menores migrantes centroamericanos en su tránsito por México." In *Riesgos en la migración de menores mexicanos y centroamericanos a Estados Unidos de América*, edited by Oscar Misael Hernández-Hernández, 155–81. Ciudad Victoria, Tamaulipas, Mexico: El Colegio de Tamaulipas, 2016.

Speed, Shannon. 2019. *Incarcerated Stories: Indigenous Women Migrants and Violence in the Settler-Capitalist State.* Chapel Hill: The University of North Carolina Press.

Torres, María de Los Angeles. 2003. *The Lost Apple: Operation Pedro Pan, Cuban Children in the U.S., and the Promise of a Better Future*. Boston: Beacon Press.

UNHCR. 2014. "Children on the Run: Unaccompanied Children Leaving Central America and Mexico and the Need for International Protection." Report published by United Nations High Commissioner for Refugees. Washington, DC. Accessed on March 15, 2014. www.unhcrwashington.org.

Vogt, Wendy A. 2018. *Lives in Transit: Violence and Intimacy on the Migrant Journey*. Oakland, CA: University of California Press.

Walsh, Shannon Drysdale, and Cecilia Menjívar. "Impunity and Multisided Violence in the Lives of Latin American Women: El Salvador in Comparative Perspective." *Current Sociology* 64, no. 4 (2016): 586–602.

Walsh, Shannon Drysdale, and Cecilia Menjívar. "The Architecture of Feminicide: The State, Inequalities, and Everyday Gender Violence in Honduras." *Latin American Research Review* 52, no. 2 (2017): 221–40. https://doi.org/10.25222/larr.73.

Williamson, John. "Democracy and the 'Washington Consensus.'" *World Development* 21, no. 8 (1993): 1329–36.

14

Colonial *Projects*

Public Housing and the Management of Puerto Ricans in
New York City, 1945–1970

VANESSA ROSA

In a memo from the New York City Mayor's Committee on Puerto Rican Affairs (MCPRA), dated September 30, 1951, the subject line reads: "Enclosed a plan detailed to try to solve the housing problem of this City in general and particularly the Puerto Ricans." While the memo refers to housing shortages, affordability, and inadequate conditions during a period of urban renewal, its framing and the phrasing—"particularly the Puerto Ricans"—falls in line with the rhetoric that shaped much of the commentary about the mass migration of Puerto Ricans to New York City and the "problems" this migration posed for an already burdened urban infrastructure. The development of public housing in New York City from the 1940s to the 1960s coincided with the displacement and migration of Puerto Ricans to the continental United States. As a result of Operation Bootstrap, a rapid industrialization program led by the US and Puerto Rican governments, more than 800,000 Puerto Ricans (around 85 percent of all Puerto Rican migrants) settled in New York City during this twenty-year period.

Initially framed as "excellent" public housing tenants by city officials (Mayor's Committee on Puerto Rican Affairs 1953), Puerto Ricans, along with African Americans, were quickly blamed for their enduring poverty and the perceived "decline" and failure of public housing projects. Oscar Lewis, the architect of the culture of poverty thesis (1966), gave scientific weight to beliefs that slum housing conditions were created by Puerto Rican families who lacked organization, structure, and a work ethic.[1] "With time," historian Sonia Song-Ha Lee writes, "public housing projects became physical embodiments of black and Puerto Rican poverty" (2014, 47). With the dramatic increase in the New York City Puerto Rican population, alongside an extreme housing shortage, I argue that public housing became a key site for the spatial articulation of Puerto Rican's racial position within US society. The colonial status of the island as an unincorporated territory and Puerto Ricans' status as second-class citizens in need of refinement, management, and surveillance was articulated and reproduced through public housing as part of a circular logic that bolstered colonial projects. The colonial subjectivity of Puerto Ricans justified truncated housing options and the monitoring and surveilling of Puerto Ricans in public housing simultaneously contributed to ideas around the racial inferiority of Puerto Ricans.

I build on scholarship that both explores the second-class citizenship of Puerto Ricans (Ramos-Zayas 2003; Rúa 2012; Staudenmaier 2017) as well as "inclusionary forms of exclusion" (Carbado 2005, 638; Espiritu 2003) rooted in Puerto Rico's status as an unincorporated territory of the United States. While critiques of urban renewal often focus on displacement (Bender 2010; Thompson Fullilove and Wallace 2011; Wyly et al. 2010), this chapter explores the housing of Puerto Ricans in public housing projects.[2] I examine demographic data, housing statistics from the New York City Housing Authority (NYCHA), and archival city documents to trace key moments in the history of Puerto Ricans in public housing in New York City from 1945 to 1970.

Since the United States established colonial rule in Puerto Rico in 1898, there has been much debate and confusion about the status of the island and the positionality of Puerto Ricans vis-à-vis US citizenship and Americanness. According to legal scholars Brook Thomas, Christina Duffy Burnett, and Burke Marshall (2001), debates addressed ". . . the meaning of the phrase 'United States'; the distinction between the status of territories and the status of their inhabitants; the differences between civil and political rights; the distinctions between 'citizens,' 'nationals,' and 'aliens'; and more" (5). Deemed an unincorporated territory under the Foraker Act (1900), Puerto Rico *was* incorporated into empire by establishing that Puerto Rico was a colonial possession with no path to autonomy or statehood. Without statehood, no path to constitutional US citizenship exists (Duffy Burnett and Marshall 2001).[3] As an unincorporated territory, the island and its residents would be indefinitely governed by US constitutional law. However, nonincorporation means that constitutional law is not evenly applied in Puerto Rico.[4]

Drawing on the work of critical race and ethnic studies scholars, I explore the structural and historical specificity of inclusion through practices of exclusion (Carbado 2005; Espiritu 2003). Critical race and legal studies scholar Devon Carbado (2005) explains, "[R]acism is a naturalization process through which people become Americans" and "[N]aturalization is simultaneously a process of exclusion and inclusion" (637). Carbado highlights how racism is foundational to Americanness—for Black people to be included in Americanness is to experience exclusion via racism. Carbado's analysis provides a structural and historical framing of everyday racial encounters (that draw on racial knowledge and racial "intelligence") and centers how the building of US empire has required racial naturalization. In reference to the Insular Cases, Carbado highlights the case of Puerto Rico "as neither foreign nor part of the United States" (2005, 643) and adds, "Blackness, in this sense, might be thought of as an insular identity; like Puerto Rico, blackness is foreign in a domestic sense" (2005, 639). Central to his argument are the legal mechanisms that most scholars of citizenship emphasize but also the social processes at play that complicate how we might think of citizenship and naturalization in the context of empire.

Critical ethnic studies scholar Yen Le Espiritu (2003) theorizes the relationship between inclusion and exclusion through her concept of differential inclusion. She defines differential inclusion as "the process whereby a group of people is deemed integral to the nation's economy, culture, identity, and power—but integral only or precisely because of their designated subordinate standing" (46). She intentionally does not use the term "exclusion" to signal how ideas around "voluntary" immigration/migration obscure the violence in US nation-building through "conquest, slavery, annexation, and the importation of foreign labor" (2003, 47).

Carbado's and Espiritu's respective frameworks inform my research by centering historical context and nuancing the binary logics of inclusion and exclusion. They shed light on the links between "inclusionary" exclusion by exploring, into what, exactly, subjects are being included and how. Such insights implore us to trouble ongoing colonial relations and nation-building projects. In the case of Puerto Ricans in public housing in New York City, Puerto Ricans were incorporated as a mechanism of the racial and spatial regulation required to maintain colonial *project*s and reinforced the island's status as an unincorporated territory.

Building on Carbado and Espiritu, I explore efforts to *incorporate* Puerto Ricans in public housing in New York City as an inclusionary form of exclusion as a starting point to examine broader dynamics of colonialism, unequal power relations, and the articulation of racial logics through urban governance structures. The housing of Puerto Ricans offers a glimpse into how Puerto Ricans were differentially incorporated in public housing in New York City as an inclusionary form of exclusion, maintaining a precarious colonial and second-class status and folding Puerto Ricans into the US racial hierarchy. Public housing *project*s were a site to further entrench the US colonial *project* and relied on deficit frameworks and ideas around a Puerto Rican culture of poverty to justify the management of Puerto Ricans in public housing.

Puerto Ricans and Public Housing in New York City

Images of poverty and discourses of "the ghetto" often dominate contemporary depictions of public housing projects in the United States. Such images and discourses become easily detached from the history of post–World War II public housing that was constructed not only to address a housing shortage and dilapidated housing but also to provide temporary and transitional housing for veterans returning from the war.[5] During this period, slum clearance initiatives facilitated the demolition of areas deemed blighted or in a state of decay by planners and city officials. Through urban renewal policy, public infrastructure, such as highways and housing projects, replaced urban "slums." The highly influential urban planner Robert Moses did not believe in the rehabilitation of deteriorated urban areas. Instead, he favored bulldozing these areas as the only way to address extreme poverty and the ailments of slum districts (Berman 1982). Moses chaired the New York City Slum Clearance Committee, along with many other city initiatives. African American and Latina/o neighborhoods were the targets of his many projects (Sánchez 2007, 102). Moses did not hold back his racist sentiments about these communities and was well known for believing that Puerto Ricans were inferior to whites (Caro 1975). Journalist and Moses biographer Robert Caro referenced an incident where Moses complained about "the scum floating up from Puerto Rico" (Caro 1975, 1168).[6] Moses wrote to Mayor O'Dwyer in December 1949, asking why Puerto Ricans were not subject to more "rigid searches and health examinations" before being permitted to travel to New York (Moses 1949). His beliefs about Puerto Ricans as unsanitary, disease ridden, and racially inferior "scum" shaped his policies and approaches to urban planning in New York City in the 1940s and 1950s. It was no secret that he favored planning that would prevent low-income people and people of color from accessing beaches and parks in and around New York City (Schindler 2015). Moses's racist preoccupations and approach to planning, however, did not fully align with other city bureaucrats. With a vacancy rate of 1.1 percent, others were trying to address a housing shortage, an affordable housing crisis, and a new labor force of Puerto Ricans in need of places to live.

In a 1949 letter the commissioner of the New York City Department of Welfare, Raymond Hilliard, urged the mayor of New York City, William O'Dwyer, to develop an advisory committee with members from key city departments, including the New York City Housing Authority, to address "the Puerto Rican problem" (September 6, 1949). This framing of the Puerto Rican *problem* would become common phrasing for city officials. In a subsequent letter establishing the advisory committee and inviting the Chairman of NYCHA to be one of the original members, Mayor O'Dwyer wrote (1949): "One of the outstanding, and at the same time least understood, problems of New York City undoubtedly concerns our 'Puerto Rican' community." The Mayor's invitation to the chairman of the housing authority to join the advisory committee signals how housing was regarded as a primary way to address "the Puerto Rican problem" in New York City. Established in 1949, the Mayor's Committee on Puerto Rican Affairs included a subcommittee on housing.

In 1949, 3.5 percent of public housing residents were Puerto Rican. By 1955, "Puerto Rican families occupied 8,571 of New York City's 80,761 public housing units" (Glazer and McEntire 1960, 148)—almost 10 percent of residents. By 1960, 18 percent of public housing tenants were Puerto Rican, while the overall Puerto Rican population in New York City was 8 percent. MCPRA viewed access to public housing as a primary way to address "the Puerto Rican problem" as indicated in a January 12, 1950 letter from an MCPRA housing subcommittee member to the Chairman of NYCHA: "The general feeling was that because most Puerto Ricans are of low income, the main source of aid was in our public housing projects." The Committee proceeded to encourage the City and NYCHA to review its method of selecting tenants in order to increase access to public housing for Puerto Ricans. With the advocacy of the MCPRA, many Puerto Rican families would become public housing residents.[7] In contrast to 24 percent of white families and 18 percent of Black families, 46 percent of Puerto Rican families displaced by slum clearance were able to move into public housing buildings (Sánchez 2007, 103).[8] The rehousing of Puerto Ricans at higher rates is tied to efforts to address the "Puerto Rican problem" and incorporate Puerto Ricans into society via public housing. In 1953, the housing authority described Puerto Ricans as "excellent" tenants and expressed its commitment to providing "modern" housing for Puerto Ricans in New York (Mayor's Committee on Puerto Rican Affairs 1953). However, these framings of Puerto Ricans as excellent tenants and city support for providing modern housing must be understood in relation to Puerto Rican migration and colonialism on the island. Puerto Ricans were incorporated into public housing through urban governance structures that were based on Puerto Rican migration framed as a problem to be managed, the second-class citizenship of Puerto Ricans, and the unincorporated status of the island.

In the same year that NYCHA described Puerto Rican's as excellent tenants, new strict tenant eligibility requirements were implemented. A list of twenty-one factors was used to determine the "non-desirability" of tenants, including clauses about the exclusion of welfare recipients, single parenthood, out-of-wedlock children, and a lack of furniture (Dagen Bloom 2008, 176).[9] Puerto Rican incorporation in public housing both relied on and furthered racist tropes about domesticity, inherent poverty, and heteronormative nuclear family structure that were mobilized on the island and justified US occupation (Briggs 2002; Suarez-Findlay 2000). While eligibility requirements were applicable to all tenants, they emerged in a period of increased migration of Puerto Ricans to New York and white flight. These institutional changes advanced a "social work" and social scientific approach to policies. Social scientific frameworks like the culture of poverty logic specifically attempted to address and explain the inferiority of Puerto Ricans.[10] Culture of poverty discourses were used to justify the exclusion of Puerto Ricans based on presumptions about inherent cultural inferiority, where culture came to stand in for race (Briggs 2000, 165). I expand upon critiques of the culture of poverty thesis that emphasize behavioral and cultural traits (as opposed to the systemic causes of poverty and colonialism), ideas about sexuality, and victim blaming (Briggs 2000; Gustafson 2015; Valentine 1969) to consider the ways in which this exclusion and racialization are produced through spatial regulation via incorporation in public housing. Anthropologist Arlene Dávila identified concrete practices by NYCHA, like interviews to determine "suitability" and hygiene inspection of units, were used to surveil tenants (2004, 31). These practices were one way to rationalize the monitoring and management of Puerto Ricans. Social scientific approaches to establishing housing requirements and policies, tenant eligibility requirements, and the framing of Puerto Ricans as a "problem" were key ways in which Puerto Ricans racial position was spatially articulated.

Despite these changes to tenancy requirements that emphasized surveillance and monitoring, a committee made up of local settlement and community organizations published "The Puerto Rican Migration: A Report" (1955) urging NYCHA to put in place more surveillance and management mechanisms to address the perceived problems of migration. The report echoed deficit ideologies that framed Puerto Ricans as a problem and the need for management and regulation. Written by the members of the Settlement Committee, the report outlined recommendations for local authorities in New York to manage the "seriousness of the migration problem" (1955, 1). Because the Settlement Committee considered housing central to assimilation and "integration," the report recommended the following directly to New York City Housing Authority: "a) More adequate screening of families to determine their readiness for apartment living. b) Adequate orientation and education as preparation for incoming tenants. c) Strict supervision of families by management to prevent overcrowding, uncleanliness, unsanitary disposal of garbage and poor relationships with other tenants" (1955, 7). The Settlement Committee's report was a call for NYCHA to better manage the perceived problem of Puerto Rican migration through increased "supervision" and "education." These recommendations came just two years after NYCHA's strict tenancy requirements and tenant surveillance—NYCHA already had similar regulations in place. The report encouraged the incorporation of Puerto Rican tenants in public housing, but only with strict surveillance mechanisms that reinforced Puerto Ricans positionality as colonial subjects who required education and monitoring.

The Settlement Committee used language comparable to Department of Welfare Commissioner Hilliard's report on "The Puerto Rican problem" and referred to the "seriousness of the migration problem." Like Commissioner Hilliard and the MCPRA, the Settlement Committee's recommendations highlighted the significance of public housing in the integration of Puerto Ricans while further emphasizing the need to manage Puerto Ricans. Whereas slum clearance advocate Robert Moses wanted more health screenings for Puerto Ricans before they migrated to New York, the Settlement Committee recommended better screening for apartment living. They recommended "*adequate* orientation and education for incoming tenants" (emphasis added, 1955, 7). They also recommended the "strict supervision of families by management to prevent overcrowding, uncleanliness, unsanitary disposal of garbage." The references to "uncleanliness, unsanitary disposal of garbage," as Kay Anderson (1991) and Jill Nelson (2002) note in the case of Vancouver's Chinatown and Halifax's Africville, respectively, target and mark communities of color as not only dirty, but also in need of regulations, and represent how space makes race and vice versa. This deficit framing once again positioned Puerto Ricans as a problem and ignored the previous policies already put in place by NYCHA. Overcrowding in apartments, much the same as overpopulation on the island, was seen as a defining characteristic of the Puerto Rican problem that legitimized colonial regulation and management of Puerto Rico and its people. Framing Puerto Ricans as a problem alongside changes to tenancy policies that increased surveillance exemplifies how incorporation in public housing, as second-class citizens from an unincorporated territory, was a way to spatially articulate and manage Puerto Ricans positionality as colonial subjects.

In 1955, six years after its inception, and two years after the peak of Puerto Rican migration, Mayor Robert Wagner dismantled the MCPRA. In a letter to the Chairman of NYCHA dated January 6, 1956, Wagner wrote,

> Now that the statutory Commission on Intergroup Relations has come into being and has been organized, it has been necessary for me to review whether there should continue to exist a separate committee dealing with only one aspect of minority problems in New York. I have reached the conclusion that continuation of the Committee on Puerto Rican Affairs after the constitution of the new Commission might lead to confusion and duplication of functions. Furthermore, it seems to me that the Committee on Puerto Rican Affairs has to a large extent carried out most effectively its basic purpose of indoctrinating the City Department on Puerto Rican affairs and of providing for coordination between official and private efforts in this field.

Suggesting that the coexistence of the MCPRA and Commission on Intergroup Relations (COIR) might cause confusion or duplication of function, Mayor Wagner cast Puerto Ricans as part of a broader "minority problem." The mayor's decision in favor of one committee—even though plans for COIR had yet to be determined—signaled the racial positioning of Puerto Ricans alongside African Americans. This positioning was codified via the structures of urban governance. The managing of intergroup relations and "minority problems" was a discursive and material way to place Puerto Ricans within the US racial logic. Even as administrative structures shifted, public housing remained a central way to manage the ongoing "Puerto Rican problem."

Conclusion

According to a section of a MCPRA interim report titled "Where the Puerto Ricans Must Live," the Housing Authority reported that it "arranged many programs to help integrate them into the communities in which they live" (MCPRA

1953). Integration "into the communities in which they live" masks the inclusion-ary exclusion and differential incorporation of Puerto Ricans in public housing as the language of integration legitimized surveillance and exclusion (MCPRA 1953). The language of integration does not necessitate addressing structural inequality or racism. Feminist scholar Sara Ahmed writes, "Being included can thus be to experience an increasingly proximity to those norms that historically have been exclusive . . . We are not then simply included by an act of inclusion. In being 'folded in,' another story unfolds" (Ahmed 2012, 164). The incorporation of Puerto Ricans in public housing projects—the folding in that Ahmed refers to—is tied to the story and lived reality of colonial subjectivity. The Foraker Act incorporated Puerto Rico into empire by declaring the island unincorporated territory, ensuring Puerto Ricans would remain second-class colonial subjects. The colonial *project* in Puerto Rico was reinforced through policies and efforts in public housing *projects* in New York City that promoted the need to manage the Puerto Rican problem through "integration," surveillance, and regulation.

In a November 17, 1959 letter to the Mayor's office, the Chairman of NYCHA, William Reid, identified multiple ways that the Housing Authority maintained a relationship with the Commonwealth of Puerto Rico. He wrote about a recent meeting *in* Puerto Rico between the NYCHA's director of Intergroup Relations and the mayor of San Juan, to emphasize the ways that NYCHA made efforts to share information about public housing with officials in Puerto Rico, further sig-naling the centrality of public housing in addressing the "Puerto Rican problem." In the letter, he described NYCHA's efforts to coordinate with the Commonwealth to ensure that those migrating to New York City were familiar with NYCHA "pol-icy, rules, and regulations." That the mayor's office would be concerned with the local housing authority's relationship with the Commonwealth of Puerto Rico, and the Housing Authority would go to the lengths of having an independent meeting with the mayor of San Juan in Puerto Rico, marks that it was a point of pride that Puerto Ricans were educated about NYCHA rules and regulations before even migrating. This suggests the many ways in which public housing was central to addressing the perceived "Puerto Rican problem." NYCHA efforts on the island to educate families migrating to the mainland about policy, rules, and regulations exemplifies how Puerto Ricans were included through exclusion in public housing—in this case, they were presumed to be deviant and in need of regulation before they even left the island or were tenants in NYCHA buildings.

While public housing was a stepping-stone for whites, it was a space of man-agement and surveillance for Puerto Ricans. Positive framings that promoted their tenancy quickly faded as they became scapegoats for the design failure of public housing that has haunted urban planning into the twenty-first century. Incorporation in public housing for Puerto Ricans was tied to rhetoric that was a material reminder of the second-class citizenship of Puerto Ricans and justified efforts to manage hygiene and cleanliness, increase surveillance, and regulate the norms of living in public housing in New York City. Public housing became a tool in the articulation of Puerto Rican racial inferiority by incorporating Puerto Ricans into public housing alongside exclusionary policies that prevented people of color from having access to equitable housing opportunities.

NOTES

1 Oscar Lewis's culture of poverty thesis (1959 and 1966) asserted that Puerto Ricans and Mexicans, had, over time, adapted to poverty, which led to the creation of a culture of poverty.

2 This includes those who lived in neighborhoods impacted by slum clearance along with those who were newly arrived and in need of housing.

3 The status of former Spanish colonies acquired by the United States was debated in a series of early twentieth-century US Supreme Court cases known as the Insular Cases. It is from these cases that the Supreme Court deemed Puerto Rico as "foreign to the United States in a domestic sense" (Duffy Burnett and Marshall 2001, 1).

4 Puerto Ricans became *legislative* US citizens in 1917 with the passing of the Jones–Shafroth Act. Drawing on political scientist Charles R. Venator-Santiago's work, historian Michael Staudenmair (2017) highlights how "the way Puerto Ricans gained citizenship status over this period only further highlighted—rather than remedied—the precarious colonial status of Puerto Ricans: with no constitutional provision granting citizenship, the right for those born on the island could be revoked simply by an act of congress" (685). Unlike territories in the Southwest that would become states and therefore offered a pathway to citizenship, the limited citizenship of Puerto Rican's intertwines with the island's status. The second-class citizenship of Puerto Ricans is an example of an inclusionary form of exclusion because it is citizenship without full rights, representational government, and just a legislative process away from repeal.

   Sam Erman's research on Gonzales v. Williams (1904), examines the question of citizenship in the Insular Cases. The Supreme Court ruled that Puerto Ricans could not be considered aliens, but they did not conclude that they were citizens. Thus, similar to Downes v. Bidwell (1901), the most prominent of the Insular Cases, Puerto Rico and Puerto Ricans were neither fully included nor excluded, leaving their status in limbo and the United States always in a position to make decisions about their colonial possession.

5 Broader critiques of housing policy during this period have explored discriminatory housing policies such as redlining, a practice that prevented certain areas in cities from accessing bank loans and home insurance (Bender 2010, Hayden 2003; Massey and Denton 1991; Schwartz 2015), which left few housing options for African Americans, Puerto Ricans, and other marginalized groups. These same discriminatory policies, which subsidized private homeownership, benefitted whites and were essential to the growth of the suburbs (Lipsitz 1995). The majority of African American and Puerto Rican (veterans, poor, and working class) were left behind in under-resourced urban neighborhoods with public housing as their subsidized housing option. But not all projects were the same, as policies and quotas maintained segregation in some NYCHA projects, particularly between African Americans and whites (Rothstein 2012). As resident demographics shifted from white to African American and Puerto Rican, public housing projects were stigmatized and racialized as vertical ghettos.

6 In a later interview, Caro reported that he was referring to Moses saying, "They expect me to build playgrounds for that scum floating up from Puerto Rico" (Caro, in Robbins 2017).

7 The Federal Housing Act of 1949, which provided funding for urban renewal and caused displacement in New York City, did have a clause that required temporary relocation and

"permanent provision" of affordable dwellings for those displaced (Housing Act of 1949). However, such policies were not often enforced, hence mass displacement (particularly of African Americans) (Hyra 2012).

8 Sánchez suggests that the MCPRA had significant political power and was able to leverage that power to provide access to public housing for Puerto Ricans (2007, 104).

9 The rules around welfare recipients were changed in 1968 after immense pressure from welfare activists.

10 The culture of poverty thesis informed the infamous "Moynihan Report" (Moynihan 1965). Similar logic can be traced to the pathologizing of Latina/o/x populations in Samuel Huntington's (2009) widely cited work.

REFERENCES

Ahmed, Sara. 2012. *On Being Included.* Durham, North Carolina: Duke University Press.

Anderson, Kay. 1991. *Vancouver's Chinatown: Racial Discourse in Canada 1875–1980.* Montreal and Kingston: McGill-Queen's Press.

Bender, Steve. 2010. *Tierra y Libertad: Land, Liberty and Latino Housing.* New York: NYU Press.

Berman, Marshall. 1982. *All that is Solid Melts into Air.* New York: Simon and Schuster.

Biro, Gregory W. "Meeting with Housing Sub-Committee, Mayors' Committee on Puerto Rican Affairs." New York City Housing Authority. January 12, 1950.

Briggs, Laura. 2002. *Reproducing Empire: Race, Sex, Science and U.S. Imperialism in Puerto Rico.* Berkeley and Los Angeles: University of California Press.

Carbado, Devon. "Racial Naturalization." *American Quarterly* 57, no. 3 (2005): 633–58.

Caro, Robert. 1975. *The Power Broker: Robert Moses and the Fall of New York.* New York: Vintage Books.

Dagen Bloom, Nicholas. "Jacob Riis Houses." In *Affordable Housing in New York: The People, Places and Policies That Transformed a City,* edited by Nicholas Dagen Bloom and Matthew Gordon Lasner, 128–30. Princeton, New Jersey: Princeton University Press, 2016.

Dagen Bloom, Nicholas. 2008. *Public Housing that Worked: New York in the Twentieth Century.* Philadelphia: University of Pennsylvania Press.

Dávila, Arlene. 2004. *Barrio Dreams: Puerto Ricans, Latinos, and the Neoliberal City.* Berkeley and Los Angeles: University of California Press.

Thomas, Brook, Christina Duffy Burnett, and Burke Marshall. 2001. *Foreign in a Domestic Sense: Puerto Rico, American Expansion, and the Constitution.* Durham, North Carolina: Duke University Press.

Espiritu, Yen L. 2003. *Home Bound: Filipino American Lives Across Cultures, Communities, and Countries.* Berkeley and Los Angeles: University of California Press.

Glazer, Nathan, and Davis McEntire, eds. 1960. *Studies in Housing & Minority Groups.* Berkeley and Los Angeles: University of California Press.

Gustafson, Kaaryn. 2011. *Cheating Welfare: Public Assistance and the Criminalization of Poverty.* New York University Press: New York.

Hayden, Dolores. 2003. *Building Suburbia: Greenfields and Urban Growth, 1820–2000.* New York: Pantheon Books.

Hilliard, Raymond. Commissioner Letter to the Mayor Wagner. "The Puerto Rican Problem" of Department of Welfare of New York. September 6, 1949.

Housing Act of 1949, Public Law 81–171 (7/15/1949).

Huntington, Samuel. 2009. The Hispanic Challenge. *Foreign Policy.*

Hyra, Derek S. "Conceptualizing the New Urban Renewal: Comparing the Past to the Present." *Urban Affairs Review* 48, no. 4 (2012): 498–527.

Lee, Sonia Song-Ha. 2016. *Building a Latino Civil Rights Movement: Puerto Ricans, African Americans and Racial Justice in New York City*. Chapel Hill, NC: UNC Press.

Lewis, Oscar. 1959. *Five Families: Mexican Case Studies in the Culture of Poverty*. New York: New York Basic Books.

———. 1966. *La Vida: A Puerto Rican family in the culture of poverty—San Juan and New York*. NY: Vintage.

———. 1968. *A Study of Slum Culture: Backgrounds for La Vida*. New York: Random House.

Lipsitz, George. 1995. *The Possessive Investment in Whiteness: How White People Profit from Identity Politics*. Philadelphia: Temple University Press.

Massey, Douglass., and Nancy Denton. 1993. *American Apartheid: Segregation and the Making of the Underclass*. London and Cambridge: Harvard University Press.

Mayor's Committee on Puerto Rican Affairs. 1949. Interim Report of the Mayor's Committee on Puerto Rican Affairs.

Mayor's Committee on Puerto Rican Affairs. 1953. Interim Report of the Mayor's Committee on Puerto Rican Affairs.

Moses, Robert. 1949. Letter to the Mayor. December 2, 1949.

Moynihan, Daniel. P. 1965. The Negro Family: The Case for National Action. Washington, DC, Office of Policy Planning and Research, U.S. Department of Labor.

Nelson, Jennifer. "The Space of Africville: Creating, Regulating and Remembering an Urban Slum." In *Race, Space, and the Law*, edited by Sherene Razack, 211–32. Toronto: Between the Lines, 2002.

New York City, Department of Welfare. 1949. Report of the Puerto Rican Problem of the City of New York Department of Welfare. September 6, 1949.

Ramos-Zayas, Ana. 2003. *National Performances: The Politics of Race, Class, and Space in Puerto Rican Chicago*. Chicago: University of Chicago Press.

Reid, W. 1959. Letter to Mr. Robert Low, Chairman of the Continuations Committee, Office of the Mayor. November 17, 1959.

Robbins, Christopher. "Robert Caro Wonders What New York Is Going to Become." *Gothamist*, February 16, 2017. https://gothamist.com.

Rothstein, Richard. "Race and Public Housing: Revisiting the Federal Role." *Poverty and Race Research Action Council*, 21, no. 6 (2012): 1–2, 13–17.

Rúa, Mérida. 2012. A *Grounded Identidad: Making New Lives in Chicago's Puerto Rican Neighborhoods*. Oxford and New York: Oxford University Press.

Rutledge, E. Letter to Philip J. Cruise, Chairman of the New York City Housing Authority. April 10, 1956.

Sánchez, José Ramón. R. 2007. *Boricua Power: A Political History of Puerto Ricans in the United States*. New York: NYU Press.

Schwarz, Alex. 2015. *Housing Policy in the United States*. New York: Routledge.

Staudenmaier, Michael. "Mostly of Spanish Extraction: Second Class Citizenship and Racial Formation in Puerto Rican Chicago, 1946–1965." *Journal of American History* 104, no. 3 (2017): 681–706.

Suarez-Findlay, Eileen. 2000. *Imposing Decency: The Politics of Sexuality and Race in Puerto Rico*. Durham, North Carolina: Duke University Press.

Thompson Fullilove, Molly., and Rodrick Wallace. "Serial Forced Displacement in American Cities, 1916–2010." *Journal of Urban Health* 88, no. 3 (2011): 381–89.

Valentine, Charles et. al. "Culture and Poverty: Critique and Counter Proposals." *Current Anthropology* 10, nos. 2–3 (1969): 181–201.

Wagner, Robert. 1949. Letter to the Chairman of NYCHA. September 8, 1949.

Wyly, Elvin, Kathe Newman, Alex Shafran, and Elizabeth Lee. "Displacing New York." *Environment and Planning A* 42 (2010): 2602–23.

15

Puerto Rico, Palestine, and the Politics of Resistance and Surveillance at the University of Illinois Chicago Circle

SARA AWARTANI

On May 11, 1978, Chicago's Jewish community gathered at the University of Illinois Chicago Circle (UICC) to commemorate thirty years of Israeli independence.[1] Over the course of several months, the university's three most prominent Zionist student organizations—Hillel, Associated Movements for Israel (AMI), and Students for Israel—worked closely with administrative officials and campus security to coordinate event logistics. Massive crowds packed the Chicago Circle Center's Illinois Room where they listened to a range of local politicians, including Mayor Albert Smith of Skokie, Illinois, Deputy Governor Ilana Rovner, and State Representative Alan Greiman, articulate their support for the state of Israel.[2]

A less congratulatory, though equally impassioned, group of approximately one hundred pro-Palestinian students gathered outside in protest against the celebration's brazen politics. For nearly forty-five minutes, demonstrators chanted "Long live Palestine!" and "Palestine is Arab land!" Twenty-five core protestors—a group of Arab, Iranian, Eritrean, and Puerto Rican students—eventually effaced police barricades intended to prevent their admission into the celebration. Upon making their way into the Illinois Room, the protestors booed and shouted while tearing down pro-Zionist posters and balloons. "We actually made arrangements to see how we could get people inside the event to protest," said Edwin Cortes, a leading member of the Union for Puerto Rican Students (UPRS). As the Mayor Smith spoke, one of the demonstrators gave a cue, prompting the others to "pop-up" chanting. "And that's when all hell broke loose," remembered Alejandro Molina, a Mexican student activist involved with the UPRS, his memories of the protest still vivid even forty years later.[3] Uniformed and plainclothes university and Chicago Police Department (CPD) officers immediately intervened, threatening arrest should the demonstrators fail to disperse. But they refused police demands. As one Palestinian member of the Organization of Arab Students (OAS) later explained to the campus newspaper, "We're against the Zionists. We don't like the fact that they stole our homeland nor the way the Zionists treat us. When a celebration is held, and they're selling 'I am a Zionist' buttons and celebrating [. . .] how could we just sit back?"[4]

Five months later, the Israeli Independence Day protest continued to animate campus politics, in large part because of the university's insistence on pursuing charges against several of the protestors—first by threatening criminal prosecution and only later settling for expulsion. News of the Israeli Independence Day protests even reached nearby Northeastern Illinois University (NEIU), prompting its UPRS chapter to publish an article strongly condemning UICC administration's decision. Written as a statement of solidarity against "30 years of Zionist occupation, repression, and expulsion," NEIU's UPRS demanded all disciplinary charges brought against the pro-Palestinian protestors be dropped. UICC's administration was actively policing political dissent; prosecution of the Israeli Independence Day protestors was simply the latest iteration in a robust history of racist and repressive administrative policies. After all, these Puerto Rican students charged, UICC's administration had long colluded with law enforcement agencies—both domestic and foreign.[5]

The political awakening and radicalization of Chicago's Puerto Rican communities emerged, in large part, as response to heavily policed spatial segregation, police brutality, and federal surveillance. But this history of Puerto Ricans' confrontations with the state, their racialization into a Third World political condition, and the coalitions these experiences of repression produced is far more diverse than historical scholarship has recognized.[6] The 1970s simultaneously witnessed the emergence of an Arab American Left who, much like Puerto Ricans, found themselves organizing with and against, as historian Salim Yaqub observes, a "national tapestry of repression and dissent," including the Operation Boulder regime, a federal program dedicated to scrutinizing and restricting Arabs and Arab Americans for possible terrorist connections.[7] The May 11, 1978 Israeli Independence Day protest erupted precisely within this historical conjuncture, wherein multiple communities of color found themselves fighting against the development of the carceral state. The Israeli Independence Day protest thus represents a more complicated moment in social movement historiography—highlighting the continued production of oppositional politics, and of heretofore unforeseen solidarities, despite the tactics of state repression and surveillance that historians have traditionally signaled as the collapse in radical political organizing. It was precisely Puerto Rican and Arab American radicals' concerns about the constitutive uses and abuses of US imperial power, domestically and abroad, that facilitated coalition building.

Drawing from interviews I conducted with UPRS activists and attorneys involved in the protests as well as archival documentation from university administrators, student journalists, and campus organizations, I demonstrate how university policing of Palestine activism was—and is—as much a story of *resilience* as it was of repression. First, I provide a detailed understanding of *how* the Israeli Independence Day protest was policed, including a particularly sinister use of surveillance technologies. Responding to rising pro-Palestinian sympathies

and solidarities, pro-Israel and Zionist students, together with UICC's administration, consistently cast Arab student activism as dangerous political propaganda. It was this volatile mixture of activism and anxiety—known colloquially
throughout campus as "minor wars"—that came to a head at the May 11, 1978
Israeli Independence Day celebration. At the same time, as the extent of disciplinary action against the Israeli Independence Day protestors became known,
a number of Puerto Rican students spearheaded broadscale coalition building
efforts in their defense. By the following quarter, the ad hoc organization Committee Against Student Repression (CASR) was formed. This alliance situated the
Israeli Independence Day protests within a larger set of political concerns ani-
mating Puerto Rican Chicago, namely revelations of Chicago Red Squad infiltra-
tions and the increasing use of grand jury repression against the independence
movement. I argue that by locating the Israeli Independence Day celebration
within a broader history of surveillance and counterintelligence, these Puerto
Rican students mobilized the protests to articulate their own relationship to an
aggressive, imperialist state.

While the Committee Against Student Repression was tentative and short
lived, its vision of solidarity—and the points of contact between communities initiated—remains its greatest legacy. To stand in solidarity with Arab and
pro-Palestinian students meant more than standing against arrests and suspen-
sion. Ultimately, it also meant understanding that such prosecutions provided
early evidence of what scholars now understand as the "sinister collaboration"
between US and Israeli security states—and the crucial role universities have
played in that nexus of politicized surveillance, harassment, and policing against
Palestine solidarity in particular, and in support of US imperialism writ large.[8] It
was partly through the struggle for Palestinian self-determination that Chicago
Puerto Ricans learned to think and operate within a revolutionary political
condition.

Let Arabs Know about Picture Taking

More than a month before the May 1978 Israeli Independence Day celebration
was scheduled to occur, Zionist students began raising concerns over protests.
"The time is drawing near for the annual Israeli Independence Day celebration
at Circle," cautioned Debbie Simon and Mark Stein, members of AMI, in a letter
published in UICC's student newspaper, the *Chicago Illini*, on April 3, 1978. "In
the past, these celebrations have been the occasion for minor wars between Jewish and Arab students." Deborah Kallick, a student planning to attend that year's
celebration, echoed these anxieties: "I dread the inevitable annual confrontation
on Israeli Independence Day."[9]

Throughout the 1970s, UICC witnessed a growth of pro-Palestinian sympathies and solidarities led by the Organization of Arab Students. Debates on the

morality and legitimacy of Zionist politics regularly saturated the pages of the *Chicago Illini*, and rallies, teach-ins, and shouting matches between students pro- liferated throughout campus.[10] But these cautions—particularly the invocations of warfare—also reflected broader anxieties over Arab political activity, namely that it constituted an extension of Palestinian political propaganda. Since the 1969 infiltration of the Organization of Arab Students' national convention, the Anti-Defamation League regularly monitored Arab campus activities. That same year, then-Congressman Gerald Ford branded Arab students as "radical agita- tors and potential terrorists" in a speech delivered to the American Israel Public Affairs Committee.[11]

On campus, these fears prompted Patti Ray, director of Hillel, to work directly with UICC's administration to maintain a watchful eye over Arab students and Palestine activism, especially as it concerned Israeli Independence Day. "I wanted to be sure that you have a full record of the concerns which were expressed by Patti Ray and a delegation of Hillel students in a meeting with [Chancellor] Don [Riddle] and me about a month ago," wrote Carol Berthold, Riddle's assistant, in an April 17, 1978 letter to Vice Chancellor Richard Ward. "I promised Patti Ray that I would double check everything to be sure that their concerns are not forgotten," she explained. Among these concerns, originally aired at a March 2, 1978 meeting, was the profound anxiety over *when*—not if—violence would erupt, a quandary posed as "What is disruptive?" What, in other words, consti- tuted legitimate political dissent? Or, at the very least, what would the university appear to tolerate before intervening?[12]

University officials turned to policing to discipline Arab students and to cur- tail any further emergence of Palestine solidarity movements.[13] Chancellor Don- ald Riddle, Vice Chancellor Richard Ward, and Oscar Miller, Dean of Student Affairs, all actively coordinated security forces for the Israeli Independence Day celebration. University and Chicago Police Department officers were expected to be on site before, during, and after the celebrations, with additional units on reserve should tensions escalate as it had in years past.[14] And at Hillel's request, a single administrative official was to be designated the "on-the-scene man." Vice Chancellor Ward was chosen for this position, and he assumed authority to deploy and direct any subsequent security should Arab students and their allies cross the university's (undefined) threshold of respectable behavior.[15]

But more concerning than the recruitment of police was the administration's use of surveillance against Arab students and their allies. University officials requested that police provide photographic documentation of the demonstra- tions. Notes from a February 21, 1978 meeting included an ominous reminder to "let Arabs know about picture taking; they risk it. (Applies to inside meeting too)."[16] And protestors did come to know of administration's plans for surveil- lance. In an attempt to curtail that year's protest, Vice Chancellor Ward met with Arab students in advance of the Israeli Independence Day celebration, issuing a stern warning that "photos could be used for deportation purposes." On the day of, a few of the protestors actively resisted this surveillance, choosing instead to hide their faces with cloth.[17] But most chose to take the risk, trusting that the university would not endanger the lives of its students, especially when those very same students had communicated just how real they feared the consequences of arrest.[18]

On the afternoon of May 11, 1978, Arab and pro-Palestinian students met the full force of university-sanctioned policing and surveillance. Nearly forty plainclothes and uniformed university and CPD officials patrolled the Chicago Circle Center, with additional units called in as the protests unfolded. In a damning exposé, the *Chicago Illini* revealed that police actively recorded protestors throughout the duration of the demonstration. Ward even went on record confirming these allegations and their motivation: to facilitate the identification and eventual arrest of pro-Palestinian students. Ward remained unapologetic. "As for the reaction he expects from students [regarding arrests]," reported the *Chicago Illini* one week later, "Ward said he knew that the University (and himself in particular) would be criticized."[19]

With the exception of Edwin Cortes—who Ward personally filed a complaint against—all disciplinary action derived from photographic evidence.[20] UICC's police department concluded its Israeli Independence Day incident report with the assurance that "photos will be viewed in an effort to obtain the names, address, and status (if student) of alleged offenders so that notices to appear or warrants may be obtained." These identifications needed to be produced quickly. At the time the initial report was filed (May 11), police had already scheduled a meeting for May 23 with Ward and several other persons wishing to file criminal complaints. Ward even personally reached out to the *Chicago Illini* for photos taken at Israeli Independence Day that might "aid him in his search for 'criminals.'" His request was denied. Still, in the supplementary report outlining the results of the meeting, university police noted that several of the complainants "brought in their own photos of the alleged offenders." Students targeted for arrest were to receive letters at their home addresses. Should any fail to turn themselves in, Ward confirmed they would be detained on campus.[21]

An Emerging Defense of "Concerned Students"

Tense debates inundated UICC as the scope and repercussions of such surveillance became known. Both AMI and Hillel encouraged disciplinary action against the pro-Palestinian students. Hillel purchased an advertisement in the *Chicago Illini* demanding prosecution. "Until they stop acting like vicious hoodlums," explained Hillel, "they do not deserve the same rights of other student organizations."[22] Other students objected to the university's insistence on filing criminal charges. Some, like the *Chicago Illini* editorial board, feared arrests could set dangerous precedents—validating administrative overreach and curtailing future free speech.[23]

Meanwhile, Arab and pro-Palestinian students articulated a more pointed critique: that threatening arrest was evidence of administrative *collusion* with US interests in the Middle East. Some, like John Pottinger of UICC's Young Socialist Alliance, argued that prosecuting the Israeli Independence Day protestors satisfied the university's long-awaited desire to quell Palestine activism. "The administration shows itself on the side of the Zionist state of Israel," he rebuked.[24] Arab students echoed these claims, emphasizing the very dangerous repercussions that yielding to Zionist propaganda could have on their lives. The OAS cited the case of Sami Esmail, a Palestinian American student at nearby Michigan State University arrested by Israeli authorities in 1977. "[I]t was reported in the press that the American student from the University of Michigan [. . .] was arrested by Israeli authorities on the basis of information provided by 'some students' in the U. of Michigan," they explained of Esmail's case. Although some details cited were incorrect—Esmail attended Michigan State—their message stood: university-sanctioned surveillance placed Arab students in the dangerous crosshairs of the Israeli state.[25]

Pro-Palestinian students quickly began demonstrating against the administration's intent to arrest. Much of this emergent defensive campaign owed its initial momentum to Puerto Rican students who leveraged their individual reputations (and organizational affiliations) in support of the Israeli Independence Day protestors. At the heart of this solidarity work was Edwin Cortés. Of course, not only had Cortés helped organize that year's (and prior years') protest, he was also among those facing arrest. But, as a student senator, Cortés occupied a unique position of power, one that he wielded willingly in defense of Palestine activism. For example, on May 24, forty students from a number of Third World student organizations demonstrated outside the Chicago Circle Center.[26] Cortés then directed a contingent of these "concerned students" to the Board of Trustees meeting where he delivered a statement on their behalf.[27]

As Cortés appealed to the Board of Trustees, he narrated a broader history of abuse and repression encountered on campus. He warned that threats of arrest were simply the most recent evidence in a dangerous pattern of administrative collusion with "repressive agencies, foreign and U.S. spies" on campus. Earlier that academic year, revelations surfaced that UICC's administration knowingly allowed the Chicago Police Department's "Red Squad" to monitor and collect information on demonstrations, campus organizations, and individuals—even classes and faculty members—for almost a decade.[28] UICC had supposedly also allowed SAVAK (the Iranian Secret Police) to operate on campus; UICC's Office of Foreign Student Affairs warned Iranian students that engaging in political demonstrations made them liable to arrest and deportation.[29] Cortés also reprimanded administration's collusion with the ongoing FBI investigation of the Puerto Rican independence movement, slamming, in particular, the decision to release student records to a federal grand jury as evidence of repressive administrative policies. He also testified to chilling experiences of intimidation among Third World student movements: "Our student leaders are continuously watched. Our phones are tapped. We are followed, step by step, through each day." But it was the nonchalant, public manner in which Ward pursued criminal charges that Cortés noted as most concerning. It functioned as intimidation against any student who might be sympathetic to Palestine activism. He implored the Board of Trustees to force administration to deal with the matter internally. "The University cannot continue to permit the UICC administration to make a mockery of academic freedom and turn this university into a police citadel," Cortés insisted.[30] "Is this the University of Illinois, or the Police State of Illinois?" Cortés asked the Board pointedly.

Expulsion Hearings, Israeli Propaganda, and the Committee Against Student Repression

By the fall quarter, the Israeli Independence Day protestors no longer faced arrest or criminal charges, only expulsion from the university. Arrests likely posed too much a liability for an administration already marred by controversy. But if administration hoped handling the matter internally would dampen any further critique of their handling of the Israeli Independence Day celebration, the opposite proved to be true. Palestinian activist Samir Odeh of the Arab Community Center swiftly secured legal representation for the prosecuted students; attorneys Michael Deutsch and Mara Seigel of Chicago's People's Law Office agreed to defend the students before UICC's Judiciary Committee. According to Deutsch, their legal defense strategy was straightforward: "We took the position that they were exercising their first amendment rights to protest and that, you know, the whole thing was kind of a propaganda exercise on behalf of Israel—that it wasn't even a proper subject for the university to take on."[31]

As the hearings commenced, Puerto Rican comrades once again took the helm in rallying students in solidarity, this time organizing under a new banner: the Committee Against Student Repression. Proceedings against the pro-Palestinian students began in September and lasted throughout the month of October. During this period, CASR spearheaded a number of educational forums meant to "provide students with an analysis of what has happened at the trials, and what our legal strategy is."[32] Folks like Edwin Cortes and Alejandro Molina leveraged their UPRS contacts at nearby NEIU to help drum up broader support for the students on trial (themselves included). Molina specifically remembers sharing information from the CASR in hopes that their analysis of the proceedings might be published in their newspaper, *Qué Ondée Sola* (QOS).[33]

CASR doubled down on earlier critiques of administrative collusion. They argued that the disciplinary hearings, like the Israeli Independence Day celebration itself, were Israeli propaganda exercises; UICC's Judiciary Committee was a "disciplinary kangaroo court."[34] Students continued to accuse administrative officials of preventing their right to protest. Edwin Cortes and Alejandro Molina, as well as attorney Michael Deutsch, all recalled stories that Oscar Miller and Richard Ward had nefarious relationships with the government—that they were rumored to be staunch Zionist supporters and involved with intelligence operations. They also believed the chairperson leading it, Maryanne Albrecht, was biased in her handling of the proceedings. For example, Deutsch and Seigel were reportedly denied permission to cross-examine witnesses or sufficiently review new evidence introduced against the protestors. Instead, Albrecht accused the defense of deliberately disrupting the proceedings and threatened to arrest the students on trial. And nor was the trial one by peers: the hearing panel included a member of a Zionist organization but no representatives of Third World student organizations. In response, CASR and the protestors on trial threatened to walk out on the hearings.[35]

Yet CASR's strongest objections stemmed from a very particular fear: that the university would record and share tapes of the hearings to "U.S. or foreign repressive agencies." How could they trust an institution that had historically worked with law enforcement agencies to surveil its own students—and that, they alleged, continued to do so?[36] CASR argued that a flawed judicial system could never bring about justice; only a coordinated offensive of direct action by radical, progressive, and Third World student organizations would succeed. "It has been the experience of students that all qualitative changes have and will come only by struggle and confrontation," explained an article published in *QOS*—the very same statement of solidarity introduced at the start of this chapter. "We urge all students to join in a united effort to drop the charges against Palestinian students and their supporters," it implored its predominately Puerto Rican and Latino audience.[37]

According to CASR, prosecuting Palestinian students and their supporters further rationalized and institutionalized UICC's intensifying entanglements with local, state, and national counterintelligence activities. Whereas five months prior, at the May 24 Board of Trustees meeting, Edwin Cortés had *insinuated* these connections, now they were being promulgated as definitive fact. That the university had allowed SAVAK to monitor and attack Iranian students; that the administration so willingly handed over student records to an FBI investigation hell-bent on destroying the Puerto Rican independence movement;[38] that the university's very own Committee on Police Surveillance verified collusion with the Chicago Red Squad.[39] These all confirmed what pro-Palestinian students had already believed to be true: the United States was an aggressive, imperialist state. Of course the university would be complicit in intelligence gathering and record keeping against politically radical students, particularly if they engaged in activities that critiqued US government policies. Surely, solidarity with Arab and pro-Palestinian students meant standing against the most immediate threat of expulsions. But for CASR, it also meant standing as comrades against a history of surveillance and repression—to stand, in other words, against the impact of US empire in their daily lives.[40]

By January 1979, UICC's Judiciary Committee reached its decision: expulsion. Still, CASR refused defeat, organizing a formal demonstration against the decision, held on January 10. Continuing to cite Richard Ward and Oscar Miller's connections to law enforcement, CIA operatives, and Zionist organizations, CASR issued the following statement on the "obvious[ly]" biased proceedings:

> The Administration's motive for this attack was to silence and remove from campus [. . .] the most active elements of support for a free PALESTINE, free from oppressive and illegal Israeli occupation. [. . .] The repressive actions taken against Palestinian students and supporters comes during a period in which the state is executing a very well organized plan to eliminate all the democratic and progressive elements at U.I.C.C. and in our communities.[41]

According to CASR, the Israeli Independence Day Celebration was no longer just an instance of Zionist collusion; it was symptomatic of a larger repressive political machine—US imperialism—in which the university was an important cog. They promised to continue building a united Third World front, one that unequivocally included Puerto Ricans and Palestinians as comrades—"brothers and sisters"—in struggle. "The Season of Struggle is our Season. FOR FREEDOM WE SHALL LAY DOWN OUR LIVES. THE STRUGGLE CONTINUES," vowed CASR.[42]

Conclusion

Despite this intensity of conviction, the Commitee Against Student Repression lasted little longer than that January. As students exited the university—whether because of graduation, expulsion, or arrests related to the FBI's investigation of the Puerto Rican independence movement—relationships between the OAS and UPRS subsided. Neither Alejandro Molina nor Edwin Cortés, whom both actively traversed organizational boundaries to facilitate alliances, were enrolled at UICC after that academic year.[43] Israeli Independence Day celebrations continued largely unhampered. The university invested more resources into securing the event, even recruiting police clad in riot gear to contain future demonstrations. Although a protest did still occur, the 1979 celebration went on with little commotion; the biggest controversy stemmed from the *Chicago Illini*'s lack of reporting, which incensed a number of students and faculty members.[44]

But pro-Palestine students' fears of administrative collusion with Zionist interests may not have been so far-fetched after all. As the academic year came to a close, Oscar Miller returned a campus survey on Arab student activism to the Anti-Defamation League. When prompted as to whether any anti-Semitic organizing occurred at UICC's campus, Miller responded affirmatively. "The Israeli Independence Day celebration appears to be the one event that brings the anti-Jewish sentiment into focus for a violent reaction, as well as providing an outlet for anti-Israel and anti-Jewish sentiment from other students," he wrote. And when asked whether this activism was indicative of a "broader and more serious condition," Miller was again in agreement. To an organization that was already involved in the surveillance of Palestinian activism, he shared:

> It is my opinion that there is a strong anti-Jewish element among some of the Marxist oriented groups as well as among the Arab students sympathetic to the PLO. These groups manage to enlist the support of some radical elements in other ethnic groups (Puerto Rican Liberation, and other Marxist or left leaning groups) and play upon some basic anti-Semitic latent in others (even on the staff of the "student newspaper"). The condition can be considered potentially serious and requires careful attention.[45]

In some ways, CASR's vision of solidarity persisted. Puerto Rican students continued to locate the Israeli–Palestinian conflict within broader analyses of colonial tactics of surveillance and political repression. Later that same year, the extradition of Ziad Abu Eain, a Palestinian residing in Chicago who Israel charged with terrorism, captivated UICC. At an October 18, 1979 lecture hosted by the OAS, Jim Fenerty, one of Eain's attorneys, linked the case to the 1978 Israeli Independence Day protests. "The same lawyers that were used by Hillel students last year in presenting a case at UICC against seven Palestinians and supporters were also the same lawyers advising the U.S. state's attorney in the Ziad case," Fenerty accused.[46] Even NEIU's UPRS responded to Ziad's case: "We want them ["the Zionists and their American imperialist sponsors"] to know that Zeyad [sic] is only one Palestinian and the rest of the Palestinians with all the oppressed people of the world will continue their march until they achieve victory and liberation."[47]

And this moment of solidarity continues to matter to both the Puerto Rican and Palestinian communities in Chicago. One of the first times I learned of this brief, yet powerful, history of coalition building between the UPRS and the OAS was during Rasmea Odeh's speech celebrating Oscar López Rivera's homecoming in May 2017. Before a large crowd gathered in Chicago's Paseo Boricua, Odeh—a Palestinian American community organizer and former political prisoner—explained:

The Puerto Ricans in this city have always been close to our community. We have faced similar grand jury repression and attacks on our activism. We've marched together in dozens of protests for immigrant rights, Palestinian independence, Puerto Rican independence, and other social justice issues. We organized together at UIC in the radical student days.[48]

Nor is Rasmea Odeh alone in celebrating this early, foundational moment of solidarity. Many of Chicago's young Arab American activists I have spoken with recounted stories they have been told of the 1978 Israeli Independence Day protest. From their perspective, the protests symbolized the enduring solidarities that can emerge in the face of surveillance and repression. "You could always rely on the Puerto Rican students to have your back," one community organizer explained to me wistfully of the lessons she'd learned from the Israeli Independence Day struggle.

Undoubtedly, Puerto Rican students, so swept up in the romanticism of 1970s Third World liberation, found in Palestine parallel experiences of colonialism and a shared ideological commitment to revolutionary struggle. But in organizing with Arab and Palestinian students, especially against the 1978 Israeli Independence Day celebrations, they came to develop grounded identifications as victims of what were, to them, very real instances of state violence perpetrated by UICC's administration and operating in tandem with the government surveillance and political repression bearing down on their respective communities.

Now, in 2019, we are again entering a renewed era of racialization and exclusions justified under the guise of national security—and of an intensifying relationship between the United States' and Israel's policing methods and technologies. The 1978 Israeli Independence Day protests provides cautionary tale of how the carceral state extends beyond physical "borders" to criminalize solidarities and the acts of protests that empower communities of color. It also demonstrates the crucial role universities play in the enactment and experience of—and resistance against—repression. In policing the boundaries of acceptable political dissent, UICC's administration willingly subjected its own students to heightened technologies of surveillance. As student activists continue to organize against border-maintaining institutions—mass incarceration, immigration, police brutality—on college campuses today, the 1978 Israeli Independence Day protests stands as history that they, too, can cull from in denouncing the universities' role in undergirding US imperialism, domestically and abroad.

NOTES

1   The institution now goes by University of Illinois at Chicago, or UIC.
2   "Israel Anniversary-Rally on Thurs," *Chicago Illini*, May 8, 1978, p. 7.
3   Edwin and Alejandro were responsible for mobilizing Puerto Rican and Latino student support for the Israeli Independence Day protests. Alejandro Molina, interview with author, October 19, 2018; Edwin Cortés, interview with author, November 10, 2017.

4 John Wasik. "Chicago Police, PLO, Hillel Clash in Illinois Room." *Chicago Illini*, May 15, 1978, pp. 1, 5.

5 "Repression and Racism at U.I.C.C." *Que Ondee Sola* (henceforth *QOS*), October 1978, pp. 2–3.

6 Much of this literature focuses on Black–Brown solidarities. See as examples: Dan Berger, "'A Common Citizenship of Freedom': What Black Power Taught Chicago's Puerto Rican Independentistas," in *Civil Rights and Beyond: African American and Latino/a Activism in the Twentieth-Century United States,* ed. Brian D. Behnken (Athens: University of Georgia Press, 2016), 127–51; Lilia Fernández, *Brown in the Windy City: Mexicans and Puerto Ricans in Postwar Chicago* (Chicago: University of Chicago Press, 2012); Jakobi Williams, "We Need to Unite with as Many People as Possible: The Illinois Chapter of the Black Panther Party and the Young Lords Organization in Chicago," in *Civil Rights and Beyond: African American and Latino/a Activism in the Twentieth-Century United States,* ed. Brian D. Behnken (Athens: University of Georgia Press, 2016), 105–26.

7 Salim Yaqub, *Imperfect Strangers: Americans, Arabs, and U.S.-Middle East Relations in the 1970s* (Ithaca: Cornell University Press, 2016), 90.

8 Lloyd Barba and Laura Pulido, "In the Long Shadow of the Settler: On Israeli and U.S. Colonialisms," *American Quarterly* 62, no. 4 (Dec. 2010): 795–809; Martha Vanessa Saldívar, "From Mexico to Palestine: An Occupation of Knowledge; a *Mestizaje* of Methods," *American Quarterly* 62, no. 4 (Dec. 2010): 821–33; Piya Chatterjee and Sunaina Maira, eds., *The Imperial University: Academic Repression and Scholarly Dissent* (Minneapolis: University of Minnesota Press, 2014); Rodrick A. Ferguson, *Reorder of Things: The University and its Pedagogies of Minority Difference* (Minneapolis: University of Minnesota Press, 2012).

9 Debbie Simon and Mark Stein, "A Suggestion for Peace in the Middle East." *Chicago Illini*, April 3, 1978, p. 9. Deborah Kallick, "Zionism is Not Racism," *Chicago Illini*, May 8, 1978, p. 13.

10 See as examples Ghada Hashem Talhami, "'Good & Evil' Redefined: An Arab Speaks out on the Mideast Crisis," *Chicago Illini*, October 22, 1973, p. 6–7; Yona Damenstein, "Mideast Crisis II: The Israeli Side," *Chicago Illini*, November 13, 1973, p. 3; Organization of Arab Students and Organization of Students for Palestine, "Demonstration: Palestine Belongs to the Palestinians. Palestine Lives!" May 5, 1976, Rec. # 059-07-12, Folder: Organization of Arab Students, University of Illinois at Chicago University Archives (henceforth UIC Archives).

11 Pamela E. Pennock, *The Rise of the Arab American Left: Activists, Allies, and Their Fight against Imperialism and Racism, 1960s-1980s* (Chapel Hill: University of North Carolina Press, 2017), 55.

12 "Israeli Independence Day Log," 1978, Rec. # 003-01-02, Series IV, Box 66 Folder 815, UIC Archives.

13 David Young, "Arabs, Jews Wage War on the Propaganda Front," *Chicago Tribune*, July 27, 1975, p. A2.

14 On the 1977 confrontations, see Mike Ostrowski, "ILLINI photographer attacked while covering Arab, Jewish confrontation," *Chicago Illini*, April 25, 1977, p. 4.

15 "Israeli Independence Day Log."

16 Ibid.

17 "Incident Report—Israeli Day Celebration," University of Illinois Police Department, May 11, 1978, Rec. # 003-01-02, Series IV, Box 52 Folder 613, UIC Archives.

18 Wasik, "Chicago Police, PLO, Hillel Clash in Illinois Room."

19 Kathy Leatherman, "Ward Reveals Plans for Student Arrests," *Chicago Illini*, May 22, 1978, p. 1.

20 Dr. Richard H. Ward, "Complaint Form: Edwin Cortes," University of Illinois Student Judiciary System, May 26, 1978, Rec. # 003-01-02, Series IV, Box 65 Folder 807, UIC Archives.

21 "Incident Report—Israeli Day Celebration"; Leatherman, "Ward Reveals Plans for Student Arrests."

22 Hillel, Associated Movements for Israel, and Israeli Student Organization, "WE PROTEST," *Chicago Illini*, May 15, 1978, p. 6.

23 "Proposed Solution to Violent Demonstrations is Nothing but a Bust," *Chicago Illini*, May 22, 1978, p. 9.

24 John Pottinger, "The Arrest of Student Dissent," *Chicago Illini*, May 22, 1978, p. 9.

25 Concerned Arab Students, "Organized Propaganda Requires Money," *Chicago Illini*, May 22, 1978, p. 9.

26 Larry Gember, "Students Protest Arrests; Demonstrate at CCC," *Chicago Illini*, May 29, 1979, p. 1.

27 Cortés's speech is also noted in the Board of Trustees meeting report. See University of Illinois, "Transactions of the Board of Trustees: Fifty-Ninth Report, 1976–78," (Urbana, IL: University of Illinois, 1978), 633.

28 Moll, "Protestors & PhD Program Vie for Trustees' Attention," *Chicago Illini*, May 29, 1978, p. 1; "'Red Squad' Spying at UICC Uncovered," *Chicago Illini*, February 27, 1978, p. 3.

29 Organization of Nigerian Students, W.F. Kuse, Anna V., Sigfrido Reyes, and Lee Webster, "Protest Arrests and Harrassment [sic]," *Chicago Illini*, May 29, 1978, p. 7.

30 Linda Moll, "Protestors & PhD Program Vie for Trustees' Attention."

31 Michael Deutsch, interview with author, August 31, 2018.

32 Committee Against Student Repression at UICC, "Fight Student Repression!" October 20, 1978, Rec. # 059-07-12, Folder: Committee Against Student Repression at UICC, UIC Archives.

33 Alejandro Molina, interview with author, October 19, 2018.

34 "Repression and Racism at U.I.C.C."

35 Michael Deutsch, interview with author, August 31, 2018; Alejandro Molina, interview with author, October 19, 2018; Edwin Cortes, interview with author, November 10, 2017.

36 Committee Against Student Repression at UICC, "Condemn Decision to Expel Students—Demonstrate January 10," ca. 1979, Puerto Rican Cultural Center, private collection.

37 "Repression and Racism at U.I.C.C."

38 In the 1970s, the FBI began compiling information on individuals suspected of affiliation with the FALN. These investigative efforts relied on subpoenaing known activists in the Puerto Rican community to appear before grand juries, casting layered shadows of suspicion and criminalization over the community.

39 "Senate to Release Files; Spying Investigation Ends," *Chicago Illini*, July 3, 1978, p. 1. See also Natalie Crohn Schmitt Papers, Rec. # 011-24-20-02, Series II & III, Box 1, UIC Archives.

40 Nadine Naber, *Arab America: Gender, Cultural Politics, and Activism* (New York: New York University Press, 2012), 39.

41 Committee Against Student Repression at UICC, "Condemn Decision to Expel Students—Demonstrate January 10," ca. 1979, p. 1, 4, Puerto Rican Cultural Center, private collection; Union for Puerto Rican Students, "Repression and Racism Part 1," *El Grito Estudiantil*. Vol. V. I, February 1979, p. 3, Rec. # 003-01-02, Series IV, Box: 54 Folder: 644, UIC Archives.

42 Committee Against Student Repression at UICC, "Condemn Decision to Expel Students—Demonstrate January 10," ca. 1979, p. 3.

43 Molina was among those expelled; Cortés had already managed to complete his degree requirements, making his expulsion irrelevant.

44 "Israeli Day Celebration," *Chicago Illini*, April 23, 1979, p. 3; Jeremy Newberger, "One Photo Coverage," *Chicago Illini*, May 14, 1979, p. 9.

45 Oscar Miller, "Campus Survey," Anti-Defamation League of B'nai B'rith, June 9, 1979, Rec. # 003-01-02, Series II, Box 163 Folder 1560, UIC Archives.

46 Mariam Zayed, "Abu Ein Case Related to UICC," *Chicago Illini*, October 22, 1979, p. 3.

47 "The Case of Zeyad Abu Eain," *Que Ondee Sola*, February 1980, p. 6, 10.

48 Odeh was deported from her home in the United States soon after the event welcoming Oscar López Rivera home. "Rasmea Odeh addresses homecoming of Oscar López Rivera in Chicago: Read her speech," Samidoun Palestinian Prisoner Solidarity Network, May 23, 2017, https://samidoun.net.

16

"Now Why Do You Want to Know about That?"

Heteronormativity, Sexism, and Racism in the Sexual

(Mis)education of Latina Youth

LORENA GARCIA

Sex education is generally designed to diminish risks for young people. But sex education also poses risks to Latina youth through its reliance on heterosexualizing lessons that are also gendered and racialized. These lessons may further disadvantage girls already encountering multiple inequalities. Focusing on the experiences of Latina youth, in this chapter I explore how heteronormativity, sexism, and racism operate together to structure the content and delivery of school-based sex education.

Heteronormativity and Queering Educational Inequalities in Schools

Sex education unfolds within a larger heteronormative educational context. As sociologist C. J. Pascoe (2007, 27) points out, "School rituals, pedagogical practices, and disciplinary processes all inform heterosexualizing processes in educational institutions, from elementary schools through high schools." Explicit and implicit lessons about (hetero)sexuality, along with gender, are routinely conveyed via students' interactions with their peers, teachers, and school administrators (Fields 2008; Fields and Tolman 2008; Fine 1988; Fine and McClelland 2006; Tolman 1994). Research has also demonstrated that race/ethnicity shapes how school authorities respond to students' embodiment of gender and sexuality, finding that Black and Latinx students' performance of heterosexuality is especially monitored and disciplined within schools. Empirical research has documented how this treatment is informed by perceptions of youth of color as adult-like rather than child or youth-like (Ferguson 2001), as sexually precocious (Fields 2008; Hyams 2006; Morris 2007; Pascoe 2007), and as potential gang members or criminals and teen mothers (Bettie 2003; Ferguson 2001; López 2003; Pérez 2006). Such scholarship underscores political scientist Cathy Cohen's (1997, 451–57) observation that heteronormativity does not evenly assign

Abridged reprint from: *Gender & Society* 23, no. 4 (2009): 520–541.

privilege and power to all individuals categorized as "heterosexual." Instead, a state-sanctioned white middle- and upper-class heterosexuality is most rewarded and used as the reference point to determine how to distribute privilege and power.

Educational research that has centered on the experiences of lesbian, gay, bisexual, transgender, and queer/questioning (LGBTQ) and gender nonconforming students has furthered our understandings of educational inequalities. Much of this scholarship has applied insights from queer theory to foreground the ways in which heteronormativity permeates educational institutions and practices (Blackburn 2007; Horn 2007; Kehily 2000; Pascoe 2007; Petrovic and Ballard 2005). This work has illuminated how teachers and administrators participate, whether deliberately or unintentionally, in sanctioning the mistreatment of LGBTQ or gender nonconforming youth, such as through heterosexist and homophobic joking with students (usually male teachers with male students) or ignoring verbal and physical harassment perpetuated by students (Khayatt 1995; Muñoz-Plaza, Quinn, and Rounds 2002; Rofes 1989; G. W. Smith 2005). Education scholar Lance T. McCready (2004) asserts that the experiences of LGBTQ and gender nonconforming students of color are underexplored because one identity (typically sexuality) is given primacy by researchers while other identities (i.e., race/ethnicity) are disregarded or treated as secondary. LGBTQ scholars of color have challenged the notion that sexual subjectivity and racial subjectivity are mutually exclusive by underscoring how these subjectivities develop interdependently, inside and outside of schools (Kumashiro 2001; Rodríguez 2003; Rust 2006).

Few scholars, however, have examined how heteronormativity, sexism, and racism coalesce in the classroom production of sex education to differentially shape students' experiences. I do so by centering the experiences of Latina youth. In what follows, I first provide a brief overview of the study on which this chapter is based on, as well as relevant background information on sex education. I then consider how ideas about gender and race are integrated into sex education lessons transmitted to Latina youth, followed by an attention to the ways in which same-sex attraction and desires were unacknowledged and silenced in their school-based sex education.

Study participants' narratives reveal that heteronormativity was central to the content and delivery of their sex education. The lessons they were provided were crafted around heterosexuality and heterosexual norms, most often discussed in relation to masculinity and femininity, whereby femininity was tightly linked to the good girl/bad girl dichotomy (Levy 2005; Schaffner 2006; Tanenbaum 1999; Tolman 1994, 2002). Moreover, the institutionalization of heterosexuality via sex education in the classroom entailed the incorporation of racialized gender stereotypes to produce specific lessons for Latina youth.

Data and Method

This chapter is based on in-depth interviews, ethnographic fieldwork, and content analysis, conducted in Chicago between September 2002 and November 2004, with Latina girls (and a subset of their mothers) about sexual identity formation (Garcia 2012). This research focused on how Mexican and Puerto Rican young women actively engage with practices and ideas pertaining to safety and pleasure in the process of constructing and negotiating their sexual identities.

I interviewed young women who met the following criteria: self-identified as (a) Mexican or Puerto Rican, (b) sexually active, (c) between the ages of 13 and 18, (d) practicing safe sex, and (e) having no children. My sample included 40 Latina youth (20 Mexican-origin and 20 Puerto Rican girls) who were recruited to participate in the study through four Chicago community organizations. Of the young women recruited for this study, 32 self-identified as heterosexual and eight young women self-identified as lesbian. The average age of participants was 16, and the majority of them were second-generation Mexican-origin and Puerto Rican girls, meaning that they are U.S.-born children of (im)migrants. All of the young women reported having working-class backgrounds. And with the exception of two girls, all of the young women who participated in this project were or had been at one point Chicago Public Schools (CPS) students.

Learning about Latina Sexuality: Latina Youth as Oversexed and Over-reproductive

Generally, sex education curricula are grouped into two broad categories: abstinence-plus (also called comprehensive sexuality education) and abstinence-only-until-marriage (also called abstinence only). Comprehensive sex education does promote abstinence, but also teaches about contraception, sexually transmitted diseases, HIV, and abortion. Abstinence-only education promotes abstinence from sex, but does not teach about contraception or abortion. When sexually transmitted diseases and HIV are referenced, it is typically to highlight the negative consequences of premarital sex. Study participants' middle school education generally occurred between 1998 and 2002, during a time when CPS had no official stance or guidelines on the content of sex education. They reported encountering both abstinence-only and comprehensive sex education in middle school, a period marked by increased federal funding for abstinence-only programs (Boonstra 2007; Irvine 2002; Luker 2006; Sexuality Information and Education Council of the United States 2008).

My discussion of Latina girls' accounts of their sex education experiences centers on themes and patterns related to heteronormativity, sexism, and racism that cut across both abstinence-only and comprehensive sex education curricula to understand the inequalities that emerge and are reinforced through sex education.

Lessons about Engaging Sex Education in the Classroom

Quite often, girls reported that boys were scolded or disciplined by teachers for misbehaving during sex education, such as "acting foolish," "not taking it seriously," or "saying ignorant things." Girls, on the other hand, were reprimanded for being "too interested" in learning about sex in the classroom. Seventeen-year-old Minerva's experience is evidence of this:

> I raised my hand up and told the [sex educator], "Is it true you can't get pregnant if you take the morning-after pill?" or something like that. Anyways, she was starting to answer me when Ms. Phyllis [her eighth grade teacher] was like, "Now why do you want to know about that, Minerva? You don't got anything to worry about if you're behaving and anyway, we are out of time."

Other respondents narrated similar interactions with their teachers and sex educators, suggesting they were perceived as "knowing girls" and perceived to be sexually active (Fields 2007, 76–77). By publicly questioning Minerva about the motives behind her question, her teacher communicated to students not only that certain questions were invalid, but also that such inquiries could shift girls to the "wrong side" of the good girl/bad girl dichotomy.[1]

Some interlocutors vividly recalled how teachers and sex educators emphasized the expectation that girls be "good girls" or "young ladies." Seventeen-year-old Imelda recounted:

> Like the woman [sex educator] was talking about sex as being a personal choice and not letting anyone pressure us, and that when we're ready we should remember to be safe, and all that, you know? And Mrs. Damenzo [8th grade teacher] is like, "Yeah, but they shouldn't be doing it, right? They should act like young ladies so that the boys will respect them."

These contradictory lessons left the girls uncertain about the information presented to them. Teachers and sex educators never appeared to warn boys that their respect was tied to their sexual behavior. These gender-specific messages implicitly communicated to girls that, despite being recipients of sex education, there were limits to the knowledge given and expectations of sexual modesty. More significantly, these gender-specific messages were fused with perceptions about these female students as Latina girls. Teachers and sex educators inscribed racialized sexual stereotypes that functioned to specify the kind of "bad girls" that Latinas should avoid becoming (e.g., the pregnant teen or the sexually pro-miscuous Latina).[2] Seventeen-year-old Olivia describes her interaction with a seventh-grade, abstinence-only sex educator:

> The lady [sex educator] talking to us was all about how true love waits. Every time I asked a question, she didn't like or whatever, she would say, "That is not something someone your age should even be thinking about." . . . I think I was annoying her cause she just said, "Maybe a lot of girls you know are having sex, but you need to be better than that. When you ask things like that, it makes people think you are like those girls."

Likewise, other Latina girls reported that teachers and sex educators assumed that they would already know "those girls," and that such girls were presumably prevalent in the students' very neighborhoods. For instance, seventeen-year-old Elvia described her eighth-grade sex educator's response to her when she questioned her suppositions about Latinas: "She got all embarrassed . . . and just said, 'Well, I'm just telling you how it is. Numbers don't lie, there are a lot of teenagers in your community who are making real poor choices when it comes to sex.'" When teachers referenced "those girls" and "a lot of teenagers" they specifically meant Latina youth.

Teachers and sex educators not only presumed that all students were hetero-sexual, but also invoked a good girl/bad girl dichotomy. Meanwhile, the boys' sexual behaviors were kept invisible and unchecked. Furthermore, this dichot-omy was inherently racialized, presenting Latinas as culturally predisposed to fall on the "bad" side of feminine sexuality (Fine, Weis, and Roberts 2000).

Lessons about "Latino Culture" and Pregnancy Prevention

Another recurrent theme in Latina girls' accounts of school-based sex education experiences was the emphasis placed on pregnancy prevention and the per-spective that young Latina teens were always at heightened risk for pregnancy. Minerva noted:

> Sometimes they come at us like we are these ghetto-ass kids who just make babies and drop out of school . . . like we all have single moms on welfare that don't show us how to be responsible so they talk down to us, like, "OK, we know that in the Hispanic culture it's OK for girls to get pregnant young and become mothers, but not in American culture, OK?"

As Minerva notes, teachers and sex educators often blamed Latina girls' risk for pregnancy on a "Latino culture." Latinas were presumed to be sexually exces-sive, while Latino men were characterized as uniquely machista and oppressive to women.[3] Sixteen-year-old Miriam explained: "She [seventh-grade teacher] started talking about Latino culture and saying that because of machismo, guys were always gonna try to control us and tell us how many babies to have, and that they were too macho to wear condoms." Miriam's experience illustrates how the heterosexual parameters of femininity are maintained through gendered and racialized sex education. Such lessons depict Latino boys as sexually manipulative and ignorant about condom use. Latina girls are taught that their goal should be to develop the skills necessary to effectively fulfill a sexual gatekeeper role (Fine 1988; Thompson 1995; Tolman 2002).

Race and gender stereotypes about Latinas in sex education were evident in discussions of Depo-Provera. Sex educators generously supplied both information and advice about the effectiveness of this particular birth control option to the girls. Maritza recounted how a sex educator introduced "the shot" to the young women in her eighth-grade class:

> So this woman [sexuality educator] has the nerve to get up there and say, "I ain't gonna spend too much time on condoms cause you probably won't use them anyway. Guys usually don't wanna wear them cause of all the machismo and stuff. So if you are gonna have sex, and you really shouldn't, then you should wear a condom and at least know about the pill or shot so you won't get pregnant."

Latina girls' narratives reveal that while they are presumed heterosexual, their bodies, read through a racial-gender lens, are interpreted as excessively reproductive and thus nonconforming to idealized heteronormative standards. Historically, racial-gender stereotypes around Latina reproductive decision-making in the United States depict them as having large families and being unable use birth control effectively. However, Latinas' sexuality and reproduction have recently been intensely scrutinized, most readily reflected in the nativist narrative around immigrant "invasion" and "anchor babies" (Chávez 2004; Gutiérrez 2008; Inda 2002). Anti-immigrant discourses and policies have fueled public stereotypes about the "hyperfertility" of Latinas. According to sociologist Elena Gutiérrez (2008), these discourses inform the development of social and body control policies with implications for racially marginalized women, such as the unethical testing of Depo-Provera on women of color in developing countries and the heavy marketing of this form of birth control to women of color in the United States (Roberts 1997; A. Smith 2005). The racialized heteronormative assumption of Latinas as potentially over-reproductive bodies often constrained access to information, particularly the possibility of exploring non-heterosexual identities in middle school.

Learning to Conceal Same Sex Desire

I now focus on the sex education experiences of respondents who identified as lesbians. These girls, while still not identifying as lesbian in middle school, described an awareness of their emerging sense of sexual identity while in middle school. Respondents who identified as lesbian did not perceive school-based sex education as a supportive context in which to explore such feelings and related questions. Except for one respondent, this group of girls did not ask questions during sex education. Seventeen-year-old Linda, the only lesbian-identified girl who reported venturing to ask a question (albeit anonymously) while in middle school, described how her teacher reacted to her question:

> She [eighth grade teacher] had us write down our questions . . . so she could pick some to give to the sex ed teacher who was going to be coming to our class the next day. . . . She started yelling, "Who asked this?! Who asked the question about books about lesbian teenagers?!" Shit, I did, but I wasn't gonna say anything! . . . She got more pissed off and was like, "I don't know who did it, but I hope it wasn't one of you girls, because you should know better than to act so immature."

The teacher's response to Linda's anonymous question shows how teachers directed gender-specific comments about acceptable sexual behavior and inquiries exclusively to girls. Such a response can also be interpreted to reflect the expectation that girls will assume "femininized responsibility" for helping maintain order within the classroom (Ferguson 2001). The dismissal of Linda's question as "immature" reflects once again an assumption that all the students were heterosexual, while reinforcing non-heterosexuality as abnormal.

The middle school classroom was not a site in which these girls felt safe exploring their sexual identity. And while these girls indicated that they were "not gonna say anything" that would draw unwanted attention to same-sex attractions, they reported making efforts to be recognized as "straight" by peers and school authorities. Eighteen-year-old Barbara recounted how and why she performed a heterosexual femininity her eighth grade:

> There was this guy in our class who everyone thought he was gay. . . . Anyway, the guys would always pick on him a lot, calling him *maricón* [queer]. During a workshop, some of the guys were being smart asses and said, "So, Manolo wants to know about having sex with other guys, cause he's a fag." Most of the class laughed and the messed up thing was that the sex educator ended up laughing too, even though she told them to be respectful. I didn't want to be treated that way, so I just acted like I was just a regular girl, you know, saying that I thought this boy and this boy were cute, even though I had a crush on a girl in my classroom.

The sex educator's laughter at the comments made about Manolo shows how oftentimes teachers support heteronormativity by both their actions and inactions in the presence of homophobia (Khayatt 1995; Muñoz-Plaza, Quinn, and Rounds 2002; Rofes 1989; G. W. Smith 2005). Like Barbara, other respondents explained that they felt intense pressure to conform to heterosexuality in school to avoid the mistreatment by peers, especially inflicted on gender nonconforming boys.

However, two girls reported instances in which they did attempt to challenge the heteronormativity they encountered in their middle school sex education, specifically the virginity pledges presented to them in abstinence-only sex education. Seventeen-year-old Arely stated that her seventh grade teacher punished her for "ripping the virginity pledge" form she was asked to sign by a sexuality educator. According to Arely, she was made to stand in the hallway during the remainder of the presentation. When I asked her whether she thought this was fair, she responded,

> I didn't care. It's not like I really wanted to listen to that bullshit about the only right way to have sex is when you are married and with a person of the opposite sex. She [teacher] never really asked me why I ripped the form. . . . I don't think she wanted to know, know what I mean?

Arely's refusal to sign a virginity pledge may have briefly created an opportunity to destabilize heteronormativity, but it was precluded by her teacher's failure to use this as a teachable moment. Arely's interaction with her teacher is further evidence that respondents' gendered racialization, as Latina girls, overdetermined the content of their sex education. The narratives of Latina girls who identified as lesbian reveal that same-sex identities, practices, and desires remained violently rejected, even if tacitly. This response to their emerging sexuality reinforced heteronormativity and ethnoracial over-determinism among Latinx students, who are already imagined as heterosexual (Guzmán 2006; Kumashiro 2001; Rodríguez 2003).

Discussion

Heteronormativity, racism, and sexism operate together to structure the content and delivery of school-based sex education for the Latina girls in my study. In their narratives of Chicago middle school sex education, respondents described interactions with teachers and sex educators rooted in heterosexualizing lessons that were not only gendered, but also racialized.

Teachers and sex educators invoked a good girl/bad girl discourse to teach girls how to be students of sex education, inscribing racial stereotypes, to provide Latina youth with a static notion of the kind of Latina girl they needed to avoid becoming. Teachers and sex educators infused sex education with personal biases about Latinxs, and disseminated and/or withheld information from them accordingly, potentially placing them at further risk of inequality. Student narratives reveal that teachers and sex educators perceived them as always precarious and on the verge of slipping onto the wrong side of a good girl/bad girl dichotomy. They are the Latina teens perpetually at risk for pregnancy because of a "Latino culture." Such perceptions are reflective of long-held stereotypes underlying assumptions about "the subculture" of the poor, most notably in anthropologist Oscar Lewis's (1961; 1968) concept of the "culture of poverty." Lewis explained poverty among the Mexican and Puerto Rican families he studied as caused by the generational transmission of "deficient" worldviews and behaviors. His focus on the supposed attitudinal and behavioral deficiencies of the poor informed U.S. poverty policy approaches.

The heterosexualizing processes Latina students encountered through their interactions with teachers and sex educators entailed the over-determination of the students' racial and gender identities.[4] The interplay of heteronormativity, sexism, and racism in Latinas girls' sex education simultaneously reproduced, normalized, and concealed inequalities (Fine 1987). In this context, Latina youth can be understood to be more broadly "at risk" of these oppressions, which arguably pose greater danger to girls than sex or pregnancy. Latina youth are taught they have control over whether they will or will not get pregnant, but that they lack the power to disrupt gender inequalities. Survival inside and outside of their schools necessitates an adherence to heteronormative imperatives; discouraging the formation and expression of Latinx queer subjectivities.[5]

When considering school-based sex education, we typically focus on the debate about whether abstinence-only or comprehensive sex education is the most appropriate and effective approach to teaching students about the subject. However, students are unevenly positioned in our current racial/ethnic, gender, class, and sexual hierarchies and this matters for the quality of their schools and education. We need to remember this when we consider the purpose and merit of school-based sex education. Most recently, the Chicago Public Schools (CPS) Board of Education approved a Sexual Health Education policy in 2013 to ensure that all students receive age-appropriate comprehensive sexual health education at each grade level. All CPS schools are to have begun implementation of this policy by fall 2016. Whether and how this has occurred across all schools remains to be seen. We need to continue to develop our understanding of the processes by which sexuality and bodies are policed within educational institutions if we are committed to offering Latina girls guidance on how to confront and disrupt the intersecting inequalities shaping their lives.

NOTES

1   Young women are most often placed on one side of the good girl/bad girl dichotomy based on others' perceptions about their sexual behavior. However, youth can also assign their own meanings to this dichotomy based on other behaviors and practices, sometimes approaching being on the "bad girl" side as an advantage, such as when being a "bad girl" becomes a strategy for addressing gender inequality and/or facilitates the ability to obtain social and cultural capital among peer groups (Garcia 2012; Jones 2010; Ramos-Zayas 2012).

2 Study participants reported that the majority of their middle school teachers and sex education instructors were women and white, but some were also Black and Latina.

3 Teachers' assumptions about "Latino culture" and their sex education lessons to students could also likely be reflective of teachers' lack of training in their teacher preparation programs about diverse students, such as students of color, as well as LGBTQ and gender-nonconforming students (see Horn et al. 2009).

4 Implementation of sex education has been guided by the perceived need either to protect the sexual innocence of youth or to protect youth from the dangers of their own sexual curiosity, often informed by race/ethnicity (Ericksen and Steffan 1999; Fields 2008; Patton 1996). While middle- to upper-class white youth are often perceived as in need of intervention to guide them through their "normally abnormal" hormone-besieged adolescence, youth of color are constructed as always "at risk" and a source of danger (Patton 1996, 43).

5 Scholars have rightfully critiqued the assumption that queer Latinxs' struggle to express their sexualities is primarily due to their families and communities being somehow more homophobic or less tolerant of queer identities (see for instance, Acosta 2013; Decena 2011).

REFERENCES

Acosta, Katie. 2013. *Amigas y Amantes: Sexually Nonconforming Latinas Negotiate Family*. New Brunswick: Rutgers University Press.

Bettie, Julie. 2003. *Women Without Class: Girls, Race, and Identity*. Berkeley: University of California Press.

Blackburn, Mollie V. "The Experiencing, Negotiation, Breaking, and Remaking of Gender Rules and Regulations by Queer Youth." *Journal of Lesbian and Gay Issues in Education*, 4, no. 2 (2007): 33–54.

Boonstra, Heather D. "The Case for a New Approach to Sex Education Mounts: Will Policymakers Heed the Message?" *Guttmacher Policy Review*, 10, no. 2 (2007): 2–7.

Chávez, Leo. "A Glass Half Empty: Latina Reproduction and Public Discourse." *Human Organization*, 4, no. 2, (2004): 173–88.

Cohen, Cathy. "Punks, Bulldaggers, and Welfare Queens: The Radical Potential of Queer Politics." *GLQ: A Journal of Lesbian and Gay Studies*, 3, (1997):437–65.

Decena, Carlos U. 2011. *Tacit Subjects: Belonging and Same-Sex Desire among Dominican Immigrant Men*. Durham: Duke University Press.

Ericksen, Julia A., and Sally A. Steffan. 1999. *Kiss and Tell: Surveying Sex in the Twentieth century*. Cambridge, MA: Harvard University Press.

Ferguson, Ann Arnett. 2001. *Bad Boys: Public Schools in the Making of Black Masculinity*. Ann Arbor: University of Michigan Press.

Fields, Jessica. 2007. "Knowing Girls: Gender and Learning in School-Based Sexuality Education." In *Sexual Inequalities and Social Justice*, edited by N. Teunis and G. Herdt., 66–85: Berkeley: University of California Press, 2007.

———. 2008. *Risky Lessons: Sex Education and Social Inequality*. New Brunswick, NJ: Rutgers University Press.

Fields, Jessica, and Deborah L. Tolman. "Risky Business: Sexuality Education and Research in U.S. Schools." *Sexuality Research and Social Policy*, 3, no. 4, (2006): 63–76.

Fine, Michelle. "Silencing in Public Schools." *Language Arts*, 64, no. 2, (1987): 157–74.

Fine, Michelle. "Sexuality, Schooling, and Adolescent Females: The Missing Discourse of Desire." *Harvard Educational Review*, 58, no.1, (1988):29–53.

Fine, Michelle, and Sara I. McClelland. "Sexuality Education and Desire: Still Missing Discourse of Desire." *Harvard Educational Review*, 76, no. 297, (2006): 297–337.

Fine, Michelle, Lois Weis, and Rosemary Roberts. "Refusing the Betrayal: Latinas Redefining Gender, Sexuality, Culture and Resistance." *Education/Pedagogy/Cultural Studies*, 22, no. 2, (2000): 87–119.

Garcia, Lorena. 2012. *Respect Yourself, Protect Yourself: Latina Girls and Sexual Identity*. New York: New York University Press.

Gutiérrez, Elena R. 2008. *Fertile Matters: The Politics of Mexican-Origin Women's Reproduction*. Austin: University of Texas Press.

Horn, Stacey S. "Adolescents' Acceptance of Same Sex Peers Based on Sexual Orientation and Gender Expression." *Journal of Youth and Adolescence*, 36, no. 3, (2007): 363–71.

Horn, Stacey S., Kathleen McInerney, Erica Meiners, Connie North, Therese Quinn, and Shannon Sullivan. 2009. *Visibility matters full report card*. Chicago: Illinois Safe Schools Alliance.

Hyams, Melissa. "La Escuela: Young Latina Women Negotiating Identities in School." In *Latina Girls: Voices of Adolescent Strength in the United States*, edited by J. Denner and B. L. Guzmán, 93–108. New York: New York University Press, 2006.

Inda, Jonathan X. "Biopower, Reproduction and the Migrant Woman's Body." In *Decolonial Voices: Chicana and Chicano Cultural Studies in the 21st Century*, edited by A. J. Aldama and N. Quinoñez, 98–112. Bloomington: University of Indiana Press, 2002.

Irvine, Janice M. 2002. *Talk about Sex: The Battles Over Sex Education in the United States*. Berkeley: University of California Press.

Jones, Nikki. 2010. *Between Good and Ghetto: African American Girls and Inner-City Violence*. New Brunswick: Rutgers University Press.

Kehily, Mary Jane. "Understanding Heterosexualities: Masculinities, Embodiment and Schooling." In *Genders and Sexualities in Educational Ethnographies*, edited by G. Walford and C. Hudson, 27–40. Amsterdam: JAI, 2000.

Khayatt, Didi. "Compulsory Heterosexuality: Schools and Lesbian Students." In *Knowledge, Experience, and Ruling Relations: Studies in the Social Organization of Knowledge*, edited by M. Campbell and A. Manicom, 149–163. Toronto: University of Toronto Press, 1995.

Kumashiro, Kevin K. 2001. "Queer Students of Color and Antiracist, Antiheterosexist Education: Paradoxes of Identity and Activism." In *Troubling Intersections of Race & Sexuality: Queer Students of Color and Anti-Oppressive Education*, edited by K. K. Kumashiro, 1–25. Lanham, MD: Rowman & Littlefield, 2001.

Levy, Ariel. 2005. *Female Chauvinist Pigs: Women and the Rise of Raunch Culture*. New York: Free Press.

Lewis, Oscar. 1961. *The Children of Sánchez*. New York: Random House.

———. 1968. *La Vida: A Puerto Rican Family in the Culture of Poverty*. San Juan: Vintage.

López, Nancy. 2003. *Hopeful Girls, Troubled Boys: Race and Gender Disparity in Urban Education*. New York: Routledge.

Luker, Kristin. 2006. *When Sex Goes to School: Warring Views on Sex and Sex Education Since the Sixties*. New York: Norton.

McCready, Lance Trevor. "Some Challenges Facing Queer Youth Programs in Urban High Schools: Racial Segregation and De-Normalizing Whiteness." *Journal of Lesbian and Gay Issues in Education*, 1, no. 3, (2004): 37–51.

Morris, Edward W. "'Ladies' or 'Loudies'?: Perceptions and Experiences of Black Girls in Classrooms." *Youth & Society* 38 (2007): 490–515.

Mufioz-Plaza, Corne, Sandra Crouse Quinn, and Kathleen A. Rounds. "Lesbian, Gay, Bisexual and Transgender Students: Perceived Social Support in the High School Environment." *High School Journal*, 85, no. 4, (2002): 52–63.

Pascoe, C. J. 2007. *Dude, You're a Fag: Masculinity and Sexuality in High School*. Berkeley: University of California Press.

Patton, Cindy. 1996. *Fatal Advice: How Safe-Sex Education Went Wrong*. Durham, NC: Duke University Press.

Pérez, Gina M. "How a Scholarship Girl Becomes a Soldier: The Militarization of Latina/o Youth in Chicago Public Schools." *Identities: Global Studies in Culture and Power*, 13, no. 1, (2006): 53–72.

Petrovic, John E., and Rebecca M. Ballard. "Unstraightening the Ideal Girl: Lesbians, High School, and Spaces To Be." In *Geographies of Girlhood: Identities in Between*, edited by P. Bettis and Natalie G. Adams, 195–209. Mahwah, NJ: Lawrence Erlbaum, 2005.

Ramos-Zayas, Ana Y. 2012. *Street Therapists: Race, Affect, and Neoliberal Personhood in Latino Newark*. Chicago: The University of Chicago Press.

Roberts, Dorothy. 1997. *Killing the Black Body: Race, Reproduction, and the Meaning of Liberty*. New York: Pantheon.

Rodríguez, Juana Maria. 2003. *Queer Latinidad: Identity Practices, Discursive Spaces*. New York: New York University Press.

Rofes, Eric. "Opening Up the Classroom Closet: Responding to the Educational Needs of Gay and Lesbian Youth." *Harvard Educational Review*, 59, no. 4, (1989): 444–53.

Rust, Paula C. "The Impact of Multiple Marginalization." In *Reconstructing Gender: A Multicultural Anthology*, edited by E. Disch, 285–292. Boston: McGraw-Hill, 2006.

Sexuality Information and Education Council of the United States. n.d. Fact sheet: Abstinence-Only-Until Marriage Q & A. www.siecus.org/ (accessed June 24, 2008).

Schaffner, Laurie. 2006. *Girls in Trouble with the Law*. New Brunswick, NJ: Rutgers University Press.

Smith, Andrea. "Beyond Pro-Choice vs. Pro-Life: Women of Color and Reproductive Justice." *NWSA Journal*, 17 (2005): 119–40.

Smith, W. George. "The Ideology of 'Fag:' The School Experiences of Gay Students." In *Beyond Silenced Voices: Class, Race, and Gender in United States Schools*, edited by L. Weis and M. Fine, 95–116. Albany: State University of New York Press, 2005.

Tanenbaum, Leora. 1999. *Slut! Growing Up Female with a Bad Reputation*. New York: Seven Stories Press.

Thompson, Sharon. 1995. *Going All the Way: Teenage Girls' Tales of Sex, Romance, and Pregnancy*. New York: Hill and Wang.

Tolman, Deborah L. "Doing Desire: Adolescent Girls' Struggles For/With Sexuality." *Gender & Society*, 8, no. 3 (1994): 324–42.

———. 2002. *Dilemmas of Desire: Teenage Girls Talk about Sexuality*. Cambridge, MA: Harvard University Press.

17

Refashioning Afro-Latinidad

Garifuna New Yorkers in Diaspora

PAUL JOSEPH LÓPEZ ORO

When I am challenged or questioned about my identity, I respond by saying that Black people exist in Central America. Some are descendants of enslaved peoples; some are not. Some speak Spanish; some do not. Some are Catholic; some are Rastas; some are Garveyites. Some are immersed in hybridized identities that include native, Asian, and African nations. And when these Black people come to the United States, they continue to be Black people from Central America, negotiating among invisibilities.[1]

In the United States, the invocation of Central America conjures a set of racial and political imaginaries that center mestizos, Indigenous cultures, revolutionary movements, civil wars, and US occupations that eclipse a discussion of race and racism in the region and its diasporas. Within Central American *mestizaje*, Blackness is relegated, alienated, and ascribed to the Caribbean coast erasing centuries of Black folks in the interior and Pacific coasts. By ascribing Blackness and Black people to Central America's Caribbean coasts, *mestizaje* constructs its imaginary in opposition and in negation to Blackness, especially when the Caribbean coast is understood to be removed from the national public spaces of mestizo governance, i.e., Managua or Tegucigalpa. Moreover, rendering and ascribing Central American Blackness as Caribbean, coming from elsewhere and not already always present prior to the formation of the Republic. More recently, Central American neoliberal multiculturalism[2] constructs Blackness as a folkloric caricature for tourist and popular culture consumption.[3] Black Central Americans doubly negotiate their invisibilities on the isthmus and in their diasporas in the United States. Despite the extensive and rich history of Africans and their descendants in the isthmus, especially their presence and contributions centuries prior to the 1821 Wars of Independence,[4] Black history and Blackness remain alien to Central American nationhood in and outside of the isthmus. This negation and erasure of Black Central Americans is produced and preserved by the dominant nationalist racial project of racial mixture or *mestizaje*. Black Central Americans transgenerationally migrate to the United States with centuries of embodied histories of anti-Black racism and violence.[5]

Vielka Cecilia Hoy's essay "Negotiating among Invisibilities: Tales of Afro-Latinidades in the United States" in the trailblazing volume *The Afro-Latin@ Reader: History and Culture in the United States*. Vielka's essay is one of three essays that is written by and from a Black Central American worldview in a 584-page volume. Born in Brooklyn, NY, Vielka Cecilia Hoy was raised in Oakland, CA, by immigrant parents, her mother is a Creole Nicaraguan woman from Bluefields and her father is an Afro-Panamanian man from Colón descendant of West Indian migrant workers. Her essay powerfully illustrates the nuances and complex ways her Black Latinidad are in perpetual conflict in a space like the West Coast, where the dominance of mestizo Mexican identities and cultures shape the Californian imaginary as a Mexican/Chicanx/Mexican American space of Latinidad. Likewise, New York City is a Caribbean Latinx city, where Afro-Latinx people are always already assumed to be Dominican, while Black Central Americans are racialized as African Americans or West Indians. Hoy's essay is striking by the multiplicity of invisibilities and contradictions she engages with. It is here in the space of negotiations, contradictions, and articulations that I engage how transgenerational Garifuna New Yorkers exist, live, and articulate their multiple subjectivities of Black, Indigenous, and Latinidad.

Garifuna are Black Indigenous peoples who are descendants of shipwrecked enslaved West Africans and autochthonous Carib-Arawak on the Caribbean island of Saint Vincent. Their exile by British colonial powers in 1797 to the Bay Islands of Honduras and their subsequent migrations to Belize, Guatemala, Nicaragua, and mainland Honduras scripts their ethnogenesis in the lesser Antillean Caribbean mark their multiple diasporas: African diaspora, Caribbean diaspora, and Central American diaspora.[6] In the mid-twentieth century with the economic collapse of the United Fruit Company, Garifuna Central Americans commenced multiple waves of transgenerational migrations to major US port cities such as New York City, New Orleans, Miami, Chicago, Boston, and San Francisco. This migration that remains present today as gang violence, government corruption, and economic instability continue to dominate the Central American region. A diasporic multiplicity that informs the complex ways in which Garifuna negotiate their multiple subjectivities in Central America and in the United States, as Central America's Caribbean coasts becomes a nostalgic site of home and whose Black Indigeneity imagines Saint Vincent as homeland.[7] Garifuna Black Indigeneity unsettles racial formations in the Americas that ascribe Blackness, Indigeneity, and Latinidad as mutually exclusive.

In the context of Belize, Guatemala, Honduras, and Nicaragua where Garifuna and Creole communities have lived prior to 1821, *mestizaje* discursively emerges as an ideological project of nation-building violently negating Blackness and the existence and contributions of peoples of African descent in its construction of a racially mixed harmonious mestizo subject. The absence of Black Central Americans[8] in Latinx studies and Central American studies is an epistemological violence inherited from Latin American *mestizaje*. The insurgence of Afro-Latinx studies is an intellectual and political response to the erasure and negation of Latinxs of African descent in the field of Latinx studies. I call for a refashioning of *AfroLatinidad* that dismantles the dangerous allure of ethnoracial nationalism (i.e., Afro-[insert nation-state]) and cartographies of Blackness into exclusionary geographies of Spanish-speaking Americas (i.e., "you must be Dominican, because you don't look Guatemalan"). Drawing on oral history interviews, visual cultures, and social media, I demonstrate how transgenerational Garifuna New Yorkers histories and politics of self-making, from the late 1950s to the present, highlight their negotiations as they perform/articulate their multiple subjectivities as Black, Indigenous, and Latinx. In the following section, I begin with a mid-nineteenth-century and early twentieth-century history of anti-Black racism on Central America's Caribbean coasts to point to how hemispheric ideological travels from South (Central America) to North (United States) shape how Garifuna New Yorkers negotiate and articulate their Blackness, Indigeneity, and Latinidad in the United States.

Central America's Caribbean Coasts: Racialized Geographies of Anti-Blackness

In Central America, Blackness and geography are intrinsically entangled with histories of Spanish colonialism, mestizo governance, and alienation of Blackness to the Atlantic coast.[9] *Mestizaje* as a racial discourse emerges in the early twentieth century in response to a larger hemispheric critique of US imperialism grounding Latin American's myth of racial democracy as a distinct marker of racial egalitarianism in the face of US Jim Crow apartheid.[10] Central American ideologies of *mestizaje* emerge in distinct geographies and historical moments, I turn to Honduras and Nicaragua in particular because of how the Caribbean coasts become an explicit demarcation of Black geography's detached from the mestizo nation-state both discursively and geographically. Political theorist Juliet Hooker (2005) charts out the absence of *costeños* (Creole/Afro-Caribbean and Indigenous Nicaraguans) in Nicaragua's formulation of *mestizaje*. She coins the term "mestizo multiculturalism" to highlight the contradictions of Nicaragua's 1987 move as to being one of the first Latin American countries to adopt multicultural citizenship reforms. These reforms assigned special collective rights to Black and Indigenous communities on its Atlantic coast while maintaining mestizo culture as the hallmark of national identity in the company of racial and cultural diversity.[11]

The Atlantic coast of Nicaragua is marked as a distinct geography in the landscape of Nicaraguan mestizo nationalism. British colonialism on Nicaragua's Caribbean coast marks a cultural, religious, linguistic, and racialized alterity to Nicaragua's mestizo nationalism. Following independence from Spain in 1821,

Nicaragua underwent a wave of domestic civil wars and governmental regimes that aimed to bring forth national unity and state formation. One of the most collectively remembered of these state-building efforts was the forcible "reincorporation" of the Atlantic coast in 1894, an act of internal colonization on Black and Indigenous communities to assimilate into mestizo culture. The forcible annexation in 1894 violently made Spanish the official language and Catholicism the official religion on the Atlantic coast. This legacy informs the vexed relationship Creole and Indigenous communities have with the mestizo nation-state, and therefore the shift to multiculturalism has been welcomed with much deserved skepticism. Despite the constitutional shift into a multicultural paradigm, peoples of African descent remain geographically and politically marked as alien, foreign, and ascribed to only exist on the Caribbean coasts removed from the interior (Pacific coast) of mestizo political power.

Historian Darío A. Euraque argues that the Honduran congressional act of 1926 to officially title the national currency to Lempira was an explicit response to the threat of Blackness by the growing banana economy on Honduras's Caribbean coast. Euraque argues:

> In the 1920s the notion of an Indo-Hispanic mestizaje represented only an emerging elite discourse. However, the 1920s effort to officially designate Lempira as the "representative" of the "other race" in "our mestizaje" involved a local racism that drew on a postindependence rejection of blackness, and especially a rejection of Garifuna blackness as a more local and immediate racial threat.[12]

Black Hondurans were a great source of anxiety at a time when the Caribbean coast was gaining financial and political independence from the capital city of Tegucigalpa through the presence of US-owned banana companies. This anxiety also fueled the deportation of thousands of West Indian migrant laborers, mostly from British Honduras (present-day Belize) and Jamaica. Honduran anti-Blackness made Garifuna and Creole communities on the Caribbean coast vulnerable to border patrol harassment and risk of deportation.[13] In Nicaragua, Honduras, and the rest of the isthmus, Blackness was (and continues to be) a great source of discursive and economic anxiety at distinct moments of nation-building.[14]

Anti-Black racism in Central America informs the political mobilization and self-making processes of Garifuna New Yorkers. Anti-Black racist histories are embodied memories that are transmitted generationally through oral histories. Garifuna New Yorkers negotiate and contradict their Blackness, Indigeneity, and Central Americanness based on that historical legacy that shapes contemporary racial and racist discourse on the isthmus and its diasporas. Central America's Caribbean coasts are present in New York City and throughout the rest of the Garifuna diaspora in the United States, directly shaping how US Garinagu engage and mobilize alongside other Black Caribbean, African American, and Latinx communities. I turn my attention to Garifuna New Yorkers of mostly Honduran and Guatemalan descent born and raised in New York City (Eastern Brooklyn and the South Bronx) and analyze their diasporic processes of self-making Garifunaness in the company of African Americans, Dominicans, Jamaicans, Puerto Ricans, and Ghanaians.

Afro-Latinx studies is a political project whose origins stand outside of the disciplinary boundaries of the academy and whose intellectual impulse is one of disrupting the absence of Latinxs of African descent in the field of Latinx studies.[15] In this following section, I grapple with questions on how transgenerational Garifuna New Yorkers negotiate and articulate their Central Americanness and Garifunaness simultaneously. How does an explicit politics of rejecting AfroLatinidad for Garifunaness reinscribe Garifuna exceptionalism and ethnoracial nationalism?

The Insurgency of Black Latinidad: Unsettling Hemispheric *Mestizaje*

"No matter your race because you know you're Latino"
—*N.O.R.E.* (October 2004)

"Si tú eres Latino, saca tu bandera."
—*Gente de Zona* (April 2015)

Latinidad in the United States is built, travels, and is performed on the ideological legacies of Latin American *mestizaje,* as a political project of racial mixture that seeks to distance itself from its northern imperial neighbor: US Jim Crow apartheid.[16] *Mestizaje* also romanticizes Spanish colonialism and caste system in its national memory of a past Indigenous culture and civilized Spanish conquest, where the gendered and sexualized violence of Spanish colonialism in the Americas is omitted from that historical memory.[17] The negation of Blackness within the project of *mestizaje* or the recovery of it, as in the example of Mexico's Third Root, both problematizes *mestizaje* as a racial project that imagines racial mixture as the solution to racism and racial inequalities. It is here in the negation, erasure, and recovery of Blackness in Latin America and US Latinidad that Afro-Latinx studies insurgency is a necessary political and intellectual project of Black political mobilization.

In the context of the United States, Mireya Navarro writes in "For Many Latinos, Race is more Culture Than Color":

the census categorizes people by race, which typically refers to a set of common physical traits. But Latinos, as a group in this country, tend to identify themselves more by their ethnicity, meaning a shared set of cultural traits, like language or customs. So when they encounter the census, they see one question that asks them whether they identify themselves as having Hispanic ethnic origins and many answer it as their main identifier.[18]

Here we see a persistent dilemma within hemispheric constructions of Latinidad: its on-going production (to borrow from Stuart Hall) is rooted in ethnic signifiers in hopes of evading racial discourse for a raceless imaginary of ethnicities. The problematic news story that argues that Latinos are so racially mixed that their ethnic differences marks them much more deeply than race in the United States. This is a narrative supported by general notions that racial discourse and racism do not exist in Latin America and the Caribbean as they do in the United States and what inequalities do exist are due to class and ethnic differences. This trope of Latinx racial exceptionalism as simply not fitting into US racial categories is a hemispheric project of *mestizaje* haunted by the mythical illusion of racial democracy (read: racial paradise) in the shadow of US Jim Crow's Black/white binary. In the United States, non-Black Latinx peoples mobilize for a census category that transcends US racial categories in distancing and opposition to the histories of racial formation by aspiring for a racialized sameness (read: Hispanic/Latino) vis-à-vis ethnoracial nationalist identities (read: Puerto Ricans, Mexican Americans, etc.) in a continued negation of Black and Indigenous Latinx peoples.

While scholarly production on Black Latin America has enjoyed a long tradition since the nineteenth century, equivalent scholarship on Black Latin Latinxs in the United States and their descendants remains absent. It is here in this absence where the political and intellectual necessity of Afro-Latinx studies, the lived experiences of Latinxs of African descent whose transgenerational migrations, routes, and lineages are located south of the US border, disrupt a homogenized Latino racial exceptionalism. Afro-Latinx studies opens a space to analyze how Black Latinxs born and raised in the United States can potentially unsettle the media-infused narrative of African American and Latinx conflict fomenting a divisive majority-minority dichotomy.

Miriam Jiménez Román and Juan Flores's groundbreaking edited volume *The Afro-Latin@ Reader: History and Culture in the United States* gives us a useful introductory definition of Afro-Latin@s as "people of African descent in Mexico, Central and South America, and the Spanish-speaking Caribbean, and by extension those of African descent in the United States whose origins are in Latin America and the Caribbean."[19] Building upon this definition, AfroLatinidad emerges as an insurgent analytic that dismantles centuries of discursive and scholarly erasure and negation of Blacks and Blackness in Latin America and unsettles US Latinidades' investment in an imagined racially harmonious project that reinscribes ethno-nationalism as exceptional transcendence of US racial formations.[20] The political significance of visibility is one used by Afro-Latinx studies to highlight our existence and trouble the legacies of anti-Black racism and colorism lived throughout the Americas. AfroLatinidad complicates Blackness in the United States as a site of rupture by making a hemispheric turn to deepen our histories, politics, and transmigrations of Blackness in the Americas.

As mode of conclusion, I turn to three moments in which transgenerational Garifuna New Yorkers negotiate and articulate their multiple subjectivities as an act of refashioning AfroLatinidad. My engagement with visual cultures, oral histories, and memoirs highlight the ways in which AfroLatinidad is not only an invocation from invisibility to visibility but an acutely intellectual and political contestation of ethnoracial nationalism in centering Blackness in and out of Latinidad.

Garifunizando AfroLatinidad: The Politics of Self-Making Garifuna New Yorkers

> Many of the terms, including Latino/a, we use today were created (or influenced) by those who've colonized us. In using the term *negra*, or *Afrodescendiente*, I'm choosing to without a doubt center Blackness. Identity isn't clear cut. It's complex and multilayered. As I journey through life, just as my current experiences influence how I identify, new encounters and knowledge will further shape it. No matter which terms I use, my pride in my African roots will forever be a constant. Let there be no confusion as to who I am: a Black woman. In the eternal words of Victoria Santa Cruz, "*Sí, soy negra. Negra soy.*"[21]

New York City is home to the largest Garifuna community outside of Central America's Caribbean coast. This geographic and demographic distinction matters for many historical and political motivations. It highlights an understudied history of Garifuna Central American transmigrations to New York City that begins in the late 1950s with the economic collapse of the US owned fruit companies, igniting a Great Migration of Black Central Americans from South of the US South.[22] The migration of thousands of Garifuna and Creole Central Americans migrating to urban port cities such as New Orleans, Miami, New York City, Houston, San Francisco, and Chicago reveal entangled and complex histories of US imperialism on Central America's Caribbean coasts. In other words, Garifuna folks are US imperial subjects before arriving to the shores of the United States. Within the broader racialized geographies of US Central Americanness, New York City is not imagined as a US Central American space with the dominance of Caribbean Latinx communities.

On February 23, 2014, the image below was posted on a popular Facebook page named "Garifuna TV Page" where news on gatherings and community events in the United States (New York City, Chicago, Houston, New Orleans, Miami, and Los Angeles), as well as in Central America, are shared. The Facebook page also promotes Garifuna culture and music, giving publicity to local Garifuna musicians, artists, and activists. The posting with the provocative caption "Be Proud

of who you are!!! Don't allow no one to change your identity!! #notupfordebate."
The posting was a response to an ongoing debate in Garifuna social media spaces
about Afrolatinidad. The statement "Do not call me Afro Latino!! & Do not call
me an Afro-Descendant because I am a Proud Garifuna" along with visuals of
Garifuna culture and traditions ranging from the symbolic presence of the Garifuna flag and its colors (yellow, white, and black), plantain mashing for a plate of
machuca (*hudutu*), rasping coconut on a board to make either bread or stew, and
carrying baskets all labor done by Garifuna women and the only male presence
in the image is one of a young boy being carried on his mother's back. All of these
Garifuna tropes are packaged to invoke nostalgia of Central America's Caribbean
coast and carry historical weight onto diasporic Garifunaness.

The image was created by Ana Castillo, a US-based Garifuna poet from Honduras whose concern for losing Garifuna culture and language to American
culture, specifically African American culture, has been an ongoing concern
of the generation of Garifuna Central American immigrants of the 1960s. The
clear rejection of AfroLatinidad and Afrodescendant in this image is a deeply
significant assertion that points to the centuries of anti-Black racism and violence experienced by Garifuna Central Americans in the isthmus. The assertion
of an exclusively Garifuna epistemology matters here as a point of disruption
into a category that does not capture Garifuna Black Indigeneity but also reveals
the political mobilization of Garifuna communities in Central America and in
the United States in preserving their culture, language, and history. A generational concern here is that something is lost in the United States; that values,
customs, language, traditions, and music are slowly being erased because of
American assimilation and families no longer living in their hometowns on
the Caribbean coasts. Both categories of Afro-Latino and Afrodescendant presented together is quite interesting and is enacting a hemispheric discourse to
convey a reinscription of Garifuna pride throughout the Americas. Afro-Latino
a term mostly used in the United States, and Afrodescendant is mostly used in
Latin America; both have parallel political projects of insurgency responding
to the erasure and absence of Blacks and Blackness in Latin America and US
Latinidad. However, here Garifuna folks are not interested in investing into a
project that from its inception has erased, excluded, and voided their existence.
The phrasing "Do not call me Afro Latino and Do not call me Afro-descendant,
I am a Proud Garifuna" is an affective political affirmation of visibility and
recognition in a moment where AfroLatinidad and Afrodescendant has taken
center stage as an all-encompassing umbrella term. Garifuna folks are uneased
by how both terms erase/silence/footnote the specific histories of Blackness in
Latinx Americas. More importantly, *I am a Proud Garifuna* builds on the political genealogies of US Black Power movements of the 1960s and 1970s, echoing
James Brown's iconic vocals in "Say It Loud, I'm Black and I'm Proud." *I am
a Proud Garifuna* is an explicit response to the historical and contemporary

Figure 17.1. Facebook post on GarifunaTv page on February 23, 2014.

manifestations of mestizo supremacy and anti-Black racism in Central America that remains present today in spite of a multicultural shift. The echo of US Black Power movement here is one that unearths the hemispheric influences of African American political thought and formations. It also exemplifies how Garifuna New Yorkers and throughout the rest of their diaspora in the United States engage directly with US Black history, culture, and politics.

In the opening epigraph of this section, Janel Martinez's invocation of her Blackness at the opening of this section is of great transgenerational diasporic importance. Her rejection on using the term of AfroLatinx especially at a moment of hyperawareness points to her individual and collective desire to center her Blackness in lieu of a racial fetish. Moreover, it speaks to the broader politics of how on Garinagu New Yorkers and those in Central America negotiate and articulate their Blackness as a political project of membership to the larger African diaspora rooted in the racialized lived experiences of being Black. Although "indigeneity" is a part of the Garifuna identity in these instances, it becomes secondary to a politics of Blackness.

"Ain't I Latina?": Negotiating Central Americanness vis-à-vis AfroLatinidad

Aida Lambert, a Garifuna woman born and raised in Honduras, came to New York City in 1964 at a time period where Central Americans—especially Garifuna folks—did not have much visibility in the ethnic pantheon of New York City's Latinidad. Aida Lambert forms part of the second-largest wave of Garifuna New Yorker transmigrants who arrived a few years prior to the economic collapse of the United Fruit Company. She first lived in Eastern Brooklyn and later, when she married, moved to East Harlem with her husband and children. In her autobiographical essay "We Are Black Too: Experiences of a Honduran Garífuna," Lambert illustrates the nuanced experiences between African Americans and Spanish-speaking immigrants. Lambert was a founding committee member of *Desfile de la Hispanidad* [Hispanic Parade]. The Annual Hispanic Parade in October emerged in the mid-1980s when NuyoRicans and recent migrants from Puerto Rico wanted to exhibit their culture, work ethic, and racial differences from their African American neighbors. Lambert's involvement developed out of her language barriers with other English-speaking Blacks and her cultural and linguistic bond with Puerto Ricans and Dominicans:

> I have found that even though you are Black, the fact that you are Latina means to them [African-Americans] that you are of another race . . . even at home in Honduras, our Garífuna culture and our language, is losing ground and becoming less and less familiar. And here it is even more so. My own children, as much as I try to keep the culture alive, they have their own lives and often forget whatever they learn. Not to mention my grandchildren, who were born here. I warn them about my experiences with African Americans, but they play with them, are influenced by them, and join them. They make friends with them, they identify with them, in the way they dress, and talk, and the music they listen to. And what can I do, I have to let them choose their own culture preferences.[23]

Figure 17.2. Aida Lambert at the *El Diario* carousel for the 2018 *Desfile de la Hispanidad* on Fifth Avenue in New York City. Photo courtesy of the author.

Lambert's *testimonio* is telling of her generation of Garifuna Central American immigrants and their engagement and inclusion with Puerto Rican and Dominican aspirations of social mobility. The generations of Garifuna New Yorkers following Lambert's arrival to Brooklyn and Harlem negotiate Latinidad in multiple ways that simultaneously reject and interject into Latinidad as a marker that makes Garifuna Blackness distinct from African Americans, while simultaneously using Garifunaness as a distancing from mestizo Latinidad and AfroLatinidad. Her feeling of rejection by Black Americans and acceptance by Puerto Ricans is a significant act of remembrance for a number reason, particularly because Garifuna Central Americans migrate to the United States at the intersections of anti-Black racism, nondemocratic governments, and economic instability. Lambert's remembering of solidarity and support from Puerto Ricans is not a universal narrative by Spanish-speaking Black immigrants who continued to experience anti-Black racism from their own country-mates in the United States. The most well-known example is Arturo Alfonso Schomburg, a Black Puerto Rican who migrated to Harlem in 1891, but, in contrast to Lambert, felt rejected by other Spanish-speaking immigrants and embraced by African Americans and Afro-Caribbeans.[24] Aida's generation resisted US labeling as African American and maintained a household mantra of "*somos negros pero no como aquellos*" ("we are Black but not like them"), the "them" being African Americans. This narrative does not remain true for second- and especially third-generation Garínagu, as their interpellation as Black Americans creates interstitial spaces between their Blackness, Garifunaness, and Latinidad, never fully belonging into any of these categories because of the United States being a dislocation of birthplace, citizenship, and fragmented home.

Janel Martínez is a Garifuna woman of Honduran descent, born and raised in the Bronx, daughter of Garifuna Honduran immigrants from the 1970s generation, and is the creator of "Ain't I Latina?" an online destination created by an Afro-Latina for Afro-Latinas inspired by the lack of representation in mainstream media as well as Spanish-language media. Martínez is a multimedia journalist whose work has been featured in both African American media sites such as The Root, Black Enterprise, Madame Noire, as well as Latinx media sites such as Cosmopolitan for Latinas, Remezcla, and NPR's Latino USA. The very question that inspires Martínez's online site, and which provocatively connects her to Sojourner Truth's "Ain't I a Woman?" shows the importance of disrupting mestizo Latinidades and how such Latinidades erase peoples of African descent. Martínez's Black Latinidad is articulated not as separate from African Americans but very much in company of African American and other non-US Black lived experiences in the United States. Her travels to her parent's hometown communities on the Caribbean coast of Honduras in Ciriboya and Iriona deepened her Garifuna political identity formation. She notes, "Garifuna was never an identity I had to unearth; it was a culture and way of being I experienced within and all around me."[25] Martínez points to her home life as a site of Garifuna self-fashioning where food, language, and traditions are preserved in the intimacies of her mother's kitchen and in family gatherings in her parents' living room. Furthermore, after her grandmother's passing and the ensuing *beluria*, a Garifuna spiritual tradition to celebrate life in and after ancestral deaths, Martínez's interest in learning about Garifuna life and history continues.

Martínez's journalistic work has examined the complexities of being raised Garinagu in the United States, where one's identity is frequently demeaned or marginalized. Grounded in her identities as Garifuna and Black Latina, Martínez

Figure 17.3. Janel Martínez on April 12, 2018, being awarded a proclamation by New York City Council Member Vanessa L. Gibson for her activism and cultural work in preserving Garifuna history and culture in New York City. Photo courtesy of the author.

explores the complexities and multiplicities of diasporic linkages with other Black Latinxs and the intersectionality of race, ethnicity, country of birth, and nationality. While Martínez acknowledges that presuming a common AfroLatinidad, especially one that does not center Blackness,[26] runs the risk of homogenizing Latinxs of African descent, her work still notes how refashioning AfroLatinidad calls for an expansive and hemispheric Blackness in the Americas not simply relying on a politics of inclusion into Latinidad.

Hemispheric Black Latinidades: Garinagu New Yorkers Presente

On July 13, 2018, I was invited to participate on a Presidential Plenary titled "U.S. Central Americans, Invisible, and Silent No More" for the Latina/o Studies Association biannual meeting. I began my comments with the following provocation to problematize the absence of Black Central Americans in the scholarship on US Central Americans:

My Central America is Caribbean. My Central America is a Caribbean Coast whose natural resources and peoples have and continue to be exploited by U.S.

imperialism. My Central America is Black, Black Indigenous to be exact whose descendant's survivors of the transatlantic slave trade and Carib-Arawak Indigeneity on the Antillean island of St. Vincent and whose marronage and exile call Central America's Caribbean Coast: home. To be Garifuna is to be Caribbean and Central American simultaneously. I am the grandchild of banana workers from Tela and Balfate, Honduras whose transmigrations to Harlem, New York in 1964 was made possible by the political mobilization of Garveyism and whose parents met in Bedford-Stuyvesant, Brooklyn in 1982. My Black Central America is also New York City.

My articulations of Black Central America on the isthmus and its diasporas builds on centuries of anti-Black racism and erasure of our existence. Aida Lambert, Janel Martínez, and Vielka Cecilia Hoy all articulate a politics of Black Central Americanness that remains invisibilized in the face of a mythical all-inclusive Latinidad. Lambert's political mobilization alongside Puerto Ricans, Dominicans, and other mestizo Latinx New Yorkers animate her desires to negotiate her Black Honduranness in the *Desfile de la Hispanidad*, where her activism allowed for a Garifuna Honduran woman to win the beauty pageant contest in 1994. Martínez's negotiation and articulation of her Black Latinidad engages a hemispheric project that centers Blackness in the Americas with an inclusionary praxis into Latinidad. Garifuna New Yorkers of Central American descent are marked by their transgenerational differences and bounded by a Garifunaness that disrupts hegemonic racial and ethnic subjectivities.

NOTES

1 Vielka Cecilia Hoy, "Negotiating among Invisibilities: Tales of Afro-Latinidades in the United States," in *The Afro-Latin@ Reader: History and Culture in the United States*, ed. Miriam Jiménez Román and Juan Flores (Durham: Duke University Press, 2009), pp. 429–430.

2 Charles R. Hale, "Neoliberal Multiculturalism: The Remaking of Cultural Rights and Racial Dominance in Central America," *PoLAR* 28, no. 1 (2005): pp. 10–28.

3 Christopher Loperena, "Radicalize Multiculturalism? Garifuna Activism and the Double-Bind of Participation in Postcoup Honduras," *The Journal of Latin American and Caribbean Anthropology*, 21, no. 3 (2016): pp. 521–22.

4 Lowell Gudmundson and Justin Wolfe, *Blacks and Blackness in Central America: Between Race and Place* (Durham: Duke University Press, 2010), 5.

5 My reference to violence here is one both physical and epistemological, pointing to the centuries of land dispossession, US imperialism, and erasure from national subjecthood. Central Americans of African descent are in the margins on the histories of transmigrations and political movements in the isthmus and their diasporas.

6 Sarah England, *Afro-Central Americans in New York City: Garifuna Tales of Transnational Movements in Racialized Space* (Gainesville: University Press of Florida, 2006).

7 Garifuna epistemology is rooted in Black Indigeneity, in one where Blackness is marooned in the Americas, as the collective memory of ethnogenesis on Saint Vincent: being descendants of shipwrecked slaves, an important marker of alterity and problematic

divorcing of plantation slavery in the Americas. Garifuna notion of maroonage is foundational to Garifuna Black Indigeneity, as it invokes an act of shipwreckedness and eventual
hybridity with Carib-Arawak Indigenous peoples on St. Vincent in the fifteenth century.

8 I reference the homogenized term Black Central Americans or Central Americans of
African descent, which does not detail the multiplicity of Black Central American communities. I do it with the political intent of affirming Blackness in a region of the Americas that
is racialized as a non-Black space.

9 Edmund T. Gordon, *Disparate Diasporas: Identity and Politics in an African-Nicaraguan
Community* (Austin: The University of Texas Press, 1998), 133.

10 Juliet Hooker, *Theorizing Race in the Americas: Douglass, Sarmiento, Du Bois, and Vasconcelos* (New York: Oxford University Press, 2017), 158.

11 Juliet Hooker, "'Beloved Enemies': Race and Official Mestizo Nationalism in Nicaragua,"
Latin American Research Review 40, no. 3 (2005): 14–39.

12 Darío A. Euraque, "The Threat of Blackness to the Mestizo Nation: Race and Ethnicity in
the Honduran Banana Economy, 1920s and 1930s," in Banana Wars: Power Production, and
History in the Americas, eds. Steve Striffler and Mark Moberg (Durham: Duke University
Press, 2003), 243.

13 Glenn A. Chambers, *Race, Nation, and West Indian Immigration to Honduras, 1890–1940*
(Baton Rouge: Louisiana State University Press, 2010), 74.

14 Even during the multicultural era, especially as Creole, Garifuna, and West Indian communities continue to fight for autonomy and inclusion.

15 I will only use the hyphen when referring to the field of study of Afro-Latinx Studies. I
explicitly use AfroLatinidad and AfroLatinx to refer to peoples, histories, and cultures,
because the hyphenation of Afro-Latinidad/Afro-Latinx is a continued violence of erasure.
A hyphen reinscribes the notion that "Black" and "Latinx" are mutually exclusive to each
other. Here I build in conversation with Omaris Z. Zamora (2016) and Yomaira C. Figueroa
(2014) that Blackness is always already present in our Latinidad. Hyphenation is a dislocation of Blackness in/distancing from Latinidad and in this context more specifically US
Central Americanness.

16 Juliet Hooker, *Theorizing Race in the Americas: Douglass, Sarmiento, Du Bois, and Vasconcelos* (New York: Oxford University Press, 2017).

17 Breny Mendoza. "De-Mythologizing Mestizaje in Honduras: A Critique of Recent
Contributions," *Journal of Latin American and Caribbean Ethnic Studies* 1, no. 2 (2006):
185–201.

18 Mireya Navarro, "For Many Latinos, Race is more Culture than Color," *New York Times*,
January 13, 2012.

19 Miriam Jiménez Román and Juan Flores, eds., *The Afro-Latin@ Reader: History and Culture
in the United States* (Durham: Duke University Press, 2010), 1.

20 Paul Joseph López Oro, "Ni de aquí, ni de allá: Garifuna Subjectivities and the Politics of
Diasporic Belonging," in Afro-Latin@s in Movement: Critical Approaches to Blackness and
Transnationalism in the Americas, eds. Petra R. Rivera-Rideau, Jennifer A. Jones, and
Tianna S. Paschel (New York: Palgrave Macmillan, 2016), 62.

21 Janel Martínez. "'Negra Soy': Why I've Moved Away from the Term Afro-Latina," *Remezcla*,
September 17, 2018, https://remezcla.com/features/culture/negra-vs-afro-latina.

22 I refer to this understudied transmigration of Garifuna and Creole folks to the United States
as a "Great Migration of Black Central Americans from South of the US South" to point to
the various hemispheric Black migrations and to disrupt the grand narrative of a US-
centered Great Migration. Throughout the Americas, there have been and continue to be
"Great Migrations" of Black communities fleeing anti-Black racism.

23 Aida Lambert, "We Are Black Too: Experiences of a Honduran Garifuna," in *The Afro-Latin@ Reader: History and Culture in the United States*, eds. Miriam Jiménez Román and Juan Flores (Durham: Duke University Press, 2009), 433.

24 Jesse Hoffnung-Garskof, "The Migrations of Arturo Schomburg: On Being Antillano, Negro, and Puerto Rican in New York, 1891–1938," *Journal of American Ethnic History* 21, no. 1 (Fall 2001): 3–49.

25 Janel Martínez, "Growing Up Garifuna." March 18, 2017, http://aintilatina.com/2017/03/18/growing-up-garifuna.

26 Janel Martínez, "Negra Soy: Why I've Moved Away from the Term Afro-Latina." September 17, 2018, https://remezcla.com/features/culture/negra-vs-afro-latina.

CRITICAL DIÁLOGO 5

Work and the Politics of "Deservingness"

The fifth critical diálogo unpacks the notion of "deservingness," by considering the material, spiritual, and emotional labor that becomes tacitly or explicitly associated with racialized and immigrant populations. The question that frames this critical diálogo is: *How have material production, capitalist accumulation, and human subjectivity become mutually constitutive in the world of Latinx work?* We view "work" as a complex series of practices that can range from the world of "reputable" paid work, activism, and religious belonging, to a world of work not readily legible to neoliberalism. To approach this question, the essays in this diálogo push against conventional understandings of work and labor. Larry LaFontaine documents the role of Puerto Rican trans activist Sylvia Rivera in LGBTQ not-for-profit work, while Sujey Vega discusses the role of Latinx members of the Church of the Latter-day Saints in immigrant activism within a Mormon context.

Centering on the role of creativity, joy, and pleasure in Latinx Studies, Albert Laguna analyzes the performances of the ludic in recasting narratives of Cuban America, while Johanna Lodoño highlights the role of professional Latinx architects, urban planners, and designers in constructions of deservingness and belonging through the built environment. Contextualizing the cultural work of Bronx Puerto Rican photographers, Sebastián Pérez sheds new light on social life in communal spaces. This new approach to "work" allows us to question dominant characterization of Latinx communities as invariably destitute and always-already pleasureless by demonstrating the place of pleasure, joy, laughter, scripture, and creativity in spatial and community building struggles.

18

The Life and Times of Trans Activist Sylvia Rivera

LAWRENCE LA FOUNTAIN-STOKES

The civil rights activist Sylvia Rivera is one of the most important global trans-gender Latinx figures, with streets and organizations such as the Sylvia Rivera Law Project (SRLP) in New York City named after her, but she is also the subject of elision and controversy.[1] Originally perceived as a homeless rabble-rouser and at times marginalized by the social movements she helped to establish, Rivera has come to be recognized as a national symbol, and in 2002 her death was noted in the *New York Times*.[2] In 2015 she became the first transgender person featured at the Smithsonian National Portrait Gallery in Washington, DC, where she appears in a photo with her partner Julia Murray and with the Puerto Rican Stonewall veteran Cristina Hayworth, who originated the first LGBTQ march in San Juan in 1991.[3] In 2019 it was announced that Rivera would be honored, together with the African American trans activist Marsha P. Johnson, with a monument in New York City, the first ever dedicated to trans persons in the United States.[4] In spite of these achievements, some commentators continue to downplay Rivera's importance, particularly questioning her presence at the Stonewall revolt.[5] In this essay, I will address some of the interpretive battles over her legacy and the challenges in assessing her sex-radical labor politics in the context of Latinx studies.

Rivera has been written about extensively since the early 1970s, at times iden-tified by her birth name, others by her adopted one.[6] She has also been portrayed in numerous films such as Nigel Finch's 1995 *Stonewall*, Roland Emmerich's simi-larly named 2015 *Stonewall*, and Tourmaline (Reina Gossett) and Sasha Wortzel's 2018 *Happy Birthday, Marsha!* Martin Duberman (1993) and Roderick A. Fer-guson (2019) have identified Rivera as a central figure in the American queer liberation movement. Who was Sylvia Rivera? And what does her story tell us about Latinx experience and about queer Latinidad in the United States, specifi-cally about transgender Latinxs, homeless Latinxs, and Latinx sex workers who are civil rights activists?

Rivera was born in 1951 in New York City to a Puerto Rican father and a Ven-ezuelan mother and raised by her maternal grandmother in a predominantly diasporic Puerto Rican environment.[7] Much like other transgender Puerto Rican youth, she ran away from home at a young age and went on to live on the street and engage in sex work in the Times Square area of Manhattan, where she was adopted, so to speak, by older Puerto Rican drag queens.[8] She became politicized in the mid- to late 1960s and early 1970s in the context of the civil rights struggle, the anti-Vietnam War movement, the women's and gay liberation movements, the Black Panthers and Black liberation movement, and the Puerto Rican movement led in New York City by the Young Lords Party, with which she collaborated (Rivera 1998).[9] She spoke frequently about her participation in the Stonewall riots of late June 1969 and became extremely involved in gay, trans, and antiviolence liberation struggles on and off until the time of her death from liver cancer at age fifty. Her intersectional approach and multidimensional commitment to varied social movements have made her a key referent for contemporary queer politics (Ferguson 2019, 18–45). I see her as a key Intralatina *transloca*, that is to say, a Latinx trans subject that embodies the multiple stigmatized meanings of *loca* in Spanish, including effeminate homosexual, madwoman, and sex worker (La Fountain-Stokes 2011, 2021).

Rivera's youth was marked by profound challenges.[10] Rivera's mother committed suicide by ingesting rat poison when Rivera was three years old, and she tried to get Sylvia to also kill herself. "Viejita," the grandmother who raised her, had mixed feelings about Rivera and became abusive when the young child started to express feminine behavior. Rivera engaged in early sexual activity with older men by age ten and was also wearing female makeup. Tensions led her to abandon her home in 1962 when she was eleven years old.

In the 1960s, Times Square was a well-known space of child and adult prostitution, and it was also a major site for working-class queer Puerto Ricans. It was here that the young Rivera obtained her new name, "Sylvia Lee."[11] This period was marked by drug and alcohol use, but also by more stable jobs in Jersey City, New Jersey and a long-term relationship with an older teenager. Rivera stated on numerous occasions that she was at the Stonewall Inn during the June 1969 riots, humorously clarifying that she threw the second, and not the first, Molotov cocktail of the evening (Rivera 2007).[12] She used the authority and respect that she received as a Stonewall veteran to raise awareness of the needs of gender nonconforming people, which she referred to in different ways throughout her life, including using the terms "street queens," "drag queens," "girlies," "STARs," "transvestites," and toward the end of her life, "transgender."[13] She also used Spanish-language terms such as *pato*, *mariposa*, and *maricones* to reference this stigmatized population (Cohen 2008, 104; Marcus 1993, 188), indicating how they were also called "scum" (Rivera 1972) as well as "freaks," "deviants," and "perverts" (Rivera 2007).

There are debates over the reliability of Rivera's Stonewall testimony. Only one or two witnesses, including the Puerto Rican drag performer Ivan Valentin, corroborated her story.[14] As in other famous interpretive struggles regarding truth-telling and sociopolitical activism—most notably, that of Guatemalan Nobel Peace Prize winner Rigoberta Menchú—defenders support Rivera's claims while detractors try to discredit and minimize her role.[15] The Puerto Rican scholar Arnaldo Cruz-Malavé (2007, 2017) has addressed the complexities of queer Latinx *testimonio*, highlighting the nature of this mode of confession/life-story telling, particularly for poor or working-class, disenfranchised, marginal subjects, highlighting how language, structural racism, and homophobia play a role in the enunciation and reception of discourse. As Cruz-Malavé indicates, "*testimonio* is the resulting textual or visual product of an individual act of witnessing and/or experiencing an abject social state that is more than individual, that is indeed collective" (2017, 228). For Cruz-Malavé, *testimonio* centers and validates "the figure of the speaker who narrates his or her story under the duress of the social order's threat of abjection, invisibility, or death" (228).

Rivera had extensive knowledge about the first night of the Stonewall riots and was able to narrate the events in the first person without a script, as she did when I invited her to a meeting of Latino Gay Men of New York (LGMNY) in June of 2001.[16] Rivera frequently explained why she marched in the New York City Gay Pride Parade with the Veterans of Stonewall, and many people recognized her for her involvement, for example gay historian Martin Duberman (1993) in his definitive account, even if journalist David Carter (2004) chose not to mention Rivera in his book on the same topic and has also written against her recognition (Carter 2019). While Rivera is not mentioned in the 2010 documentary *Stonewall Uprising* (dir. Kate Davis and David Heilbroner), she is included in the New York Public Library's *The Stonewall Reader* (2019) and in Marc Stein's *The Stonewall Riots: A Documentary History* (2019); Stein highlights the controversies regarding Rivera and includes several documents in his book that showcase her role in early 1970s LGBTQ activism.[17]

Rivera is also a key figure for trans activists, artists, and scholars such as Leslie Feinberg, Jessi Gan, Tourmaline (formerly known as Reina Gossett), Jack Halberstam, Dean Spade, Susan Stryker, and Riki Wilchins, all of whom have highlighted Rivera's foundational role in the trans rights movement; Feinberg interviewed Rivera about Stonewall, to which Rivera responded, "We were fighting for our lives" (Feinberg 1998, 97).[18] Part of the challenge is precisely the overdetermined status of the Stonewall revolt as the foundational moment of the contemporary LGBTQ movement, an overvaluation of one incident above and beyond previous and later equally important ones.[19]

Soon after the Stonewall riots, Rivera became extremely involved in the gay rights struggle, but she was not always well received, as journalist and Gay Activist Alliance (GAA) member Arthur Bell documented in detail in his memoir *Dancing the Gay Lib Blues* (1971a). In his book *Stonewall*, Duberman cites Bell on how "the general membership [of GAA] is frightened of Sylvia and think she's a troublemaker. They're frightened by street people," highlighting Otherness as a mark of Rivera's alterity, emphasizing her sociopolitical, economic, and behavioral inappropriateness ("wrong ethnic group," "wrong side of the tracks," "wrong clothes") and other markers linked to race and colonialism (Brown-ness, being dark skinned), her language ("her passionate, fractured English"), her comportment and manners (anarchic), and her pose ("her sashaying ways") that ruptured and countered hegemonic WASP decorum and order and that also challenged assimilationist and radical feminist conceptions of appropriate gen-der expression (Duberman 1993, 235–36). Rivera's difference generated fear for those who were uncomfortable with having to engage with a "Hispanic street queen," that is to say, a radical Latinx trans homeless person who had worked in prostitution and who at times consumed alcohol and drugs, particularly one who was perceived as aggressive and pushy, unlike Marsha P. Johnson, who had a less confrontational stance.

Rivera's activism blossomed in the early years after Stonewall, after she joined the Gay Activist Alliance. She was arrested in April of 1970, while petitioning for signatures in Times Square to bar "antigay discrimination and repeal exist-ing sodomy laws" (Duberman 1993, 263); her court case became a major site for gay activism and media coverage, in part due to the efforts of Arthur Bell (1971a, 60–64), who encouraged Rivera to pursue justice and not accept a misdemeanor charge. On Sunday, June 28, 1970, Rivera participated in the first Christopher Street Liberation Day march: "And right up front, leading the cheers all along the sixty-block route, was Sylvia" (Duberman 1993, 276). In early September 1970, she participated in the Revolutionary People's Constitutional Convention orga-nized by the Black Panther Party in Philadelphia, where Rivera spoke with Black Panther leader Huey Newton.[20] Later that month, she was profiled by Bell in the *Village Voice* for her participation in a building takeover at New York University; the Weinstein Hall protesters were evicted by the Tactical Police Force, receiving major news coverage.[21]

Immediately after the NYU takeover, and facing general hostility and mar-ginalization in GAA, Rivera and her comrade in arms, the African American activist Marsha P. Johnson, established STAR (Street Transvestite Action Revo-lutionaries) and STAR House, which was a homeless shelter for young street queens.[22] According to Arthur Bell: "STAR, short for Street Transvestite Action Revolutionaries, is mainly into whoring and radical politics . . . They're a sub-culture unaccepted within the subculture of transvestism and looked down at in horror by many of the women and men in the homosexual liberation move-ment" (1971b, 1). As a radical political organization committed to intersectional struggles, STAR participated in events with the Young Lords, as Rivera discussed in an interview with trans activist and journalist Leslie Feinberg:

> Later on, when the Young Lords came about in New York City, I was already in GLF (Gay Liberation Front). There was a mass demonstration that started in East Harlem in the fall of 1970. The protest was against police repression and we decided to join the demonstration with our STAR banner. That was one of the first

times the STAR banner was shown in public, where STAR was present as a group. I ended up meeting some of the Young Lords that day. I became one of them. (Rivera 1998, 108)

Feinberg (1998, 123) also identifies Rivera as one of the founding members of the internal Lesbian and Gay Caucus of the Young Lords in New York City. This information does not coincide with Young Lords Party member Iris Morales's recollections, but Morales does reference Rivera's involvement with the Puerto Rican group as part of her broader discussion of LGBT Young Lords (2016, 63–66); so does the Puerto Rican scholar Darrel Wanzer-Serrano (2015, 117–18). Both Morales and Wanzer-Serrano cite Feinberg's interview as their main source.

Housing was a major concern for Rivera and for the members of STAR. Initially they lived in a trailer truck in a parking lot but then transitioned to fixing up an abandoned building located at 213 East Second Street that belonged to Mike Umbers, a local businessman with Mafia connections.[23] To pay the rent, Rivera and Johnson worked in prostitution, but they also organized a dance party fundraiser, requesting the assistance of GAA and GLF; some GLF members helped. Rivera cooked at STAR House for the young street queens and encouraged them to join her for prayers. Both Bell and Duberman highlight Rivera's religiosity, indicating that Rivera "'worked with the saints.' Devoted from childhood to Santería, and convinced that St. Barbara was the patron saint of gay Hispanics, Sylvia set up an altar in STAR House, complete with incense and candles, around which everyone would gather and 'pay tribute' before they left the house" (Duberman 1994, 253). Other sources describe Rivera's practice as closer to folk Catholicism, with an affinity for the emotive services of Pentecostal churches. Rivera and her brood eventually got evicted by Umbers in 1971 due to nonpayment of rent.[24]

In 1972, Rivera published a short piece titled "Transvestites: Your Half Sisters and Half Brothers of the Revolution" in *Come Out!*, the newspaper of the Gay Liberation Front.[25] Rivera begins by demanding recognition of the bias faced by her group (10). She then positions transvestites as prescient agents of radical transformation who have "liberated themselves from this fucked up system that has been oppressing our gay sisters and brothers" (10). In this early piece, Rivera establishes the centrality of trans persons at Stonewall and alludes anonymously to her own activism being arrested on Forty-Second Street and participating in the NYU sit-in. Her column concludes with a plea ("So sisters and brothers remember that transvestites are not the scum of the community"), reaffirming the foundational role of this group, and it offers information about STAR meetings.

Overcoming accusations of being "scum" is no easy task, particularly for homeless trans sex workers of color, even ones actively involved in the early 1970s gay liberation movement. Rivera's participation in the 1973 New York City

[handwritten margin note at top: even @ celebration honoring queer ppl, they felt were not accepted]

Christopher Street Liberation Day march and rally cemented her position in trans history; she describes the rejection she felt as a type of death: "We died in 1973, the fourth anniversary of Stonewall. That's when we were told we were a threat and an embarrassment to women because lesbians felt offended by our attire, us wearing makeup" (Rivera 2002, 82). According to Randy Wicker, Rivera experienced several confrontations during the march route and narrowly missed being arrested.[26] At the rally, the lesbian GAA leader Jean O'Leary attempted to block Rivera from addressing the audience; failing to do so, O'Leary would go on to speak after her, giving a "statement on transvestites . . . attacking men who 'impersonate women for reasons of entertainment and profit,' saying they 'insult women'" (Clendinen and Nagourney 1999, 172).[27] O'Leary's anti-trans position corresponds to what is now identified as trans-exclusionary radical feminism (TERF), led by "biology-based/sex-essentialist" cisgender women who do not acknowledge transgender women as actual women.[28] After O'Leary spoke, the drag performer and activist Lee Brewster denounced O'Leary as biased (172), stating that while he did not approve of Rivera's tactics, he endorsed Rivera's social justice message.[29] Rivera posed a major challenge, and did so visibly and articulately, as Bell (1973) wrote at the time in the *Village Voice*.

The speech that Rivera gave, documented and included in films and videos such as *The Question of Equality* (Dong 1995), *Sylvia* (Mateik 2002), and *The Death and Life of Marsha P. Johnson* (France 2017), portrays an activist hell-bent on challenging racist, classist, and gender-based exclusions within the lesbian and gay movement; she is also fully committed to an intersectional radical critique of incarceration that anticipates the more recent prison abolition movement analyzed by scholars such as Angela Y. Davis and Ruth Wilson Gillmore.[30] The strength and impact of Rivera's message had to do as much with her physicality and portentous voice as it did with her words; the scholar Ruth Osorio identifies this as "*parrhesia*, or truth telling," investigating "the role of delivery in Rivera communicating her truth" (2017, 152).[31] I agree with Osorio's claim: Rivera's struggle to get to the microphone and her physical and emotional exhaustion and strength were crucial, and they are what makes her speech powerful to this day.

[handwritten margin note: such a commitment to ppl who are incarcerated, homeless ppl, generally ppl who are deemed disposable by society which is rly important]

Rivera's discourse was structured around complex rhetorical strategies, focusing on the situation of incarcerated street queens who wrote to STAR and who were ignored by the leading gay and lesbian groups. Rivera goes from describing their plight being subjected to violence in prison, including rape, and unable to save money for "sex changes" in order "to become women of the women's liberation [movement]" to speaking from personal experience and challenging those who are listening to her, the same ones who booed her when she got on stage. She concludes by getting the audience to participate in a collective cheer, inviting them to spell out the words "gay power," her voice faltering in exhaustion toward the end. Rivera employed similar rhetorical strategies in the 2001

LGMNY speech at the Lesbian and Gay Community Services Center, juxtaposing her personal experience and those of her community to the experience of her listeners.[32]

Rivera advocated for the radical transformation of structures such as the police and the lesbian and gay movement. She supplemented this with an impetus for the creation of alternative spaces such as STAR and STAR House. Shunned in 1973, she withdrew for over two decades from activism. While she became involved in AIDS awareness, despair also marked her life, as when homeless and depressed, she attempted suicide in 1995 by walking into the Hudson River and ended up in the day room of the psychiatric wing of Saint Joseph's Hospital in Yonkers (Kaufman 1995). As the *Village Voice* columnist Michael Musto noted, her celebrity was nearly meaningless as she continued homeless barely a year after she was feted in Stonewall 25: "Stars of the early gay movement, Sylvia and Marsha fell through the cracks of liberation as they got older, lonelier, and more neglected" (1995, 25).

But Rivera was nothing if not resilient. By 1996, back in Manhattan, she was organizing queer homeless encampments near the Hudson River. In 1997, Rivera moved to Brooklyn and joined the Transy House Collective (Bronski 2002). By the late 1990s, she restarted STAR and embraced the possibilities of effecting change and offering services through the Metropolitan Community Church (MCC), becoming the coordinator of their food pantry (Dunlap 2002). As a social services provider, Rivera channeled the energy that she had expended previously in activism and other jobs (including prostitution) into a more mainstream, stable, and recognizable vital practice. Throughout, Rivera's thought, activism, and labor focused on the advancement of poor, disenfranchised drag queens, transvestites, homeless queer youth, and trans women of color.

How did Sylvia Rivera become the symbol she is today? Rivera's pioneering activism was recognized immediately after Stonewall by activists such as Arthur Bell, who also became a collaborator, penning a piece on "forced psychiatric institutionalization, gender coercion, self harm and the prison industrial complex" (Bell and Rivera 1970). Rivera was also recognized by Randy Wicker (1973) and by later historians and journalist/activists such as Martin Duberman (1993), Eric Marcus (1993), and Leslie Feinberg (1998), and many archival sources have been made easily accessible online by Tourmaline.[33] Rivera published a limited number of columns in radical publications and many saw her give impassioned speeches. As early as 1972, her collaborator Marsha P. Johnson spoke about Rivera when interviewed by Karla Jay and Allen Young for their pioneering anthology *Out of the Closets: Voices of Gay Liberation*.[34] In the late 1980s, when very few people were interested in or even remembered who Rivera was, Dave Isay interviewed her for NPR to celebrate the twentieth anniversary of the Stonewall riots. Rivera received some recognition during the twenty-fifth anniversary of Stonewall in 1994 yet was quickly forgotten until her suicide attempt

[handwritten marginalia: "seems so ridiculous to shun others from activism when the loss of this think is accessibility u ll"]

[handwritten marginalia: "yes! such a good summary sentence!"]

in 1995. In 1996, back in New York City and homeless, she was interviewed by Randy Wicker. In 2000, Rivera was honored at World Pride in Rome, Italy, and in 2001, LGMNY invited her to our meeting, where she shared her frustrations about how the murder of Amanda Milan, an African American trans woman, was not being addressed, and how demanding justice was at the heart of her current activism.[35] After her death in 2002, her funeral included a huge memorial celebration and horse-drawn carriage procession down Christopher Street, which was attended by hundreds.[36] Her legacy has been celebrated in the names of streets in New York City and San Francisco; organizations such as the Sylvia Rivera Law Project, which was established by leading trans activist and lawyer Dean Spade; and through portraits and now plans for a public sculpture. She has even had her articles and speeches anthologized by an anarchist press without attribution of sources and published in English and Spanish (*Street Transvestite Action Revolutionaries* 2013); Untorelli Press's editions have made Rivera's writings widely available but have also obscured the work of multiple journalists and scholars such as Tourmaline and myself (and of my students), who have labored to make this archive available.

All efforts to remember and memorialize are motivated by particular interests and complex politics. The documentary *Sylvia Rivera: A Tribute* directed by trans videomaker Tara Mateik and Denise Gaberman (2002) is a good example. This twenty-minute film distributed by Video Data Bank in Chicago under the title *Sylvia* features interviews with a variety of individuals who knew Sylvia, particularly gay white men such as Bob Kohler and Randy Wicker, trans white women such as Chelsea Goodman and Rivera's partner Julia Murray, and the white lesbian MCC pastor Pat Bomgardner.

Sylvia has the virtue of condensing Rivera's life and experiences, offering a rich community portrait, albeit one marked by the absence of people of color as interview subjects; in this sense, it falls into the pitfalls identified by Jessi Gan (2007), Tim Retzloff (2007), and Benjamin Shepard (2004b). At the same time, Mateik and Gaberman's video decenters and deromanticizes the strangely alienating portrayal effected by the actor Guillermo Díaz in his role of La Miranda in Nigel Finch's 1995 film *Stonewall*, and it insists on the current relevance of Rivera's activism at the end of her life, such as her struggles to pass the New York State Sexual Orientation Non Discrimination Act (SONDA) and her spiritual life ministering to homeless people, particularly trans youth.[37] The film also allows Julia Murray, her transgender partner, and their friends, to talk about Murray and Rivera's romantic relationship, that of two transgender women.[38]

Other memorializations of Rivera have caused major scandals. One example is Roland Emmerich's major Hollywood film *Stonewall*, which generated an enormous controversy due to its elision and whitening of key figures of the Stonewall riots (Barnes 2015). At the same time, the character of Ray/Ramona played by

Puerto Rican actor Jonny Beauchamp shares Rivera's birth name (Ray); Beauchamp has stated publicly that he based his performance on what he knew about
Rivera (Crummy 2015). David France's 2017 film *The Death and Life of Marsha P.
Johnson* also caused great debate, particularly due to Tourmaline's accusations of
appropriation; as of 2020, it is the best documentary source on Rivera.[39] Tourmaline and Sasha Wortzel's 2018 short film *Happy Birthday, Marsha!* also features
a very limited fictional representation of Sylvia Rivera, interpreted by the Cuban
American trans actress Eve Lindley.[40]

Rivera's life, activism, and political thought raise very uncomfortable issues
regarding Latinidad that truly challenge assimilationist paradigms. One example
is Rivera's focus on sex work (including that of children) as the only type of
employment available to marginalized trans subjects:

[handwritten marginal note: — So many "taboo" topics especially for Latinx community]

> Everybody thinks that we want to be out on them street corners. No we do not. We
> don't want to be out there sucking dick and getting fucked up the ass. But that's the
> only alternative that we have to survive because the laws do not give us the right to
> go and get a job the way we feel comfortable. I do not want to go to work looking
> like a man when I know I am not a man. I have been this way since before I left
> home and I have been on my own since the age of ten. (Rivera 2007, 121)

While Rivera's work with the Metropolitan Community Church at the end of her
life would seem to sanitize her legacy, it is crucial to remember that Rivera was
unashamedly a *puta*, to use a disparaging term that the radical Latinx scholar
Juana María Rodríguez (2015) has embraced and critically reclaimed; in this
sense it is necessary to affirm that sex work, whether on the streets or in pornog-
raphy, is a legitimate form of labor. In many respects, the complexity of Rivera's
activist legacy is still well beyond many Latinx studies scholars' grasp. These are
issues that have still not been resolved, nearly two decades after Rivera's death.

NOTES

1 See Gan (2007); Retzloff (2007); Shepard (2004, 2013).
2 Dunlap (2002). Also see Bronski (2002); Wilchins (2002).
3 See Perry (2015).
4 See Jacobs (2019).
5 A leading example is Carter (2019).
6 Important sources on Rivera are Bell (1971a); Duberman (1993); Marcus (1993). For
   extremely thorough accounts of her life and work see Cohen (2008); Phillips and Olugbala
   (2006).
7 See Cohen (2008); Duberman (1993, 20–24); Marcus (1993).
8 See Duberman (1993, 65–71).
9 Also see Duberman (1993, 251).
10 Duberman (1993, 20–24, 65–71); Marcus (1993, 187–89).
11 See Cohen (2008, 101–02).
12 Also see Feinberg (1998); Marcus (1993); Rivera (1998, 2002).

13 On "STARs" and "girlies," see Bell (1971b, 1).

14 See Cain (2004); Carter (2019); Shepard (2004a); Stein (2019, 17).

15 Cruz-Malavé (2007, 2017) offers valuable insights regarding Menchú and truth-telling in *testimonio*.

16 See Rivera (2007). This speech has been reprinted without attribution in sources such as *Street Transvestite Action Revolutionaries: Survival, Revolt, and Queer Antagonist Struggle* (Untorelli Press 2013), which is also available in Spanish.

17 See Stein (2019, 17–18).

18 Also see Feinberg (1996, 1998a, 2006); Gan (2007); Gossett (2012a, 2012b); Halberstam (2018); Stryker (2017); Wilchins (2002).

19 See Armstrong and Crage (2006); Ferguson (2019).

20 Duberman (1993, 259); Rivera (1998).

21 See Bell (1970).

22 See Bell (1971a, 1971b); Cohen (2008); Duberman (1993, 251); Rivera (2002, 81).

23 Bell (1971b, 1973).

24 Bell (1971b); Duberman (1993, 254–55).

25 Also reprinted in Stein (2019, 213).

26 Wicker's (1973) account was published in the leading gay periodical *The Advocate*. This article also appears in Stein (2019, 294–96).

27 On O'Leary's attack, also see Cohen (2008); Duberman (1993, 236); Rivera (2002, 82).

28 See Williams (2016).

29 "Drags and TVs Join the March" (1973, 44).

30 A transcription of Rivera's 1973 speech appears in Cohen (2007, 158–59).

31 Clendinen and Nagourney's description of the event is rather jarring and potentially inaccurate (1999, 171).

32 See Rivera (2007).

33 See Gossett (2012a, 2012b).

34 See Johnson (1992).

35 See Rivera (2007); Shepard (2002, 2004a, 2004b).

36 Bronski (2002).

37 For a critique of Finch's *Stonewall*, see Mayora (2018).

38 Feinberg (1998) discusses and challenges these assumptions about compulsory trans heterosexuality.

39 See Ennis (2018).

40 See the *Happy Birthday, Marsha!* website.

BIBLIOGRAPHY

Armstrong, Elizabeth A., and Suzanna M. Crage. "Movements and Memory: The Making of the Stonewall Myth." *American Sociological Review* 71 (October 2006): 724–51.

Barnes, Henry. "Stonewall Sparks Boycott Row after Claims Film 'Whitewashes' Gay Struggle." *Guardian*, August 7, 2015. www.theguardian.com.

Bell, Arthur. "Sylvia Goes to College: 'Gay Is Proud' at NYU." *Village Voice*, October 15, 1970: 61. http://thespiritwas.tumblr.com/post/16872982696/sylvia-goes-to-college-tw-transphobia (partial).

———. 1971a. *Dancing the Gay Lib Blues: A Year in the Homosexual Liberation Movement*. New York: Simon and Schuster:

———. "STAR Trek: Transvestites in the Street." *Village Voice*, July 15, 1971b: 1, 46. https://thespirit was.tumblr.com/post/18264877034/star-trek-sylvia-star-house-leave-the-lower.

———. "Hostility Comes Out of the Closet." *Village Voice*, June 28, 1973: 1.

Bell, Arthur, and Sylvia Rivera. "Chris: Gay Prisoner in Bellevue." *Gay Flames*, November 14, 1970: 1, 2, 7. https://thespiritwas.tumblr.com/post/44308523726/sylvia-rivera-star-and-arthur-bell-gay-activist.

Bronski, Michael. "Sylvia Rivera: 1951–2002. No Longer on the Back of the Bumper." *Z Magazine*, April 1, 2002. https://zcomm.org.

Cain, Paul D. "David Carter: Historian of The Stonewall Riots." *Gay Today*, July 1, 2004. http://gaytoday.com.

Carter, David. 2004. *Stonewall: The Riots that Sparked the Gay Revolution*. New York: St. Martin's Press.

———. "Exploding the Myths of Stonewall." *Gay City News*, June 27, 2019. www.gaycitynews.com.

Clendinen, Dudley, and Adam Nagourney. 1999. *Out for Good: The Struggle to Build a Gay Rights Movement in America*. New York: Simon and Schuster.

Cohen, Stephan L. 2008. *The Gay Liberation Youth Movement in New York: An Army of Lovers Cannot Fail*. New York: Routledge.

Crummy, Colin. "Stonewall's Jonny Beauchamp Is 'A Trans and Queer Ally.'" *i-D*, November 6, 2015. https://i-d.vice.com.

Cruz-Malavé, Arnaldo. 2007. *Queer Latino Testimonio, Keith Haring, and Juanito Xtravaganza: Hard Tails*. New York: Palgrave Macmillan.

———. "Testimonio." In *Keywords for Latina/o Studies*, edited by Deborah R. Vargas, Nancy Raquel Mirabal, and Lawrence La Fountain-Stokes, 228–32. New York: New York University Press, 2017.

Dong, Arthur, dir. *The Question of Equality*. 1995; CA: KQED Video. Video.

"Drags and TVs Join the March." 1973. *Drag*, 3, no. 11: 4–11, 44. https://archive.org/stream/drag311unse#page/4/mode/2up.

Duberman, Martin. [1993] 1994. *Stonewall*. New York: Plume.

Dunlap, David W. "Sylvia Rivera, 50, Figure in Birth of the Gay Liberation Movement." *New York Times*, February 20, 2002. www.nytimes.com.

Emmerich, Roland, dir. *Stonewall*. 2016; Santa Monica: Lionsgate.

Ennis, Dawn. "Inside the Fight for Marsha P. Johnson's Legacy." *Advocate.com*, January 23, 2018. www.advocate.com.

Feinberg, Leslie. 1996. *Transgender Warriors: Making History from Joan of Arc to Dennis Rodman*. Boston: Beacon Press.

———. 1998. *Trans Liberation: Beyond Pink or Blue*. Boston: Beacon.

———. "Street Transvestite Action Revolutionaries." *Workers World*, September 26, 2006. www.workers.org.

Ferguson, Roderick A. 2019. *One-Dimensional Queer*. Medford, MA: Polity.

Finch, Nigel, dir. *Stonewall*. 1999; New York: Fox Lorber Home Video. Film.

France, David, dir. *The Death and Life of Marsha P. Johnson*. 2017; Submarine. Film.

Gan, Jessi. "'Still at the Back of the Bus': Sylvia Rivera's Struggle." *CENTRO: Journal of the Center for Puerto Rican Studies* 19, no. 1 (Spring 2007): 124–39.

Gossett, Reina. "Sylvia Rivera 10 Year Memorial." *The Spirit Was . . .*, February 18, 2012a. https://thespiritwas.tumblr.com/post/17831883099/sylvia-rivera-10-year-memorial.

———. "Ten Posts for Sylvia Rivera's Ten Year Memorial." *The Spirit Was . . .*, July 31, 2012b. https://thespiritwas.tumblr.com/post/19399849610/ten-posts-for-sylvia-riveras-ten-year-memorial.

Gossett, Reina (Tourmaline) and Sasha Wortzel, dir. *Happy Birthday, Marsha!* 2018; Star People LLC. Film.

Halberstam, Jack. 2018. *Trans*: A Quick and Quirky Account of Gender Variability*. Berkeley: University of California Press.

Isay, Dave, with Michael Schirker, prod. *Remembering Stonewall. Story Corps*. 1989. https://storycorps.org.

Jacobs, Julia. "Two Transgender Activists Are Getting a Monument in New York." *New York Times*, May 29, 2019. www.nytimes.com.

Johnson, Marsha P. "Rapping with a Street Transvestite Revolutionary: An Interview with Marcia Johnson." In *Out of the Closets: Voices of Gay Liberation*, edited by Karla Jay and Allen Young, 112–20. 2nd ed. New York: New York University Press, [1972] 1992.

Kaufman, Michael T. "Still Here: Sylvia, Who Survived Stonewall, Time and the River." *New York Times*, May 24, 1995. www.nytimes.com.

La Fountain-Stokes, Lawrence. "Translocas: Migration, Homosexuality, and Transvestism in Recent Puerto Rican Performance." *emisférica* 8, no.1 (Summer 2011). https://hemisphericinstitute.org.

———. 2021. *Translocas: The Politics of Puerto Rican Drag and Trans Performance*. Ann Arbor: University of Michigan Press.

Marcus, Eric. "The Drag Queen: Rey 'Sylvia Lee' Rivera." Interview. In *Making History: The Struggle for Gay and Lesbian Equal Rights, 1945–1990 (An Oral History)*, 187–96. New York: HarperPerennial, 1993.

———. "Interview with Ray Rivera, Saturday, December 9, 1989." ("Sylvia Rivera Discusses the Stonewall Riots in a Never-Heard-Before Interview.") *Out.com*, October 13, 2013. www.out.com.

Mateik, Tara, and Denise Gaberman, dir. *Sylvia*. 2002; Chicago: Video Data Bank. Video. www.youtube.com/watch?v=ybnHoHBolqc.

Mayora, Gabriel. "Her Stonewall Legend: The Fictionalization of Sylvia Rivera in Nigel Finch's *Stonewall*." *CENTRO: Journal of the Center for Puerto Rican Studies* 30, no. 2 (Summer 2018): 452–77.

Morales, Iris. "Women Organizing Women." In *Through the Eyes of Rebel Women: The Young Lords 1969–1976*, edited by Iris Morales, 43–85. New York: Red Sugarcane Press, 2016.

Musto, Michael. "Lost in Yonkers. Sylvia Rivera May Be the Rosa Parks of Gay Rights, But on the Streets, She's Just Another Homeless Queen." *Village Voice*, May 30, 1995: 25.

New York Public Library, ed. 2019. *The Stonewall Reader*. New York: Penguin Books.

Osorio, Ruth. "Embodying Truth: Sylvia Rivera's Delivery of *Parrhesia* at the 1973 Christopher Street Liberation Day Rally." *Rhetoric Review* 36, no. 2 (2017): 151–63.

Perry, Ana. "Sylvia Rivera: Activist and Trailblazer." *Smithsonian Institution National Portrait Gallery*, October 26, 2015. http://npg.si.edu.

Phillips, Layli, and Shomari Olugbala. "Sylvia Rivera: Fighting in Her Heels: Stonewall, Civil Rights, and Liberation." In *The Human Tradition in the Civil Rights Movement*, edited by Susan M. Glisson, 309–34. Lanham, MD: Rowman and Littlefield, 2006.

Retzloff, Tim. "Eliding Trans Latino/a Queer Experience in U.S. LGBT History: José Sarria and Sylvia Rivera Reexamined." *CENTRO: Journal of the Center for Puerto Rican Studies* 19, no. 1 (Spring 2007): 140–61.

Rivera, Sylvia. "Transvestites: Your Half Sisters and Half Brothers of the Revolution." *Come Out* 2, no. 8 (Winter 1972): 10.

———. "I'm Glad I Was in the Stonewall Riot." In *Trans Liberation: Beyond Pink or Blue* by Leslie Feinberg, 106–9. Boston: Beacon, 1998.

———. "Queens in Exile, The Forgotten Ones." In *GenderQueer: Voices from Beyond the Sexual Binary*, edited by Joan Nestle, Clare Howell, and Riki Wilchins, 67–85. Los Angeles: Alyson Publications, 2002.

———. "Sylvia Rivera's Talk at LGMNY, June 2001, Lesbian and Gay Community Services Center, New York City." *CENTRO: Journal of the Center for Puerto Rican Studies* 19, no. 1 (Spring 2007): 116–23.

Rodríguez, Juana María. "Pornographic Encounters and Interpretative Interventions: *Vanessa del Rio: Fifty Years of Slightly Slutty Behavior.*" *Women and Performance* 25, no. 3 (2015): 315–35.

Shepard, Benjamin. "Amanda Milan and the Rebirth of the Street Trans Action Revolutionaries." In *From ACT UP to the WTO: Urban Protest and Community Building in the Era of Globalization*, edited by Benjamin Shepard and Ronald Hayduk, 156–63. London: Verso, 2002.

———. "History or Myth? Writing Stonewall." *Lambda Book Report* 13, no. 1/2 (August/September 2004a): 12–14.

———. "Sylvia and Sylvia's Children: A Battle for a Queer Public Space." In *That's Revolting!: Queer Strategies for Resisting Assimilation*, edited by Mattilda, a.k.a. Matt Bernstein Sycamore, 97–112. Brooklyn: Soft Skull Press, 2004b.

———. "From Community Organization to Direct Services: The Street Trans Action Revolutionaries to Sylvia Rivera Law Project." *Journal of Social Service Research* 39, no. 1 (2013): 95–114.

Stein, Marc. 2019. *The Stonewall Riots: A Documentary History*. New York: New York University Press.

Street Transvestite Action Revolutionaries: Survival, Revolt, and Queer Antagonist Struggle. 2013. n.p.: Untorelli Press. https://untorellipress.noblogs.org.

Stryker, Susan. 2017. *Transgender History: The Roots of Today's Revolution*. Revised ed. New York: Seal.

Wanzer-Serrano, Darrel. 2015. *The New York Young Lords and the Struggle for Liberation*. Philadelphia: Temple University Press.

Wicker, Randy. "Gays Pour Through New York." *Advocate*, July 18, 1973: 3–5.

Wilchins, Riki. "A Woman for Her Time: In Memory of Stonewall Warrior Sylvia Rivera." *Village Voice*, February 27, 2002.

Williams, Cristan. "Radical Inclusion: Recounting the Trans Inclusive History of Radical Feminism." *TSQ: Transgender Studies Quarterly* 3, no. 1–2 (May 2016): 254–58.

19

"Blossom as the Rose"

Exploring a Politics of Worthiness for Millennial Latina/o Latter Day Saints

SUJEY VEGA

It was called *Como la Rosa*, like the rose . . . it is like this idea in the scripture in Doctrine and Covenants that Lamanites will "blossom like a rose" and so we took that on as a play on words, *como la rosa* . . .
—Armando. Interview by author, June 2016[1]

To Latinas/os, and Mexicans in particular, the rose holds significant cultural and religious symbolism. Much like the rocky hill of Tepeyac in Mexican Catholicism, the Church of Jesus Christ of Latter-day Saints (LDS church) has its own connection to roses: "Jacob shall flourish the wilderness, and the Lamanites shall blossom as the rose" (Doctrine & Covenants 49:24). Armando, a millennial LDS Latino, referenced this passage when recalling his time in an immigrant rights group. The group's name was a play on words, or direct critique, of LDS theology. Rather than blossoming as a result of Mormon conversion, Latina/o LDS activists reframed the concept to illustrate their coming to conscious. In forming *Como La Rosa*, activists challenged the politics of worthiness implicit in Mormonism.

For Latina/o Saints, one's worthiness manifests in various navigations with state and church apparatuses. Living in a state of constant surveillance and doubt of one's legal belonging, Latina/o Saints position themselves in good standing in their faith as a way to counteract immigration politics. For some millennials, this constant performance of worthiness to their church and the nation became increasingly frustrating. The following focuses specifically on Latina/o LDS millennials and their activism to understand how they were influenced by their religious training to fight for social justice.

Table 1 depicts the correlation of age with critique toward the LDS Church. Millennials (ages nineteen to forty) were more likely to critique the church's patriarchal whiteness, meaning the system of power and privilege that positions males and Mormons of European descent with certain prestige in the church. Because priesthood authority and major decision-making roles are only granted to men, millennials additionally utilized intersectional arguments against sexism

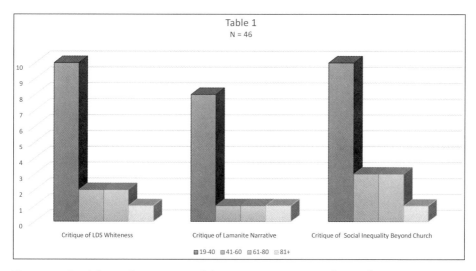

Figure 19.1. Breakdown of age groups and their respective critiques of LDS whiteness, Lamanite narrative, and social inequality beyond the church. Courtesy of the author.

and racism in the church. Thus, exploring their narratives accounts for the way millennial Latinas/os merged faith and activism to address the politics of worthiness in the twenty-first century.

Of the Latina/o millennials interviewed, nine out of twelve (75 percent) were involved at some point with advocating on behalf of undocumented immigrants. This particular subsection of LDS Latinas/os grew up in the church, believed wholeheartedly in the scriptural lessons they received, and felt particularly called to defend Latino undocumented immigrants against the rhetorical and material violence of the twenty-first century. These Latina/o millennial Saints both advocated on behalf of undocumented immigrants and voiced concerns with the structural inequality observed in the LDS church.

LDS Latina/o Immigrant Activists

Though Gaby lived in Utah during Arizona's infamous SB 1070 debate in 2010, she still felt troubled by the political attention to immigration. Popularly known as the "show me your papers" bill, 1070 sanctioned racial profiling by requiring law enforcement to check the immigration status of anyone based on "reasonable suspicion." Law enforcement was not supposed to use racial/ethnic measures to determine suspicion, but in practice discrepancy arose in the way the bill was enforced. Gaby, like many Latina/o Mormons in Utah, moved with her parents to the Salt Lake City precisely because of how it centered their faith.

Flanked with LDS temples and worship spaces throughout, Latino families soon realized that, like Arizona, Utah offered little to no protection from the larger politics of immigration. Bishop storehouses (pantries) were readily available to families in need, but the church stopped short of defending undocumented families from deportation. With rhetoric and political actions bubbling to the surface in the state just south of Utah (Arizona), immigrant activist like Gaby grew fearful they may be next.

Undocumented at the time, Gaby inquired with members of her ward (Mormon congregations), "Honestly I feel like the turning point for me was when [Pearce] introduced the Arizona Papers Law and then that's when I started asking the people in the ward . . . some of them were a little indifferent about it." Much to her disappointment, her church meetinghouse was not a safe space. Instead, leaders she spoke to attempted to veil the growing fears of their members. Within the walls of the meetinghouse discussions centered around faith and the gospel; however, the immigration politics just beyond the doors of their ward directly challenged aspects of the gospel. To make matters worse, the sponsor of SB 1070, Russell Pearce, was LDS and claimed to have the church's backing. Pearce cited the "the rule of law" in LDS doctrine as justification. This emphasis with "the law" stemmed from attacks on Mormons as polygamists in the nineteenth century. As a result, the church promoted the image of Mormons as law-abiding citizens (no longer polygamists). The resulting emphasis on being good model citizens melded patriotic performance within LDS gospel well into the twenty-first century.

That Pearce himself was Mormon necessitated action according to Gaby. Her ward refused to address the situation; "they were a little indifferent about it." Other wards, those with leaders who weekly fielded tearful requests for assistance from undocumented members, found ways to respond. As Josefina, who lived in Pearce's district in Arizona, mentioned, "my husband knew he shouldn't, but he snuck in the importance of getting along and acceptance during one of the sacrament meetings." Importantly, sacrament meetings were part of Sunday services. This was when the entire ward gathered and passed the sacrament. This was the main part of Sunday service and often lasted a full hour. Once this hour was over, members often split off into specific instruction meetings based on gender and/or age. Josefina's husband utilized this collective moment to emphasize a message of love and acceptance.

Shortly after SB 1070 was signed into law, *Salt Lake Tribune* reporter Kristen Moulton sought the perspective of Latino Saints in Utah. She interviewed Tony Yapias and Alfredo Gallegos, who addressed the double standards of welcoming folks on Sunday and denying them rights "Monday through Saturday" (2010). Latino activists in Utah gathered over 100 signatures to send to the Mexico, asking them to deny visas to LDS missionaries (Montero 2011). They argued that a church unwilling to stand up on this issue should not be allowed to proselytize in a country targeted by such cruel legislators. Additionally, a coalition of Latinas/os and non-Latinas/os created the "Utah Compact" that called for a humane compassionate response and suggested resolving the broken immigration system ahead of criminalizing families. Caught between staunch conservative members like Pearce and their efforts to welcome Spanish-speaking converts, the LDS church finally released an official statement in June 2011, a full year after SB 1070 was passed. The statement utilized the church's own history of persecution to draw parallels with undocumented families:

> The history of mass expulsion or mistreatment of individuals or families is cause for concern especially where race, culture, or religion are involved. This should give pause to any policy that contemplates targeting any one group, particularly if that group comes mostly from one heritage.

This church statement, the Utah Compact that preceded it, and the countless efforts of Latina/o and non-Latino members to promote a more compassionate approach toward immigration all provided an alternate narrative to Pearce.

The church's response was a step forward in bridging understanding and advocating compassion, but it stopped short of condemning the politics of exclusion in the immigration debate. Like Gaby earlier, eight out of ten (80 percent) Latino LDS millennials interviewed expressed disappointment with the way the church handled the xenophobia of members toward immigrants. Raúl reflected through tears how he was "heartbroken," and it was a "slap in the face" when LDS leadership did not more forcefully advocate for the undocumented.

Raúl's wife was undocumented, and this made him more aware of the power of silence to slow down change. The lack of involvement from the church led to a faith crisis for Raúl. Like a majority of millennials in this study, Raúl joined the church as a child when his parents converted to the faith. He grew up with a determined sense of faith and testimony that carried Raúl into early adulthood.[2] Still, once married, he began to see discrepancies in what the church said it believed and how the faith was actually enacted. Outright dismissals and microaggressions toward Latinas/os caused Raúl's final decision to leave the church:

> I started to learn how heated the immigration debate was in the United States through my wife. I learned that sometimes White folks don't like Brown folks even if they're church members and that's what really opened my eyes to the church. I started getting a bad taste in my mouth. Here's my wife, a good girl, but all of a sudden, the gospel is not important anymore because of the law. You know "the law says" and "God tells us the laws are important" and yada yada, all the bullshit they tell you in Sunday school.

Raúl's eyes were opened to the problems with "the law" and the unjust handling of undocumented individuals. Once Raúl recognized the injustice undergirding

American laws, he viewed the Mormon devotion to the United States with disgust. He did not understand how his church, the faith he was so dedicated to in his youth, could blindly sanction such a flawed political system.

Unlike Raúl who chose to leave the faith altogether, other Latino millennials preferred to operate from within. Returning to Armando, activists in *Como La Rosa* wanted to educate their brethren. They sought to humanize the experience and use the church's own theology in support of undocumented families. As Isaac explained, "You know I'm undocumented, I'm unafraid, here's my story. Quit labeling me you know. Cause we wanted to put a face on the issue." Like the rest of the nation, Dreamers within the LDS church were eager to come out of hiding and put a face to the experience. As Gaby suggested, "We had this vision to expose members that were unaware of the undocumented within their wards, that we are just like them and that we are not criminals and that we are not taking anybody's place in heaven." Distancing oneself from criminality is critical here. Though many activists challenge playing into the binary of "good" versus "bad" immigrant,[3] playing on these tropes was significant to LDS doctrine. As mentioned, an adherence to "the law" positioned undocumented immigrants as disobedient. In this turn, undocumented immigrants were unworthy of salvation if they continued to break the law. Gaby sensed feelings of resentment from White members based on this "legal" dictate and felt a need to explain that undocumented immigrants were not taking advantage or taking the place of someone who was "more" righteous.

Officially, the church tried to thread the political needle. They claimed to accept all of God's children, but in practice were less inclined to advocate on behalf of undocumented members. As Armando shared, "We wanted them to change their official statement of 'we want to be compassionate but follow the laws of the country.' It was very contradictory at points. We love you, but you're still breaking the law, quote unquote." To shift the paradigm, young activists utilized a main doctrinal underpinning of the church to place a mirror onto these contradictions.

A significant part of Mormon theology includes the notion that families can be together forever. According to LDS principles, once a couple is sealed in a temple ceremony, they and their children are eternally bound to one another. This ensures that death on earth does not sever the covenant between wife and husband, parents and children. Instead, the family unit is reestablished in heaven and is together for all eternity. *Como La Rosa* organizers were raised in the church and believed in this doctrine; thus, Armando described how *Como La Rosa* coordinated in 2015 to create the hashtag #TogetherWithoutBorders to reflect the importance of family in the gospel. As Armando reflected, "Yes, it is very churchy, but it's all strategic right. That's what we wanted to do, talk about family, talk about your experience, and why the LDS church needs to get involved." Similar to Raúl's earlier disappointment with silence from the LDS church, Armando was frustrated that the church did not stand up for undocumented families. Even before Donald Trump entered the debate, activists across the country protested Obama policies that deported a record number of immigrants.[4] For Armando and fellow activists, the political became personal when religious lessons on family unity were muted in church's dealings with national politics.

Most disappointing was how conservative fervor convinced otherwise friendly LDS members to chastise undocumented brethren. As Ester so passionately stated, "That's actually one of the things that like I do hold against people that are LDS who say shit about immigration that are just like 'oh send them back' and it's like who the fuck, like what kind of faith do you have, you know?" Ester eventually went inactive and openly critiqued what she perceived as the hypocrisy of the church. Everything she was taught as a child about Christ's love and the power of the gospel seemed to capsize in the face of conservative members who ignored articles of the faith. Though she still held some connection to a higher power, the antagonism Ester faced within the LDS church led her to withdrawal from such perverse interpretations of God's love.

Ester was attracted to the church by the notion of a predestined divine. You were chosen, before birth, to lead and renew the true gospel. In my research, Latino families mentioned the importance of sealing one's family in the afterlife. Knowing that they eternally tied to each other regardless of borders or boundaries was enticing for many. The issues, however, remained here in one's earthly experience. For Ester and others, being tied to one's loved ones in the afterlife was not enough. They needed each other here on Earth too. Ester began to lose her connection to faith once it was obvious that prayer alone would not guarantee the safety of her family. Other remained active to "do things within the system that might change an outcome." Remaining active meant they had a place at the table to engage in topics that would otherwise not be addressed. These Latina/o LDS millennials had faith, but it was the church and its actions that they struggled with; thus, they chose to stay. They felt committed to being the thorn on the side of their leadership and do their part to complicate the conservative ideologies already infiltrating their faith.

LDS Doctrine and Social Justice

Latina/o millennials emphasized how their faith shaped their sense of social justice. Lali asserted, "I started getting involved in activism because that's what the scriptures would say, you know you have to tend . . . to the ones that need help you know and like the kingdom of God was for everyone." LDS faith begins with the

Book of Mormon and the story of Nephites and Lamanites in order to emphasize the need to bring God's children together. Establishing the church with the story of Lehi (father), Nephi (son), and Laman (wayward son) set the stage for the need to bring together all of God's children to receive His grace. Mormon theology prioritizes the "restoration of the gospel" and sharing the Book of Mormon across the world. The LDS Jesus foretold of a time when the Book of Mormon will be shared with all in order to fulfill his second coming. Rather than doctrine based on fear, rapture, or being left behind, the LDS Jesus bequeathed a responsibility onto Latter-day Saints to restore the gospel everywhere so that all will have an opportunity to rejoice in the eternal ever after. From its inception, the LDS church is ideally based on notions of almsgiving as a means of sharing the gospel. Though certainly not always practiced as such, in the ideal this meant that every human had the right to hear the restored gospel and should be welcomed to the table. This ideology was threatening to antebellum America as some have argued that it is precisely this welcoming spirit and missioning among Native and Black populations that led to persecution in Missouri and Illinois.[5]

Lali was immersed in this altruistic message. She appreciated how LDS doctrine nurtured a responsibility to act but felt troubled with the patronizing approaches disguised as benevolence. Similarly, Ester recalled, "They always mention in a lot of the lessons like service for others, like doing service for others. What does that mean though?" Ester questioned the kind of "service for others" she witnessed in the church. Since 2015, the LDS church offered immigration services with free legal clinics, cultural adaption classes, emergency family planning, and pro bono legal services. This would seem a step in the right direction, but these official church-sponsored resources did not replace the weekly need to discuss concerns, anxieties, and fears at the local level. Ester hungered for a bishop who would openly recognize the immigration concerns of members.

Neither Lali nor Ester went on a mission, but those who did expressed the importance of being in fellowship with community. For these millennials, their commitment to faith translated to deep connections with people and not, like their fellow White missionaries, the number of baptisms accumulated. Julia expressed that instead of baptisms, "it was the personal connections and being of service to the people that mattered." Similarly, Armando described missioning as

> the numbers game or 'elder you got to baptize more' and I'm like I don't care about that, I really didn't care about that. I got to work with people, that's what I really cared about . . . to me the gospel was an attempt to show another human that we love you.

Latino millennials who went on a mission typified the biblical directive that "they will know you by your good works." Missionaries financially pay their own way and are called locally and abroad for eighteen months (women) to two years (men). Young missionaries (nineteen to twenty-one) are often sponsored by their families. This financial burden is made more precarious for undocumented youth who serve in the United States rather than abroad to avoid immigration issues. In the past, ethnicity and race were used to determine location in order to facilitate acceptance in the receiving communities.[6]

LDS Latinas/os in this study who went on a mission were often assigned to a Spanish-speaking community. They identified with the community on multiple levels and in spite of the pressures toward baptisms, their focus was supporting the people and building lasting relationships. For instance, Camilo noted that during his mission "the most impactful thing was really seeing how people lived and the real challenges that they had. In ways that were totally invisible from me before. And really like developing a commitment to social justice and saying like this is not right." Citing his knowledge of liberation theology, Camilo further asserted that he preferred to model the Christ who blessed the meek and denounced those who ignored the poor. Camilo read about liberation theologians in Guatemala and El Salvador and identified with the priests and laypeople whose faith ground their challenge to oppression.

Similar to liberation theologians, Mormon Latino millennials grew frustrated with a church that promoted prayer instead of action. Ester, for instance, recalled being advised to simply trust God in the fight for immigration reform:

> I reached a point where hoping was not enough . . . I'm done with only praying, like some people now are just like you know how did you forget God? And da da da. It's just like listen, you can pray but there needs to be action and so that's when I was like I had to do something because I love my family so much (starts crying).

As the first person in her family born in the United States, Ester felt responsible for fighting on behalf of her siblings and parents who were still undocumented. The fate of her siblings and parents was real, was raw, and could not depend simply on uttering some words of hope. She needed to do something, she needed to get the attention of politicians in Utah and in Washington, DC, so that they, too, could face the realities she and her family dealt with daily. For Ester, her faith taught her that if one feels passionately about their testimony, they need to vocalize it and share it with the world so that they, too, might know the true gospel. Ester's testimony included her faith, but it also included the love she had for her family and the need to keep them safe and united. Similarly, Rafael noted, "Within Mormon faith, community is so important, family is important . . . So our faith really supplied the motivation to be involved, it was very church focused." Under their theology, the cohesion of the family supplanted the rule of law, and if the law meant severing the family then it was the law, not the family, that was to blame. Rafael, Ester, and others grew increasingly disappointed that the church did not take this stance.

Latina/o millennials active in immigration rights noticed the irony of the church's silence in this particular political moment. As Sandra noted, "When Proposition 8 was going on they were basically saying vote for the values that you believe the church stands for and for your families . . . the church has sent political messages from the pulpits . . . [and] for immigrants they said nothing." Activists pleaded with their church to respond and advocate for the unity of the family, a major tenant of the faith, to little or no avail. Raúl explained he "was surprised to see how much money and how much political muscle the church had exercised to make sure that the people of the gay community couldn't get married." LDS Latina/o millennials were keenly aware of the church's overreach with California's Proposition 8 and knew the church's political influence.

The separation of families due to deportation and asking children to condemn LGBT parents ran counter to the supposed dictates of putting family first.[7] In 1995, the LDS church released its "Family: A Proclamation to the World," which detailed the divine destination of "law-abiding" heterosexual families and affirmed "marriage between a man and a woman." In this faithfully followed edict, some families are worthy of value and others condemned. When it came to defend undocumented and mixed-status families, Raúl felt the church deemed his family disposable. They only offered platitudes and never utilized their might, as they had with Prop 8. The juxtaposition of the church's role in California politics with their inaction toward undocumented families was too cruel to ignore. Rampant homophobia in the name of "the family" was the first crack in Raúl's faith journey; however, their lack of protecting families from deportation (especially his own) was the final death knell. Raúl figured that if such a central tenant such as the family could be manipulated in some instances but disregarded in others than the rest of the church's theology had to be called into question as well.

Armando was equally disillusioned with the role homophobia played over undocumented families, "They allow people to say its gay marriage that is destroying the family, I'm like dude its fucking deportations that are destroying families. . . . I think they distract committed members of the congregation with other issue that they feel are important and moral to talk about." Indeed, none of the millennials interviewed vocalized support for the homophobia encouraged by the church in 2008. Within the group of activists, two identified as queer themselves and the rest were accepting of the LGBTQ community. When compared to the rhetoric espoused by the church on Prop 8, the avoidance to speak about immigrant policies was remarkable. Ester recalled when she asked her bishop if they could hold a "Know Your Rights" workshop or at least plan a meeting to talk to members and acknowledge their anxiety surrounding the

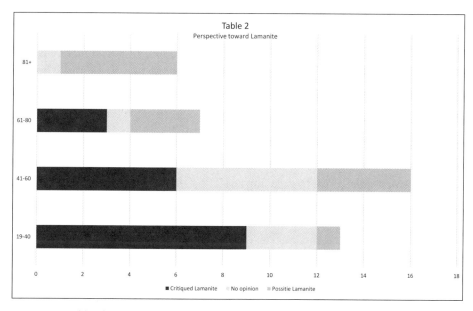

Figure 19.2. Table of perspective toward lamanites categorized by age group.

anti-immigrant rhetoric. Instead, the response was, "We can't do politics you know, we can't talk about politics I'm sorry." Like Raúl, Ester felt the church demonstrated how homophobia mattered more than their doctrinal commitment to the family. Just a few years prior, rhetoric from the LDS church positioned LGBTQ rights as an attack on the family, but here was a direct juridical threat to undocumented families, and they refused to coordinate their members against these laws. Latino families were actually harmed by a national deportation regime, not marriage equality; moreover, it was Mormons themselves who introduced and championed these bills. The hypocrisy opened a wound for Latino millennials who lost faith in their church and the nation.

Conclusion

Members of *Como La Rosa* utilized their faith to plead for just and comprehensive immigration reform. Regretfully, unlike Proposition 8, the church steered clear from actually promoting any legal resolutions to the situation. Indeed, in 2016, 61 percent of Mormons voted for the Republican candidate (Martínez and Smith 2016). They voted for a known philanderer who proudly joked about sexually assaulting women; they voted for white nationalism over their faith's notion of morality. Latina/o activists saw this result coming. Since 2010, Latina/o activists have known that their interventions were not enough to contest the white supremacy beneath the surface. Scriptures that promoted blossoming into a "white and delightsome" sainthood and multiple microaggressions about "following the law" pushed out incredibly gifted LDS Latina/o millennials. LDS Latina/o activists were outraged by the discrepancies of the church and lost faith in the potential of the doctrine. Still, commitment to social justice issues grew out of their training and sometimes in spite of the hierarchal modeling of the church.

Latina/o LDS millennials came of age knowing their rightful place in both. Still, they faced countless encounters where their families were positioned beyond the realm of worthiness. Having to constantly prove oneself became too taxing for many of the Latina/o LDS millennials interviewed for this study (only three remained fully active in the Church). Latina/o millennial Saints embodied what it meant to live the gospel. The talent and moral acumen of these young members was a testament to how faith evoked courage to act against injustice. Instead of adopting the cult of "the law," LDS Latina/o millennial activists embodied the restored gospel. They, more than any, proved what it meant to live out one's faith and act in the name of love.

NOTES

1 All names in this chapter are pseudonyms.

2 Testimony, in this context, refers to a deeply spiritual sign or confirmation that the LDS church is the one true gospel. Mormons speak of their testimony as proof of how they know the LDS church to be truer than other faiths.

3 See Escobar (2016) for more critique on the good/bad binary and the criminalization of undocumented immigrants.

4 Lopez and González-Barrera (2013).

5 See Mueller (2017) and Harris and Bringhurst (2015) on the abolitionist history of the church and resulting persecution in 1830s–1840s. Note the irony of a church that initially welcomed Black converts and was abolitionist in the beginning but eventually succumbed to the racism present within its leadership and banned Black men to the priesthood between 1852 and 1978.

6 Between 1940 and 1990 Native Hawaiian Mormons were strategically sent to Navajo country to aid in the missioning effort. It was believed that the Diné would more willingly accept the gospel from a Native Hawaiian rather than a White missionary. For more, see King (2019).

7 In 2015 the LDS church barred children of LGBTQ couples from faith rituals unless they publicly disavowed their parents' sexuality. In April 2019 the church changed course and went back to allowing children of same-sex couples to perform rituals of the church.

BIBLIOGRAPHY

Boxer, Elise. "The Lamanites Shall Blossom as the Rose": The Indian Student Placement Program, Mormon Whiteness, and Indigenous Identity. *Journal of Mormon History* 41, no. 4 (2015): 132–76.

Church of Jesus Christ of tLatter-day Saints. Doctrine & Covenants, 49. 2013. Salt Lake City, Utah. www.churchofjesuschrist.org.

Escobar, Martha D. 2016. *Captivity beyond Prisons: Criminalization Experiences of Latina (Im)migrants.* Austin: University of Texas Press.

Harris, Mathew L., and Newell G. Bringhurst. 2015. *The Mormon Church and Blacks: A Documentary History.* Baltimore: University of Illinois Press.

Hokulani, Aikau. 2012. *A Chosen People, A Promised Land: Mormonism and Race in Hawai'i.* Minneapolis: University of Minnesota Press.

King, Farina N. "Aloha in Diné Bikéyah: Mormon Hawaiians and Navajos, 1949–1990 Farina Noelani King." In *Essays on American Indian and Mormon History*, edited by Jane Hafen and Brenden Rensink, 161–82. Salt Lake City: University of Utah Press, 2019.

López, Mark Hugo, and Ana González-Barrera. "High Rate of Deportations Continue under Obama Despite Latino Disapproval." Pew Research Center, September 19, 2013. www.pewre search.org.

Martínez, Jessica, and Gregory A. Smith. "How the Faithful Voted: A Preliminary 2016 Analysis." Pew Research Center, November 9, 2016. www.pewresearch.org.

Montero, David. "Latino Activist Urges Mexico to Halt LDS Missionary Visas." *Salt Lake Tribune*, February 13, 2011. https://archive.sltrib.com.

Moulton, Kristen. "LDS Latinos Amp Up Pressure on Church on Immigration." *Salt Lake Tribune*, June 8, 2010. https://archive.sltrib.com.

Mueller, Max Perry. 2017. *Race and the Making of a Mormon People.* Chapel Hill: University of North Carolina Press.

Pew Forum on Religion & Public Life & *Pew* Research Center. "U.S. religious landscape survey, 2014." Washington, DC: Pew Research Center, September 4, 2014. www.pewforum.org.

20

Guillermo Alvarez Guedes and the Politics of Play in Cuban America

ALBERT SERGIO LAGUNA

Early in my career, as I worked my way through the bibliographies of race, ethnic, and Latinx Studies in particular, I can remember asking myself a simple question: Where are the jokes and laughter? It is perhaps not shocking to learn that Latinx Studies has not produced a significant body of scholarship on the ludic broadly defined.[1] Histories of imperial violence, institutional racism, and the pain that often accompanies deracination and migration don't immediately call for a light touch. Then there is the fact that comedy has long played a central role in the production and reinforcement of racial hierarchies in the United States— minstrelsy, political cartoons, and crude stereotypes in film since the dawn of Hollywood, to name a few examples. Finally, there are institutional considerations that make the ludic a difficult topic in the field. Latinx Studies, along with race and ethnic studies more broadly, were made possible by the rise of protest movements. Institutional recognition has always been a fight, and maintaining a tenuous foothold in the university has been a constant challenge. Focusing on pleasure and play would seem to run counter to the "real" work at hand. As the struggle for representation continues, the need for "serious" scholarship that legitimizes the field has inadvertently created an imbalance in how we study the lives of racialized subjects.

The lack of scholarship on the ludic was especially striking to me in the context of Cuban America. Most scholarship equated exile with melancholy, anger, and bitterness—the guiding affective logic being that Cubans began coming to this country in the 1960s and '70s not because they wanted to but because of the politics of Fidel Castro's revolution.[2] Where was the focus on the kind of quotidian pleasures that are the reward for a long workweek?[3] The bawdy satirical comedy playing at a local theatre in Little Havana or jokes shared over coffee? Of course, life in the exile community wasn't one big conga line down Calle Ocho in Little Havana. But popular culture was always there to inspire not only the laughter that keeps you from crying but also a ludic sociability that helped shape narratives of a community. Searching for a way to make sense of a profound disconnect between scholarly focus and lived experience, I turned to jokes in an attempt to laugh my way to greater clarity.

After hours of listening to the comedy of Cuban exile Guillermo Alvarez Guedes, I came upon a moment from his eleventh standup album recorded live in Miami in 1980 that would become the point of departure for my focus on the role of pleasure and play in Latinx communities. Before he could begin the second half of his set, a man in the audience interrupted the crowd's attentive silence by directly addressing the comedian: "Aren't you going to talk about Mariel?" At the time of the recording, Miami was a city in chaos roiled by racial tension and the Mariel boat crisis. Cubans had stormed the Peruvian embassy in Havana in hopes of securing political asylum. In an effort to take control of the narrative, Fidel Castro allowed people to leave via the port of Mariel. Castro claimed that he was ridding Cuba of its "undesirables"—criminals, homosexuals, and others categorized as socially deviant. The *Miami Herald*, voice of the white establishment and hostile against the Cuban population at the time, played a key role in disseminating these characterizations. The depressed state of the Miami economy, conflicting opinions about the *marielitos* within the exile community, and the backlash of the white establishment due to the growing Cuban population created an atmosphere of heightened tension for *all* Cubans in Miami at the time.

So when a man in the audience prompted Alvarez Guedes to address the unfolding crisis during his set, the air was instantly sucked out of the room, leaving an anxious silence in its wake. After hesitating, Alvarez Guedes replied:

> No man, I don't see the humorous angle to that. That is very dramatic. Because they are using the Cubans again, the communists. They are taking advantage. They know that the lovers of freedom also love their families and so they are taking advantage of the circumstances.[4]

Remarkably, Alvarez Guedes successfully reversed the building tide of tension through a seamless shift back into his comic persona. He ended his commentary on the boatlift with the following quip about the difficult conditions Cubans endured while awaiting passage: "What they [Cuban price gougers] charge is outrageous: ten dollars for a gallon of water, fifteen for a beer, thirty for a steak. Even to take a shit you have to pay seven bucks! Two for the bag and five for the guy who has to get rid of it!" This unexpected comic shift instantly dispelled the unease in the room and the crowd erupted in laughter. In a span of fifty-five seconds, Alvarez Guedes rerouted his audience's affective bearing toward Mariel from anxiety to a state of relieved comic pleasure.

When prompted to talk about Mariel, the comedian first responded with a grave tone consistent with exile political talking points. Indeed, the initial tone and language Alvarez Guedes deployed were consistent with dominant representations of the exile community as a no-nonsense collective when it comes to the topic of Cuba and communism. But the wheezing of audience members catching their breath amidst their laughter in response to Alvarez Guedes's comic twist communicates an intensity of experience that demands attention. There is a choral quality to the laughter as it commingles to produce a sonic invitation to the listener that says, "Join us." This laughter is marked by the shared understanding of that historical moment, the setup and twist, and a recognition of how Alvarez Guedes's performance *feels* Cuban as a result of his accent, tone, word choice, and the scatological framework for his punchline. This moment signaled to me another way for thinking about the relationship between affect, politics, and everyday life. What if, instead of quickly moving from the humor to the somberness surrounding Mariel, we lingered on that ludic intensity? What are the possibilities that arise when we understand this joke not just as an animated interruption in the usual discourse surrounding tense moments in Cuban diasporic history but as an example of the ludic as a consistent strategy for narrating the present and what it means to be Cuban *off* the island?

By focusing on *momentos de diversión* like the one I have just described—moments of diversion, of play, of laughter—I seek to provide an affective complement to Cuban American and Latinx studies more broadly by shifting critical emphasis away from feelings that so often dominate academic conversations around minoritarian experience—the anger, pain, loss, and disappointment expressed in the first part of Alvarez Guedes's response to the question about Mariel. That pain is also part of my scholarship with diversión serving as a means to process and manage it, but I am more interested in foregrounding the critical possibilities that arise in those bursts of laughter. In that laughter, I "hear" the long history of humor as both an object of study in the Cuban intellectual tradition and as a key component in cultural production on and off the island.[5] I can hear a mode of relationality, a ludic sociability, echoed throughout the history of the Cuban diaspora and fostered by the consumption and circulation of popular culture. By paying close attention to that laughter and the language and performance that produce it, I engage a basic question that I will address in this essay: What do ludic popular culture and the feelings it inspires *do* in the diasporic context?

To answer this question, I return to Alvarez Guedes and his comic material at a moment in the history of the exile community rarely discussed in playful terms: the late 1970s and 1980s. The Mariel crisis, domestic terrorism against alleged Castro sympathizers, racial tensions, and the rise of the drug trade in Miami created strife and turned the tide of public opinion against Cuban Americans. Far from simply serving as a cathartic release from the tensions roiling Cuban Miami, Alvarez Guedes's performances also illustrate the role of diversión in forging a narrative of Cuban exile identity that privileged whiteness and heterosexuality while simultaneously speaking back to discrimination from Anglo Miamians.[6] By making the politics of pleasure and laughter the focus of my analysis, this essay will, in turn, highlight the critical potential of the ludic for

Latinx Studies. I argue that a focus on ludic popular culture makes possible an understanding of transnational continuities not only around cultural forms such as styles of humor (in the Cuban case, *choteo*) but also targets of comic discourse. This most clearly manifests itself in comedy that is dominated by men and utilizes representational strategies inflected with racism, homophobia, and sexism that have currency on and off the island. It is in exploring this basic dynamic—that feeling good can come at the expense of others—that we can grasp the intersecting, and at times contradictory, narratives that affect how communities come to imagine themselves across spaces. Examining ludic popular culture allows for a more nuanced conversation about our often-fraught attachments to popular culture, its transnational movements, and the way it can challenge and reify normative ideologies.

Alvarez Guedes, "The Natural"

Guillermo Alvarez Guedes was a mainstay of the Cuban American entertainment scene for decades. He hosted radio programs, published books, and produced and starred in a number of television, music, and film projects. He is best known among Cubans for his thirty-two live stand-up comedy albums released over the course of three decades. While these albums quickly became hits among exiles, success did not come immediately for the comedian after leaving the island. In a 2007 interview, he describes the difficulty in finding work in the Spanish-language entertainment industry during the 1960s and 1970s: "To make a living as an actor in those days, you had to be an actor in television soap operas, and to work in television soap operas, you had to have what they called a neutral accent . . . I have a Cuban accent; I don't know what it means to speak neutrally."[7] This hostility to the entertainment industry's demand that he tame his tongue created the foundation for his career in exile. Throughout this interview, Alvarez Guedes constantly refers to his commitment to performing "naturally" through a performance practice marked by his use of Cuban vernacular, specifically the corpus of "bad words" that he believed to be authentically Cuban.

The "naturalness" that commentators have attributed to Alvarez Guedes is due in part to sonic aspects of his performance such as his accent, tone, and the words he uses. But it is not simply a matter of a one-to-one relationship between sound and ethnic identification. The "naturalness" is a product of *how* he tells his jokes. This practice can be best described as falling under the tradition of *choteo*. Choteo is a form of humor and mockery common among the masses and articulated through the idiomatic specificity of Cuban popular culture. As Cuban critic Jorge Mañach wrote in his 1928 essay "Indagación del choteo" ("Investigation of Choteo"), it is "a form of relation typically ours."[8] It is a recognizable, culturally specific form of diversión and interaction that acts as a way to filter serious or distressing experiences in a nonserious, anti-authoritarian, and irreverent

Figure 20.1. Album cover for *Alvarez Guedes 8*, 1978.

manner and thereby also provides an alternative, critically ludic perspective on topics that would not otherwise be objects of jest. The "naturalness" of Alvarez Guedes's choteo, then, becomes a way to help make the "unnatural" state of exile legible, perhaps even bearable in quotidian life.

Alvarez Guedes's diversión deployed through his use of choteo and performance practice are not the sole reasons for his designation as a "natural" performer. Implicitly informing this naturalness is his whiteness. Though his fans primarily experienced his comedy by listening, his likeness was never far behind. It is featured on each of his album covers. Encoded within his "naturalness" is a narrative that manifests itself in jokes that assert whiteness as part of the communal narrative of exile cubanía. In what follows, I examine jokes from the 1970s and '80s as sites for understanding how the Cuban exile community reconciled attitudes about race from Cuba with US perspectives. Though jokes about race in no way represent the majority of the content on his albums, when they do arise these comic bits shine a light on the ongoing project to articulate a cultural identity in exile and its normative boundaries at historical moments when definitions and the privileges of whiteness were being hotly contested.

Comedy and Racial Politics

Treated as political refugees fleeing communism rather than economic migrants, Cubans arriving in South Florida in the 1960s and 1970s received unprecedented support from federal and local governments in the form of generous benefits, resettlement programs, and most importantly, legal status through the Cuban Adjustment Act of 1966—benefits that make the reception of Cubans unique in the history of migration from Latin America to the United States.[9] Despite this warm welcome, Cubans quickly realized that their social positions in Miami would not be the same as in Cuba. Once at the top of the racial hierarchy on the island, the mostly white Cuban exiles were subject to discrimination from the Anglo majority in South Florida. Nevertheless, the majority of exiles did not align themselves with other groups who had and continue to face discrimination in Miami, such as the Black community composed of Afro-Caribbeans and African Americans.[10] Instead, they aimed to redeploy their "possessive investment in whiteness" cultivated in Cuba to help define exile cubanía.[11] Claims to whiteness were essential components for imagining an exile cubanía that was drawn from Cuban racial ideologies and reinforced by Cold War rhetoric, which together positioned these exiles as white victims of communism.

While discrimination experienced on the ground complicated this narrative of whiteness and privilege, there was little interest in identifying as an oppressed minority.[12] Instead, Cuban exiles drew from a long history of racist humor from the island to assist in the crafting of a communal narrative about the place of the exile community in the social hierarchy of South Florida. Jokes about Blacks can be found throughout Alvarez Guedes's albums but are most prevalent in material from the tumultuous 1970s and early 1980s—decades marked by racial uprisings in Miami provoked by experiences of racism, discrimination, and anti-Black violence. These jokes and performances capture the role diversión played in solidifying and patrolling the boundaries of a white, heteronormative, politically enfranchised exile identity while simultaneously demonstrating the transnational melding of Cuban and US racial ideologies.

It is not surprising that race-based humor has long existed on an island where histories of slavery, colonialism, and capital have always intersected. What is so fascinating is the way in which the themes and ideological preoccupations encoded within Cuban race-based humor reappear in the popular culture of the post-1959 exile community. In her study of blackface performance in nineteenth-century Cuba, a cultural form that continues to shape the Cuban comic imagination, Jill Lane explains the ideological projects of *teatro bufo*: "This blackface humor works discursively at two levels: it controls and limits the otherwise menacing significance of Blackness at the same time that it renegotiates the meanings of whiteness in a colonial hierarchy that privileged Spanish peninsulares [literally, "peninsulars," those born on the Iberian peninsula] over white criollos [descendants of Spanish colonists born in Cuba]."[13] Like nineteenth-century *bufo*, Alvarez Guedes's race-based material functioned as a means to negotiate Cuban whiteness and its relationship to Blackness.[14] I read his jokes as part of an ongoing project for negotiating Cuban whiteness in the context of United States racial politics at a time of great anxiety about Blackness in Miami and a moment when Cuban racial self-definitions were under fire from Anglos wary of the Cuban influx into South Florida.

The following joke from *Alvarez Guedes 2* (1974) speaks to the kind of humor inspired by racial politics in the United States:

> A black guy commits a traffic violation in Alabama and they condemn him to die in the arena with the lions. He only ran a red light but they condemned him to die with the lions. They take him to a stadium and they bury him in sand up to his neck. Twenty thousand blond, green-eyed spectators fill the stands. They release the lion and it quickly attacks the black guy who can't defend himself because his head is the only part of his body above the sand. But when the lion gets close enough, the black guy bites the lion's leg. The twenty thousand spectators stand up and scream: FIGHT FAIR YOU BLACK SON OF A BITCH!

In this joke, Alvarez Guedes positions the audience to see the racial drama of the United States from an outsider perspective with Alabama as the symbolic site. As in Cuba, racism against Blacks is fodder for humor. In this joke, the Black man is the silent victim whose last-ditch effort at resistance is read as consistent with stereotypical understandings of uncivilized Blackness. The fifteen seconds of uninterrupted laughter following the delivery of the punchline signal the audience's enjoyment and alignment with a comic perspective that routinely uses racist violence as a means to entertain.

Is it possible to read the Alabama joke as an indictment of racial violence? While it is important to leave that possibility open, historical context makes such a reading less convincing. Alvarez Guedes invites white Cubans to laugh at the racial politics of the United States at a moment when anxiety about Blacks in Miami was high. Bruce Porter and Marvin Dunn detail what they call thirteen separate racially charged "miniriots" in 1970s Dade County—violence that reached a climax with the uprising of 1980 sparked by the acquittal of four white police officers in the beating death of a Black man named Arthur McDuffie (1984, 18–22).[15] These uprisings were rooted in the long history of discrimination, unequal power relations, and segregation in Miami and would have been visible to the growing Cuban community. The vast majority of Cubans in Miami at the time this joke was performed in 1975 had little interest in casting their lot with the Black communities of South Florida and the challenges they faced.

Focusing on how narratives of whiteness circulate in popular culture is essential for understanding race relations not only among Cuban Americans but across Latinx groups. While race and ethnicity in the Latinx context is often discussed as in conflict with United States regimes of white supremacy, scholarship has examined the place of whiteness and anti-Black sentiment within Latinx communities.[16] More of this work is necessary. Attention to ludic popular culture can provide access to those notions around race that circulate within a community, perhaps unsaid in "serious" discourse yet understood among cultural insiders.

Cubano–Americano Tensions

Alvarez Guedes's comedy was not just a means to claim an abstract, privileged whiteness. Instead, exiles were invested in a distinctly *Cuban* whiteness that also resisted Anglo assimilationist paradigms. Built into the rhetoric of exile is the notion of forced departure and the fantasy of return. These two elements of the exile narrative strongly informed the desire to maintain Cuban cultural characteristics and the performances of cultural nationalism that permeate Alvarez Guedes's comedy. Unsurprisingly, this led to tensions between exiles and the Anglo majority throughout the 1970s and 1980s in Miami. The frustrations of "native" Miamians reached a boiling point in 1980 with the circumstances surrounding the Mariel crisis. The *Miami Herald* railed against President Carter's undefined policy regarding Mariel and the exile community's desire to facilitate the exodus to Miami. In the time leading up to and after the boatlift, the *Miami Herald* effectively agitated the non-Cuban population in Miami. With the white establishment bent on asserting power in a time of rapid change, the modern English-only movement was born in Miami with an antibilingual referendum. It passed, and in November 1980, the ordinance changed the policies of biculturalism and bilingualism in Dade County instituted in the early 1970s.[17] It is out of these tensions that Alvarez Guedes's most popular and recurring targets for the anti-authoritarianism of choteo surfaces, "*los americanos.*"

With all these events roiling Miami, Alvarez Guedes performed regularly and continued to release his albums, cementing his popularity in the exile community. Much of his comedic production during this time addressed the hot-button language issue of the day and the general culture clash well underway in Miami. As the inflammatory rhetoric and tension between Anglos (referred to as los americanos) and the exile community escalated, so did the tone and aggression of his material. Choteo's antihierarchical strain became a means to confront

Anglo political power while simultaneously attempting to consolidate an exile cubanía founded on national characteristics, anti-Castro sentiment, cultural expressions, and whiteness.

In 1982, Alvarez Guedes released his best-selling, and certainly most unique, album titled *Alvarez Guedes 14: How to Defend Yourself from the Cubans*. What makes this album so exceptional is that it is the only one that features him performing primarily in English. On this album, non-Spanish speakers are identified as those who need to "defend" themselves by learning Spanish. If they do not, they risk being unable to navigate a Miami that has undergone radical change with the influx of immigrants from Latin America, especially Cubans:

> I've been watching very closely what's been happening in Miami lately and I believe that something has to be done in favor of those who can't speak Spanish in this area. They have to learn to defend themselves. They have to learn Spanish because they need the goddamn language. They need it. It is the only language you hear everywhere. I don't care where you are. Wherever you are, in Miami, there are Cubans . . . Sometimes we take advantage because since we know that you don't speak Spanish, we talk of you [sic] in front of you and you don't know it.

He follows this up by imagining situations in which an americano would have to defend himself from Cubans. Every example describes the americano as being on the outside looking in and incapable of understanding when Cubans are talking badly about him. Choteo has changed the stakes of the game through a clear inversion of power relations. Cuban culture on this album becomes center, while the non-Spanish-speaking americanos are marginalized by their inability to understand what has been classified as "foreign" for so long.

This positing of Cuban culture as moving from minor to major indicates a shift in how "defense" has evolved in Alvarez Guedes's repertoire. On earlier albums, "defender" was invoked to describe one's ability to at least "get by" in English. The covert aggression of this first class used choteo to "level" the linguistic power relations in Miami by creating an imagined scenario wherein Spanish was an important, equal part of the "bi" in "bilingual" city. As the political situation in Miami became more intense with the Mariel crisis and the antibilingual referendum, "defense" took on a more military connotation—defense as offense. These narratives stress how the Cuban and Latin American presence is a powerful force politically and economically by pointing out the pervasiveness of Spanish throughout the city. Alvarez Guedes goes on the attack on these albums, using choteo to speak out against the Anglo establishment and its attempts to discredit the community. On *How to Defend Yourself from the Cubans*, the Cuban community, and by extension, Spanish, is positioned as dominant. The burden of defense is now upon los americanos in a Miami where English is becoming more marginal.

Adding to the comic effect of this album is Alvarez Guedes's deployment of Spanish. When he uses Spanish, it is only to "teach" his "American audience" how to use certain vulgar words to defend themselves from Cubans in the situations mentioned above. But when he does explain how to fire back against these Cubans, his Spanish is inflected with an English accent. He mispronounces words, puts the accent on the wrong syllable, and generally sounds like the stereotypical gringo attempting to roll a pair of *R*s with little success. In contrast to the gringo-inflected Spanish, Alvarez Guedes's speech reflects a relative mastery of English. His ability to speak both Spanish *and* English, to be functionally bilingual, is a statement against the tensions surrounding language in Miami at the time of this album's release. To perform in English to an audience that understands the jokes as they shift from English to Spanish is to enact the community's attempt at mastering the codes of the dominant culture while simultaneously retaining culturally specific forms like the Spanish language and choteo as powerful, pleasurable ways of narrating experience.

Although the performance is all about displacing the need for defense onto los americanos of Miami, teaching an "American audience" how to defend themselves against the linguistic threat of Cuban Spanish is, once again, a form of defense for a community at a particularly hostile moment in time. National poll results after the Mariel crisis showed the country's extremely low opinion of the Cuban community in the United States.[18] The repeal of bilingualism laws, together with negative views of the Cuban community, created a need to perform a certain brand of cultural solidarity and even superiority. By performing his mastery of the English language and simultaneously invoking the familiar language and codes of choteo, Alvarez Guedes makes a defiant statement against American assimilation models and stresses the vitality of the exile community through an emphasis on Cuban cultural practice.

In a time of domestic terrorism among Cubans in Miami in the form of bombings and threats, generational shifts, political infighting within the community, and the most intense anti-Castro sentiment, diversión played an instrumental role in establishing the "common ground" of exile cubanía throughout the 1970s and 1980s. Alvarez Guedes's material during this time reveals the utility of popular culture for "analyzing the consciousness of the past."[19] His performances and his widespread appeal reveal how the community made sense of its place in Miami's social hierarchy through a ludic discourse that combined the racial and ideologies of Cuba and the United States to inform a narrative of exile cubanía. The history of choteo and its racial preoccupations on the island aligned with social hierarchies and discriminatory rhetoric in the United States and provided a convenient transnational continuity for exiles getting their bearings. When Anglos in Miami attempted to enclose the exile community in the realm of "otherness" and its attendant disenfranchisement, the community answered with a brash assertion of a Cuban cultural identity that simultaneously insisted on the privileges inherent in whiteness and heteronormativity. This manifested itself in popular culture and, as the 1980s progressed, increased visibility and power in local and, eventually, national government.

Alvarez Guedes's comedy is a telling example of the role of popular culture in the production of a ludic sociability upon which social relations and communal identifications can be built and projected. His albums playing in the background of a family party or on long car rides. People use Alvarez Guedes "one-liners" in conversations where they function as an understood, broadly held cultural currency to describe a person or situation. Alvarez Guedes's jokes provide the texture of everyday experience; they are samples of those mininarratives that are so memorable, reproduced and repeated in everyday interactions that disseminate and reinforce the ideological codes within them through repetition. And yet, forms of diversión are often ephemeral as well. A standup comedy album or half-remembered joke, for instance, will often fall outside the usual archival logics of the academy. But for the scholars who take the time to uncover and reconstruct these archives, there is potential to develop a more nuanced understanding of how Latinx communities narrate their experiences by and for themselves and produce a shared context for relationality.

NOTES

1 There are, of course, exceptions, but across Latinx Studies the ludic has generally received little attention. For scholarship that does this work, see Gutiérrez-Jones (2003) Habell-Pallán (2005); Reyes (2005); González and Rodríguez y Gibson, (2015); Hernández, (1991); Paredes, (1993); Pérez (2016).

2 Cuban America has changed a great deal politically and culturally due to generational turnover and increased migration from Cuba since the 1990s. See Laguna (2017) for a book-length analysis of these changes.

3 Roberto Fernández's novel *Raining Backwards* (1988) and José Esteban Muñoz's *Disidentifications* (1999) were notable exceptions that made me hopeful about the potential of this ludic line of inquiry in Cuban American Studies.

4 All translations from Spanish to English are mine.

5 See Mañach (1991); Ramos (1995); Ortiz (1985, 1986).

6 In *Diversión* (2017), I spend significant time throughout the book examining the sexual politics of ludic popular culture alongside race. Because of space constraints, I am limiting my focus to race in this essay.

7 Evora (2007), 172.

8 Mañach (1991), 54.

9 García (1996).

10 For scholarship on the relationship between Cuban exiles and Miami's established Black communities, see Aja "Intra-Immigrant"; López (2012); Gosin (2019).

11 Lipsitz (2016).

12 According to Torres (2001, 85), exiles were also wary about discussing discrimination they faced because it could potentially fuel Fidel Castro's criticism of the United States and his propaganda war against the exile community.

13 Lane (2005), 15.

14 See Rivero (2005) for an analysis of how comedy negotiated the broader politics around race on Puerto Rican television in the twentieth century.

15 Porter and Dunn (1984) *Riot*, 18–22. One of the officers involved was Cuban American. For an excellent reading of the McDuffie case and racial politics in Cuban America, see López (2012).

16 This is by no means an unexamined area of inquiry, but more is necessary given the role of anti-Blackness in political and social formations. See Almaguer (2012), "Race"; Hernández (2003); Jiménez Román and Flores (2010) Torres-Saillant (2003).

17 Castro (1992).

18 Portes and Stepick (1993), 31.

19 Moore (1998), 9.

WORKS CITED

Aja, Alan. "The Intra-Immigrant Dilemma." *New Politics* 10, no. 4 (Winter 2006).

Almaguer, Tomás. "Race, Racialization, and Latino Populations in the United States." In *Racial Formation in the 21st Century*, edited by Daniel Martinez HoSang, Oneka LaBennett, and Laura Pulido, 143–61. Berkeley: University of California Press, 2012.

Alvarez Guedes, Guillermo. *Alvarez Guedes 11*. 1996 (originally released in 1980). AG Enterprises, compact disc.

Alvarez Guedes, Guillermo. *Alvarez Guedes 14*: *How to Defend Yourself from the Cubans*. 1996 (originally released in 1982). AG Enterprises, compact disc.

Castro, Max. "The Politics of Language in Miami." In *Miami Now!: Immigration, Ethnicity and Social Change*, edited by Guillermo J. Grenier and Alex Stepick, 109–32. Gainesville: University of Florida Press, 1992.

Evora, José Antonio. "Guillermo Alvarez Guedes, El Natural." *Encuentro de la cultura cubana* 44 (2007): 171–80.

Fernández, Roberto. 1988. *Raining Backwards*. Houston: Arte Público Press.

García, María Cristina. 1996. *Havana USA: Cuban Exiles and Cuban Americans in South Florida, 1959–1994*. Berkeley: University of California Press.

González, Tanya, and Eliza Rodríguez y Gibson. 2015. *Humor and Latina/o Camp in Ugly Betty: Funny Looking*. Lanham: Lexington Books.

Gosin, Monika. 2019. *The Racial Politics of Division: Interethnic Struggles for Legitimacy in Multicultural Miami*. Ithaca: Cornell University Press.

Gutiérrez-Jones, Carl Scott. "Humor, Literacy and Chicano Culture." *Comparative Literature Studies* 40, no. 2 (2003): 112–26.

Habell-Pallán, Michelle. 2005. *Loca Motion: The Travels of Chicana and Latina Popular Culture*. New York: New York University Press.

Hernández, Guillermo. 1991. *Chicano Satire: A Study in Literary Culture*. Austin: University of Texas Press.

Hernández, Tanya Katerí. "'Too Black to be Latino/a:' Blackness and Blacks as Foreigners in Latino Studies." *Latino Studies* 1, no.1 (2003): 152–59.

Jiménez Román, Miriam, and Juan Flores, eds. 2010. *The Afro-Latin@ Reader*. Durham: Duke University Press.

Laguna, Albert Sergio. 2017. *Diversión: Play and Popular Culture in Cuban America*. New York: NYU Press.

Lane, Jill. 2005. *Blackface Cuba: 1840–1895*. Philadelphia: University of Pennsylvania Press.

Lipsitz, George. 2006. *The Possessive Investment in Whiteness: How White People Profit from Identity Politics*. Philadelphia: Temple University Press.

López, Antonio. 2012. *Unbecoming Blackness: The Diaspora Cultures of Afro-Cuban America*. New York: New York University Press.

Mañach, Jorge. 1991. "Indagación del choteo." Miami: Ediciones Universal. First published in 1928.

Moore, Robin. 1998. *Nationalizing Blackness: Afrocubanismo and Artistic Revolution in Havana, 1920–1940*. Pittsburgh: University of Pittsburgh Press.

Ortiz, Fernando. 1985. *Nuevo Catauro de Cubanismos*. Havana, Cuba: Editorial Ciencias Sociales. First published in 1923.

———. 1986. *Entre Cubanos: Psicología Tropical*. Havana, Cuba: Editorial de Ciencias Sociales. First published in 1913.

Paredes, Américo. 1993. *Uncle Remus con Chile*. Houston: Arte Público Press.

Pérez, Raúl. "Brownface Minstrelsy: "José Jiménez," the Civil Rights Movement, and the Legacy of Racist Comedy." *Ethnicities* 16, no.1 (2016): 40–67.

Porter, Bruce, and Marvin Dunn. *The Miami Riot of 1980: Crossing the Bounds*. Lexington, KY: Lexington Books, 1984.

Portes, Alejandro, and Alex Stepick. 1993. *City on the Edge: The Transformation of Miami*. Berkeley: University of California Press.

Ramos, José Antonio. 1995. *El manual del perfecto fulanista*. Miami: Editorial Cubana. First published in 1916.

Reyes, Israel. 2005. *Humor and the Eccentric Text in Puerto Rican Literature*. Gainesville: University Press of Florida.

Rivero, Yeidy. 2005. *Tuning Out Blackness: Race and Nation in the History of Puerto Rican Television*. Durham: Duke University Press.

Torres, María de los Angeles. 2001. *In the Land of Mirrors: Cuban Exile Politics in the United States*. Ann Arbor: The University of Michigan Press.

Torres-Saillant, Silvio. "Inventing the Race: Latinos and the Ethnoracial Pentagon." *Latino Studies* 1, no. 1 (2003): 123–51.

21

Urban Designers and the Politics of Latinizing the Built Environment

JOHANA LONDOÑO

There are barriers that can be built in key places, which are legitimate . . . a sovereign nation has a right to . . . radar and blimps, and other devices for measurement of human traffic . . . the country *deserves* to have security on the border. Most democrats agree with that. Most Americans agree with that. The question is, what is the *form* of it? The wall has become a sort of a symbol, an outside symbol of something completely different, [like] the Berlin wall and other walls in history that separated people [emphasis mine].[1]

In a February 2019 interview with Fox Business, Henry Cisneros, former Secretary of the Department of Housing and Urban Development (HUD) under the Clinton administration, remarked on one of the latest public debates framing Latin American immigrants as a threat to the United States.[2] President Donald Trump had claimed that only a "beautiful" wall on the US–Mexico border could resolve the crisis presented by immigrants and asylum seekers. Having placed his bets on an electoral base galvanized around anti-immigrant hate and white supremacy, Trump emphasized the wall for its ability to divide and exclude. In the interview, Cisneros, now chairman of the infrastructure investment firm American Triple Partners LLC, did little to assuage the fears over immigration that FOX, resonating with Trump, was wont to enflame. Though he did point out that a wall "from sea to shining sea" was not feasible, Cisneros largely opted for a nonconfrontational approach. His strategy was like that of many other Democrats and echoed his previous remarks, made elsewhere, that immigration reform must be bipartisan.[3]

Unsurprisingly, Cisneros narrowed in on the built environment to make his political compromise on immigration. His suggestion that "barriers," "blimps," and "radars" be used as tools for appeasing the anxieties of nativists while also challenging the very need of a "wall" that signified exclusion was in line with a long-term preoccupation with "form" and a career founded on the idea that design can be used for social engineering. At the same time, his support for border security, which he believes the nation "deserves," contradicts a career in which, at least if taken at face value, he promoted the inclusion of marginalized residents in the construction of new housing.

It was the latter inclusive work that first attracted me to Cisneros. I was researching architects, urban planners, and designers, some of whom continued the 1960s legacy of representing barrios in a positive light. Their representations contrasted the dominant view of people of color as poor, abject, and without cultural value and of their urban spaces as unmodern, unclean, and a socio-economic problem. These representations were, however, few and far between. Generally, Latinx designers rarely appear in scholarly writing or in the archives.[4] The Latino-Hispanic Design archive at the Cooper Hewitt, Smithsonian Design Museum, the only one of its kind, includes a limited selection of designers, some whom were raised in Latin America and do not identify as Latinx/Hispanic. In large part, the omission of Latinx designers in academic literature can be explained by the fact that they represent a very small number in the mostly non-Latinx white industries of architecture, planning, and urban design. At the end of the aughts, Latinxs represented about less than 10 percent of the total employee population for each architecture and urban planning employee categories, compared to about 80 percent for non-Latinx whites.[5] Moreover, some individuals, such as Cisneros, may be counted under other employment categories by virtue of their interdisciplinary work. Latinx designers also represent a departure from multidisciplinary scholarship in Latinx Studies that emphasizes builders who are working-class or nonconforming to white normative landscapes. Histories of Mexican railroad construction workers in the late nineteenth century and early twentieth century show the central role they played in the building of a landscape that allowed the nation to move, expand, and thrive economically.[6] Accounts of working-class vernacular architecture and murals describe how communities resisted late-twentieth-century urban renewal and policies of neglect.[7] Latinx workers in the twenty-first century Los Angeles landscaping industry maintain gardens for wealthy homeowners, while Latinxs struggle to keep their community gardens alive in neighborhoods undergoing heightened gentrification.[8] It makes sense that working-class builders are emphasized. During the same period in which data on urban designers was collected above, Latinxs represented 24 percent of the construction industry, the second-highest percentage of Latinx workers after agriculture.[9]

Yet urban designers are important to study because of how they convince buyers and users to experience and inhabit urban culture. Moreover, because of the knowledge and skills acquired in formal education, designers are viewed by professionals in cognate industries as having authority. The manual "work" of designers may be limited to drawings, plans, and mockups, but the way they "work" the built environment and its users through the power of discourse and representation is deemed valuable. They have a say as to what extent the built environment becomes a site for inclusion, exclusion, racialization, or resistance. Latinx designers, in particular, are often put in a position of representing Latinx and low-income communities while negotiating with elites in the building, public sector, and development industries. Cisneros, for example, referred to his intertwined role of planner, city official, and public persona as "a bridge between the community and resources, power structures," a process in which he tried "to be an honest interpreter and broker."[10]

In examining Cisneros, I found myself "studying up," an approach that looks at the middle-class and wealthy sectors of society to examine a fuller range of power relations.[11] For Latinx designers, however, privilege is not always cut and dry. Though born into a middle-class military family, Cisneros grew up in the Latinx West Side of San Antonio. He accumulated cultural capital at elite schools and professional appointments. With several urban policy related degrees from Harvard and George Washington University, and an MA in urban and regional planning from Texas A&M, Cisneros has occupied multiple positions where he has had the power to regulate and modify, if not erect, built environments. As mayor of San Antonio in the 1980s, he was the first Latino to govern a large US city in the twentieth century. During the Clinton administration he was the first Latino to hold the position of Secretary of HUD. By serving in majority white professional contexts, he amplified his role as a cultural broker but also, in the process, his privilege.

Further complicating their privileged position, some of the designers that I study maintain what I call a "barrio affinity" that compels them to draw inspiration from low-income, racialized landscapes.[12] After conducting interviews in Miami, New York City, San Antonio, and Southern California with Latinx designers of multiple national backgrounds, I found that those most inspired by barrios, including Cisneros, are Mexican American. They had grown up in or regularly visited barrios where the 1960s and '70s Chicana/o movement's uplifting of barrio culture had created murals, organizations, and inspired urban designers who applied their expertise to marginalized neighborhoods.[13] One interviewee, Henry Muñoz, the Mexican American head of one of the largest minority-owned design firms in Texas, had grown up in the suburbs of San Antonio but regularly visited the barrios in the city where his relative, Willie Velásquez, was a well-known Chicana/o movement organizer. Muñoz's experiences in the city influenced his barrio-inspired design projects in the public sector. Urban planner James Rojas grew up in a suburb of Los Angeles, but his Mexican family had roots in East Los Angeles, and it was this barrio that would influence his urban planning career.[14]

Other interviewees similarly observed the willingness of Mexican American designers to engage with and uplift the barrio in their design practice. A Miami-based Cuban American architect noted in our interview that when he received my request to talk about design and barrios, he immediately assumed that I had been interviewing Mexican American identified designers in California or the Southwest. "Cuban Americans will probably answer 'no' to the question of whether barrios inspire design," he said.[15] The assumption that large Latinx groups with roots in 1960s and '70s activism, such as Mexican Americans, would have an interest in barrio-associated design, did not easily translate to discussions about the Puerto Rican diaspora, the second-largest historic Latinx subgroup, and their engagement with the built environment. During our interview, a Mexican-raised architect spoke about the recent revitalization of a Nuyorican *casita*—one of the small house-like structures built in abandoned lots of 1970s deindustrialized New York City and a prominent example of Nuyorican barrio architecture—and insisted that the *casita* was not specific to Puerto Rican culture.[16] Thus, this designer argued, it was not necessary to keep the *casita*'s Nuyorican connections in the lot's redevelopment.[17] A Puerto Rican designer I spoke with who had redesigned a Nuyorican *casita* with the local community in mind thought of their design work as a transnational artifact rather than as part of an inner-city barrio structure.[18] In contrast, the Mexican Americans I spoke with reified the origins of the spatiality and culture of the barrio.

Cisneros came of age during San Antonio's Chicana/o movement and the emergence of important organizations such as the Mexican Youth Organization. His politics of representation echo the movement's interest in augmenting the value of barrio spaces. Importantly, however, Cisneros's commercial interests represent a deviation from the movement's primary objectives. In a neoliberal era of multiculturalism that commodified Latinidad, Cisneros's post-HUD heralding of barrio spaces as "Latino New Urbanism" lifestyles worthy of inclusion in a middle-class housing market benefitted urban elites more than others. Moreover, the barrio-inspired built environments planned by Cisneros have wider, not all-Latinx, audiences and spaces in mind. His politics of representation echo the politics of the professional-oriented LULAC (League of United Latin American Citizens) that encouraged the assimilation of Mexican Americans and other Latinxs. Urban planner and Chicana/o studies scholar David Diaz has claimed that "the cultural impact of *el barrio* has superseded its historic center and is at the precipice of influencing urban society more broadly."[19] Although probably not the kind of impact that Diaz imagined, Cisneros, as I describe below, expected to expand the role of barrio-inspired design at a national level. As such, his work is a good example for analyzing the connections between the politics of Latinx belonging and the built environment.

In this essay, I focus on how Cisneros manipulated the built environment throughout his lengthy career. I start by briefly discussing how his replacement of low-income high-rise buildings with smaller scale traditional architecture was a precursor to his Latinx-specific design that melded aspects of poor, barrio spaces with traditional building styles. I end by connecting this career trajectory to his more recent support for border barriers. I make these connections to better understand how design is put at the service of a politics of respectability that encourages Latinx belonging, albeit in limited, mainstream ways. In the case of Cisneros, it is evident that national anti-immigrant and anti-poor discourses inform these politics. I elucidate how Cisneros's urban design created marketable Latinized built environments that allow those invested in maintaining a white-dominant landscape feel safe and at ease.

Whitewashing Aesthetics of Urban Poverty

Cisneros's time at HUD set a precedent for the barrio-inspired designs that he would pursue after leaving the position. During his tenure, Cisneros revived and promoted architect Oscar Newman's 1972 concept of "defensible spaces" that sought to curb crime in public housing.[20] By parceling land into smaller units, the "defensible space" approach encouraged residents to perform ownership of land by surveilling it. Cisneros integrated defensible space with New Urbanism, a design theory that embraced low-rise building scales and traditional design styles, such as Victorian and colonial revival. Proponents of New Urbanism opposed modern architecture's austere aesthetics, superblock layouts removed from the street, and high-rise buildings, precisely the design style of much post-war public housing. From the mid-1990s and well into the first decade of the 2000s, the principles of both defensible space and New Urbanism gave shape to the new low-rise, mixed-income developments erected in place of the nation's "most blighted public housing."[21] The new housing was known as HOPE VI, short for the Urban Revitalization Demonstration program that was part of the Homeownership and Opportunity for People Everywhere (HOPE). Though approved a few years before Cisneros's arrival at HUD, it became a hallmark of his career.[22]

Some celebrated the new architecture as a long-awaited revitalization of low-income neighborhoods and a way to generate aesthetic parity among low-income and middle-class residents. No longer, proponents suggested, would low-income public housing tenants be stigmatized for living in cold, detached, high-rise buildings. Living in HOPE VI developments would make housing assistance inconspicuous and possibly, it was anticipated, lead low-income tenants to become homeowners. Supporters applauded the mixed-income strategy and smaller scale as a way to deconcentrate poverty.

Detractors, however, thought HOPE VI framed the preexisting, low-income neighborhoods as sites of moral corruption and social alienation and their low-income residents as criminals in need of landscapes that regulated their behavior and uplifted their social standing.[23] Because of the smaller scale, new developments could not house all of the residents formerly living in high-rise buildings. HOPE VI made matters worse for public housing residents forced out of their communities. As geographer James Hanlon put it, "the aestheticization of HOPE VI revitalization conceals the human costs of its implementation."[24] Geographer Jason Hackworth made the consequences of displacement clear, writing that HOPE VI made national urban policy "a more effective instrument at facilitating gentrification."[25] It would be better, some critics thought, if HUD invested in moribund public housing instead of replacing it with new public-private complexes intended to make low-income neighborhoods appear visually safe and suburban-like and restore traditional white urbanism. The issues that made New Urbanism controversial carry over to Cisneros's post-HUD work, even if researchers have rarely examined this later stage of his career.

Whitewashing Barrio Aesthetics

After leaving HUD, Cisneros hitched his wagon onto private housing developments geared toward a Latinx homebuyer. At the time, Latinx urban planners, urban elites, and scholars argued that New Urbanism paralleled Latinx lifestyles in the United States.[26] That it took New Urbanism to set the stage for a serious national conversation on how to include Latinx representations in designed spaces is unsurprising given that the modernist aesthetic that New Urbanism denounced avoided cultural difference for the sake of a universal architectural language. Taking a market-friendly approach, urban planner Michael Méndez coined the term "Latino New Urbanism" to describe how a "spicier" New Urbanism could draw the attention of a growing consumer base of socioeconomically mobile Latinx homeowners.[27] Cisneros, the most high-profile advocate of "Latino New Urbanism," furthered this latter notion by claiming that Latinxs living in barrios had specific cultural and spatial preferences for mixed-use and family-orientated housing that could appeal to private real estate and urban development.[28]

His most prominent medium for promoting Latino New Urbanism was the coedited volume *Casa y Comunidad: Latino Home and Neighborhood Design.*[29] In a large format, the glossy pages of *Casa y Comunidad* depict Spanish colonial building styles, adobe-like exteriors, and colorful facades—the safe Latinx parallels to white Victorian and Classical Revival architecture. The text described a Latinx preference for houses that could fit large multigenerational families. *Abuelita/os* were, as suggested in the book's images of elderly couples with small children, crucial members of the Latinx household. Images, some sourced from stock photography agencies, only showed white or light Brown Latinxs. The book rehashed well-worn ideas about Latinxs and their lifestyles that neglected Black Latinxs and nonheteronormative and nonnuclear families.[30] If the aesthetics of New Urbanism had ushered in a white revitalization of low-income urban neighborhoods, the aesthetics and marketing of Latino New Urbanism proposed a white and normative Latinx landscape.

Casa y Comunidad's release in 2006 coincided with a housing boom disproportionately fueled by Latinx and African American homebuyers. Groups historically left out of discriminatory housing markets became easy targets of risky, high-interest—subprime—loans that promised to deliver on the American dream of homeownership. A year after the book's publication, the nation was in a housing crisis. Millions were about to foreclose on their homes after missing a payment or more on the subprime mortgages they had recklessly been given. In light of this, and with the advantage of hindsight, Latino New Urbanism became another dimension of predatory housing markets that took advantage of Latinx desires to buy into the dream of homeownership. *Casa y Comunidad* was published by BuilderBooks, the publisher of the National Association of Home Builders, with the sponsorship of Freddie Mac, the government-chartered mortgage corporation later accused of being involved in the foreclosure crisis. The Latino New Urbanism celebrated in the pages of *Casa Y Comunidad* thus not only furthered Latinx stereotypes, it was also implicated in one of the worst recessions in decades, one that put a significant dent on Latinx wealth accumulation. Legal scholar Steven Bender holds that the Latinx spatial experience is one marked by a "legacy of loss" that began with land theft during and after the Mexican American war and was perpetuated by spatial inequalities and racial discrimination.[31] While Latino New Urbanism was seemingly an aesthetic form of inclusion, it was also part of a legacy of loss in line with a history of white appropriation of land.

Working the Built Environment

Besides restoring whiteness in the built landscape, what geographer Neil Smith has described as "revanchism," there were many other similarities between the HOPE VI and Latino New Urbanism projects. For one, as part of the Clinton administration's neoliberal reconstitution of welfare, Hope VI symbolized the privatization of public housing and thus was part of the private housing market in which Latino New Urbanism developed. Second, similar to his promotion of Latino New Urbanism, at HUD Cisneros participated in "ethnic advocacy" on behalf of Latinx housing tenants in places such as rural Texas.[32] Third, and especially pertinent to this essay, both HOPE VI and Latino New Urbanism aestheticized and sanitized the housing of two groups of hyperurbanized and racially othered subjects—low-income public housing tenants who could be of any race but were often Black or Latinx and Latinx homeowners, who, even as middle-class buyers, were assumed to have an origin in and affinity for lifestyles observed in barrios. Both HOPE VI's New Urbanism's "traditional" design style and Latino New Urbanism's emphasis on Spanish colonial design and "tropicalized" colorful exteriors were Eurocentric renderings of the urban spaces of low-income and racially marginalized people that did not always improve the lives of residents.[33]

Little scholarship has discussed the role of sanitized built environments in marking marginalized people as deserving of urban belonging. Instead, scholarship has analyzed liberal narratives that emphasize the importance of being a hard worker for carving out a space of belonging.[34] Yet, work, it turns out, is not enough. For people of color, work does not always rehabilitate them. It does not reverse racist notions of human worth that have defined their character. Nor does it always make them appear worthy of benefits, respect, and of a full life. For nearly a century Latinxs have been thought of as undeserving, despite their hard work and the jobs they fill.

The urban design that Cisneros and other designers promoted implied that they, too, realized that work—long at the heart of a US capitalist myth about achievement and upward mobility—would not alone generate belonging. Rather, their designs suggested that the way Latinxs present themselves and their spaces are key to proving their worth. Latino New Urbanism, in particular, gave the impression that Latinxs could be included in the urban fabric of the nation insofar as they assimilated into traditional housing landscapes and aspired toward the ideal of homeownership. The approach Cisneros took during his interview with CNN in early 2019 was thus not new. With the rise of Latinx designers and a multicultural recognition that representation matters, the form of the built environment became a vehicle with which to establish a nonconfrontational, assimilated belonging.

This way of working the built environment reaffirms racial and class notions of safe, clean, and pleasant urban spaces. I want to return to the quote that opens this chapter because it highlights who Cisneros excludes from these normalized landscapes of deservingness. Cisneros's belief that Latinxs are to be included in housing developments may seem to contradict his claim, evoking tired ideas of US exceptionalism, that the nation "deserves" to build landscapes that exclude Latin American immigrants, but I argue that a similar anti-poor immigrant logic informs the two statements. After all, the subjects that Latino New Urbanism caters to are not the same subjects barred from crossing the border—the too poor, undesirable, undeserving, and supposedly criminal immigrant. The ideal resident of Latino New Urbanism, by virtue of being future occupants of normative housing, is deserving of space and thus of belonging to the nation. Their way of life, the spaces they inhabit, are carefully disciplined commodities visually crafted to conform. The same can't be said of the racialized and maligned immigrant crossing the border whose movement and settlement is too unpredictable to be visually disciplined by the built environment, with the glaring exception, of course, of border security. Indeed, the border "barriers," such as "radars and blimps," that Cisneros calls for in the quote at the beginning of this essay and the designs of Latino New Urbanism are two sides of the same coin. It behooves designers shaping the urban built environment to move from mainstreaming practices that regulate the urban belonging of poor and Latinx residents to actions that accept the diversity of needs and tastes and tackle head on the structural limitations of making the city an inclusive place.

NOTES

1 Henry Cisneros, "America deserves to have security on the border: Fmr. HUD Secretary Henry Cisneros," filmed February 5, 2019 at FOX Business, video, 7:13, https://video.fox business.com/v/5998832748001/#sp=show-clips.

2 Ibid.

3 "Henry Cisneros: Immigrants are key to nation's success," Arizona State University, November 15, 2016, https://asunow.asu.edu.

4 Not all of these designers identify as Latina/o/x. Instead of using the umbrella term, some identify by their national and ethnic group. But for the sake of brevity I am using that term here.

5 In 2009, of the total 204,000 employed architects, 6.9 percent was Latinx and over 80 percent was white. Data on employed architects can be found in the 2009 Household Data published by the U.S. Bureau of Labor Statistics, "Employed persons by detailed occupation, sex, race and Hispanic or Latino ethnicity," 2009 Annual Averages-Household Data-Tables from Employment and Earnings. The Bureau of Labor Statistics does not offer a racial and ethnic breakdown for employed planners because, at less than fifty thousand people, they consider the population too small. However, the American Planning Association (APA), the leading national association for urban planning, indicates that over 90 percent of its membership was non-Latinx white in 2004. This data on membership may include retired architects and urban planners. Leonardo Vazquez, "Lagging Behind: Ethnic Diversity in the Planning Profession in the APA New York Metro Chapter Area," 2001 *American Planning Association*, www.nyplanning.org.

6 See, for example, Jeffrey Marcos Garcilazo, *Traqueros: Mexican Railroad Workers in the United States, 1870–1930* (Denton, TX: University of North Texas Press, 2016); Erasmo Gamboa, *Bracero Railroaders: The Forgotten World War II Story of Mexican Workers in the U.S. West* (Seattle, WA: University of Washington Press, 2018).

7 See, for example, Luis Aponte-Parés, "Casitas Place and Culture: Appropriating Place in Puerto Rican Barrios, *Places*, 11, no. 1 (1997); James Rojas, "The Enacted Environment: The Creation of 'Place' by Mexicans and Mexican Americans in East Los Angeles" (Master's thesis, Massachusetts Institute of Technoloy, 1991); Raúl Homero Villa, *Barrio Logos: Space and Place in Urban Chicano Literature and Culture* (Austin, TX: University of Texas Press, 2000).

8 Pierrette Hondagneu-Sotelo, *Paradise Transplanted: Migration and the Making of California Gardens* (Berkeley: University of California Press, 2014)

9 "Hispanic Workers in Construction and Other Industries," The Center for Construction Research and Training, accessed Sept. 1, 2019, www.cpwr.com.

10 Interview with Henry G. Cisneros by the author, May 2011.

11 Anthropologist Laura Nader first made the appeal to "study up." See Laura Nader, "Up the Anthropologist: Perspectives Gained from Studying Up," in *Reinventing Anthropology*, ed. Dell H. Hymes (New York: Pantheon Books, 1972).

12 See also Johana Londoño, "Barrio Affinities: Transnational Inspiration and the Geopolitics of Latina/o Design," *American Quarterly*, vol. 66, no. 3 (2014); Johana Londoño, "Barrio Affinities and the Diversity Problem," in *Abstract Barrios: Visualizing the Crises of Latinx Belonging in Cities* (Duke University Press, 2020).

13 In 1970 Los Angeles, recent college graduates dreamed of being "the architects and planners for Chicano neighborhoods" and founded the nonprofit Barrio Planners Inc. George Ramos, "Drawing the Line: Planners Meld Activism, Urban Projects Incomplete Source," *Los Angeles Times*, June 5, 1988; Barbara Goldstein, "Harvest the Sun," *Progressive*

Architecture, 63, no. 4 (1982). Non-Chicano/a examples include the Architects' Renewal Committee in Harlem, started in 1965 and eventually run by J. Max Bond, Jr., an African American architect. Brian D. Goldstein, "'The Search for New Forms': Black Power and the Making of the Postmodern City," *Journal of American History*, 103, no. 2 (2016): 375–399. The Real Great Society Urban Planning Studio (RGS/UPS), founded in 1968 by Puerto Rican youth in East Harlem to promote "community self-determination." Luis Aponte-Parés, "Lessons from El Barrio—the East Harlem real great society/urban planning studio: A Puerto Rican chapter in the fight for urban self-determination," *New Political Science*, 20, no. 4 (1998), 409.

14 James Rojas, "Latino Placemaking: How the Civil Rights Movement Reshaped East LA," Project for Public Spaces, March 4, 2014, https://www.pps.org/article/latino-placemaking-how-the-civil-rights-movement-reshaped-east-la.

15 Interview with author, March 2015.

16 Interview with author, June 2015.

17 Ibid.

18 Interview with author, July 2017.

19 David R. Diaz, *Barrio Urbanism: Chicanos, Planning and American Cities* (New York: Routledge, 2004).

20 Henry G. Cisneros, "Defensible Space" Deterring Crime and Building Community," US Department of Housing and Urban Development, January 1995, Washington, DC.

21 Henry G. Cisneros and Lora Engdahl, ed., *From Despair to Hope: Hope VI and the New Promise of Public Housing in America's Cities* (Washington, DC: The Brookings Institution, 2009).

22 Peter Calthorpe, "Hope VI and New Urbanism," in *From Despair to Hope: Hope VI and the New Promise of Public Housing in America's Cities* (Washington, DC: The Brookings Institution, 2009), 49–64; Henry G. Cisneros, "Defensible Space."

23 James Hanlon, "Success by design: HOPE VI, new urbanism, and the neoliberal transformation of public housing in the United States," *Environment and Planning A* 42 (2010): 94.

24 Hanlon, "Success by design," 93.

25 Jason Hackworth, *The Neoliberal City: Governance, Ideology, and Development in American Urbanism* (Ithaca: Cornell University Press, 2007), 130.

26 See, for example, urban planner and scholar David Diaz, who insists that "what is being claimed as 'new urbanism' is in reality 'barrio urbanism' or 'Chicana/o urbanism.'" David Diaz, *Barrio Urbanism: Chicanos, Planning and American Cities* (New York: Routledge, 2005), 73.

27 Michael Méndez coined the term in his 2003 Master's thesis. Michael Méndez, "Latino Lifestyle and the New Urbanism," (Master's thesis, Massachusetts Institute of Technology, 2003). Mendez refers to Latino New Urbanism as a "spicier new urbanism" in Michael Anthony Mendez, "Latino New Urbanism," in *Casa y Comunidad: Latino Home and Neighborhood Design*, ed. Henry G. Cisneros and John Rosales (Washington, DC: Builder Books, 2006), 104.

28 Phone interview with Henry G. Cisneros conducted by the author, May 2011.

29 Henry G. Cisneros and John Rosales, ed., *Casa y Comunidad: Latino Home and Neighborhood Design* (Washington, DC: Builder Books, 2006).

30 For more on stereotyped racial representations of Latinxs in marketing see Arlene Dávila, *Latinos, Inc.: The Marketing and Making of a People* (Berkeley: University of California Press), 111–12.

31 Steven Bender, *Tierra y Libertad: Land, Liberty, and Latino Housing* (New York: NYU Press, 2010).

32 "Henry Cisneros Oral History, Secretary of Housing and Urban Development," Transcript, Presidential Oral Histories, Bill Clinton Presidency, Miller Center, University of Virginia, Nov. 21, 2005, https://millercenter.org.

33 For more on "tropicalization" as a colonial projection onto Latin American and Latinx culture see Frances R. Aparicio and Susana Chávez-Silverman, eds., *Tropicalizations: Transcultural Representations of Latinidad* (Dartmouth College Press, 1997).

34 Ideas of how work determines the deservingness and nondeservingness of poor people of color have long informed national politics. See Michael B. Katz, *The Undeserving Poor: America's Enduring Confrontation with Poverty*, second Edition (New York: Oxford University Press, 2013), 3. The concept of deservingness was revived in the 1990s while Cisneros was at HUD. The Clinton administration's welfare reform redistributed aid in favor of the "working poor" versus the nonworking, undeserving poor. More recently, DACA (Deferred Action for Early Childhood Arrivals) and its supporters defend conferring citizenship rights to undocumented immigrant on the grounds of their consumption, college education, and military service. Even the poor and out-of-school youth left out of the "good" immigrant category underlying DACA practice a politics of deservingness to gain community recognition. For more on the latter see Eric Macias, "Negotiating Citizenship: Undocumented (and Afraid), 'Drop-out,' and Serving Their Community," paper presented at *The Society for Latin American and Caribbean Anthropology*, Santo Domingo, Dominican Republic, April 11–13, 2019.

REFERENCES

Aparicio, Frances R., and Susana Chávez-Silverman, eds. 1997. *Tropicalizations: Transcultural Representations of Latinidad*. Lebanon, NH: Dartmouth College Press.

Aponte-Parés, Luis. "Casitas Place and Culture: Appropriating Place in Puerto Rican Barrios." *Places*, 11, no. 1 (1997): 54–61.

———. "Lessons from El Barrio—the East Harlem Real Great Society/Urban Planning Studio: A Puerto Rican Chapter in the Fight for Urban Self-Determination." *New Political Science*, 20, no. 4 (1998): 399–420.

Bender, Steven. 2010. *Tierra y Libertad: Land, Liberty, and Latino Housing*. New York: NYU Press.

Calthorpe, Peter. "Hope VI and New Urbanism." In *From Despair to Hope: Hope VI and the New Promise of Public Housing in America's Cities*, edited by Henry G. Cisneros and Lora Engdahl, 49–64. Washington, DC: The Brookings Institution, 2009.

Cisneros, Henry G. "America Deserves to Have Security on the Border: Fmr. HUD Secretary Henry Cisneros." Filmed February 5, 2019, at FOX Business. Video, 7:13. https://video.foxbusiness.com/v/5998832748001/#sp=show-clips.

———. "Henry Cisneros: Immigrants are Key to Nation's Success." Arizona State University, November 15, 2016. https://asunow.asu.edu.

———. "Henry Cisneros Oral History, Secretary of Housing and Urban Development." Transcript, Presidential Oral Histories, Bill Clinton Presidency, Miller Center, University of Virginia, Nov. 21, 2005. https://millercenter.org.

Cisneros, Henry G., and Lora Engdahl, eds. 2009. *From Despair to Hope: Hope VI and the New Promise of Public Housing in America's Cities*. Washington, DC: The Brookings Institution.

Cisneros, Henry G., and John Rosales, eds. 2006. *Casa y Comunidad: Latino Home and Neighborhood Design*. Washington, DC: Builder Books.

Gamboa, Erasmo. 2018. *Bracero Railroaders: The Forgotten World War II Story of Mexican Workers in the U.S. West*. Seattle, WA: University of Washington Press.

Garcilazo, Jeffrey Marcos. 2016. *Traqueros: Mexican Railroad Workers in the United States, 1870–1930*. Denton, TX: University of North Texas Press.

Dávila, Arlene. 2012. *Latinos, Inc.: The Marketing and Making of a People*. Berkeley: University of California Press.

Diaz, David R. 2004. *Barrio Urbanism: Chicanos, Planning and American Cities*. New York: Routledge.

Goldstein, Barbara. "Harvest the Sun." *Progressive Architecture* 63, no. 4 (1982).

Goldstein, Brian D. "'The Search for New Forms': Black Power and the Making of the Postmodern City." *Journal of American History* 103, no. 2 (2016): 375–99.

Hackworth, Jason. 2007. *The Neoliberal City: Governance, Ideology, and Development in American Urbanism*. Ithaca: Cornell University Press.

Hanlon, James. "Success by design: HOPE VI, new urbanism, and the neoliberal transformation of public housing in the United States." *Environment and Planning A* 42 (2010): 80–98.

"Hispanic Workers in Construction and Other Industries," The Center for Construction Research and Training, accessed September 1, 2019. www.cpwr.com.

Hondagneu-Sotelo, Pierrette. 2014. *Paradise Transplanted: Migration and the Making of California Gardens*. Berkeley: University of California Press.

Katz, Michael B. 2013. *The Undeserving Poor: America's Enduring Confrontation with Poverty*. Second Edition. New York: Oxford University Press.

Londoño, Johana. "Barrio Affinities: Transnational Inspiration and the Geopolitics of Latina/o Design." *American Quarterly*, vol. 66, no. 3 (2014).

———. "Barrio Affinities and the Diversity Problem." In *Abstract Barrios: Visualizing the Crises of Latinx Belonging in Cities*. Durham, NC: Duke University Press, 2020.

Macias, Eric. "Negotiating Citizenship: Undocumented (and Afraid), 'Drop-out,' and Serving Their Community." Paper presented at *The Society for Latin American and Caribbean Anthropology*, Santo Domingo, Dominican Republic, April 11–13, 2019.

Méndez, Michael. "Latino Lifestyle and the New Urbanism." Master's thesis, Massachusetts Institute of Technology, 2003.

Méndez, Michael Anthony. "Latino New Urbanism." In *Casa y Comunidad: Latino Home and Neighborhood Design*, edited by Henry G. Cisneros and John Rosales, 101–28. Washington, DC: Builder Books, 2006.

Nader, Laura. "Up the Anthropologist: Perspectives Gained from Studying Up." In *Reinventing Anthropology*, edited by Dell H. Hymes, 284–311. New York: Pantheon Books, 1972.

Ramos, George. "Drawing the Line: Planners Meld Activism, Urban Projects Incomplete Source." *Los Angeles Times*, June 5, 1988.

Rojas, James. "Latino Placemaking: How the Civil Rights Movement Reshaped East LA." Project for Public Spaces, March 4, 2014. https://www.pps.org/article/latino-placemaking-how -the-civil-rights-movement-reshaped-east-la.

Rojas, James. "The Enacted Environment: The Creation of 'Place' by Mexicans and Mexican Americans in East Los Angeles." Master's thesis, Massachusetts Institute of Technology, 1991.

U.S. Bureau of Labor Statistics, "Employed persons by detailed occupation, sex, race and Hispanic or Latino ethnicity." 2009 Annual Averages-Household Data-Tables from Employment and Earnings.

U.S. Department of Housing and Urban Development. *"Defensible Space" Deterring Crime and Building Community*, by Henry Cisneros. Washington, DC, January 1995.

Vazquez, Leonardo. "Lagging Behind: Ethnic Diversity in the Planning Profession in the APA New York Metro Chapter Area." 2001 *American Planning Association*. www.nyplanning.org.

Villa, Raúl Homero. 2000. *Barrio Logos: Space and Place in Urban Chicano Literature and Culture*. Austin, TX: University of Texas Press.

22

The Bronx in Focus

The Visual Politics of En Foco, Inc.

SEBASTIÁN PÉREZ

En Foco, Inc. was among the first organized arts collectives founded by Puerto Ricans dedicated to photography in New York City. It grew from a small collective of Puerto Rican photographers in the 1970s South Bronx to a cultural organization pushing at the boundaries of fine art and documentary photography and the inclusion of photographers of color in the mainstream art world throughout the late-twentieth century.[1] From 1974 onward, En Foco developed an antiracist aesthetic visual politics to organize photographers of color; provided a collective space for the critique, circulation, and promotion of their work; and sent out photographers to teach and work in their South Bronx communities. Collectively, En Foco's on-the-ground practices, gallery shows, and publications worked against mainstream art discourses that prioritized objectivity, rather illustrating that compelling, formally innovative, and beautiful photographic art could be and was made by the very photographers whose practice was informed by their experiences as minoritized subjects.

In this essay, I examine the emergence of En Foco and the radical potential of their position of being *in focus*. I turn to the visual economy of New York Puerto Rican visibility throughout the late twentieth century across the cultural industries from popular films to social scientific literature as a comparative lens from which to trace En Foco's visual politics. Insisting on seeing the mainstream representations of Puerto Ricans as a visual economy, I emphasize the differential currency of stereotypical imagery and its value in supporting a racist political order and worldview, particularly with respect to images of spectacle.[2] By centering En Foco's street galleries and visual literacy classes, as well as an overview of the organization's print culture manifested by their journal *Nueva Luz*, I underscore the point that the South Bronx became and remains a site for the differential articulation of a racialized and minoritized consciousness in support of a collective recognition of dignity for Puerto Ricans and Latinx subjects. This consciousness found its expressions and validity in the occurrences of everyday life in the barrio. En Foco mined this fertile ground to make art, an art whose roots lay in the collective communal struggles of communities in the Bronx, New York City's poorest and most stereotyped borough.

Such an aesthetic declaration ran counter to the ways in which the borough had been symbolized since the 1960s. By the time of En Foco's founding, the South Bronx had become synonymous with "urban crisis." A toxic alchemy of urban renewal policies and discriminatory municipal management called "Planned Shrinkage" imposed austerity on the borough. Officials suspended sanitation routes and shuttered firehouses. They laid the groundwork for the borough to burn. According to the data from the time period, the city closed seven fire companies in the South Bronx in 1968 while laying off thousands more firefighters and fire marshals as the 1970s wore on.[3] In just over ten years, seven different census tracts in the borough lost more than 97 percent of their buildings to fire and abandonment; 44 tracts lost more than 50 percent. Most of these census tracts were concentrated in the South Bronx.[4]

Simultaneously, the city's Puerto Rican population continued to expand and concentrated itself in its greatest numbers in these very South Bronx neighborhoods. Of the nearly one million Puerto Ricans residing in the city in 1970s, over a quarter called the Bronx home.[5] While the Puerto Rican population of Manhattan dropped by about twenty thousand inhabitants between 1970 and 1980, the Puerto Rican population of the Bronx grew, albeit marginally, to over 320,000 by the end of the decade.[6] As the borough burned, Puerto Ricans continued to make it their home. Historian Evelyn González puts individuals' commitments to staying in the South Bronx bluntly, stating, "People moved to the South Bronx out of necessity, not choice, often installed there by the welfare authorities. All who could move away did so."[7] Yet despite these conditions of privation, I look to En Foco as a site from which to reevaluate the totalizing negativity of these dire conditions for the borough's Puerto Ricans.

En Foco's Art Activist Practice

Three New York Puerto Rican photographers, Charles Biasiny-Rivera, Phil Dante, and Roger Cabán, founded En Foco in 1974, though its iteration as the not-for-profit national photographic arts organization under analysis in this essay did not take shape until 1978.[8] A federal Comprehensive Employment and Training Act (CETA) program, the largest federally funded arts program since the New Deal, allowed the group to set up shop in an off-campus building donated by Lehman College in the Bronx.[9] From here, the mission of the group coalesced. It began with the recruitment of Latinx artists to lead their photo-based instruction programs in two South Bronx public schools. By making themselves visible as mentors in the Puerto Rican and African American communities of the South Bronx, they utilized their En Foco Street Galleries and street portrait studios to exhibit their work, which contained the images of local families, friends, and community members.[10] This affirmation of the quotidian brought photographers like David González and Perla de León into spaces where the camera and the still image became technologies of an expansive visibility. This visibility did not shy away from the conditions of poverty and the degradation of the South Bronx built environment. It made room for moments of laughter, play, and intimacy whose texture made possible the survival and resilience of the Puerto Rican, African American, and West Indian communities archived within En Foco's rolls of film.

In this vein, En Foco chipped away at the gatekeeping of the formal art world, how its boundaries operated to keep a space like the South Bronx apart from and outside of the categories of mainstream artistic representation. En Foco recalibrated the spaces of the everyday to produce an alternative photographic vision of the creative energy being harnessed by ordinary residents of the borough to live and work toward a better community. Here I am thinking alongside, but slightly departing from, what Latinx and Latin American art, media, and cinema scholar Colin Gunckel has termed the "Chicano photographic," whereby the Chicana/o movement served as an organizing principle for viewing, interpreting, and archiving the expansive trove of images produced by Chicana/o photographers of protests, social gatherings, and public art projects in 1960s Southern California.[11] He illustrates just how critical a role photography played in the preservation of repertoires of protest and cultural survival for the Chicana/o movement and its numerous forms of representation from the site of the body, to street art, to print culture. My inquiry into the early history and social art practices of En Foco answers the natural follow-up question to the motivations of Gunckel's project: How do we understand photography produced by and about Latinx subjects in the absence of a coherent social movement, photography that dwells in the daily lives of people who do not enact the prototypical poses of protest and resistance for the lens?[12] As hinted at by the very name of the organization and its journal, En Foco and *Nueva Luz* suggest a renewed vision for both seeing and enacting what historian Lorrin Thomas has referred to as a "politics of recognition" for the diasporic Puerto Rican residents of New York City.[13] However, it was on the streets of the South Bronx where this vision took place.

En Foco published its debut biannual photography journal in 1985. Entitled *Nueva Luz*, its name complemented the *in-focus* mission of the organization. The journal's style and from, using news print and in the format of a tabloid newspaper, adapted the aesthetics of photojournalism, questioning the claims to the "truth" of the newspaper. As both a form of news and an art publication, it blurred the lines between the journalistic and the aesthetic, possibly closing the distance between "truth" and fabrication whose very tension produces the shaky ground upon which photographic critique attempts to solidify. Read from the perspective of theorist Walter Benjamin, perhaps this type of mechanical reproduction of art could infiltrate and coopt the mainstream forms of news and perhaps lay greater claim to its subjects "aura," the representation of people, places, and things typically outside the realm of accurate representation.[14]

In choosing a name in Spanish, En Foco made itself intelligible to community members who only or primarily spoke Spanish and resisted the desires for English-language dominance expressed by those anxious about the failure to incorporate Puerto Ricans into the body politic of the United States. This connection of the visual with the linguistic aligned En Foco's work with the histories of Puerto Rican and Latinx organizing around education since their arrival to the city. Symbolized most notably by the work of the feminist educator, social worker, and activist figure of Antonia Pantoja, alongside organizations like the NAACP, they contested the discriminatory practices of the United States education system for decades, calling for bilingual education and a shift in state and municipal funding to support the infrastructure of schools in the so-called "inner city."[15] En Foco's occupation of two South Bronx public schools for their visual literacy classes is part of this larger history in which Puerto Rican organizations such as ASPIRA, founded in 1961, focused on training young people in leadership and community organizing. Beyond the neighborhoods of New York City, the neoconservative turn in US American politics symbolized by necessitated for Latinx service, arts, and educational organizing. As art critic and writer Lucy Lippard shared in *Nueva Luz*'s twenty-fifth anniversary commemorative issue, "Artists were inspired by the repressions and racism of the Reagan-Bush administration to fight back and start new groups. Central America was a preeminent issue, which served to jolt Latino photographers in particular . . . At the same time, photography was taking on a new role in the art world . . . the medium that most closely parallels the activist impulse."[16] En Foco activated this impulse to train young people and Latinx community members in the critical function of seeing differently, of using the visual to translate their experiences and make sense of their world outside of the mechanisms that sowed hopelessness into the fabric of neighborhoods like the South Bronx.

The Visual Economy of Puerto Rican Visibility in New York City

"*NOT* West Side Story," commented Charles Biasiny-Rivera when reflecting on the founding and original mission of En Foco.[17] In an article celebrating the organization's thirty-fifth anniversary, Biasiny-Rivera incisively articulated the stakes of cultural representation at En Foco's inception in the mid-1970s and its inherent links to space and place in the city.

This time is perhaps most well known, at least with respect to Puerto Ricans, for Rita Moreno's Academy Award–winning performance as Anita in the 1961 film adaptation of *West Side Story*. The popularized lyrics of Anita's signature performance of "America" in which she laments Puerto Rico's poor economy and exponentially growing population, gained academic traction in Oscar Lewis's National Book Award–winning sociological text *La Vida: A Puerto Rican Family in the Culture of Poverty—San Juan and New York* published in

1967.[18] In the sphere of popular music, salsa exploded with remarkable popularity as the Fania All Stars sold out clubs and dance halls while salsa boomed out beyond Manhattan as a globalized musical and dance practice. These contending and often contradictory modes of representation of New York Puerto Ricans relied on the visual and/or cinematic image to convey their symbolic value and meaning, or perhaps their lack of meaning, in a turbulent time for the city.

With respect to *La Vida*, Oscar Lewis's 1966 article in *Scientific America* entitled "The Culture of Poverty" predates the publication of the book. It uses photography as visual evidence of Puerto Ricans' supposed location within a culture of poverty that is defined both racially and spatially. A photograph foregrounds the slums of San Juan against the backdrop of modern apartment and office buildings in another segment of the city. Another presents aerial shots of San Juan and El Barrio in a visual hierarchy that supports the assertion that Puerto Ricans belong to a separate culture and geography, that they remain, despite migration to the city, as unassimilable and problematic subjects.[19] On one of the only pages where actual people are photographed, an image of Puerto Rican boys playing in an Upper East Side Manhattan schoolyard, the caption reads, "The culture of poverty does not cherish childhood as a protected and prolonged part of the lifestyle."[20] The circulation of these portraits of unruly Puerto Rican bodies made Puerto Ricans hypervisible for all of the wrong reasons, as a cultural problem at the end of the 1960s.

With respect to the prevailing salsa boom, Puerto Ricans would become recognizable for libidinal excess as desirable and performative bodies preserved in films like *Our Latin Thing* (1972) or in the coverage of the Fania All-Stars sell-out concert in Yankee Stadium in 1973.[21] From *West Side Story* and the Fania All-Stars to the Culture of Poverty thesis, image and narrative worked together to distinguish New York Puerto Ricans as "other" and dissonant, while reifying them as commodified cultural beings, readily extractable from the discourses of rights and citizenship.

Biasiny-Rivera's directive that opens this section invites the question of where to shift our gaze(s). If not toward *West Side Story* and its affiliated forms of popular culture, then where? Where might we look for alternative renderings of the Puerto Rican experience in New York City? En Foco grounded it early mission by focusing their gaze on the Puerto Rican communities of the Bronx and New York City at large, toward themselves. As Biasiny-Rivera himself wrote, "We started out as a few New York-Puerto Rican photographers, displaying our work at block parties in the South Bronx. The initial reason we formed En Foco was that we noticed that we were not visible as Puerto Rican photographers. So we decided to make ourselves visible by organizing exhibitions and creating events. We were interested in *identifying ourselves to ourselves*" (italics mine). [22] His reflections speak to the underlying sense of alienation experienced by Puerto

Figure 22.1. Photograph of Perla de León teaching young boys to use a camera, David González, Fall 1979.

Rican photographers in the struggle to gain even the most basic sense of visibility, that of self-recognition.

The Street Gallery and Visual Literacy

A critical component of En Foco's early life in the 1970s were its street galleries and visual literacy classes.[23] As previously mentioned, photographer Perla de León taught young people how to use cameras and to make images in the classrooms of South Bronx public schools (Figure 22.1). The street galleries took this pedagogical imperative to the street, where community members could see themselves on En Foco's mobile wall installations. They likewise offered lessons on instant camera photography in street studios, which they would erect on opposite ends of streets during block parties. Following sociologist Avery Gordon, these image-making practices hold space for the *complex personhood* inherent in their subjects, a reminder "that even those who live in the most dire circumstances possess a complex and oftentimes contradictory humanity and subjectivity that is never adequately glimpsed by viewing them as victims or, on the other hand, as superhuman agents."[24] She suggests that an appropriate way to view or to see complexly is to mediate between the grotesque and abstract, to play with the focus.

David González's portrait of several Bronx boys, entitled *Pistoleros*, emblematizes the complexities of the in-focus work enacted by Puerto Rican photographers affiliated with En Foco (Figure 22.2). Taken in August of 1979 in the Mott Haven section of the Bronx, only several blocks south of the most dev-astated area in the borough, the boys clamor among each other to be in the frame and show off their water pistols, of which they are clearly proud.[25] Faces, eyes, hands, and water guns predominate as the in-focus elements of the image, the depth of field of González's camera rendering the background of the street fair occupying this particular thoroughfare in the neighborhood blurry. For a place infamous for its degradation, to soften the built environment of the South Bronx in this image is to deny its power to overdetermine the lives of its inhabitants and specifically of those in the frame of the photograph. Each with his finger on the trigger of their plastic pistols, they pose with a raucous humor.

Gun, face, gun, face and gun, face . . . the image juxtaposes humanity with instruments of death placing them on similar planes as the tips of guns meet eyes and vice versa. It is evident that the guns are toys, their translucency apparent as their water levels can be accounted for in the gradations of contrast within the photograph. The visual interruption of the guns may obscure the real intimacy at play between these kids with their curly hair and arms interlocked, and it is this very tension between intimacy and violence in which the photograph sits and occupies. Recalling the 2014 case of Tamir Rice when police or the state see toy guns as evidence enough to shoot and kill, this image takes on a spectral quality made all the more intense by the multiplicity of gazes and sightlines made mani-fest by this collective of boys.[26]

Figure 22.2. *Pistoleros*, David González, August 1979.

To make such an image, González had to crouch down and be level with his subjects, rather than photograph at a downward angle to cast the instrument of the camera as a technology of power and surveillance, perhaps evident of the training he received as a photographer for En Foco. He also had to get close to them, eschewing the possibility of zoom, to create such a crisp depth of field that focuses our attention on the hailing at play in the image. The majority of the boys appear to perform for the camera, perhaps loosened into silliness by the intimacy between photographer and subject, between Puerto Rican young man and Puerto Rican boy. Yet one boy hails back, his gaze piercing the frame of the photograph, even-keeled and intense. Electric eyes emphasized by the precise reflection within his pupils, he seems to issue a challenge for how we might read him and imagine him alongside his friends. Do you see a gang? Are you frightened? Or do you see me? *Can* you see me? Can you imagine my future? Adorned with rosary beads, he takes on a simultaneous elegiac and wondrous character, endowed with a spirit that holds a consciousness of this South Bronx world that abounded with life when many were consigned to a premature death.

These boys and numerous other people, families, friends are preserved in the film of En Foco's photographers, many of which have only been in circulation for the past decade. Although the subjects and communities rendered remain precarious, the conditions of possibility made manifest by the social life of photography in the South Bronx of the late 1970s can serve as a starting point for considering alternative narratives beyond the frame that allows us to *see* rather than simply *look* at the people who comprise our families and reside in our neighborhoods. Writing about these tenuous possibilities in the photo essay in which *Pistoleros* appears, González states,

> The children we encountered that day were like so many others from those years. They would ask—if not demand—that you take their picture. They all had their poses, filled with mock bravado or impish charm.
>
> I have no idea what became of them. Maybe the boys got caught up in the insane violence that swept the area when crack wars broke out on those same streets, riddling hallways and passers-by with volleys of bullets. Maybe the girls became mothers before they became high school graduates.
>
> Then again, maybe not.[27]

The Print Culture of *Nueva Luz*

Tracing the genealogy of *Nueva Luz* and those of several of the hundreds of photographers featured within its pages for its over thirty-year print run quite literally illuminates and expands the spaces considered peripheral to not only the mainstream art world but also to Latinx cultural production, especially as it emerged in the 1970s and 1980s. *Nueva Luz* sutures the photographic with the literary as a mobile text designed to circulate beyond the streets and interiors of the organization's aesthetic practices in the South Bronx. En Foco's use of a renewed light within the context of the South Bronx's visuality in the 1970s is suggestive of the need for a new vision of the borough and its people. For a place such as the South Bronx to be the center of an imaginary of urban blight, a condition that could be described as a particular kind of overexposure, divergent formal choices about the production of alternative images became necessary as matter of artistic necessity and community survival. Whereas En Foco endeavored to sharpen the focus of an emergent class of multiethnic photographers and teach communities the science of seeing differently, *Nueva Luz* provided the location within which those visions could exist as *art*, the street gallery made material. Overexposed as a harrowing caricature of the urban and awash in the firelight of burning buildings, the desire for a new type of light to organize, collect, and curate images from a position of difference coalesced in the form of *Nueva Luz*.

Within the frames or planes of vision of society, we can understand light as illuminating what is within the visual field that the light touches, while the ideas that structure what appears to be more visible cover certain spaces in darkness. That darkness is treated as a fascination, a locus of desire to see that and those placed in sparsely lit realms, lightly touched by the modern but without a place within that frame. If Latinxs, Black peoples, Asian Americans, and Native Americans are indeed at the margins of this plane of vision, the new light of photography in the hands of those subjects works to uncover the potential of those spaces for revising the terms upon which mainstream ways of looking have operated. And if the study of Latinx photography has remained "peripheral" to the "marginality" of their place within the body politic of the United States, to borrow the words of Silvio Torres-Saillant, *Nueva Luz* mines that peripherality as a sight of an alternative aesthetics that can hold multiplicity and relationality among and between mediums within its pages.[28] Given that art galleries and art markets remained closed to these photographers, the politics at the core of *Nueva Luz* opened up a space for the needed conversation between artists sharing their subaltern status as racial, ethnic, and linguistic others in the United States.

Speaking of *Nueva Luz*'s first issues, specifically its premier issue in Winter 1985 and its second issue in Winter 1986, the curatorial choices of the photographers featured belie the foundational geographies and multiethnic solidarities of the Bronx-born publication and its New York Puerto Rican editorial team. The first issue featured the Puerto Rican woman portraitist Sophie Rivera, the Cuban photographer Tony Mendoza, and Japanese American photographer Kenro Izu, whose landscape and ruin photography of Egypt and Mexico found compelling analogue in the scarred terrain of the South Bronx. The Winter Issue of 1986 ran Coreen Simpson's portrait *Barry* on its cover, and its three featured photographers were all Black and African American.[29] Given that anti-blackness in the Puerto Rican and Latinx community is something ever present but rarely discussed, *Nueva Luz* confronted these tacit issues of racial discrimination and black erasure by making black art visible and present at the grassroots level. According to *Nueva Luz*'s associate editor, Betty Wilde-Biasiny, the journal was the among the first homes for some of the most successful and notable photographers and critics of color, writing "For Carrie Mae Weems, Dawoud Bey, Albert Chong, Héctor Méndez-Caratini and numerous others, publication in *Nueva Luz* predated their eventual mainstream recognition."[30] Perhaps a radical move for a bilingual publication at the time, *Nueva Luz* often featured black photographers and images of black daily life critiqued by Puerto Rican editors or alongside Latinx photographers.

Nueva Luz's multiracial visual politics set it apart from other photographic publications at the time. It existed at the vanguard of circulating images of daily life for peoples of color across the United States, with the Bronx as a critical node in the circulation and production of such images. The African American artist and photography scholar Deborah Willis, who served as a guest editor for *Nueva Luz*, writes, "Publications like the *Black Photographer's Annual* and En Foco's *Nueva Luz* were established to inform their own communities as well as the larger public about the works of photographers of color. To most Americans, these various posed images of black Americans were virtually unknown."[31] Of the radical reorientation of visions that *Nueva Luz* participate in, she goes on to note how "for years, images depicting black life were virtually nonexistent outside black communities . . . The photographic image played a key role in shaping black people's ideas about themselves and was considered as powerful as the written word to persuade the American public to change their notions about race and equality."[32] Throughout its print run and continuing today, *Nueva Luz* remained committed to creating spaces for aesthetic solidarities to form between artists and communities of color. Blackness and everyday life became critical sites of articulation for a visual politics that revised the critique and production of fine art photography. The pages of *Nueva Luz* worked against hierarchies, placing the work of photographers of color in relation to arrive at a sharper critique and enunciation of power expressed through visual mediums.

The twenty-fifth anniversary commemorative issue of *Nueva Luz*, which debuted in 2001, stands out among their journals for its aesthetics and contextualization of En Foco's worked since its founding in the 1970s. This edition temporarily diverged from the periodical form of previously published volumes and issues of *Nueva Luz*, which was made possible by a major grant from the Rockefeller Foundation, the New York City Department of Cultural Affairs Challenge Grant, the National Endowment for the Arts, and the New York State Council on the Arts. En Foco's recognition in these circles of arts funding spoke to its longstanding role in reshaping the art world from the grassroots.

For the first time, this issue of *Nueva Luz* featured high-gloss reproductions of work from some of the journals' most notable photographers and artists since it debuted in 1984. Staying true to its Puerto Rican roots, the cover featured a mixed media collage of Afro-Puerto Rican and Nuyorican artist Juan Sánchez, entitled *Victoria de Samotracia (Afro-Taína)* from 2000. For only fifteen dollars, the journal mimics the form of expensive and difficult to access fine art texts that appear on the shelves of museum gift shops for more than triple that cost.

Within its pages, notable art historians, critics, and photographic practitioners offer in-depth perspectives on the role of En Foco and *Nueva Luz* in the visual arts. From fine art and abstract photography to documentary images in black and white and others in full color, the issue presents the work of such notable photographers and artists as Albert Chong, Frank X. Méndez, Sophie Rivera, Laura Aguilar, Graciela Iturbide, Dawoud Bey, and Adal Maldonado. Its existence as a material artifact is representative of a coming out moment for En Foco and *Nueva Luz* anticipating the journal's eventual shift to a full-gloss production in the mid-2000s. Currently, *Nueva Luz*'s issues from 2004 to the present can be accessed online through En Foco's online archive and website. Over the course of its print run since 1984, the price for a single issue has only increased by twelve dollars. It remains accessible and dedicated to continuing foster alliances through aesthetics between communities of color and to dignifying the creative capacities of artists and the places from which they create. And it's still from the South Bronx.

En Foco's street galleries, visual literacy classes, and print culture expand the archive of Puerto Rican cultural production from New York City, which has primarily been traced through literature, poetry, and theater within Puerto Rican and Latinx Studies over the last twenty years. In accounting for the South Bronx as site of emergence and coherence for a visual politics oriented toward racial solidarity and focused on the daily lives of Latinx and Afro-Latinx individuals, families, and communities, the work of En Foco counteracts the totalizing narratives that have rendered the South Bronx as an irredeemable slum since the fires of the 1970s. Their pedagogical and artistic lenses serve as aesthetic interruptions to a racialized urban power that has historically looked to surveille and incarcerate rather than serve and support. By elevating daily life and creating a platform for photographers of color since the 1970s, En Foco reveals the centrality of the visual arts and photography to how communities of color communicate and participate in practices that dignify their places within the world. From the streets of the South Bronx to the pages of *Nueva Luz*, we bear witness to the fertile spaces of the still image, its creation and composition revealing far more complexity for the Latinx subjects within and beyond the frame.

NOTES

1   *En Foco's Street Gallery*, 1978, https://enfoco.org.

2   Krista Thompson's discussion of the visual economy of images in colonial and contemporary Jamaica provide the schematic for how I work with images of Puerto Rican "hypervisibility" in New York City. Her insight on the *value* of images of black servitude in their support of a white, colonizing, and touristic gaze is especially important for analyzing the circulation of images and their representational politics in their association with dominant narratives of power and subjectivity. See Thompson, "Introduction," in *An Eye for the Tropics* (Durham: Duke University Press, 2006).

3   Jeff Chang, *Can't Stop Won't Stop: A History of the Hip-Hop Culture* (New York: St. Martin's Press, 2005), 14.

4   The burnings are visualized in a hauntingly beautiful map drawn by the cartographer Molly Roy. The areas of darkest red and orange illustrate that those areas experienced nearly 75 to 100 percent housing stock loss. See Molly Roy, *Burning Down and Rising Up: The Bronx in the 1970s*. Nonstop Metropolis: A New York City Atlas, www.mroycartography.com.

5   Evelyn González, *The Bronx* (New York: Columbia University Press, 2006), 110, 113.

6   Maurice Carroll, "Migration Change by Puerto Ricans," *New York Times*, December 12, 1982, sec. N.Y. / Region, www.nytimes.com.

7   González, *The Bronx*, 121.

8   Charles Biasiny-Rivera, "Editorial," *Nueva Luz* 7, no. 2, Commemorative Issue (2001): 4.

9   Ibid.

10 Ibid.

11 Colin Gunckel's, "The Chicano/a Photographic: Art as Social Practice in the Chicano Movement," *American Quarterly* 67, no. 2 (June 11, 2015): 377–412.

12 This question is motivated by visual culture scholar Tina Campt's provocations to think about how diasporas settle. She writes, "For although it begins with migration or displacement from a home elsewhere, diaspora *is not* an endless trajectory that perpetually overwrites its arrival *somewhere*." Dwelling then becomes a distinct form settlement with its own conditions for visibility. See Tina M. Campt, "Family Matters: Diaspora, Difference, and the Visual Archive," *Social Text* 27, no. 1 98 (March 1, 2009): 83–114.

13 Puerto Rican demands for "recognition" emerged consistently in the 1960s. For Puerto Ricans, such claims are inherently tied to the ongoing colonial status of the island and the colonial conditions of Puerto Rican migration to the United States. It is precisely this call for "recognition" that delimits the promises of citizenship and places Puerto Rican activism within larger world historical discourses of human rights and dignity since the 1960s. See Lorrin Thomas, *Puerto Rican Citizen: History and Political Identity in Twentieth-Century New York City* (Chicago: University of Chicago Press, 2010), 5.

14 See "Art in the Age of Mechanical Reproduction" in Walter Benjamin, *Illuminations* (New York: Schocken, 2007).

15 For an account of Dominican educational organizing and protest in New York City, see Jesse Hoffnung-Garskof, *A Tale of Two Cities: Santo Domingo and New York after 1950* (Princeton: Princeton University Press, 2010); for a comprehensive historical overview of the struggles that animated African American and Puerto Rican social justice organizing, see Sonia Song-Ha Lee, *Building a Latino Civil Rights Movement: Puerto Ricans, African Americans, and the Pursuit of Racial Justice in New York City* (Chapel Hill: The University of North Carolina Press, 2014); Chapter 5 of *Puerto Rican Citizen* historicizes Puerto Rican student and educational activism see Lorrin Thomas, *Puerto Rican Citizen: History and*

Political Identity in Twentieth-Century New York City (Chicago: University of Chicago Press, 2010).

16 Lucy R. Lippard, "Contact Lenses, Corrected Vision," *Nueva Luz* 7, no. 2, Commemorative Issue (2001): 19.

17 "Changing the Art World, One Image and Viewer at a Time: En Foco Inc.'s Thirty-Fifth Anniversary," September 11, 2009, https://enfoco.org.

18 Silver Screen Collection, *Rita Moreno, West Side Story*, January 1, 1961, Moviepix, www.gettyimages.com.

19 Oscar Lewis, "The Culture of Poverty," *Scientific American* 215, no. 4 (1966): 20, 22, 24.

20 Ibid, 24.

21 Marisol Negrón, "Fania Records and Its Nuyorican Imaginary: Representing Salsa as Commodity and Cultural Sign in Our Latin Thing," *Journal of Popular Music Studies* 27, no. 3 (September 21, 2015): 274–303.

22 "Changing the Art World, One Image and Viewer at a Time."

23 David González, *Untitled*, 1979, Photograph, Slide 1 of 9, "From the Archive: Bronx Street Art," https://lens.blogs.nytimes.com.

24 Avery F. Gordon, *Ghostly Matters: Haunting and the Sociological Imagination* (Minneapolis: University of Minnesota Press, 2008), 4.

25 David González, *Pistoleros*, 1979, https://loeildelaphotographie.com.

26 In 2012, twelve-year-old Tamir Rice was shot and killed by police officer in a park in Cleveland, OH. He was playing with a toy gun. As a black boy playing with a fake gun in a public space, those who called 911 in addition to the police officer who shot Rice twice in the chest acted upon the too-easy racist association of blackness with criminality, blackness as a threat to life. See Damon Young, "12 Year Old Killed By Police; Darren Wilson Preps For TV Interview," Very Smart Brothas, accessed September 9, 2019, https://verysmartbrothas.theroot.com.

27 David González, "In the Bronx, Capturing Beauty in the Bad Old Days of 1979," *The New York Times*, August 21, 2009, sec. N.Y. / Region, www.nytimes.com.

28 Silvio Torres-Saillant, "La Literatura Dominicana En Los Estados Unidos y La Periferia Del Margen," *Cuadernos de Poetica*, no. 21 (1993): 7–26.

29 Coreen Simpson, *Barry*, 1985, in *Nueva Luz* 1, no. 2, featured photograph on cover.

30 Betty Wilde-Biasiny, "Introduction," *Nueva Luz* 7, no. 2, Commemorative Issue (2001): 7.

31 Willis, "Photography and Black America," 61.

32 Ibid.

BIBLIOGRAPHY

Campt, Tina M. "Family Matters: Diaspora, Difference, and the Visual Archive." *Social Text* 27, no. 1 (98) (March 1, 2009): 83–114.

Carroll, Maurice. "Migration Change by Puerto Ricans." *New York Times*, December 12, 1982, sec. N.Y. / Region. www.nytimes.com.

Chang, Jeff. 2005. *Can't Stop Won't Stop: A History of the Hip-Hop Culture*. New York: St. Martin's Press.

"Changing the Art World, One Image and Viewer at a Time: En Foco Inc's Thirty-Fifth Anniversary," September 11, 2009. https://enfoco.org.

González, David. "In the Bronx, Capturing Beauty in the Bad Old Days of 1979." *New York Times*, August 21, 2009, sec. N.Y. / Region. www.nytimes.com.

González, Evelyn. 2006. *The Bronx*. New York: Columbia University Press.

Gordon, Avery F. 2008. *Ghostly Matters: Haunting and the Sociological Imagination*. Minneapolis: University of Minnesota Press.

Gunckel, Colin. "The Chicano/a Photographic: Art as Social Practice in the Chicano Movement." *American Quarterly* 67, no. 2 (June 11, 2015): 377–412.

Hoffnung-Garskof, Jesse. 2010. *A Tale of Two Cities: Santo Domingo and New York after 1950.* Princeton: Princeton University Press.

Lee, Sonia Song-Ha. 2014. *Building a Latino Civil Rights Movement: Puerto Ricans, African Americans, and the Pursuit of Racial Justice in New York City.* Chapel Hill: The University of North Carolina Press.

Lippard, Lucy R. "Contact Lenses, Corrected Vision." *Nueva Luz* 7, no. 2, Commemorative Issue (2001).

Lewis, Oscar. "The Culture of Poverty." *Scientific American* 215, no. 4 (1966): 19–25.

Negrón Marisol. "Fania Records and Its Nuyorican Imaginary: Representing Salsa as Commodity and Cultural Sign in Our Latin Thing." *Journal of Popular Music Studies* 27, no. 3 (September 21, 2015): 274–303.

Roy, Molly. "Burning Down and Rising Up: The Bronx in the 1970s." Nonstop Metropolis: A New York City Atlas, n.d. www.mroycartography.com.

Thomas, Lorrin. 2010. *Puerto Rican Citizen: History and Political Identity in Twentieth-Century New York City.* Historical Studies of Urban America. Chicago: University of Chicago Press.

Thompson, Krista A. 2007. *An Eye for the Tropics: Tourism, Photography, and Framing the Caribbean Picturesque.* Durham: Duke University Press.

Torres-Saillant, Silvio. "La Literatura Dominicana En Los Estados Unidos y La Periferia Del Margen." *Cuadernos de Poetica*, no. 21 (1993): 7–26.

Walter Benjamin. 2007. *Illuminations.* New York: Schocken.

Wilde-Biasiny, Betty. "Introduction." *Nueva Luz* 7, no. 2, Commemorative Issue (2001).

Willis, Deborah. "Photography and Black America." *Nueva Luz* 7, no. 2, Commemorative Issue (2001).

Young, Damon. "12 Year Old Killed By Police; Darren Wilson Preps For TV Interview." Very Smart Brothas. Accessed September 9, 2019. https://verysmartbrothas.theroot.com.

Citizenship Subjects and "Illegality"

The sixth critical diálogo tackles a US discourse of "illegality," a politics of worthiness, and national belonging, as these condition the everyday routines and community practices of US-born Latinxs and Latin American and Caribbean populations. A guiding question for the critical diálogo in this section is: *What forms of self-fashioning become important survival strategies to challenge dominant narratives of "illegality" and criminality, and carve belonging and worthiness in contexts of social abandonment and differential inclusion?*

In this critical diálogo, Lisa Marie Cacho focuses on the devaluation of the racialized dead subject who fails to comply to neoliberal expectations, while Gina Pérez examines US citizenship practices and subjectivities through JROTC in predominantly Latinx public schools. Elena Machado Sáez, moreover, analyzes "worthiness" in Broadway theatrical representations of Latinx barrios like Washington Heights and US national patriotic figures like Alexander Hamilton. Finally, Elena Sabogal explores alternative connections between "illegality" and social class through the experiences of undocumented middle-class Peruvians immigrants in South Florida. Taken together, these essays show forms of agency and subjectivity within the constraints of US citizenship.

23

Racialized Hauntings of the Devalued Dead

LISA MARIE CACHO

On March 24, 2000, my cousin Brandon Jesse Martinez died in a car accident in San Diego, California. He was nineteen. When Brandon was alive, he frustrated teachers, counselors, employers, and even his friends and family. He took drugs sometimes, drank sometimes, and sometimes slept all day. He liked low-rider car culture and Tupac Shakur. He was quick witted and too clever, thoughtful and impulsive, well intentioned as well as reckless. His teachers thought he was "lazy" and a "troublemaker"; he proved them right by never graduating from high school. He lied on job applications and didn't pay his bills on time. He believed that one day he would go to prison even though he never planned to commit a criminal offense. He didn't donate his free time to religious or social activism. Instead, he smoked a lot, drank a lot, and joked a lot. These were the memories Brandon left me, his parents, his sister, and the others who loved him. They made it hard to share stories about him that didn't also characterize him as a "bad kid," a "deviant subject," or an "unproductive citizen."

Our conflicting memories and feelings about Brandon's "deviance" evoked deeply felt tensions at the memorial service and the gatherings afterward as we struggled but failed to ascribe value to Brandon's life and life choices. We were nostalgic for the days of his childhood, and we were very upset over losing his future and the person that he would never become. Our most recent memories— his teenage and young adult years—were shared in fragments with obvious omissions. For some of us, his death became the pretext for teaching moral lessons: Don't drink and drive. Go to school. Listen to your parents. Pray. These lessons attributed meaning and purpose to Brandon's death. His death could be instructive for his friends and cousins because for those he left behind "it was not too late." But these lessons also taught us to devalue his life because they were dependent upon understanding Brandon as an example never to emulate or imitate. His life was narrated as important because he provided us with a constructive model to evaluate, judge, and reject. The first line of a poem written by his sister Trisha Martinez echoed loudly, persistently, and honestly in the space of his haunting: "You just don't know how much he meant." In many ways, we didn't

Abridged reprint from: *Strange affinities: The gender and sexual politics of comparative racialization* (2011): 25–52.

because we didn't know how to valorize the choices we warned him not to make or how to value the life we told him not to live. How could we explain to others and ourselves "how much he meant" when his most legible asset was his death?

We couldn't translate his value into language. We couldn't talk about Brandon as valuable not only because he was marked as "deviant," "illegal," and "criminal" by his race and ethnicity but also because he did not perform masculinity in proper, respectable ways to redeem, reform, or counter his (racialized) "deviancy." Even if we had attempted to circumvent the devaluing processes of race and gender by citing other readily recognizable signs and signifiers of value, such as legality, heteronormativity, American citizenship, higher education, affluence, morality, or respectability, we still would not have had evidence to portray him as a productive, worthy, and responsible citizen. Ascribing social worth to the racially devalued *requires* recuperating what registers as "deviant" and "disreputable" because societal value is ascribed through explicitly or implicitly disavowing their relationships to the already devalued and disciplined categories of deviance and nonnormativity.

As Lindon Barrett reminds us, the "object" of value needs an "other" of value as its "negative resource."[1] The act of ascribing legible, intelligible, and normative value is inherently violent and relationally devaluing. To represent Brandon as the "object" of value, we would need to represent ourselves as the devalued "other." On some level, the *violence* of Brandon's death was perversely and disconcertingly a source of value for us because it valorized the life choices that each of us made but he did not. It naturalized how and why he died while simultaneously reaffirming our social worth and societal value. His violent death validated the rightness of our choices and the righteousness of our behaviors, thereby illustrating Lindon Barrett's insight that "relativities of value [are] ratios of violence."[2] Examining how "value" and its normative criteria are naturalized and universalized enables us to uncover and unsettle the heteropatriarchal, legal, and neoliberal investments that dominant and oppositional discourses share in rendering the value of nonnormativity illegible. Processes of valuation and devaluation are tangled, intersecting, differential, contingent, and relational. The choices we made to become valuable members of society validated U.S. society's exclusionary methods for assigning social value and worthlessness.

Although Brandon was disciplined by many of us many times, we never disowned, abandoned, or rejected him, so his absence left us raw and uncertain because the ready-made reasons for his death were hurtful and heartbreaking rather than healing. Hence, the empty space he left behind in each of us *necessarily destabilized* the binaries and hierarchies of value that formed the foundations for each of our lives. Brandon was profoundly valued, but we could not tell you why. Still empty, the space of his absence holds ruptural possibilities, where we must reckon with what has always been unthinkable.[3]

Wreck in the Road

When Brandon died in a car crash with his two friends, Vanvilay Khounborinh and William Christopher Jones, news media coverage of their accident criminalized them and the racial masculinities that they each embodied. They became part of the pre-existing news narrative that devalued their lives when they were alive. On March 25, 2000, the *San Diego Union-Tribune* printed an article about Brandon's car accident entitled, "Three Men Killed When Speeding Car Hits Trees; a Fourth Walks Away," with the subtitle, "Drinking Suspected; Auto Was Traveling without Headlights."[4] Journalist Joe Hughes described Vanvilay's driving as reckless and irresponsible joyriding and reported that witnesses corroborated police officers' suspicions that the car was "speeding and may have been racing other cars."[5] Vanvilay was driving Brandon's 1984 Mustang, which was not a racing car and, in fact, was not even a car that ran very well. It did not seem to matter to police, witnesses, or the reporter whether or not the examiner's report would reveal alcohol in Vanvilay's blood; even if he was not legally intoxicated, he was definitively represented as driving recklessly and (if not, then as if) drunk. The accident was framed as inevitable and deserved through construing their "illegal" behaviors (underage drinking and driving) as a daily pattern, connoting both immorality and criminality. As Hughes reported, "In addition [to detectives learning that the four had been drinking that evening], alcoholic containers and mixing beverages were found in the car's mangled remains."[6]

Oftentimes, "official" accounts of death and dying such as news media or police records do not acknowledge particular racialized tragedies in terms of collective loss. In fact, the deaths of Brandon, Vanvilay, and William Christopher were represented by the journalist as not-losses and not-tragedies through what Diana Taylor calls a "performance of explicit non-caring."[7] Not only was public sympathy for them not evoked, it was explicitly refused. This refusal compels us to juxtapose the limited "official" archive of the written, recorded accounts of their deaths with the ephemeral performances of their friends' and relatives' mourning, their explicit performances of love, care, and grief beyond words.

Privileging "anecdotal and ephemeral evidence," as José Esteban Muñoz explains, "grants entrance and access to those who have been locked out of official histories and, for that matter, 'material reality.'"[8] Brandon's friends and relatives created what Ann Cvetkovich calls "an archive of feeling," an archive constituted by the lived experiences of mourning and loss, ephemeral evidence that is now anecdotal.[9] It is an archive of the felt traces and sticky residue their deaths left behind in everyone's chests. These feelings were temporarily incarnated and took various visual forms: a roadside memorial, T-shirts, and the wrecked car. Witnesses would be left with fleeting imprints etched somewhere in their memories, raw material their unconscious might use for dreams. When the story about the value of lives cannot be told, the visual can be an alternative mode of expression. It is akin to the way in which Karla Holloway examines performances of mourning as central to African American culture. Holloway argues that "visual excess expressed a story that African America otherwise had difficulty illustrating—that these were lives of importance and substance, or that these were individuals, no matter their failings or the degree to which their lives were quietly lived, who were loved."[10]

While the official, limited archive of Brandon's death functioned primarily to repudiate him, this "archive of feeling" documented a different way to measure value. There was no attempt to make this grief universal, and, in fact, the particular and specific was all that mattered. His name was Brandon. He died in *this* car on *this* road. We created our own publics to witness our grief. In doing so, we resisted the erasure of our loved ones and made a statement: These were valuable young men and they are missed. Our audiences were not given the opportunity to ask why.

Soon after the crash, on the median of Calle Cristobal, friends and relatives erected a roadside memorial, overflowing with flowers, brightly lit by candles, and replete with personal messages, mementos, tributes, and items the deceased might need, such as rosaries, oranges, water, boxes of their favorite cigarettes, and cans of menudo. Brandon's sister, Trisha, attached her poem to the site's tree, the memorial's center, reminding us all of the need for alternative meaning-making at the base, or the core, of the tragedy: "You just don't know." Noticeable from both sides of the road, the makeshift memorial mourned and remembered Brandon, Vanvilay, and William Christopher, but it also functioned to reactivate the "scenario" of their deaths, forcing roadside spectators to become witnesses and participants.[11] This particular memorial was staged in such a way that pedestrians and drivers would have to actively and consciously not notice it. Because the memorial was located on the median of Calle Cristobal, people who wanted to contribute to it had to run across the road that claimed the young men's lives.

One of the young men's best friends, Shawn Essary, who declined to go out with them that night, created four hundred T-shirts and fifty caps in their memory. In his design three open roses are connected by thorny vines, symbols of love and death connected by the pointed pains of suffering, violence, and redemption (see figure 1). The shirts bear their pictures, birthdays, and death-day, and all the clothing is boldly underscored by "R.I.P." (see figure 2). Worn in public by the young men's family members and friends long after the funerals were over, the clothing unerased our racialized dead as our "other/ed" bodies helped Brandon, Vanvilay, and William Christopher transgress another border, the one between the living and the dead.

Figure 1: Front of T-Shirt. Photo by David Coyoca.

The roadside memorial and clothing were especially important in enabling friends of Brandon, Vanvilay, and William Christopher to participate directly in honoring their dead with dignity. Their friends had limited resources to express their grief and no control over the mourning rituals or funeral preparations and needed to negotiate the pain of losing three people all at once. Fusing three distinct religious and cultural backgrounds, they held their ceremonies in the middle of the road: It happened *here*. They used their bodies to display the communal tombstone that they would have written, walking around in silent protest: Our chests hurt *here* where Brandon, Vanvilay, and William Christopher Rest In Peace. They carried their grief heavy on their backs, like living altars with so much symbolism: I got your back.

Figure 2: Back of T-Shirt. Photo by David Coyoca.

The visual performance of explicit caring also was vital for my aunt and uncle, Christine and Jesse Martinez, Jr., who made brief appearances on the news and gave speeches at high schools. Saving the car in its wrecked form, they towed it to and erected it on several San Diego high school campuses. Their activism narrated Brandon's death as illogical and preventable, as tragic and avoidable. Rather than warning people *of* young men like Brandon, Vanvilay, and William Christopher, they cautioned young people *like* Brandon, Vanvilay, and William Christopher. They recognized that one's life circumstances can be unforgiving but never have to be all determining. Directing their rage and intense sadness into anti–drinking-and-driving activism ensured that Brandon's death had a purpose. They refused to let him die in vain, speaking their story and leaving behind his name like an echo. Here is the car, and this was his name. Perhaps at the next party their teenage audiences would attend, fleeting imprints of a wrecked car and a parent's tears might be resurrected, a reminder and a remainder: Hand over the keys.

This "archive of feeling" evidenced the human, familial, and social value of Brandon, Vanvilay, and William Christopher as their friends and family publicized their private pain. They were important alternative representations that helped us to mourn and work against the young men's absolute erasure. But Brandon's picture on a T-shirt, a poem by his sister, the red box of cigarettes he smoked, and a lonely funeral card were not enough pieces of his lost life to reassemble into a proper eulogy to tell *you* why he mattered, to tell you why you have lost out, too, because the life he led and the future he would have had were your loss, too. The emotive power of this archive of feeling also was limited precisely because it relied upon feeling; it was dependent upon grief and survival guilt. And it was all we had to ascribe value to Brandon; how much we hurt was evidence of how much he was valued.

Dead Ends and Detours

What we wanted to tell you was why Brandon was a valuable human being who did not deserve to die so young, and lacking a narrative that could convince others why Brandon mattered hurt us all. When he died, it seemed as if he did not hold the attitudes, values, desires, or work ethics that would have eventually enabled him to have a decent paying job that could take care of a future wife and future children in a nice suburban neighborhood. This "American Dream" framed how our middle-class, mixed-race families grieved. Because our parents, aunts, and uncles wanted this dream and this future for their children, Brandon was narrated as a bad example to follow but a good lesson to learn. We either devalued his life by demonizing the same "deviant" qualities we missed and mourned, or we harshly disciplined ourselves for not diverting his "delinquency" early enough.

We all wanted a better life for Brandon, but no one could guarantee it, and so his death also became understood and talked about as everyone else's private failures and the incomprehensible "will of God." I found myself wanting to argue with my family that the "inevitability" of Brandon's death could not be solely attributed to his decisions, the choices his parents made, the personal moments we each failed him, or God's will. Brandon could not be completely blamed for his decisions because there were so many options he never had and so many second chances he was never given. How could Brandon, his parents, or his friends and relatives be held accountable for making the "wrong" choices when the "right" opportunities never arose?

Weren't most resources withheld from Brandon, Vanvilay, and William Christopher? Economic restructuring and capital flight eradicated the blue-collar jobs that these young men did not have to go to the next morning.[12] Poorly funded schools in segregated communities provided them with inadequate educations to attend a four-year college.[13] Gang profiling marked them as potential criminals and gang members by law enforcement.[14] The widespread exploitation of both professional and unskilled immigrants makes it more profitable for companies to hire immigrants than to train the racialized working class.[15] The long history of U.S. militarism and imperialism in Asia, Latin America, Mexico, and Africa makes it more profitable for companies to relocate to countries economically devastated from structural adjustment policies because it is more profitable to exploit, abuse, and dehumanize racialized women and children in the global South than it is to pay decent salaries, provide insurance, and follow health and safety regulations at home.[16]

Brandon, Vanvilay, and William Christopher were surplus labor, not needed then, but presumably always already desperate enough to take a job. What they did in the meantime was live with their parents and sleep late in the morning. They drank beer while everyone else was sleeping and talked about dreaming their way out of their respective depressions, about how one day there would be a day when their lives would be different. Socializing over a few beers can be imagined as either an innocent, harmless recreational activity (e.g., after a long day at work) or an indicator of criminality. Which one is evoked depends on the color of your skin, your gender, your age, your drinking company, where you live, where you drink, and whether you have a job to go to the next day. Brandon, Vanvilay, and William Christopher were a racially mixed group of unemployed and insecurely underemployed young men of color (Chicano, Laotian, and African American, respectively) who were fostering their homosocial relationships with each other in a predominately middle-class suburban neighborhood. The recreational practices they shared as well as the individual work activities they lacked marked them all as "lazy" and "immoral," potentially "criminal," and always "illegal." When they died, their lives were not on the way to middle-class status, marriage, property ownership, or white-collar careers, and their (in)activities already fit a media and law enforcement profile that criminalizes Latino, Southeast Asian, and African American masculinities.[17] Read and represented as irresponsible and reckless, their social practices are rendered deviant, understood as needing discipline by the military or requiring punishment by and containment within the prison industrial complex. Could Brandon, Vanvilay, and William Christopher really be blamed for not making better decisions when the only institutions recruiting them were prison or the military?[18]

Before Brandon died, the story of racial exclusion and racial exploitation always seemed so sensible. For me, its primary purpose is to evoke sympathy for the people that many Americans are quick to devalue. This is not an easy task even though it seems as if it should be. To evoke public sympathy, we need to appeal to U.S. norms and values; doing so, however, requires obfuscating all the evidence that might suggest a person or population deserves devaluation if evaluated by those norms. This means re-presenting young men of color who lead unsympathetic lives—gang members, drug users, or risk-takers—as latent law-abiding, hard-working, family-oriented men who have been "unfairly" excluded from the resources and opportunities that would lead to responsible, normative choices. If we concede that economic opportunities will not necessarily integrate marginalized men of color into legal and moral economies, we run the risk of unwittingly validating conservative policies. In other words, to blame structural forces for Brandon's death requires that I take away his agency, so that I could represent him as an innocent and pure victim of a racist economy. To do so, I have to ignore his decision to not make decisions and erase his talent for choosing nonoptions.

It would be untrue to Brandon to script him as a victim who was unable to access a better life, so I tried to reimagine how his choices were empowering. I imagined that it was a form of empowerment for him to perform Mexican American masculinity through hip-hop music, lowered cars, and baggy clothes. Although his attitudes and his attire could sometimes be read as stereotypical, they could also be read as evidence of an "oppositional social identity."[19]

Performing racial masculinity could be read as a form of resistance if we read culture as political: "'Politics' must be grasped," as Lisa Lowe and David Lloyd assert, "as always braided within 'culture' and cultural practices."[20] Robin D. G. Kelley insists that reserving the category of "resistance" for activists, organizations, and leaders underestimates and depreciates everyday forms of resistance, such as strategies to subtly subvert exploitation or artistic approaches to reclaim and "redecorate" public space. Even though leisure activities are created for pleasure, they often become or can be read as "political" in relation to where and when they take place.[21] Intention doesn't always matter. Brandon didn't need to be devoted to radically progressive politics to be valued by the kinds of epistemologies that motivate anti-racist, anti-capitalist projects and scholarship.

Yet like the story of racial exclusion, the narrative of resistance wasn't quite the right analytical framework for making sense of Brandon's life. Although this perspective decriminalizes and depathologizes nonnormative racial masculinities, it ascribes value to his potential rather than his present. An effect of rereading Brandon's actions and attitudes as evidence of his potential to become an anti-capitalist, anti-racist "revolutionary-to-be" is that value can be attributed to him only by arbitrarily divorcing the person he was from the imagined, idealized person he could have been. What did it mean that I had to recast who he was into someone he might never have become in order to narrate him as someone who should be valued?

"A Politics of Deviance"

He was only nineteen. Sometimes, his age makes it difficult to ask the questions I have been asking. My analysis can seem imposing because, at nineteen, he was an unreliable predictor for the adult he might have been at age thirty-eight or sixty-two. But the expectations for the adult he was supposed to become not only disciplined him for most of his life; they also provided ways to measure his value after he died—as if "'living' is something to be *achieved* and not *experienced*."[22]

So much of life and its supposed "seminal" moments are organized according to the universalized expectations of the family and its gendered roles in naturalizing private property (buying your first home), wealth accumulation (passing down inheritance), and the pleasures of domestic consumption (planning weddings and baby showers). The milestones of heteronormative life that Brandon would never be able to experience rendered his life tragic. He would not have children to carry on his family's name, and his death deprived his parents and sister of significant life moments with him.

It is difficult to value Brandon by the quality of his life experiences when time and space are organized through heteronormativity and dictated by capital accumulation.[23] However, by situating him in a "queer time and place," we can find ways of being and frameworks for valuing that "challenge conventional logics of development, maturity, adulthood, and responsibility."[24] As Jack Halberstam argues, "Queer subcultures produce alternative temporalities by allowing their participants to believe that their futures can be imagined according to logics that lie outside of those paradigmatic markers of life experience—namely birth, marriage, reproduction, and death."[25] Denaturalizing (hetero)normative time, space, and the life achievements they universalize enables us to extend value to—or at least suspend judgment of—all kinds of people who live outside the logics of capital accumulation and bourgeois reproduction. A queer of color analysis makes sense of Brandon's life without condemning or celebrating who he was or who he could have been.

Imposing a normative framework onto Brandon's aspirations made his goals and desires difficult to decipher because he wanted to be unremarkable and live his life a little on the lazy side. He was only lackadaisically defiant, but we all read him as rebellious because he kept diligently deferring or sabotaging what was supposed to be his "American Dream." For example, before we found out that Brandon would not graduate from high school, he asked me to tutor him. We met once a week for a couple of months, but even though he was receiving A's and B's on the assignments we worked on together, his overall grades weren't improving. I explained that the tutoring would work only if he did his homework every day, not just once a week with me. He apologized for wasting my time, and our tutoring sessions stopped. It never crossed my mind to ask him why he wanted tutoring.

It was not until after he died that I realized he just wanted to talk. He talked about pressures to graduate, get a good job, move out of the house, and become responsible. He talked about how he thought the students at his high school racially segregated themselves voluntarily and how he and his few close friends of different colors didn't have a group to join, a place to fit. He talked about how police were always following him, and he told me about how he felt left out and left behind when his parents became part of the middle-class. We talked about wishing we knew our fathers' languages because we felt there were things our grandparents wanted to tell us that English could not communicate. We talked about growing up with white mothers and growing out of internalized racism. We talked about West Coast rap music and the different car cultures of Mexicans and Filipinas/os in Southern California. I talked about the future I wanted him to have: college, MEChA, and ethnic studies classes. He listened.

He told me he wanted to be a lifeguard in the first (and last) essay we worked on together in our study sessions. The assignment was to pick a career and research a path to achieve his goals. He decided he would like to be a lifeguard. It was an interesting choice because, at least the way I saw it, being a lifeguard would not change his life all that much. He wouldn't have much disposable income; he'd have to continue living at home; and the only upward mobility the job could offer was becoming a lifeguard II. This is why contextualizing Brandon's life choices through his exclusion from decent-paying blue-collar work is inadequate; it implies that access to good-paying jobs or higher education would have

Figure 23.1. T-Shirt commemorating Brandon, Chris, and Van. Photo credit to the author.

enabled him to make different choices. But as his essay on the future he would never have suggests, he didn't really want a nuclear family with a house in the suburbs. He might not have taken one of those decent-paying blue-collar jobs even if they were still available. At the same time, Brandon constructed himself not only as someone who was not productive but also as someone who was not useless: "I am not quite sure but when you save a person's life I bet it makes you feel very good inside that is something I could see myself doing. Plus just being around the water and people all the time seems like something good for me."[26] He didn't want to work to pull himself up a corporate ladder; he wasn't interested in raises or promotions. He wanted to spend his time on the beach, feeling good on the inside if someone needed help, feeling good on the outside when everyone was safe. He wanted to be accountable to everyone and responsible for everyone.

It was as if he followed a logic all his own—and maybe that was the tutoring lesson I was supposed to learn. Maybe I failed because I looked in all the wrong places to find methods, narratives, and strategies for ascribing social worth to his personhood, trying to make him fit into my over-researched reasons and rationales rather than making an effort to remember what he might have been trying to teach me.

I think he wanted to teach me how to make sense of what Cathy Cohen terms "a politics of deviance."[27] A politics of deviance makes sense of deviations from the norm differently rather than defensively. Such a politics would neither pathologize deviance nor focus most of its energies on trying to rationalize why people choose deviant practice over proper behavior. Rather than repudiating nonnormative behavior and ways of being, we would read nonnormative activities and attitudes as forms of "definitional power" that have the potential to help us rethink how value is defined, parceled out, and withheld.[28] Cohen argues that "ironically, through these attempts to find autonomy, these individuals, with relatively little access to dominant power, not only counter or challenge the presiding normative order with regard to family, sex, and desire, but also create new or counter normative frameworks by which to judge behavior."[29] Sometimes defiant or deviant practices critique the rules of normality but don't necessarily break them; they might direct us toward necessarily nonnormative criteria for recognizing social worth even if they don't model or theorize alternative ways of living.

Recuperating those deemed deviant means trying to make others' lives more acceptable and sympathetic, but *reckoning* with those who live in the spaces of social death means individually changing ourselves and collectively changing the world that made us all. As Avery Gordon writes, "Reckoning is about knowing what kind of effort is required to change ourselves and the conditions that make us who we are, that set limits on what is acceptable and unacceptable, on what is possible and impossible."[30] Brandon's unintelligible ethics of deviance might be neither unapologetically normative nor radically transformative, but it is definitely a way of living that interrogates and elucidates how normative understandings of morality and ethicality may sometimes mitigate oppositional politics and scholarship. When we take Brandon and others like him seriously, we are expected to suspend judgment of those who choose to drive down fatal roads because there is value as well as apprehension in taking risks and living differently—even if it means actively, accidentally, and unthinkably leaving the

Figure 23.2. Image of Brandon, Chris, and Van. Photo credit to the author.

rest of us behind, empty and haunted. As Rubén Martínez reminds us, "The road may kill us in the end, but it's also the only way to get to where we're going."[31]

NOTES

1 Lindon Barrett, *Blackness and Value: Seeing Double* (Cambridge: Cambridge University Press, 1999), 19, 21.

2 Ibid., 28.

3 Avery F. Gordon, *Ghostly Matters: Haunting and the Sociological Imagination* (Minneapolis: University of Minnesota Press, 1997), 202.

4 Joe Hughes, "Three Men Killed when Speeding Car Hits Trees; a Fourth Walks Away," *San Diego Union-Tribune*, March 25, 2000.

5 Ibid.

6 Ibid.

7 Diana Taylor, *The Archive and the Repertoire: Performing Cultural Memory in the Americas* (Durham: Duke University Press, 2003), 147.

8 José Esteban Muñoz, "Ephemera as Evidence: Introductory Notes to Queer Acts," *Women and Performance: A Journal of Feminist Theory* 8, no. 2 (1996): 9.

9 Ann Cvetkovich, *An Archive of Feelings: Trauma, Sexuality, and Lesbian Public Cultures* (Durham: Duke University Press, 2003).

10 Karla F. C. Holloway, *Passed On: African American Mourning Stories: A Memorial* (Durham: Duke University Press, 2003), 181.

11 Taylor, *The Archive and the Repertoire*, 33.

12 Mike Davis, *Prisoners of the American Dream: Politics and Economy in the History of the U.S. Working Class* (London: Verso, 1986), 208; Manuel Castells, *The Informational City: Information Technology, Economic Restructuring, and the Urban-Regional Process* (Oxford, UK: Blackwell, 1989), 308; Masao Miyoshi, "'Globalization,' Culture, and the University," in *The Cultures of Globalization*, ed. Fredric Jameson and Masao Miyoshi (Durham: Duke University Press, 1998), 255.

13 Jonathan Kozol, *Savage Inequalities: Children in America's Schools* (New York: HarperPerennial); Clarence Y.H. Lo, *Small Property Versus Big Government* (Berkeley and Los Angeles: University of California Press); Gary Orfield, Susan E. Eaton, and Elaine R. Jones, *Dismantling Desegregation: The Quiet Reversal of Brown v. Board of Education* (New York: New York University Press).

14 Richard T. Rodríguez, "On the Subject of Gang Photography," *Aztlán: A Journal of Chicano Studies* 25, no. 1 (2000): 109–143; Edward J. Escobar, *Race, Police, and the Making of a Political Identity: Mexican Americans and the Los Angeles Police Department, 1900–1945* (Berkeley: University of California Press, 1999); Jerome G. Miller, *Search and Destroy: African-American Males in the Criminal Justice System* (Cambridge: Cambridge University Press, 1997).

15 Philip L. Martin, "The United States: Benign Neglect toward Immigration," in *Controlling Immigration: A Global Perspective*, ed. Wayne A. Cornelius, Philip L. Martin, and James Hollifield (Stanford: Stanford University Press, 1994), 94.

16 Bello, *Dilemmas of Domination*.

17 Herman Gray, *Watching Race: Television and the Struggle for "Blackness"* (Minneapolis: University of Minnesota Press, 1995); Tang, "Collateral Damage"; Rodríguez, "On the Subject of Gang Photography."

18 Jorge Mariscal, "Military Targets Latinos: Tracked into Combat Jobs," *War Times / Tiempo de Guerras*, November 2003, 3, www.war-times.org/issues/13art5.html; Jorge Mariscal, "The Future for Latinos in an Era of War and Occupation," *CounterPunch*, April 18, 2003, www.counterpunch.org/mariscal04182003.html; *Population Representation in the Military Services: Fiscal Year 2002* (Washington, DC: Department of Defense, 2004), Appendix B-25, Appendix B-30. *California Prisoners and Parolees 2009* (Sacramento: California Department of Corrections and Rehabilitation, 2010), 19.

19 Beverly Daniel Tatum, *"Why Are All the Black Kids Sitting Together in the Cafeteria?" A Psychologist Explains the Development of Racial Identity*, 5th ed. (New York: Basic Books, 2003), 61.

20 Lisa Lowe and David Lloyd, "Introduction," in *The Politics of Culture in the Shadow of Capital*, ed. Lisa Lowe and David Lloyd (Durham: Duke University Press, 1997), 26.

21 Robin D.G. Kelley, *Race Rebels: Culture, Politics, and the Black Working Class* (New York: Free Press, 1994), 47, 166.

22 Sharon Patricia Holland, *Raising the Dead: Readings of Death and (Black) Subjectivity* (Durham: Duke University Press, 2000), 16.

23 Judith (Jack) Halberstam, *In a Queer Time and Place: Transgender Bodies, Subcultural Lives* (New York: New York University Press, 2005). As Halberstam explains, "queer temporality disrupts the normative narratives of time that form the base of nearly every definition of the human in almost all our modes of understanding" (152).

24 Ibid., 13.

25 Ibid., 2.

26 Brandon Martinez, paper assignment for Mira Mesa High School, San Diego, California (1997), 2.

27 Cathy J. Cohen, "Deviance as Resistance: A New Research Agenda for the Study of Black Politics," *Du Bois Review: Social Science Research on Race* 1, no. 1 (March 2004): 34.

28 Ibid., 38.

29 Ibid., 30.

30 Gordon, *Ghostly Matters*, 202.

31 Rubén Martínez, performance of "Wreck in the Road" with Los Illegals on April 22, 2000, at Espresso Mi Cultura in Los Angeles, California.

24

"Citizenship Takes Practice"

Latina/o Youth, JROTC, and the Performance of Citizenship

GINA PÉREZ

For those interested in understanding how young people imagine themselves as citizen subjects, they would do well to examine carefully growing student involvement in Junior Reserve Officer Training Corps Programs (JROTC) in American public high schools. Since its inception in 1916, JROTC has been promoted as vital program for developing in young people allegedly much-needed moral and physical discipline necessary for good citizenship. And while JROTC's presence in American public schools has waxed and waned throughout the 20th century, the program has experienced unprecedented expansion since the 1990s and now has approximately 557,643 participating in 3,405 units nationwide. JROTC's principal mission is to "motivate young people to be better citizens," a motto that is ubiquitous in the program's promotional materials, educational texts, posters, handbooks, and that infuses conversations with students, administrators, family members, and the broader community alike.[1] But what kind of citizens are JROTC students invited to become? And what exactly does citizenship mean? How do working-class youth, and in particular young Latinas/os and their families, define citizenship? What kind of citizenship are they invited into? And why does the language of citizenship resonate with them so powerfully? These are some of the questions that emerged as a result of a decade's worth of research into the experiences of Latina/o youth in JROTC. This chapter takes up these questions by focusing on the ways that JROTC invites young people to imagine themselves as citizens and the work they do as valuable citizenship acts that demonstrate their worthiness. For Latina/o youth who are not only enmeshed in what anthropologist Leo Chavez refers to as "the Latino Threat Narrative" that questions their rightful belonging and place in the nation, but whose marginal economic and social position also positions them as allegedly deficient in citizenship, imagining oneself as a valued member of the national community through their association with respected military programs like JROTC is no small matter. Indeed, for many Latina/o youth, their participation in JROTC is one of

This chapter is an abridged version of Chapter 5, "'Citizenship Takes Practice': Service, Personal Responsibility and Representing What Is Good about America," in my book *Citizen, Student, Soldier: Latina/o Youth, JROTC, and the American Dream*. New York University Press, 2015.

many examples of how they and their family members have used their relationship with the U.S. military to lay claim to full citizenship rights. Here I focus on the experiences of Latina/o youth participating in Fairview High School's Army JROTC program in Lorain, Ohio, and demonstrate the ways they strategically deploy their participation in the program to challenge pernicious narratives that stigmatize them and their families and how they advance, instead, a vision of citizenship that values their role in self-improvement, personal responsibility, and community uplift.

Citizenship in Practice and Theory in the International City

Located approximately 30 miles east of Cleveland along the shores of Lake Erie, the city of Lorain has a population of 64,097 residents and is the tenth largest city in Ohio.[2] According to the 2010 census, more than a quarter of the city's population is Latina/o (25.2%) with African Americans (17.6%) and Whites (55%) largely comprising the remainder of the city's population.[3] Puerto Ricans are the largest Latina/o subgroup in Lorain, with nearly 13,000 currently living in the city. And while Mexican-Americans, like Puerto Ricans, have a long history in the city, their numbers are smaller yet growing, with 2,900 Mexican-origin residents in Lorain in 2010. Fairview High School is located in South Lorain, the largely Puerto Rican area of the city that, according to local historian Gene Rivera, is home to some of *La Colonia's* pioneering Puerto Rican institutions from the 1950s. Beginning in the late 1940s, Lorain's robust economy was an important draw for thousands of Puerto Ricans who migrated not only from the various island communities, but also rural and urban centers in New York, New Jersey, and Pennsylvania and rural towns. As a workforce that was largely built through a contract labor system that ensured a reliable and highly regulated workforce, Puerto Rican arrivals in Lorain joined thousands of other migrant labors and their families from Mexico, Poland, Hungary, and Slovenia. Like much of region, however, the city of Lorain has suffered from the consequences of deindustrialization in dramatic ways beginning in the 1970s with a particularly devastating impact in the past two decades. Residents in the city suffer from high unemployment, with approximately 16.2% unemployment rate compared to nearly 7.3% in Ohio and 9.5% nationally, according to the 2008–2012 American Community Survey.[4] Nearly 30% of households in Lorain live below the poverty line, compared with 15.4% in Ohio and 14.9% nationally.[5] 22% of Puerto Ricans in Lorain live in poverty, and have lower educational attainment compared to other city residents, with 56% of Puerto Ricans attaining a high school degree or higher versus 74% for the population at large. The past decade has been particularly challenging for residents in the region, with plant closings in the auto industry and other manufacturing limiting employment opportunities for well-paying jobs.[6]

JROTC students are acutely aware of the limited economic opportunities available to them and their families, and they often talk about the ways that participating in the program opens up important possibilities that allow them to help them meet their own as well as their families' needs. JROTC instructors are also aware of their students' economic circumstances and help them in their efforts to find for afterschool jobs and remind them of their important role as members of a program that is committed to community service and helping others. This emphasis on their unique and important role as cadets was one that First Sergeant Milano, one of Fairview's JROTC instructors, often returned to in his conversations with students during class and beyond. On one icy, grey February morning, he stood before Charlie Company at the beginning of class and encouraged them to bring in donations—toothbrushes, toothpaste, soap, lotions, trail mix, and other nonperishable snacks—to help support local veterans groups assembling care packages for U.S. soldiers in Afghanistan and Iraq. First Sergeant managed to make this JROTC-sponsored event into a school-wide service opportunity, with dozens of Fairview students stopping by the JROTC classroom to donate items to "support the troops." Charlie Company, apparently, was lagging behind the other classes, and First Sergeant was trying to motivate them. "Everything you do in life makes a difference," he explained. He was encouraging them not only to participate, but also to lead the school by their own actions, saying:

> In order to get something done, you need to lead. I'm asking you to lead this school. You. My own cadets. The best in the business. You are the best at community service. You go to nursing homes. You escort guests for school events, like the one tonight. You do something positive other students do not. You are generous and do so much. We do so many good things in the community because if we don't care for our people, who will? So, *please*. Participate. *Please*. Get involved.

Students nodded attentively, familiar with the ways they are compared favorably with others in the school and frequently reminded that they are exceptional and should lead others by their exemplary behavior. Impassioned speeches such as this were what endeared First Sergeant to many of the students, who would often roll their eyes and smile as he delivered sermon-like exhortations to get involved in their school and local communities; to lead by example; to be disciplined and work hard; and to recognize and appreciate the good they do through their participation in JROTC. His unwavering belief in them and in the program, as well as his mentorship and discipline-based approach to school and life, were admired and appreciated by students, parents, and those who worked with JROTC both in the school and in the community.

First Sergeant's appeal invited students to reflect on other examples in which people make a difference in their communities. In the most recent election, for example, a school funding levy failed to pass by a slim margin. According to First Sergeant, the levy lost by just one vote:

> If just *one more* person voted, then there would be money for sports, for buses, for teachers. Now they are going to have to cut many of these things if the absentee ballots don't reverse the decision. *One vote* made the decision. Your participation in community life makes a difference. When you get involved, it makes a difference. It only takes a few to change the world. Just look at Reverend Martin Luther King. That's *one man*. And he made a difference. You can and have made a difference too.

First Sergeant didn't hide his disdain for the outcome of the local election, not only because he disagreed with the voters' failure to support local schools, but also because it demonstrated the kind of apathy and lack of engagement he indefatigably combatted in his daily interactions with students.

From the very first days in JROTC, students are encouraged to get involved through drill teams, community service, working with local veterans organizations, and fieldtrips. They are told that participating in extracurricular activities is not only good for them (it's fun, it helps boost their resume, and it provides important opportunities for them to learn and lead), but it is also good for their communities. Like other students in the school, JROTC cadets are reminded of those who have made a difference in the lives of others—Reverend Martin Luther King Jr. and military veterans, for example—and are invited to think of themselves as catalysts for making the world a better place. But what seems to distinguish JROTC students from others is the way the program consistently binds up "making a difference" with the duties and obligations of good citizenship. First Sergeant Milano's comments that morning, therefore, were neither new nor surprising; indeed, they are recurring themes highlighting one of JROTC's core tenets: Citizenship takes practice.

Citizenship talk permeates all facets of JROTC. And while inculcating particular visions of citizenship have informed JROTC since its inception, its prominence in the JROTC curriculum, promotional materials and social media connect the current moment with various citizenship campaigns directed at the nation's growing immigrant populations in the early 20th century.[7] Large posters featuring an undulating American flag at dusk, with the words: "Mission Statement: To Motivate Young People To Be Better Citizens," are displayed prominently in JROTC classrooms and drill competitions. The motto also appears in promotional literature, in the JROTC workbooks, videos, and in bold red lettering at the top of each page of the Army JROTC website. In both formal interviews and casual conversations with students and JROTC staff, citizenship is invoked to explain various behaviors and attitudes. Throughout my time working with students at Fairview High School and the many years I have read and researched JROTC, it is has become increasingly clear to me that talk about citizenship is like water: It gets in everywhere.[8]

Students, parents, as well as program staff and supporters of Fairview's JROTC program all invoked citizenship in surprising ways. For many, citizenship is grounded in a sense of duty and obligation to serve others in the community. Toy drives, fundraisers, cleaning up parks, volunteering for community events, working with veterans organization, and collecting goods to send to deployed troops abroad are examples of the community service JROTC students perform. In addition to these activities, young people also conveyed more affective visions of citizenship that were bound up with a sense of duty to promote collective betterment and community uplift.[9] This was particularly true for Latina/o students who, as sociologist Lorena Garcia and other Latina/o scholars have documented, are acutely aware of the challenges facing their neighborhoods and families and how they are characterized in the broader society.[10] Puerto Rican and Latina/o youth from Lorain often conveyed frustration, disappointment, and anger both about the problems facing their communities, as well as the enduring stereotypes they believed failed to capture the complexity and pride of South Lorain, the area of town that is largely synonymous with Puerto Rican Lorain.

These questions of citizenship are also of significant scholarly concern. In September 11th's wake, writers from across the political spectrum have debated the meaning of citizenship and have struggled to define its contours. For some, citizenship is an urgent question about boundaries and edges, about who belongs and who is excluded. This vision of citizenship narrowly focuses on legal definitions of belonging and, as Linda Bosniak notes, "boundary-focused citizenship is understood to denote not only community belonging but also community exclusivity and closure."[11] Others, such as anthropologist Leo Chavez, have called for more inclusive notions of citizenship that acknowledge how social practices, culture, and transnational activities have transformed "what a sense of belonging and community membership mean today."[12] And writers such as historian Andrew Bacevich have called for Americans to return to a notion of citizenship in which "privileges entail responsibilities."[13] Given the range of meanings attached to citizenship, careful attention to the ways young people learn, conceptualize, and enact citizenship in their daily lives is both timely and necessary. According to most of the young people I worked with, JROTC was *the first and only* place where they were actively invited to think of themselves as citizens.[14] This raises important questions about what kind of citizenship they are imagining and participating in, as well as the ways they are enacting citizenship in their daily lives.

According to political theorist Judith Shklar, "There is no notion more central in politics than citizenship, and none more variable in history, or contested in theory."[15] Ongoing debates about citizenship attest to Shklar's observation as scholars theorize the shifting meanings of citizenship, particularly in response to sustained attacks on everything from the legitimacy of birthright citizenship to the right of elected Congressional leaders of color to engage in dissent *as* Americans.[16] These experiences are deeply troubling and represent what Leo Chavez characterizes as "the contemporary crisis in the meaning of citizenship."[17] Indeed, while citizenship usually refers to a sense of democratic belonging and inclusion that invokes a sense of equality and solidarity, Linda Bosniak observes that in practice, "this inclusion is usually premised on a conception of community that is bounded and exclusive . . . [that] can also represent an axis of subordination itself."[18] In a post-9/11 world, citizenship-as-subordination has taken many forms, including virulent, anti-immigrant legislation tendentiously justified by the need to secure U.S. borders in the name of National Security.[19] These policies have had a particularly devastating effect on Latina/o communities who are defined not only as outside the nation, but also as a destructive force undermining the "the privileges and rights of citizenship for legitimate members of society."[20]

It is precisely the contradiction between egalitarian ideals of national solidarity and the reality of subordination bound up within notions of citizenship that contributes to a palpable sense of unease and anxiety about the meaning of citizenship in contemporary American society. Perhaps this is why I was so surprised with the clarity and ease with which students, teachers, parents, and community members alike, most of whom were working-class Puerto Rican, Mexican, and white, invoked the language of citizenship to refer to their activities, their identities, and their aspirations for themselves and their communities. Rather than expressing a critical stance vis-à-vis citizenship or a rejection of how it is often deployed to marginalize them as poor, working-class, and communities of color, JROTC students embraced and fashioned understandings of citizenship that were expansive, inclusive, and hopeful. Their embrace and insistence on an expansive vision of citizenship reflects Bosniak's observation: "Citizenship is a word of the greatest approbation. To designate institutions and practices and experiences in the language of citizenship is not merely to describe them, but also to accord them a kind of honor and political recognition."[21] Students described cleaning local parks, aiding disabled veterans, overcoming adversity, taking responsibility for oneself and improving the experiences and reputation of one's community as examples of good citizenship, as emotionally resonant acts they were deeply invested in and were publicly honored and praised for doing. These actions were not taken lightly, nor were they random or episodic. Rather, they reflect habituated behaviors that exemplified not only students' understandings of what citizenship is (solidarity and belonging), but also where it takes place (profoundly local) and who can be a citizen (anyone chooses to actively participate).[22] While social theorists have identified rights, legal status, political participation, and collective sentiment and identity as core concerns of citizenship, JROTC cadets regard these last two categories—participation and collective sentiment/identity—as the most valued examples of citizenship that inform their behaviors and actions within JROTC and beyond.[23]

For Fairview's youth, whose class, ethnic, racial, employment, and legal status have placed them and their families at various moments in time at the margins of society, the possibility of being positively associated with the most admired qualities and privileges of national membership is no small matter. Both in the past and in contemporary political discourse, for example, we witness how the ability to be freely employed, productive, earn money, and be financially independent is central to our understandings of full citizenship. Those who are unable to do so—the poor, those who rely on public aid, the "underclass" or, borrowing from 2012 Republican Presidential candidate, Mitt Romney, the forty-seven percent—are "not quite citizens."[24] Similarly, because, as Lisa Cacho reminds us, "social value is assigned and denied on racial terms," Puerto Ricans' struggle for full citizenship rights has often rested on their military service, both as a mechanism for economic and racial justice as well as to proof of their "worthiness" and "deservingness of inclusion into the US nation-state."[25] Yet despite the vitriolic national debates about citizenship and belonging, painful histories of exclusion, and powerful attempts to continue to define the poor, immigrants, and communities of color outside the nation, the largely Latina/o, African American, immigrant, and low-income students who comprise the bulk of Fairview's JROTC program proudly embrace the label of citizenship to describe themselves and their actions. In doing so they simultaneously expand definitions of citizenship in order to challenge stigmatizing images and labels characterizing their communities.[26]

Learning Citizenship in the JROTC Classroom

So, how do JROTC cadets come to think of themselves as citizens and identify many of their activities as citizenship acts? Three key features of JROTC instruction—the classroom curriculum, public performances and competitions, and community service—are designed to provide citizenship education and to link these insights with embodied practice. From very early on in the JROTC curriculum, students are introduced to extensive discussions about the origins, meaning, duties, and responsibilities bound up with citizenship through course readings, lectures, in-class video screenings, online video clips on the JROTC website, and through promotional literature, posters, and invited speakers. Ritualized practices, such standing and reciting the Pledge of Allegiance as well as the Cadet Creed each morning at the beginning of class, also reinforce a sense of citizenship and national belonging. The Cadet Creed is particularly important both because it invites students to identify with seven specific attributes that define them as an Army JROTC cadet, and it does so by explicitly invoking the language of citizenship, patriotism, loyalty, family, and nation.

I am an Army Junior ROTC Cadet

I will always conduct myself to bring credit to my family, country, school and the Corps of Cadets

I am loyal and patriotic

I am the future of the United States of America

I do not lie, cheat or steal and will always be accountable for my actions and deeds

I will always practice good citizenship and patriotism

I will work hard to improve my mind and strengthen my body

I will seek the mantle of leadership and stand prepared to uphold the Constitution and the American way of life

May God grant me the strength to always live by this creed[27]

The Creed's emphasis on acting in ways that "bring credit" to others and demonstrate how they are "accountable" for actions and deeds, resonate with notions of neoliberal citizenship emphasizing personal responsibility and reliability. Like weekly uniform inspections, reciting the Cadet Creed daily is a powerful example of how schools play a key role in ritualizing "the production of responsible, reliable student-citizens" through quotidian embodied practices.[28] The JROTC curriculum reinforces these ideas about citizenship, obligation to family, community, school, and nation and is an important site for understanding not only how they develop an understanding of citizenship that is about "giving back" and community uplift, but how these ideas shape student aspirations and social reproduction.[29]

At the beginning of each academic year, JROTC cadets are provided with a Leadership, Education and Training (LET) workbook that provides readings, course objectives, key terms, and exercises that are the core of JROTC's course of study. While questions of citizenship suffuse all three LET instruction levels, it has an especially prominent role in LET II and LET III, with more than half of LET II's curriculum dedicated to the unit, "Citizenship in American History and Government." Notably, the very beginning and ending of this long unit is dedicated to what the book describes as "citizenship skills" and "citizen roles." Citizenship skills are described as the "basic human values the Founding Fathers envisioned when they drafted the Constitution," and are derived directly from the Preamble of the United States Constitution. According to the text, "Individual values, which are also important to the success of our nation, are inferred from the Preamble," and are the basis for these seven citizenship skills that define "what good citizenship should be."[30] These seven skills include cooperation, patience, fairness, respect, strength, self-improvement, and balance and are described as interdependent and in need of constant vigilance and practice.[31] While each citizenship skill has an extensive and distinct explanation, both of its specific origin in the Preamble as well as the way it is a skill one can enact on a daily basis, the ideas of practice and individual agency are recurring themes connecting the seven skills. This analysis and the review questions at the end of the lesson all reinforce the core tenets of JRTOC: Citizenship takes practice and requires self-improvement.

The final chapter on citizen roles makes a similar point—emphasizing the ways students can be good citizens "in your school, community, country and the world"—and also makes explicit comparisons between American notions of citizenship and those in totalitarian or dictatorial regimes. Because this final section explicitly locates U.S. citizenship within a broader global context, it also addresses questions about naturalization, alien residents, the changing nature of citizenship in a multicultural and increasingly transnational world. Like the previous discussion about citizenship skills, the lessons in this final section emphasize both the rights and duties of citizens, and highlights the imperative to be actively involved by identifying problems (such as violence in urban and rural American) and promoting solutions to these problems on a local and broader level. "Citizens," according to the workbook, "are made, not born."[32] People *learn* citizenship through their daily activities beginning at an early age. And while the lesson makes the important distinction between political and social action, many of the examples presented focus on social action and the ways one learns citizenship and enacts it at home, in classrooms, in communities, and in the nation. Again, these notions, while explicitly linked to concerns about the "common good" and the need to promote and support a collective sense of the common good, rest primarily on self-knowledge, balancing self-interest with service to others and personal accountability. This tension between "enlightened self-interest" and promoting the "common good," is not an unfamiliar one. Indeed, as the text points out, it represents an enduring conundrum in American civic life that often (erroneously) pits discourses of natural rights against classical republican virtue. The ultimate lesson JROTC provides, however, is an opportunity to reflect on the possibilities to reconcile these visions of citizenship, while simultaneously encouraging students to engage in those behaviors that enhance self-esteem, self-improvement, and accountability. While JROTC clearly advances this vision of citizenship in its readings, videos, and lectures, the program's popular extracurricular offerings, including drill competitions and community service, provide additional vehicles for self-modification, improvement, and discipline for both personal and group success throughout the year.

Conclusion

Students in JROTC receive messages about their exceptional citizenship on a regular basis. In school, in their communities, and especially in emotionally charged events like drill competitions, they are constantly praised for their hard work and for being part of something positive that brings pride to them, their families, schools, and communities. Public performances like marching in the local Memorial Day Parade, posting colors at city-wide sporting events, and drill competitions are highly ritualized events that reinforce some of the key tenets of citizenship including discipline, self-improvement, accountability to others, and working for the common good. These events are also important because they strengthen group solidarity and belonging, not just to others in one's unit or community, but also to the military whose ubiquitous presence is seen as a catalyst for good in their lives. If citizenship takes practice, JROTC's myriad activities are important sites for habituating the virtues and actions required for enacting good in the world. They are also valued spaces where students and their supporters are publicly recognized for their efforts. After a regional drill competition in Toledo, Ohio, that brought together hundreds of JROTC cadets together from Indiana, Illinois, Michigan, and Ohio, Fairview's JROTC competed successfully and the students and their family members basked in the praise JROTC leaders like Major Newsome during the closing ceremony. Standing in front of hundreds of weary cadets, alumni, parents, active and retired military personnel, and JROTC supporters she congratulated the students for all their hard work. "It may be that others make fun of you for being in JROTC. But today everyone looks at you with respect and envy. You have made people proud. And you are an example of what youth can do today." While none of the praise was new or surprising, students savored the JROTC exceptionalism that was particularly meaningful coming from military personnel who, as Andrew Bacevich and others observe, "enjoy respect and high regard."[33] At a moment when neoliberal governance has privatized service provision for the poor and socially marginalized and abdicated responsibility to the market, private interest, and the work of non-profits, JROTC is a space where the state's presence is highly visible, welcomed, and woven into the fabric of their daily lives. These very same students and their families are already familiar with the way the state embeds itself in their everyday lives, frequently through their experiences with punitive social control.[34] Associating oneself with the military is both a corrective to these painful experiences as well as an opportunity to forge another kind of relationship to the state. In doing so, students not only draw on the language of citizenship to gain recognition and standing for what they do, but they also deploy notions of citizenship, duty, and uplift to challenge stigmatizing labels and raise questions about the role of government to address the causes of enduring inequality that face their families and communities.

NOTES

1 According to Coumbe and Harford, this mission statement was adopted in 1987 and originally stated JROTC's mission was to create "good" citizens and was later changed to "better" citizens (1996, 269).

2 http://factfinder.census.gov; www.geonames.org/US/OH/largest-cities-in-ohio.html.

3 http://quickfacts.census.gov/qfd/states/39/3944856.html, accessed January 8, 2014.

4 http://factfinder2.census.gov/faces/tableservices/jsf/pages/productview.xhtml?pid=ACS_12
   _5YR_DP03, accessed January 8, 2014.

5 http://factfinder2.census.gov/faces/tableservices/jsf/pages/productview.xhtml?pid=ACS_12
   _5YR_DP03, accessed January 8, 2014.

6 http://factfinder.census.gov/servlet/ACSSAFFFacts?_event=ChangeGeoContext&geo
   _id=16000US3944856&_geoContext=&_street=&_county=Lorain&_cityTown=Lorain&_
   state=04000US39&_zip=&_lang=en&_sse=on&ActiveGeoDiv=&_useEV=&pctxt=fph
   &pgsl=010&_submenuId=factsheet_1&ds_name=ACS_2005_SAFF&_ci_nbr=null&qr_name
   =null&reg=null%3Anull&_keyword=&_industry.

7 See Barlett and Lutz 1998.

8 An evocative metaphor I borrow from a conversation with Tedra Osell many, many years ago.

9 Lauren Berlant 1997 and 2011.

10 Garcia, 151.

11 Bosniak 2006: 2.

12 Chavez 2008: 177.

13 Bacevich 2013: 190.

14 See Levinson 2014 for a discussion of the failure of public schools to not only engage
   students with civic education, citizenship, and histories of civic empowerment, but also how
   in failing to do so, schools contribute to what she calls a "civic empowerment gap."

15 Shklar, 1.

16 While the Trump administration is not the progenitor of such attacks, they have taken on a
   particularly visible and vicious form with his ongoing efforts to undermine birthright
   citizenship, a constitutional right protected by the Fourteenth Amendment, as well as his
   exhortation that Congresswomen Ocasio Cortez, Omar, Pressley, and Tlaib should "go
   back" to the countries they came from given that their critiques of particular policies are
   allegedly evidence that they are not "capable of loving our country." See for example Jon
   Swain, "Trump Renews Racist Attack on Squad," *The Guardian*, July 21, 2019. www.the
   guardian.com/us-news/2019/jul/21/
   trump-racist-squad-democrats-omar-ocasio-cortez-tlaib-pressley.

17 Chavez, 4.

18 Bosniak, 1.

19 See Hector Amaya's (2013) discussion of citizenship excess for a more thorough analysis of
   the ethnoracial terms of these legal and political exclusions.

20 Chavez 177.

21 17.

22 Bosniak argues that questions about citizenship fall into three overlapping categories of
   what, where, and who is a citizen (17).

23 Bosniak, 35. Others whose scholarship has been extremely helpful in thinking through
   questions of citizenship include Shklar 1991; Chavez 2008; Oboler 2006; Ngai 2004; Amaya
   2013; Ramos Zayas 2012; Cacho 2012.

24 Shklar 1990, 22.

25 Cacho 2012 4; Ramos-Zayas 2012, 116–117. See also Kimberley Phillips' (2012) thorough
   analysis of African American military service and freedom struggles for a discussion of
   military service and race and economic justice.

26 Fairview students' ability to take on a citizenship identity clearly reflects the demographic
   composition of the Latina/o population, which is largely Puerto Rican and second and
   third generation Mexican with very few recent migrants from Mexico and Central
   America. This, however, is changing. But at the time of this research, questions of legal
   status did not appear to be a significant issue for students or school administrators.

27 www.usarmyjrotc.com/overview-of-jrotc. The Cadet's Creed follows the form and tenets of the Soldier's Creed. See www.army.mil/values/soldiers.html. Accessed October 29, 2014.

28 Davidson 51.

29 Davidson, 21. Davidson provides an excellent discussion of how the emphasis on presentation skills, physical comportment, and team building exercises are key in producing reliable and responsible student-citizens and how this is a key mechanism in social reproduction for working-class Latina/o youth. Cox (2013) makes a similar observation about self-presentation skills and comportment among low-income African American girls in Detroit.

30 LET II 2005, 158 and 166.

31 LET II, 159. The seven citizenship skills are: cooperation, patience, fairness, respect, strength, self-improvement, and balance.

32 Ibid, 335.

33 Bacevich 2013, 11.

34 Rios 2011, 21.

REFERENCES

Amaya, Hector. 2013. *Citizenship Excess: Latino/as, Media and the Nation*. New York: New York University Press.

Bacevich, Andrew. 2013. *Breach of Trust: How Americans Failed Their Soldiers and Their Country*. New York: Metropolitan Books.

———. 2005. *The New American Militarism: How Americans Are Seduced by War*. Oxford University Press.

Bartlett, Lesley and Catherine Lutz. 1998. "Disciplining Social Difference: Some Cultural Politics of Military Training in Public High Schools." *Urban Review* 30(2): 119–136.

Berlant, Lauren. 2011. *Cruel Optimism*. Durham, NC: Duke University Press.

———. 1997. *The Queen of America Goes to Washington City: Essays on Sex and Citizenship*. Durham, NC: Duke University Press.

Bosniak, Linda. 2006. *The Citizen and the Alien: Dilemmas of Contemporary Membership*. Princeton, NJ: Princeton University Press.

Cacho, Lisa. 2012. *Social Death: Racialized Rightlessness and the Criminalization of the Unprotected*. New York: New York University Press.

Chavez, Leo. 2008. *The Latino Threat: Constructing Immigrants, Citizens and the Nation*. Stanford, California: Stanford University Press.

Davidson, Elsa. 2011. *The Burdens of Aspiration: Schools, Youth, and Success in the Divided Social Worlds of Silicon Valley*. New York: New York University Press.

Garcia, Lorena. 2012. *Respect Yourself, Protect Yourself: Latina Girls and Sexual Identity*. New York: New York University Press.

Levinson, Meira. 2014. *No Citizen Left Behind*. Cambridge, MA: Harvard University Press.

Oboler, Suzanne, editor. 2006. *Latinos and Citizenship: The Dilemma of Belonging*. New York: Palgrave Macmillian.

Phillips, Kimberley L. 2012. *War! What Is It Good For?: Black Freedom Struggles and the U.S. Military From World War II to Iraq*. Chapel Hill: University of North Carolina Press.

Ramos-Zayas, Ana Y. 2012. *Street Therapists: Race, Affect, and Neoliberal Personhood in Latino Newark*. Chicago: University of Chicago.

Rios, Victor M. 2011. *Punished: Policing the Lives of Black and Latino Boys*. New York: New York University Press.

Shklar, Judith. 1991. *American Citizenship: The Quest for Inclusion*. Cambridge, MA: Harvard University Press.

25

In Pursuit of Property and Forgiveness

Lin-Manuel Miranda's Hamilton *and* In the Heights

ELENA MACHADO SÁEZ

Lin-Manuel Miranda's musicals, *In the Heights* and *Hamilton*, are the product of a complex negotiation with the institution of Broadway and its historic (mis)representation of people of color. The musicals ambivalently balance a counter-narrative to a history of stereotype on the Broadway stage with the goal of convincing the predominantly white, highly educated tourists in attendance that the "other" is one of "us."[1] Both musicals display an ambivalence about the efficacy of the affective strategies used to educate the spectator. The symbolic conflict between the value of community versus property becomes articulated using literal and rhetorical references to Blackness. The dynamics of choosing profit over people within the geopolitical locale of New York City ultimately trouble the work of creating audience affiliation within Lin-Manuel Miranda's *In the Heights* and *Hamilton*.

Academic criticism often contrasts Miranda's *In the Heights* with *Hamilton*, arguing that they are on opposite ends of an ideological continuum in terms of audience dynamics.[2] These readings configure *Hamilton* as affirming the politically conservative and/or racist assumptions of white spectators while positioning *In the Heights* as more progressive and resistant. For example, historian Lyra Monteiro explains that "doing really mainstream founding fathers' history" in *Hamilton* "seemed like a really weird choice for somebody who had done something that I thought was so revolutionary in *In the Heights*, in terms of [. . .] non-white immigrants" (*Onion* 2016). Monteiro draws a contrast between the two Broadway shows on the grounds that they depict populations with differing relationships to racial privilege and dominant historical narratives. While Monteiro maintains that *Hamilton*'s racial politics and cross-casting reinforce conservative notions of nation building, she views the Latinx neighborhood in *In the Heights* as groundbreaking because it undermines racial stereotypes. Performance studies scholar James McMasters also argues that the musicals are at odds with each other in terms of how they depict immigration and property ownership: "While *Hamilton* celebrates settler-colonists as patriots for stabilizing

Abridged reprint from: *Studies in Musical Theatre* 12, no. 2 (2018): 181–97.

stolen land into a new nation, *In the Heights* is a *critique* of the violence of gentrification [and] colonization" (original emphasis).

I push back on this interpretation of the musicals by making the case for how Miranda's depiction of a contemporary community in Washington Heights sets the stage for his historical vision of the American Revolution. The stories of *In the Heights* and *Hamilton* share an investment in private property as a defining facet of the American Dream and, by extension, national belonging. At the same time, both musicals display an anxiety about the terms of such belonging. The themes of property acquisition and dispossession are accompanied by a constant plea for forgiveness for who gets sacrificed by the "free" market in order to facilitate the upward mobility of the rest. In both works, the audience is asked to empathize with the struggles of a model citizen defined by his relationship to property. The individualistic freedom of the protagonists is constructed in relation to a disavowed community of Others. *In the Heights* posits the U.S. Latinx business class as a normative ideal even as the song "Blackout" references the underlying violence that necessitates the erasure of Other Latinidades. The blackout's literal Blackness in *In the Heights* is a precursor to the rhetorical Blackness in *Hamilton*. The embodiment of the white founding fathers with a multicultural cast alludes to how the musical's emplotment necessitates the silencing of the Other founders: enslaved Africans. The musical consequently inherits a model for audience affiliation as well as an ambivalence regarding representation and staging from *In the Heights*.

Trafficking in Latinx Stereotypes

In contrast to the Good Neighbor era, the latter half of the twentieth century saw the equation of Latinx residents and immigrants with criminality on the Great White Way following the success of *West Side Story* (1957). As cultural studies critic Frances Negrón-Mutaner notes in *Boricua Pop* (2004), the musical is a foundational fiction that defines "Puerto Ricans as criminals (men) and victims (women)" (62). The legacy of *West Side Story* is such that its narrative "remains a constitutive site for AmeRican ethno-national identifications" by visualizing Puerto Ricans as a U.S. ethnicity (58). Negrón-Mutaner argues that the musical "can be dubbed the diaspora's trauma" because Puerto Ricans are forced to wrestle with the shame and valorization associated with the musical's portrayal (58). Brian Eugenio Herrera expands upon her analysis in *Latin Numbers* (2015) by explaining how the film consolidated the stereotype of criminality: "the Latino gang member as a stock character in US popular performance" (121). The transition from stage to screen magnified an ethnic-specific stereotype into a pan-Latinx one. That "racialized stock character" (127) would serve as a measure by which to interpret Latinx creative work on Broadway. In *José, Can You See?* (1999), Alberto Sandoval-Sánchez reveals how this specter of criminality haunted the first US Latinx-authored plays on Broadway: *Short Eyes* in 1973, *Zoot Suit* in 1979, and *Cuba and His Teddy Bear* in 1986. While each portrayed a different Latinx population (Nuyorican, Chicano, and Cuban-American, respectively), the reception by "general audiences" construed the dramatic works as "embodiment[s] of derogatory stereotypes of US Latinos/as" (115). Broadway as a gatekeeping institution placed a "burden of representation" upon U.S. Latinx theatre to reproduce *West Side Story*, from its urban setting to the depiction of working-class populations engaged in illicit or illegal activities (115). The first Latinx dramatic works to cross over to the Broadway stage therefore "easily perpetuate[d] the stereotyping of US Latinos as delinquents, gang members, criminals, drug users" (115). The expectation that a Latinx dramatic performance address limited facets of "ghetto life" in order to claim any cultural authenticity and be seen as a viable investment for a Broadway production inevitably led to the reinforcement of a white audience's prejudices.

Lin-Manuel Miranda often refers to how the staging of stereotypes about Latinidad shapes his understanding of himself as a Latinx artist. Miranda points to a specific formative experience in high school that inspired *In the Heights*, the "perfect storm" of directing *West Side Story* at the same time that *Capeman* made its debut on Broadway (Brown 2015). Miranda recalls the marketing of *Capeman* as the show that was "going to be the great brown moment in musical theater" and his disappointment that "it was us as gang members in the '50s, again" (Brown 2015). The confluence of staging *West Side Story* while witnessing the floundering of *Capeman* "fueled" Miranda's "creative fire" with the ethical imperative of portraying Latinx characters "onstage without a knife in our hand," of creating a "show with Latino people where we aren't gang members and drug dealers, because that's been super well represented already" (Brown 2015). *In the Heights* is shaped by this desire to focus on alternative narratives of Latinidad, moving away from the depiction of poverty and working-class populations. Miranda emphasizes his hope that "this musical will correct" the stereotypes of the "knife fight" and "drug deal" by making the case that "You know, these people are just like you, and they're getting priced out of Manhattan just like you are, and we're all just trying to get by" (Anon. 2007). The work of cultural translation aims to educate the audience, to undermine the inherited stereotype about Latinx criminality, by drawing spectators into an affective identification with the entrepreneurial U.S. Latinx characters depicted in *In the Heights*.

Unruly Offstage Others in the Heights

The song "Blackout" from *In the Heights* is an important precursor to *Hamilton*'s depiction of a Caribbean immigrant as model citizen. Aiming to produce empathy for the Latinx experience, Miranda stakes a claim in the universalism of entrepreneurship in order to transform the "you" of the audience into a "we" bonded by struggle. *In the Heights* articulates the shared concern of property loss by opening with Usnavi lamenting the neighborhood's gentrification and rising living costs (Machado Sáez "Bodega Sold Dreams" 2018). The blackout scene that concludes Act 1 marks a pivotal shift in the musical's class hierarchy. The musical's desire to counter the Broadway stereotypes of criminality translates into the invisibility of such bodies onstage during the blackout—we never see the population attacking the bodega and other businesses. The song "Blackout" expresses the concerns of the business-class Latinx population, inviting the spectators to identify with the emotional turmoil generated by the blackout's challenge to property ownership.[3] The absence of the bodies perpetrating the violence is paired with the transformation of Graffiti Pete and Abuela Claudia. We witness the conversion of Graffiti Pete from a thug violating personal property to an artist employed by the bodega to paint a mural (Machado Sáez "Bodega Sold Dreams" 2018). Meanwhile, Abuela Claudia gives her lottery winnings to Usnavi for safekeeping and then promptly passes away. Since Latinx populations have historically been depicted as inherently criminal, the musical cannot imagine a space for the poor or working class on the Broadway stage that does not reinforce such stereotypes. The blackout's literal Blackness acts as temporal break in the musical and invokes the specter of the unruly poor in order to position the business class as the truly disempowered population. Graffiti Pete ultimately resolves the tension of the class competition and reverts the narrative back to the more comfortable emotional terrain of heteronormative romance.

The blackout's enveloping darkness aligns the perspective and positionality of the audience with that of the Latinx characters. In the scene leading into the blackout, Usnavi, Benny, Vanessa, and Nina are out at a club when the revelry suddenly escalates into violence. A character, Club Guy, grabs the two women who were previously dancing with Usnavi. Benny finishes the contest over women's bodies by punching Club Guy. As the fight escalates, the staging and choreography create an anonymous blur of bodies, preparing the audience for the great equalizer of the blackout. The club dance scene becomes "intense, crazy" and the dancing transforms into a "whirlwind of movement, a release of stress, when suddenly: the power goes out" (86). The stage is plunged into "complete darkness" (86). The performers onstage and their spectators temporarily find themselves downwardly mobile, navigating the absence of light. The gaze of the audience eventually becomes oriented on the individual faces that emerge out of the Blackness, with the characters in the club illuminated by "cell phone light" while a "flashlight comes on" in the Rosario Car service (86) and at the bodega, showing Sonny "holding a baseball bat, protecting the storefront" (87). Via these spotlights, the audience adopts the perspective of the Latinx business class facing the threat of vandalism during the blackout.

The "Blackout" lyrics articulate the concerns of the barrio businesses and how the blackout jeopardizes their profitability. Piragua Guy is the first to sing

"Oye Que Pasó" (86) with Usnavi responding "Blackout, Blackout!" (87). The power struggle in the club over women's bodies is transferred to the urban landscape. At Usnavi's bodega, Sonny declares that "I gotta guard the / store make sure / that nothing's / going wrong" (88). Sonny's voice joins that of Kenny and Camila, the owners of the Rosario Car service, and the Piragua Guy to sing "We are powerless!" (89). The temporary downward mobility of the US Latinx business class is paired with references to invisible chaotic bodies. Graffiti Pete responds to the chorus of concern by warning about "people lootin' / and shootin'" who do not appear onstage (89). Previously described by Usnavi as a "punk" who needed to be "chase[d] away" in order to protect the bodega (1), Graffiti Pete is enlisted by Sonny during the blackout to defend Usnavi's property. Graffiti Pete offers "a couple of roman candles" to "distract the vandals" (90). The explosion of fireworks also distracts the chorus of singers, providing them and the audience with an upward gaze that is tied to renewed hope in the barrio's economic future. Usnavi, Nina, Vanessa, Daniela, the Piragua Guy, and others repeat, "Look at the fireworks / Light up the night sky" (90, 92, 93, 94). The vision of the characters and the audience is reoriented, so that the glow of Graffiti Pete's fireworks reframes the attack on businesses as backdrop for a romantic kiss between Benny and Nina. The (dis)articulation of class conflict central to *In the Heights*, with the song of "Blackout" foregrounding the tension between the business class onstage and the stereotypes of criminal hoards offstage.

In this power struggle over representation, the musical weighs in on the side of the property owners over that of the have-nots, but it nevertheless acknowledges the legacy of class and racial stereotypes on Broadway. During the penultimate scene of Act 2, the musical situates a financial exchange between Sonny and Graffiti Pete in "a shady alleyway" (146). Since "Sonny whispers into Graffiti Pete's ear," the audience is not privy to why Sonny is sharing his lottery winnings (146). Sonny explains that "no one knows about this but you and me," so the audience is left to imagine the parameters of the "business proposition" (146). The reason for secrecy is left open to interpretation, including the possibility that Sonny's lottery winnings are shared with Graffiti as part of an illicit transaction. The encounter invokes the Broadway stereotype of Latinxs as "gang members and drug dealers" (Brown 2015), which is corroborated by Usnavi in the final scene of the musical. Usnavi responds to Graffiti Pete's reappearance by reminding Sonny of his previous warning regarding "this punk" (150). Sonny counters by stating, "You have to commission an artist while his rate is good" (150). Sonny resolves the troublesome implications of a covert payment in the barrio, with the translation of Graffiti Pete from a property-destroying punk to a "legitimate," as in commissioned, artist. Graffiti Pete is transformed from a street artist outside the capitalist economy to wage labor once he is paid to complete a "huge graffiti mural of Abuela Claudia" (150).

Abuela Claudia embodies an earlier generation of Latinx-Caribbean immigration, arriving in New York in 1943 work as a domestic (62). During the blackout, Abuela Claudia entrusts Usnavi with the lottery winnings she has kept secret up to this point, asking him to "guard this with your life" (92). When the neighborhood next bonds together during Act 2's "Carnaval Del Barrio," Abuela Claudia is absent. With her sudden death announced at the end of the song, her legacy of lottery winnings passes onto Usnavi and Sonny, securing their ownership of the bodega, in the face of rising living costs. Even though Abuela Claudia's death provides the funds that allow for Graffiti Pete's art and Usnavi's change of heart at the end of the musical, the emotional valence of the community's loss is centered on Usnavi. The members of the barrio mourn Abuela Claudia with the song "Alabanza," but she is ultimately a vehicle for the reintegration of Usnavi into the neighborhood, so that he can stake his claim of property ownership despite gentrification. The audience is encouraged to identify with his troubles and the community's fear that he too will move up and out. Abuela Claudia's death is ultimately a positive development, whereas Usnavi's planned abandonment of the bodega and migration to the Caribbean is equated with the true death of the barrio. Regardless of whether they end up reformed or eliminated, working-class characters have no future in the musical's Washington Heights—only those who contribute to the market(ability) of the neighborhood can combat stereotype and embody hope on the Broadway stage.

Ghostly Presence of the Enslaved in *Hamilton*

Miranda's second musical, *Hamilton*, has a different educational imperative: to showcase the centrality of the immigrant to the American nation-building enterprise. The show counters the stereotype of the unassimilable immigrant with the characterization of Hamilton as a model citizen. In order to frame Alexander Hamilton as a working-class Caribbean immigrant, the musical wrestles with the forced movement of enslaved people. As Toni Morrison argues in *Playing in the Dark*, "Africanism is the vehicle by which the American self knows itself not enslaved, but free" (52). The historical reality of people as property shadows Hamilton's characterization. In Act 1, slavery is explicitly acknowledged as a system defining the boundaries of freedom and enslavement. Freedom is framed as the rationale for the American Revolution, aligning the US colonies and their leaders with the enslaved. In Act 2, the successful declaration of independence shifts the function of slavery as a context. The emotional valence of oppression is abandoned, with slavery humorously invoked to position Thomas Jefferson as a foil to Alexander Hamilton. The comedic performance of Jefferson's hypocrisy emphasizes the contradiction between his democratic ideals and the profit he derives from enslavement. Slavery is made to work as comic relief; invoked and then safely regarded as a problem of the past as opposed to a historical legacy that continues to shape American identity and values. The metaphorical invocation of Blackness haunts the musical's project of historical revisionism and bespeaks the limits of whose stories get "fleshed out" and can appeal to the spectator for empathy and affiliation. *Hamilton* therefore inherits the ambivalence from *In the Heights* about the efficacy of its own corrective project of representation.

The song opening Act 1, "Alexander Hamilton," introduces its main character as a mystery of upward mobility: "How does a bastard, orphan, son of a whore and a / Scotsman [. . .] / Impoverished, in squalor / Grow up to be a hero and a scholar?" (16). The musical offers itself as an answer to this question, suggesting that it rectifies a historical silence about "how" Hamilton's journey from periphery to center was accomplished. Hamilton is introduced as a symbol of the American Dream, a "self-starter" (15), "comin' up from the / bottom" (16), crediting his initiative and drive for his transformation into the architect of American democratic capitalism. Slavery is depicted as an important inspiration for Hamilton's ambition and upward mobility. The song explains that Hamilton "struggled and kept / his guard up" while "slaves were being / slaughtered and carted / away across the waves," implying that seeing this injustice created a divide between his public and private self (15). His struggle over the morality of human enslavement does not get articulated in the song. Instead, Hamilton's individualistic desire to belong is conveyed: "Inside he was longing for something to be / a part of" (16). The audience is tasked with valorizing Hamilton's embodiment of a marginalized underclass, of empathizing with his desires to overcome his illegitimate background and poverty. At the same time, Hamilton makes sense of his individualism as a white male through a contrast with the enslaved. Historian Lauren Isenberg analyzes how Hamilton's "Caribbeanness, is somehow conflated with abolitionism" in the musical, despite contradictory historical evidence: "Hamilton purchased slaves" (298). This conflation implies that Hamilton empathizes with the enslaved because he was born in the Caribbean, because of his outsider status to the US.

The portrayal of Hamilton as a working-class immigrant from the Caribbean is first developed in "My Shot." The discourse of class struggle is intertwined with the metaphor of Blackness to narrate a white founding father's migration and his American Dream of capitalist individualism. The discourse of slavery is deployed to position Hamilton-the-immigrant as the embodiment of the ideal American.[4] Rapping with the Marquis de Lafayette, Hercules Mulligan, and John Laurens, Hamilton conflates the project of independence with that of abolition, labelling the group "a bunch of revolutionary manumission abolitionists" (27). Laurens in turn proclaims that "we'll never be truly free / until those in bondage have the same rights / as you and me" (27). The concern for equality, however, is not a question of social justice but a matter of economic freedom from England's empire. Hamilton asks: "If we win our independence? 'Zat a guarantee of freedom for our descendants?" (29). The securing of freedom is limited to "handling our financial situation" (29). The slippage from human bondage to economic independence makes clear that the "we" of the nation does not refer to the enslaved. Rather, the unbroken lineage of white patriarchy traces itself from King George to Alexander Hamilton to the Broadway audience, rather than the ancestral lineage of the actors onstage. The plan for rebellion, to "hatch a plot blacker than the kettle callin' the pot" (27) translates into "roll[ing] like Moses, claimin' our promised land" (29). Abolitionist discourse structures the imaginary of American anticolonialism, but ultimately the musical is not concerned with the rebellion of the enslaved Black and Brown colonial subjects. During the last song in Act 1, "Non-stop," Hamilton announces that he has moved on to different concerns following the end of the American Revolution: "I've seen injustice in the world and I've corrected it. / Now for a strong central democracy" (137–38). With the moral imperative of independence fulfilled, Hamilton argues that the next important project is to establish the political and economic structure of the nation.

The second half of the musical is more concerned with absolution than abolition. In Act 2, the project of nation-building becomes disconnected from abolitionism, with slavery only invoked in relation to Thomas Jefferson. The songs "What'd I Miss" and "Cabinet Battle #1" depict Jefferson as ignorant of the contradiction between his articulation of freedom and role as slave owner. Upon his return from France, Jefferson gazes "at the rolling / fields" of his plantation and exclaims "I can't / believe that we / are free" (152). The invisible bodies laboring on the plantation are given a ghostly presence; the ensemble dancers mimic the actions of domestic slaves, for example, wiping the floor. One member performs the role of Sally Hemings, the sole enslaved person named in *Hamilton*. The audience is not encouraged to empathize with her position or view her as a subject. Rather, Hemings is an object of humorous critique: she does not speak and her body is merely relevant in relation to Jefferson as a means of poking fun at his hypocrisy. Jefferson finds "a letter from the President," which prompts him to ask, "Sally be a lamb, darlin', won'tcha open it?" (152). The Hemings-persona follows Jefferson's request and showcases the imaginary letter to him and the audience, so that the spectators are aligned with his gaze as slaveholder. After Jefferson informs the audience that the letter "says the President's assembling a cabinet," the actress returns to the ensemble cast to become one of many dancing bodies (152). The staging evokes the anonymity of the blackout from *In the Heights*, since the ensemble member is dressed in the same uniform as the rest of the dance cast, rendering her interchangeable.

The indictment of Jefferson during Act 2 is the vehicle by which the musical can symbolically resolve its silencing of the enslaved, the ghost of slavery haunting the birth of the nation. The critique levelled at Jefferson liberates the musical from the ethical obligation it articulates at its start—that the independence of the nation and its subjects are intertwined—and assuages the liberal guilt of the audience as well. During "Cabinet Battle #1," Jefferson demands that Hamilton not "tax the South cuz we got it made in / the shade," in other words that the region should not be punished for being financially profitable. Hamilton responds by highlighting that such profit is derived from an unjust system: "A civics lesson from a slaver. [. . .] / Your debts are paid because you don't pay for / labor" (161). In the libretto's sidebar footnote to "Cabinet Battle #1," Miranda confesses, "I cannot tell you how cathartic it is to get to express this to Jefferson every night. The audience's reaction is similarly cathartic" (161). The release is tied to the acknowledgement of how people are enslaved as property: "we know who's really doing the planting" (161). Hamilton is not the enslaved, but he is tasked with speaking for them and deconstructing Thomas Jefferson's authority. The audience is emotionally freed from the burden of identifying with a corrupt founding father by offering Hamilton as an enlightened critic of the Enlightenment. At the same time, the audience is released from affective affiliation with the enslaved. The troublesome ghost that haunts the foundational fiction of freedom can be put to figurative rest, since it has been acknowledged in a light-hearted, comedic manner. The enslaved are rhetorically excluded from that community, even as the bodies of the actors function as symbols for those who have been silenced in American history.

Additionally, the imagery of Blackness almost disappears during Act 2. "The Room Where it Happens," which centers on an inaccessible historical moment, contains the most noteworthy mention of darkness. The song highlights the status of Washington, DC as the nation's capital and Hamilton's role in establishing the national debt, but is primarily dedicated to the problematic vacuum of historical knowledge. Burr emphasizes that "no one really knows how the game is played" because "no one else was in / the room where it / happened" (186). Burr's concern is an individual one, his ambition is thwarted because he has not been invited to be a power broker. However, the audience becomes aligned with Burr, bonded in a shared ignorance about the "art of the trade," of political compromise (187). What the contemporary spectators of the musical inherit from the founding fathers is a legacy of decontextualization, knowing what happened but not how. The affective alliance between the spectators and Burr is based on the desire to access the secrets of historiography, how we come to know what happened. The affiliation of the audience with Burr nevertheless assumes that the audience would not be in danger of being traded, of being categorized as property.

The song's final dialogue between the company and Burr declare that the audience's vulnerability lies in the appeal of heroism, of expecting a narrative where "our leaders save the day" and provide a "dream of a brand new start" (190). However, the birth of this new nation is facilitated by a historical silencing. Because "we don't get a say in what they trade / away" in order to produce the dream of American exceptionalism, of heroic revolutionaries fighting for freedom, the audience is told that "we dream in the dark for the most part / dark as a tomb where it happens" (190). Burr asks Hamilton to reveal "what did they say to you to get you to sell New York City down the river" (188). What is unknown is how Hamilton balanced his self-interest with that of the city that made him anew, giving him the opportunity to thrive and rise up. New York is personified as an enslaved subject via the expression of "being sold down the river." The NPR CodeSwitch podcast researched the etymology of this phrase, finding that it refers to a shift in the US slave trade after importation of Africans ceased in 1808, when enslaved persons were sold and shipped down the Ohio and Mississippi Rivers to endure plantation work in the Deep South (Ghandi 2014). While the expression is used to "signify a profound betrayal" (Ghandi 2014), it is rooted in American slavery's betrayal of humanity. Hamilton faces Burr to confess, "God help me and forgive me / I wanna build something that's gonna / Outlive me" (188). Acknowledging that ambition outweighed his moral compass, Hamilton offers an emotional apologia on behalf of the Revolutionary Fathers. Hamilton's political success and history's enshrinement of American leadership are dependent upon the support of slavery's immoral enterprise and a vacuum of empathy. The rise of American capitalism is indebted to the unpaid labor and violent objectification of enslaved Africans. The dark trade of negotiation obliquely references slavery as the original sin that must be forgotten in order to maintain the American Dream myth: the immigrant who through hard work achieved class mobility—or at least his face on the ten-dollar bill.

Conclusion

Hamilton closes with the song "History Has Its Eyes on You," which warns that, "You have no control / Who lives, who dies, who tells your story" (280). The "you" is explicitly Alexander Hamilton, the figure who the musical's revisionist history seeks to recover. Nevertheless, *Hamilton* suggests that it is equally concerned with the "you" who listens to this story and how the presence of a specific audience shapes the storytelling. Usnavi closes *In the Heights* by asserting his role as translator for the audience, as the one who "illuminate[s] the stories of the people in the street" (151) and "keeps our legacies" (152). He apologizes to the spirit of a deceased Abuela Claudia for locating home in Washington Heights rather than the Caribbean, explaining that Manhattan is true home because of its capitalist institutions. Usnavi declares "It's a wonderful life that I've known— Merry Christmas, you ol' building and loan! / I'm home!" (153). Invoking the 1946 movie *It's A Wonderful Life*, Usnavi makes the debt economy central to his belonging in Washington Heights. The uncanny resemblance between Usnavi and Hamilton lies at the intersection of American individualism with the US banking industry. The musicals counter stereotypes of the Latinx resident and immigrant using a neo-liberal logic that defines the American Dream as the pursuit of life, liberty, and property. The rags-to-riches prototype makes the figures of Usnavi and Hamilton palatable to a predominantly white audience as well as figures for identification and empathy. The rhetorical moves the musicals make to foster a dynamic of audience affiliation are haunted by the voices and bodies that cannot be assimilated into such neat narratives.

NOTES

1 According to Broadway League reports on demographics when *In the Heights* and *Hamilton* premiered, audiences became slightly whiter (74% to 77% white) and significantly more educated, an elite cohort that was not representative of either New York City or broader national trends.

2 For a detailed discussion of how the academic reception defines the politics of Miranda's aesthetics, see the longer version of this essay entitled, "Blackout on Broadway," in *Studies in Musical Theater*.

3 Christian Krohn-Hansen asserts in *Making New York Dominican* (2013), the economic realities of Dominican employment in the New York tri-state area are complex and varied. I therefore read *In the Heights* as an ambivalent product of Miranda's negotiation of who is an "appropriate" or "representative" Latinx subject for the contemporary Broadway stage, rather than interpreting the musical as an anthropological text that comments on lived Dominican-American experience.

4 By contrast, the historical Hamilton and his Federalist party advocated an "unrelenting anti-immigrant policy" (Isenberg 2017: 302).

REFERENCES

Anon. "Interview—*In the Heights*' authors, Lin Manuel-Miranda & Quiara Alegría Hudes." *Broadway Bullet* (13 March 2007): www.broadwaybullet.com/?p=272. Accessed 15 May 2017.

Broadway League. "The demographics of the Broadway audience: 2008–2009 season." *New York Times* (2009): http://static01.nyt.com/packages/pdf/arts/NY2008-09revised.pdf. Accessed 15 May 2017.

———. "The demographics of the Broadway audience: 2015–2016 season." *Official Website of the Broadway Theater Industry* (2016): www.broadwayleague.com/research/research-reports/. Accessed 15 May 2017.

Brown, Rembert. "Genius: A conversation with *Hamilton* Maestro Lin-Manuel Miranda." *Skewed & Reviewed* (29 September 2015): http://grantland.com/hollywood-prospectus/genius-a-conversation-with-hamilton-maestro-lin-manuel-miranda/. Accessed 7 January 2016.

Carp, Benjamin L. "World wide enough: Historiography, imagination, and stagecraft." *Journal of the Early Republic* 37:2 (2017): 289–94.

DiGiacomo, Frank. "Hamilton's Lin-Manuel Miranda on finding originality, racial politics (and why Trump should see his show)." *Hollywood Reporter* (12 August 2015): www.hollywoodreporter.com/features/hamiltons-lin-manuel-miranda-finding-814657. Accessed 16 February 2017.

Ghandi, Lakshmi "What does "sold down the river" really mean? The answer isn't pretty." *Code Switch Podcast: Race and Identity, Remixed* (27 January 2014): www.npr.org/sections/codeswitch/2014/01/27/265421504/what-does-sold-down-the-river-really-mean-the-answer-isnt-pretty. Accessed 16 February 2017.

Herrera, Brian Eugenio. *Latin Numbers: Playing Latino in Twentieth-Century US Popular Performance.* Ann Arbor, MI: University of Michigan Press, 2015.

———. "Miranda's manifesto." *Theater* 47:2 (2017): 23–33.

Isenberg, Nancy. "Make 'em laugh: Why history cannot be reduced to song and dance." *Journal of the Early Republic* 37:2 (2017): 295–303.

Krohn-Hansen, Christian. *Making New York Dominican: Small Business, Politics, and Everyday Life*. Philadelphia: University of Pennsylvania Press, 2013.

Lindley, Courtney. "The *Hamilton* cast's message to Mike Pence will give you a little bit of hope today." *Bustle* (19 November 2016): www.bustle.com/articles/196007-the-hamilton-casts-message-to-mike-pencewill-give-you-a-little-bit-of-hope-today. Accessed 30 November 2017.

Machado Sáez, Elena. "Bodega Sold Dreams: Middle-class Panic and the Crossover Aesthetics of *In the Heights*." Eds. Carlos Gallego and Marcial González. *Dialectical Imaginaries: Materialist Approaches to U.S. Latino/a Literature*. Ann Arbor, MI: University of Michigan Press, 2018: 187–216.

———. "Blackout on Broadway: Affiliation and audience in *In the Heights* and *Hamilton*." *Hamilton: A Special Issue*. Guest Ed. Peter C Kunze. *Studies in Musical Theater* 12.2 (2018): 181–197.

McMasters, James. "Why *Hamilton* is not the revolution you think it is." *HowlRound* (23 February 2016): http://howlround.com/why-hamilton-is-not-therevolution-you-think-it-is. Accessed 21 August 2017.

Miranda, Lin-Manuel and Hudes, Quiara Alegría. *In the Heights*. Milwaukee, WI: Applause Theatre & Cinema Books, 2013.

Miranda, Lin-Manuel and McCarter, Jeremy. *Hamilton: The Revolution*. New York: Grand Central Publishing, 2016.

Monteiro, Lyra D. "Race-conscious casting and the erasure of the black past in Lin-Manuel Miranda's *Hamilton*." *Public Historian* 38:1 (2016): 89–98.

Morrison, Toni. *Playing in the Dark: Whiteness and the Literary Imagination*. New York: Vintage, 1992.

Nathans, Heather S. "Crooked histories: Representing race, slavery, and Alexander Hamilton onstage." *Journal of the Early Republic* 37:2 (2017): 271–78.

Negrón-Mutaner, Frances. *Boricua Pop: Puerto Ricans and the Latinization of American Culture*. New York: NYU Press, 2004.

Nerenson, Ariel. "An unfinished symphony with a stutter (beat)." *American Quarterly* 68:4 (2016): 1045–59.

Onion, Rebecca. "A Hamilton skeptic on why the show isn't as revolutionary as it seems." *Slate* (5 April 2016): www.slate.com/articles/arts/culturebox/2016/04/a_hamilton_critic_on_why_the_musical_isn_t_so_revolutionary.html. Accessed 19 February 2017.

Sandoval-Sánchez, Alberto. *José, Can You See?: Latinos On and Off Broadway*. Madison, WI: University of Wisconsin Press, 1999.

26

Leaving Lima Behind

The Immigration of Peruvian Professionals to Miami

ELENA SABOGAL

Camila, a preschool teacher, and Pedro, a pharmaceutical sales manager, both in their forties, left Peru in 2000 after being unemployed for two consecutive years. The constant pressure of having to deal with an uncertain future became too difficult to handle. The economy was weak, and finding a good job was almost impossible. Criminal violence and political unrest heightened their sense of fear and insecurity. Concerned about their future and that of their children, they decided to leave Peru. They considered Washington, DC, but settled on Miami because family and friends offered them a place to stay and could provide guidance on the fundamental things they needed to know to begin a new life in the United States. They also thought that their lack of English skills would be less of a problem in Miami, and the weather would be more attractive. Although they arrived with tourist visas, they viewed Miami as a place full of long-term possibilities where they felt comfortable and safe. However, their initial sense of security would soon change.[1]

Starting in the late 1980s, many older, highly trained Latin American middle-class professionals migrated to Miami without legal work status[2] or English skills. Political instability and economic insecurity throughout Latin America contributed to their decisions to uproot their lives and families and move to the United States.[3] Their experiences are rarely documented in academic literature, where Latin American immigrants are usually portrayed as following one of two trajectories: as professional immigrants who encountered fewer barriers because they came to the United States legally[4] or as unauthorized migrants forced to take unskilled jobs because of their lack of education and legal status.[5] Neither of these groups include highly trained professionals who came to the United States with modest financial resources but without legal status or previously arranged employment, such as Camila and Pedro.[6] Nor did these immigrants fit the pattern of young unauthorized migrants.[7] Most chose to immigrate in their forties and fifties, when middle-class individuals are assumed to be established in their careers.[8] Pierre Bourdieu's multiple forms of capital (economic, social, and cultural) can help address this gap in the literature by providing a framework for contextualizing the neglected immigration experiences of displaced Latin American professionals.[9] As Bourdieu notes, economic capital is measured in terms of money and material possessions; cultural capital includes tangible attributes such as education and professional credentials as well as intangible attributes such as manners, taste, and how one projects one's social class; and social capital comprises one's social network and social relationships.[10] Latin American middle-class professionals migrated with all three forms of capital. They sold their homes, cars, and other assets, which combined with their depleted savings financed their ability to migrate. Upon arrival, while they were not initially able to capitalize on their cultural or social capital, their education, professional experience, and social networks eventually enabled them to overcome the obstacles they faced because of their lack of English skills and legal status.

In this chapter, I explain the economic and political circumstances that led Peruvian professionals to leave their country in search of a life in a new one. I then discuss the city of their reception—Miami, the most successful Latino city in the United States—using the stories of Camila, Pedro, and other professional Peruvians who settled there. Finally, I highlight how their language, legal status, and perceptions of insecurity shaped their experiences of migration and settlement, along with the role that "Miami,"[11] a space characterized by its plethora of Latino populations, played in the process of community building.

Peruvian Immigration to the United States

In his seminal study of Peruvian migration, Teófilo Altamirano argued that Peruvian migration had multiple and overlapping historical roots.[12] Growing urban poverty, few employment opportunities, the Peruvian government's inability to satisfy basic needs, political upheaval, and increasing violence and human rights violations periodically generated uncertainty and instability, creating strong incentives for Peruvians to leave their country in search of better opportunities. The preferred destination was the United States. Peruvian migration can be traced to the early 1930s.[13] By the 1950s, Peruvians from different geographical regions and class backgrounds began migrating to New York, New Jersey, California, Florida, Chicago, and Washington, DC.[14]

The magnitude of this migration changed dramatically after 1987, during the government of Alan García (1985–1990), when the implementation of structural adjustment policies such as privatization, devaluation of Peruvian currency against the US dollar, and lifting of price controls caused Peru to become a "nation of emigrants."[15] These policies significantly increased unemployment and inflation, pushing the country into economic and political turmoil.[16] Over the next decade, under Alberto Fujimori's presidency (1990–2000), Peru underwent another series of economic reforms aimed at curbing inflation and attracting foreign capital. The "Fuji-shock" devaluations of the Peruvian currency caused a 40 percent decrease in income levels.[17] More structural adjustment policies led to privatization of government enterprises, hundreds of thousands of government workers being fired, and the arrival of foreign-made goods that put Peruvian firms out of business. Squeezed by unemployment and a lack of social programs, 60 percent of the population fell into poverty.[18] Although much of the burden affected the poorest segments of the population, the middle class also suffered tremendously.[19] Massive numbers of Peruvians of all ages left the country during the 1990s, including older Peruvians with higher levels of education.[20]

In the years preceding this economic collapse, Lima, the capital city, had experienced massive internal migration, which Peruvian anthropologist Jose Matos Mar defined as a "desborde popular" in which traditional "Official Peru" was flooded by the "Other Peru"—people from the Andes.[21] This "overflow" of Andean migrants fragmented Lima along racial and class lines.[22] In Peru, race combines cultural and social markers not exclusively based on skin color.[23] Populations of Andean origins are seen as inferior and labeled with the derogatory term *cholo*.[24] In Lima, a class-segregated city, middle-class Peruvians remained within their familiar traditional neighborhoods, while deeming areas of the city where internal migrants settled as "unsafe."

The perception of living in a dangerous city increased in the 1980s with the emergence of Shining Path, a terrorist group that originated in the Peruvian highlands that quickly made its presence felt in Lima. To instill fear in the population and demonstrate that the government was not in control, Shining Path blew out electrical towers, leaving entire areas in the dark. These blackouts generated a heightened sense of insecurity, and even middle-class neighborhoods became dangerous and unfriendly. The middle and upper classes could no longer depend on the basic services and amenities they had taken for granted. Without electricity, nothing worked except the radio, which became a lifeline for learning what was happening in the city, which neighborhoods were affected by blackouts, and how long these neighborhoods would have to wait for power to be restored. A general distrust led to an even more fractured capital city.[25] With the constant threat of terrorism, Lima was no longer a safe place to live, and all its residents viewed migration as the only option for a better future. Any Peruvian who could afford to leave the country, did.[26] Destinations were chosen based on access to economic and symbolic capital.

Arriving in Multiethnic Miami

In the 1990s and early 2000s, middle-class Peruvians arrived in Miami with the intention of staying. In their view, Miami was a desirable destination, far away from the chaos and insecurity they had experienced in Lima.

The arrival of Cubans had transformed Miami's landscape in the 1960s, making it an attractive place for other migrating Latin Americans. Peruvians perceived the city as immigrant friendly. According to the US Census, 49.2 per-cent of Miami's population in 1990 was Hispanic. Cubans represented 29.1 percent of the population, and non-Cuban Hispanics, 20.1 percent.[27] Over the next two decades, the combination of "white flight" and an increase in the non-Cuban Hispanic population contributed to Miami's Latino cultural diversity.[28] By 2017, the percentage of Hispanics in the city increased to 68.6 percent.[29] Carib-bean, Central, and South Americans had steadily made their way to the city, solidifying the connection between the United States and the rest of the Americas.

Miami has been described as a "city on the edge," a "multiethnic city," and more recently, a "city in flux."[30] Cubans as well as Colombians, Nicaraguans, Peruvians, and other Latino groups transformed Miami into a unique space attracting a large number of import and export companies, banks, restaurants, and other businesses from all over Latin America. The image of Miami as a vacation and retirement destination furthermore built the city's reputation as a transient place. For example, geographer Jan Nijman argues that Miami, with its "constant coming and going of people," serves as "merely an interlude in [individuals'] unfolding lives."[31] However, as Elizabeth Aranda, Sallie Hughes, and Elena Sabogal show, for Latin Americans, "Miami is a place that is close to home and feels like home. [Transnational I]mmigrants can be back home in just a few hours; use their native language for daily activities; engage in famil-iar leisure, religious, or ceremonial practices; [and] find people from their own country."[32] Latin Americans of diverse backgrounds, ethnicities, and class status have relocated to and built community in Miami. The city's neighborhoods are emblematic of the cultural diversity of Latin America and the Caribbean. There are currently an estimated 86,640 Peruvians in Miami, making them the ninth-largest Latino group and the third-largest South American group after Colom-bians and Venezuelans.[33]

Notwithstanding Miami's positive attributes, the decision to leave Lima behind[34] was not easy for the Peruvian professionals in my study. Many of the immigrants I interviewed discussed the anxiety they experienced as they weighed the advantages and disadvantages of immigrating to the United States without work permits. The expectations associated with middle-class life in Lima, such as employing domestic workers to clean, cook, and take care of chil-dren, and sending children to private schools and universities would be unsus-tainable in the United States.[35] Frequently, parents informed their adult children that they would need to contribute to the household economy upon arrival in South Florida.[36]

Peruvians had access to social networks of family or friends already living in Miami who communicated seductive fragments of life in the United States.[37] Once in Miami, Peruvian migrants realized that they did not have the exten-sive or enduring social networks they had come to associate with the Cuban exile community, for instance.[38] Yet smaller Peruvian social networks were still important in helping middle-class Peruvians find housing and employment. These social networks also played a role in guiding them in their transition from a temporary to a more permanent immigrant status, while also reassuring them of their self-worth and identity. Arriving in Miami with sufficient economic capital generated from the sale of their homes and possessions in Lima, they were able to rent or to buy houses comparable to those they left behind. Peruvians settled into diverse middle-class areas alongside other Latino populations, further contributing to the unique cultural fabric of Miami, even when Peruvians have not claimed a specific geographical space within the city.[39]

As M. Cristina Alcalde has noted, middle- and upper-class Peruvians establish space boundaries along racial and class lines both within and outside Peru.[40] In Miami, Peruvians continue to socialize within these boundaries. When meeting other Peruvians, individuals acknowledged these cultural and symbolic markers by asking questions that socially located their compatriots, such as asking about the Lima neighborhoods where they had grown up or schools they had attended.[41] These markers remained paramount in reinforcing their sense of space and belonging regardless of their postmigration economic or legal status or how others perceived them in Miami.

Peruvians did not socialize or crafted forms of social capital necessarily in relationship to their Peruvian identity, but based on markers imported from their middle- and upper-middle premigration lives in Lima. Hailing from a radically heterogeneous country, in which even the Spanish language[42] could not be framed as intrinsic to a Peruvian identity, Peruvians in Miami did not seek a unifying Peruvian national identity as an exclusive criterion for building social networks. The traditional middle-class Peruvians in my research spoke only Spanish, and while this was a critical factor in their choice of Miami, they had underestimated how much of a problem their lack of English would become.

Spanish Miami or Bilingual Miami?

Emblematic of a convergence of Latin American and Caribbean populations, Miami is widely perceived as a Spanish-speaking city. Whether in Key Biscayne (an upper-class neighborhood) or Hialeah (a lower-income neighborhood),[43] "[d]ifferences in vocabulary, accent and . . . slang that are associated with country of origin and class status"[44] are commonly heard. Miami is one of the few places in the United States where speaking Spanish has become naturalized and normative.[45] While Cecilia Menjívar notes that in certain areas of the country, "Spanish fluency is often associated with poverty, undesirable occupations, a recent arrival and even undocumented status,"[46] in Miami, *not* speaking Spanish is "a disadvantage."[47]

Most participants in my research had previously visited Miami as tourists and, based on these experiences, believed it was unnecessary to speak English in South Florida. Indeed, one participant, Melissa, explained, "We chose to come to South Florida because of . . . our language difficulties, we knew that in other places it would be harder for us." Yet, unbeknownst to them, it is English–Spanish bilingualism, rather than being a Spanish speaker, that accrued social, cultural, and economic capital in Miami. Linguists Phillip Carter and Andrew Lynch have suggested that Miami is probably "the most bilingual city in all of the Americas."[48]

Upon arrival, the Peruvians in this study realized that being bilingual was essential and only unskilled jobs were available for those lacking English proficiency. One participant, Manuel, left his job as an accountant at a power utility company in Lima to find himself working as a custodian at age fifty-four. Like other Peruvians, Manuel had underestimated the language barrier. He commented: "It never occurred to me that speaking English might be crucial, for example to get a job that was more or less well paid." Luisa, a married forty-four-year-old who had a successful private law practice in Lima but migrated because of her husband's inability to find employment, also failed to anticipate the importance of English in Miami: "In Lima, everyone thinks that in Miami everyone speaks Spanish. . . . I disagree with that because even though many people speak Spanish, it is necessary to speak English."

Some Peruvian migrants assumed that learning English would enhance their cultural capital and labor market opportunities. They therefore tried to learn English, even when demanding work schedules, family responsibilities, and limited resources made this difficult. My interviews challenged the assumption that people not proficient in English lack a formal education.[49] While an ability to speak English was important for securing a professional position in Miami, legal status was indispensable.[50]

Legal Insecurity in "America's Most Miserable City"

Although middle-class Peruvians perceived Miami as a place of economic opportunities, urban researchers Richard Florida and Steve Pedigo note that income inequality in Miami is comparable to that found in some Latin American countries.[51] Miami consistently ranks as one of the poorest metropolitan cities in the United States, and in 2012, Forbes named Miami "America's most miserable city."[52] Most of the Miami workforce (47.8 percent) is in the service economy, with contingent jobs largely represented in the tourism, hospitality, food services, retail, and domestic work sectors.[53] Essentially, Miami is a geographical region divided by class. Elites and affluent Latinos gravitate toward neighborhoods along the coast, while their middle-class and lower-income counterparts could only afford to settle inland, in areas such as Kendall and Hialeah.[54]

Upon arrival, Peruvians and other immigrants faced this stark economic reality of a city divided between rich and poor, discovering to their shock that they were no longer associated with the privileged side of this divide. Liliana and her husband, former small business owners in Peru, initially had trouble securing jobs. They started painting houses for friends, something they had never done. Money was hard to come by, so Liliana took a job in a cleaning company earning less than minimum wage:

> When I arrived, I worked for a cleaning service. I didn't let them mistreat me because I told them, "no more," and I think that my knowledge and my education are worth more than for me to let another person abuse me. That has been my only obstacle, them knowing that you don't have papers, so they pay you less than the $5.50 minimum wage and with that money, I had to buy the cleaning materials.

After resigning from the cleaning company, with the help of friends she found cleaning jobs in the area where she lived. Eventually, she found a job as an office manager. It offered only slightly higher pay and did not include benefits, as she worked "off the books." Yet the job provided the emotional benefit of working in an office setting and an opportunity to build her social network. Marta, a former teacher and business owner, was not so lucky. During our interview, she claimed "there is no such thing as undignified work," but she would have preferred to stop cleaning houses. Back in Lima, Marta had a maid and only cleaned on the maid's day off. Her education contributed to her emotional turmoil and cognitive dissonance in taking orders as a subordinate: ". . . me, a Catholic University graduate, cleaning bathrooms!" When I interviewed her, she was working in five different houses, five days a week, and she was always tired because cleaning was physically demanding. Her husband had two jobs and worked six days a week just to be able to meet their expenses. In coming to terms with her new marginalized position, Marta attempted to rationalize her situation:

> The type of jobs that you never had to do before and were never used to doing, obviously you do because you have no other choice. Nevertheless, your aspirations are not to remain cleaning houses because you have a profession. My limitation is language, but I can (teach) anywhere. I also have all the skills to do it and the only thing I need is the language.

At the time, Marta's mistaken aspirations of returning to a professional career clashed with the reality of her unauthorized status and lack of English skills. Despite her and her husband's dependence on unskilled work, they continued to maintain their middle-class identity. Both of their adult children contributed to the family finances, enabling them to rent a three-bedroom condominium in a gated community. Families often pooled their salaries together to support their American middle-class lifestyle, allowing them to project many of the markers associated with Peruvian middle-class status: a nice neighborhood, how they entertained, and with whom they associated. Attending dinner parties and social events with other middle-class Peruvians, they were able to benefit from their social capital while reinforcing their sense of worth and belonging. Legal status was openly discussed. Advice, strategies, and contacts were shared in the hopes of helping find sponsorships for work visas. Presumably, these strategies would eventually enable them to return to office jobs. These gatherings were both social and informative. However, the tenor of their conversations changed when a Peruvian family facing deportation became the lead story on the Spanish local news. The public focus on unauthorized status brought back the fears, uncertainty, and insecurity the respondents had previously experienced in Lima.

The Beginnings of Fear in Miami: The Sandivar Case

After September 11, 2001, unauthorized immigration became a major threat to national security in the United States. New enforcement policies were implemented under the guise of keeping US citizens safe. The newly created Department of Homeland Security (DHS) chose Miami, along with Detroit and Anchorage, for testing a highly controversial electronic monitoring program. On January 11, 2004, the *Miami Herald* reported the case of Lourdes Sandivar, a Peruvian immigrant in Broward County who was ordered by the DHS to wear an electronic monitoring device on her ankle. She was one of thirty people wearing the ankle devices as part of this controversial program. Lourdes and her husband, Jose, had arrived in Miami with tourist visas in 1993, and one year later, they requested political asylum. Their asylum was denied, and they lost an appeal in 2002.[55] After living ten years in South Florida, the Sandivars had thirty days to pack up their lives and prepare for deportation. Although the Sandivar children were born in the United States and were US citizens, they were deported along with their parents on February 7, 2004.[56]

The Sandivar case was highly visible in the South Florida media—in both English and Spanish—as well as in Peru, and it was followed closely by the participants in my research. The Sandivar case exposed the vulnerability of their situation and brought the issue of race to the forefront. When they first arrived, these immigrants commonly believed that the authorities ignored unauthorized workers provided they otherwise respected US laws. Marta recounted her sister's advice: by respecting the laws, not committing any crimes, and not driving drunk, you can live happily in the shadows. Now, for the first time, Peruvians were in the news, and their belief that staying below the radar was safe had been shattered.

Increased surveillance of Latinos and the implementation of pilot policies in Florida created anxiety and uncertainty among Miami's immigrant population in 2003 and 2004. Constant rumors of people getting in trouble if stopped by police were rampant. Media coverage exacerbated this fear, and news stories in the

Spanish media led to the respondents' sense of vulnerability and exposure. Their daily lives were impacted by "legal violence," a term coined by Cecilia Menjívar and Leisy Abrego that explains the suffering they were experiencing caused by laws that enabled authorities to unnecessarily intrude into their lives, regardless of whether they were law-abiding members of their communities or not.[57] My interviewees perceived that the US government was targeting them but were convinced that a chance to legalize their status would solve all their problems.

While race had not previously been a salient factor in their lives, suddenly it was dominant, and they had now become visible and racialized.[58] They were racialized as "Latinos," and, in Miami, this racialization was determined primarily by their legal status.[59] The real threat of deportation became the source of their greatest emotional distress. Like unauthorized families in other areas of the country, those living in South Florida lived in constant fear of police officers.[60] Without legal status, they had to live clandestine lives. Nearly everyone I interviewed preferred to keep a low profile to avoid being noticed.

The Sandivar case brought new, but different, worries. The streets were once again dangerous, but not because of crime committed against them, as in Lima. Now, because of their unauthorized status, everyday routines—shopping, walking, or driving—could lead to being stopped, questioned, and potentially deported because they were perceived as "criminals."

In Miami to Stay

A year after arriving in Miami, Pedro was able to secure a work sponsorship with the help of a friend who owned a cleaning supply company. Pedro's lawyer was then able to file a work visa on his behalf.[61] Throughout the years, Pedro and Camila lived in an "in-between" legal status relying on lawyers that, despite charging them thousands of dollars, made multiple paperwork errors resulting in costly delays.[62] With the deadline approaching on the expiration of Pedro's work visa and still unable to adjust their status, they reluctantly left Miami.

While happy to reconnect back with family in Lima, they never quite felt "at home." Camila felt that many of the problems that initially led to their departure remained. She continued to feel unsafe and never lost hope of returning to Miami. In Lima, Pedro discovered that his application had been approved a few months after they left the United States. They immediately returned to Miami to reactivate the case and were finally able to get legal permanent status fifteen years after their initial arrival. Camila was able to validate her degree in Early Childhood Education and secure a job as a teacher in a private preschool, where her bilingual skills were valued and parents recognized the advantage of their children learning Spanish.

The experiences of professional Peruvians were similar to those described by Central Americans, Colombians, and other Latinx professionals who, because of their "in-between" legal status, were vulnerable to legal violence in various areas of their lives.[63] Many of the Peruvians I interviewed in 2003 eventually became legal residents of the United States. Although their path to legalization took many years and was fraught with setbacks, the forms of capital they possessed such as their economic and symbolic resources proved critical in helping them secure the legal resources that eventually allowed them to regularize their situations. While overstaying their visas created a legal problem, they were still able to pursue legal status through employer sponsorships, marriages, and family reunifications. However, the path to legal status is much more complicated for marginalized and working-class Peruvians who depended on *tramitadores* or migration brokers to obtain the documents necessary to leave the country.[64] This is because once in the United States, any documents misrepresenting their identities reduced the likelihood of securing legal status. In this respect, the importance of the economic, cultural, and social capital that the professional class brings with them and embody cannot be underestimated.

The middle-class professionals in my study made the choice to immigrate to South Florida misjudging the importance of speaking English. In the end, however, choosing Miami as a Spanish-friendly city became an advantage. Arriving with a modest financial safety net and utilizing their cultural and social capital to reinforce their sense of belonging, they ultimately achieved the security they desired. For them, this is where they want to be, at home in Miami.

NOTES

1 This research is part of a larger study I conducted with Elizabeth Aranda and Sallie Hughes about immigrants of seven nationalities who arrived in Miami after 1986. The study included in-depth interviews with 101 participants and fifteen focus groups composed of 110 participants conducted between 2003 and 2006. The research for this chapter includes the in-depth interviews with twenty Peruvian immigrants and two focus groups. I also conducted follow-up in-depth informal interviews in 2013 and 2019 with eight of the participants in the original study.

2 They arrived by plane with tourist visas, which did not authorize them to work in the United States.

3 Aranda, Hughes, and Sabogal, *Making a Life*; Sabogal, "Denaturalized Identities."

4 Portes and Rumbaut, *Immigrant America*.

5 Chavez, *Shadowed Lives*; Coutin, *Legalizing Moves*; Hagan, *Deciding to Be Legal*; Hagan and Rodriguez, "Resurrecting Exclusion."

6 For discussions of unauthorized migration by Brazilians, see Beserra, *Brazilian Immigrants* and Margolis, *Invisible Minority*.

7 Sassen, *Labor and Capital*.

8 Sabogal, "Viviendo en la Sombra."

9 Bourdieu, "Forms of Capital."

10 Ibid.

11 The Miami region is generally referred to as Greater Miami, Metro Miami, or the Tri-state area: Miami Dade, Broward, and Palm Beach counties.

12 Altamirano, *Los que se fueron*.

13 Paerregaard, *Return to Sender*.

14 Altamirano, *Los que se fueron*; Paerregaard, *Peruvians Dispersed*.

15 Durand, "Peruvian Diaspora," 12.

16 Crabtree and Durand, *Peru*.

17 Massey and Capoferro, "Salvese Quien Pueda."

18 Garcia, "Peru and Bolivia."

19 While structural adjustments and opening the country to international competition curbed inflation, these did not create jobs, even a decade after the first shock treatment. Unemployment rates in metropolitan Lima steadily increased from 7.8 percent in 2000 to 8.8 percent in 2001 and 9.7 percent in 2002, with higher percentages for the younger population. The rates of underemployment—people working less than full-time or beneath their level of education and experience—were also much higher. See Alvarez, "Jóvenes en la cola" and INEI, Encuesta Nacional de Hogares, 2000–2002.

20 Durand, "Peruvian Diaspora"; Sabogal, "Viviendo en la Sombra."

21 Matos Mar, *Peru*.

22 Gandolfo, *City at Its Limits*.

23 Alcalde, *Peruvian Lives Across Borders*; Golash-Boza, "Had They Been."

24 In Peruvian society, the term *cholo* has racial, social, and cultural connotations. It alludes to particular physical features but also to one's belonging to a lower and less prestigious social class.

25 Martucelli, *Lima y sus arenas*.

26 Oboler "South Americans."

27 Aranda, Hughes, and Sabogal, *Making a Life*.

28 Ibid.

29 See 2017 American Community Survey 1-Year Estimates.

30 Aranda, Hughes, and Sabogal, *Making a Life*; Portes and Armony, *Global Edge*; Portes and Stepick, *City on the Edge*.

31 Nijman, *Miami*, 118.

32 Aranda, Hughes, and Sabogal, *Making a Life*, 314.

33 See 2017 American Community Survey 1-Year Estimates.

34 In common parlance, when referring to Peru, middle- and upper-class Limeños tend to substitute "Lima" for "Peru." Historically, Lima has been the seat of political, economic, and cultural power in Peru.

35 Sabogal and Núñez, "Sin Papeles."

36 Sabogal, "Viviendo en la Sombra."

37 Massey and Capoferro, "Salvese Quien Pueda"; Tilly, "Transplanted Networks."

38 Portes and Stepick, *City on the Edge*.

39 Miami has no "Peruvian enclave" like the one in Paterson, New Jersey, which is generally referred to as "Little Lima" because of the proliferation of Peruvian businesses and restaurants in a downtown area recently designated as "Peru Square."

40 Alcalde, *Peruvian Lives Across Borders*.

41 Ibid.

42 In addition to Spanish, there are forty-seven native languages spoken in Peru.

43 Carter and Callesano, "Social Meaning of Spanish."

44 Aranda, Hughes, and Sabogal, *Making a Life*, 299.

45 Miami was the birthplace of the first contemporary English-Only movement. An antibilingualism ordinance was passed in 1980 and remained in effect until it was repealed in 1993. See Castro, "The Politics of Language in Miami."

46 Menjívar, "Living in Two Worlds?" 544.

47 Mahler, "Monolith or Mosaic?" 13.

48 Carter and Lynch, "Multilingual Miami," 369.

49 Sassen, *Labor and Capital*; Waldinger and Lichter, *The Other Half*.

50 Portes and Rumbaut, *Immigrant America*; Waldinger and Lichter, *The Other Half*.

51 Florida and Pedigo, "More Inclusive Region."

52 Aranda, Hughes, and Sabogal, *Making a Life*, 115.

53 Florida and Pedigo, "More Inclusive Region."

54 Ibid.

55 Eckland, "Ankle Lock."

56 For more information on the Sandivar case, see Berg, "El Quinto Suyo," and Sabogal, "Viviendo en la Sombra."

57 Menjívar and Abrego, "Legal Violence."

58 Omi and Winant, *Racial Formation in the United States*.

59 Aranda, Chang and Sabogal, "Racializing Miami."

60 Hagan and Rodriguez, "Resurrecting Exclusion."

61 Pedro received an H-1B nonimmigrant visa that authorized him to work. H-1B visas are temporary but provide a path to legal permanent status. Camila received an H-4 dependent visa, which, at the time, allowed her to reside but not to work in the country.

62 See Menjívar, "Liminal Legality."

63 Menjívar, "Liminal Legality;" Menjívar and Abrego, "Legal Violence;" and Aranda, Hughes and Sabogal, *Making a Life*.

64 Berg, *Mobile Selves*; Sabogal and Núñez, "Sin Papeles."

BIBLIOGRAPHY

Alcalde, M. Cristina. 2018. *Peruvian Lives across Borders: Power, Exclusion, and Home*. Urbana: University of Illinois Press.

Altamirano, Rua Teófilo. 1990. *Los que se fueron: Peruanos en Estados Unidos*. Lima: Pontificia Universidad Católica del Perú.

Alvarez, Juan. "Jóvenes en la cola." *La República*. (January 11, 2004): 12–16.

Aranda, Elizabeth, Rosa E. Chang, and Elena Sabogal. "Racializing Miami: Immigrant Latinos and Colorblind Racism in the Global City." In *How the United States Racializes Latinos: White Hegemony and Its Consequences*, edited by Jose A. Cobas, Jorge Duany, and Joe R. Feagin, 149–165. Boulder: Paradigm Publishers, 2009.

Aranda, Elizabeth, Sallie Hughes, and Elena Sabogal. 2014. *Making a Life in Multiethnic Miami: Immigration and the Rise of a Global City*. Boulder: Lynne Rienner Publishers.

Berg, Ulla D. "El Quinto Suyo: Contemporary Nation Building and the Political Economy of Emigration in Peru." *Latin American Perspectives* 37, no. 5 (September 2010): 174.

———. 2015. *Mobile Selves: Race, Migration, and Belonging in Peru and the U.S.* New York: New York University Press.

Beserra, Bernadete. 2003. *Brazilian Immigrants in the United States: Cultural Imperialism and Social Class*. New York: LFB Scholarly Publishing LLC.

Bourdieu, Pierre. "The Forms of Capital." In *Handbook of Theory and Research for the Sociology of Education*, edited by J. Richardson, 241–48. New York: Greenwood, 1986.

Carter, Phillip M., and Salvatore Callesano. "The Social Meaning of Spanish in Miami: Dialect Perceptions and Implications for Socioeconomic Class, Income, and Employment." *Latino Studies*, 16, no. 1 (2018): 65–90.

Carter, Phillip M., and Andrew Lynch. "Multilingual Miami: Trends in Sociolinguistic Research." *Language and Linguistics Compass* 9, no. 9 (2015): 369–85.

Castro, Max. "The Politics of Language in Miami." In *Miami Now!: Immigration, Ethnicity, and Social Change*, edited by Guillermo J. Grenier and Alex Stepick III, 109–32. Gainesville: University Press of Florida, 1992.

Chávez, Leo R. 1992. *Shadowed Lives: Undocumented Immigrants in American Society*. Fort Worth: Harcourt Brace Jovanovich College Publishers.

Coutin, Susan Bibler. 2003. *Legalizing Moves: Salvadoran Immigrants' Struggle for U.S. Residency*. Ann Arbor: The University of Michigan Press.

Crabtree, John, and Francisco Durand. 2017. *Peru: Elite Power and Political Capture*. London: ZED Books Ltd.

Durand, Jorge. 2010. "The Peruvian Diaspora: Portrait of a Migratory Process." Translated by Mariana Ortega Brena. *Latin American Perspectives* 174, vol. 37, no. 5 (September 2010): 12–28.

Eckland, Emily T. "Ankle Lock: Success and Sorrow." *Herald* (January 11, 2004): B1.

Florida, Richard and Steve Pedigo. "Toward a More Inclusive Region: Inequality and Poverty in Greater Miami." 2019. http://carta.fiu.edu.

Gandolfo, Daniella. 2009. *The City at Its Limits: Taboo, Transgression, and Urban Renewal in Lima*. Chicago: The University of Chicago Press.

Garcia, Jose Z. "Peru and Bolivia." In *Latin America: Its Problems and Its Promise*, edited by Jan Knippers Black, 475–94. New York: Westview, 1998.

Golash-Boza, Tanya. "'Had They Been Polite and Civilized, None of this Would Have Happened': Discourses of Race and Racism in Multicultural Lima." *Latin American and Caribbean Ethnic Studies* 5, no. 3 (November 2010): 317–30.

Hagan, Jacqueline. 1994. *Deciding to be Legal: A Maya Community in Houston*. Philadelphia: Temple University Press.

Hagan, Jacqueline, and Nestor Rodriguez. "Resurrecting Exclusion: The Effects of 1996 U.S. Immigration Reform in Communities and Families in Texas, El Salvador, and Mexico." In *Latinos: Remaking America*, edited by Marcelo M. Suarez-Orozco and Mariela M. Paez, 190–201. Berkeley: University of California Press, 2002.

INEI (Instituto Nacional de Estadística e Informática). 2000–2002. Encuesta Nacional de Hogares. Electronic Document.

Mahler, Sarah J. "Monolith or Mosaic? Miami's Twenty-First-Century Latin@ Dynamics" *Latino Studies* 16 (2018): 2–20.

Margolis, Maxine. 1998. *Invisible Minority: Brazilians in New York City*. Boston: Allyn and Bacon,.

Martucelli, Danilo. 2015. *Lima y sus arenas: Poderes sociales y jerarquías culturales*. Lima: Cauces Editores SAC.

Massey, Douglas S., and Chiara Capoferro. "Salvese Quien Pueda: Structural Adjustment and Emigration from Lima." *The Annals of the American Academy of Political and Social Science, Chronicle of a Myth Foretold: The Washington Consensus in Latin America* 606 (July 2006): 116–17.

Matos Mar, Jose. 2012. *Peru: Estado Desbordado y Sociedad Nacional Emergente*. Lima: Universidad Ricardo Palma, Centro de Investigacion.

Menjívar, Cecilia. "Living in Two Worlds? Guatemalan-Origin Children in the United States and Emerging Transnationalism." *Journal of Ethnic and Migration Studies*, 28, no. 3 (July 2002): 531–52.

———. "Liminal Legality: Salvadoran and Guatemalan Immigrants' Lives in the United States." *American Journal of Sociology* 111, no. 4 (January 2006): 999–1037.

Menjívar, Cecilia, and Leisy Abrego. "Legal Violence: Immigration Law and the Lives of Central American Immigrants." *American Journal of Sociology* 117, no. 5 (March 2012): 1380–421.

Nijman, Jan. 2011. *Miami: Mistress of the Americas*. Philadelphia: University of Pennsylvania Press.

Oboler, Suzanne. "South Americans." In *The Oxford Encyclopedia of Latinos and Latinas in the United States*, edited by Suzanne Oboler and Deena González, 146–58. New York: Oxford University Press, 2005.

Omi, Michael, and Howard Winant. 2015. *Racial Formation in the United States*. Third Edition. New York: Routledge.

Paerregaard, Karsten. 2008. *Peruvians Dispersed: A Global Ethnography of Migration*. Lanham: Lexington Books.

———. 2014. *Return to Sender: The Moral Economy of Peru's Migrant Remittances*. Woodrow Wilson Center Press, Washington, DC: University of California Press.

Portes, Alejandro, and Ariel C. Armony. 2018. *The Global Edge: Miami in the Twenty-First Century*. Oakland: University of California Press.

Portes, Alejandro, and Ruben G. Rumbaut. 1996. *Immigrant America: A Portrait*. Second Edition. Berkeley: University of California Press.

Portes, Alejandro, and Alex Stepick. 1993. *City on the Edge: The Transformation of Miami*. Berkeley: University of California Press.

Rincón, Lina. "The Indelible Effects of Legal Liminality among Colombian Migrant Professionals in the United States." *Latino Studies* 15 (September 2017): 323–40.

Sabogal, Elena. "Viviendo en la Sombra: The Immigration of Peruvian Professionals to South Florida." *Latino Studies* 3, no. 1 (April 2005): 113–31.

———. "Denaturalized Identities: Class-Based Perceptions of Self and Others among Latin American Immigrants in South Florida." *Latino Studies* 10, no. 4 (Winter 2012): 546–65.

Sabogal, Elena, and Lorena Núñez. "Sin Papeles: Middle and Working Class Peruvians in Santiago and South Florida." *Latin American Perspectives* 37, no. 5, issue 174 (September 2010): 88–105.

Sassen, Saskia. 1988. *The Mobility of Labor and Capital: A Study in International Investment and Labor Flow*. Cambridge: Cambridge University Press.

Tilly, Charles. "Transplanted Networks." In *Immigration Reconsidered—History, Sociology, and Politics*, edited by Virginia Yans-McLaughlin, 79–95. New York: Oxford University Press, 1990.

US Census. 2017 American Community Survey 1-Year Estimates. Sept 13, 2018. https://factfinder.census.gov.

Waldinger, Roger, and Michael I. Lichter. 2003. *How the Other Half Works: Immigration and the Social Organization of Labor*. Berkeley: University of California Press.

Disciplining Institutions, Evicting Regimes

The seventh critical diálogo analyzes the institutional structures that condition US Latinx everyday lives and processes of (im)mobility, at the levels of the body, the neighborhood, the nation, and the transnational. Considering a range of disciplinary regimes—from housing and shelter systems to a draconian deportation machinery and for-profit carceral industries—this diálogo more directly documents Latinx lives in a white supremacist state. This critical diálogo focuses on the commonalities and differences of these various forms of institutional control, social regulation, and surveillance practices while remaining attentive to how racial, national, gendered, and generational distinctions might yield an array of diverse outcomes. A central question that frames this critical diálogo is: *What do we gain when we consider a variety of US institutions as interdependent, mutually enforcing pieces of a system that is not abstract or distant but integrated into every aspect of Latinx daily life?*

The interconnectedness of these interdependent, mutually reinforcing US institutions range from the racial projects on which legal systems in Latin America and the United States have been solidified, and which Tanya Hernández documents to the gendered experience of homeless shelters as surveillance and policing institutions in Odilka Santiago's ethnographic work. Ulla Berg focuses on the afterlife of the US deportation regime as it impacts members of the US Peruvian diaspora who have been returned to Peru. Likewise, drawing from Latinx Studies paradigms, Bahia Munem examines the resettlement practices of Palestinian refugees throughout the Americas, by considering the (im)mobility experienced by a Palestinian extended family. Finally, Angela García extends discussions of the transformations of inheritance by centering on the life of Hispanos in New Mexico, while connecting land ownership to the embodiment of land dispossession through drug addiction. Although all the diálogos in this volume gesture to the broader connections between Latinx Studies and other disciplinary and interdisciplinary traditions, this seventh critical diálogo foregrounds more explicitly the impact of fields like Latin American Studies and Arab American Studies to what we consider the intellectual, intersectional, and comparative future of a more global Latinx Studies.

27

Latino Anti-Black Bias and the Census Categorization of Latinos

Race, Ethnicity, or Other?

TANYA KATERÍ HERNÁNDEZ

For the last few years the Census Bureau has been considering a proposal to add "Latino" and "Hispanic" to the list of government-defined races on its decennial population survey questionnaire, amongst other changes. This would be a marked shift from treating Latino/Hispanic as an ethnicity to instead treating it as a race. Since the 1980 census, "Hispanic origin" has been part of a separate ethnicity question rather than being listed as an option in the "what race are you" question on the census (Cohn 2010). Such a two-part formulation in 2010 enabled Latinos to indicate their ethnic origin as "Hispanics" and simultaneously indicate their racial identity as White, Black, Asian, American Indian, or Native Hawaiian. Yet, much to the dismay of the Census Bureau, Latinos more than any other group indicate that their race is "some other race" while writing in responses such as "Mexican," "Hispanic" or "Latin American." Thirty-seven percent of Latinos did so on the 2010 census, as did 42 percent on the 2000 census (Parker et al. 2015). In preparation for the 2020 census, the 2018 American Community Survey of 2018, estimates a 25.8 percent Some Other Race reporting rate for Latinos. The Census Bureau prefers to diminish the numbers of Latinos and others who use the Some Other Race option out of concern for how the capaciousness of the "Some Other Race" option presumably hinders the ability to make empirically precise data comparisons across years. The federal government proposes to solve this "problem" by removing the Hispanic-origin ethnicity question, and instead inserting the Hispanic/Latino category into a single race question listing of possible "races" a respondent can self-select. Despite the fact that the 2020 Decennial Census Program decided to continue to use the existing two separate question format, the Census Bureau remains interested in supporting a change to the single question format in the future.

Significantly, because so many Latinos have used the Some Other Race category option, the Census Bureau believes that Latinos are confused by the array of North American constructed racial categories (Frank, Akresh, and Lu 2010).

Reprint of Book Chapter "Latino Anti-Black Bias and the Census Categorization of Latinos: Race, Ethnicity or Other?" in the book *Antiblackness* (Duke Univ Press, 2021 eds. Moon-Kie Jung & João H. Costa Vargas).

The Census Bureau presumes that Latinos do not comprehend the stark census racial categories because of their Latin American fluid approach to racial identity and racial mixture. And there is certainly plenty of Latino rhetoric for asserting such a position, despite the fact many Latinos refuse to avail themselves of the opportunity to fluidly enumerate their multiple racial ancestries by checking multiple census racial categories (Hitlin, Brown, and Elder, Jr. 2007).

The large majority of Latino "Some Other Race" census category respondents are from Central America (Hogan 2017). It is possible that some of those Central American Latinos select the "Some Other Race" census category as a mechanism for denoting their indigenous ancestry, inasmuch as the census category "American Indian" seemingly excludes them with its instruction to print the name of the enrolled tribe or principal tribe with which they are affiliated. As a result, Latino respondents of indigenous origin may very well view the American Indian race box demand for enrolled tribe status as pertaining solely to persons of North American indigenous ancestry.

Yet, an overall examination of Latino responses to the census and other racial data collections contravenes the notion that Latinos never or cannot view race in stark terms. When provided the ability to check as many racial boxes as apply in ways that could reflect a fluid mixed-race identity, the majority of Latinos instead prefer to solely check White. For example, on the Census Bureau's 2018 annual American Community Survey, 68.61 percent of Latinos still elected to choose a single racial category apart from the Some Other Race response, and the single race chosen 95.4 percent of the time was White. Moreover, when Latino census respondents alter their choice of racial categories from one census decade to another, they primarily do so by moving from "some other race" to White. For instance, 2.5 million respondents who said they were Hispanic and "some other race" on the 2000 census, later told the census in 2010 that they were Hispanic and White (Cohn 2014). In their pursuit of Whiteness, Latinos are the largest race or ethnic group to alter their selection of racial categories from one census year to another.

Similarly, when recent Latino immigrants are surveyed and not given the option of choosing Some Other Race, 79 percent choose the single White category regardless of skin color (Frank et al. 2010). Moreover, those Latinos who are most integrated into U.S. society (based on the duration of residence in the United States and English language proficiency) are more likely than others to not choose an enumerated racial category. In short, a recently arrived cultural confusion with presumably U.S. racial categories is not the driving explanation for the Latino use of Some Other Race responses.

It is the preference for Whiteness and its twin flight from Blackness that is a more accurate reflection of any presumed "Latino" cultural expression on the census form. In contrast to the many reports of a Latino preference for mixed-race census racial categories, there is a strong Latino preference for the White racial category and some Latino groups like Cubans disproportionately select the White racial category (Darity, Jr., Hamilton & Dietrich: 2010). Moreover, a closer study of Latino racial preferences across generations in the United States from 1989–1990, entitled the Latino National Political Survey, found that a substantial majority of respondents chose to self-identify as White (Golash-Boza and Darity, Jr. 2008). The study indicated that the White racial category is particularly preferred by recent immigrants of all skin color shades. And when later generations do move away from the White racial category, they do so in favor of collective national ethnic labels like "Latino" or "Hispanic."

Census data from Latin American countries show the same proclivity for the White racial category regardless of actual skin color in response to the Latin American disdain for African and indigenous ancestry (Telles 2014). Latin American census experiences suggest that the United States Latino "Some Other Race" selection may instead be an outgrowth of the cultural preference for Whiteness and its companion disdain for indigeneity and Blackness. A brief consideration of the Latin American racial context will help illuminate how the Census proposed reform to treat Latinos as a racial category rather than an ethnic one may become another mechanism for refusing to officially acknowledge indigenous and particularly African ancestry within the Latino community.

Latin American Racism Comparison

Racism and in particular anti-Black racism is a pervasive and historically entrenched fact of life in Latin America and the Caribbean. Over 90 percent of the approximately 10 million enslaved Africans brought to the Americas were taken to Latin America and the Caribbean, whereas only 4.6 percent were brought to the United States (Jiménez Román: 1996). And so the historical legacy of slavery is pervasive in Latin America and the Caribbean.

In Latin America and the Caribbean, like the United States, having lighter skin and European features increases the chances of socioeconomic opportunity, while have darker skin and African/Indigenous features severely limits such opportunity and social mobility (Hernández 2013). Predictably the poorest socioeconomic class is populated primarily by Afro-Latinos, the most privileged class is populated primarily by Whites, and an elastic intermediary socioeconomic standing exists for some light-skinned mulattos (mixed-race Blacks) and mestizos (mixed-race Indigenous persons). For instance, until the Cuban revolution in 1959, certain occupations used explicit color preferences to hire Mulattos to the complete exclusion of dark-skinned Afro-Cubans, based on the premise that Mulattos were superior to dark-skinned Afro-Cubans but not of the same status as Whites (Rout 1976). Such White supremacy is deeply ingrained and continues into the present in Cuba and the rest of the region (Cleland 2017; Sawyer 2006).

For instance, in research conducted in Puerto Rico, the overwhelming majority of college students interviewed described "Puerto Ricans who are 'dumb' as
having 'dark skin'" (Hall 2000). Conversely, the same interviewees correlated
"light" skin color with a description of "Puerto Ricans who are physically strong."
Such negative perspectives about African ancestry are not limited to the college
study participants. In 1988, when the presiding Governor of Puerto Rico publicly
stated that "[t]he contribution of the black race to Puerto Rican culture is irrelevant, it is mere rhetoric," it was in keeping with what social scientists describe
as the standard paradox in Puerto Rico: Puerto Ricans take great pride in the
purported claim of being the Whitest people of the Caribbean islands, while
simultaneously asserting themselves as non-racist. The pride of being a presumably White population is a direct reaction to the Puerto Rican understanding
that "black people are perceived to be culturally unrefined and lack ambition"
(Torres 1998: 297). More recent research on racial segregation in Puerto Rico
only confirms these racialized attitudes (Dinzey-Flores 2013 & Godreau 2015).
The Puerto Rican example is emblematic of the racial attitudes throughout the
Caribbean and Latin America (Hernández 2013).

As in the United States, the disparagement of Black identity is not limited to
Mulattos and Whites, but also extends to darker-skinned Afro-Latinos who can
harbor internalized racist norms. The internalization manifests itself in a widespread concern among Afro-Latinos with the degree of darkness in pigmentation, width of nose, thickness of lips, and quality of one's hair—with straight,
presumably European hair denominated literally as "good" hair. This concern
with European skin and features also influences Afro-Latino assessments of
preferred marriage partners. Marrying someone lighter is called "adelantando
la raza" (improving the race) under the theory of "blanqueamiento" (whitening), which prizes the mixture of races precisely to help diminish the existence
of Afro-Latinos (Martínez-Echazabal 1998). Even familial affection has been
observed to be influenced by the extent of one's Black appearance (Bonilla-Silva
2010). It should not be so surprising then, that migrants from Latin America and
the Caribbean travel to the United States with their culture of anti-Black racism
well intact along with all other manifestations of their culture (Torres-Saillant
2002). And that in turn this facet of Latino culture is transmitted to some degree
to younger generations along with all other transmissions of Latino culture in
the United States.

Afro-Latinos in the United States

For Latinos in the United States "being, or becoming, anything other than black
is preferable" (Cruz-Janzen 2007: 83). Furthermore, the Latino imaginary consistently identifies a White face as the quintessential Latino (DiFulco, 2003:86).
Even for those Latinos who do acknowledge their African ancestry, there is a

cultural pressure to publicly emphasize their Latino ethnicity as a mechanism for distancing themselves from public association with the denigrated societal class of Anglo-Blacks (Pessar 1995: 44). This truism is highlighted by the popular refrain "The darker the skin, the louder the Spanish," (Howard 2001: 114–115). Thus, compounding the Latin American cultural legacy of anti-Blackness, is the Latino resistance to a United States framework in which Latinos of all shades are often viewed as non-White depending on the context.

While commentators in the United States are seemingly oblivious to the native anti-Black racism of Latinos, the one arena in which Latino anti-Black racism has been discussed in the United States, is with respect to the apparent racial caste system of Spanish-language television that presents Latinos as almost exclusively White (Fletcher, 2000). In fact, because of the scarce but derogatory images of Afro-Latinos in the media, activists even considered a lawsuit against the two major Spanish-language networks to challenge their depiction of Afro-Latinos. Some Latino activists see a direct parallel between the Whiteness of Spanish-language television and Latino politics. One such activist states:

> Latino leaders and organizations do not want to acknowledge that racism exists among our people, so they have ignored the issue by subscribing to a national origin strategy. This strategy identifies Latinos as a group comprising different nationalities, thereby creating the false impression that Latinos live in a color-blind society. (Flores 2001:30–31)

But many concrete examples demonstrate that Latinos are not color-blind and nor do they emanate from color-blind contexts. To begin with, Afro-Latinos in the United States consistently report receiving racist treatment at the hands of other Latinos in addition to being perceived as outsiders to the construction of Latino identity. For example, Afro-Latinos are frequently mistaken for African Americans in their own communities and upon identifying themselves as Afro-Latinos are told, "But you don't look Latino" (Comas-Diaz, 1996). Indeed the 2002 National Survey of Latinos sponsored by the Pew Hispanic Center and the Kaiser Family Foundation indicated that Latinos with more pronounced African ancestry, such as many Dominicans, more readily identify color discrimination as an explanation for the bias they experience from other Latinos (Pew Hispanic Center & The Kaiser Family Foundation 2002). Moreover, the 2010 National Survey of Latinos found that after immigrant status, skin color discrimination is the most prevalent perceived form of discrimination for Latinos. The 2019 Pew Research Center survey of Latinos found that Latinos with darker skin are more likely to experience discrimination than those with lighter skin (González-Barrera 2019). Indeed, the skin tone bias has been empirically connected to a strong wage penalty for darker skin Latin American immigrants that is often nonexistent or much less pronounced among other national-origin populations

(Rosenblum et al. 2016). Moreover, employment discrimination cases involving Latinos often implicate anti-Black bias in Latino discrimination against Afro-Latinos and African Americans (Hernández 2007). Even the presumably more enlightened spaces of academia are not immune, as Afro-Latino college students report that "Latino spaces have always been the most violent" on college campuses (Haywood 2017).

Furthermore, Latino life circumstances are influenced not only by the social meaning of being of Hispanic origin but also by how facial connections to Africa racialize a Latino as also Black. Studies suggest that the socioeconomic status of Afro-Latinos in the United States is more akin to that of African Americans than to other Latinos or White Americans. Latinos who identify themselves as "Black" have lower incomes, higher unemployment rates, higher rates of poverty, less education, and fewer opportunities and are more likely to reside in segregated neighborhoods than those who identify themselves as "White" or "other" (Logan 2003; López and González-Barrera 2016; Monforti and Sánchez 2010).

In addition, despite the fact that Afro-Latino health behaviors are similar to the Latino ethnic groups they pertain to culturally, Afro-Latino health outcomes in meager access to health insurance and health services are racially distinctive and more in line with the racially disparate health outcomes of African Americans (LaVeist-Ramos et al. 2012). Even high blood pressure rates have been observed to vary with socially perceived racial differences unrelated to actual scientific degrees of pigmentation, such that those perceived as Afro-Puerto Rican have higher blood pressures and rates of hypertension than Puerto Ricans socially perceived as more European descended (Gravlee, Dressler, and Bernard 2005). Furthermore, socially perceived Blackness is more predictive of Latino mental health status than Latino racial self-identification (López et al. 2017). Given the significance of how much African phenotype, hair and skin shade influence the socioeconomic status of Latinos, some studies indicate that interviewer observations of racial appearance provide the most accurate tool for monitoring discrimination among Latinos of varying shades (Roth 2010).

In fact, sociologist Nancy López notes that there is mounting evidence that there are distinct social outcomes in terms of intermarriage, housing segregation, educational attainment, prison sentencing, and labor market outcomes that vary for Latinos according to externally perceived racial status (López 2013). Thus, the ability to document the racial disparity within Latino ethnic communities is fundamentally advanced by having Census data that separately asks Latinos to indicate both their Hispanic-origin ethnicity and their racial ancestry (López 2013). Treating Hispanic-origin ethnicity as a homogeneous group signifier obscures the complexity of the socioeconomic racial hierarchy that exists across Latino communities that census racial data was designed to help measure.

Equality Law Census Racial Data Uses

The Office of Management and Budget (OMB) racial and ethnic classifications that the Census Bureau uses were devised in 1977 for the specific purpose of facilitating the enforcement of civil rights laws. Census racial data is principally used to enforce the civil rights mandates against discrimination in employment, in the selling and renting of homes, and in the allocation of mortgages. The U.S. Department of Housing and Urban Development uses census racial data to determine where to locate low-income and public housing. Census racial data is also used in voting-rights redistricting to improve the political participation of people of color. In short, when the census collects racial data, the primary concern is not with how a person individually identifies, but rather with how society differentiates that person for the purpose of measuring any possible racial disparity.

For this reason, the Census Bureau consideration to modify the census demographic questions so as to remove the Hispanic/Latino option as an ethnic choice and instead have it presented as a racial category distinct from Black and all others, has been viewed with alarm by Afro-Latino activists (Reyes 2014). Collapsing Latino and Hispanic ethnic identity into the list of racial categories with Black in particular, risks obscuring the number of Afro-Latinos and the monitoring of socio-economic status differences of Latinos across race that exist.

Unfortunately, many Latino leaders assert Whiteness as a key component of their identity and this is especially apparent in their lack of concern with the need to monitor racial disparity amongst Latinos (Haney López 2003). For instance, the National Association of Latino Elected and Appointed Officials (NALEO) Educational Fund, the Mexican American Legal Defense and Education Fund, and the National Council of La Raza all publicly endorsed the Census Bureau recommendation to treat Hispanic as a homogeneous racial category, with the assertion that there would be very little loss in necessary data since Afro-Latinos could always elect to check both the Hispanic race box and the Black race box to indicate their Afro-Latino identity (NALEO 2017).

What such a perspective under-appreciates is how over time Latino anti-Black bias will inhibit the count of Afro-Latinos in ways that the Census Bureau experiments with test questions could not readily appreciate. When "Hispanic" is juxtaposed as a racial category distinct from others, Latinos perceive the other categories as pertaining only to non-Hispanics. This helps to explain why Puerto Ricans in Puerto Rico differ in their use of the Some Other Race box compared to Puerto Ricans living in the mainland United States. Only 11 percent of Puerto Ricans in Puerto Rico selected "Some Other Race" or "Two or More Races" on the 2010 census, as compared with the 30.8 percent of mainland Puerto Ricans that selected Some Other Race or Two or More Races (Hogan 2017). On the island of Puerto Rico, Puerto Ricans can view the racial categories as pertaining to themselves and not exclusively to North American census takers. As a result, over 75 percent of Puerto Ricans on the island self-identified as White on the 2010 Census, and only 3.3 per cent of respondents indicated Two or More Races (Allen 2017).

The island Puerto Rican embrace of Whiteness despite the contestation as to whether White appearance is empirically as dominant as the Puerto Rico Census numbers suggest also raises a parallel hindrance to the count of Afro-Latinos—the Latino cultural flight from Blackness. Juxtaposing Hispanic as a race distinct from others also situates Blackness as uniquely African American inasmuch as Latinos historically prefer to view Blackness as always situated outside of their national identities (Hernández 2003). The distancing of Blackness in Puerto Rico thus enables Puerto Ricans to view Blackness as imbued primarily in their Dominican neighbors, while Dominicans instead view Blackness as imbued primarily in their Haitian neighbors (Duany 2002). A similar racial distancing happens in other Latin American countries where Blackness is presumed to be contained to geographically limited spaces rather than being a fundamental part of the nation state (Minority Rights Group 1995). Latino Blackness is never within but instead displaced elsewhere. For U.S. based Latinos, "real" Blackness is only imbued in African Americans along with English speaking Afro-Caribbeans and Africans. Again, Blackness is always somewhere else. Even in Miami, Florida's large Caribbean population, Blackness is often exclusively associated with African-Americans, such that Afro-Cubans consistently report not feeling welcomed by their fellow White Cuban residents (Gosin 2017).

Collapsing Hispanic ethnicity into the Census racial categories rather than having it remain a separate ethnicity question shields Latinos from confronting their own possible Blackness. In contrast, retaining two separate questions enables all Latinos to demarcate their Hispanic origin as an ethnicity with the first question, and then reflect on their racial origins with the second question specifically on race. Forcing the confrontation with the racial question on the census form can be a very productive navigation of the Latino cognitive dissonance with Blackness. This is borne out by the narratives of Afro-Latinos relating how the census race question brings out from the shadows family discussions of Blackness and race (Hoy 2010).

The concern of Latino leaders that the current two-question ethnicity/race census survey framework may hinder the ability to use census data to accurately portray and challenge the societal exclusion of Latinos qua Latinos, misapprehends how Equality Law jurisprudence assesses anti-Latino discrimination. The Supreme Court enforces the constitutional protections against racial discrimination for all Latinos, not because they are viewed as a "race" but because Latinos are a group distinguished by bias in "the attitude of the community" despite not being uniformly distinguishable based on race or color (Hernández v. Texas 1954). Civil Rights statutory protections against racial discrimination are also accorded to Latinos because "race includes ethnicity" when Latino ethnicity is subject to adverse differentiation compared to Anglo Whiteness or other racial and ethnic groups (Village of Freeport v. Barrella 2016: 598). When allegations of anti-Latino discrimination are presented in court, claimants are thus authorized to use the census count of Hispanic-origin ethnicity responses with which to compare their disparate exclusion.

In short, what this chapter has attempted to demonstrate is that the Latino use of the Some Other Race category need not be viewed by the Census Bureau as a "problem" that needs to be solved. Rather, the Some Other Race usage provides relevant information about the persistence of Latino anti-Black bias in the flight from considering race. That insight should be viewed as an invitation to provide a forum for confronting race and its social salience.

REFERENCES

"2010 National Survey of Latinos," Washington, DC: Pew Research Center Hispanic Trends Project (www.pewhispanic.org).

Allen, Reuben. 2017. "Investigating the cultural conception of race in Puerto Rico: residents' thoughts on the U.S. Census, discrimination, and interventionist policies." *Latin American and Caribbean Ethnic Studies* 12: 201–226.

Bailey, Benjamin. 2001. "Dominican-American Ethnic Racial Identities and U.S. Social Categories." *International Migration Review* 35: 677–708.

Cleland, Danielle Pilar. 2017. *The Power of Race in Cuba: Racial Ideology and Black Consciousness during the Revolution*. New York, NY: Oxford University Press.

Cohn, D'Vera. 2010. "Census History: Counting Hispanics." Pew Research Center Social & Demographic Trends (www.pewsocialtrends.org).

Cohn, D'Vera. 2014. "Millions of Americans changed their racial or ethnic identity from one census to the next." Pew Research Center: Fact Tank News in the Numbers. Retrieved August 16, 2019 (www.pewresearch.org).

Comas-Diaz, Lillian. 1996. "LatiNegra: Mental Health Issues of African Latinas." In *The Multiracial Racial Borders as New Frontier*, edited by Maria P.P. Root, 167–90. New York: Sage Publishers.

Cruz-Janzen, Marta I. 2007. "Madre Patria (Mother Country): Latino Identity and Rejection of Blackness." *Trotter Review* 17: 79–92.

Darity, Jr., William, Darrick Hamilton & Jason Dietrich. 2010. "Passing on Blackness: Latinos, race and earnings in the USA." *Applied Economics Letters* 9: 847–853.

De Genova, Nicholas and Ana Y. Ramos-Zayas. 2003. *Latino Crossings: Mexicans, Puerto Ricans, and the Politics of Race and Citizenship*. New York, NY: Routledge.

DiFulco, Denise. 2003. "Can You Tell a Mexican from a Puerto Rican?" *Latina*, August 2003 8(1): 86–88.

Dinzey-Flores, Zaire Zenit. 2013. *Locked In, Locked Out: Gated Communities in a Puerto Rican City*. Philadelphia, PA: University of Pennsylvania Press.

Duany, Jorge. 2002. *The Puerto Rican Nation on the Move: Identities on the Island and the United States*. Chapel Hill, NC: University of North Carolina Press.

Dzidzienyo, Anani, and Suzanne Oboler, eds. 2005. *Neither Enemies nor Friends: Latinos, Blacks, Afro-Latinos*. New York: Palgrave Macmillan.

Ennis, Sharon R., and Merarys-Rios Vargas, Nora G. Albert. 2010. *The Hispanic Population: 2010*, Washington, DC: United States Census Bureau (www.census.gov).

Fletcher, Michael A. 2000. "The Blond, Blue-Eyed Face of Spanish TV." *Washington Post*, Aug. 3, 2000, A01.

Flores, Carlos. 2001. "Race Discrimination Within the Latino Community." *Diálogo, Center for Latino Research DePaul University*, Winter/Spring 2001(5): 30–31.

Frank, Reanne, Ilana Redstone Akresh, and Bo Lu. 2010. "Latino Immigrants and the U.S. Racial Order: How and Where Do They Fit In?" *American Sociological Review* 75(3): 378–401.

Godreau, Isar P. 2015. *Scripts of Blackness: Race, Cultural Nationalism, and U.S. Colonialism in Puerto Rico*. Champaign, Illinois: University of Illinois Press.

Golash-Boza, Tanya and William Darity, Jr. 2008. "Latino racial choices: The effects of skin colour and discrimination on Latinos' and Latinas' racial self-identifications." *Ethnic and Racial Studies* 31: 899–934.

González-Barrera, Ana. 2019. "Hispanics with darker skin are more likely to experience discrimination than those with lighter skin." Pew Research Center Fact Tank: News in the Numbers. Retrieved August 15, 2019 (www.pewresearch.org).

Gosin, Monika. 2017. "'A bitter diversion': Afro-Cuban immigrants, race, and everyday-life resistance." *Latino Studies* 15: 4–28.

Gravlee, Clarence C., William W. Dressler, and H. Russell Bernard. 2005. "Skin Color, Social Classification, and Blood Pressure in Southeastern Puerto Rico." *American Journal of Public Health* 95: 2191–2197.

Grieco, Elizabeth M. 2010. *Race and Hispanic Origin of the Foreign-Born Population in the United States: 2007* Washington, DC: U.S. Census Bureau.

Haney López, Ian F. 2003. "White Latinos." *Harvard Latino Law Review* 6: 1–7.

Haywood, Jasmine M. 2017. "'Latino spaces have always been the most violent': Afro-Latino collegians' perceptions of colorism and Latino intragroup marginalization." *International Journal of Qualitative Studies in Education* 30(8): 759–82.

Hernández v. Texas, 347 U.S. 475, 479–80 (1954).

Hernández, Tanya Katerí. 2003. "'Too Black to Be Latino': Blackness and Blacks as Foreigners in Latino Studies." *Latino Studies* 1: 152–159.

Hernández, Tanya Katerí. 2007. "Latino Inter-Ethnic Employment Discrimination and the 'Diversity' Defense." *Harvard Civil Rights-Civil Liberties Law Review* 42: 259–316.

Hernández, Tanya Katerí. 2013. *Racial Subordination in Latin America: The Role of the State, Customary Law, and the New Civil Rights Response*. New York, NY: Cambridge University Press.

Hitlin Steven, J. Scott Brown, and Glen H. Elder, Jr. 2007. "Measuring Latinos: Racial vs. Ethnic Classification and Self-Understandings." *Social Forces* 86: 587–611.

Hogan, Howard. 2017. "Reporting of Race Among Hispanics: Analysis of ACS Data." Pp. 169–191 in *The Frontiers of Applied Demography*. Cham, Switzerland: Springer International.

Howard, David. 2001. *Coloring the Nation: Race and Ethnicity in the Dominican Republic*. Boulder, CO: Lynne Rienner Publishers, Inc.

Hoy, Vielka Cecilia. 2010. "Negotiating among Invisibilities: Tales of Afro-Latinidades in the United States." Pp. 426–430 in *The Afro-Latin@ Reader: History and Culture in the United States*, edited by Miriam Jiménez Román and Juan Flores. Durham, N.C.: Duke University Press.

Jiménez Román, Miriam, and Juan Flores, eds. 2010. *The Afro-Latin@ Reader: History and Culture in the United States*. Durham, N.C.: Duke University Press.

Jorge, Angela. 1979. "The Black Puerto Rican Woman in Contemporary American Society." Pp. 134–141 in *The Puerto Rican Woman*, edited by Edna Acosta-Belén. New York: Praeger Publishers.

LaVeist-Ramos, Thomas Alexis, Jessica Galarraga, Roland J. Thorpe Jr., Caryn N. Bell, and Chermeia J. Austin. 2012. "Are Black Hispanics Black or Hispanic? Exploring disparities at the intersections of race and ethnicity." *Journal Epidemiological Community Health* 66: 1–5.

Logan, John R. 2003 "How Race Counts for Hispanic Americans." Lewis Mumford Center, University at Albany, State University of New York. (mumford.albany.edu).

López, Gustavo and Ana González-Barrera. 2016. "Afro-Latino: A deeply rooted identity among U.S. Hispanics." Pew Research Center Fact Tank: News in the Numbers. Retrieved August 15, 2019 (www.pewresearch.org).

López, Nancy. 2013. "Killing two birds with one stone? Why we need two separate questions on race and ethnicity in the 2020 census and beyond." *Latino Studies* 11: 428–438.

López, Nancy, Edward Vargas, Melina Juarez, Lisa Cacari-Stone and Sonia Bettez. 2017. "What's Your 'Street Race'? Leveraging Multidimensional Measures of Race and Intersectionality for Examining Physical and Mental Health Status among Latinx." *Sociology of Race and Ethnicity* 1–18.

Martínez-Echazabal, Lourdes. 1998. "Race and National Identity in the Americas." *Latin American Perspectives* 25: 21–42.

Minority Rights Group, ed. 1995. *No Longer Invisible: Afro-Latin Americans Today*. London: Minority Rights Publications.

Monforti, Jessica Lavariega and Gabriel Sánchez. 2010. "The Politics of Perception: An Investigation of the Presence and Sources of Perception of Internal Discrimination Among Latinos." *Social Science Quarterly* 91(1): 245–265.

NALEO (National Association of Latino Elected and Appointed Officials) Education Fund. 2017. Policy Brief: "The Census Bureau's Proposed "Combined Question" Approach Offers Promise for Collecting More Accurate Data on Hispanic Origin and Race, but Some Questions Remain" (http://d3n8a8pro7vhmx.cloudfront.net).

Parker, Kim. 2015. *Multiracial in America: Proud, Diverse and Growing in Numbers*. Washington, DC: Pew Research Center. Retrieved November 20, 2017 (http://assets.pewresearch.org).

Pessar, Patricia R. 1995. *A Visa for a Dream: Dominicans in the United States*. Needham Heights, MA: Allyn and Bacon, a Division of Simon and Schuster.

Pew Hispanic Center & The Kaiser Family Foundation. 2002. "National Survey of Latinos." Retrieved August 15, 2019 (www.pewresearch.org).

Reanne Frank, Ilana Redstone Akresh, and Bo Lu. 2010. "Latino Immigrants and the U.S. Racial Order: How and Where Do They Fit In?" *American Sociological Review* 75: 378.

Reyes, Raúl A. 2014. "Afro-Latinos Seek Recognition and Accurate Census Count," *NBC News*, Sept. 21, 2014 (www.nbcnews.com).

Rosenblum, Alexis, William Darity, Jr., Angel L. Harris, and Tod Hamilton. 2016. "Looking through the Shades: The Effect of Skin Color on Earnings by Region of Birth and Race for Immigrants to the United States." *Sociology of Race and Ethnicity* 2(1): 87–105.

Roth, Wendy D. 2010. "Racial Mismatch: The Divergence Between Form and Function in Data for Monitoring Racial Discrimination of Hispanics." *Social Science Quarterly* 91: 1288–1311.

Rout, Jr., Leslie B. 1976. *The African Experience in Spanish America*. Princeton, NJ: Markus Wiener Pub.

Sawyer, Mark. 2006. *Racial Politics in Post-Revolutionary Cuba*. New York, NY: Cambridge University Press.

Telles, Edward. 2014. *Pigmentocracies: Ethnicity, Race, and Color in Latin America*. Chapel Hill: University of North Carolina Press.

Thomas, Piri. 1967. *Down These Mean Streets*. New York: Knopf.

Torres-Saillant, Silvio. 2002. "Problematic Paradigms: Racial Diversity and Corporate Identity in the Latino Community." Pp. 435–455 in *Latinos: Remaking America*, edited by Marcelo M. Suarez-Orozco and Mariela M. Paez. Berkeley, CA: University of California Press.

Torres, Arlene. 1998. "La Gran Familia Puertorriqueña 'Ej Prieta de Belda' (The Great Puerto Rican Family is Really Really Black)." Pp. 285–306 in *Blackness in Latin America and the*

Caribbean, vol. 2, edited by Arlene Torres and Norman E. Whitten, Jr. Bloomington, IN: Indiana University Press.

U.S. Census Bureau. 2015. "2020 Census Operational Plan" (www2.census.gov).

U.S. Census Bureau, 2018. "American Community Survey Table of Hispanic or Latino Origin Population by Race" (https://data.census.gov).

Village of Freeport v. Barrella, 814 F.3d 594, 598 (2nd Cir. 2016).

28

Regulating Space and Time

The Disciplining of Latina and Black Sheltered-Homeless Women in NYC

ODILKA S. SANTIAGO

While accompanying Deana, a Black and Puerto Rican single mother, and her son to their shelter unit in a six-story private building on the Upper West Side of Manhattan, we were greeted by two security cameras. One faced the entrance of the building and the other the stairs descending to the basement. Underneath one of the cameras, a sign read "No Loitering." A security guard "peace officer"[1] sat at the entrance with the sign-in sheet. He made sure that Deana and her son did not return with contraband and were in the building by the 9:00 p.m. curfew. If a resident missed curfew without a pass more than three times, they would be kicked out. Visitors are not allowed inside the building. "This is more like a prison than a shelter," Deana complained. "I am like a prisoner." The level of monitoring that sheltered-homeless people like Deana experience ranges from security guards and metal detectors to regularly giving out their private information to social workers.

Constituting three-quarters of NYC's homeless shelter population, Black and Latina[2] families are the fastest-growing demographics in the city's shelter system. Housing insecurity and homelessness are racialized problems; 58 percent of shelter residents are African American, and 31 percent are Latinx (Coalition for the Homeless 2019a). While there are more white women using welfare, Latina and Black women are treated more punitively. Black and Latina women have been disproportionately kicked off the roll for "socially unacceptable reasons," like having children out of wedlock or for having the father of their children in prison (Piven and Cloward 1971; Roberts 1997).

This chapter illustrates the role of the state in disciplining racially marginalized populations through surveillance practices in homeless shelters and welfare offices. Welfare assistance and shelter are available only for those who work for it. The shelter system's infrastructure, punitive rules, monitoring, and long wait periods are designed to discipline sheltered-homeless women into accepting structural inequalities (Piven and Cloward 1971, 7, 45) and racialized class divisions (Neubeck and Cazenave 2001; Willse 2015). The presumed equal access to public services obscures the penal and punitive conditions that Latina and Black women experience in shelters and welfare offices. The homeless shelter system requires that individuals forfeit all rights to privacy and time.

The conditions and practices in shelters and welfare offices in NYC convey to clients that they should comply and accept poverty as their fault, as an individual problem. For example, a popular phrase repeated when first meeting women and asking to interview them during outreach in the summers of 2017 and 2018 was: "I'm not like these women," or "This is just a bad time but this [situation] is not *me*." They become institutionalized into the shelter system and must navigate through many time-consuming obstacles to qualify for basic services like housing and food. The twists and turns through the shelter system divert attention away from the larger problem of housing insecurity and un/underemployment while delaying the process of finding permanent housing.

This chapter is based on in-depth interviews with twenty-five Latina and Black sheltered-homeless women in New York City during the summers of 2017 and 2018. These women had lived in a shelter for at least a year. Previously some lived in an apartment without being on the lease or had a lease that was not renewed. Others had moved from elsewhere following a promise of housing by a friend, family member, or contact, only to have that promise gone unmet. Others had escaped domestic violence. Homeless outreach organizers use the term "sheltered-homeless" to describe a person housed in a municipal shelter, in contrast to the "street-homeless" who sleep outside. This distinction in terms is important for homeless grassroots organizations fighting for housing and civil rights for all varieties of homeless people, like Picture the Homeless (PTH) in East Harlem. Volunteering and doing outreach with this organization from 2017 to 2019 has greatly informed this chapter. I also interviewed staff at nonprofit organizations. The shelter system's punitive rules and practices, like curfew, mandatory meetings, and long waiting lines, do not necessarily provide permanent housing but instead reinforce the state's control over these women's bodies.

Scholarship on Homelessness

While there has been a significant growth of Black and Latina women and families entering homeless shelters, few studies address the experiences of these populations. The valuable literature on poverty that critically examines welfare policy, social regulation, and gender (Abramovitz 1988; Piven and Cloward 1967, 1971) and race (Neubeck and Cazenave 2001; Roberts 1997, 2001) says little about homelessness or homeless shelters. Gentrification studies that attend to homelessness generally focus on policy changes, class relations, surplus labor, and spatial politics (Bratt, Hartman, and Meyerson 1984; Chronopoulos 2011; Marcuse 1978, 2016; Willse 2015). Qualitative studies of homelessness only offer the personal experiences and perspectives of homeless men and women living on the street (Carter and Duneier 1999; Liebow 1993). Other scholarship situates homelessness within examinations of health and hygiene (Jones 2016; Riis 1957).

An important contributor to the scholarship on homelessness is cultural studies scholar Craig Willse (2015), who argues that homelessness and housing insecurity are technologies of state racism. Willse argues that homelessness as a problem has obscured the material conditions that produced housing deprivation and techniques that have expanded insecurities (54). Likewise, anthropologist Aimee Cox (2018) explores how young Black women resist and disrupt exclusionary practices in a Detroit shelter. Faced with stereotypes and the real, material degrading experiences of homelessness, poverty, abandonment, and shame, these young Black women use "choreography" as a method to challenge popular discourses that marginalize them. They create transformative and empowering responses that challenge talk of them as "undesirable, dangerous, captive or out of place" (29). Thus, Cox provides a valuable framework to think about different forms of agency that sheltered women exercise.

Within Latina/o/x studies, numerous scholars have focused on gentrification and displacement (Betancur 2005; Muñiz 1988; Pérez 2002; Rúa 2017) but with little, if any, mention of the homeless. The scholarship that does attend to Latinx homelessness concentrates mainly on the street homeless in relation to migration, employment, language cultural barriers, and community support (Baker 1996; Chinchilla and Gabrielian 2019; Conroy and Heer 2003). The lack of scholarship on the sheltered-homeless in Latinx studies could be due to Latinxs avoiding homeless shelters out of fear of deportation, past experiences of discrimination, or lack of Spanish translators (Chinchilla and Gabrielian 2019). This chapter ventures outside of these approaches by focusing on the disproportionate way Latina and Black homeless women who seek public shelter are socially regulated, policed, and surveilled.

Surveillance is defined here as a technology and technique of governance aimed at producing disciplined bodies through potential constant state control. This technology of governance is part of the state apparatus developed during the transition to modern capitalism. In 1791, English philosopher Jeremy Bentham proposed surveillance through the "the panopticon," as a model through which the built environment operates to instill discipline, "good" behavior, and efficiency. French philosopher Michel Foucault (1977) goes further. He suggests that surveillance is a physics of power that makes its populations knowable for the sake of subjecting them to social regulation and discipline. With the potential gaze of an authority figure, the prisoner, the student, or the worker would act appropriately. Broadly understood, surveillance and knowledge collection are used by the state to exercise power over its population. However, this gaze is not equally distributed. Conventional surveillance scholarship generally examines prison, state security, policing, risk-assessment, and management but rarely considers the role of race or gender (Browne 2015; Cole 2002; McCoy 2009; Parenti 2003; Rao and Pierce 2006). Latina and Black homeless women are generally left out of this scholarship. However, the monitoring of marginalized Latina and Black women directly relates to how the state surveils so-called problem populations, like the undocumented or criminals, because they can disrupt the capital (re)production of the state.

Knowledge-based techniques or "dataveillance," which include data collection by institutional staff (Foucault 1977, 196–197; Lyon 2003; Monahan 2010; Parenti 2003), has also become part of what we understand as the contemporary surveillance apparatus. With the exception of Simone Browne (2015), there has been scant attention to the state-sanctioned punishment and monitoring of women of color in surveillance studies. The few studies that consider the surveillance of Latinx populations concentrate on border control, immigration, and antiterrorist security in the United States (Monahan 2010; Parenti 2003) or the surveillance of political activists, like, for instance, the Young Lords Party in the 1970s (Fernández 2011). As I also highlight in this essay, space and technology are inherently racialized, gendered, and unequally administered depending on the nature of public spaces, digital spaces, and the body.

Latina and Black women navigate the disciplinary landscape of the homeless shelter system as they assert their agency, personhood, and dignity. Since Ronald Reagan's 1976 presidential campaign, racially charged invocations of the infamous "welfare queen"—a fraudulent, lazy, freeloading welfare system cheat— have been deployed to justify invasive home monitoring and surveillance of Black and Brown women and to inform the discriminatory practices of welfare caseworkers (Briggs 2002; Katz 1986; Neubeck and Cazenave 2001; Piven and Cloward 1971; Roberts 1997). The purpose of telling these stories is to expand popular understandings of surveillance beyond national security and domestic terrorism. Instead, I focus on the containment of so-called "problem populations," particularly homeless Latina and Black women.

Conditions of Shelters

A casualty of Hurricane Sandy in 2012, Lucy, a forty-eight-year-old African American woman, has lived in multiple private hotels and public and private shelters for the past six years. After the hurricane destroyed her apartment in Brooklyn, and her landlord decided to sell the building rather than repair damages, she lived at a Holiday Inn for a year. Commercial hotels have become more commonly used for the long-term shelter instead of as emergencies. A year later, Lucy and her family were moved to a private cluster housing unit, which Department of Homeless Services (DHS) contracted to private landlords. Despite DHS paying landlords an average of $3,000 per unit, cluster shelters are poorly maintained physically and generally roach and/or rodent infested. Lucy recalled one cluster site where she stayed during a summer that had no windows or central air in the apartment, making it difficult to breathe.

Since 1981, New York City has been legally mandated to house anyone found legitimately homeless, either through public shelters, private landlords, or hotels. The Department of Social Services (DSS)—through the Department of Homeless Services (DHS) and the Human Resources Administration (HRA)—distributes funds to multiple nonprofit agencies, private landlords, and corporate hotels to provide welfare and homeless services. DHS does not follow the "housing first model,"[3] which is a proposal by housing rights advocates to provide affordable permanent housing immediately and unconditionally. Instead, DHS shelters in NYC require that clients also sign up with HRA for at least food stamp assistance. Shelter-unit decisions are not determined on the first day of the application process. A person in need of shelter must endure a heavily bureaucratized punitive welfare system. Once she receives shelter, that person becomes a *client* of the state and nonprofit organization so long as she follows certain rules.

After hours of waiting at an intake center, applicants are bused with their possessions to an overnight emergency shelter, which they must vacate the next day, possessions in hand, sometimes as early as 6:00 a.m. The women and families in my study had to enter either Prevention Assistance and Temporary Housing (PATH) in the Bronx or the Adult Family Intake Center (AFIC) in Queens. After walking through a metal detector, applicants must provide a valid ID and contact information for friends, family, or other potential support. A social worker from the intake center calls people on the contact list to ask whether they can provide a room, couch, or even the floor, granting shelter admission only as a very last resort. After ten days, if an applicant is deemed ineligible and decides to appeal, the entire process is restarted.

While living in a cluster site in the Bronx, Deana's son became ill with lead poisoning at the age of two. Recently he was diagnosed with Attention Deficit Hyperactive Disorder (ADHD) and a speech disability. The DHS worker said that Deana could not prove it was from their site. There was no investigation, and no repairs made to this private shelter in the Bronx. To avoid further poisoning, she moved to an apartment above her pay grade. In less than a year, Deana and her son reentered the shelter system. Lucy currently lives in a former elementary school turned shelter. She complained that there is no space to talk freely: "The director didn't want anyone talking to each other." "There was a camera in the building, and if she seen anyone in the hallway talking . . . a staff would come and say, 'no talking in the hallway!'" she said. Sheltered-homeless individuals are extra vulnerable to state intervention because there is no demarcation between private and public spaces in shelters. The sheltered-homeless have no privacy inside or outside the shelter. Nonprofit organizations' personnel or security can freely search through their personal belongings in their rooms at any time without their permission. Some women told multiple stories about their personal items being confiscated or moved without their consent; some items were stolen.

There are increased reports on the unsafe and hazardous conditions of NYC homeless shelters. An October 2017 incident that made local news headlines was of two baby girls scalded to death from a busted radiator in a Bronx cluster unit (Fanelli 2017). The sheltered-homeless, rather than being protected, are punished with random inspections, metal detections, curfews, and placed in unsafe housing. These conditions reinforce that they are unworthy and irresponsible and need to be overseen by staff before ensuring permanent housing. Popular sentiment favors that shelters should not be *too comfortable*; otherwise, *those people* will stay and milk the welfare system. However, my research shows that despite conditions worsening, the length of time in shelters is increasing. This increase is due to the lack of real affordable housing in NYC and elimination of subsidized housing. Helen, a staff member who has overseen numerous shelters for several decades, blames the arrangements former Mayor Bloomberg made with private developers for the homeless crisis in NYC. She said that there was time when

> New York City Housing Authority and Section 8 people who were homeless and from shelters got priority for vouchers and NYCHA interviews. And under [former mayor] Giuliani, that priority decreased and under Bloomberg that simply went away. No applications were accepted from people who were homeless. There were no longer any priorities and the applications were just stopped.

Helen has seen three generations (re)enter the shelter system and blames the lack of housing resources. Latina and Black women remain in precarious shelter housing situations for more prolonged periods because of the lack of viable housing options due to political decisions. They would have nowhere else to turn but to the street.

Regulation of Time as a Form of Disciplining

> You're supposed to give assistance up to 35 hours a week of your life. Like a job. So, if you don't take on a job you will sit in room or work on resume. It's very insulting to people who had a job or have been to school because they even test you.
> —Marissa

Sheltered-homeless women need to report and verify how they spend their days, a disciplining structure and practice of the shelter system. A participant in the Work Employment Program (WEP) in 2015, Marissa, a Dominican woman in her midthirties, had to take the Test of Adult Basic Education (TABE). The disagreeable experience made her feel as if she was back in high school. TABE assesses high school level reading, writing, and math proficiency. Marissa has a high school diploma and some community college class credits but has had to take the TABE assessment twice upon reentering the shelter system. She firmly believes these tests are a waste of time and do not help to find jobs.

Making sheltered-homeless women wait and perform tasks that neither provide permanent housing nor jobs serve to discipline them. Waiting is a disciplinary tool: sheltered-homeless women have no control over their time; their plans and mobility are at the mercy of state personnel. From the moment of applying for shelter, individuals must give up the right to control how they spend their time. It begins with something as common and benign as waiting for routine appointments with caseworkers or housing specialists. It continues with waiting in line at the Housing Resources Administration (HRA) office or waiting to attend mandatory Back-to-Work programs. Despite popular beliefs, a third of homeless people in shelters are currently employed in New York City (Coalition for the Homeless 2019). Depending on one's employment status and the kind of assistance received (cash and/or food[4]), there is an obligation to attend meetings, workshops, and accept unpaid jobs.

The time that sheltered-homeless women spent going to mandatory meetings or reporting their personal information to various personnel disciplines them into accepting their marginality as a personal fault. Unlike the time spent by full-time, nonsheltered homeless workers at work or in meetings, sheltered-homeless women have no idea how long they will have to wait for or in a meeting. If they do not know how long it will take to be seen by a social worker, they cannot plan out their day or week accordingly. They are stuck in limbo and in a constant state of anxiety.

Shawna, an African American and in her forties, described mandatory programs like WEP as a "waste of time." She discovered after she had been moved from one shelter site to another that her case was dropped, which meant she had to start the whole process from scratch. "I can't with this, worrying about today and tomorrow, I can't rest properly," she said. "I participated in the Back-to-Work program but I ain't never follow through because they [DHS] kept moving you around. So when I got to Back-to-Work there, I was excited, and out of nowhere, they closed my case . . . Every time you move, you have to start over the Back-to-Work program. Why you gotta start over, why you gotta erase, and start the paperwork over again?" Sheltered-homeless women not only have no sense of their own time but are also continually shuffling from one office to the next. It's not a transparent wait. Clients cannot know that there is progress in the time they put in because there are no guaranteed results of permanent housing or jobs from these meetings.

Marissa had to attend WEP for thirty-five hours per week to receive cash assistance. "They want people who get SNAP [Supplemental Nutrition Assistance Program] to work 20–30 hours a week. For 192 dollars they want you to work for your stipend." WEP[5] began in 1995 under Mayor Giuliani in order to recruit and train for job preparation with, for example, assistance with resumes. She cannot leave because to receive the assistance she has to put in twenty-five to thirty-five hours of required hours. Marissa continues:

They had me working the train station, cleaning the train station, that was really disgusting . . . They say you can get the job after . . . Yeah, basically. Well they didn't say it was free because I was still getting food stamps and cash for them, so it wasn't really free . . . but I had time that I owed them in order to get that.

Similar to the welfare-workfare program, recipients like Marissa must work for housing doing temporary jobs like cleaning for the Parks Departments for her "free" stipend. She accepted the temporary work for her housing and stipend because staff presented it as a possible permanent employment opportunity that could pay a real living wage. That never happened. State assistance is treated as charity from the state (Hall 1979), no longer a right fought for by the working class. Individuals must work to show that they are worthy of charity.[6] The conditions of volunteer work, waiting, "doing time" at mandatory meetings, or reporting how one spends her time does not necessarily connect welfare recipients to potential employers or a permanent job. Instead, these tactics coerce sheltered-homeless women to comply with the state's power to control their bodies. Marissa, for example, would rather clean a train station for her assistance than sit and wait in a room all day. After a year and a half of doing WEP, Marissa took a sales representative position at a clothing store for ten dollars an hour, making her ineligible for the Family Homelessness and Eviction Prevention (FHEPS) housing supplement. She could not afford her rent without the assistance and had to return to a homeless shelter. Her housing voucher depends on her remaining poor enough to qualify. Currently, Marissa does not make more than $8,000 a year to meet the requirements of the FHEPS housing supplement and food stamps program for her and her son. With these strict regulations in place, she cannot accept more work hours or a promotion because any slight increase in wages would bar her from these programs. Marissa works—even though her work options are desperately restricted—because she prefers working to being stuck in a room all day. Nonetheless, Marissa is essentially stuck.

A sheltered-homeless person who opts out of using the job programs office, but remains in the shelter and receives food assistance, has to prove that she is working. Angie, who is Puerto Rican and Dominican, worked as a barista at a Starbucks for ten dollars an hour. Her employment spared her from ten hours a week of "doing time" in the waiting room. Angie, however, had the burden of going from her job in Manhattan to the Bronx—a more than forty-minute commute (one way) on the subway—to get her work-verification form signed by a staff member. She complied to continue receiving food assistance while in the shelter with her one-year-old son.

Sociologist Javier Auyero (2012, 4) draws attention to how waiting, as a tool of the welfare system in Argentina, inculcates domination with consent. "Domination works," he writes, "through yielding to the power of others . . . waiting hopefully and then frustrated for others to make decisions, and in effect surrendering to the authority of others" (4). Waiting for an unknown amount of time without the guarantee of progress is one method used by the state to make marginalized and dependent bodies obedient. Waiting is punitive. A regimen of waiting is prescribed to produce and control compliant subjects. If sheltered-homeless women do not wait patiently and quietly, if they speak out or resist some of these humiliating practices, they are vulnerable to brute force as happened to Charise, a forty-five-year-old Black woman.

Charise was frustrated. For more than two hours, she sat waiting in the Human Resources Administration (HRA) building for her number to be called. The number display had not gone in chronological order. Charise got up from her seat to walk out. On her way out, she complained: "I started talking about all the problems they're having in the welfare center." A DHS peace officer left her post and scolded, "Would you shut the fuck up, nobody wants to hear that." Defending herself, Charise responded, "I could talk all day if I want, as long as I'm not being violent or talking to a caseworker. . . . I can speak all day. I got freedom of speech." Two officers pushed Charise to the ground, kicked her in the ribs, and later kicked her out of the HRA building. She filed a grievance against one of the officers, who was subpoenaed but did not show up for court. The case was dismissed. Reflecting on the experience, Charise told me: "She got to assault me, and nothing ever happened. If it had been the other way and I assaulted her, I would've been locked up right now. They treat us like animals. Go in your cage, can't leave your cage at this time, and if you leave your cage three times then we're going to kick you out." There are countless stories of physical abuse in waiting rooms and inside shelters by security peace officers employed by DHS.

When the monitoring of time and a regimen of waiting is not met with compliance, physical violence is often used to reestablish discipline. Because Charise did not remain silent and complained, she was subject to brute force. These practices produce new ways of convincing individuals to accept conditions of subordination. The episode reinforced for Charise that in the eyes of the state her body is worthless, even disposable. Charise has since left the shelter, living from house to house. According to the staff member at a nonprofit organization, many sheltered-homeless individuals leave because they are traumatized (Coalition for the Homeless, 2019). Currently, Charise works as an organizer with several grassroots organizations advocating for more affordable housing in New York City.

Conclusion

By paying attention to the everyday experiences of those navigating the shelter system, we can see how Black and Latina women experience social regulation.

State surveillance practices divert attention from real factors that contribute to homelessness among women of color—unaffordable housing, un/underemployment, and low wages. If Black and Latina sheltered-homeless women internalize the shame of *their* experiences being homeless, then housing insecurity and socioeconomic inequalities remain ignored. And if this is ignored, there is no dialogue about how the capitalist state relies on social hierarchies of race, class, gender, and nationhood for labor divisions, exploitation, and profit making.

While the state does not formally criminalize and confine sheltered-homeless persons in prison, many have described the shelter system and shelters as prisonlike. Latina and Black women in homeless shelters are disciplined and surveilled through the physical layout of the shelter buildings, the record keeping of case workers and peace officers, and the monitoring of their time. A regimen of waiting—endless appointments; long lines for basic services; providing itemized, detailed information to different state bureaucrats—and the constant shuffling from place to place without any certainty of receiving needed assistance ultimately exacerbates homelessness and the precarious lives of Black and Latina women. The punitive treatment of sheltered-homeless women of color works to silence them and make them accept inequality and internalize shame. Even so, there are moments of individual resistance, albeit without much structural impact. Operating as a white supremacist structure, the shelter system undermines the possibility for collective action.

NOTES

1 Since 1997, DHS has had peace officers serve as security. The NYPD officially does not intervene unless there are cases of robbery or assault.

2 Blacks and Latinxs are grouped together because they experience similar material conditions of poverty and discriminatory treatment by state workers and law enforcement; more specifically, Nuyoricans, Puerto Ricans, Dominicans, Mexicans, and other South/Central American diasporas living in the New York. Similarly, in *Prisons of Poverty* (2009), Loic Wacquant shows that Latinos that live in urban (ghetto) conditions are more closely related to African Americans.

3 Homeless people are provided housing unconditionally regardless if they are using or engaging in risky behavior like drug use. However, this is available for only a fraction of sheltered-homeless previously diagnosed with mental illness.

4 All sheltered-homeless have to receive food assistance like the Supplemental Nutrition Assistance Program (SNAP).

5 Steve Banks, then commissioner of HRA and now director of DHS, phased out WEP in 2016 with contracts to three other partnerships, Youth Pathways, Career Compass, and Career Advance and noted the failures of the Clinton administration's Personal Responsibility and Work Opportunity Act (PRWOA) implemented in 1996 due to its punitive structure.

6 The practice of working for public assistance is not new. It can be traced back to poor houses in mid-nineteenth-century New York, where work tests were required to receive housing (Eubanks 2018, 19). In 1934, President Roosevelt's Work Progress Administration (WPA) replaced the Federal Emergency Relief Administration (FERA) as a means to mitigate middle-class fears of the poor not having an incentive to work (Eubanks 2018, 25).

REFERENCES

Abramovitz, Mimi. 1988. *Regulating the Lives of Women: Social Welfare Policy from Colonial Times to the Present*. USA: Routledge.

Acthennerg, Emily, and Peter Marcuse. 1986. "The Causes of the Housing Problem." In *Critical Perspectives in Housing*, edited by Rachel Bratt, Chester Harman, and Ann Meyerson, 4–11. Philadelphia: Temple University Press.

Auyero, Javier. 2012. *Patients of the State: The Politics of Waiting in Argentina*. Durham, NC: Duke University Press.

Baker, S. G. 1996. "Homelessness and the Latino Paradox." In *Homeless in America*, edited by Jim Baumohl, 134–140. Phoenix, AR: Oryx. Press.

Betancur, John. 2005. "Gentrification before Gentrification." The Plight of Pilsen. Chicago: Nathalie P. Voorhees Center for Neighborhood and Community Improvement, Voorhees Center White Paper (2005).

Boyd, Michelle. "The Downside of Racial Uplift: Meaning of Gentrification in an African American Neighborhood." *City & Society* 17 (June 2008): 265–88. https://doi.org/10.1525/city.2005.17.2.265.

Bratt, Rachel G.; Hartman, Chester; and Meyerson, Ann, eds. *Critical Perspectives on Housing*. Philadelphia: Temple University Press, 1984.

Briggs, Laura. 2002. *Reproducing empire: Race, sex, science, and US imperialism in Puerto Rico*. Vol. 11. Berkeley: University of California Press.

Browne, Simone. 2015. *Dark Matters: On the Surveillance of Blackness*. Durham & London: Duke University Press.

Carter, Ovie, and Mitchell Duneier. 1999. *Sidewalk*. New York: Farrar, Straus & Giroux.

Chinchilla, Melissa, and Sonya Gabrielian. "Stemming the Rise of Latino Homelessness: Lessons from Los Angeles County." *Journal of Social Distress and the Homeless* (September 5, 2019). https://doi.org/10.1080/10530789.2019.1660049.

Chronopoulos, Themis. "Robert Moses and the Visual Dimension of Physical Disorder: Efforts to Demonstrate Urban Blight in the Age of Slum Clearance." *Journal of Planning History* 13, no. 3 (May 14, 2013): 207–33.

Chronopoulos, Themis. "Commentator: 'Carthage Must Be Destroyed': Health, Housing and the New Deal." *Paper Presentation by Betty Livingstone Adams at the Rutgers Centre for Historical Analysis* (2011).

Coalition for the Homeless. 2019a. "New York City Homelessness: The Basic Facts." Accessed September 20, 2019. www.coalitionforthehomeless.org/.

Coalition for the Homeless. 2019 b. "FAQ & Myths." Accessed August 2019. www.coalitionforthehomeless.org.

Cohen, Stanley. 1985. *Visions of Social Control*. Cambridge: Polity Press.

Cole, Simon A. 2002. *Suspect Identities: A History of Fingerprinting and Criminal Identification*. USA: Harvard University Press.

Conroy, Stephen J., and David Heer. "Hidden Hispanic Homelessness in Los Angeles: The "Latino Paradox" Revisited" *Hispanic Journal of Behavioral Science* 25, no. 4 (Nov. 1 2003): 530–38. https://doi.org/10.1177/0739986303258126.

Cox, Aimee Meredith. 2018. *Shapeshifters: Black Girls and the Choreography of Citizenship*. North Carolina: Duke University Press.

Donzelot, Jacques. 1977. *The Policing of Families*. New York: Pantheon Books.

Edwards, Anne R. 1988. *Regulation and Repression: Studies in Society*. New Zealand: Allen & Unwin.

Eubanks, Virginia. 2018. *Automating Inequality: How High-Tech Tools Profile, Police, and Punish the Poor*. New York: St. Martin's Press.

Fanelli, James. "Shelter Operator of Bronx Apartment Where Baby Girls Died No Longer Runs Cluster-Sites." *New York Daily News*. October 25, 2017. Accessed September 20, 2019. www.nydailynews.com.

Fernández, Johanna. 2011. "The Young Lords and the Social and Structural Roots of Late Sixties Urban Radicalism." In *Civil Rights in New York City: From World War II to the Giuliani Era*, edited by Clarence Taylor, 141–60. New York: Fordham University.

Foucault, Michel. 1977. *Discipline and Punishment: The Birth of the Prison*. New York: Vintage Books.

———. 2007. *Population, Security and Territory. Lectures at the Collège de France, 1975–76*. New York: Picador.

Hall, Stuart. 1979. *Drifting Towards a Law and Order Society*. London: Sage Publishing.

INCITE. 2017. *The Revolution Will Not Be Funded: Beyond the Non-Profit Industrial Complex*. Cambridge, MA: Duke Press.

Jones, Marian Moser. "Does Race Matter in Addressing Homelessness? A Review of the Literature." *World Medical & Health Policy* 8, no. 2 (June 2016): 139–56. MA & Oxford: Wiley Periodicals.

Liebow, Eliot. 1993. *Tell Them Who I Am: The Lives of Homeless Women*. New York: Free Press.

Lyon, David. 2003. *Surveillance as Social Sorting: Privacy, Risk, Digital Discrimination*. New York: Routledge.

Marcuse, Peter. 1978. "Housing Policy and the Myth of the Benevolent State." In *Critical Perspectives in Housing*, edited by Rachel Bratt, Chester Harman, and Ann Meyerson, 248–63. Philadelphia: Temple University Press.

McCoy, Alfred. 2009. *Policing America's Empire: The United States, the Philippines, and the Rise of the Surveillance State*. University of Wisconsin Press: Wisconsin.

Monahan, Torin. 2010. *Surveillance in the time of Insecurity*. New Jersey: Rutgers University Press.

Muñiz, Vicky. 1988. *Resisting Gentrification and Displacement: Voices of Puerto Rican Women of the Barrio (Latino Communities: Emerging Voices—Political, Social, Cultural and Legal Issues)*. USA: Routledge.

Muzio, Rose. "The Struggle Against Urban Renewal in Manhattan's Upper West Side and the Emergence of El Comité." *Centro Journal* XXI, no. 2 (2009): 109–41. New York: The City of New York. www.redalyc.org/.

Neubeck, Kenneth J., and Noel A. Cazenave. 2001. *Welfare Racism: Playing the Race Card Against America's Poor*. New York & London: Routledge.

Parenti, Christian. 2003. *The Soft Cage: Surveillance in America from Slavery to the war on Terror*. New York: Basic Books.

Pérez, Gina M. "The Other 'Real World': Gentrification and the Social Construction of Place in Chicago." *Urban Anthropology and Studies of Cultural Systems and World Economic Development* 31, no. 1 (2002): 37–68. JSTOR, www.jstor.org.

Picture the Homeless Committee. n.d. "The Business of Homelessness: Financial & Human Costs of the Shelter-Industrial Complex." Accessed November 27, 2018. http://picturethehomeless.org.

Piven, Frances Fox, and Richard A. Cloward. 1967. *The Breaking of the American Social Compact*. New York: The New Press.

———. 1971. *Regulating the Poor: The Functions of Public Welfare*. USA: Vintage.

Qu, Gensis, and Stephanie Lai. "Latino Homeless Population Found to Be at Disadvantage in Outreach Programs." *Daily Bruin*, February 18, 2019. https://dailybruin.com.

Rao, Anupama, and Steven Pierce, eds. 2006. *Discipline and the Other Body: Correction, Corporeality, Colonialism*. North Carolina: Duke University Press.

Riis, Jacob A. 1957. *How the Other Half Lives.* New York: Garrett Press.

Roberts, Dorothy. 1997. *Killing the Black Body: Race, Reproduction and the Meaning of Liberty.* NY: First Vintage Books.

Roberts, Adrienne. 2017. *Gendered States of Punishment and Welfare: Feminist Political Economy, Primitive Accumulation and the Law.* London and New York: Routledge.

Rúa, Mérida, and Ivis Garcia. "Our Interests Matter': Puerto Rican Older Adults in the Age of Gentrification." *Urban Studies* 55, no. 14 (November 22, 2017): 3168–84. https://doi.org/10.1177/0042098017736251.

Sánchez, José Ramón. 1986. "Residual Work and Residual Shelter Housing Puerto Rican Labor in NYC from WW11 to 1983." In *Critical Perspectives in Housing,* edited by Rachel Bratt, Chester Harman, and Ann Meyerson, 202–20. Philadelphia: Temple University Press.

Spitzer, Steven. "The Rationalization of Crime Control in Capitalist Society." *Contemporary Crises* 3 (1979): 187–206. doi:10.1007/BF00729229.

Vasudevan, Alexander. 2017. *The Autonomous City: A History of Urban Squatting.* New York: Verso.

Wacquant, Loïc JD. 2009. *Prisons of poverty.* Vol. 23. Minneapolis: University of Minnesota Press.

Willse, Craig. 2015. *The Value of Homelessness: Managing Surplus Life in the United States.* Minneapolis & London: University of Minnesota Press.

29

The Afterlife of US Disciplining Institutions

Transnational Structures of (Im)mobility among Peruvian Deportees

ULLA D. BERG

The lunch hour rush was peaking in El Callao's Aventura Mall food court when JZ arrived. His broad smile, imposing height, and friendly demeanor could disarm even the crankiest lunch guest. He had been running errands that morning in between clients at the barbershop and arrived sweaty and with hardware purchases under his arm. JZ had grown up in New Jersey since age nine. His parents had migrated to North Newark in 1990 to join a large extended family already living there. Aside from the pioneering migrant grandmother, her seven children, and their spouses, JZ also had around twenty-five cousins, nieces, and nephews. Most of the foreign-born family members became citizens long ago, but JZ, in his youthful invincibility, and despite being eligible, never bothered to take the citizenship test. Little did he know that this *descuido* would come back to haunt him.

JZ's story had similarities to the experiences of other Peruvian deportees and of urban Black and Latinx youth who are pushed out of public educational systems and funneled into the criminal justice system (Flores 2016; Ríos 2011; Rosas 2012). But JZ's life in Lima after his deportation unfolded along a different path than most deportees I met during my fieldwork there.[1]

JZ was first deported in 2005 after serving a nine-month prison sentence for charges of possession and eluding and then subsequently losing his immigration case.[2] Provisions in the 1996 immigration act IIRIRA had made deportation mandatory for both lawful permanent residents (LPRs) and unauthorized immigrants who had been convicted of a serious crime, and permanent residents like JZ could be stripped of their green cards overnight and deported even for minor crimes committed in the past. With little family left in Lima and no work opportunities, JZ attempted to return to the United States after six months in Peru. He was arrested at the US–Mexico border and charged with reentry. Because of his prior felony conviction, he was sentenced to four years in federal prison, but the sentence was later reduced based on good conduct. After two years he was transferred into immigration custody and deported. JZ knew then that this was it; that his life in the United States belonged in the past.

Eventually a relative in El Callao got him a job at a phone company, and later he found other jobs. JZ now works full time as a barber, a skill he learned from

Dominican friends in Newark. When I first met him, he told me proudly: "I used to braid my own hair and Peruvians here like the urban style that I brought from over there," and then he showed me his Instagram with hundreds of pictures of elaborate urban hairstyles. The recognition he received as a barber in Lima, leading to invitations to fairs and competitions all over Peru, was due to his ability to capitalize on the global fascination of aestheticized forms of US Blackness as a symbol of urban style and cosmopolitanism (Ramos-Zayas 2012). JZ also married his Peruvian girlfriend, and they have two young kids. "This life keeps me busy now," he laughed while sipping his *chicha morada*, a popular Peruvian soft drink.

JZ's accomplishments stand as the exception to the rule when compared to the more common deportation story of unemployment, poverty, ongoing criminalization, shame, and feelings of personal failure; in which the afterlife of US disciplining institutions continues to live on in the social practices and structures of feeling of individuals and communities who have been produced, ghettoized, and trashed by these institutions and later banished through deportation. Writer and literary scholar Saidiya Hartman's theorization of the "afterlife of slavery" is useful to think about how deportees, too, are the afterlife of the very institutions that destroyed their lives and sentenced them to a future of lasting adverse effects. Hartman argues that slavery withstands as an issue in the political life of Black America because Black lives continue to be "imperiled and devalued by a racial calculus and a political arithmetic that were entrenched centuries ago" (2008, 6), one that manifests today in poor life chances and lack of access to proper health care and education. While deportation in many ways is different from the forced "migration" that was slavery, its continued disfigurement of lives over time is akin to the complication of links between places and between the past and the present that Hartman so powerfully describes. The racialization and criminalization that 1.5 generation youth of color experience in places like New Jersey not only produces the condition that lead to their detention and deportation but also haunts their present once they are forced into exile.

JZ's experiences of racialization and criminalization in US schools, prisons, and immigration detention lives on in his daily practices and ways of relating to others in Lima; they taught him to internalize racial knowledge and cultivate an acute awareness of the always-present moral judgement by others as the result of a perceived and negatively coded "Americanization." Anthropologist Ana Ramos-Zayas has described how return migrant youth in Brazil and Puerto Rico are characterized by local youth in both places as "emotionally defective," a reaction based on local emotional epistemologies that insist that life in the US makes you depressed, aggressive, and detached (2012, 308). Similarly, deportees in Lima had to confront local perceptions of their presumed embodied "foreignness" and criminality in their countries of birth. JZ knew all too well that despite his circumstantial fame as a wizard of urban black "coolness" through elaborate haircuts, the only way to survive "the blows of deportation," as he called them, and to challenge its afterlife, was to personify the form and affective registers of neoliberal personhood that deportees were typically seen as lacking: that of hard work, entrepreneurism, personal responsibility, emotional self-regulation, and family values cast in a language of respectability. "I make really good money here," JZ told me. "It's gotten me to the point where I can support my family. I care about my kids, about them being healthy. I'm building my house here too. Right now, I work for somebody, but my goal this year is to open my own barbershop." Evidently, JZ strived to compensate for his "foreignness" and worked hard to reinvent himself as an entrepreneurial, Spanish-speaking, and respectable family man whose belonging in the middle-class section of Callao where he now lived would never be questioned. But JZ's outward compliance with the expectations of neoliberal productivity in Peru's urban environment did not prevent him from privately airing the hurt and frustration he felt regarding his deportation and how these experiences continued to shape his life in the present: "It's still hard though. I can tell you everything is great now, but sometimes it's still like *man*, I wish I could take that plane and go back. I've lived in the U.S. my whole youth. I left a lot of love and people over there. Going through everything I went through there, being locked up, seeing different characters, different stuff, I would never wish that on no one. It has taken a lot outta me and changed me a lot."

Drawing on ethnographic fieldwork with Peruvian deportees in Lima and Callao, and with family members in the United States (mainly New Jersey and New York), this chapter examines the central place of institutional structures affecting Latinx lives and communities by viewing them through the transnational lens of detention and deportation. Based on participant observation and life history interviews with Peruvians who were deported from the United States between 2009 and 2017, I show how the lives of these ex-US residents continue to be shaped by the institutional structures that produced their precarity and ultimately lead to their banishment from the United States. Through an ethnographic study of deportation as a transnational social system that enables race and white supremacy to operate across time and space, I reveal the enduring effects of US disciplining institutions and regimes across borders and timespaces. The chapter also substantiates the assertion that Latinx Studies as a field of critical inquiry must decenter its dominant focus on the United States and be more attentive to hemispheric social, economic, and racial processes that both extend but also sometimes begin beyond the borders of the United States. Latin American Studies, in turn, must be more attentive to the complex racial and class dynamics that shapes the lives and expectations of Latinx populations deported or returning from the United States. Operating at the intersection of Latinx and Latin American Studies, the ethnographic approach to deportation taken here thus requires concurrent analysis of the particular national and racial projects in Latin America and the United States that render individuals "deserving" or "unworthy" of membership and recognition based on their potential for generating capital, participating in local versions of respectability politics, and rendering themselves legible in multiple and very different contexts. But most importantly, the approach taken here shows exactly *how* deported lives for the most part remain deeply entangled with and imperiled by the effects of US institutional structures and disciplinary regimes despite the passing of time.[3]

South American Entanglements with US Deportation Policy

Deportation to Latin America from the United States is hardly a novel phenomenon. As a mechanism of immigration control, the use of deportation has fluctuated in US history according to prevailing political doctrine and US labor needs. Throughout the twentieth century, Latin Americans and other foreign citizens sympathetic with anarchist and socialist ideologies were cast by the US government as subversive and deported through highly politicized deportation proceedings. During the McCarthy era, similar politically motivated deportations were based on fear of communist immigrants infiltrating the US government (Kantstroom 2007). Additionally, deportation policy has also been mobilized to regulate labor supply and demands. For example, Mexican migrants recruited to the United States during both World Wars to fulfill the war economy's labor needs were deported, first during the Great Depression and then again during the infamous Operation Wetback in 1954, a military-style removal initiative that became a controversial point in US–Mexico relations (García 1980). But such labor regulation is not only accomplished by actual deportations. Anthropologist Nicholas De Genova (2002) has argued that it is the awareness among undocumented migrant populations of the *possibility* of being detained or deported, rather than deportation itself, that creates a large, cheap, and docile labor force, unable to challenge highly repressive labor regimes, racial orders, xenophobia, and systematic forms of exclusion preventing these populations from claiming any social, civic, and political rights.

Peruvians and other South Americans were not particularly targets of US deportation policies until the 2000s. Before the 1990s, Peruvian migration to the United States was largely elite or middle-class skilled professionals and, in Latin American Studies scholar Elsa Chaney's words, "aliens by choice" (1976). According to anthropologist Suzanne Oboler (2005), these Peruvians had inserted themselves as "honorary whites" into mainstream US society, facilitated by their race, education, and class status. Working-class Peruvians, on the other hand, had been migrating to New Jersey since the 1950s and 1960s to work in the textile industry when work was still plentiful in Paterson's factories (Altamirano 1990) and, by mid-decade, the Immigration Reform Act of 1965 further favored Latin American migration.[4] While several working-class Peruvians were able to bring their close relatives through the law's family reunification provisions, Peruvians of all backgrounds continued to arrive in the 1980s and 1990s through different travel modalities, without visas or with tourist visas that were later overstayed (Berg 2015). It was this cohort of migrants whose 1.5 generation immigrant children would end up in the deportation pipeline a decade or two later. Their stories are all variations on these multigenerational migrations and transnational family projects.

Postwar-era deindustrialization and growing unemployment in the 1970s and 1980s gave rise to common urban problems like poverty, crime, racial tension, and white flight. Encouraged by American Dream mythology, earlier generations of immigrants aspired to leave gateway cities and move to the suburbs or affluent towns of New York and New Jersey, but poor and working-class populations had no real option than to stay in their now segregated and criminalized neighborhoods, work long hours, put their children in underserved schools, and hope for the best. The passage of the 1986 Immigration Reform and Control Act (IRCA) legalized close to three million immigrants nationally, but it also brought about greater interior enforcement. Factories employing undocumented workers became new zones of insecurity for Latin American migrant populations.

The most significant shift toward the current path of permanent criminalization of Latin American immigrants and US Latinx populations, and of detention and deportation as the United States' de facto immigration policy, happened in 1996. That year the Clinton administration approved the Illegal Immigration Reform and Immigrant Responsibility Act (IIRIRA) and the Antiterrorism and Effective Death Penalty Act (AEDPA), which transformed US immigration law by establishing an ever more restrictive and punitive approach that made mandatory the detention and deportation of both lawful permanent residents (LPRs) and unauthorized immigrants who had been convicted of a serious crime. The law also expanded the list of offenses that qualified as "serious crimes" for immigration purposes (Morawetz 2000). Consequently, since 1996, an increasing number of immigrants, including LPRs, have been detained and deported for an ever-proliferating list of minor offenses now reclassified as serious crimes. These laws laid the ground for further securitization of immigration after 9/11, where immigration in no uncertain terms was recast as a matter of national security. This Bush and Obama-era trend continued with President Trump who, soon after his election, and despite a period of revision of enforcement priorities during Obama's second term, directed federal agencies to employ "all lawful means" against "all removable aliens," not only those convicted but also those who had just been charged with a criminal offense (Pierce 2019).

The vast majority of the hundreds of thousands of migrants detained and deported from the United States each year continue to be Mexican and Central American men (Golash-Boza and Hondagneu-Sotelo 2013), yet the number of South Americans who have been removed by Immigration and Customs

Enforcement (ICE) via interior enforcement or returned from the US–Mexico border area by Border Patrol has been significant in the last decade and a half. Between 2003 and 2020, a total of 15,405 Peruvians have been deported.[5] Each statistic represents not only a personal experience but also an intersection of individual biography with collective histories of racialization, criminalization, incarceration, and immobilization rooted in the specific US communities and neighborhoods where the deportees had hoped to live their lives as well as in the Peruvian communities they are now facing and challenged to adopt as their own.

The School-to-Prison-to-Deportation Pipeline

Like JZ, Jefferson had spent most of his adolescent and adult life in the United States. His uncle was the first in the family to migrate and later brought Jefferson's mother after she divorced Jefferson's father, an abusive alcoholic. When his mom left for the United States, Jefferson, then age four, stayed with his grandmother in el Callao until his mother sent for him and his brother in 1988. At age ten, Jefferson arrived in New York City. He began his schooling in Queens and later moved to Paterson, NJ, where his mother was offered a better-paying job. Jefferson's grandmother, brother, aunt, and little cousin all came along. The family eventually received their green cards. Life was looking promising. Jefferson finished middle school in Paterson and enrolled in high school. His mother remarried a Peruvian from Paterson, "a good man," in Jefferson's opinion. But the guy, who Jefferson now refers to as his father, wasn't acting as his father back then. "He couldn't really tell me too much because he had just met my mother, so you know, he wasn't really my father. He didn't tell me yo, you can't do this, you can't do that. So I was in detention a lot, cuz I wasn't comin to school, you know playin hookin party, goin out with my friends. My ma often told me over and over 'you gotta get yourself straight.' Finally, I passed my high school, but I was 20 then."

After high school Jefferson took classes at a training school and started working in an auto body shop. He also took a stab at construction work with his uncle in New York, but spent most of his free time on the streets of his Paterson neighborhood:

> So in 2010 I started gettin serious. I had already been in the streets a lot, you know, sellin drugs, doin drugs, robbing people, stealin cars, mostly just to get high. When you get high you don't care about nothing. My life just got too quick. I got connected with my cousin and we started sellin pounds of weed, and crack, and we started getting real good money. But more money, more problems. The other blocks would get jealous because we brought in more money . . . I got, not famous, but I got known on the block. 'Oh this guy, nice cars, everything.' At the same time, you have to learn to save your money cause when you get locked up you got no money. You ain't nothin.

Dealing drugs taught Jefferson several useful things, including how to save money, but he wasn't done learning about the consequences of not choosing the life options that the US state and normative social and racial regimes deems worthy. In fact, just like Ethnic Studies scholar Lisa Marie Cacho writes about her "troublemaker" cousin Brandon who her family lost to drunk driving, Jefferson too had "a talent for choosing life's nonoptions" (Cacho 2012, 165).

Jefferson first got caught in 2011 with a pound of weed and served an eighteen-month sentence. After his release, he returned to working in construction and moved in with his girlfriend, a US citizen, but "half Peruvian," as he put it. They had fallen in love before his incarceration and stayed together throughout his time in jail. The girl had lost both her parents and lived with a great aunt. Soon after they met, she was diagnosed with cancer. Jefferson was there for her and remembers feeling needed, appreciated, and loved. Life was good despite its challenges. He had a job and a girl he cared about and who cared about him. But when the owner of the construction company died unexpectedly, the company was sold and most workers laid off. With his girlfriend's mounting medical bills, Jefferson was desperate to make money. His cousin came to the rescue and they started selling ecstasy. Jefferson eventually got busted when trying to sell to an undercover cop. Since he knew the importance of setting money aside when working in the drug economy, he was able to get out on bail.[6]

Back in the neighborhood, the hustling got more violent, and drug market interactions often involved confrontations with competitors. In one of these encounters, Jefferson lost his best friend in a shoot-out. He was stricken with grief and wanted revenge. One evening he got high and went looking for the people who killed his friend. He was arrested that same evening and later charged with robbery, weapon possession, and attempted murder. Jefferson served seven months in the county jail and two and a half years in federal prison before he was transferred into ICE custody. Economic struggles, poor schooling, addiction, and lack of access to health care and any real job opportunities culminated in his deportation to Lima in 2014. Jefferson was thirty-six years old then and had not been back since he left Peru at age ten in 1988. "When I first got here I couldn't believe that I was really in Peru. Everything seemed so different from what I remembered," he said. He only had four hundred dollars in savings, accumulated from working for two dollars a day while in prison. His mother's best friend picked him up at the airport and helped him with food, lodging, and the basics for almost a year.

"After that year I was really stressing out, trying to fit into society, trying to know the streets, speak the language, trying to know the money they pay here, trying to know how much the minimum wage is. All this stuff. It was bad. At one point I was thinking about hanging myself up." Jefferson was not alone in his despair. His anguish was echoed in the stories of other deportees I met who experienced serious mental health consequences and profound existential crises as a result of the disorientation, poverty, and difficulties adjusting to the new environment and to life after deportation.

With little formal schooling and no significant transferable skills, Callao's drug economy emerged as one of the few viable livelihood options. Jefferson started hustling, but quit after an incident where he almost got caught. Despite their experiences with the US prison and detention system, most deportees were genuinely afraid of ending up in a Peruvian prison. When I met him, Jefferson had been back for four years, and after working all sorts of odd and poorly paid jobs he landed a job as a security agent in the port of Callao. The job paid the minimum wage rate of 930 soles a month (circa $282). However, Jefferson really wanted to open a small business, but for someone without a credit history it was almost impossible to get a bank loan. Some instead borrowed from informal loan sharks or local money laundering schemes but had to be wary of impossible debt cycles. Ultimately, this made deportees dependent on family members in the United States to lend them money or give up on their entrepreneurial dreams altogether. When asked if he would consider selling drugs again Jefferson replied: "Nah not anymore, I don't want to sell, but I want to work, and keep busy. I'm trying to save money in a different way, cause I'm trying to go to Europe." The lack of opportunities or failure to meet the expectations of the neoliberal economy often led urban deportees in Peru to either attempt returning to the United States or, like Jefferson, dream about trying their luck elsewhere. But few could escape the structures of violence that had led to their deportation and that continued to trouble them in the very place they were now obliged to call home.

Violence and Alternative Social Structures

Paco and his brother had grown up in the care of relatives in Callao from a very young age because their biological mother, a victim of domestic and sexual violence, was too young and traumatized to take care of two small children. When Paco was thirteen he was brought to Paterson, NJ, by the Peruvian women who had raised him in Callao before migrating to the United States. She enrolled him in high school and hoped for the best. High school was tough for a recent immigrant kid who spoke limited English. According to Paco, there was a lot of bullying and discrimination against the South Americans who were seen by the Puerto Rican and Dominican kids as less savvy and lacking street credentials (cf. Ramos-Zayas 2012). On one occasion, Paco got mugged and beaten by a group of teens on his way home from school. The beating was so bad that he ended up in the hospital. Shortly after this incident, he became involved with the Latin Kings chapter in Paterson. The gang had other Peruvian and some Ecuadorian members and, according to Paco, "We would go out and beat someone up when we had to protect or defend a member, but mostly it was like a family." In the midst of attempts to carve out a space and a group to belong to, gang member-ship provided Paco with a much-needed social and familial structure and group of friends.[7]

When not at school, Paco hung out with a group of kids in the primarily Afri-can American neighborhood where he grew into adulthood. He told me it was thanks to this mostly African American group of friends, not the ESL program at his high school, that he learned English. They also taught him the ways of the street in Paterson. He learned to sell drugs, tried some, but didn't use much then. He also played soccer and he was good at it. When he graduated from high school, he had several sports scholarship offers from universities in the area, including Rutgers and Montclair State University, but when these institu-tions realized that he didn't have papers they rescinded their offers on claims of ineligibility.

Paco's deportation story is a classic tale of someone who is successively pushed out of public educational systems and funneled into the criminal justice system. When the possibility of a sports scholarship disappeared, Paco started working at a car wash. His girlfriend at the time was a US citizen born to a Peruvian mother. They met when Paco was eighteen and she was sixteen and still a Catholic school student. Despite the fact that the age for sexual consent in New Jersey is sixteen, the relationship resulted in other complications in Paco's life that ultimately con-tributed to his deportation. Paco became a father at age twenty, but the baby was taken away by social services because the mother had an addiction problem (later the child was placed with the maternal grandparents). When they sepa-rated, Paco faced several penalties as a result of his failure to pay child support and also served jail time for domestic violence charges. His girlfriend called the police on him numerous times but never showed up in court, and as a result he had been mostly able to get out on bail. Only the last time did the judge ask him to produce papers. Paco lied about his immigration status and never returned to court out of fear of deportation. He managed to stay in the shadows until one evening in 2009 when he was arrested in a street fight in Passaic. When his criminal record was checked against his immigration status and produced "a hit," he was transferred into ICE custody and deported. Paco was twenty-four years old then.

Paco arrived in Lima without a cent in his pocket. His many prison tattoos prevented him from getting a job in the formal service economy despite being fluent in English. He first stayed in his adoptive mother's family home in Cal-lao, but eventually her relatives asked him to leave. He had been homeless for stretches of time, sleeping under the bleachers in a nearby open-air stadium, without a job, and battling an addiction. When I first met him he had tried to detox by associating himself with a Pentecostal group who administered a cen-ter for troubled homeless youth in Callao (aka La Casa), many of them drug addicts and *sicarios*, or people hired to kill. As one of the older guys at La Casa and thanks to the knowledge of group dynamics acquired through gang membership in New Jersey, Paco quickly rose as a leader. This entailed new responsibilities of looking out not only for himself but for others. He found the daily activities including going to el Mercado and ask for food for the youth at La Casa both grueling and humiliating. La Casa resembles the unregulated residential treatment centers for addiction called *anexos* in Mexico City described by anthropologist Angela Garcia who discusses how and why violence seems so intimately linked to projects of recovery among the urban poor. The answer García offers resonates with Paco's experience: "Neither vulnerability nor cure is sought; instead, what is at stake is a different way of expressing and managing the pain of the self and community" (2015, 468). Paco tried to leave La Casa and disassociate a few times, but it was harder said than done. "Every time they see me on the street they approach me. Last night I got a little crazy. I had bought a bag of coke and wanted to use it, so I was sitting in a park nearby and of course they come and begin singing and stuff and I was desperate because I just wanted them to leave me alone to do my drugs!"

The last time I saw Paco before this chapter went into print, he was still struggling with addiction. He had left La Casa and slept on the couch in a distant aunt's living room. Everyone who lived there took drugs regularly. His son, who was now a teenager and still living with the grandparents in Paterson, had started to display his own signs of troubled adolescence, and Paco felt sick with worry. He talked a lot about death at our last encounter. He had been working as a lookout for a local gangster in drug transactions and had almost gotten himself killed twice. Caught in a transnational web of violence, precarity, pain, and addiction, and without the means to envision a way out of this predicament, Paco saw his life spiraling downward. It seemed only to be a matter of time before the very structures of transnationalized violence that engulfed his socially encumbered personhood would catch up with him and claim his life.

Concluding Remarks

Stories about the dehumanizing effects of detention and deportation on mostly Latin American migrants has recently received increased attention in both mainstream media and interdisciplinary scholarship. Yet once off the radar of spectating US publics, the lives of those who are subjected to detention power and deportation regimes fade into the unknown. This chapter has examined the afterlife of US disciplining institutions in the lives of Peruvian deportees in Lima through its haunting effects on their forced displacements. The stories of JZ, Jefferson, and Paco impart how deportation and the disciplinary institutions and policy that produce it operate across time and space as a diachronic and profoundly disrupting transnational structure of *im*mobility through which migrant personhood becomes uncertain, questionable, and under siege within unevenly distributed fields of power. While each life impacted by deportation is different, all must deal with its lingering effects. JZ was able to silence the stigma of his deportation by conforming to neoliberal expectations of what it meant to lead a productive and moral life in the eyes of those surrounding him. Jefferson and Paco were less compliant. Their ongoing personal and collective dramas illustrate how Black, Latinx, and immigrant youth are not only pushed out of US public educational systems and funneled into the criminal justice system, but ultimately propelled into a future that was conditioned before it was lived. Studying the afterlife of US disciplining institutions through the perspective of deportee experiences thus illustrates how both Latinx and Latin American Studies can be mobilized to further bring into focus the hemispheric social and economic processes and transnational social and racial systems that continue to shape the lives and biographies of people who once called the United States their home.

NOTES

1 The fieldwork discussed here is from the research project "(Im)mobile Lives? The Detention and Deportation of South Americans from the U.S.," supported by the Wenner-Gren Foundation (GR-9518).

2 Eluding or attempting to flee from the police can become a second-degree offense in New Jersey if the attempt to elude creates a risk of death or serious injury to another person.

3 Transnational migration studies focusing especially on the Caribbean and Mexico have since the 1990s studied how migrants maintain links over time with their communities of origin (Glick Schiller et al. 1995; Massey et al. 1994). This approach advanced important critiques of earlier scholarship, which had framed immigration as a one-directional movement of cultural and racial outsiders coming into the United States (for a discussion of these debates, see Berg 2015, 10–11). Rarely, however, did the transnational migration scholarship consider deportation as part of its object of study.

4 The 1965 law replaced the previous quota system established in 1924 with a preference system focusing on the skills of immigrants and exempted close relatives of US citizens from country quotas (Ngai 2014).

5 In comparison, 25,177 Ecuadorians were deported in this same period. These numbers are compiled by the author from DHS Yearbooks of Immigration Statistics between 2003 and 2018.

6 A bondsman posted his $80,000 bail in full, with a bail premium of 10% that Jefferson paid with "money set aside."

7 Paterson has many gangs and most of them were represented at Paco's high school: Dominicans Don't Play (DDP), the Trinitarios, the 4K Bloods, the Crips, the Ñetas, and a number of smaller autonomous gangs.

BIBLIOGRAPHY

Altamirano, Teófilo. 1990. *Los que se fueron: peruanos en Estados Unidos*. Pontificia Universidad Católica del Perú, Fondo Editorial.

Berg, Ulla D. 2015. *Mobile Selves: Race, Migration, and Belonging in Peru and the US*. New York: NYU Press.

Cacho, Lisa Marie. 2012. *Social Death: Racialized Rightlessness and the Criminalization of the Unprotected*. Vol. 7. New York: New York University Press.

Chaney, Elsa M. "Colombian Migration to the United States (Part 2)." *The Dynamics of Migration: International Migration* (1976): 87–141.

De Genova, Nicholas. Migrant "Illegality" and Deportability in Everyday Life. *Annual Review of Anthropology* 31, no. 1 (2002): 419–47.

Flores, Jerry. 2016. *Caught Up: Girls, Surveillance, and Wraparound Incarceration* (Vol. 2). Berkeley, Los Angeles, and London: University of California Press.

García, Angela. "Serenity: Violence, Inequality, and Recovery on the Edge of Mexico City." *Medical Anthropology Quarterly* 29, no. 4 (2015): 455–72.

García, Juan Ramón. 1980. *Operation Wetback: The Mass Deportation of Mexican Undocumented Workers in 1954*. Contributions in Ethnic Studies, No. 2. Westport, Connecticut: Greenwood Press.

Glick Schiller, Nina, Linda Basch, and Cristina Szanton Blanc. "From Immigrant to Transmigrant: Theorizing Transnational Migration." *Anthropological Quarterly* 1 (1995): 48–63.

Golash-Boza, Tania, and Hondagneu-Sotelo, Pierette. "Latino Immigrant Men and the Deportation Crisis: A Gendered Racial Removal Program." *Latino Studies* 11, no. 3 (2013): 271–92.

Hartman, Saidiya. 2008. *Lose Your Mother: A Journey along the Atlantic Slave Route*. New York: Farrar, Straus, and Giroux.

Kantstroom, Daniel. 2007. *Deportation Nation: Outsiders in American History*. Cambridge, MA: Harvard University Press.

Massey, Douglas S., Luin Goldring, and Jorge Durand. "Continuities in Transnational Migration: An Analysis of Nineteen Mexican Communities." *American Journal of Sociology* 99, no. 6 (1994): 1492–533.

Morawetz, Nancy. "Understanding the impact of the 1996 deportation laws and the limited scope of proposed reforms." *Harvard Law Review* 113, no. 8 (2000): 1936–962.

Ngai, Mae. M. 2014. *Impossible Subjects: Illegal Aliens and the Making of Modern America-Updated Edition* (Vol. 105). Princeton: Princeton University Press.

Oboler, Suzanne. "Introduction: Los Que Llegaron: 50 years of South American Immigration (1950–2000)—An Overview." *Latino Studies* 3, no.1 (2005), 42–43.

Pierce, Sarah. 2019. *Immigration-Related Policy Changes in the First Two Years of the Trump Administration*. Washington, DC: Migration Policy Institute.

Ramos-Zayas, Ana Y. 2012. *Street Therapists: Race, Affect, and Neoliberal Personhood in Latino Newark*. Chicago: University of Chicago Press.

Ríos, Victor M. 2011. *Punished: Policing the Lives of Black and Latino Boys*. New York: NYU Press.

Rosas, Gilberto. 2012. *Barrio Libre: Criminalizing States and Delinquent Refusals of the New Frontier*. Durham, NC: Duke University Press.

30

Wars, Diasporas, and Un/Re-Rooted Familial Geographies

From Springfield, Massachusetts, to São Paulo, Brazil, and Beyond

BAHIA M. MUNEM

Eu sou brasileiro, palestino, nascido no iraque, MUÇULMANO, com avós nos estados unidos. Ei, é legal, né?/I'm Brazilian, Palestinian, born in Iraq, MUS-LIM, with grandparents in the US. It's cool, right? (interview with the author, Springfield, MA, January 2018)

In January 2019, the president of the United States claimed that Muslim prayer rugs had been found on the US–Mexico border, casting Muslimness and Latinidad as incompatible by indicating that Latin Americans weren't the only ones attempting to cross into the country (Qiu 2019). The declaration, via tweet, came less than three months after he claimed "criminals and unknown Middle Easterners" had infiltrated a large group of migrants who had been making their way to the country's southern border (Qiu 2019). The material representation of Islam and thus purported multitudes in the group also alluded to a visual imperceptibility of differences among the Brown bodies that were journeying to the border. This familiar Orientalist rehearsal of Islam and Middle Easterners as always already dangerous and in the midst of Latin Americans, who, too, are stereotyped and criminalized, operated as further justification for increased militarization of the border, including building a wall, foreclosing the possibility of migrant entry into the United States, and separating and incarcerating families. On the one hand, the troubling conflation of people and places is primal in (neo)imperialist and (neo)colonialist logics and migration discourses. On the other, there is a long history of Middle Eastern communities (Christian and Muslim) in Mexico (Alfaro-Velcamp 2007), Honduras and El Salvador (Foroohar 2011), Chile (Baeza 2014), Brazil (Hamid and Munem 2017; Karam 2007), other Latin American countries, and the Caribbean and the United States (Alsultany and Shohat 2013; Logroño-Narbona, Pinto, and Karam 2015) dating back to the Ottoman period and intensifying during times of war, conquest, and political instability in the twentieth and twenty-first centuries. Moreover, similar events have destabilized and compelled Latin Americans to migrate. This in turn has tangibly amplified ethnic identities and categories and historically and contemporarily put in diálogo Latinx and Latin American and Arab American

Studies and communities. In the United States, migrants from these geographies and diasporas are similarly disciplined, scrutinized, racialized, surveilled, and separated by immigration and police regimes, impacting families and kinship formations.

In 2008, boasting the long history of Arab migration and its inextricable connections to Brazilianness, President Lula's administration granted asylum to over one hundred Muslim Palestinian–Iraq War refugees.[1] While conducting preliminary research on this group in São Paulo in late 2009, I met the Soleiman family. Marwan, aged fifteen and quoted in the epigraph, is one of its members. He became a refugee as a three-month-old infant. Amira, Marwan's mom, emerged as a primary interlocutor in an ethnographic project that spanned several years. Having documented the resettlement of these refugees in Brazil elsewhere (Munem 2014), my aim in this chapter is to develop what I call *un/re-rooted familial geographies*. I utilize this term to capture the displacement and emplacement of transnational refugee families in scattered locations because of military conflict, (neo)colonialism, immigration regimes, and their refashioned kinship, identity, and belonging. My focus on the specific case of the Soleimans considers a family separation that began in 2003. Following the US invasion of Iraq, some of its members had been relegated to a desert camp, Ruweished, for nearly five years after attempting to flee to Jordan and being denied entry at the border. They remained in the camp, administered by the United Nations High Commissioner for Refugees (UNHCR), until Brazil's humanitarian overture. The Soleimans continued their dispersion in various in-between places from 2003 to 2017 and maintained familial connections while anchoring their lives in different locations. The family presents a microcosm of multiple dispersions, institutions that emplaced them, and the networks that animate and sustain them in their new local contexts, specifically in Springfield, MA, and São Paulo. While Brazil and the United States are the nexus of these exchanges, these familial geographies encompass the contexts of Lebanon, Syria, and Australia and also reflect and dialogue with familial dispersions of Latinx communities. Moreover, Brazilians often claim an ambivalent positionality in US Latinidad (Ramos-Zayas 2012), which in part reflects Brazil's distinct Portuguese colonial legacy in Latin America and then attributes this distinction to a privileged and hierarchized difference. Despite these fraught and layered relations, my aim isn't to unravel these dynamics here, but to instead consider how systems of US empire and white supremacy, particularly immigration regimes, similarly discipline the day-to-day lives of members of diasporic communities.

Marwan's reflection, with which I begin this chapter, registers a harmonious multiplicity of his Latino/Palestino/Muslim personhood. At once he recasts the Brazilian nationalist mythology of "racial democracy," premised on a convivial plurality of race and difference, and simultaneously erases the arduous journey this multidisplaced Palestinian family has endured—fragmented by war, settler-colonialism, and ongoing dispossession. In January 2018, he and his mother visited her parents in Springfield, Massachusetts, where Marwan's grandparents had been recently resettled. This marked the first time Marwan was meeting his maternal grandparents (Sameera and Ali) in person. His grandparents had also fled Baghdad during the US invasion and managed to reach Beirut, where they awaited asylum for over thirteen years and were restarting their lives in Springfield.

Diasporic Histories in Springfield, MA

The city of Springfield in western Massachusetts has long been a center for diasporic communities. It has the second-largest Latinx population in the state, which constitutes nearly 40 percent of the city's residents. Over 85 percent are Puerto Ricans (US Census Bureau 2010) who began to migrate to the area in the early 1950s and worked predominantly in agriculture and factories (Cruz 2002). Because of ongoing US colonial domination of Puerto Rico and industrialization projects that extracted labor and propelled migration, this diasporic community significantly increased in the middle of the twentieth century. More recently, there has been notable Puerto Rican migration into the Springfield metropolitan area, including Holyoke, which has the largest population of Puerto Ricans per capita anywhere in the United States (Centro Data Brief, Hunter CUNY) because of the economic crisis on the island and the devastating effects of Hurricane Maria in 2017.

Although Puerto Ricans specifically represent the largest diasporic community in the area, Springfield has also been a resettlement hub for many Iraq War, Syrian Civil War, and Palestinian refugees among these. All share in common the up/re-rooted familial geographies stemming from old and new colonial and imperial regimes. Organizations in Greater Springfield, such as Enlace de Familias and Ascentria Care Alliance, have been designated by the Massachusetts Office of Health and Human Services as points of entry for families displaced by natural disasters such as Hurricane Maria and Middle East war refugees, respectively. Both provide direct services and partner with local organizations to locate housing and offer English language instruction, legal services, workforce entry, and other assistance. However, these services, especially for refugees admitted into the United States, mark the final steps of a process that is often years in the making. There is an initial application, usually to UNHCR, then a rigorous vetting procedure through the US State Department. Next, in consultation with the Departments of Homeland Security and Health and Human Services, the resettlement process is coordinated with local agencies, such as Ascentria. As is the case with the Soleiman family, adult members of a single family, between the process of applying for asylum and being granted refugee status, may be denied entry into one country and granted asylum in another. Moreover, these processes can change depending on national leadership regimes and immigration policy, such as Donald Trump's 2017 executive order, which banned persons with origins from seven Muslim-majority countries and outwardly denied all Syrian refugees entry, even those who had gone through the multiyear vetting process.

While Springfield is also an economic hub in the region, about a third of its residents live below the poverty line, including many migrants. Ascentria, in an effort to integrate resettled persons in the workforce, frequently connects them to local businesses, such as plant nurseries, landscaping, and service industry jobs. Persons with limited or no English proficiency can more easily be placed in these positions. However, earning a living wage through them is more difficult. As much as there are differences between and among these diasporic groups, there is also relatedness—a kinship of and in displacement.

Kinship Near and Far

"Um Muhammad, fadi? UM MUUUHAMMMAD, faaadi? /Muhammad's mom, are you free? Are you free?" A small but clear voice bellowed down the stairs and through the closed kitchen door. "3t fadhali ya Zuzu"/ "Come on in Zuzu." I could hear faint but deliberate footsteps taking one stair at a time coming from the wooden stairwell outside the kitchen door—the same staircase that led upstairs to the neighbor's apartment. The doorknob wiggled as though the hands on the other side weren't strong enough to fully turn it in one direction or another, so "Muhammad's mom" (Sameera) helped out and opened the door, and in walked an under-three-foot-tall bespectacled little girl, dazzling in her pink outfit: pink skirt, white tights, pink sweater, with a matching pink necklace and pink eyeglass frames, encasing the lenses to correct her strabismus. She took a quick inventory of the people in the kitchen and leaned into her much older friend's leg, pointed her little index finger at me and asked, "Who's that?" Her verbal fluency and articulation betrayed her size and age—she wasn't yet three years old. Zuzu had forged an unlikely but strong friendship with her downstairs neighbor, who was nearly seventy. They had become fast friends. Filling in for absent relations, they formed an endearing kinship. Sameera's six grandchildren don't live near. Two live in Brazil with her daughter, Amira, and four live in Sydney with her eldest son Muhammad. Zuzu became for Sameera the grandchild she hadn't had the opportunity to coexist with or occasionally visit. For Zuzu, her downstairs neighbor was the *fun* grandmother. The one who danced, sang, and loved to engage in any foolishness that would double Zuzu over in infectious belly laughter. Her paternal grandmother, the one she lives with, doesn't horse around much. Sameera's and Zuzu's bond highlights the productions of kinship in new locations that are part of refugees' un/re-rooted familial geographies. Separated families outside of their home locations restructure affective bonds, engaging in kin-making through affiliation, not filiation.

Sameera was born and raised in Burj al-Barajneh, a Palestinian refugee camp located in southern Beirut. Her parents were among over 750,000 Palestinians displaced in 1948 upon the establishment of Israel, and today they and their descendants constitute the largest and most protracted refugee situation in the globe. Over the years, the camp—one of fifty-eight in the Middle East officially recognized as a Palestinian camp—transformed from a makeshift outpost, lined with UN tents sheltering people who thought their displacement was temporary, into concrete, fixed structures. Because the camp's physical boundaries were clearly delineated, the only way to accommodate its increasing population was to build upward, not unlike the iconic Brazilian favelas. With a current population of approximately eighteen thousand, Burj al-Barajneh is densely populated and has precarious infrastructure: "The water is salty; the electricity is not only unreliable but also often jerry-rigged" (Feldman 2016, 42). Death rates by electrocution are disproportionately high.

After marrying her Iraqi husband and moving to Baghdad, Sameera thought her status of refugee had shifted, "I'm 70 years old and it has been a persistent shadow." The "it" here is the protracted condition of "refugeeness" for Palestinians, together with the fact that her husband and children became refugees because of the Iraq War. Her four children were now scattered around the globe. The eldest two had been married with families of their own when the war broke out. One was resettled in Brazil and the other in Australia. Sameera's youngest daughter, Reem, was granted asylum with her in the United States, but her youngest son, Bilal, was living with her mother, his grandmother, while awaiting resettlement by UNHCR in the place Sameera had longed to escape as a child. The newly fueled anti-immigrant, anti-refugee, and anti-Muslim policies ushered in by the Trump administration had drastically reduced the likelihood of resettlement with his family in Massachusetts.

Zuzu, like her much older friend, was born in a refugee camp in Beirut. Her parents and grandparents fled the Syrian Civil War and made their way to Lebanon, where they were confined in a camp while awaiting resettlement in a third country. Zuzu was named after her twenty-seven-year-old paternal aunt, Zuleika, who was killed in Syria along with her six-year old son. Zuzu's actual grandmother, Um Yassin, was shot in the shoulder during that same street battle. Her deceased aunt left behind a set of twin four-year-old girls, who were still living in Syria with their father. Her grandmother was quick to show photos of her smiling granddaughters, then a photo of the daughter and grandson she lost. "Allah yerhamhum"—may God bless their souls—she said, as her face softened and saddened. When I asked her if they were Syrians or Palestinians who'd been living in Syria, she said, "We're Syrians, but we're the same people. It's just that the people want to make us different. Look at all of us in this house, we're the same." In this context, "the same" meant that everyone there had experienced war, dispossession, and dispersion but also fostered kinship. There was a palpable bond between the two refugee families who were displaced by two separate wars yet found kinship in a place of estrangement. The house they occupied was animated with layered histories, multiple trajectories, and interconnecting life stories. Springfield, as a multiethnic, urban, working-class space, with its Latinx, immigrant, and refugee histories, facilitated and cultivated these ties.

Transnational Familial Un/Re-Rootings

Transnational families have been overwhelmingly framed within the scope of economic migrants who seek work in the Global North to provide for their families in the Global South. Over the past two decades, we have seen a significant growth in scholarship documenting the separation of families due to global divisions of labor, which induce movements across borders to provide remittances for families in home locations (Hondagneu-Sotelo and Avila 1997; Parreñas 2001). Because of these cross-border movements, transnational families have become an increasing form of family arrangement. The specificities of these formations have been compellingly documented (Abrego 2014; Baldassar 2007; Baldassar and Merla 2013; Berg, 2015; Nuñez 2010). These families struggle to "do kinship" over time and place, as new technologies often facilitate interactions and help negotiate absences (Berg 2015). This literature mostly traces family separation whose provenance is in Latin American countries, like El Salvador, Mexico, Peru, among others, and has a direct impact on Latinx communities in the United States. Yet it can also be extended to consider familial dispersions in Middle Eastern diasporic communities who also grapple with the reach of US empire and are similarly racialized in the United States and subjected to immigration regimes that impact families and mobility. Moreover, economic migrants (documented or undocumented) as a designation, especially for Central Americans, has been used even for those who meet the criteria for refugee status (Menjívar and Abrego 2012). For instance, Salvadorans who fled a civil war in the 1980s largely fomented by the United States' political and material support of a military regime, which killed an estimated seventy-five thousand civilians, were granted Temporary Protected Status (TPS) instead of political asylum (Abrego 2014, 13–15). TPS does not offer a path to permanent residency and must be renewed every eighteen months. The precarity of this status was revealed in 2018 when the Trump administration vowed not to renew TPS for over three hundred thousand people effective September 2019, impacting nearly two hundred thousand Salvadorans.

Anthropologist Didier Fassin argues that the high rates of rejections in asylum cases leads to questioning whether actual protections are still offered by the 1951 Refugee Convention of the Status of Refugees, which is the principal international code that allows signatories to determine who is a refugee, to establish their rights, and to prescribe the standard of treatment and legal obligations the state has to refugees in its national territory. Fassin claims that often those seeking refugee status and resettlement are regarded with suspicion, and the process of granting asylum has transformed from "legal entitlement" to "selective humanitarianism" (2016). This is apparent with Middle East war refugees as well as those asylum seekers at the US–Mexico border. Most are from Latin American countries and have been broadly criminalized, families split and placed in detention camps indefinitely, and children separated from their parents and, in some cases, made virtually untraceable. What Fassin alludes to is that the 1951 Convention and its full doctrine of rights was created during mass movement of Europeans after World War II, and as mobilities have increasingly entailed Black and Brown people from the Global South seeking asylum and protection, selections have diminished.

Global governance institutions such as UNHCR and nation-states, through resettlement partnerships with international organizations, decide whether to maintain refugee families together. If kinship relations do not fit into normative Western conceptualizations of a family unit, individuals are often separated across multiple countries, as in the case of Sameera and her children. To remain together in traditional refugee resettlement, kin must fit narrow definitions of "family" produced by oversight institutions. Heteronormative nuclear family structures, parents with unmarried children under the age of twenty-one, are privileged. This sometimes leads to turning down placement offers. For instance, Amira, Sameera's eldest daughter, and her husband Nasser, had been among fifty refugees from the Ruweished camp to be vetted and selected for resettlement in Canada. Since the Canadians did not select Nasser's parents, however, the young couple opted against leaving behind the elderly couple, who had already undergone multiple displacements and experienced health problems. Eventually Brazil extended asylum to all of them.

In refugee camps, such as Ruweished, with echoes of the policing that takes place in the Southern borderlands of the United States, resettlement teams decide whether an individual or family being reviewed will be able to integrate into what would be their host society, based on factors such as employability, education, state of health, and age. While enshrined in humanitarian discourses, the selection process operates within a neoliberal framework of self-reliance and self-sufficiency. These practices align with current measures by the Trump administration to deter border crossing and overhaul the immigration system. The latter would base obtaining residency on a person's ability to "carry their own weight" (Shear, Jordan, and Dickerson 2019). In August 2019, the acting head of US Citizenship and Immigration Services announced this new proposed "public-charge" rule would make central self-sufficiency and apply to all migrants.

As noted above, Sameera's two older married children were assigned resettlement, via UNHCR, in disparate countries. Because her younger children were in their early teens at the time (the family was originally displaced in 2003), she, her husband, and her kids all awaited resettlement through UNHCR in Beirut. However, the total length of time it took for them to be resettled in a third country was over thirteen years. By that time, her kids had aged out of nuclear family resettlement, but Sameera still hoped they would all be placed together.

When the Soleimans were informed by UNHCR that they had been selected for resettlement in the United States, they were also told that their youngest daughter, Reem, twenty-six, would be considered for placement with them. Reem was fluent in English and could mitigate difficulties with language barriers. Moreover, both Sameera and Ali suffered from chronic health problems. Their daughter would be invaluable to the family's transitional negotiations with health care, housing, and day-to-day living necessities. After days of uncertainty and preparing for the possibility of another familial dispersion, Reem received notification that her application had been approved. She would be resettled in Springfield with her parents. However, Sameera's twenty-eight-year-old son's application was still pending.

Family Reunion

In January 2018, I headed to Springfield to meet up with Amira for the first time in five years and also witness the Soleiman family reunion, nearly six years in the making. Amira and Marwan were visiting from Brazil, and Amira's brother, Muhammad, Sameera's oldest son, was visiting from Australia with his wife and four kids.

The level of immersion in the local contexts in which the family members were emplaced was highlighted by the languages they spoke, with their various lilts, and the cultural-specific references from their current "home" locations. Marwan, who had arrived in Brazil when he was five, spoke with a Portuguese-accented Arabic to his grandparents, aunt, and uncle. When he spoke with his mother, he would often code-switch between Arabic and Portuguese, which he spoke with native fluency. His wide-eyed impassioned discussions of the Paulista soccer team, Corinthians, made him indistinguishable from many teenagers in São Paulo, where, like in other parts of Brazil, "futebol" is culturally central. Given the large immigrant Brazilian population in the greater Boston area, two hours east of Springfield, it didn't make him much different from youth there, either. Muhammad's four kids, on the other hand, communicated with one another in Aussie English. Three of four had been born in Sydney. The adults spoke primarily Arabic, and all but Sameera and Ali spoke the languages of the places in which they had been emplaced with differing levels of proficiency. These exchanges illuminate facets of their un/re-rooted familial geographies.

Because of their multiple dispersions, it seemed like the only common place Sameera's adult children occupied together was their past. The connection was in the histories they recalled of a place they once inhabited together. Amira and Muhammad had each obtained citizenship in Brazil and Australia, respectively, and had rebuilt their lives. Reem's command of English, employment, and general savvy repositioned her as the head of household in the United States. Her parents now showed her deference for the very things which in Iraq and Beirut positioned them at the top of the family hierarchy. Reem was able to navigate institutions that required a keen awareness of their functioning, such as the Social Security Administration. Much like Amira, whose rather quick acquisition of Portuguese had enhanced her status in an otherwise heteropatriarchal family, in the United States Reem became parentified. She accompanied her parents to doctors' appointments, translated documents for them, paid bills, sought out services, and advocated for their needs and her own. In a phone conversation shortly after her arrival in Springfield, Reem explained: "It's very hard. I don't have any of my siblings here to help, so everything falls on my shoulders" (personal communication, January 2017). Resettlement in the United States, unlike other traditional resettlement countries, entails refunding the government for one's airline ticket within six months of arrival. Reem was concerned about paying the government back. As she put it, she and her parents had been received with a "welcome to America, you've been through war and survived bill for $3,045." For Sameera, the dispersal of her children, and the transformation of family dynamics as a result, produced new, queer family arrangements. That is, in the context of diaspora and dispersal of filiation, transnational families, such as the Soleimans, are restructured across time and space, challenging traditional kinship configurations. Fictive kinships coalesce, animated by the experience of war, loss of home, and filiation. Sameera's relationship with Zuzu and Zuzu's family attests to this. However, the idea of having her adult kids in close proximity made Sameera pressure Amira and Muhammad to relocate to the United States.

Amira expressed anxiety about her mother's insistence that she and her family move from Brazil. According to Amira, her mother was failing to see how difficult it would be for her to uproot and come to the United States after living for nearly ten years in Brazil.

> It was so *hard*. I worked so hard to get through dental school. How many times am I going to rebuild my life? I'm not twenty anymore. She thinks it's because I don't want to. But, honestly, my English is horrible. I'd have to retake all dentistry board exams IN ENGLISH! I get exhausted just thinking about it. It's not even that we're steady there. Eventually I want a practice of my own. (personal communication, January 14, 2018)

The personal difficulties Amira encountered when she resettled in Brazil were plentiful, and she recalled them with dread. When she entered the country at twenty-eight, she was pregnant and lost the fetus in the third trimester. The complications from the miscarriage led to a hysterectomy. Feeling vulnerable with doctors and hospitals, she resolved to learn Portuguese at all costs.

In São Paulo, Amira faced discrimination for wearing the veil, both at work and in school. When the restaurant where she worked changed management, she was told to either remove the veil or leave. She was getting paid under the table, so she felt she had no legal recourse and left. When Amira began dentistry school, a professor asked her to remove the veil because she thought it posed a "contamination" risk. She removed her outer veil but not the headdress beneath it. After lab class, she went directly to the dean. In his office she rehearsed the much-touted Brazilian nationalist discourses of racial democracy and harmonious plurality that had been echoed time and again by politicians and resettlement authorities when Amira arrived in the country with the other hundred-plus Palestinian Iraq War refugees. She told the dean Brazil was not France[2] and expressed concern over the professor's suggestion that she was dirty and her veil a contaminant. The dean sent out a faculty-wide email regarding personal and religious rights. Veiling never again emerged as an issue in school.

Amira had gone back to school, obtained a degree in dentistry, and was employed in a dental clinic in São Paulo. As a mother of two teenaged sons, the idea of uprooting them seemed too great a sacrifice. After all, as she conceded, "Eles são brasileiros" (they are Brazilians). Marwan had entered Ruweished as an infant, and her older son was three years old. Both had survived five formative years in the desert camp. These were some of the hardships Amira had endured and the efforts she made to rebuild a life in São Paulo.

Likewise, Muhammad had made a life with his wife and four children in Australia. With his bachelor's degree in accounting, his wife's degree in primary education, and their one child at the time, they had a nuclear family and profile for self-reliance that a traditional resettlement country like Australia looks for in emplacing refugees. Since English initially proved difficult for Muhammad, he resolved to abandon accounting and worked in construction where language proficiency was not necessary. His wife, however, used her degree to teach in a private Muslim school.

Unlike his sister's gendered experience in Brazil, in Sydney, where Muhammad lives, there is a significant Muslim population with social and political capital. They eagerly participate in Muslim organizations. His wife is in a women's Quranic chant group, and he is an active member in the coed Muslim Scouts, a religious subsidiary of Scouts Australia, which offers a social-religious outlet for the family. It's also a space where he can impart a Muslim ethos valorized by the nation-state. Such clear civic and personal sense of belonging in Australia also operates as a mechanism of disciplining Aussie Muslim subjects, even as an apparatus of internal surveillance in the community.

The Scouts, they give us a number to call if we see something is wrong. Because kids repeat things they hear at home. The majority of kids don't come up with ugly ideas on their own. Usually there is an adult behind it. The scouts teach you to be good, to do good, and to enjoy life. I like very much to take the kids [camping] in the bush. They don't have cell phones or video games. I'm the only one, and the other scout too, who has a special emergency phone . . . When you go to the bush, you can talk to kids about nature, Islam, and the right way. (interview, January 14, 2018)

Muhammad is at once domesticating and being domesticated into a desirable and worthy citizen subject, while also being implicated in new technologies of surveillance.[3]

For Reem and her parents, in the local context of the Springfield metro area and diasporic hub, being "different" racially, religiously, and linguistically was more normative than not. It was common to hear multiple languages in the soundscape, particularly Spanish because of the large Latinx population, specifically Puerto Ricans. The multiethnic, urban social milieu made differences and interactions unremarkable. When asked whether she had experienced discrimination for wearing the hijab or speaking Arabic, Reem said she had not. "Everybody is from some place in this area." Her response speaks to the uprootings and re-rootings of families and members of the community and the multiplicity of place. While living in one area, people also belong to other places. Reem's command of English created the opportunity to work directly as a translator with the local resettlement agency, Ascentria, and made her a critical ally to Arabic-speaking refugees whom she met through the organization, which broadened her social networks.

Conclusion

The Soleiman family offers a microcosm of the complex, layered life worlds of multiple members of a single refugee family that is in direct dialogue with the experiences of Latinx communities and Latin American migrants while elaborating un/re-rooted familial geographies. Utilizing this framework, I capture the dispersion and restructuring of transnational refugee families because of war while also considering immigration regimes that triage desirable bodies and govern resettlement processes. Belonging and intimacies are refashioned through the structure of the nation, fictive kinships are cultivated in new locations, and filial ties are sustained across time and space. The family's separation and Bilal's inability to gain entry to the United States because of Orientalist immigration policies that racialize and criminalize Muslims and Arabs further points to interconnections with the criminalization of Latin Americans attempting to cross the Southern border and the impact these policing and immigration regimes have on Latinx communities in the United States.

Institutional and state policies shape mobility and reinforce US-centric white supremacy, which have diverse consequences for transnational families in these communities and in their day-to-day lives. Although seemingly distinct, these populations are similar in heterogeneity and complexity and are sometimes coconstituted. This not only intertwines experiences but also offers a possibility for (un)disciplining Latinx and Latin American and Arab American Studies in favor of hemispheric frameworks, emphasizing transnational connections and comparative (neo)colonialisms. Here Euro-American regimes would be decentered by interconnecting previously disparate histories and resignifying migration, belonging, and pan-ethnic identity, while also amplifying and enriching dialogues, analyses, and movements for social justice.

NOTES

1 Most were second- and third-generation Palestinians who had been living in Iraq as refugees and originally dispossessed in 1948 during Israel's formation.
2 This was a reference to the 2004 French law that banned wearing "conspicuous religious symbols" in public schools—often referred to as the headscarf ban.
3 My aim here is not to undermine the networks that this organization provides for people who have been resettled. Instead, it is important to consider how people within them are instrumentalized by mechanisms of the state. As the state already has preformulated ideas of "good" versus "bad" Muslim immigrants and refugees.

REFERENCES

Abrego, Leisy J. 2014. *Sacrificing Families: Navigating Laws, Labor, and Love Across Borders*. Stanford: Stanford University Press.
Alfaro-Velcamp, Theresa. 2007. *So Far from Allah, So Close to Mexico: Middle Eastern Immigrants in Modern Mexico*. Austin: University of Texas Press.
Alsultany, Evelyn and Ella Shohat, eds. 2013. *Between the Middle East and the Americas: The Cultural Politics of Diaspora*. Ann Arbor: University of Michigan Press.
Baeza, Cecilia. "Palestinians in Latin America: Between Assimilation and Long-Distance Nationalism." *Journal of Palestine Studies* 43, no. 2 (Winter 2014): 59–72.
Baldassar, Loretta. "Transnational Families and the Provision of Moral and Emotional Support: The Relationship Between Truth and Distance." *Identities: Global Studies in Culture and Power* 14, no. 4 (October 2007): 385–409.
Baldassar, Loretta, and Laura Merla, eds. 2013. *Transnational Families, Migration, and Care Work*. London: Routledge.
Berg, Ulla D. 2015. *Mobile Selves: Race, Migration, and Belonging in Peru and the U.S*. New York: New York University Press.
Cruz, José E. "Latino Politics in an At-Large System: Springfield." In *Latino Politics in Massachusetts: Struggles, Strategies, and Prospects*, edited by C. Hardy-Fanta and J. Gerson, 153–75. New York: Routledge, 2002.
Fassin, Didier. "From Right to Favor: The Refugee Question as a Moral Crisis" *Nation*, April 5, 2016.
Feldman, Ilana. "Humanitarian Care and the Ends of Life: The Politics of Aging and Dying in a Palestinian Camp." *Cultural Anthropology* 32, no. 1 (2016): 42–67.
Foroohar, Manzar. "Palestinians in Central America: From Temporary Emigrants to Permanent Diaspora." *Journal of Palestine Studies* 40, no. 3 (2011): 6–22.

Hamid, Sonia, and Bahia Munem. "A Política do Discurso Humanitário Brasileiro: Reflexões a Partir do Reassentamento de Palestinos no Brasil." In *Migrações Internacionais: Abordagens de Direitos Humanos*, edited by Carmem Lussi, 119–36. Brasília: CSEM, 2017.

Hondagneu-Sotelo, Pierrette, and Ernestine Avila. "'I'm Here, But I'm There': The Meaning of Latina Transnational Motherhood." *Gender and Society* 11, no. 5 (1997): 548–71.

Hunter College's Centro de Estudios Puertorriquenos "Far and Away: Hurricane Maria's Impact on Puerto Rican Communities in the United States." September 2020. https://centropr.hunter.cuny.edu.

Karam, John Tofik. 2007. *Another Arabesque: Syrian-Lebanese Ethnicity in Neoliberal Brazil.* Philadelphia: Temple University Press.

Logroño-Narbona, Maria del Mar, Paulo G. Pinto, and John Tofik Karam, eds. 2015. *Crescent over Another Horizon: Islam in America, the Caribbean, and Latino USA.* Austin: University of Texas Press.

Menjívar, Cecilia, and Leisy Abrego. "Legal Violence: Immigration Law and the Lives of Central American Immigrants." *American Journal of Sociology* 117, no. 5 (2012): 1380–421.

Munem, Bahia. "Expulsions and receptions: Palestinian Iraq war refugees in the Brazilian nation-state." PhD diss., Rutgers University-Graduate School-New Brunswick, 2014.

Núñez Carrasco, Lorena. "Transnational Family Life among Peruvian Migrants in Chile: Multiple Commitments and the Role of Social Remittances." *Journal of Comparative Family Studies* 41, no. 2 (2010): 187–204.

Parreñas, Rhacel Salazar. 2001. *Servants of Globalizaton: Women, Migration, and Domestic Work.* Stanford: Stanford University Press.

Qiu, Linda. "Trump's Evidence-Free Claims about the Migrant Caravan," *New York Times*, October 22, 2018. www.nytimes.com.

———. "Trump's Baseless Claims of Prayer Rugs Found at the Border," *New York Times*, January 18, 2019. www.nytimes.com.

Ramos-Zayas, Ana Y. 2012. *Street Therapists: Race, Affect, and Neoliberal Personhood in Latino Newark.* Chicago: The University of Chicago Press.

Shear, Michael, Miriam Jordan, and Caitlin Dickerson. "Trump's Policy Could Alter the Face of the American Immigrant," *New York Times*, August 14, 2019. www.nytimes.com.

31

Regeneration

Love, Drugs, and the Remaking of Hispano Inheritance

ANGELA GARCIA

Since the early 1990s, New Mexico's Española Valley has had one of the highest rates of heroin addiction and overdose in the United States. Between 1995 and 2000, this network of rural, Spanish-speaking communities saw over one hundred deaths attributed to heroin overdose. Heroin addiction in the Española Valley primarily affects Hispanos, who trace their ancestry to Spanish colonial settlers. While the majority of Hispanos are mestizos, with Spanish, Native American, and Mexican ancestry, many differentiate themselves from other "Hispanic" and "Latino" communities on the basis of their deep historical ties to the land in which they live. These ties are evident in Hispano culture and language. For example, the Hispano idiom for inheritance, *querencia*, blends the Spanish term for love (*querer*) with heritage (*herencia*). Traditionally *querencia* described Hispanos' attachment to land. Today, *querencia* also refers to an attachment to heroin.[1]

Indeed, among Hispanos, heroin addiction is commonly experienced across multiple generations of kin, who often live in a single, shared household. This arrangement reflects Hispano traditions and ideals of family as cohesive, self-reliant, and enduring. It also reflects—and to a degree offsets—conditions of entrenched poverty, including high rates of unemployment, chronic health problems, and lack of health care, among others. Studying daily household activities, including using heroin and caring for addicted family members, offers insight into how Hispano kinship is embedded in, and expressive of, complex rhythms of connection and disconnection, as well as broader relations of social and political inequality. In exploring family narratives that reflect this tension, I've tried to understand how intergenerational heroin use sustains a sense of continuity by generating familial ties of injury and care, which are put into motion by the rhythms of addiction itself.

In what follows, I reflect on intergenerational heroin addiction for its insights about the remaking of Hispano inheritance. Drawing on narratives of Hispano family life, my goal is to offer a textured ethnographic account of the complex relations that converge around past and present configurations of *querencia* and to show its implications for anthropological understandings of addiction, kinship, and the embodiment of Hispano history. To begin, let us first consider the losses Hispano families have endured over time. This history is a critical for understanding the politics and ethics of inheritance enacted through intergenerational addiction.

Genealogies of Loss

The Española Valley is often described as the "heart" of New Mexico. Located in Rio Arriba County, it sits at the center of a triangle whose corners are the wealthy tourist meccas of Santa Fe and Taos, and the techno-military center Los Alamos. The town of present-day Española is the site of the first Spanish colonial settlement in the United States. Extending outward are tightly knit villages whose Hispano residents locate their ancestry not in an official township but in a locality comprised of multiple generations of kin (Pulido 1998). Thus, one lives not in the village of Chimayó but in "Los Martinezes" or "Los Luceros," for example. These localities evolved out of the historical context of successive struggles over land expropriation and sociopolitical domination—first by Spain, then Mexico, and finally by the United States (Dunbar-Ortiz 2007).

Two Native American pueblos are located in the valley, Ohkay Owingeh and Santa Clara. When New Mexicans speak of the Española Valley, however, they tend to refer to villages established by the Spanish colonists. The majority of the inhabitants of these villages consider themselves "Spanish" or "Hispano," and the Spanish language is still spoken in many households.

Land was not a commodity in the Spanish colonial system. Rather, land tenure was based on grants dedicated to families for settlement and agricultural production. Spanish and later Mexican settlers were allotted land for an individual home, an irrigable plot for family farming, and the right to share common land with other settler families. According to the deeds, personal allotments could be sold as private property but common lands could not; they were to be preserved for family and community survival (Briggs and Van Ness 1987). As descent was calculated bilaterally, practices of land inheritance traditionally involved bequeathing land to male and female heirs, resulting in plots of equal but diminishing size, all of which remained in the family lineage. This system enabled kin to live in close proximity and work collectively as farmers. Such practices were aimed at creating and sustaining crucial social, material, and affective connections. Indeed, these connections assumed a lexical structure of kinship as represented in the idiom *la tierra es madre* (land is mother), as well as the agricultural terms *acequia madre* (mother ditch) and *sangrías* (literally "bloods," or smaller ditches), which relate to the distribution of water to family fields. Imbued with emotional connotations of a bodily connection between mother and child, land was fundamental in imagining and enacting kin relations (Rivera 1999; Zentella 2009).

The expropriation of Hispano settlers from the land began in 1848, when the United States violated the Treaty of Guadalupe Hidalgo, which was to affirm land-grant titles upon the United States' seizure of present-day New Mexico from Mexico. Women were the first to lose their inheritance and communal property rights, as well as their rights to hold contracts and testify in court (Montoya 2005). Many women sold their property to male kin in order to keep it within the family. However, homes based in agricultural rhythms were quickly replaced by a cash economy propelled by railroads, mining, and tourism. This new economy forced Hispano men to seek work outside their village and home, while women struggled to maintain a remnant of their family's land (González 2001).

By the time New Mexico entered the union in 1912, Anglo settlers controlled 90 percent of the land that had sustained generations of Hispano farmers. Millions of acres have since been transformed through powers of eminent domain into the National Labs and the US National Forest. Today, over 70 percent of Rio Arriba County, where the Española Valley sits, is classified as federal land.

Memories and sentiments regarding land loss remain powerful tropes, not only for Hispano land-grant activists who continue to struggle to regain land but for the population more broadly. As Jake Kosek writes, Hispanos' "lost" or "stolen" lands produce "a shared idiom of longing that has become central to cohesiveness and boundaries of both community and individual identity. People remember and remake the past through acts of memory that bring the meaning of the past to bear on conditions and politics of the present, and vice versa" (2006, 60). In the Española Valley, land has been an emblematic figure for Hispano experiences of loss. Over the past twenty years, the aggrieved discourse has come to index increase rates of heroin addiction and overdose. Heroin users and their families are likely to weave details about the dispossession of their land and property into intimate stories about loved ones who died of heroin overdose or their own struggles with addiction.

Today, most Hispanos are forced to commute long distances to work low-wage service-sector jobs. Whatever inherited land remains is increasingly sold to survive, creating tensions within many families. Between 2002 and 2007, Hispano land holdings declined by four million acres, reflecting the stark economic pressures they face (US Census 2011). The land, ever present but out of reach, produces an idiom of loss and longing that expresses both the cohesiveness and fissures of family life. Indeed, it is a witness to another time and to the death of a way of life.

To a certain extent, today's multigenerational household is a form of connection that seems to have survived this collapse, as it enables kin to continue to live together and contribute to the care of the household and each other. But this traditional living arrangement has been enmeshed in pressures from property loss and high rates of incarceration, addiction, and institutional neglect. Against the backdrop of these pressures, these households carry an overwhelming responsibility for the survival of its members.

In my research, mother-daughter and father-son dyads of intergenerational heroin use were more common than mother-son or father-daughter. This pattern could be related to a range of factors, including household composition, gender norms, sex differences in employment, and rates of incarceration, among others. However, both Hispano men and women framed addiction as a phenomenon of loss, connection, and love. This framing folds the past into the present, affect into materiality, mobilizing each for different purposes. As I describe below, it is through the simultaneity of objects (land and drugs), emotions (loss and love), and generations (parent and child) that heroin addiction emerges as a form of *querencia*.

Presence in the Flesh

Heroin in the Española Valley can be traced back to the 1940s, when some Hispano men, stripped of their land and livelihood, sought temporary work in Los Angeles. Culturally marked, they tended to live in Mexican American barrios where heroin was prevalent. During interviews with me, a few of them, now well into their seventies, recounted returning to the Española Valley with an addiction to heroin. Others recalled returning home from the Vietnam War a generation later, also addicted to heroin.

The Española Valley's first epidemiological studies of heroin addiction were conducted in the early 1990s, coinciding with the escalation of the nation's "War on Drugs." During this time, the western-US heroin market became dominated by very pure and highly addictive Mexican "black tar" heroin. Significantly, the Española Valley is part of the old Camino Real, the colonial trade route that connected Mexico City to the northernmost outposts of New Spain. Now referred to as I-25, it transports products from Mexico to the United States, including heroin.

From 1974 onward, in a series of stops and starts, addiction recovery programs were established in the Española Valley. Many of these programs were led by land-grant activists, pointing to their leadership roles in community affairs as well as the valley's improvised response to the problem of drug addiction. These land-activist-turned-addiction providers proposed a connection between the region's history of dispossession and its growing problem of addiction. They developed a discourse of causality through idioms of agrarian struggle. Addicted youth were "untended fields," and "lost sheep," both references to the Hispano working landscape a generation or more removed. Such discourse enabled a connection between past and present struggles. It might be tempting to dismiss such narratives and to retreat to prevailing discourses of personal choice and individual responsibility, as some Hispanos do. But, as one land-activist provider poignantly described, "We are surrounded by beauty that we can no longer see . . . [because] we have been blinded by drugs, despair and private property." Such an observation demands a broader response to addiction, one that includes economic exploitation and social disintegration as causal factors.

The connection between dispossession and addiction is sometimes alluded to in scholarly and public discourses but is rarely a central concern (Reichelt 2001; Trujillo 2009). Perhaps this is because there is no smooth translation between the political sphere of the Hispano past and its embodied present. Yet we might approach heroin addiction as a kind of psychic protest to, or symptom of, the erosion of the boundaries between past and present, the political and the corporeal. Indeed, it is in the context of persistent experiences of dispossession and the disintegration of longstanding genealogical ties central to Hispano kinship, especially land inheritance, that intergenerational heroin use emerges as a practice and principle of connection, even repair. It is, however, a practice that perpetuates the very injuries it seeks to remedy, for familial property in the traditional sense (land, houses) is often the precondition for new addictive properties (drugs, heroin-related scars). For many families in the Española Valley, kin relations are now attached to and routed through these new associations of property and forms of inheritance that travel via heroin. In this shift, "addiction" functions as the heritable "thing," linking (and often separating) family members.

Blood Relations

Like many cultures, Hispano configurations of kinship are primarily based on ideas of "blood" (Franklin and McKinnon 2001; Schneider 1980 [1968]). But blood conjures up a constellation of symbols, social relations, and historical referents that are not especially concerned with issues of kinship, per se. For example, Hispanos speak of carrying the land in their blood (*llevar la tierra en la sangre*), thereby connecting the materiality of the physical body with that of land. Blood is also presented as the vehicle through which cultural traditions are transmitted from one generation to the next. In this sense, "blood" is a metaphor for the endurance of ideas and practices of belonging, not a biological process.

It is no coincidence that images of blood suffuse the local landscape: the mountains that hug the Española Valley are named the *Sangre de Cristo* (Blood of Christ) Mountains; irrigation ditches are *sangrias* (veins), tree sap is *sangre* (blood), to name a few examples. Regional proverbs also draw upon the rich symbolism of blood. For example, *la primavera la sangre altera* (literally, the sap rises in the spring) celebrates the advent of spring after long winter months. Or, *la sangre sin fuego hierve* (literally, blood boils without a fire), alludes to the strength of family bonds. These examples illustrate the significance of blood and the way it is elaborated in the context of natural and domestic worlds.

The phenomenon of heroin addiction has multiplied blood's symbolic and affective meanings. Hispanos typically inject heroin directly into a vein. The rituals of injection (finding a vein, getting a bit of blood to flow into the syringe before injecting, "shooting" the heroin into the vein) often take place within the household. Users often describe the physiological effects of this process as a force of "love," with heroin "embracing" the body (*me abraza*), relieving pain and promoting feelings of belonging and well-being. Heroin may thus be understood as a substance that nourishes and strengthens the bonds between kin. In this process, negative feelings and associations accompanying drug use are lessened, a transfer put into motion by the very rhythms of addiction itself. Commemorative and generative, the physical marks and scars that result from heroin use materialize the connection between kin.

Yet veins may collapse or become permanently scarred, leading to sickness and negative associations. Indeed, the physical damage associated with heroin injection is sometimes analogous with damaged personal relationships and the existence of "bad blood" between kin. Here the interpenetration of physiological and metaphorical meanings of blood highlights how heroin is simultaneously a source of vitality and danger, connection and disconnection.

The multiple symbolic registers of blood intersect and amplify in other ways as well. Bobby, a young, heroin-addicted father from the Española Valley, described blood's constitutive role in Hispano's identification with the land as well as the connectedness of kin. "When I was little I believed soil flowed through our veins. That's what my pops said to me back then. *Lleva el suelo en las venas, mijo.*"

As Bobby described the story of his father's life, it became clear how heroin use was oriented to healing loss and pain, and that its potentially stabilizing force was directed to strengthening links to the past and family members. For example, Bobby recalled how his father left home before sunrise to work at a gravel mine. Like many Hispanos, Bobby's father loathed the mine, which he believed compromised the agricultural nature of the region as well as the health of those who labored in it. Although his father often spoke about "leaving the pit," local jobs were in short supply and his skills were agricultural, which no longer provided a means to make a living. Moreover, Bobby's father suffered from debilitating rheumatoid arthritis, which had mutilated his hands. "My pops could drive a tractor but he couldn't pick an apple," Bobby said plaintively.

Eventually, the gravel mine closed. To make ends meet, Bobby's father sold the remaining three acres of land he had inherited from his own father. After the sale, his father began to use heroin. Bobby vividly described how, at the age of fourteen, he learned to cook heroin and inject his father with the drug.

According to Bobby, heroin relieved his father's pain and improved their relationship. Under the effects of the drug, Bobby's father taught him to cultivate the sliver of land that was on the side of their modest adobe house.

We planted some corn, some chile. He'd sit or sleep between the crops. Rest in the little rows, *you know*? Sometimes I'd sit with him and he'd tell me about the old days. Like about what his pops grew, or going out hunting or cutting wood in the *Sangres* [Sangre de Cristo Mountains].

Bobby began injecting himself with heroin when he was seventeen years old, his father by his side. Like blood or land, heroin became a generative "substance" that bound Bobby and his father together in enduring ways.

In what follows, I reflect in more detail on the nuances of love and loss and their connection to intergenerational heroin addiction. Concretized in practices and expressions associated with intergenerational heroin use, I argue familial configurations of addiction are far from determinable as moral failing or biogenetic disorder, as they are often defined by law and medicine. Rather, I show how intergenerational addiction emerges as a threshold between rupture and continuity, injury and care. My focus is a mother and daughter, Eugenia and Bernadette. Without filling out a complete picture of their relationship, I hope to show how it opens up horizons for contemplating the possibilities and risks of a form of inheritance that functions through addiction.

Reunion

I began this investigation in 2004, shortly after Bernadette was charged with a felony-level offense related to drugs. Prior to her trial, she was ordered to the rural drug recovery program where I worked as an ethnographer and clinical staff. While she was there, I observed Bernadette's month-long stay during my work on the night shift and often attended to her basic needs, like providing food or medications or dialing the telephone for her outgoing calls. It was during casual conversations at the clinic that I first learned that Bernadette's mother was also addicted to heroin.

Upon Bernadette's release from the clinic, an electronic monitoring bracelet was attached to her ankle and she was confined to her trailer until her trial. I visited Bernadette often during this period; I brought her groceries and cigarettes, and she told me stories about her life. These stories often centered on "another time," well before she started using heroin, when she and Eugenia still lived in their ancestral village and home. Bernadette spoke lovingly about the home and the happy events that took place within it. But the bucolic image of the house and the quaint memories of it stood in tension with the other stories Bernadette eventually told me: her recollections of her mother's declining mental health, their deepening poverty, and her own growing loneliness and worry.

When Bernadette was twelve, Eugenia sold the ancestral property and rented a trailer in a neighboring town. At the age of thirteen, Bernadette began working in order to contribute to the running of the new household. At the time, there was only one drug recovery program in the area and no mental health services, despite the growing heroin problem. Thus, mother and daughter crafted their own services by caring for each other. In interviews, Bernadette described how she watched and cared for Eugenia during her bouts with *las malias* (literally, maladies)—pains that are produced through and treated with heroin. This meant scoring *medicina* (heroin) for her mother, often from a relative. Bernadette said everything would "go back to normal" once her mother was high—Eugenia would stop crying, hold Bernadette, and promise that things would get better. Her narrative reveals the affective and bodily polarities of addiction and the reparative nature of heroin in family relations. Heroin sutured pain and fear, guilt and hope, while casting a profound shadow that tied mother and daughter together ever more tightly.

At sixteen, Bernadette began smoking heroin with a boyfriend. Soon she began injecting the drug intravenously, at which point her mother became her primary drug partner. Many second-generation addicts described the transition from using heroin with non-kin to a parent as a "natural" or "normal" one. That is, their drug use was bound up in a familial and thus familiar world that, while often precarious, nevertheless persisted—unlike the more fleeting and often threatening relations with lovers and friends. It was through kin relations that heroin users were most able to experience their addiction as "normal."

For the next fifteen years Eugenia and Bernadette used heroin together. Bernadette described:

> It [heroin] brought us closer together. Because she's my mother and she understands me and I understand her . . . She gets my whole body, the highs and lows, gets me when I feel down for needing this [heroin] . . . We feel these things together. It's just a very close feeling. It's very close and very heavy . . . This is how life is for us. It's heavy but it's close.

The closeness and heaviness described by Bernadette is an intermediate space where suffering, stigma, and release intertwine. Traversing these states together, mother and daughter negotiate a space between injury and repair, addiction and love, revealing these to be mutually constitutive, not agonistic. The renewal of shared recognition and feeling—enabled by drugs and the rituals involving them—underwrites fidelity between heroin-using kin. This hold is as much ethical as it is biological. Over time, it becomes a strategy for living.

Bernadette was incarcerated in 2005. I spoke with and visited her and her mother on several occasions during their period. "Tell her I love her," one would say of the other—pressing into my hand a letter, a photo, or money for me to deliver. These transactions had powerful affective resonance and I observed how this resonance (the words, the things) at once collapsed and highlighted the distance between the two women. Like heroin, the objects were meant to offer some comfort, but they carried with them an acknowledgement of the very injuries they sought to relieve, especially the pain of loss and separation.

Bernadette was paroled in 2008 and reunited with her daughter. Shortly after returning to the Española Valley, she resumed using heroin with Eugenia. The three generations lived together in a small apartment in a sprawling low-income complex in Española, located a few miles west of the Martinez's ancestral home. Although it had been over twenty years since they had lived there, the home lived on in photographs taped to the apartment's thin walls.

Despite their heroin use, Eugenia and Bernadette consistently attended the local women's recovery group, which I often observed as a part of my research. One meeting in particular stands out in my mind. It took place on a hot, late-summer evening. About twenty women were crammed into a small room, sitting on tattered couches and chairs. The conversation turned to the topic of the red-dish abscess, or the *corona* (literally "crown"), on Bernadette's arm. The group's facilitator lectured the women on safe-injection practices, wound prevention, and care—measures already well known. While she spoke, Bernadette traced her *corona* and quietly countered that she was "born" this way—that is, born addicted and, presumably, with heroin-induced scars. Her interpretation of her *corona* as a kind of unchosen gift emphasized how her story was profoundly entangled with the stories of others situated similarly, especially her mother. This density of narrative, these histories and affinities, had claimed and enshrined themselves in her body in ways that she could not imagine, or perhaps even hope, to undo.

During this exchange another woman revealed her skin, which was also scarred from years of injecting heroin. She admitted that she took comfort in her scars because they connected her to family members she loved and lost to her-oin. In both accounts, injured skin is far more than infected skin to be prevented through behavioral modification. Rather, abscesses are jewels, passed from one generation to another, imbued with family history, memory, and emotion.

It was an especially intense meeting. At the end of it, Bernadette asked if I could drive them back to their apartment in Española. We piled into my car, Eugenia beside me in the passenger seat, and Bernadette in the back, where she quickly fell asleep. As we approached a fork in the road, Eugenia asked me to slow down and then to stop. I pulled to the side of the road. We were parked across the street from the house that Eugenia had inherited from her father, Eugenio. Eugenio worked as a weaver and a farmer, selling his wares from his home. Both were trades he had inherited from his own father who had also inherited them—and so the story goes for generations. However, Eugenio was the first of the Martinezes who had not inherited the land upon which these inherited practices were based.

We stared at the house's peeling adobe walls, the dented tin roof, and the neglected trees in the front yard that still bore fruit. Eugenia was born in the house her father had inherited. Her mother died in it when Eugenia, the eldest and only daughter, was a child, making her *la dueña*, the "woman of the house." She raised Bernadette there until she was twelve years old. The house materialized affective and political histories and a multigenerational struggle to construct what Eugenia often described as a "decent life" in the face of increasing economic scarcity.

Sitting beside Eugenia as she stared at her ancestral home, I was struck by the connections between the losses that the Martinez family had endured and by their attempts to keep memory, family, and continuity itself alive. These memories and the feelings associated with them are anchored in histories (of loss and struggle), sites (a village and home), feelings (of love and longing), and in the physical wounds that appear on the bodies of kin (the *corona*). A new notion of inheritance to be bequeathed and received had come into being, and it emerged through heroin itself.

Family Ties

In her story "Family Ties," Clarice Lispector writes about the recognition of the forces that bind one to kin. In a passage about a woman creating the same affective bonds with her young son that she shares with her own mother, Lispector writes, "Who would ever know at what moment the mother transferred her inheritance to her child. And with what morose pleasure. Now mother and son were understanding each other within the mystery they shared" (1972, 123).

It would be easy to interpret the scene in recovery group and the nature of the addictive ties that are being bestowed in the Española Valley as mere dysfunction—more morose than pleasure. However, in considering these ties, we benefit from the implications of Lispector's double-edged notion of inheritance and the valences of *querencia*. Lispector brings the mystery and emotion of connection back into inheritance, and *querencia* opens it up as an ethical space calling for reflection. Both have much to teach us about blurring the lines that have become sharpened in contemporary explanations of addiction as the result of biology or disposition on the one hand, or politics and history on the other. We might also read this blurriness as a move toward greater clarity, where addiction and love are revealed as vital forms of connection that link kin together via the past and present worlds.

Recall that *querencia* denotes love and heritage. From land and labor, to loss and addiction, *querencia* shifts over time. But if we look closely, there are moments when the past and present mix, bringing into view overlapping objects, desires, and relations. Like a child resting in a garden with his heroin-using father or a woman perceiving kinship in her heroin-related wounds. In ethnographically attending to these scenes, we see that the domains of loss and inheritance, like love and addiction, cannot be kept separate.

NOTE

1   The families I followed as a part of this research were selected because they were contending with intergenerational heroin addiction. They are not intended to be representative of Hispano family life or addictive experience writ large. My intention is to how specific Hispano families, with whom I have worked for over a decade, live meaningful and connected lives under extremely difficult circumstances. For more on this work, see Garcia 2010.

REFERENCES

Briggs, C., and Van Ness, J. 1987. *Land, Water and Culture: New Perspectives on Hispanic Land Grants*. Albuquerque: University of New Mexico Press.

Dunbar-Ortiz, R. 2007. *Roots of Resistance: A History of Land Tenure in New Mexico*. Norman: University of Oklahoma Press.

Franklin, S., and McKinnon, S., eds. 2001. *Relative Values: Reconfiguring Kinship Studies*. Durham: Duke University Press.

Garcia, Angela. 2010. *The Pastoral Clinic: Addiction and Dispossession along the Rio Grande*. Berkeley: University of California Press.

González, Deena. 2001. *Refusing the Favor: The Spanish-Mexican Women of Santa Fe, 1820–1880*. Oxford: Oxford University Press.

Kosek, J. 2006. *Understories: The Political Life of Forests in Northern New Mexico*. Durham: Duke University Press.

Lispector, Clarice. 1972. *Family Ties*. Austin: University of Texas Press.

Montoya, Maria. 2005. *Translating Property: The Maxwell Land Grant and the Conflict of Land Over the American West*. Wichita: University of Kansas.

Pulido, L. "Ecological Legitimacy and Cultural Essentialism: Hispano Grazing in Northern New Mexico." In *Chicano Culture, Identity, Politics: Subversive Kin*, edited by D. Peña, 121–40. Tucson: University of Arizona Press, 1998.

Reichelt, L. 2001. *Substance Abuse, Culture and Economics in Rio Arriba County, Northern New Mexico: An Analysis of Impacts and Root Causes*. Española Valley, NM: Rio Arriba Department of Health and Human Services.

Rivera, J. 1999. *Acequia Culture: Water, Land, and Community in the Southwest*. Albuquerque: University of New Mexico Press.

Schneider, David. 1980. *American Kinship: A Cultural Account*. Chicago: University of Chicago Press.

Trujillo, M. 2009. *Land of Disenchantment: Latina/o Identities and Transformations in Northern New Mexico*. Albuquerque: University of New Mexico Press.

US Census Bureau 2010. Households and Families: 2010. Retrieved September 15, 2013. www.census.gov.

Zentella, Y. 2009. "Hispano Attachment to and Loss of Land." *Cultural Psychology*, Vol. 15, no. 2: 181–200.

Latinx Kinship and Relatedness

The eighth critical diálogo foregrounds the trope of the "extended family" and how imaginaries around the familial arguably supply one of the leading characterizations of Latinx communities and Latin American and Caribbean populations more broadly. A presumed familial and fictive kinship render Latinxs as oriented toward community, in contradistinction to the more "individualistic" US Anglo culture. Peeling through layers of simplistic portrait of the patriarchal or matrifocal Latino family, this critical diálogo centers around the question: *What happens when we reframe conversations about "family" away from the biopolitics of kinship and normative US ideals and into the cultural practices of relatedness in Latinx communities?*

In this section, Jennifer Jones highlights the relational contexts of "minority linked fate" in the New South, while Jillian Hernández documents the hyperfemininity in Latinx iconography as an alternative practice of relatedness and belonging. Examining scriptural documents and photographs, Lloyd Barba's groundbreaking work recasts Mexican Pentecostalism in agricultural labor circuits in rural United States. Finally, Frances Aparicio critically contemplates "mourning" and decolonial healing through diasporic relatedness and sonic practices in the aftermath of Hurricane Maria in Puerto Rico.

32

Blackness, Latinidad, and Minority Linked Fate

JENNIFER A. JONES

What do you mean people don't know there are black Mexicans?
Then take me home with you! I'll pretend I'm your auntie and nobody will
know!
—Linda, Afro-Mexican resident of Cuajinicuilapa

Scholars have conceived of *Latinidad* as a racial paradox. While initially developed as part of a political project that highlights pan-ethnic connections to Latin America, it is racialized but not a racial category. It exists as part of a political and social counternarrative to whiteness and empire, and yet its meaning is derived, in part, through claims of proximity to whiteness and empire. *Latinidad* is a concept that is born out of US race relations and politics, and yet is embedded historically, socially, and politically in transnational and hemispheric relations. And, as a plurality of scholars has noted, despite its construction as a category that can be of "any race," it is emphatically not Black. For these reasons, teasing conversations like the one I had with Linda are possible. The idea that she could walk through an airport with ease and accompany me—an African American woman—from Mexico to Chicago without incident, is emblematic of this paradox. Black and Latinx, in the collective imaginary, do not coexist.

In this essay, I show how this two-pronged problematic of *Latinidad*—in which it both excludes Blackness and is constructed as proximate to whiteness—produces two fundamental problems. The first is that it upholds white supremacy and creates space for within-group anti-Blackness. The second is that it misses the lived experiences of many Latinx people who increasingly experience and understand *Latinidad* through race.

In what follows, I outline the genealogy of this paradox not merely as a critique but as an opening to consider the political power of the alternative. That is, what would it mean to think of *Latinidad* as proximate to and/or inclusive of Blackness? Below, I consider the advantages of this reconstruction, theoretically, empirically, and politically. I then illustrate this through two case studies, Afro-Mexicans in Mexico and Latinx immigrants in North Carolina. I conclude by considering the implications of these findings for political projects.

Critical Genealogies of Latinidad

Conceptions of *Latinidad* are rooted in hemispheric efforts to redefine Latin America as a modern, civilized region. In the colonial era, racial difference was defined in the Americas as it was throughout the West. Europeans were dominant, Indigenous populations destroyed, and Africans were imported as slaves to extract wealth. In order to maintain political and economic domination, a color hierarchy was established.

As the colonial period gave way to independence movements in the nineteenth and twentieth centuries, Latin American leaders found themselves contending with leaders in Europe and the United States who applied this same color hierarchy to civilization as a whole, arguing that countries with numerous Afro-descendant and Indigenous people lacked the capacity for nation-building and self-governance (Cook-Martín and Fitzgerald 2014). In response, Latin American scholars and leaders attempted to carve out new racialized spaces for themselves, asserting that *mestizaje,* on both a national level and an individual one, was an asset (Martí 1977; Vasconcelos 1993 [1925]).

In practice, while *mestizaje* replaced straightforward color hierarchies, in which the presence of Blackness or Indigeneity did not automatically disqualify one from citizenship and national belonging, this new formulation of race still considered whiteness the most valued attribute (as evidenced by many national programs to attract European migrants). This ethnonationalist project was so effective that it reshaped racial politics and social life in Latin America (Oboler and Dziedzienyo 2005). Indeed, until the 1990s, most Latin American countries refused to acknowledge that Afro-descendants existed within their borders (Hooker 2005). They were effectively erased.[1]

In the US context, as demographic changes in the post–civil rights era reconfigured the demographic landscape, expanding and diversifying the Latinx population, Latinx Studies scholars in the 1970s and 1980s embraced *mestizaje* and its qualities of fluidity and ambiguity as defining parts of the Latinx experience. Popularized most effectively by scholar, feminist poet, and activist Gloria Anzaldúa (1987), *Latinidad* was politicized as a concept of the borderlands, a kind of mixedness that Mexican philosopher José Vasconcelos (1925) championed with a racial orientation toward whiteness and away from Blackness that went unproblematized.

As a result, just as *mestizaje* was challenged in Latin America, scholars of US Latinxs borrowed from *mestizaje* to argue that there is something uniquely mixed about Latinxs that both gives them collective meaning and transcends national origins (Anzaldúa 1987). This vagueness was reproduced in both scholarly and political settings, laying the foundation for a unique categorical position in the US Census and an assertion of flexibility within the US hierarchy.

Thus, unlike the position of Blackness as a visible and named axis of difference that justified exploitation, denigration, and abuse, the racial project of *Latinidad* was intended to obfuscate (Omi and Winant 1994). *Latinidad* is, by definition, vague (Grosfoguel 2003; Mora 2014; Padilla 1985). It avoids the conventional status hierarchy even as it asserts meaning within it; it claims racial meaning and value as it refuses to acknowledge race; it resists conventional categorization even as it participates in the elevation of whiteness and erases Blackness and Indigeneity (Candelario 2007; Torres-Saillant 2003).[2] In constructing *Latinidad* in this way, scholars in particular (but also citizens) have bought into a racial project by attempting to avoid race.[3]

Scholars acknowledge and assert a kind of globalized racism, and indeed, rightly cry foul at how they have been positioned. But rather than attempt to dismantle the system, *Latinidad* has been constructed by scholars to embrace an assimilationist approach, reproducing, rather than calling into question, the existing racial hierarchy (Guinier and Torres 2002). As Silvio Torres-Salliant, a scholar of Latino and Latin American Studies, argues, in the United States, "the ambivalent rapport of Latinos with this country's existing racial categories . . . suggests an idea of themselves as non-racial selves. Among other likely consequences, such a hesitant self-definition has the potential for nurturing the resilience of the white supremacist ideals that historically have influenced the ways Latinos construct their identity" (2003, 137).

Under *Latinidad* historically, then, claims to mobility, power, and achievement were made through an assertion of proximity to whiteness—in biology, in ability, in ambition, and in cultural superiority. Yet assimilation is not possible for Black and Brown bodies (Gotanda 1995; Kim 1999). Like colorblind projects in the United States (Jung 2015), in official discourse, *Latinidad* primarily operates as a deracialized concept. Therefore it fails to acknowledge and address the ways that Latinxs are subject to racialized exclusion in daily life.[4]

In refusing acknowledgment of racialized exclusion in everyday life, common uses of *Latinidad* are conceptually distanced from the status realities of Latinxs who are increasingly positioned alongside Black people in the US racial hierarchy. And in rendering Afro-Latinx people invisible within the conception of *Latinidad*, the concept itself fails to achieve its broadly inclusive aims. In sum, *Latinidad* as an ideology has not historically provided Latinxs with the power to challenge the consequences of a racialized position in the US hierarchy and has precluded, by definition, the possibility of a *Latinidad* that is compatible with Blackness and, by extension, race.

The Importance of Afro-Latinidad

Afro-Latinxs and Afro-Latin Americans not only exist but are part of the historical and contemporary fabric of Latin America. Their longstanding marginalization throughout the continent has translated to the US context, in which Blackness is perceived as incompatible with *Latinidad* (Oboler and Dzidzienyo 2005). As a result of these assumptions, Afro-Latinxs have been marginalized from mainstream Latinx discourse, both political and academic. It is this alienation that prompted Miriam Jiménez Román and Juan Flores' assertion that *Afro-Latinidad* requires a "triple consciousness." Building on Du Bois's conception of double consciousness in the United States, they posit that *Afro-Latinidad* adds another challenging layer to the racialized experience, underlining dominant notions of *Latinidad*, Blackness, and Americanness as incompatible identities. Triple consciousness clarifies how, as race and legal scholar Tanya Katerí Hernández argues, Afro-Latinxs, and therefore Blackness, remain unintelligible within our understandings of *mestizo Latinidad* and therefore outside of the Latinx imaginary (2003).

The categories of "Latinx" and "Black" do not meaningfully make space for Afro-Latinx identity formation. Because Latinx is understood as *mestizo*, and therefore inclusive of race mixture, but emphatically not Black—and Black is understood as inclusive of any proportion of African ancestry as *only* Black, changes to the US Census would continue to exacerbate the purportedly neat division between Black and Latinx where relatively few US residents currently identify as both Black and Latinx. And yet the importance of integrating Afro-Latinxs into both scholarly and public conceptions of *Latinidad*, as Hernández (2003) and others have argued, cannot be overstated. Doing so is important on empirical, theoretical, and political grounds.

Empirically in the US, Black Latinxs have the lowest incomes and highest rates of poverty among Latinxs (Logan 2010). Such socioeconomic disparities indicate the need to understand the specific experiences of Black Latinxs as distinct from the *mestizo* majority. Our deep understanding of colorism, different citizenship trajectories, and sending contexts suggests that the omission of Black Latinxs from our broader assessments of racial inequality undermines the power of this work.

Or these data may be indicators of the complicated ways in which race works—those who identify as Black recognize the anti-Black global hierarchies they operate in and how structural barriers may shape their lives in more impactful ways than a blanket Latinx designation. Political scientist Atiya Stokes-Brown finds that race is a significant predictor of political attitudes, suggesting that Blackness is an important but undertheorized axis of meaning for making sense of *Latinidad* (2012).

Theoretically, acknowledgment and integration of Afro-Latinx people, as well as an affirmation of Blackness within the broader category of *Latinidad*, is necessary for a complete understanding of how Latinx people are positioned and understood within the US context. As political scientist Mark Sawyer and sociologist Tianna Paschel note, their ommission is part of a hemispheric anti-Blackness regime that undermines our ability to understand Latinx people as a whole. "In the Dominican Republic, Puerto Rico, and the United States, there are people, natives as well as migrants, both documented and undocumented, who are perceived and treated as Black. However, despite the complexity within each of these contexts, Blackness routinely marks a person as outside the nation, as some version of an unwanted outsider" (2007, 304).

Finally, the integration and understanding of race, Blackness, and Afro-Latinx people into our broader conventional and scholarly understandings of *Latinidad* is a political project. As Katerí Hernández argues, the Latinx image of "enlightened racial thinking by virtue of their racially mixed heritage" is undermined by the negation of Afro-Latinx existence and a pursuit of whiteness (2003, 156). To effectively challenge the position of Latinx people as racialized foreigners, the concept of *Latinidad* must be radically reworked to acknowledge, embrace, and build a politics from their denigrated status.

Despite its problematic history and present, *Latinidad* holds within myriad possibilities for social change if it can be transformed to account for Blackness. Such a move would mean a shifting of *Latinidad* to a distinctly racialized formulation, one which articulates a form of *Latinidad* that is proximate to or inclusive of *Blackness* and therefore can serve as a basis for political mobilization and solidarity. I suggest that an embrace of Blackness, as a basis of meaning-making *and* as a source of solidarity among multiple Latinx populations, holds possibilities for the transformation of *Latinidad* into a genuine and open political collectivity.

To understand the possibilities of such a transformation in the meaning of *Latinidad*, I briefly offer two case studies that help illustrate the gaps in our current conventional usage of the term and the possibilities when *Latinidad* is recast as a racialized concept, connected to histories of migration, inclusive of Black populations and cognizant of the realities of racial hierarchies. I turn to the experience of Afro-Mexicans to highlight the importance of including overlooked populations and the experience of immigrant Latinxs in North Carolina to illustrate the ways in which what it means to be Latinx is changing in real time. I conclude by highlighting some of the political implications of an inclusive *Latinidad*, in which the acknowledgment of Black populations and shared status creates opportunities for the kind of political, antiracist mobilization that sociologist Felix Padilla (1985) and others call for.

Cases

In these two cases, I examine Mexicans and their relationship to Blackness. Through a brief examination of Afro-Mexican migration, I show how transnational circulation matters for shaping racial identities and outcomes in both the US and Mexico, working to excavate racial meanings, identities, and practices among populations who, by virtue of this interstitial racial location, are either purposively ignored and invisiblized, as has historically been the case for Afro-Mexicans in Mexico, and rendered invisible through hegemonic racial meanings, as is the case for Afro-Mexicans in the United States.

And, through a case study of mestizo Mexicans that have settled in a Black community, I also examine how racial meanings and practices shift across time and space considering how, in the case of the United States, anti-Black frameworks often serve as a place of social convergence, in which denigration, by definition, is located in Blackness. In a moment in which Latinxs are increasingly othered and criminalized on the one hand and finding a space to claim meaning and rights as proximate to Blacks on the other, Blackness, *Latinidad*, and *Afro-Latinidad* are being transformed.

Afro-Mexico

From the colonial period until 2015, when Afro was finally added as a category on the Mexican Census, Afro-descendants were erased from Mexico's history and national imaginary. Despite this erasure, Afro-Mexicans engaged in the project of race-making, frequently finding meaning in their identity through transnational circulations, primarily migration. Until the mid-1990s, few Afro-Mexicans migrated to the United States. The North Atlantic Free Trade Agreement (NAFTA), however, was detrimental to the residents of rural towns that rely on subsistence agriculture, including many Afro-Mexican pueblos. Because NAFTA drove down prices, flooded the market with US agricultural surplus, and closed opportunities for small loans, rural coastal Mexicans who had never previously migrated have left their homes in large numbers, primarily for North Carolina (Jones 2013).

Though Afro-Mexicans have historically been poor farmers, many are now upwardly mobile as remittances from the United States have increased. Meanwhile, when they return to Mexico from the United States, migrants are forced to bring their regional identities into discussion with national ones, creating spaces for new forms of racial formation. This process of increased physical mobility has put Afro-Mexicans in the position of having to explain and justify their origins for the first time, emphasizing their sense of invisibility. In addition to being perceived as outsiders due to their official erasure, a pervasive lack of knowledge regarding Afro-Mexican origins, culture, and history have forced migrants to examine their understandings of Blackness, even when they had previously been disinclined to do so. Similarly, Mexicans leaving their pueblos encounter for the first time not only American ideas about Blackness but also ideas about Mexicanness.

Migration, combined with increasing streams of African American visitors from the United States, shifted the structural and ideological fields in which both Afro-Mexican migrants and nonmigrants constructed their identities (Jones

2013). Moreover, these dialogues forced Afro-Mexicans not only to put their transnational identities in conversation with local ones but to question their invisibility in urban contexts and, by extension, national ideologies.

These same processes mattered for how Afro-Latinx identity was being shaped in the US context. Though Afro-Latinxs have long resided in New York, Boston, and Chicago, increased migratory streams and settlement across the United States of Latin Americans from a wide variety of backgrounds and skin tones in a context of anti-Latinx paranoia has in many cases changed the way that Latinxs think about *Latinidad* in new localities and, increasingly, on a national level. Through this process of being racialized as "other" and in being systematically denigrated and deprived of rights and privileges, Latinxs have found themselves increasingly linking their experiences to those of African Americans, building political coalitions, and articulating a sense of linked fate. For Afro-Mexicans in particular, these simultaneous exclusions as Afro and as Latinx created new opportunities for both identity formation and politics that would not exist without migration and the politics that shape it on both the sending and receiving ends.

For example, Jorge, a young Afro-Mexican man who's lived in Winston-Salem for approximately fifteen years, informed me: "I've got a lot of black friends. We listen to the same music. We have the same outlook, you know, we are the same, like family . . . Black people here, they treat you like a friend, like a brother. White people here, they just treat you like a stranger, like just some guy."

For the Afro-Mexicans in my study, who were settling into places like North Carolina where Blackness was long established and highly visible, but *Latinidad* was something new, creating and recreating localized racial meanings meant grappling not just with histories of Black oppression but encountering Black solidarity for the first time and attempting to make sense of what civil rights organizations, for example, might offer Black Latinxs who were settling in those communities. While these experiences had a significant impact on how Afro-Mexicans and mestizo Mexicans situated African Americans in their localized racial schemas, such encounters, I was told, were also formative for Afro-Mexicans who then returned to the Mexican context, bringing with them a new perspective on their racial identity construction.[5] Indeed, while I was in Cuajinicuilapa, a small town in Mexico, in the region of the Costa Chica, known for its Afro-descendants, a shop owner explained that he participated in an exchange with a school in Detroit. He noted: "We sent a group of youth there to do cultural performances and learn about the city there. It was so important for that generation [of young people], because they learned a lot about the history and about slavery, and they brought that knowledge back with them."

The specifics of these circulations, termed "racial remittances" by sociologist Sylvia Zamora, played an essential role in shaping the meanings and identities brought with them. This pattern of meaning through migration and circulation is critical to our understanding of *Latinidad*. But it is also crucial to the ways in which Blackness shapes *Latinidad*, pushing back against mestizo nationalism through diasporic engagement.[6] Afro-Mexicans, in my study, came to understand not only what it meant to be Black but also the significance of *Latinidad* being constructed as *not* Black. Ultimately, these experiences resulted in a broader shift, politicizing Afro-Mexican existence, and forcing, eventually, the Mexican government to reckon with their presence as well the inequalities they experience. For example, pressure to finally include Afro-descendants in the Mexican Census came from grassroots organizations with the backing of the United Nations.

Similarly, migrants who settled in North Carolina, regardless of phenotype, also engaged in new meaning-making processes as a result of migration and circulation. For them, new social experiences and political contexts changed the meaning of Latinx itself, situating Latinxs alongside African Americans, not necessarily in terms of skin color but status and political identity.

North Carolina

The Afro-Mexican migrants who were part of the wave of post-1990 immigration joined a larger wave of Mexican and increasingly Central American origin population shifts across the United States. Before the 1990s, Latinx immigrants settled overwhelmingly in traditional gateway cities, such as Los Angeles, Chicago, New York, and Miami. By mid-decade, however, the convergence of economic stagnation on the West Coast and Mexico and growth in the US South pulled new migrants to the region. As a result, by 2000, the population of foreign-born residents in many Southern cities and towns increased by threefold.

Rapid economic expansion at first was welcome and necessary for economic growth in North Carolina. Unemployment remained low, and in counties where working-class whites and African Americans were upwardly mobile, Latinxs filled a significant economic void. Indeed, from 1990 to 2000, local and state policy toward immigrants, as well as the community-level reception, was positive. However, over the next few years, the reception quickly chilled.

Many states increasingly pursued policies that would restrict the rights of noncitizens, particularly undocumented immigrants. Post-9/11, new immigration initiatives frequently framed noncitizens as threats to US security and culture. As a result, the connection of undocumented immigration with security at the national level dramatically altered the discourse on immigration all over the country, shifting attention to Latinxs—primarily Mexicans—as threats to the state. This linking of immigration and security by the federal government not only instigated a general sense of panic and anti-immigrant sentiment throughout the United States, but it also inspired a fundamental change from the 1996 laws, which ultimately cleared the way for states and municipalities to take on the task of immigration enforcement. This shift happened just as Latin American migrants were arriving in unprecedented numbers to regions like the South.

ICE sponsored programs such as Secure Communities, 287(g) partnerships, and statewide, anti-immigrant measures, such as banning undocumented students from state community colleges, produced an onslaught of negative repercussions for Latinx immigrants in North Carolina and throughout the region.[7] As a result, most Latinxs in the area articulated a sense of being suddenly targeted for discrimination as racialized minorities (Jones 2019a). This growing sense of fear and marginalization, while detrimental to the well-being of Mexicans, was essential to building bridges between Blacks and Mexicans through what they perceived as their collective experience of racism and discrimination.

For example, Diego, an undocumented mestizo immigrant from Guerrero, indicated that he had poor experiences with whites in comparison to Blacks. He said, "In some places that I go, in a restaurant, or in a store, I've had more bad experiences with the whites. With people of color, no."[8] I asked him if he would explain further with an example.

An example is if I ask them [whites] for something and, or I ask them something, they don't answer me. They look at me and turn around. There are some white people who, if I park my car next to them, they turn on the security alarm on in their car. They think I'm going to rob them [laughs]. This is what I've noticed many times, many, many times. And, well, it's easy to understand what they are doing, what they want me to understand, with these things that they do. Or they clutch their bags.

INTERVIEWER: Oh?

DIEGO: It's the same thing you see with someone of color. They do the same thing.

INTERVIEWER: White people do it to people of color?

DIEGO: Yes, of course, of course. And with people of color, I've never noted it. Never have I seen someone close their bag or clutch their purse because they see me walking next to them. So.

Diego's noting of the parallels between both groups being viewed as criminal are strong signals of what he perceives as both a shared commonality with Blacks and a distance from whites. From his perspective, whites feared both Mexican immigrants and African Americans, viewing them as criminals, while Mexicans and African Americans never perceived each other in this denigrating way.

This growing sense of discrimination as the result of both negative attitudes and policies not only produced a sense of minority status in Latinxs but also triggered a perspective of *shared* status, and to an extent, linked fate, with African Americans. Importantly, community leaders played a pivotal role in reinforcing Mexicans' sense of shared racial status with Blacks.

The city's human relations commission, led by African American and Latinx city bureaucrats with support of the NAACP also proactively sought to connect minority concerns and build good community relations through its popular Beyond Soul and Salsa forums, initiated in 2005, by highlighting a myriad of topics faced by Winston's minority communities. At one forum, a Latina woman in the audience asked the police captain:

> Hispanics are more and more receiving the kind of treatment that African-Americans are getting on the street from police, and I speak from personal experience, but it was frightening and I was terrified. What is frightening is that both communities are identifiable by color, most of the time, and that makes them targetable. And the difference between the two is that Hispanics are perceived to be from a different country.

These public expressions of concern regarding issues that face both the Latinx and African American communities were not isolated incidents. Instead, they were part of an ongoing effort to build coalitions around their shared issues as minorities. Black leaders in the area argued from the pulpit and elsewhere that as civil rights leaders, they must speak out against the situation facing Latinxs in their communities, in part because their experiences are not so different from the racism they suffered less than a generation ago (Jones 2019b). Certainly, conflicts did exist. However, they were outweighed by conciliatory efforts by community members. Moreover, city leadership and community organizers made a point of tamping down conflict in favor of building positive relations (see Jones 2019b).

The experience of institutional discrimination, combined with a sense that African Americans empathize with that experience and support them, was vital in producing connections between the two groups. Such findings suggest that a re-creation of *Latinidad* that acknowledges and highlights a shared racial status can be not only liberating in terms of identity and meaning but also holds within it new political possibilities anchored in antiracist solidarity.

Minority Linked Fate

In their analysis of racialization and racial solidarity projects, legal scholars Lani Guinier and Gerald Torres note that we often fail to consider the fullness of racialization projects (2002). That is, we emphasize racial boundaries, the significance of phenotype, and the privileges and penalties associated with racial identity and ascription. Guinier and Torres argue, however, that race also contains possibilities for liberation projects. They argue that because race is not merely historical or cultural, but political, political projects that undermine the power structures that distribute privileges to some and punishments to others along racial lines will require *political racial projects*. They call for a politics that asks "with whom do you link your fate," arguing that cross-racial political projects are the key to achieving social change (2002). The idea of political race as a "democratic social movement aimed at bringing about constructive change within the larger community" relies on the actualization of what I call *minority linked fate*.

As Stokes-Brown notes, "If racial identity can serve as the basis for coalitions, then identification with Blackness among African-Americans, Afro-Latinxs, and Latinxs may serve a more cohesive and durable foundation, due in part to perceptions of common or linked fate" (2012, 9). Similarly, sociologist Sylvanna Falcón calls for a "mestiza double consciousness" as a lens through which transnational solidarity work can be forged. *Minority linked fate*, I argue, is at the crux of a revised understanding of *Latinidad*, one that is proximate to or inclusive of Blackness, and therefore serves as a basis for solidarity both within the Latinx population and between Latinxs and other marginalized groups. Such a framework or perspective is not new. The social histories of Afro-Latinos everywhere provide numerous illustrations of a race-centered *Latinidad*. For example, at the turn of the twentieth century, due to Jim Crow, Afro-Cubans settled in Florida alongside African Americans, rather than their white Cuban counterparts (Mirabal 2003). Evelio Grillo, an Afro-Cuban American writer, recounts in his memoirs experiences of attending segregated schools in Ybor City in the 1920s and '30s and being absorbed into the Black community, which later influenced his work as a civil rights organizer (Grillo 2000). Yet, too frequently, these lived realities are hidden from our conventional understanding of *Latinidad*.

NOTES

1 Sociologist Ginetta Candelario points to the Dominican Republic as an important exception tat proves the rule. Unique in its proximity to Haiti and its specific history of Spanish colonization, ethnoracial identity in the Dominican Republic nevertheless can be described as an ideological erasure of Blackness and elevation of whiteness and Indigeneity as an assertion of privilege (2000).

2 *Latinidad*, like *mestizaje,* was a conceptual project aimed at challenging a Eurocentric notion of whiteness and superiority, both throughout the hemisphere and within the context of the United States. Scholars and activists intended *Latinidad* and *mestizaje* to articulate a sense of meaningful identity and experience that challenged the status quo, centering Brownness, mixedness, and transnational meaning. I do not argue that *Latinidad* was a conservative project. However, scholars and the public have not fully reckoned with Black erasure and with how white privilege operates through *Latinidad*.

3 This is not specific to the United States but endemic to the hemisphere where political leaders and everyday citizens deny racism, discrimination, and in many cases, the existence of Afro-descendants themselves (Dultitzky 2005).

4 Scholars have highlighted that the perception of Latinxs as perpetual foreign threats racializes Latinxs (Chávez 2008; Cobas et al. 2009; Rumbaut 1997). Positioned as neither morally valorous nor as insiders, Latinxs are in some ways more structurally and socially marginalized than other groups (Kim 1999).

5 Some scholars have found that return migrants are perceived as criminal in part due to their association with US-born African Americans and Latinos (see Ramos-Zayas 2012). While it is the case that many return migrants in Cuaji were deported as the result of criminal convictions, this was not associated with Blackness, perhaps in part because Cuaji has large populations of Afro-descendants. Some elders did complain of the growing visibility of African American cultural forms, but this was framed as a differential form of Blackness and loss of the traditional cultural ways.

6 Certainly, the paradox of Black identity and mestizo nationalism is not specific to Mexicans. Garifuna from Honduras, Afro-Peruvians, and Afro-descendants from Nicaragua, for example, likely have parallel experiences. While these cases are beyond the scope of this essay, see Hooker (2005), López Oro (2016), and Falcón (2008) for more on these populations.

7 In 2010, 8.4 percent of the population of North Carolina was Latinx, and 61 percent of the Latinx population in the state was of Mexican origin (Census 2010). In Winston-Salem, the Latinx population was 14.9 percent, and just under 70 percent of the Latinx population was of Mexican origin (Census 2010).

8 Elsewhere in the conversation, he clarifies that by people of color, he means African Americans.

REFERENCES

Anzaldúa, Gloria. 1987. *Borderlands: La Frontera*. Vol. 3. San Francisco: Aunt Lute.

Candelario, Ginetta E. B. 2007. *Black Behind the Ears: Dominican Racial Identity from Museums to Beauty Shops*. Duke University Press.

Candelario, Ginetta. "Hair Race-ing Dominican Beauty Culture and Identity Production." *Meridians* 1, no. 1 (September 1, 2000): 128–56.

Chávez, Leo Ralph. 2008. *The Latino Threat: Constructing Immigrants, Citizens, and the Nation*. Palo Alto: Stanford University Press.

Cobas, José, Jorge Duany, and Joe R. Feagin. 2009. *How the United States Racializes Latinos: White Hegemony and Its Consequences*. Boulder: Paradigm.

Cook-Martín, David, and David Fitzgerald. 2014. *Culling the Masses: The Democratic Origins of Racist Immigration Policy in the Americas*. Cambridge: Harvard University Press.

Dultitzky, Ariel E. "A Region in Denial: Racial Discrimination and Racism in Latin America." In *Neither Enemies Nor Friends: Latinos, Blacks, Afro-Latinos*, edited by Anani Dzidzienyo and Suzanne Oboler, pp. 39–59. New York: Springer, 2005.

Falcón, Sylvanna M. "Mestiza Double Consciousness: The Voices of Afro-Peruvian Women on Gendered Racism." *Gender & Society* 22, no. 5 (October 2008): 660–80.

Flores, Juan, and Miriam Jiménez Román. "Triple-consciousness? Approaches to Afro-Latino Culture in the United States." *Latin American and Caribbean Ethnic Studies* 4, no. 3 (2009): 319–28.

Gotanda, Neil. "Other Non-Whites in American Legal History: A Review of Justice at War," *Columbia Law Review* 85 (1995): 1186–92.

Grillo, Evelio. 2000. *Black Cuban, Black American. A Memoir*. Houston: Arte Publico Press.

Grosfoguel, Ramón. 2003. *Colonial Subjects: Puerto Ricans in a Global Perspective*. Berkeley: University of California Press.

Guinier, Lani, and Gerald Torres. 2002. *The Miner's Canary: Enlisting Race, Resisting Power, Transforming Democracy*. Cambridge: Harvard University Press.

Hernández, Tanya Katerí. "'Too Black to be Latino/a: 'Blackness and Blacks as Foreigners in Latino Studies." *Latino Studies* 1, no. 1 (2003): 152–59.

Hooker, Juliet. "Indigenous Inclusion/Black Exclusion: Race, Ethnicity, and Multicultural Citizenship in Latin America." *Journal of Latin American Studies* 37, no. 2 (2005): 285–310.

Jones, Jennifer A. "From Open Doors to Closed Gates: Intragenerational Reverse Incorporation in New Immigrant Destinations." *International Migration Review* 53, no. 4 (2019a): 1002–31.

Jones, Jennifer A. 2019b. *The Browning of the New South*. Chicago: University of Chicago Press.

Jones, Jennifer Anne Meri. "'Mexicans Will Take the Jobs That Even Blacks Won't Do': An Analysis of Blackness, Regionalism, and Invisibility in Contemporary Mexico." *Ethnic and Racial Studies* 36, no. 10 (2013): 1–18.

Jung, Moon-Kie. 2015. *Beneath the Surface of White Supremacy: Denaturalizing US Racisms Past and Present*. Stanford University Press.

Kim, Claire Jean. "The Racial Triangulation of Asian Americans." *Politics & Society* 27, no. 1 (1999): 105–38.

Logan, John. "How Race Counts for Hispanic Americans." In *The Afro-Latin@ Reader: History and Culture in the United States*, edited by Miriam Jiménez Román and Juan Flores, 471–84. Duke University Press, 2010.

López Oro, Paul Joseph. "Ni de aquí, ni de allá: Garifuna Subjectivities and the Politics of Diasporic Belonging" in *Afro-Latinos in Movement: Critical Approaches to Blackness and Transnationalism in the Americas*, edited by Petra R. Rivera-Rideau, Jennifer A. Jones, and Tianna S. Paschel, 61–83. New York: Palgrave Macmillan, 2016.

Martí, José. 1977. *Our America: Writings on Latin America and the Struggle for Cuban Independence*, edited by Philip S. Foner. New York: Monthly Review Press.

Mirabal, Nancy Raquel. "'Ser de aquí': Beyond the Cuban Exile Model." *Latino Studies* 1, no. 3 (2003): 366–82.

Mora, G. Cristina. 2014. *Making Hispanics: How Activists, Bureaucrats, and Media Constructed a New American*. Chicago: University of Chicago Press.

Oboler, Suzanne, and Anani Dzidzienyo. "Flows and Counterflows: Latinas/os, Blackness, and Racialization in Hemispheric Perspective." In *Neither Enemies nor Friends: Latinos, Blacks, Afro-Latinos*, edited by Anani Dzidzienyo and Suzanne Oboler, 3–35. New York: Palgrave MacMillan, 2005.

Omi, Michael, and Howard Winant. 1994. *Racial Formation in the United States: From the 1960s to the 1990s*. New York: Routledge.

Padilla, Felix M. 1985. *Latino Ethnic Consciousness: The Case of Mexican Americans and Puerto Ricans in Chicago*. Notre Dame: University of Notre Dame Press.

Ramos-Zayas, Ana Y. 2012. *Street Therapists: Race, Affect, and Neoliberal Personhood in Latino Newark*. Chicago: University of Chicago Press.

Rumbaut, Ruben G. "Assimilation and Its Discontents: Between Rhetoric and Reality." *International Migration Review* 31, no. 4 (1997): 923–60.

Sawyer, Mark, and Tianna Paschel. "'We Didn't Cross the Color Line, The Color Line Crossed Us': Blackness and Immigration in the Dominican Republic, Puerto Rico, and the United States." *Du Bois Review* 4, no. 2 (2007): 303–15.

Stokes-Brown, Atiya Kai. 2012. *The Politics of Race in Latino Communities: Walking The Color Line*. New York: Routledge.

Torres-Saillant, Silvio. "Inventing the Race: Latinos and the Ethnoracial Pentagon." *Latino Studies* 1, no. 1 (March 1, 2003): 123–51.

US Census Bureau. "American Fact Finder: Winston-Salem, North Carolina." US. Census Bureau, 2010 Census. Accessed July 17, 2019. https://factfinder.census.gov/.

Vasconcelos, José. 1993 [1925]. *La Raza Cósmica*. Mexico City: Centro de Estudios Latinoamericanos (CELSA), Universidad Autonomia de Mexico.

Zamora, S. "Racial Remittances: The Effect of Migration on Racial Ideologies in Mexico and The United States." *Sociology of Race and Ethnicity* 2, no. 4 (January 2016): 466–81.

33

Chongivity Activity

Latinx Hyperfemininity as Iconography, Performance,
and Praxis of Belonging

JILLIAN HERNÁNDEZ

Loud, assertive, and stylistically spectacular. The working-class figure of the *chonga* embodied by young Latina women in Miami inspires both admiration and denigration among her fellow residents. Her no-nonsense attitude commands respect, but her fashion sense, marked by large gold hoop earrings, tight spandex outfits, and dramatic makeup, is often mocked as excessive. The *chonga's* comportment and sexual body presentation are read as gender nonconforming, and her performances of ethnicity (heavily accented Spanglish, stylistic citations of Blackness, indifference to assimilating into whiteness) as aberrant. Above all other characterizations, the *chonga* is defined by her hyperfemme aesthetics, as famously depicted by the Latina creators of the viral "Chongalicious" YouTube video of 2007, Mimi Davila and Laura Di Lorenzo, who at the time were theatre students in an arts magnet high school in Miami. In it, they parody the *chonga's* style by using stick glue for hair gel and Sharpie pens for lip liner. Despite the numerous ways that *chongas* are policed for their transgressions of gender, ethnic performance, and fashion, their bodies nevertheless signal ethnic belonging and are sometimes celebrated among residents for how they mark Miami as a site of undisciplined performances of Latinidad. The city, like *chongas*, is also perceived in the wider US imaginary as aesthetically, ethnically, and sexually over the top.

While young women like *chongas* and *cholas*, their West Coast counterparts, are perceived as having antagonistic relationships with other women through infighting, as represented in popular culture through works such as the film *Mi Vida Loca* (1993) and the "Chongalicious" video, these tropes occlude how Latinx have activated working-class Latina hyperfemininities as a relational practice. The forms of relation I center on in this essay would be called *chongivity activity* by Latinx in Miami, who use the term when observing the collaborative trouble-making behaviors of *chongas*. Chongivity activity describes the shameless and often gender-nonconforming actions that *chongas* and other rebel Latinx engage in together. These activities can range from public disturbances such as tagging a public wall or dancing on a pool table at a bar, to creating cultural work such as art and YouTube videos. It often entails practices of makeup and dress undertaken with the help of one's homegirls, and it is this aspect that my commentary will center on.

I use chongivity activity as a framework for analyzing how a range of women and queer Latinx cultural producers use makeup and other forms of working-class, feminized, and criminalized forms of aesthetic labor to sustain relations with each other. Consideration of these practices provides a critical understanding of how women and queer Latinx exchange *through* hyperfemininity to collaboratively execute projects that push back against gendered and racialized sociocultural exclusions and create alternative spaces and representations. These activities tend to agitate norms of racialized gender within and outside of Latinx communities. Additionally, chongivity activity performs an organic archiving of feminized cultural practices that would otherwise face erasure, as they are not perceived as meriting historical value by dominant US nationalist narratives and masculinized tropes of Latinx resistance, as femme aesthetic body practices are often viewed as apolitical and unproductive wastes of time and money.

My analysis and theorizing are inspired by the unique styles and gender performances of Miami *chongas* but extends the meaning of the colloquial phrase "chongivity activity" to encompass a range of artistic and vernacular practices engaged by Latinx situated in various geographic locations within the United States. These artists and cultural workers have disparate gender, ethnic, and (trans)national identifications. I do not intend to subsume important historical and social particularities as it relates to these vectors of difference but rather work to name shared aesthetic and relational affinities across Latinidades in time and space. Beyond showing how chongivity activity brings women and queer Latinx together, I will also show how it challenges mainstream white feminist and homonormative politics through place-making.[1]

Tracing the Activity

Plotting the beauty marks of chongivity activity, I gather an archive comprised of various scenes—historical moments and projects that trace the circuits of Latinx aesthetic relationality across time and geographies. Studying this archive involves various affective registers, ranging from giddy, slapstick humor to righteous anger, and the feelings of mutual care shared between friends and community members, particularly those that cross generational divides. The embodied aesthetics of chongivity activity both reflect and give rise to these affects, moving through interiority and surface as they manifest in enfleshed feelings. As Latina femmes line their eyes and lips, they stir up feelings of strength, sexuality, and social rebellion while simultaneously expressing them (Mahmood 2011). Chongivity activity results in what Chicanx studies scholar Marie "Keta" Miranda terms "the publicization of the private," (2003, 5) in her study of Chicana girl gang members in Oakland, California, where intimacies between the girls shape the social landscape. Chongivity activity makes intra-Latinx recognition, affection, and place-making possible. Yet, because its unruly affects and flashy aesthetics are viewed as disreputable, it also impedes sociabilities that are forged through respectability politics, heteronormativity, and white-identification/aspiration.

I provide textual snapshots of these aesthetic relations accompanied by visual illustrations to serve as documentation culled from my visual analysis, research, and interviews with artists and cultural producers as I have traversed living Latinidad on the East and West coasts of the United States. I begin by examining how Chicana artists in the 1970s such as Judith F. Baca and Yolanda M. López engaged in chongivity activity to connect with young Chicana women in the sphere of visual art making. Baca and López's projects provide a context for more recent iterations of chongivity activity. In this archive I include the performances of self-described *chonga* drag queens Juliesy Inbed and Karla Croqueta, which resulted in the creation of Counter Corner, a monthly queer party in Miami, Florida. Counter Corner has become a significant site of sociality for queer and trans people of color in the city. By bringing these provocateurs of chongivity activity into conversation, I aim to forge radical genealogies of Latinx relation that are based on the transformative potential of cultural practices rooted in femme and queer, or *queerly femme*, practices of the body.

Chola Vanity Disrupts the Woman's Building

In 1976, artist Judith F. Baca, known for her politically radical, large-scale, community-based mural work in Southern California, was part of a collective that organized the first exhibition dedicated to showcasing Chicana art in the United States. The exhibition, titled *Las Chicanas: Las Venas de la Mujer*, was presented at the feminist art space the Woman's Building in Los Angeles. The idea for the project was prompted by the relocation of the Woman's Building to Lincoln Heights, LA, a poor and working-class immigrant enclave with a large Chicanx population. In response to the social particularities of their new site, the founders of the Woman's Building wrote a grant to support Latinas organizing their own exhibition centering on experiences of work (Indych-López 2018, 94).

While some artists in the exhibition addressed issues such as Latina sweatshop labor, Baca's project in the exhibition centered on the more intimate, yet no less public, work of Chicana self-fashioning, particularly through makeup. Baca presented *Las Tres Marias* (1976), a multimedia project that included installation, sculpture, and performance. In the performance titled *Vanity Table*, Baca transformed herself into a 1940s *pachuca*, the highly stylized, zoot-suit-wearing Chicana street girl, by applying makeup and styling her hair at a vanity table. The project also included the critically acclaimed sculpture *Las Tres Marias*, a nearly life-size triptych in which two drawings of Chicana women flank a mirror. One

Figure 33.1. Judith F. Baca as La Pachuca, 1974. Photographed by Donna Deitch and used with permission from SPARC.

side depicts the artist in the dress of a 1940s *pachuca* with teased hair, severely lined eyes and brows, and long nails. The panel on the opposite side depicts a young Chicana in the less feminized but nonetheless stylized dress of 1970s *cholas* that incorporated menswear. Baca has described how the title refers to the three dominant tropes of femininity available to Chicanas: the whore, the mother, and the virgin. The mirror in the center of the sculpture serves as a third space for Chicana women to reimagine themselves within this representational matrix.

While the gender politics of *Las Tres Marias* has been expertly addressed elsewhere (Gaspar de Alba 1998; Indych-López 2018; Ramírez 2009), here I am interested in the ghostly presence and chongivity activity of Baca's often-unacknowledged collaborators in the project. Namely, the Chicana girl gang members from Baca's neighborhood of Pacoima, California, who called themselves the Tiny Locas. Baca recruited the girls to work with her in painting a backdrop for the *Vanity Table* makeup performance. On the wall against which Baca's vanity table prop was set, the girls painted a large heart, akin to the Catholic iconography of the sacred heart, and emblazoned the center of it with "Mi Varrio Pacoima" with black spray paint in large graffiti script. The thick, tentacle-like veins that protruded from the heart were scrawled with the girls' varying individual tags. Save for a few nickname tags like "Smiley" and "Chula," much of the text is indecipherable, demonstrating the skill and practice of *chola* demarcation and delineation that literature scholar Mónica Huerta has theorized as gendered expressions of control (2018, 112). It is clear that this is their semiotic terrain.

In her monograph on Baca's oeuvre, art historian Anna Indych-López describes how the artist often recruited young women gang members to work on

Figure 33.2. Judith F. Baca standing in front of the installation of *Vanity Table* at the Woman's Building. September 1976. Copyright Judith F. Baca.

her mural projects, but *Las Tres Marias* entailed a different process. "Here, rather than work with gang youth in the streets, she brought the street to a gallery space at a moment when graffiti still signaled class warfare and was not yet accepted by the art establishment. Yet the gesture transgressed more than just the boundaries of high and low art. Although their participation in the Woman's Building was fleeting—perhaps intentionally so, to mirror real-life experiences—the presence of the Tiny Locas disrupted the cultural, class, and racial boundaries of the white feminist movement (the point of the show), even as Baca herself was grappling with these blurred and fluid boundaries (2018, 96)."

Photo documentation of *Vanity Table* in existing publications show the painting in Baca's Woman's Building installation, but the Tiny Locas are absent. Baca appears in these images, but tentatively, often looking elsewhere. She often emerges from the edges of the frame, consumed with thought or in the midst of working. Given the limits of the documentation, the tags on the wall stand in for the Tiny Locas' bodies, generating a haunting presence in the archive. As a result, Baca's *Vanity Table* makeup performance as a *pachuca*, the *chola*/Tiny Loca's predecessor, could be read as a palimpsest, an incarnation of the Tiny Locas' absent presence through incorporation.

In the *Las Tres Marias* project Baca put chongivity activity to work, not only in inviting the Tiny Locas to occupy the space but in then extending their aesthetic labor to the *Vanity Table* performance, where her *pachuca* transformation embodied a similarly undisciplined Chicana femininity. Latinx cultural studies scholar Leticia Alvarado has described this performance of gender as that of the *malflora*, the bad flower that is perceived as lesbian and gender nonconforming. Alvarado notes that the *malflora*, like the *chola*, *chonga*, and *pachuca*, is "oppositional, but also connective, reaching out with intimate touch and direct gazes that challenge normative stereotypes, but also suggest queer connectivity" (2017, 101). A reading alert to the power of chongivity activity would suggest that Baca was *led by* her relations with the Tiny Locas and their connections with each other, as fomented by aesthetic work, to examine her own positionality within the complex terrain of Chicana gendered embodiment and subjectivity. This dynamic is echoed in artist Yolanda M. López's work with the Mujeres Muralistas de San Diego.

Makeup as Creative Calling

Faced with increasing displacement due to urban development in San Diego in the 1960s, residents of Barrio Logan, the oldest Chicanx neighborhood in the city that is located near the US–Mexico border, occupied and claimed the area under the construction of the I-5 freeway. The freeway project demolished homes and disintegrated the neighborhood, forcing the removal of many residents. In

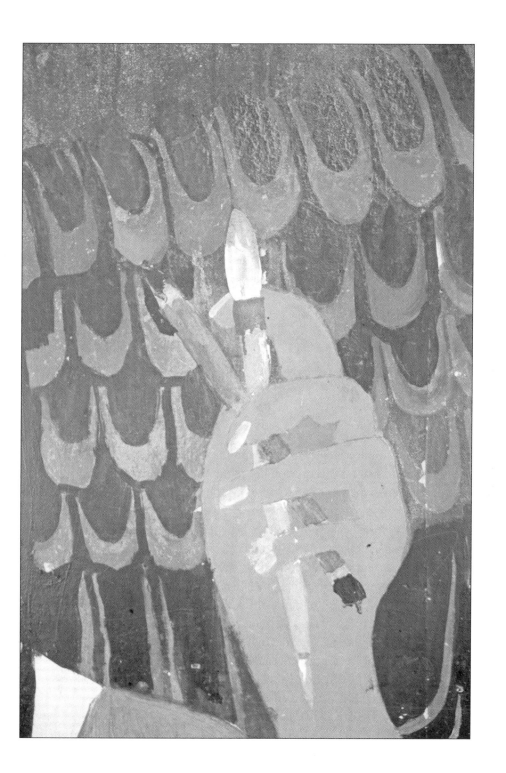

Figures 33.3, 33.4, 33.5, 33.6, and 33.7. Chicanas/Escuelas Mural at Chicano Park by Mujeres Muralistas de San Diego (Julietta A. García-Torres, Cecilia de la Torre, and Eva C. Craig) with Yolanda López. Photographed and copyright by Katherine Steelman and Jillian Hernández.

response, community members demanded that the areas below the freeway be used as a public space. Direct action began on April 22, 1970, with activists forming a human chain around bulldozers, and the land was formally designated as Chicano Park by government authorities in 1971. In 1973, local artists seized on the massive highway structure as a monumental surface upon which to inscribe Chicanx/Mexicanx histories and manifestos of resistance.

The Chicano Park mural project was spearheaded by Chicanx men and marginalized women's contributions (Lovell 2018). Artist Yolanda M. López, known for the feminist reimaginings of La Virgen de Guadalupe she fashioned in the 1970s, was from Barrio Logan and assisted with early mural efforts. She has discussed how she was never invited to contribute her own mural by the men leading the project, and due to the palpable gender dynamics she did not press the issue (Mulford 1989). Yet she was approached by a group of local high school girls who wanted to paint a mural there. In the documentary *Chicano Park* (Mulford 1989), López states, "The idea of working with young women was really thrilling to me so I said, 'Ok, we'll do it! Our enthusiasm for each other was really contagious'" (ibid). The mural was titled *Chicanas/ Escuelas* and was completed in 1978 by López and the high school students, who named themselves Mujeres Muralistas de San Diego (Julietta A. García-Torres, Cecilia de la Torre, and Eva C. Craig).

A lot of Mexican-Americans don't know about their own culture,

So we showed an Indian and a Cholo together,

to see how students dress,
how girls change themselves

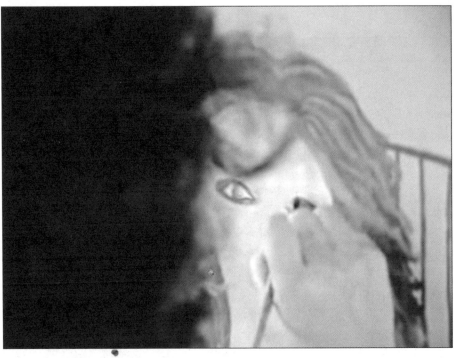

Figures 33.8, 33.9, 33.10, and 33.11. Stills from *Chicano Park* documentary featuring the Mujeres Muralistas de San Diego.

Their mural depicts a scene that traverses past and present. The horizontal diaphragm of the freeway structure is framed with a depiction of a large black eagle in Aztec style. The eagle has a snake in its mouth and is set against a vibrant rainbow in the background. A portrait of an ancient Mayan in profile is pictured on the extreme left of the structure, and a contemporary Chicano, which the muralists described as a cholo (Mulford 1989), bookends the mural on the extreme right. The two figures face each other. An Aztec girl displaying an ear of corn appears in the left-center of the composition and is paired with a young contemporary Chicana on the right. The Chicana wears red lipstick, has long fingernails, and displays a pencil and paintbrush in her hand, marking her as a student, artist, and high femme.[2] The column supporting the diaphragm depicts four young women in close proximity to each other, defiantly sprouting from stalks of corn against the dystopic backdrop of a school building that resembles a prison. Their made-up faces and otherworldly blue and purple skin tones contrast with the state architecture, declaring undisciplined femininity and radical difference in the face of displacement and discipline.

Above the grouping of girl students, the eagle displays an open book that is inscribed with cursive lettering that reads, "Ya basta! [Enough!] The schools are not teaching us. Over 50 percent of us Chicanos are pushed out of school. If we want to make it, we have to surrender our language. They want to make us coconuts—brown on the outside and white on the inside!" Like the bold lettering and semiotic markings that the Tiny Locas made at Judith Baca's *Vanity Table* installation, the text by the Mujeres Muralistas de San Diego amplifies the imagery, with the exclamation marks and bold, direct phrasing conveying the rousing affect of homegirl truth telling.

Beyond the relational praxis of López serving as what she describes as a "facilitator and teacher" to the girls, I am compelled by how the girls' vision for their mural was sparked by the Latina femme body practice of makeup. In describing the inspiration for the mural in the *Chicano Park* documentary (Mulford 1989), one of the girls stated that she arrived at the idea by observing how the students at her high school dressed, specifically how the girls "se transformavan pintando sus caras" ("would transform their faces with makeup"). In other words, the girls felt compelled to document their peers' chongivity activity and used the mural to extend the activity to disrupt the masculinist iconography of many of the murals in Chicano Park, which feature social realist depictions of figures such as Emiliano Zapata and Che Guevara. In addition to wanting to portray Chicana girls of her own generation, the student also discusses a desire to depict Chicanx women ancestors "como no usaba, no makeup antes" ("the way they didn't use makeup before"). Here, makeup serves as a temporal marker between past and present embodiments of feminine Indigeneity, Mexicanidad and Chicanidad, yet without hierarchies of valuation. In the Chicanx student artist's view, makeup and its absence indicate generational difference, not gendered/ethnic deviance or (in)authenticity.

The documentary footage of the girls talking about and working on their mural is striking, for it captures the dramatic *chola* makeup they wore themselves. In much of the footage that depicts them working, they are shown painting thick eyeliner on the faces of the young women students they depict in the mural. By engaging in chongivity activity, young Chicanx women inspired by each other's makeup enlisted Yolanda López to work with them in executing a visionary critique and representation of gendered survivance and belonging in a contested site.[3] Next we consider the more recent, makeup-fueled relationalities engendered by *chonga* drag performers in Miami, Florida.

The Place-Making Potential of *Chonga* Drag

Drag performers Juliesy Inbed and Karla Croqueta have an established following in Miami. Their signature aesthetic of tight spandex clothing and garish makeup, coupled with gaudy jewelry and their thick dark beards, have made them the unlikely darlings of the Miami nightlife scene. They are often booked to host various parties in the city in both queer and straight venues, to which they bring their raucous, *chongalicious* sense of humor in engaging participants. The way Giovanni Profera (Juliesy) and Josué García (Karla) came together to become Juliesy and Karla, and the effects it has had on Miami's queer social landscape, embody the connective and place-making potential of chongivity activity.

Profera and Garcia are two queer men who were longtime neighborhood friends. They grew up together in the working-class Cuban American enclave of Hialeah in Miami. In my individual interviews with the performers[4], they described how they came about their chongivity activity as many *chongas* do— in response to being broke. One night they wanted to go out partying but did not have money to buy drinks, so they decided to crash a lesbian ladies' night by donning drag. Gathering their outfits on the fly, Garcia wore a rain poncho with a sequined tube top worn as crop top, paired with what he describes as a "Tina Turner wig." Profera wore a tube top paired with his underwear, adding, "It took three hours to put on our makeup, we looked horrible. It was so bad. The precision wasn't right, we didn't know what the fuck we were doing." Despite being kicked out of the bar for dancing on the pool table, Garcia giddily recalls that Profera looked at him and said, "I look like such a chonga, I feel like a chonga. Did you feel that? That was amazing." The lingering high of their chongivity activity led them to repeat their performance as Juliesy and Karla that same week at the gay Latinx night club Azúcar in Miami, where they performed a rendition of Destiny's Child's song "Say My Name" during Drag Wars night.[5] They recount that no one clapped, and they were ridiculed for what was perceived as a failed drag performance. Juliesy and Karla's bearded *chonga*-drag aesthetic dramatically departs from the more conventional modes of drag popular in the Miami nightlife scene, which aim for glamour, feminine realness, and celebrity

Figure 33.12. Drag performers Juliesy InBed and Karla Croqueta. Photographed by Daniella A. Rascón. Permission to use from Daniella A. Rascón.

impersonation. This is an aesthetic that Juliesy and Karla's working-class and ethnic penchant for discount fashion store spandex getups and *chonga* makeup markedly departs from. Though they felt discouraged by this initial rejection in the gay nightclub scene, they nevertheless decided to take their *chonga* performance to the streets when prompted by mutual friend Will González, an amateur filmmaker who wanted to feature them in a series of videos.

The resulting YouTube videos, titled "Hialeah's Finest," feature Juliesy and Karla engaging in various forms of chongivity activity. In "Episode One"[6] they cause a commotion by getting into a mock argument with each other at a bus stop in Hialeah during rush hour traffic. Profera recalls, "People honked. 'Perra!' [Bitch] 'Sucia!' [Dirty whore] The best one was 'Traga leche!' [Cum swallower]." While some passersby joked along with them in good humor, these loaded sexist and homophobic epithets revealed how their performance also agitated respectable conventions of Latinx gender and sexuality through their queerly hyperfeminine *suciedad* (dirtiness). Latinx cultural studies scholar Deborah Vargas describes *suciedad* as a "trope for feminine-gendered subjectivities associated with seedy working-class Latino spaces including queer femmes, nonnormative working and underclass women of color, and travesty and transgender Latinas"

(2014, 717). The sucia's gender nonconformity is read through tropes of contamination, they are subjects to be sanitized and/or expelled from the social.

The "Hialeah's Finest: Episode One" video was shot in close proximity to Profera and Garcia's neighborhood, which made them vulnerable to being seen by family members. The video captures Profera receiving an angry phone call from his mother while he and Garcia flirt with men in the Westland Mall parking lot as Juliesy and Karla. Garcia shared, "Gio gets a call from his mom. 'Your son is on 49th street dressed like a hooker and he's with a fat hooker!'" Minutes later, Profera's mother appears in the parking lot shouting at the performers from her red Jeep, yelling "Ustedes son machos!" ("You are men!"). This unscripted scene reveals the multilayered forms that the policing of *suciedad* takes, from street harassment to family disapproval, all of which Profera and Garcia appear to take in stride. In fact, they draw energy from these agitated responses (García Hernández 2017) and use them to extend their comedic performances further.

Juliesy and Karla's improvised enactments and guerilla documentations of *chonga* identity inspire both laughter and disgust. Though they take up the oppositional practice of *chonga* femininity, their practice is not invested in presenting a restorative representation. Like the viral cholafied.com Tumblr page that features celebrity faces like Jay Z transformed into cholas through digital makeovers, Juliesy and Karla's drag performances signal a "barbed affection" for *chongas* and "seeks an aesthetic posture besides denigration, without the explicit hopes of reconstitution or 'humanizing.' There's no innocence in these made-up images. It's why there could be laughter" (Huerta 2018, 112).

The laughter induced by performances such as the queer spatial appropriation enacted by Juliesy in "Episode Two"[7] as she scales and planks a public city sign that reads "Hialeah, The City of Progress" (recalling the Mujeres Muralistas' taking up of space at Chicano Park) fomented a local audience for their *chonga* drag through the circulation of the "Hialeah's Finest" series on YouTube. As Profera elaborates, "Alongside and through the videos everyone learned how to accept us, so we got more acceptance in the night life scene. I'm starting to get the higher clientele, the ones that want to have a good time, a different vibe." The eager consumption of the Juliesy and Karla personas parallels the commodification of *chonga* embodiment that occurred in the wake of the viral "Chongalicious" video of 2007, which branded the young performers as upcoming Latina "starlets" with crossover potential. Like the "Chongalicious" creators Dávila and Di Lorenzo, Profera and Garcia created these performances in the context of their leisure time together as friends and they did not set out to create a product. Yet the spectacular embodiments and performances of *chonga* identity they authored have nevertheless been received as such, prompting these performers to draw what cultural and material capital could accrue from an identity that in vernacular contexts often constitutes a liability to social, educational, and economic success in a neoliberal context (Ramos-Zayas 2012). Spurred by the local

Figures 33.13, 33.14, and 33.15. Juliesy and Karla plank the City of Hialeah sign in the YouTube video "Hialeah's Finest: Episode Two."

coverage they received following the posting of the "Hialeah's Finest" videos by publications such as the *Miami New Times*, Juliesy and Karla started booking steady gigs at straight clubs where, rather than a social atmosphere, their performances were received more like a "circus act," according to Garcia, who quickly added, "It pays the bills. I ain't complaining."

Performing in gay venues was not a vastly different experience, as their performances were often mocked. As Profera explains, "We had to move away from the [Miami] Beach to get the opportunity. When we moved out of the Beach we went to Wynwood, now we're with all of these artists." Leaving the homonormative club scene in Miami Beach led the performers to the Wynwood arts district, and to collaborations with local queer artists like Sleeper, who suggested that they collaborate on organizing their own queer night at The Corner bar, a straight venue.

They established Counter Corner, a queer party night, in 2014, and it continues to feature emerging drag talent on the third Sunday of every month. The parties have become so popular that the venue can barely hold attendees. The space has also fomented a decidedly genderqueer and tropicalized, Miami-specific mode of drag aesthetic innovated by performers such as Queef Latina, Miss Toto, and Jupiter Velvet. As Profera explains, "Counter Corner is a strictly queer party and I do that for the community. Because I love that scene. It's young artists that just need self-expression they are not getting in their day to day lives so they dress up." In reflecting on the unprecedented growth of Counter Corner Garcia reflects, "The first time we hosted there were very few people. Now you get there and you can't even move. I cry almost every single Counter Corner. People say, 'Thank you for creating this judgement-free space. I don't feel like I'm gonna be harassed.' Trans, straight, queer—I have gotten to know people on a personal level. Everyone there is woke as fuck. It's become a safe space." Garcia and Profera juxtapose Counter Corner to the more mainstream gay venues in the city that operate on a homonormative framework that is exclusionary to femme, larger-bodied, and trans queers. Their cocreation of this place, amid the rapid gentrification of downtown Miami, mirrors the queer spatial appropriation they performed when planking the "Hialeah: City of Progress" sign. Counter Corner signifies an alternative urban narrative of "progress" that thrives on *suciedad*.

Through their friendship and *chonga* aesthetic, Profera and Garcia put chongivity activity to work in creating an alternative queer space in the midst of increasing gentrification and displacement of working-class communities of color, primarily Black, and artists in Miami. As sucias extradonaire, Juliesy and Karla exhibit how "sucia genders signal possibilities of a queer sustenance within rapidly aggressive moves to destroy alternative imaginaries of joy and intimacy and care. Such sustenance requires a dedication to labor, love, and loss in lo sucio: socialities, kinship, and nightlives that cultivate daily divestment and sustainability of what [queer theorist José Esteban] Muñoz has described as 'that which is not yet here' within the worlds of hetero- and homonormative fictions of comfort and inheritance" (ibid. 718). For the performers, *chonga* hyperfemininity served as an iconography of relation, a practice, and, importantly, as Profera describes, a feeling: "All of our stuff is impromptu. We'd have little pin points to hit, but it was all on feeling. We know the song. We created these characters, and it's been an amazing experience. Like, I don't know where I'd be in my life without Juliesy. She's a part of me, you know? That chonga bro, and I get to express that and people think it's fucking hilarious. I think it's fucking hilarious. And when it's not funny to me anymore, I'll stop."

Through various acts of gender, aesthetic, and sexual troublemaking, chongivity activity, as enacted by this intergenerational group of cultural producers, draws on the power of Latinx hyperfemininity to foment mutual recognition, belonging, and place-making among women and queer Latinx who navigate hostile social contexts. While engaging in chongivity activity can make one the target of policing and denigration both inside and outside of Latinx communities, its ethos of collaboration opens avenues for cultural and social formations that celebrate and make possible radical forms of performing Latinidad.

NOTES

1 My thinking on place-making draws from Paola Bacchetta, Fatima El-Tayeb, and Jin Haritaworn's critical intervention "Queer of Colour Formations and Translocal Spaces in Europe," which defines QPoC place-making as "concrete strategies of resistance and disturbance that disrupt, however momentarily, the exclusionary coherence of spaces assumed to be white and/or straight" (2015, 775).

2 The red of the lipstick has significantly faded over time but can be seen in early documentation of the mural.

3 My thinking on Latina survivance draws from Juana María Rodríguez's (2016) analysis of the complex negotiations of power Latina porn star Vanessa Del Rio narrates in her *testimonio 50 Years of Slightly Slutty Behavior.*

4 My interview with Giovanni Profera was conducted in Miami in August 2015. The interview with Josue Garcia occurred in Miami in July 2016.

5 The performer's access to these spaces were facilitated by Profera's networks in the Miami nightlife scene. He had garnered a local following after playing the role of a flamboyant gay pageant coach in the short independent film *La Pageant Diva* (2011).

6 "Hialeah's Finest: Episode One," accessed May 26, 2019, www.youtube.com/watch?v=2A05OmiWETU.

7 "Hialeah's Finest: Episode Two," accessed May 26, 2019, www.youtube.com/watch?v=-xF9BtEcrC4.

REFERENCES

Alvarado, Leticia. "Malflora Aberrant Femininities," In exh. cat. *Axis Mundo: Queer Networks in Chicano L.A.* Los Angeles: University of Southern California Libraries, 2017.

Bacchetta, Paola, Fatima El-Tayeb, and Jin Haritaworn. "Queer of Colour Formations and Translocal Spaces in Europe." *Society and Space* 33, no. 5 (2015): 769–78.

García Hernández, Yessica. "Que Alboroto Traen Conmigo:' Theorizing Agitated Responses to understand the Phenomenon of Jenni Rivera's Haters." Specialty Paper. San Diego: University of California, 2017. (Unpublished manuscript).

Gaspar de Alba, Alica. 1998. *Chicano Art: Inside/Outside the Master's House*. Austin: University of Texas Press.

Hernández, Jillian. "'Miss, You Look Like a Bratz Doll': On Chonga Girls and Sexual-Aesthetic Excess." *NWSA Journal* 21, no. 3 (2009): 63–90.

Huerta, Mónica. "The Queer Digital Touch of Racial Sight." *Women and Performance: A Journal of Feminist Theory* 28, no. 2 (2018): 104–20.

Indych-López, Anna. 2018. *Judith F. Baca*. Minneapolis, MN and London: University of Minnesota Press.

Lovell, Kera N. "'Everyone Gets a Blister': Sexism, Gender Empowerment, and Race in the People's Park Movement." *WSQ: Women's Studies Quarterly* 46, nos. 3 & 4 (2018): 103–19.

Mahmood, Saba. 2011. *The Politics of Piety: The Islamic Revival and the Feminist Subject*. Princeton: Princeton University Press.

Miranda, Marie. 2003. *Homegirls in the Public Sphere*. Austin: University of Texas Press.

Mulford, Marilyn. *Chicano Park*. 1989. Produced by Marilyn Mulford and Mario Barrera. New York: Cinema Guild.

Muñoz, José E. 2009. *Cruising Utopia: The Then and There of Queer Futurity*. New York: New York University Press.

Ramírez, Catherine S. 2009. *The Woman in the Zoot Suit: Gender, Nationalism, and the Cultural Politics of Memory*. Durham and London: Duke University Press.

Ramos-Zayas, Ana Y. 2012. *Street Therapists: Race, Affect, and Neoliberal Personhood in Latino Newark*. Chicago: University of Chicago Press.

Rodríguez, Juana Maria. "Pornographic Encounters and Interpretive Interventions: Vanessa Del Rio: Fifty Years of Slightly Slutty Behavior." *Women and Performance: A Journal of Feminist Theory* 25, no. 3 (2016): 315–35.

Vargas, Deborah R. "Ruminations on Lo Sucio as a Queer Latino Analytic." *American Quarterly* 66, no. 3 (2014): 715–26.

34

Capturing the Church *Familia*

Scriptural Documents and Photographs on the Agricultural Labor Circuit

LLOYD BARBA

The declining labor opportunities in Tulare and the adverse circumstances affecting the church compelled me to go to the Imperial Valley where there was much *hermandad* and seasonal laborers to pick crops. *Los hermanos* would talk about how the church in Brawley was blessed by the Lord and they assured me that I would greatly rejoice there. The trip from Tulare to Brawley was long, but the material necessities made it so that people would move to wherever there was work so they could subsist . . . [O]ne evening in 1927, upon returning tired from work and after bathing and eating dinner, I went to relax under some trees. There, while I was relaxing, I began to consider the struggles deep in my heart such as being far away from my family members and how I could not win them to Christ. All of the contempt and the bitterness that my mother had caused me passed through my mind, but I felt comforted as I remembered how God had allowed me to return and find peace among the Christian *hermandad*.[1]

—José Ortega

I liked it. Shortly after on the first day that I went to the church, I liked it. I had been left for five years as an orphan [in Mexico], so I joined them [Mexican Pentecostals]. I talked with them, and we worked together. It reminded me of the small town I was from in Sinaloa. I came here and they were very affable, very friendly, very sincere, very helpful, and I wouldn't hear any swear words; they did not drink or smoke, none of that; I liked it all, very, very much.[2]

—Aniceto Ortiz

Enter the worlds of José Ortega and Aniceto Ortiz in the fields of California, 1927 and 1950, respectively. Here, the alienating force of industrial agriculture blurred the lines between labor and anything else in a migrant farmworker's life. This dizzying built environment represented a time and place largely responsible for the wholesale objectification of Mexicans as "workers."[3] The infamous "factories in the fields" constituted a social no-man's land, and prior to the farmworker reforms of the 1960s, the industrialized agricultural system comprised the state's own "peculiar institution."[4] In these crop-combed fields, we see the production of an iconic and ironic sight of "American" labor: stooped-over Mexican families toiling to feed a nation. The state's agricultural circuit had been designed, and indeed relied, upon a dispossessed migrant labor force.[5]

While the photographs of journalists shed light on either the efficacy or the exploitative nature on the circuit, photographs taken by farmworker families themselves captured sacred and social endeavors. Where the former connoted a sense of unbelonging, the latter articulated a radical welcoming into a collective body that made homes and crossed boundaries.[6] The names of many of the millions of workers in the early and mid-twentieth century did not survive in ledgers, nor were most even accounted for, and neither can we generally learn the names of people in the photographs taken by journalists. The "racial scripts" of the time would read in favor of keeping Mexican (especially workers) in the margins.[7] Growers, hoping to maintain a steady flow of workers through the border, assuaged concerns of mass Mexican immigration by invoking the powerful full-fledged myth that the faceless and nameless farmworkers were merely "birds of passage" who would not settle in the state.[8]

A record produced and preserved by Mexican Pentecostal farmworkers flew in the face of this myth. The migrating body of believers comprised an imagined religious and ethnic family that I have termed the "church *familia*."[9] The term "*familia*" (family) rather than "*comunidad*" (community) is the more common descriptor among Mexican Pentecostals and better captures the intimate social dynamics. Within the church *familia*, members addressed one another as either *hermano* or *hermana* (even to the extent that references in writings to actual biological siblings become ambiguous).[10] The church *familia* included the nuclear, extended, and local church family as well as members of the larger denomination. The closeness of the church *familia* could either complement or compete with one's biological family. As Ortega remarked in the epigraph, he was one of many whose conversion resulted in alienation from his biological family but integration into the "church *familia*," a type of "fictive kin."[11] Where do we find "families" and how does its representation compel us to imagine a more capacious concept of family in the spiritual, migrant, and labor contexts of Latina/o life? To better understand the texture of Latina/o church life in the context of migratory labor and how the faithful claimed public space by making it sacred, this chapter works toward a broader definition of family.[12]

A migrant repertoire of "scripturalized documents" (baptismal certificates and letters of recommendation) and photographs (family photo albums) afforded migrant workers subjectivity within a growing movement of Mexican Pentecostalism. While the pen of church history largely failed to inscribe individuals like Ortega and Ortiz in the annals of American religion, other media, such as baptismal certificates, letters of recommendation, and photographs in part account for how migrants belonged to a larger network of religious and ethnic kinship embedded in the labyrinth of California's agriculture.[13]

Compounded Unbelonging: Race and Religion at the Border

Mexican Pentecostalism emerged in California in the early twentieth century, steadily gaining momentum shortly after the heyday of the Los Angeles–based Azusa Street Revival (1906–1908), a formative movement in the growth of multiethnic Pentecostalism.[14] The broader Pentecostal movement in the United States splintered into many small and a select few large denominations by the late 1920s, an era described by one historian as "the golden years of Pentecostalism."[15] Today, the Pentecostal movement figures among the most rapidly growing segment of Christianity globally. Direct encounters with the Holy Spirit that manifest in bodily ecstasy, speaking in tongues, and such spiritual gifts are among the hallmark features of Pentecostalism. Scholars point to the movement's theological emphasis on bodily healing as a key reason for growth in regions such as the borderlands.[16] The Apostolic Assembly of Faith in Christ Jesus (AAFCJ), a Oneness Pentecostal denomination organized in the late 1920s (and chartered in 1930), stands as a flagship Latino Pentecostal movement in the United States and the Americas. *Apostólicos* (that is, in this study, members of the AAFCJ) emerged among the many Pentecostal movements from *la frontera quemada* (a religious "burned-over border"), which offered fertile social soil for a host of new religious movements to flourish.[17] The labor diaspora, indeed, assumed religious dimensions. As former Mexican states, California, Arizona, New Mexico, and Texas claimed the largest population of Mexicans and also witnessed the largest influx of migrant laborers pushed out of Mexico due to the country's revolution and subsequent sociopolitical upheaval. North of the border, rapidly expanding sectors of agriculture, railroad work, construction, and mining pulled in millions of Mexicans. The working-class faithful spread Pentecostalism rapidly across this region.[18]

Apostólicos bore the brunt of compounded unbelonging. Their placement within a minoritized religio-racial community (as Mexican, Spanish-speaking, nonwhite, non-Catholic, and non-Trinitarian) set them in an inauspicious position to carry out a local, much less a lasting, binational movement. As Mexicans, they shouldered the racial inequities placed on them in a disempowering colonial labor system in California's shifting racial fault lines.[19] As Pentecostals, their radical scriptural interpretations regarding miracles and salvation and emphasis on spiritual gifts set them at odds with many of their religious contemporaries. Most of the conformist pressure came from the Mexican Catholics (the Mexican majority) and the mainline Protestants (the US religious majority), the latter of whom had evangelized aggressively in the US southwest but only with limited numerical success.[20]

Most Mexicans identified as Catholic (the two identities at times seemingly inextricable) but of a radically different extraction from their Anglophone counterparts in the United States. To not be Catholic in the context of the Mexican diaspora meant largely renouncing deeply embedded cultural symbols that increasingly marked Mexican identity. This often resulted in the ridicule of converts for having forsaken their traditional ways.[21] Even within Pentecostalism, Oneness Pentecostals comprised a minority camp of believers, as they rejected the classical notion of the Trinity and developed instead a univocal/unitarian view of the Father, Son, and Holy Spirit (hence the moniker "Oneness").[22] Both on account of race and religion, there were few places where they, as a minoritized religio-racial movement, could belong. It is their doctrinal heterodoxy and high-tension piety that gave the movement its distinct ritual and familial elements.[23]

Compounded Belonging: The Scripturalized Documents and Photographs of the Church *Familia*

The stories of Ortega and Ortiz are indicative of a well-known aspect of labor at this time and place, namely that most agricultural workers were adult males. Further solidified by the Bracero program (1942–1964), this dominant portrayal of the male worker obscures another understated phenomenon of the Mexican labor migration, that Mexicans were the first and most extensive agricultural labor force in California to travel in families.[24] While the manner in which individual family units navigated everyday life on the circuit has been only minimally documented, even paler by comparison is how more capacious notions of family arose in these grim contexts. Beyond the shared plight of economic exploitation, *Apostólicos* invested themselves individually and as a church *familia* to further their religious mandates as part of a "migrating faith."[25] While men certainly comprised the majority of workers in the fields, women outnumbered men in Pentecostal churches, a phenomenon attested to across diverse contexts in the United States.[26] That workers should stake out their own religiously and culturally inflected sense of belonging worked against the system's design of keeping them uprooted and afoot on the circuit. These dizzying conditions no doubt bred a seemingly unshakeable sense of unbelonging in public life. To remediate this alienation, *Apostólicos* carved out a socio-familial religious existence, in part, through a system of scripturalized documentation made memorable by ritual and incorporated practices.[27]

Religious studies scholars have developed a pliable concept of "scripturalization" to describe the semiosphere (that is, the "social-psychological-political discursive structure") in which communities actively engage.[28] Jacqueline Hidalgo's definition of scriptures as "centering texts used by and in order to define communities" provides a supple theoretical starting concept to understand Chicanx religious expressions and spaces of displacement.[29] The process of scripturalization then is the manner in which these "scriptures" are made, used, and reflect how dominated communities orient themselves toward existing power relations.

Apostólicos drew from a robust and carefully curated set of scripturalized documents (baptismal certificates and letters of recommendation) and photographs (of church *familias*) to emplace themselves as part of a larger imagined religious ethnoscape.[30] The photographs and documents assume a "scriptural" valence, shedding light on of the hidden publics of Latina/o religious life, illuminating for us the kinds of social texts that accord a spiritual and social sense of belonging within these insular communities. More generally, this approach offers researchers new conceptual tools to excavate the buried discourses of Latina/o religious life.

One became part of the church *familia* by partaking in the hallmark ritual of initiation: baptism. Because of the ritual and salvific gravitas afforded to the baptismal event, I suggest we think of the accompanying baptismal certificate as a scripturalized document, that is, in this context, a document that affords an individual a sense of divine social belonging.[31] The practice of baptism became the sine qua non condition for salvation and signaled an affirmation into an imagined religious community rather than to a specific congregation.[32] As both a ritual and a set of incorporated bodily practice (of singing, praying, and rejoicing), baptisms stand out as marquee moments of finding belonging in a community.[33] In most photographs of outdoor baptisms in rivers, streams, and canals, chances were that the baptizee's recent acquaintances from the church outnumbered close family and friends. Congregants expected that the newest addition to the church *famlia* would, too, proselytize.

Amid the vagaries of migrant life, *Apostólicos* developed a parallel economy of sociability and accountability, namely a protocol system of letters of recommendation for the transient faithful to deliver to pastors wherever work took them. This epistolary system guaranteed a sense of community upon arrival and attested to an individual's moral character and standing in previous congregations. The letter of recommendation established for migrant folks the bona fides needed to fully participate in the church life. In a ritual act of hospitality, congregations joined together to formally welcome newcomers by singing "Bienvenidos Seáis, Hermanos":

Cada Cristiano que ama / Every Christian who loves
A su hermano de corazón / His brother from his heart
No ve fronteras, va por / Does not see borders, and goes
La tierra sembrando amor / Through the land sowing love

Bienvenidos, seáis hermanos / Welcome, brethren
En el nombre de Cristo Jesús / In the name of Jesus Christ
Hoy reunidos nos gozamos / We gather today, rejoicing
Al saber que nos une su amor / knowing we are united by his love
Bienvenidos, bienvenidos / Welcome, welcome

En el nombre de Cristo Jesús / In the name of Jesus Christ
Porque sólo Jesús, nos da vida y salud / For only Jesus gives us life and
  health
Y la gloria al que lleva su cruz / And glory to whom carries his cross[34]

The letters of recommendation themselves and the accompanying ritual singing provide a glimpse into systems of hospitality, accountability, and a radical
welcoming for members of a population alienated from social life in the public
sphere. *Apostólicos* cultivated a community wherein one could tap into a network of resources that included housing, employment opportunities, and food.[35]
Like the preeminent ritual of baptism, "Bienvenidos Seáis, Hermanos" welcomed
the otherwise strangers with the all-important phrase "in the name of Jesus."[36]
Historian Daniel Ramírez's findings on letters of recommendation offer a clear
portrait of the regaining of subjectivity offered through the epistolary system:

> The ritual reading of a letter of recommendation in the congregation's hearing—
> and the expected public salutation by the individual—transformed the otherwise
> ordinary document into an empowering credential. Thus, an immigrant held in
> low esteem (and meagerly compensated) by a capitalist society during the day (or
> on the graveyard shift) regained a large measure of self-esteem when gathered with
> spiritual kin for spiritual fellowship and bread breaking.[37]

The letter of recommendation assumed an especially significant role in the
summer months as coreligionists from the state's border region of the Imperial
Valley, for example, would fill churches beyond capacity in sites such as Sanger
and San Jose. Congregants in various northern California churches knew full
well to expect and how to welcome their migrant counterparts from Texas, Arizona, New Mexico, and Mexico, as some returned routinely, year after year.[38]
    The strenuous conditions of work and sense of physical and social deracina-
tion constituted two major troubles of life on the circuit. To remedy this when
possible, several *Apostólico* communities took matters into their own hands and
forged *micro-colonias* to help families find stability within the larger church
familia. Photographs of congregations and church *familias* comprise a large part
of the photographs taken and preserved by *Apostólicos* in family photo albums.
The counternarrative of togetherness in the bonds of religious unity account for
a type of scripturalization through photographs, as the albums serve as "homing
devices" to historically displaced people.[39]
    Photographs especially expose the laden power dynamics always at play in
these familial contexts. At the turn of the twentieth century, and certainly by
midcentury, photographs offered visual evidence of what certain spaces (homes
and churches, for example) ought to look like. Historian Laura Wexler describes
this "regime of sentiment" as "a private practice of representing family and

domesticity that in turn became an aggressive popular social practice." She asserts that the regime of sentiment "aimed not only to establish itself as the gatekeeper of social existence, but also aimed at the same time to denigrate all other people whose style or conditions of domesticity did not conform to the sentimental model."[40] The migrant labor camps in California exemplified the kinds of social and domestic conditions that needed reform. How could the Pentecostal proletariat claim a sense of belonging in such spaces?

Apostólicos throughout the state lived in dilapidated farm camps. But the manner in which they reflect on life in the camps is largely influenced by a greater ultimate concern: the efficacy of evangelism. As an economic engine with sacred horizons in mind, the church *familia* came together to support one another and evangelize others. The formation of the church *familia* in *micro-colonias* transpired in at least two modes: the collective purchase of common property and the collective evangelism at labor camps.

A brief memoir dictated by early *Apostólico* founder of churches in northern California, Pedro Banderas, offers us a case in point of the collective purchase of property toward the formation of a *micro-colonia*:

> One day I felt the desire to go to San Jose and look for a lot to build a temple. I only had $5, which had been earned by my wife Mercedes. As I looked for a lot, I found one for sale on San Antonio Street. It was like a dump there, filled with branches, rocks, etc. The neighborhood had not yet been populated. I returned joyfully to Half Moon Bay to notify my *hermanos* about the lot that I had found. They immediately gathered $60. And early one day they packed up their tents and we all went to San Jose, around the season for apricot work. We went directly to San Antonio Street and the *hermanos* started cleaning so they could set up their *tents*. Meanwhile, I went to pay for the lot. And there we pitched our tents and set up camp.[41]

Banderas had been founding small church works (*obras*) in northern California since the mid 1920s. By the end of the decade, leaders had established the budding denomination's de facto hub in the Imperial Valley where, as Ortega commented, "much of the *hermandad* and laborers would go to pick during seasons of harvest."[42] Leaders established the Northern District in 1930 to more strategically evangelize agricultural towns in California north of the Tehachapi Mountains. In the Imperial Valley, Banderas rubbed elbows with José Ortega, who, after years of wandering and worshipping along the migrant labor circuit, later carved out a decades-long successful ministerial career in both the United States and Mexico. Several families joined Banderas in his move to San Jose in 1928. They settled in the notorious Mayfair district of San Jose, a blighted tent-city area at the time becoming increasingly populated by ethnic Mexicans (and, to some degree, Puerto Ricans).[43] Banderas later relays in the account how the families that followed him pitched their tents around the church tent, which would later materialize as an adobe-brick temple. In such a living arrangement, the male-led households would typically follow the decisions made by the pastor about piety (in terms of proper forms of prayer, dress, and behavior), and women generally performed a wide range of labor for the church including aesthetic, emotional, and intimate labor.[44] This close-knit living is evidenced in the study of one 1950s researcher who noted how "Pentecostal sects" in the Mayfair district would "form cliques in the community as a result of their social semi-isolation from their neighbors. They tend to constitute a socially distinct group and take little part in community life."[45] The founding of the San Jose church, like many others *Apostólico* churches, came as a church *familia* affair rooted in the where-withal of migrant families to cobble together sufficient resources to build homes and cross boundaries.

Just south in Salinas, the local church formed under similar circumstances. A photograph of the Salinas congregation in the 1940s, seen in figure 34.1, is one of several which captures the church *familia* as part of an intensive-labor system. Their struggle evidence both religious and familial strivings, as demonstrated in images captured and produced by farmworkers themselves.

Work and worship coalesced in these spaces. The Spreckels Sugar company gained foothold in Salinas in the 1940s as contractors recruited a massive

Figure 34.1. Salinas *Apostólicos* harvesting: The church *familia* of Salinas paused their work for a midday photograph that captured them in their everyday activities. Unlike many migrant workers in photographs whose names were not recorded, photographs of the church *familia* afford workers a stronger sense of subjectivity and belonging.[46]

Mexican labor force, among whom were *Apostólicos*. Mexican workers in Salinas solidly occupied the bottom of the socioeconomic ladder. The perennial strikes over wages and conditions throughout California and in Salinas brought to the surface the deep racist antipathy toward Mexican workers. Nevertheless, the larger agricultural empire in Salinas relied on Mexican labor as early as the 1930s. The irony of poor food producers did not elude historian Lori Flores who noted about Mexican workers in the Salinas Valley, "[t]hough they were feeding the nation through their labor, they were not nourished themselves."[47] Over the next four decades, housing covenants (kept intact in Salinas well after they had been deemed illegal), segregation in public institutions, and violence marked the landscape. As a direct consequence, Mexican settlements lay segregated into the margins of the growing city.[48] The people in figure 1 lived in their own *micro-colonia* even further out than the major Mexican neighborhoods.

Year-round residency at the Spreckels farm allowed some families to establish semipermanency and to therefore put down roots in the form of housing and permanent structures. What we do not see in figure 34.1 are the houses that surround the first temple built in the fields, a years-long undertaking of the church *familia*. Pastor Juan Amaya ventured north to work for Spreckels and launch a church *obra* in Salinas in 1942, an endeavor that assumed religious meaning and labor, and place-claiming tactic. There, ranchers recruited Amaya and asked him to invite other *Apstólicos* to work in the fields. After much labor, they saved enough to purchase a ten-acre lot in the outskirts, "high up and beautiful, free of the city's congestion." They secured it at an inexpensive price, as it was all they could afford since the "*hermanos* were poor."[49] They built a small temple and approximately nine homes, a few of which were surplus Quonset military homes. Such an arrangement of an adobe brick temple, brick-and-mortar homes, and former military homes exemplifies how the church *familia* pulled together resources in hopes of creating *micro-colonias*. For the church *familia* pictured in figure 34.1, the *micro-colonia*'s crowning moment occurred decades later when, in an unusual move, the city granted their petition to change the name of the street where the church and houses were located to "Apostolic Lane."[50] The street exists to this day and has cemented the legacy of the church *familia* fighting to claim space and make it sacred.

Families fostered a sense of reliability for the church and labor contractors alike. In fact, some growers preferred *Apostólicos* and their large families because they could count on dutiful abstemious men and, like in most places, provide less remuneration for women and children.[51] *Apostólicos* cashed in on their reputation for exemplifying moral rectitude in order to forge ties with growers and to bring the church *familia* into the circuits of farm labor. Some contractors, privy to behavioral codes of *Apostólicos*, invited them to work in their fields. Escalon grower George Driscoll of the famous Driscoll strawberries noted the sense of camaraderie among *Apostólicos* and how they worked as family units. Knowing

Figure 34.2. *Apostólicas* at the Driscoll Strawberry camp. Here two young women workers pose for a photograph on the steps of a camp housing unit. The small quarters commonly housed large families. Despite the size of these dwellings, *Apostólicos* held prayer meetings and small worship gatherings in these homes.[52]

that *Apostólicos* practiced sobriety and proved to be dutiful workers, Driscoll contracted a large number of them to work the strawberry fields of Escalon in the late 1940s. On the camp, they lived in cramped quarters as seen in figure 34.2.

The church *familia* lasted at the Driscoll Strawberry camp for five years until Driscoll ended the project for a lack of sizeable crops. During that time, *Apostólicos* comprised the majority of families at that camp, and for a short while they used the small family homes on the camps as places to gather for worship. They later set up a tent in nearby Riverbank to host church services in the late 1940s. In 1952 they built the First Apostolic Church of Modesto, which would serve as the "mother church" of the area. Those involved in this effort took immense pride in the outcome of the humble *obra*.[53]

Fewer than twenty miles southwest of Modesto, in Patterson, the testimony of Aniceto Ortiz, the once lonely *bracero*, took shape. There, *Apostólico* evangelism efforts had been carefully orchestrated at a farm labor camp overseen by *hermano* Isaac Sánchez. He and Isobel Banda took on jobs as labor contractors and recruited Mexican laborers to work in the camps in the greater Modesto area. Among the many Bracero program laborers, they also recruited *Apostólico* families. David Banda, a lay member in the church and son of Isobel Banda, recalls how the church family offered a radical new sense of belonging for migrant workers:

> The common thing among the regular worker is that 'you're in it for yourself and your survival' so everybody else is doing the same thing as your competition. In the Apostolic [world], you are my brother and instead of competing, they were working together to unite, to help network . . . that was the difference. That's using the biblical principles. . . . Not alone, but they all worked together. All the *hermanos* worked together. There was a whole group of families that learned to work together.[54]

Men comprised the majority of farmworkers but relied on the extensive labor of women to sustain the camp. Adelina Banda, for example, led a group of women in cooking for nearly four hundred workers during the summer harvests. The congregation at the labor camp initiated a food sharing program to decrease food insecurity. Families shared and passed along meals in communal space and left portions at designated locations for others.[55] The *micro-colonia* adjusted to the fluctuating number of families who would enter the community for varying durations. While *Apostólicos* primarily grew by converting fellow laborers, they fully expected incoming fellow *Apsotólico* families to sustain the ongoing economic and religious endeavor.

Isaac Sánchez allowed the church *familia* in Patterson to bring the *micro-colonia* to its ultimate spatial and sacred centrality when members set up a house of worship in the middle of the camp. The material composition of the houses of

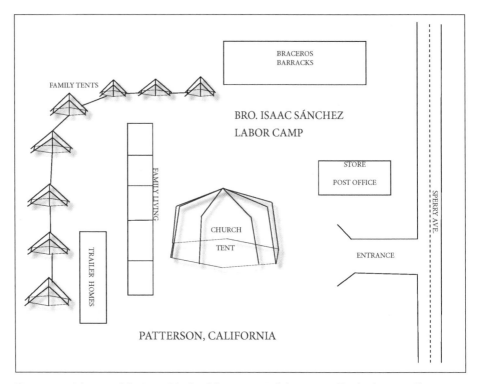

Figure 34.3. A layout of the Isaac Sánchez labor camp. While not its official title, *Apostólicos* referred to the camp as "Isaac Sánchez's labor camp." The camp followed a layout much like most camps with the exception of the house of worship at the center.[56]

worship varied from tarp tents (*carpas*), small adobe brick temples (known as "*templecitos*"), and full-fledged temples. Figure 34.3 demonstrates how the church *familia* spatially arranged the Isaac Sánchez labor camp around a consecrated *carpa*.

In this configuration, the *carpa* occupied the coveted central position where normally the camp store, post office, dance hall, or school (i.e., governmental or recreational building) would have stood in the camp. The *carpa* came as an early effort of the Modesto congregation to branch out into nearby Grayson and Patterson, both rural towns replete with farmworkers, especially those contracted through the Bracero program. Figure 34.3 outlines how Bracero workers lived in barracks near the temple, while the families (many of them *Apostólico*) occupied small homes and trailers adjacent to the Bracero's quarters and the *carpa*. The spatial arrangement of this labor camp represents the genius of the church *familia*. As bricoleurs, *Apostólicos* constructed sacred space in the placement of the *capra* at the heart of the labor camp, a privilege not afforded to other religious groups. *Carpas* would never enjoy the spatial privilege afforded to mainline Protestant churches in the center of town. But a vision of spatial centeredness, nevertheless, became a reality in the Isaac Sánchez labor camp.

They continued a similar arrangement in the 1960s when the church *familia* under the auspices of the Self-Help Enterprise, a state program designed to assist eligible migrant workers with raw materials to build homes if they proved capable of building it themselves, built homes around a church they purchased in nearby Grayson.

Conclusion: More than Meets the Eye

Former residents of the *micro-colonia* in the Patterson-Grayson area will often pass by the now sun-scorched homes in Grayson when they attend funerals at the Patterson District Cemetery. Beginning in the 1960s, several *Apostólicos* have been, and continue to be, laid to rest there, with their nuclear and church *familia* in the land where they once worked with their hands, cultivated kinships, and staked out space.

Tales of the past uncover social and embodied memories buried beneath the morass of misrepresentation. Historian Simon Schama maintains how through "an excavation below our conventional sight-level" we might be able "to recover veins of myth and memory that lie beneath the surface." These veins are "often hidden beneath the layers of the commonplace."[57] The impersonal nature of industrial agriculture was captured in the Southwest's visual regime of agriculture, which portrayed Mexican laborers as fixtures of the landscape: stooped-over, faceless, nameless silhouettes in the fields. But how can we look beyond the surface of this representation and find personhood, belonging, and *familia*?

By borrowing the media tools (specifically scripturalized documents and photographs) utilized by migrants themselves, we can unearth fragments of family and religious life in spaces designed to deny them any semblance of belonging. We uncover legacies of the church *familia* and the spaces of belonging they carved out through the establishment of *micro-colonias* on collectively purchased land and labor camps. Beneath the conventional sight level, we can capture a glimpse of the church *familia*.

NOTES

1   José Ortega, *Mis Memorias en la Iglesia y la Asamblea Apostólica de la Fe en Cristo Jesús* (Indio, CA: José Ortega, 1998), 78–79; all translations, unless otherwise noted, are my own.

2   Aniceto Ortiz interview with the author, May 2014. Translation mine.

3   Emma Pérez, *The Decolonial Imaginary: Writing Chicanas into History* (Bloomington: Indiana University Press, 1999), 19–22.

4   Carey McWilliams, *Factories in the Field* (1935 repr.; Santa Barbara: Peregrine Smith Books, 1978); Carey McWilliams, *California the Great Exception* (1949 repr.; Santa Barbara: Peregrine Smith Books, 1976), 150–170.

5   Several autobiographical writings capture elements of Mexican life on the agricultural circuit in California; see Francisco Jiménez, *The Circuit: Stories from the Life of a Migrant Child* (Boston: Houghton Mifflin Company, 1999); Frances Esquibel Tywoniak and Mario T.

Garcia, *Migrant Daughter: Coming of Age as a Mexican American Woman* (Berkeley and Los Angeles: University of California Press, 2000); José Antonio Villareal, *Pocho* (1959 repr.; New York: Anchor Books, 1989).

6 Here I am drawing on Thomas Tweed's fluid definition of religion as "confluences of organic-cultural flows that intensify joy and confront suffering by drawing on human and suprahuman forces to make homes and cross boundaries." See Thomas Tweed, *Crossing and Dwelling: A Theory of Religion* (Cambridge: Harvard University Press, 2006), 54.

7 Natalia Molina, *How Race is Made in America: Immigration, Citizenship, and the Historical Power of Racial Scripts* (Berkeley and Los Angeles: University of California Press, 2014).

8 Camille Guerin-González, *Mexican Workers & American Dreams: Immigration, Repatriation, and California Farm Labor, 1900–1939* (1994 repr.; New Brunswick, NJ: Rutgers University Press, 1996), 24–27.

9 The combination of English and Spanish in the term is offered in order to reflect how the children in the church *familia* germinated seeds of bilingualism that later flourished on an official platform with a generation of youths who came of age in the latter period (1950s–1960s) of this study. The insertion of the Spanish also serves to disambiguate it from the term "church family" used in studies on Black church life; see Anthea Butler, *Women in the Church of God in Christ: Making a Sanctified World* (Chapel Hill, NC: University of North Carolina Press, 2007), 48–50.

10 I have left untranslated the term *hermanos* and *hermandad* since they articulate this imagined kinship between women and men in ways that literal gendered translations do not.

11 Carol Stack, *All Our Kin: Strategies for Survival in a Black Family* (San Francisco: Harper and Row, 1976).

12 On Mexican American women and families claiming space see Vicki Ruiz, *From Out of the Shadows: Mexican American Women in Twentieth Century America* (1998 repr.; New York: Oxford University Press, 2008).

13 Upon being baptized, ministers of local congregations regularly offered baptismal certificates. Baptism symbolized the initiation into the heterodox body of Pentecostal believers. Members of the denomination carried letters of recommendation as they traveled from one church to another. While not necessary to become a church member, the letters established one's bona fides upon joining a new congregation as a seasonal or permanent member. The corpus of photographs I reference are primarily those held by longtime members in photo albums of their family and church as well as those published in commemorative volumes. As will be seen later, the two photographs in this chapter come from private collections.

14 Gastón Espinosa, *Williams J. Seymour and the Origins of Global Pentecostalism: A Biography and Documentary History* (Durham, NC: Duke University Press, 2014); Gastón Espinosa, *Latino Pentecostal in America: Faith and Politics in Action* (Cambridge: Harvard University Press, 2015); Cecil Robeck, *The Azusa Street Mission and Revival: The Birth of the Global Pentecostal Movement* (Nashville: Emanate Books, 2006).

15 Arlene Sánchez-Walsh, *Pentecostals in America* (New York: Columbia University Press, 2018), xxi.

16 Daniel Ramírez, *Migrating Faith: Pentecostalism in the United States and Mexico in the Twentieth Century* (Chapel Hill, NC: University of North Carolina Press, 2015) 155–158; Hector Avalos, "María Atkinson and the Rise of Pentecostalism in the U.S.-Mexico Borderlands," *Journal of Religion and Society* 3 (2001), 1–20; Espinosa, *Latino Pentecostals*, 64–67.

17 Rudy Busto's concept of "*la frontera quemada*" borrows from the term coined by Second Great Awakening preacher Charles Finney, who in the heyday of nineteenth-century revivals labeled parts of New York the "burned-over district" because of the widespread

religious fervor and founding of new religious movements that arose from the revivals. For more on the US Southwest as a *"frontera quemada"* see, Rudy Busto, *King Tiger: The Religious Vision of Reies López Tijerina* (Albuquerque: University of New Mexico Press, 2005), 87.

18 Ramírez, *Migrating Faith*; Lloyd Barba, "Farmworker Frames: *Apostólico* Counter Narratives in California," *Journal of the American Academy of Religion* 86, no. 3 (September 2018): 691–723.

19 Mario Barrera, *Race and Class in the Southwest: A Theory of Racial Inequality* (South Bend, IN: University of Notre Dame Press, 1979); Tomás Almaguer, *Racial Fault Lines: The Historical Origins of White Supremacy in California* (Berkeley and Los Angeles: University of California Press, 1994).

20 Statistics on the number of farm laborers in California at this time are unreliable, and an estimate of the number of Catholics and Protestants is difficult to ascertain. At best it can be established that since Mexico remained well over 90 percent Catholic for the majority of the twentieth century, that migrants to the United States would have comprised a similar number, especially since many hailed from staunchly Catholic states such as Jalisco and Guanajuato. *Apostólicos*, however, became more statically relevant in the agricultural towns of northern California since Mexican Catholic missions had not made robust inroads in the agricultural towns of northern California. One official roster of the first convention of the *Apostólicos* (later organized as the AAFCJ) in 1925 lists three churches in northern California (all in agricultural communities). A 1966 record accounts for forty-six AAFCJ temples in that same region. Catholic and Protestant literature from the early twentieth century hints at this competition in the fields. By WWII, Catholic clergy reacted to the proselytization efforts of Pentecostals; see Gráinne McEvoy, "Operation Migratory Labor: Braceros, Migrants, and the American Catholics Bishop's Committee for the Spanish Speaking," *U.S. Catholic Historian* 34, no. 3 (2016), 77–83; on examples of Protestant and Pentecostal growth in San Jose California, see Antonio Robert Soto, "The Chicano and the Church in Northern California, 1848–1978: A Study of an Ethnic Minority within the Roman Catholic Church" (PhD diss., Stanford University, 1978); on Protestant conformist pressures, see Vinson Synan, *The Holiness-Pentecostal Tradition: Charismatic Movements in the Twentieth Century* (Grand Rapids, MI: William B. Eerdmans Publishing Company, 1997), 146–148.

21 Ruiz, *From out of the Shadows*, xvi.

22 Lloyd Barba and Andrea Johnson, "The New Issue: Approaches to Oneness Pentecostalism in the United States," *Religion Compass* 10, no. 12 (October 2018).

23 A common pattern seemed to be that workers only found belonging in churches and not in other social institutions. It should, however, be noted that the sectarian and primitivist tendencies of Mexican Pentecostal churches, especially those of the AAFCJ, generally required that members shy away from secular organizations requiring oaths of loyalty. To suggest that *Apostólicos* then comprised a sectarian religious community is not beyond the common consensus of the literature of the time. The term "sectarian" and its variations, however, are freighted with meaning that often reveals more about the attitudes and prejudices of the dominant describing majority than the actual group target group. And the classical Weberian notion of sect-to-church does not lend a thorough explanatory scope in this case. Although the term sectarian lends a descriptive understanding to mean insular religious groups that demand particular religious experiences, we may better think of Oneness Mexican Pentecostals incarnating heterodoxy in belief and high-tension piety in practice. On heterodoxy, see Ramírez, *Migrating Faith*, 42–49; on high-tension faith, see Roger Finke and Rodney Stark, "The New Holy Clubs: Testing Church-to-Sect Propositions,"

Sociology of Religion 62, no. 2 (Summer, 2001) 175–189; and on the application of high-tension piety to Pentecostalism see Sánchez-Walsh, *Pentecostals in America*, 28, 37–42.

24 Richard Stevens Street, *Photographing Farmworkers in California* (Stanford: Stanford University Press, 2004), 54.

25 I borrow the term "migrating faith" from Daniel Ramírez, *Migrating Faith*; the shared social, economic, and cultural standing of many congregants lends itself to a reading of church *familias* and churches as a type of "congregational homophily" as observed in more modern times in the work of Sarah Stohlman; see Sarah Stohlman, "At Yesenia's House . . . : Central American Immigrant Pentecostalism, Congregational Homophily, and Religious Innovation in Los Angeles," *Qualitative Sociology* 30 (2007): 61–80.

26 The numbers bear out in the US *Religious Bodies Census* of 1936, in which a sample of seventeen (non-immigrant) Pentecostal denominations averaged 35.3 men to every 100 women; see United States Department of Commerce, Bureau of the Census, "Religious Bodies, 1936." Spanish-language Pentecostal denominations are not listed in the census; Judith Casselberry, *The Labor of Faith: Gender and Power in Black Apostolic Pentecostalism* (Durham: Duke University Press, 2017).

27 Paul Connerton, *How Societies Remember* (1989 repr.; New York: Cambridge University Press, 1996).

28 Vincent L. Wimbush, *White Men's Magic: Scripturalization as Slavery* (New York: Oxford University Press, 2012); on the concept of scriptures also see various essays in Vincent L. Wimbush ed., *Theorizing Scriptures: New Critical Orientations to a Culture Phenomenon* (New Brunswick, NJ: Rutgers University Press, 2008); Vincent L. Wimbush ed., *MisReading America: Scriptures and Difference* (New York: Oxford University Press, 2013),

29 Jacqueline Hidalgo, *Revelation in Aztlán: Scriptures, Utopias, and the Chicano Movement* (New York: Palgrave, 2016), 5, 17.

30 On ethnoscapes and imagined worlds, see Arjun Appadurai, *Modernity at Large: Cultural Dimensions of Globalization* (Minneapolis: University of Minnesota Press, 1996), 3.

31 The system of baptismal records keeping throughout Latin America carries with it a fraught history of colonialism, religious violence, and the erasure of identities. The record keeping of baptisms became a way to account for and control populations. We would be mistaken, however, to assume that the Mexican Pentecostal baptismal certificates bore much resemblance at all to Catholic baptismal records, as the former carried no kind of legal or demographic import. Above all, they were social documents that bore one's name and spiritual tie to a spiritual rebirth (often in the United States.). On outdoor baptisms, see Barba, "Farmworker Frames."

32 As in the case of classical imagined communities, members will not necessarily ever know or even meet each other, but "in the minds of each lives the image of their community." See Benedict Anderson, *Imagined Communities: Reflections on the Origins and Spread of Nationalism* (New York: Verso, 2000), 6. *Apostólicos* used particular rituals and beliefs to project an image of their community.

33 On ritual and bodily practices, see Connerton, *How Societies Remember*; singing reinforced the group's heterodoxy and commitment to a life of high-tension piety. Popular *cantos* including "Seguiré a Mi Jesús" ("I Will Follow My Jesus") and "El Nombre del Mesías" ("The Name of the Messiah") became part of the liturgical singing at baptisms, Ramírez, *Migrating Faith*, 58–59.

34 Lyrics found in Ramírez, *Migrating Faith*, 141.

35 David Banda interview with the author, March 2018.

36 David Reed, *In Jesus Name: The History and Beliefs of Oneness Pentecostals* (Blandford Forum: Deo Publishing, 2007); Barba and Johnson, "The New Issue."

37 Ramírez, *Migrating Faith*, 133.

38 Ortiz interview; Manuel J. Gaxiola, *La Serpiente y la Paloma: Análisis del Crecimiento de la Iglesia Apostólica de la Fe en Cristo Jesús de México* (South Pasadena, CA: William Carey Library, 1970) 163.

39 Hidalgo, *Revelation in Aztlán*, 4.

40 Laura Wexler, "Seeing Sentiment: Photography, Race, and the Innocent Eye" in Marianne Hirsch (Ed.), *The Familial Gaze* (Hanover, NH: The University Press of New England, 1999), 256.

41 Pedro Banderas, "Memorias." July 23, 1966 (unpaginated, copy in author's files). Translation mine.

42 Ortega, *Mis Memorias*, 78. Translation mine.

43 Stephen Pitti, *The Devil in the Silicon Valley: Northern California, Race, and Mexican Americans* (Princeton: Princeton University Press, 2004), 89. Puerto Ricans had begun to arrive in the area around this time; see Margaret Clark, *Health in Mexican American Culture: A Community Study* (Berkeley: University of California Press, 1970), 13.

44 For a contemporary study on how Pentecostal women of color operate in these various domains of labor, see Casselberry, *The Labor of Faith*.

45 Clark, *Health in Mexican American Culture*, 117.

46 Manuel Vizcarra Apostolic Archives of the Americas Collection, David Allan Hubbard Library, Fuller Theological Seminary.

47 Lori A. Flores, *Grounds for Dreaming: Mexican Americans, Mexican Immigrants, and the California Farmworker Movement* (New Haven: Yale University Press, 2018), 52; "Nuestra Historia: Salinas," (Papers of Manuel Vizcarra, David Allan Hubbard Library, Fuller Theological Seminary, Pasadena, California).

48 Flores, *Grounds for Dreaming*, 12–107.

49 "Nuestra Historia: Salinas."

50 Manuel Ares interview with the author, August 2018.

51 Eugenia Manzano interview with the author, November 2013; Guerin-Gonzales, *Mexican Workers*, 15.

52 Photograph courtesy of Eugenia Manzano.

53 Manzano interview.

54 David Banda interview with the author, March 2018.

55 Ibid.

56 Schematic layout hand drawn by Irma Perez and digitally drafted by Eva M. Díaz.

57 Simon Schama, *Landscape and Memory* (New York: Alfred A. Knopf, 1995), 14.

BIBLIOGRAPHY

Almaguer, Tomás. 1994. *Racial Fault Lines: The Historical Origins of White Supremacy in California.* Berkeley and Los Angeles: University of California Press.

Anderson, Benedict. 2000. *Imagined Communities: Reflections on the Origins and Spread of Nationalism.* New York: Verso.

Appadurai, Arjun. 1996. *Modernity at Large: Cultural Dimensions of Globalization.* Minneapolis: University of Minnesota Press.

Ares, Manuel. Interview with the author. August 2018.

Avalos, Hector. "María Atkinson and the Rise of Pentecostalism in the U.S.-Mexico Borderlands." *Journal of Religion and Society* 3 (2001): 1–20.

Banda, David. Interview with the author. March 2018.

Barba, Lloyd. "Farmworker Frames: *Apostólico* Counter Narratives in California." *Journal of the American Academy of Religion* 86, no. 3 (September 2018): 691–723.

Barba, Lloyd, and Andrea Johnson. "The New Issue: Approaches to Oneness Pentecostalism in the United States." *Religion Compass* 10, no. 12 (October 2018).

Barrera, Mario. 1979. *Race and Class in the Southwest: A Theory of Racial Inequality*. South Bend, IN: University of Notre Dame Press.

Butler, Anthea. 2007. *Women in the Church of God in Christ: Making a Sanctified World*. Chapel Hill, NC: University of North Carolina Press.

Cantú, Ernesto, and Jose Ortega. 1966. *Historia de la Asamblea Apostolica de la fe en Cristo Jesús, 1916–1966*. Mentone, CA: Sal's Printing Service.

Casselberry, Judith. 2017. *The Labor of Faith: Gender and Power in Black Apostolic Pentecostalism*. Durham: Duke University Press.

Clark, Margaret. 1970. *Health in Mexican American Culture: A Community Study*. Berkeley: University of California Press.

Connerton, Paul. 1996. *How Societies Remember*. New York: Cambridge University Press.

Espinosa, Gastón. 2014. *Williams J. Seymour and the Origins of Global Pentecostalism: A Biography and Documentary History*. Durham, NC: Duke University Press.

———. 2015. *Latino Pentecostals in America: Faith and Politics in Action*. Cambridge: Harvard University Press.

Finke, Roger, and Rodney Stark. "The New Holy Clubs: Testing Church-to-Sect Propositions." *Sociology of Religion* 62, no. 2 (Summer 2001): 175–89.

Flores, Lori A. 2018. *Grounds for Dreaming: Mexican Americans, Mexican Immigrants, and the California Farmworker Movement*. New Haven: Yale University Press.

Gaxiola, Manuel J. 1970. *La Serpiente y la Paloma: Análisis del Crecimiento de la Iglesia Apostólica de la Fe en Cristo Jesús de México*. South Pasadena, CA: William Carey Library.

Guerin-González, Camille. 1996. *Mexican Workers & American Dreams: Immigration, Repatriation, and California Farm Labor, 1900–1939*. New Brunswick, NJ: Rutgers University Press.

Hidalgo, Jacqueline. 2016. *Revelation in Aztlán: Scriptures, Utopias, and the Chicano Movement*. New York: Palgrave.

Jiménez, Francisco. 1999. *The Circuit: Stories from the Life of a Migrant Child*. Boston, Houghton Mifflin Company.

Manuel Vizcarra Apostolic Archives of the Americas Collection, David Allan Hubbard Library, Fuller Theological Seminary.

Manzano, Eugenia. Interview with the author. November 2013.

McEvoy, Gráinne. "Operation Migratory Labor: Braceros, Migrants, and the American Catholics Bishop's Committee for the Spanish Speaking." *U.S. Catholic Historian* 34, no. 3 (2016): 75–98.

McWilliams, Carey. 1976. *California the Great Exception*. Santa Barbara: Peregrine Smith Books.

———. 1978. *Factories in the Field*. Santa Barbara: Peregrine Smith Books.

Molina, Natalia. 2014. *How Race is Made in America: Immigration, Citizenship, and the Historical Power of Racial Scripts*. Berkeley and Los Angeles: University of California Press.

Ortega, José. 1998. *Mis Memorias en la Iglesia y la Asamblea Apostólica de la Fe en Cristo Jesús*. Indio, CA: self-published.

Ortiz, Aniceto. Interview with the author. May 2014.

Pérez, Emma. 1999. *The Decolonial Imaginary: Writing Chicanas into History*. Bloomington: IN: University Press.

Pitti, Stephen. 2004. *The Devil in the Silicon Valley: Northern California, Race, and Mexican Americans*. Princeton: Princeton University Press.

Ramírez, Daniel. 2015. *Migrating Faith: Pentecostalism in the United States and Mexico in the Twentieth Century*. Chapel Hill, NC: University of North Carolina Press.

Reed, David. 2007. *In Jesus Name: The History and Beliefs of Oneness Pentecostals*. Blandford Forum: Deo Publishing.

Robeck, Cecil. 2006. *The Azusa Street Mission and Revival: The Birth of the Global Pentecostal Movement*. Nashville: Emanate Books.

Ruiz, Vicki. 2008. *From out of the Shadows: Mexican American Women in Twentieth Century America*. New York: Oxford University Press.

Sánchez, George J. 1993. *Becoming Mexican American: Ethnicity, Culture, and Identity in Chicano Los Angeles, 1900–1945*. New York: Oxford University Press.

Sánchez-Walsh, Arlene. 2018. *Pentecostals in America*. New York: Columbia University Press.

Schama, Simon. 1995. *Landscape and Memory*. New York: Alfred A. Knopf.

Soto, Antonio Robert. "The Chicano and the Church in Northern California, 1848–1978: A Study of an Ethnic Minority within the Roman Catholic Church." PhD diss., Stanford University, 1978.

Stack, Carol. 1976. *All Our Kin: Strategies for Survival in a Black Family*. San Francisco: Harper and Row.

Stohlman, Sarah. "At Yesenia's House . . . : Central American Immigrant Pentecostalism, Congregational Homophily, and Religious Innovation in Los Angeles" *Qualitative Sociology* 30 (2007): 61–80.

Street, Richard Steven. 2004. *Photographing Farmworkers in California*. Stanford: Stanford University Press.

Synan, Vinson. 1997. *The Holiness-Pentecostal Tradition: Charismatic Movements in the Twentieth Century*. Grand Rapids, MI: William B. Eerdmans Publishing Company.

Tweed, Thomas. 2006. *Crossing and Dwelling: A Theory of Religion*. Cambridge: Harvard University Press.

Tywoniak, Frances Esquibel, and Mario T. Garcia. 2000. *Migrant Daughter: Coming of Age as a Mexican American Woman*. Berkeley and Los Angeles: University of California Press.

United States Department of Commerce, Bureau of the Census, "Religious Bodies, 1936."

Villareal, José Antonio. 1989. *Pocho*. New York: Anchor Books.

Wexler, Laura. "Seeing Sentiment: Photography, Race, and the Innocent Eye." In *The Familial Gaze*, ed. by Marianne Hirsch, 248–75. Hanover, NH: The University Press of New England, 1999.

Wimbush, Vincent L. 2008. *Theorizing Scriptures: New Critical Orientations to a Culture Phenomenon*. New Brunswick, NJ: Rutgers University Press.

———. 2012. *White Men's Magic: Scripturalization as Slavery*. New York: Oxford University Press.

———. 2013. *MisReading America: Scriptures and Difference*. Oxford University Press.

35

Aguanile

Critical Listening, Mourning, and Decolonial Healing

FRANCES R. APARICIO

The song brought comfort to my life, the song showed me the path back to life, the song helped me in my sorrow more than any words. And as death changes life, it also changed the message of that song.
—Sirpa, quoted by Tuija Saresma (2003, 612)

After Hurricane María on September 20, 2017, Puerto Rico joins other countries in Latin America and the Global South that collectively memorialize and mourn the thousands who have died at the hands of state violence. In Puerto Rico, 4,654 lives were lost to the politics of colonial neglect and abandonment by the US Federal government, FEMA, and the inefficacy and corruption of the Puerto Rican government after the storm.[1] As a national community, Puerto Ricans now face the pain of acknowledging the *desaparecidos* among us, not only those who migrated or fled, but those who passed during and after the storm. In the light of these innumerable deaths, it is imperative to reflect critically on the process of mourning, bereavement, and grief. How do we process this mourning individually and collectively? How do we accept these deaths, clearly preventable had there been a sustained infrastructure of support and recovery? While Puerto Rico continues to struggle to survive politically and economically as a debt state, in terms of food access and economic sustainability, it is in the arts, broadly defined, that Puerto Ricans are turning for healing and grieving. For instance, young Puerto Ricans have returned to agriculture, including artisanal coffee ventures and growing fruit crops such as guavas, as a practice of healing and recovery. For artists such as Antonio Martorell, the visual arts serve as a channel for healing, as in his *Es que la . . .* exhibit, or the *Circo de la Ausencia* exhibit staged by the Y no había Luz theater troupe from San Juan (also installed at the National Puerto Rican Museum in Chicago), the dancing on the streets of Old San Juan, or the songs being rewritten as forms of affective survival immediately after the hurricane. In addition, communal interventions such as Ritmos Resilientes by capoeira master, Kojo X. Johnson, or the dancing of bomba in Afro-Puerto Rican neighborhoods, constitute important tools in soothing depression, anxiety, and despondency after the hurricane. A most poignant example is the song composed and performed by Bad Bunny, iLe, and Residente for the Paro Nacional in summer 2019, "Afilando los Cuchillos," which has become a political anthem for the power of *el pueblo* in the call for a new government. The imperative for a collective acknowledgement regarding the lives lost in Maria and for mourning is possible through the visual arts and through sounds, music, dance, and literature, what Carlos Rivera Santana has described as the process of "catharsis" in "posthurricane art" (Rivera Santana 2019, 179–180).[2]

My proposed reading of "Aguanile" integrates music and literature as a path for grieving and mourning the deaths and the trauma post-María. As Finnish cultural studies scholar Tuija Saresma argues for the need to discuss and analyze the "experiences of bereavement and the healing powers of arts and writing" (Saresma 2003, 603), she shares the experience of Sirpa, a young mother who lost her baby daughter and who finds solace in a song entitled "The Most Beautiful Sea" written by Turkish writer, novelist, and screenwriter Nâzim Hikmet. I share Sirpa's words in the epigraph to this chapter in order to foreground the role of music and the arts in the requisite process of mourning and bereavement. The ocean and water specifically are also embedded in Saresma's own mourning for her younger brother, who took his life by drowning in the sea. Saresma's exploration of mourning and grief, mediated by songs and writing, allows her to explore the ways in which the arts serve to remember those who have passed and to mourn collectively as well.

These elements—water, memory, and collective mourning—are a central part of my analysis in this chapter. Approaching mourning through a sonoroliterary reading of Amina Gautier's (2014) short story, "Aguanile," where sounds and written words inform each other, allows me to engage the textualizing processes of mourning and loss within the intergenerational tensions of the diasporic family of the Afro-Puerto Rican *nieta*/narrator and, concomitantly, for all Boricuas after the hurricane. More specifically, I highlight the process of critical listening that the *nieta*/narrator engages of the Nuyorican salsa singer Héctor Lavoe's song, entitled "Aguanile," by now globalized and mainstreamed.[3] If listeners mostly engage with popular music as entertainment, escape, or for a sense of pleasure, the act of *critical listening* requires an analytical process through which the listener grapples with and acknowledges the potential meanings of the song in his/her social and personal world and also structurally, thus acquiring a new and empowering awareness of life and social identities. For the *nieta*/narrator in the story, as I will discuss later, listening to the song "Aguanile," as performed by Lavoe, becomes a liberatory moment for her as a granddaughter and as a Black woman in the United States diaspora. The element of water, encapsulated in the Yoruba-based title of the song (*Aguan* = cleansing thru water; *ile* = house), reaffirms the two simultaneous meanings of the word in African communities: "I'm home" and "healing with water" (from a personal conversation with Professor

Tosin Mgobi). The word, also reclaimed as an African signifier "A Wa Nilé" in Afro-Cuban poet's Soleida Ríos's (2017) poetry collection, becomes the title of Amina Gautier's eponymous short story in *Now We Will be Happy* (2014). More specifically, I read the short story as a textualization of the healing meanings of the song "Aguanile" in the face of the death of a loved one. I propose that reading Gautier's short story in 2019 returns "Aguanile," the globalized song, back to the sphere of family, of community, and of the local and national, that is, a return home. A current reading of "Aguanile" as both sonic and literary text allows us to find a language for mourning after María and, possibly, a space for relationality between the island and the diaspora, between gender subjectivities (as embodied in the *nieta*'s difficult yet loving relationship with her grandfather), and among Puerto Ricans of diverse generational identities. I also explore the symbolic connections between the narratives about the power of the hurricane, of "*agua*," as a potentially healing energy that has allowed Puerto Ricans to find a sense of "home" and sustainability, and the ensuing decolonial awareness of and collective confidence that Puerto Ricans felt in their power to bring about change and eventual sovereignty immediately after Hurricane María, a power reaffirmed in el Paro Nacional two years later. In the words of Christine Nieves, an organic intellectual on the island, post-María has been "the moment when things shifted from despair to possibility" (Klein 2018, 70). Following the *nieta*/narrator's own dilemmas as a diasporic subject, I also share a personal reflection on my own academic life and on the dilemmas of finding home and belonging as a displaced Puerto Rican. As an Island Puerto Rican who has become a US Latina scholar, Latinx studies, as a field, embodies for me the decolonial space that I claim as home, a collective and critical site that allows healing through decolonial knowledge production.

On Critical Listening and Belonging

"Aguanile," Amina Gautier's short story, is told from the point of view of the Afro-Puerto Rican *nieta*, a young woman who has recently bought her own house in Philadelphia but whose family resides in Brooklyn, New York. The story highlights the intergenerational impact of family traumas informed by the politics of masculinity, the transnational lives of Puerto Rican families, and the potential for healing and reconciliation. More specifically, the *nieta*/narrator shares the special relationship she had with her maternal Puerto Rican grandfather who lived on the island after having abandoned the African American grandmother for another woman and, eventually, moving back to Puerto Rico and starting a second family. The story is structured around the phone calls between the *nieta*/narrator and the grandfather, with some specific scenes emerging as flashbacks from the past that reiterate for the reader the vexed location of the grandfather within the *nieta*'s nuclear family. The final phone call, which triggers the narrative itself, is to inform the *nieta* about the passing of the grandfather. After that call, the *nieta* remembers, through the healing power of memory, the moment when her grandfather played Héctor Lavoe's "Aguanile" to her. It is through this act of critical listening and sonic memory that the *nieta/* narrator, as an Afro-Latina, finds a space of belonging through the sounds and rhythms of blackness performed within the song.

Framed through voice and sound, "Aguanile" is structured around three phone calls notifying us about the death of salsa musicians. The first, which opens the story, is the grandfather calling to let his *nieta* know that Charlie Palmieri, one of the early pioneering salsa musicians from New York who performed *charangas* and boogaloos, and who, with Lavoe, shared a strong presence in both the island of Puerto Rico and the diaspora in New York City, had died. At the time, the *nieta* and her family are waiting for Hurricane Gilbert to arrive to the East Coast from Jamaica, where it had devastated the island, a reference that roots the story in 1988 and that ironically foreshadows the reality of Maria in 2017. If hurricanes stand symbolically for both destruction and possibility for the *nieta/*narrator and for Puerto Rican subjectivities, likewise "writing about the dead is always both an end to a relation and the possibility of a new beginning" (Saresma 2003, 615).

The second call refers to Héctor Lavoe's death in 1993, when the grandfather travels to New York to attend Lavoe's wake and funeral procession, a public ritual on the streets of New York that memorialized the Puerto Rican singer as both a cultural hero and a singer for and of the people (Valentín-Escobar 2001, 208). Again, these phone calls concretized the affective consequences of what critics have called "*la salsa y sus muertes*"/"the deaths of salsa," that is, the collective demise of the foundational interpreters and musicians (Moreno 2015, 29; Rondón 2008, 283–308) The irony, of course, for the *nieta* narrator, is that for her estranged grandfather, Lavoe's wake was much more meaningful as a ritual of mourning than his former wife's funeral, which he did not attend. Unaware that salsa music had established a sense of collective affiliation and a sense of belonging among so many Puerto Ricans of his generation, the *nieta* responds to her grandfather: "'I'm sorry to hear that,' I said, baffled by his ability to grieve for a stranger" (Gautier 2014, 2). While the female narrator reveals her discomfort at her grandfather for grieving for salsa stars whom he never met, she is also recognizing that her grandfather is modeling for her the possibility of grieving collectively. Her grandfather, who is a persona non grata in her immediate family, is able to mourn for Salsa musicians because of the ways in which this generation of salseros formed a communal space and a sense of belonging for Puerto Rican listeners, and, most poignantly, for Puerto Rican males like the grandfather. Thus, while masculinity allows for this constructed collectivity through the sonic spaces of salsa, it opens up the possibility of collective mourning. Gautier exhorts her readers to reflect on the process of mourning, as music theorist Jairo Moreno asks in his analysis of "la salsa y sus muertes": "¿Cómo pensar el duelo más allá de lo privado, es decir, como una posibilidad política y de colectividad?" ("How do we rethink mourning beyond the private, that is, as a political and collective possibility?") (Moreno 2015, 32) and as Puerto Rican cultural studies scholar Jason Cortés has interrogated in his own work: "Could mourning, in effect, be categorized as a kind of resistance? Could it carry enough political value and weight to be intrinsically liberatory?" (Cortés 2018, 363). If the emergence of these artistic texts for mourning in the wake of Hurricane María's deaths constitute one more iteration of arts as resistance and healing within Latin America—the *arpilleras* in Chile and Argentina, protest songs in Cuba and Chile, the bossa nova in Brazil, the Abuelas de la Plaza de Mayo in Argentina, among numerous other instances—for Puerto Rico the systematic loss of life after the storm in 2017 has produced expressions of collective healing as never seen before (Rivera Santana 2019, 178–182).

The gender politics of this collective mourning emerge as we learn about the grandfather's estranged status from his former family: he was "the husband [my] grandmother had chosen not to remember, the father my mother and uncles refused to claim" (Gautier 2014, 3). As the story unfolds, we learn that the *nieta/* narrator was the bridge between him and the rest of her family, that she had been sent to spend a summer with him in Puerto Rico as "a peace offering" (Gautier 2014, 3) and that during that visit the grandfather introduced her to the sounds of salsa, to musicians like "Blades, Colón, Lavoe, Nieves, Palmieri, Puente," "who meant nothing to me [her]" (Gautier 2014, 5). The intergenerational dynamics that structure Gautier's story are central to understanding the shifting meanings of salsa music, which vary among the elders, the middle-aged, and the youth. The fact that the *nieta/*narrator "discovered" the iconic salsa singers through her grandfather signals the central role of elders in reclaiming the past for the present and the future. The wedding scene in the story, in which Chali, the son from the *abuelo's* second family, who is the groom, refuses to play Héctor Lavoe songs for the grandfather, highlights these generational gaps in sonic traditions. The grandfather thus complains to his *nieta*: "'Chali says he's not going to play anything by *him.*' My grandfather announced this as if it were a personal affront, something his son had done just out of spite" (Gautier 2014, 10). Yet, echoing the long continuity of Afro-Caribbean rhythms and sonic traditions as a collective form of resistance, that is, from the bomba to salsa, from salsa to reggaetón, the grandfather's act of introducing his *nieta* to the salsa greats is not merely an act of masculinist nostalgia but a gesture of reconciliation, a tool for decolonization and long-term resistance.

The third phone call, from one of her aunts in Puerto Rico, and which serves as the closing framework for the narrative, is to inform the *nieta* that her grandfather has passed. As the narrator remembers her grandfather in Puerto Rico, she textualizes her own memory of having listened to "Aguanile" during her visit with him. Indeed, the intersemiotic translation of the sounds, lyrics, arrangements, and performance of "Aguanile" allow the *nieta* to give closure to the narrative as much as she is giving closure to her own affective dilemmas with her estranged grandfather. Through her sonic memory of the song, the *nieta* begins to give meaning to "Aguanile" and to her own identity as an Afro-Puerto Rican woman. She finally "knew what he [the grandfather] meant. The chant of the song provided the means to chase the *demons* all away" (Gautier 2014, 15). As the lyrics, inflected with the Yoruba language and the long traditions of healing and cleansing through Santería, have long been articulated in the innumerable performances of the song, likewise Gautier's *nieta*/narrator also deploys the song as a language that allows her to find home with and through her grandfather. The *nieta*/narrator finally acknowledges the healing power of the song to exorcise the grandfather's demons, those very "demons" which also characterized Héctor Lavoe's singing and which remit us to the ways in which colonialism and dispossession affect Puerto Rican men[4] (Aparicio and Valentín-Escobar 2004, 87–88). The intergenerational tension is acknowledged, although not resolved; so are the gender politics that allow her, as a young woman who owns her own home and who refuses to marry, to forgive the grandfather's toxic masculinity, having abandoned her African American grandmother to poverty, illness, and isolation. She realizes, "He was using me to get through to them and—that night—I allowed myself to be used." Thus, she acknowledges and embraces her role as a medium that bridges the late grandfather to her mother, uncles, aunts, and siblings. She thus expresses through words the sonic memory of listening to "Aguanile":

> The song was slow to start. It began as if it were in a jungle or a forest, with the sounds of birds cawing, chirping, tittering, and screeching. Elephants trumpeted. In the distance, drums spoke and voices chanted, putting me in the mind of what I guessed African music sounded like. The song went on like this, growing without words. Then the horns kicked in, followed by a man's voice singing one lone word, stretching it to its limit, repeating it and pulling everything and more from the word he sang over and over. Without warning, drums rolled and all the instruments seemed to come in at once. I'd never heard any kind of song like it. Beneath the familiar instruments, I heard the sound of one I didn't know, a clanging like that of the small noisemakers sold on New Year's Eve. My grandfather identified it as the clave, the key, the rhythm, the heartbeat of all salsa. (Gautier 2014, 14)

This sonic memory unfolds into critical listening, as the *nieta*/narrator finds home and a sense of belonging and identity in its sounds and instrumentation. She highlights the way in which the song, "growing without words," begins as an uninterrupted instrumental crescendo then leads to "a man's voice singing one lone word" (Gautier 2014, 14) (the word "Aguanile," which is uttered through elongated and repeated syllables, from the initial "A" to the final "nile."] The *nieta*'s ears situate these opening sounds as "what I guessed sounded like African music," thus acknowledging her initial lack of knowledge about Black sonic and rhythmic traditions. Yet through critical listening she allows herself to find a sense of belonging and home in them. The *nieta* likewise notes her ignorance of the "clave" as "the sound of one I didn't know," yet immediately recalls her grandfather defining the "clave" as "the key, the rhythm, the heartbeat of all salsa." This is immediately followed by a reference to "the drums" which "drove the beating of my heart" and which, the *nieta* acknowledged, allowed her to feel that she "was moving." Thus, through this intersemiotic translation of an act of critical listening and sonic memory, the *nieta*/narrator is able to acknowledge not only her place in the family, but to situate herself within the longer genealogies of the Black diaspora and of her roots in Africa. It allows her as well to trace a longer genealogy of Afro-Puertorriqueñidad through the song's previous iterations and performances. The song itself, its sounds and the long history of Puerto Rican community building that "Aguanile" invokes as a classic of the Nuyorican moment of salsa music, is what allows the *nieta*/narrator to understand the value of her grandfather: "With the music between us, I could *almost* forget that he was the man who should have been in Brooklyn with us but had abandoned us and had a whole other family who got all of his time, care, and attention" (Gautier 2014, 11). In symbolic ways, for the *nieta* the *abuelo* embodies the abandonment of the diaspora and of the African American identities of his first family, the *nieta*'s mother and grandmother, and herself, whose Afro-Puerto Ricanness has been long elided and silenced within the island's mainstream constructions of cultural identity. If, as critics have noted, Gautier's short stories emphasize the "ambiguities" of the "concept of happiness," suggested by the inclusion of the adverb "almost," "Aguanile" the story does portray "ordinary lives in their full measure—courageous, flawed, utterly human" (Brown 2016). The inclusion of the adverb "almost" also suggests that the *nieta*/narrator will not totally forget the consequences of her grandfather's abandonment on her family and thus the healing power of sounds, rhythms, and of this particular song will always remain incomplete and imperfect, at best. Yet her acknowledgement of the collective power of salsa music as a sonic tradition is clearly liberatory for her. As she states at the end of the short story, "When I listened to 'Aguanile' that night, I knew what he [the grandfather] meant" (Gautier 2014, 15).

In closing, reading "Aguanile" in a reverse temporality allows me to illustrate the reconciling power of music and literature during this critical moment for Puerto Ricans, both on the island and in the diaspora, specifically in 2019, as the mourning after Hurricane María has transformed itself into collective political mobilization. A critical listening of "Aguanile" allows us to acknowledge the healing power of the hurricane itself, which, like water and the powers of Yemayá, "unveiled" a new sense of confidence among Puerto Ricans on the island who have engaged in grassroots organizing as a form of survival and change, as the Paro Nacional of 2019 has illustrated. After getting organized locally, regionally, and transnationally, Puerto Ricans have recognized that they did not need to depend on either the local nor the federal government for survival, but on themselves and on each other. As the Paro Nacional and the national protests in Puerto Rico demanding the resignation of Governor Ricky Roselló suggest, most Puerto Ricans, despite party affiliations, are beginning now to acknowledge the need for decolonization in the face of the abandonment by the US federal government. Could we acknowledge that the rains and waters from María not only destroyed but also allowed Puerto Ricans to begin to heal together? The photo included here beautifully illustrates the power of water as a healing force during the Paro Nacional in 2019. As Carmen Yulín Cruz stated: "I hate to say anything positive about Maria. But what the hurricane did was force us to look at the realities of life here and how our dependency on the outside weakens our ability to ensure our people are taken care of. Maria made it evident that we need agricultural sovereignty" (Adler 2018). Sylvia de Marco, a collaborator of Tara Rodriguez Besosa's farming projects also stated: "After the hurricane, even people who didn't care about food started to care. It really opened people's eyes: that we have to depend on our soil, not shipping containers" (Adler 2018). This collective recognition, a sort of decolonial *anagnórisis* for all Puerto Ricans, is also echoed by organic intellectual Christine Nieves:

> This process of discovering the latent potential in the community has been like opening your eyes and all of a sudden seeing "Oh wait, we're humans and there's other ways of relating to each other now that the system has stopped." (Klein 2018, 68)

In brief, as the rich and powerful presence of music, reggaetón, dancing (as the queer *perreo* that took place in front of the Cathedral in Old San Juan), and other forms of visual and performative arts such as the act of banging on *cacerolas* made evident during the Paro Nacional and afterward, the post-María reconstruction period in Puerto Rico has opened up the possibilities of reconciliation between the island and the diaspora, among Puerto Ricans of different generations, like the *nieta* and her grandfather, and among those with conflicting gender politics, as in Amina Gautier's short story. The political events in July 2019, which integrated individuals from such different social and political positionalities, highlighted the potential for an alternative collectivity—a way of being puertorriqueñx—that defies traditional and mainstream notions of national belonging and that were made possible by the decolonizing and healing power of the arts. For Boricuas connected with each other, on the island and throughout the diaspora, literature, music, and the visual and performative arts allow us to reimagine the possibilities for decoloniality and for collective empowerment. I hope that this critical reading of "Aguanile" contributes to the larger process of public healing, a collective experience that cannot be disconnected from our own intimate family stories of loss after the hurricane as from the field of Latinx Studies as a site that allows for such affective reconciliations.

Figure 35.1. Photo Credit: Fabián Rodríguez Torres on Instagram.

Un Adiós

In contrast to many fellow Puerto Ricans who love the island and who visit frequently to share with relatives and loved ones, I left the island to escape the dysfunctionality of my parents, my socioeconomic status, and the limitations I faced as an emerging feminist in a social world where Catholic mandates and sexual repression curtailed my own intellectual development and personal freedom, a sort of "sexile," we could say. After more than forty years in the United States, where I found the individual freedom to become a feminist and a scholar, and after becoming a United States Latina, my relationship to the island became greatly reduced—limited to the occasional visit to my aging parents' home in Guaynabo, a suburban region easily associated with well-to-do families, whiteness, and gated communities. Given my self-exile, I left behind my own sense of belonging on the island to reimagine myself otherwise. However, after the hurricane, my connection and strong reactions to its devastation reminded me of my own national identity as a Boricua and that, after all, the island was still home. The anxiety that my sisters and I shared after September 20 of not being able to communicate for weeks with my mother, who has advanced dementia, kept me from sleeping at night. After four long months, I was able to visit—to witness the sights and sounds that traced the physical destruction—a painful reminder of what my compatriots had endured. Light posts lying next to roads, trees without leaves and browned from the force of the winds, numerous homes still without roofs, boats capsized against the coast in the biophosphorescent bay of La Parguera, piles of tree branches still waiting to be picked up and cleaned, electric wires hanging loose from posts throughout residential neighborhoods, and so many other images that will never be erased, not to mention, of course, the pain, despondency, and desperation of so many *compatriotas*. Having participated in numerous fundraisers and collective interventions to aid those negatively affected by the natural and unnatural disasters on the island, I believe that my puertorriqueñidad cannot be measured by the numbers of years I have been absent from my home country, but by what we do to reimagine ourselves as part of a larger entity and by my solidarity with those on the island. Moreover, my puertorriqueñidad today can only survive wherewith it intersects the spaces of Latinidad that I have carved in the United States. Given the limitations and repressions I faced within the privileged social world of my family, no feelings of nostalgia for an idealized past on the island, nor illusions or myths about the so-called magical island, will inform my loyalty to Puerto Rico. Rather, I hope to continue to be there to support my friends, loved ones, and strangers who love Puerto Rico and all things Puerto Rican. As "Aguanile" the short story reminds me, while I was not one of the Boricua fans of Lavoe when he was alive, I can still claim a sense of puertorriqueñidad in my own critical work as a listener of salsa, and better yet, like the *nieta*/narrator, as a feminist listener of salsa.

Before moving to graduate school, my former undergraduate mentor asked me to consider the difference between being an intellectual and being a "*carrerista*." He asked me to always remain the former. Despite all the competitiveness and the power games of academia that I have been surrounded with and have engaged, I have tried always to honor the integrity of engaging in the world of ideas while remaining committed to social justice through Latinx Studies, an academic space that cannot but be, always, a decolonial and political intervention. Mentoring the brilliant graduate students during the 1990s at Michigan, at UIC, and now at Northwestern has been nothing but a gift to me and it is now, upon retirement, that I realize the critical value of academic legacies. My PhD students each inspired me, taught me, and allowed me not to feel alone in the world. They strengthened my resolve to continue to make a difference to others, to speak out, to have a voice. For Puerto Rican and Latina women of my generation, establishing a public voice was essential for our own liberation. It has been a profound privilege to have been able to write during these decades, to have my articles included in course readings across the United States, and to have younger Latinx students reflect on their own lives and discover their own power to reimagine themselves through our writings.

Latinx Studies, as a field of study, should offer each of us—students, scholars, and community members—a collective space that allows us, as a racialized community, to reclaim our histories, our cultures, and our political and social struggles through embodied knowledge. Just like critically listening to "Aguanile," Latinx Studies should always continue to imagine itself collectively as a space that offers us a sense of belonging and home.

NOTES

1   The 4,645 deaths were reported by the Harvard University study conducted in 2018. See Kishore et al. (2018). This estimate represents "more than 70 times the official estimate" of the Puerto Rican government of sixty-four deaths. In addition, as Emery (2018) indicates, the George Washington University study, commissioned by Governor Ricardo Roselló, was of 2,975 deaths. These various estimates unveil the ways in which official history and the state erase and minimize the magnitude of these losses in colonized societies such as Puerto Rico.

2   In his chapter, "Si no pudiera hacer arte, me iba: The Aesthetics of Disaster as Catharsis in Contemporary Puerto Rican Art," Rivera Santana defines "using art for social catharsis" as "an aesthetic process in which people can collectively express the complex or contradictory social, cultural and political situations that confront them" (179). By transfiguring complex realities, such as the disaster and destruction of Hurricane María, into "another intelligible form or medium," the numerous artistic expressions that emerged after the storm evinced the need for the arts to serve as healing. For Rivera Santana, the healing suggests a decolonial sensitivity to the effects of the hurricane as artists "tell the complex story of the entanglements among Hurricane María, capitalism, and colonization" (179).

3   The song "Aguanile" was originally performed by Héctor Lavoe in New York in 1972, the early years of salsa music. After the release of the film El Cantante in 2006, in which Marc Anthony performs as Lavoe, the song assumed more mainstream popularity. Not only has Marc Anthony popularized "Aguanile" for years as the opening song for many of his concerts, but in 2011 he performed it on American Idol with Jennifer López and accompanied by Sheila E in the timbales. Most recently, "Aguanile" served as background rhythms and music to the short dance ice skating performance by the German couple, Kavita Lorenz and Joti Polizoakis, during the Winter Olympics in January 2018. Clearly, the song has circulated transnationally and globally by now, suggesting shifting social and political meanings.

4   Frances Aparicio and Wilson Valentín-Escobar discuss the ways in which Héctor Lavoe and La Lupe's own condition of abjection reminded racial minorities of our own vulnerabilities

to be always already criminalized by US dominant society and the state. Both Lavoe and La Lupe's lives were "fraught with personal tragedy and suffering, elements that allowed their Latino audiences to confront their own struggles and marginalization as a result of structured social inequities" (87–88).

BIBLIOGRAPHY

Adler, Tamara. "The Young Farmers behind Puerto Rico's Food Revolution." *Vogue*, June 20, 2018. Accessed on June 22, 2018. www.vogue.com.

Anthony, Marc. "Aguanile." YouTube video. October 29, 2007. www.youtube.com/watch?v=4Nx8URjepjo.

Anthony, Marc, and Jennifer López. "Aguanile" on *American Idol*. YouTube video. May 26, 2011. www.youtube.com/watch?v=tK2s1E5-ByU.

Aparicio, Frances, and Wilson Valentín-Escobar. "Memorializing La Lupe and Lavoe: Singing Transnationalism, Vulgarity and Gender." New York: *Centro Journal* 16, no. 2 (2004): 78–101.

Brown, Julia. "Interview with Amina Gautier." *Mosaic Magazine*, Bee Ideas LLC. May 5, 2016. https://mosaicmagazine.org.

Cortés, Jason. "Necromedia, Haunting and Public Mourning in the Puerto Rican Debt State: The Case of 'Los Muertos.'" *Journal of Latin American Cultural Studies* 27, no. 3 (2018): 357–69.

Emery, David. "What Was the Actual Death Toll from Hurricane María in Puerto Rico?" *Snopes*, June 4, 2018. www.snopes.com.

Gautier, Amina. 2014. *Now We Will Be Happy*. Lincoln and London: University of Nebraska Press.

Ichaso, León, dir. *El Cantante*. New Line: 2007. Film.

Kishore, Nishant, M.P.H, Domingo Marqués, Ph.D., et al. "Mortality in Puerto Rico after Hurricane María." *New England Journal of Medicine* 379 (July 12, 2018): 162–70.

Klein, Naomi. 2018. *The Battle for Paradise: Puerto Rico Takes on the Disaster Capitalists*. Chicago, Illinois: Haymarket Books.

Lavoe, Héctor. "Aguanile." YouTube video. 1972. www.youtube.com/watch?v=pz650EkJFKc.

Miliken Institute of Public Health, George Washington University. "Ascertainment of the Estimated Excess Mortality from Hurricane María in Puerto Rico." Project Report, 2018. Washington, DC. In collaboration with the University of Puerto Rico Graduate School of Public Health.

Moreno, Jairo. "La Salsa y sus Muertes." In *Cocinando Suave: Ensayos de Salsa en Puerto Rico*, edited by César Colón-Montijo, 29–38. Caracas, Venezuela: Fundación Editorial el Perro y la Rana, 2015.

Ríos, Soleida. 2017. *A Wa Nilé*. Havana, Cuba: Editorial Letras Cubanas.

Rivera Santana, Carlos. "Si no pudiera hacer arte, me iba: The Aesthetics of Disaster as Catharsis in Contemporary Puerto Rican Art." In *Aftershocks of Disaster: Puerto Rico Before and After the Storm*, edited by Yarimar Bonilla and Marisol Lebrón, 178–90. Chicago: Haymarket Books.

Rondón, César Miguel. 2008. *The Book of Salsa: A Chronicle of Urban Music from the Caribbean to New York City*. Translated by Frances R. Aparicio with Jackie White. Chapel Hill: The University of North Carolina Press.

Saresma, Tuija. "'Art as a Way to Life': Bereavement and the Healing Power of Arts and Writing." *Qualitative Inquiry* 9, no. 4 (2003): 603–20.

Valentín-Escobar, Wilson. "Nothing Connects Us All but Imagined Sounds: Performing Trans-Boricua Memories, Identities, and Nationalisms through the Death of Héctor Lavoe." In *Mambo Montage: The Latinization of New York City*, edited by Arlene Dávila and Agustín Laó-Montes, 207–34. New York: Columbia University Press, 2001.

CRITICAL DIÁLOGO 9

Community Engagement, Critical Methodologies, and Social Justice

The final critical diálogo of the anthology foregrounds the centrality of pedagogy and activism to the scholarship and methodologies of Latinx Studies. The scholars in this section have been very explicitly and actively involved in engaging diverse communities and student populations—many Latinx, first-generation students who have direct expertise in some of the very debates and diálogos we have discussed in this anthology. A question that guides this critical diálogo is: *What does Latinx Studies look like when we shift the gaze of thematic expertise from faculty to students; from university centered to community focused?*

The scholars in this section discuss their own strategies for surfacing the applied, institutional, and communal value of the themes, paradigms, methodologies, debates—in fact, the critical diálogos—of "Latinx Studies." Mari Castañeda and Joseph Krupczynski do this by considering the influence of Latinx communities in academic praxis, while Lorgia García Peña discusses possibilities for bridging community activism and teaching modalities in Latinx Studies, even at elite institutions. Salvador Vidal-Ortiz deploys critical auto-ethnography as methodological and epistemological technique to examine whiteness in the context of Latinidad through the concept of "white person of color." Alisha Beliso-De Jesús examines how feminist-of-color scholarship is deployed by an unbound collective of brujx spiritual activists and students. Rather than drawing any definitive or conclusive guidelines, this final diálogo serves to incite new approaches to knowledge production, creative methodologies, and innovative epistemologies that honor the depth and breadth of Latinx populations.

36

The Power and Possibilities of a Latinx Community-Academic Praxis in Civic Engagement

MARI CASTAÑEDA AND JOSEPH KRUPCZYNSKI

In this moment when Latinx communities are increasingly targeted and policed, there is a greater need within university civic engagement efforts to emphasize a community-academic praxis that centers social justice, equity, reciprocity, and the importance of Latinx voices in creating a more just world. There is no denying that the future of the United States is intimately linked to Latinx futurities, and thus educational settings, especially higher education, are deeply critical sites to engage "hope and harness its power to move social justice forward . . . [as well as] reject poisonous ideologies and stereotypes that get in the way of humanizing education" and communities (Nieto and López 2019, 43–45). As Paulo Freire (1970) once noted, education has the enormous potential to enact the practice of freedom, *concienciación*, and humanization, and as a result, "the oppressed liberate themselves and their oppressors as well" (44). Similarly, we see civic engagement and community service learning as critical pedagogical methods that have the potential to transform social relations between students, faculty, and communities and also create new forms of understanding community empowerment and liberation. Ultimately, we believe that enacting a Latinx community-academic praxis in civic engagement beneficially alters how students and faculty engage with Latinx communities and the ongoing efforts to decolonize education.

It is important to note that these efforts are not new, but build on a long history of social movements in higher education that aimed to create more representative, equitable, and accessible institutions of higher learning. The student movements that called for and created Chicana/Latino Studies, African American studies, and ethnic studies were centered on profound ideological, political, and material struggles over resources and the production of meaningful scholarship that directly responded to vital community issues. It is also the result of communities rallying for the right to representation and promising futurities within and outside of academic spheres as well as the need to challenge the teaching laboratory approach to communities that scholars historically applied with regards to communities of color (Darder and Torres 2004; De la Torre and Pesquera 1993). These movements in higher education also included scholars from underrepresented communities who documented the value and depth of marginalized communities that are often left out of academia's narratives about what counts as knowledge production. Within Latino Studies, the field of education (both K–12 and college level) were especially adept at formulating new ways of engaging with Latinx communities and utilizing a Latino Studies framework as the basis for transformative work (Bedolla and Fraga 2012; Cammarota and Romero 2009; Hurtado 1994; Padilla 1997). The acknowledgement of culture and the value of *testimonios* and lived experiences are important aspects of civic engagement that a Latinx community-academic praxis can operationalize to challenge western models of engagement as well as provide new formulations that can potentially influence engagement with other marginalized communities.

In fact, the intersection of scholarship, pedagogy, and activism has always been an important attribute of Latinx Studies since the ideology of "*saber es poder*" continually fuels the motivation of scholars of color to view and occupy institutions of higher education as spaces that must be transformed and reclaimed for student and community empowerment. And such transformations occur not only through broader civic engagement and engaged scholarship but, more importantly, for Latinx faculty in particular, through courses that include community-based and service learning initiatives that are anchored in social justice, reciprocal learning, and lived experiences. When faculty and students work in Latinx communities these core characteristics, as well as intersectional ways of understanding that are at the center of Latinx studies frameworks, provide new ways to implement and enhance civic engagement and community service learning praxis. Consequently, a Latinx community-academic praxis aims to transform the social relations between communities and academic institutions and develop a reciprocal relationship in which faculty, students, and communities can learn from each other in productive, challenging, and transformative ways (Castañeda and Krupczynski 2018; Mitchell 2016). We see the goal as one in which Latinx studies faculty and students foster a decolonized approach to the university and develop their engagement with local communities as pathways for liberation and transformation (Noguera, Pierce, and Ahram 2016; Pedraza and Rivera 2005). The symbolic and physical violence against Latinos, especially immigrants, makes these endeavors more critical than ever.

Engaging Communities through Academia

What are higher education's obligations to academic civic/community engagement? As colleges and universities increasingly define and characterize their missions as "engaged" and responsive to societal challenges, they continue to be confronted by systemic limitations as institutions caught up in their own histories of inequities that enhance systems of privilege rather than critique or dismantle them. How can higher education work to deconstruct systems of power in support of underrepresented communities? What histories can we trace to find the basis for a critical approach to civic engagement and service learning and its potential for transforming the world? Concerns about doing "good" in local communities and providing resources for empowerment often shape the ways in which faculty and students form learning opportunities with community members. While John Dewey's concept of engaged and experiential learning (Dewey 1916) are often noted as being instrumental in connecting higher education environments and community settings, scholars of critical service learning build on the work of Paulo Freire and his popular education model that draws on the lived experiences of the learner, critical-thinking and dialogic processes that allow for an exploration and understanding of root causes of underlying injustice (Freire 1970, 1994). As Randy Stoecker notes, "while experiential education certainly contrasts with traditional pedagogy, Freire's critique goes beyond simply method to also critique the content of traditional pedagogy" (Stoecker 2016). In addition, efforts around popular education in the United States developed by Myles Horton of the Highlander Folk School intersected with the social movements of the 1960s and the activation of new social/political spaces on campuses as well as alternative forms of exchange and communication that challenged the repressive and organizational structures of capitalist consumer culture.

As more first-generation, working-class, Black, Indigenous, Asian, and multiracial Latinx students and faculty entered academia, there was also a growing demand to critically examine the historical and ongoing systematic exclusion and discrimination that occurred on university campuses against communities of color (Torres 2009). Students and scholars of color insisted that their communities were multifaceted, capable of knowledge production, teachers in their own right, and deserving of having their collective memories and lived experiences taken seriously within the walls of the ivory tower (Aguirre and Martínez 1993). Additionally, community members partnered with activist students to hold public institutions of higher education accountable for how they utilized communities as laboratories, denied access to education, and misrepresented their histories, social interactions, and cultural practices. Kevin Johnson and George Martínez (1998) note, for instance, that during the civil rights era, Mexican American scholar-activists worked closely with communities to fight against "racial discrimination, poor education, and the lack of equal opportunity. The Chicana/ student movement saw Mexican-Americans dramatically walk out schools throughout the southwest" in response to racist educational structures (1153).

The hard-fought struggle to institutionalize Chicana/o, Puerto Rican, and later Latinx Studies in colleges and universities across the United States not only established these scholarly spaces but also engendered a third space in which the practice of radical pedagogy could facilitate partnerships between community members and scholar-activists in order to hold institutions of higher education accountable for how they utilized communities as laboratories, denied access to education, and misrepresented their histories, social interactions, and cultural practices. As Francis Aparicio (1999) explains,

> the agenda in the 1960s and 1970s called for Puerto Rican Studies programs that, first, would problematize the relationship between power and knowledge; secondly, that would serve as spaces for decolonization through an alternative and culturally-based production of knowledge and through critical, radical pedagogies; and, third, that would dismantle individualism through collective work; finally, more than producing articulations between academia and the community, it would strive to make the non-academic community a central subject and agent in the production of Latino scholarship. (14)

This is exactly what today's efforts toward a Latinx community-academic praxis aim to achieve, that is, a continuation of the critical pedagogy first promoted by Paulo Freire, the activist possibilities of education, and the academic third spaces cultivated by Latinx scholars that recognizes and centers the valuable "knowledge is power" contributions that diverse Latinx communities are making in everyday life. Thus, "*saber es poder*" is not merely a catchphrase but rallying cry that continues to inspire Latinx faculty, students, and communities to confront the "monopoly over knowledge and its institutionalization [by] white supremacist, imperialist patriarchal power" (Candelario 2018, 196).

Centering Community Voices

Challenging and confronting the assumptions about whose voices matter in academia, and centering the stories of Latinx communities that have historically been marginalized, have always been key political and scholarly practices of civic engagement within Latinx Studies. The strategic and cooperative aspirations for educational and community liberation, most notably demonstrated through the social movement work of the Young Lords, Brown Berets, and Chicana/o Movement activists, and more recently by young undocumented DREAMers, all point to the ways in which Latinx communities have historically continued to create collaborative connections and relationships between students and faculty in order to instigate radical social change and decolonized forms of understanding. The application of Latina/o critical theory, critical race theory, and Chicana feminism, in particular, within classroom environments and in relationship to community partnerships, are some of the epistemological ways in which traditional civic engagement models and community-based learning approaches have been decolonized, challenged, and reimagined (Deeb-Sossa 2017; Deeb-Sossa and Boulware 2018; Huber 2009). One productive ontological outcome that has occurred in this process has been the centering of Latinx faculty and student experiences and the recognition that examining the complex richness of diverse Latindades has deep value for understanding our broader social world. While it is important to acknowledge that not all civic engagement partnerships integrate the voices of community members, as Velia García (2007) asserts,

> Today the Latino faculty embraces community-based learning, social justice, and civic engagement because for the most part this is very familiar territory . . . community was a main point of reference and a vast repository of knowledge; we gained access to the knowledge by doing and learning–hence praxis. Praxis and community empowerment are enduring values that continue to motivate and give greater purpose to our students. (220)

Additionally, by using critical race theory to reimagine the notion of cultural capital and the role of racial capitalism in shaping a community's access to resources, it allows faculty members to recognize as well as encourage a range of cultural knowledge, skills, abilities, and contacts held by students of color that can be brought into the classroom through an intersectional, historical, and decolonial framework. As Dolores Delgado Bernal (2002) notes, "critical race and LatCrit theorists acknowledge that educational structures, processes, and discourses operate in contradictory ways with their potential to oppress and marginalize and their potential to emancipate and empower" (109). Consequently, not only do students and community members bring lived experiences into university environments, but by acknowledging and explicating their forms of cultural knowledge, they theorize and make sense of their place in the world. In doing so, they reinforce their own and the community's strength and power and thus work collectively toward, as Tara Yosso (2005) notes, the "larger purpose of struggle toward social and racial justice" (69).

The authoring of Latinx community counternarratives have become especially fruitful through the use of *testimonio*. This process of self-reflection creates a powerful space to share stories of oppression and liberation as well as connections of solidarity in order to produce social justice change (Elenes 2001). In addition to being utilized as a research method, it has also become a transformative praxis for reflecting on the processes and experiences of civic engagement and community-based learning in diverse Latinx communities. For instance, the engagement with *testimonio* has been present in the work by Linda Prieto and Sofía Villenas (2012) in teacher education classrooms; Judith Flores Carmona (2014) in partnerships with Latina mother activists; and Mara Chávez-Díaz (2015) in the context of social justice healing. Thus, "*testimonio* can contribute to the growing scholarship on critical race methodologies which seeks to disrupt the apartheid of knowledge in academia, moving toward educational research guided by racial and social justice for communities of color" (Huber 2009). This aforementioned scholarship and others like it have built on previous generations of Puerto Rican and Chicana studies scholars who also utilized *testimonio* as well as other advocacy-oriented epistemological and pedagogical tools in order to engage politically and ethically with Latinx communities. Scholars such as Suzanne Oboler (1995), Felix Padilla (1997), and Pedro Cabán (2003), to name a few, have produced foundational pedagogical practices and scholarship that provide frameworks and examples of how to continue with the hard work of Latinx civic engagement to life our spirits and existence. This vast body of work from which we build upon has also inspired other innovative forms of engagement and community-based research including story circles, methodologies of the heart, restorative justice, performance auto/ethnography, and critical partnership praxis (Delgado Bernal, Burciaga, and Flores Carmona 2012; Gutiérrez-Pérez 2017; Saavedra and Pérez 2014). In addition to voicing experiences that are often made silent or invisible in academia, these methodological innovations are also transforming the ways in which Latinx students and communities became cocreators of new knowledge, and their participation in research and engagement needed to begin with the voices of those who have historically been left out or misrepresented in the scholarly record (Delgado Bernal and Alemán 2017). Therefore, what we are now calling a Latinx community-academic praxis builds on this deeply rich scholar-activist work and continues with the tradition of keeping communities at the very center of social justice teaching and research.

Contemporary Examples of a Latinx Community-Academic Praxis

In bell hooks's influential essay "Choosing the Margin," she articulates the space of the "margin" as a central location of a counter-hegemonic discourse founded on everyday practices. It is a space that is not understood as a marginality to escape from but a space that, by its very location outside of the center, nourishes a capacity to resist, to construct radical perspectives, and from "which to see and create, to imagine alternatives, new worlds" (hooks 1990). A Latinx community-academic praxis has the same potential to expand and recenter critical conversations about engagement as well as integrate and complicate our understanding of what it means to teach and produce research for and with diverse Latinx communities. How we acknowledge the potential that is possible working from the margins—not from a marginalized position, but from an uncentered center—holds the key to exploring redistributed power relations, decolonizing practices, and workable strategies to bridging the community and university divide.

Using the themes from the recent book, "Civic Engagement in Diverse Latinx Communities: Learning from Social Justice Practices in Action" (Castañeda and Krupczynski 2018) we can distinguish ways in which students, activist scholars, and communities are critically addressing these issues through three frameworks: (1) rethinking community and civic engagement; (2) community voices and the politics of place; and (3) expanding the media and cultural power of communities. Highlighted in each of these sections are scholar-activists who have developed higher educational courses and community-based research projects that not only engage students as partners in knowledge production but also creatively cultivate ways in which youth, elders, mothers, first-generation students, workers, farmworkers, media producers, local historians, and residents of Latinx communities can play a reciprocal role in the coconstruction of knowledge.

Latinx scholar-activists have always worked to restore, to rejuvenate, and to value non-Western, Indigenous, Black, and Latinx modes of understanding and being (Castellanos and Jones 2003; Delgado 2015; Nagar 2017). In the context of the first framework, rethinking community and civic engagement, scholar-activists work to incorporate deeply rooted cultural/community practices and to create an understanding of cultural heritage as a complex matter of "becoming" as well as of "being." These are practices and understandings that, when imaginatively investigated, belong to the future as much as the past (Hall 1994). When these critical understandings are linked to experiential learning and social justice education, dominant and destructive social narratives about Latinx communities can be subverted and community agency catalyzed.

In professor Antonieta Mercado's courses on media studies and intercultural communication, she grounds much of her engaged teaching through the Indigenous practice of *tequio*, which is derived from the Náhuatl term *tequitl*, meaning community work and service. With *tequio* she develops a practice that aligns with the "service" practices that are at the origin of community-based learning as an educational discipline (Mercado 2018). But instead of grounding her work to the common epistemologies of service learning—which are often rooted in western and race-blind ideals of service, democracy, and education as well as Christian/religious forms of charity—the restoration of this Indigenous practice allows deeper connections with communities. This shift in values works to create another way to understand and participate in a meaningful and reciprocal educational enterprise. It elevates an Indigenous practice and connects it to a Latinx community-academic praxis that allows higher-education students and programs to collaborate with immigrant and Indigenous communities in building sustainable bonds, reciprocal trust, and transformative learning.

The second framework we wish to discuss is the role community voices and the politics of place, shape, reclaim, and contest the spaces and places where Latinx communities make their homes and where they build their lives. As the growing population of Latinos/as becomes an important demographic, political, and cultural force in the United States, Latinx communities are transforming the cities, neighborhoods, suburbs, small towns, and rural areas that they inhabit. The creative resilience of Latinos/as and the transformative power of making spaces of belonging is often made visible through quotidian practices, through the transformation of a front yard, through creative bilingualism and code-switching, through the construction of alternative and informal economies, through the cultivation of the home as site of alternative education and cultural memory keeping, through the coproduction of knowledge in spaces/places that often are founded on exclusion and racial privileging. These newly created settings, hybrids of tradition and innovation, are some of the ways in which Latinx communities reshape their surroundings and create narratives from which to undo the demonization and destructive othering that the powerful strain of historical—and current—white supremacy produces.

For instance, Professor Jonathan Rosa's approach to working with Latinx communities is not as test sites for academic study, as they are often treated in the academy, but rather important sites for intellectual collaboration. Such social-justice-oriented partnerships, like the "community as campus" model (Rosa 2018), reimagine new places/spaces of belonging and learning by valuing the knowledge creation and cultivation that happens in bilingual communities. This work also aims to critique and dismantle the misguided trope that the language practices of Latinos/as are education impediments. This deficit perspective is in direct opposition to the expansive and creative potential of bilingualism and language exploration that contest structures of power. Activist scholars who recognize the creative potential of these innovations are also able to plug in to and find ways to amplify community voices and support community actions that claim space, challenge exclusion, and makes meaningful spaces of belonging. Scholars such as Rina Benmayor (1991) produced critical community-based research that set the foundation for much of the civic engagement work being conducted today. In her popular education project in East Harlem, Benmayor argued for the importance of acknowledging local knowledge, the agency of communities, language as an asset and not as a deficit, and the potential as well as the challenges of university-community partnerships. This work along with others such as Adela de la Torre and Beatríz Pesquera (1993), Frances Aparicio and Suzanne Chávez-Silverman (1997), and Juan Flores (2000), to name a few, are important for how they helped create a scholarly context in which community voices were taken seriously. Questions of how we can engage Latinx communities as intellectual collaborators grow out of these historical scholarship and critical reevaluations and point to models that "enhance our capacity to create scholarship that identifies, analyzes, and contributes to the eradication of contemporary inequities" (Rosa 2018). Thus, when we reimagine the Latinx community as active participants in the construction of their own realities, places like homes and community center become sites of strategic actions, holders and producers of community-based knowledge.

Lastly, the third way in which scholars, students, and community activists are enacting a Latinx community-academic praxis is through efforts to expand the media and cultural power of communities. For example, media literacy is a form of civic engagement that encourages people to see themselves as actors rather than consumers—producers and agents within a regulatory process. Media inequality perpetuates stereotypical media content and acts as a barrier to access as producers. Media literacy can provide context and depth to the complex dynamics of diverse Latinx identities and can be used to understand root causes of media inequality and to develop critical visual literacy skills for both Latinx and white communities.

Professor Katynka Z. Martínez has developed a reciprocal relationship with the bilingual San Francisco newspaper *El Tecolote* as an effort to further extend the newspaper's counternarratives about the lives of Latinas/os and work with students so that they may "link their own acts of resilience and organizing to a legacy of self-determination" (Martínez 2018). Within the current political landscape—where Latinx communities are demonized and othered—it is difficult to maintain a nonpolitical/nonpartisan stance within service-learning projects. Engagement with Latinx community organizations and initiatives cannot easily accommodate a neutral stance if it is to counter/challenge the false and deficit-driven narratives of Latinx people in the mainstream media discourse. Latinx community media, which advocates on behalf of the community in order to monitor and challenge mainstream media narratives, offers a model with broad implications. Postcolonial and critical race theories also provide a theoretical grounding for counternarratives to become visible. If higher education has a great need for education to counteract the hegemonic narratives of otherness and connect to values of humanity over corporatization, then these models of critical theory and practice hold great potential as models of transformation.

The broader lesson for critical service learning and engaged learning practitioners is that whiteness, if left unacknowledged, can reduce the experiences within an engaged-learning course to a surface investigation of privilege and avoid key issue of race and ethnicity. Decentering whiteness within service-learning pedagogies (Mitchell 2017) is particularly important for Latinx and other students of color, as it makes spaces for those students to engage with their community partners on their own terms and from their own positionality. Indeed, activist scholars do not simply observe and analyze but create intellectual processes that transform the realities they observe (or participate in) to challenge paradigms of oppression and structural inequalities that are often framed as social pathologies and racialized tropes by mass media, policy makers, law enforcement, and sometimes even educational institutions.

Conclusion

From storytelling that is communal, dialogic, and intrapersonal to the acknowledgment of communities of color immense knowledge production, a Latinx community-academic praxis seeks to support social change and racial justice to create access to higher-education and participate in the project of social justice that contests the systematic oppression and racialized understandings that undermine our work and hopes in a neoliberal educational context (Castañeda 2013). We see a Latinx community-academic praxis as a method that meaningfully values the coproduction of community-based and Indigenous knowledge as well as a means for its recovery and resurgence. Scholar-activists, who are often members of communities they are engaged with, are at the center of this movement to reclaim Indigenous and community-based knowledge and produce innovative and transformative scholarship. The development and expansion of what we call a Latinx community-academic praxis not only fills a critical void in community and civic engagement practices and scholarship, it also works to advocate and harness the power and share the knowledge already present in Latinx communities as well as encourage college students to think critically of transformational capacities of Latinx communities.

As members of an academic community, we can reshape the purpose and practice of education to be more responsive to community-based and Indigenous knowledge, but to also have that knowledge transform our practices, which prioritize the cocreation of research agendas and pedagogy. Intellectual perspectives that work to create alternative frameworks of knowledge production can point the way toward engaged scholarship with meaningful community impacts—as well as transformative educational prospects. Our critical engagement with several academic traditions, such as Latinx studies, Black studies, ethnic studies, women's studies, engaged/public sociology, and critical borderland studies are all aligned with the desire for, and the ability of, knowledge creation to be in service to community empowerment. This is at the source of key questions about how one comes to a community—to learn not only about its history and future, but from it.

In the current political and social moment, where waves of hate and the undermining of public policy on immigration are contexts that are in direct opposition to the mission of an engaged university, we must urgently rededicate ourselves to a broad range of knowledge creation—both on and off campus—and support critical thinking and reflective actions that counter the prevailing currents of hate, oppression, and exclusion. If we are true to the missions of the universities that are our homes to promote engaged learning with our students and community partners, and to work collectively for a more just world, then those goals are both challenged and made more essential by today's political circumstances. Thus, the exploration of how a Latinx community-academic praxis can work in solidarity with the communities, organizations, and movements that we partner with and create pathways for social justice, mindfulness, and equity that define our values and meet our aspirations is the challenge that is before us—and one that we must passionately engage.

REFERENCES

Aguirre, Adalberto, and Ruben O. Martínez. 1993. *Chicanos in Higher Education: Issues and Dilemmas for the 21st Century*. Washington, DC: ERIC Clearinghouse on Higher Education.

Aparicio, Frances R. "Reading the 'Latino' in Latino Studies: Toward Re-imagining Our Academic Location." *Discourse: Berkeley Journal for Theoretical Studies in Media and Culture* 21, no. 3 (1999): 3–18.

Aparicio, Frances R., and Susana Chávez-Silverman, S. 1997. *Tropicalizations: Transcultural Representations of Latinidad*. Hanover, New Hampshire: Dartmouth College, University Press of New England.

Bedolla, Lisa G., and Luis R. Fraga. "Latino Education, Civic Engagement, and the Public Good." *Review of Research in Education* 36, no. 23 (2012): 23–42.

Benmayor, Rina. "Testimony, action research, and empowerment: Puerto Rican women and popular education." *Women's Words: The Feminist Practice of Oral History* (1991): 159–74.

Bernal, Dolores D. "Critical Race Theory, Latino Critical Theory, and Critical Raced-Gendered Epistemologies: Recognizing Students of Color as Holders and Creators of Knowledge." *Qualitative Inquiry* 8, no. 1 (2002): 105–27.

Cabán, Pedro A. "Moving from the Margins to Where? Three Decades of Latina/o Studies." *Latino Studies* 1, no. 1 (2003): 5–35.

Cammarota, Julio, and Agustine Romero. "A Critically Compassionate Pedagogy for Latino Youth." *Latino Studies* 4, no. 3 (2006): 305–12.

Cammarota, Julio, and Augustine F. Romero. "A Social Justice Epistemology and Pedagogy for Latina/o Students: Transforming Public Education with Participatory Action Research." *New Directions for Youth Development* 123 (2009): 53–65.

Candelario, Ginetta, Paul Hengesteg, and Alade S. McKen. "Interview with Dr. Ginetta Candelario." *Journal of Critical Thought and Praxis* 7, no. 1 (2018).

Carracelas-Juncal, Carmen. "When Service-Learning Is Not a 'Border-crossing' Experience: Outcomes of a Graduate Spanish Online Course." *Hispania* 96, no. 2 (2013): 295–309.

Castañeda, Mari. "¡Adelante!: Advancing Social Justice through Latina/o Community Media." In *Media and Social Justice*, edited by Susan Curry Jansen, Jefferson Pooley, and Lora Taub-Pervizpour, 115–30. New York: Palgrave Macmillan, 2013.

Castañeda, Mari, and Joseph Krupczynski, eds. 2018. *Civic Engagement in Diverse Latinx Communities: Learning from Social Justice Partnerships in Action*. New York: Peter Lang Publishers.

Castellanos, Jeanett, and Lee Jones, eds. 2003. *The Majority in the Minority: Expanding the Representation of Latina/o Faculty, Administrators, and Students in Higher Education*. Sterling, VA: Stylus Publishers.

Chávez-Díaz, Mara. "Social Justice Healing Practitioners: Testimonios of Transformative Praxis and Hope." 2015.

Costa, Leeray M., and Karen J. Leong. "Introduction Critical Community Engagement: Feminist Pedagogy Meets Civic Engagement." *Feminist Teacher* 22, no. 3 (2012): 171–80.

Darder, Antonia, and Rodolfo D. Torres. 2004. *After Race: Racism after Multiculturalism*. New York: NYU Press.

Delgado Bernal, Dolores, and Enrique Alemán. 2017. *Transforming Educational Pathways for Chicana/o Students: A Critical Race Feminista Praxis*. New York: Teachers College Press.

Delgado Bernal, Dolores, and Octavio Villalpando. "An Apartheid of Knowledge in Academia: The Struggle Over the 'Legitimate' Knowledge of Faculty of Color." *Equity and Excellence in Education* 35, no. 2 (2002): 169–80.

Delgado Bernal, Dolores, Rebeca Burciaga, and Judith Flores Carmona. "Chicana/Latina testimonios: Mapping the methodological, pedagogical, and political." *Equity & Excellence in Education* 45, no. 3 (2012): 363–72.

Delgado, Melvin. 2015. *Community Practice and Urban Youth: Social Justice Service-Learning and Civic Engagement*. New York: Routledge.

Deeb-Sossa, Natalia. 2017. *Doing Good: Racial Tensions and Workplace Inequalities at a Community Clinic in El Nuevo South*. Tucson, AZ: University of Arizona Press.

Deeb-Sossa, Natalia, and Janet Boulware. "'We Are Not a Token!': Cultural Citizenship and Transformational Resistance in Higher Education." *Urban Education* (2018) 1–32.

De la Torre, Adela, and Beatríz M. Pesquera. 1993. *Building with Our Hands: New Directions in Chicana Studies*. Berkeley, CA: University of California Press.

Dewey, John. 1916. *Democracy and Education: An Introduction to the Philosophy of Education*. New York: The Macmillan Company.

Elenes, C. Alejandra. "Transformando Fronteras: Chicana Feminist Transformative Pedagogies." *International Journal of Qualitative Studies in Education* 14, no. 5 (2001): 689–702.

Flores Carmona, Judith. "Cutting out their tongues: Mujeres' testimonios and the Malintzin researcher." *Journal of Latino/Latin American Studies* 6, no. 2 (2014): 113–24.

Flores, Juan. 2000. *From Bomba to Hip-Hop: Puerto Rican Culture and Latino Identity*. New York: Columbia University Press.

Flores, William V., and Rina Benmayor. 1997. *Latino Cultural Citizenship: Claiming Identity, Space, and Right*. Boston: Beacon Press.

Freire, Paulo. 1970. *Pedagogy of the Oppressed*. New York: Herder and Herder.

———. 1994. *Pedagogy of Hope: Reliving Pedagogy of the Oppressed*. London: Continuum.

Garcia, Velia. "Social Justice and Community Service Learning in Chicano/Latino/Raza Studies." In *Race, Poverty, and Social Justice: Multidisciplinary Perspectives through Service Learning*, edited by José Z. Calderón, 202–24. Sterling, VA: Stylus Publishing, 2007.

Gutiérrez-Pérez, Robert. "Bridging Performances of Auto/Ethnography and Queer Bodies of Color to Advocacy and Civic Engagement." *QED: A Journal in GLBTQ Worldmaking* 4, no. 1 (2017): 148–56.

Hall, Stuart. "Cultural Identity and Diaspora." In *Colonial Discourse and Post-Colonial Theory*, edited by Patrick Williams and Laura Chrisman, 223–45. New York: Columbia University Press, 1994.

hooks, bell. 1990. *Yearning: Race, Gender, and Cultural Politics*. Boston: South End Press.

Huber, Lindsay Pérez. "Disrupting Apartheid of Knowledge: 'Testimonio' as Methodology in Latina/o Critical Race Research in Education." *International Journal of Qualitative Studies in Education* 22, no. 6 (2009): 639–54.

Hurtado, Sylvia. "The Institutional Climate for Talented Latino Students." *Research in Higher Education*, 35, no. 1 (1994): 21–41.

Johnson, Kevin R., and George A. Martinez. "Crossover Dreams: The Roots of LatCrit Theory in Chicana/o Studies Activism and Scholarship." *University of Miami Law Review* 4 (1998): 1143–99.

Martínez, Katynka Z. "'I Exist Because You Exist': Teaching History and Supporting Student Engagement via Bilingual Community Journalism." In *Civic Engagement in Diverse Latinx Communities: Learning from Social Justice Partnerships in Action*, edited by Mari Castañeda and Joseph Krupczynski, 215–28. New York: Peter Lang Publishers, 2018.

Medina, Catherine, and Luna, Gaye. "Narratives from Latina Professors in Higher Education." *Anthropology and Education Quarterly* 31, no. 1 (2000): 47–66.

Mercado, Antonieta. "Engagement: Learning from Teaching Community Praxis." In *Civic Engagement in Diverse Latinx Communities: Learning from Social Justice Partnerships in*

Action, edited by Mari Castañeda and Joseph Krupczynski, 21–36. New York: Peter Lang Publishers, 2018.

Mitchell, Tania D. "Teaching Community On and Off Campus: An Intersectional Approach to Community Engagement." *New Directions for Student Services* 157 (Spring 2017): 35–44.

Mitchell, Tania D., David M. Donahue, and Courtney Young-Law. "Service Learning as a Pedagogy of Whiteness." *Equity and Excellence in Education* 45, no. 4 (2012): 612–29.

Nagar, Richa. 2017. *Muddying the Waters: Coauthoring Feminisms Across Scholarship and Activism*. Chicago: University of Illinois Press.

Nieto, Sonia, and Alicia Mariana López. 2019. *Teaching: A Life's Work: A Mother-Daughter Dialogue*. New York: Teachers College Press.

Noguera, Pedro A., Jill C. Pierce, and Roey Ahram, eds. 2016. *Race, Equity, and Education: Sixty Years from Brown*. New York: Springer International Publishing.

Oboler, Suzanne. 1995. *Ethnic Labels, Latino Loves: Identity and the Politics of (Re)presentation in the United States*. Minneapolis, MN: University of Minnesota Press.

Padilla, Felix. 1997. *The Struggle of Latina/o University Students: In Search of a Liberating Education*. New York: Routledge.

Padilla, Raymond V., and Rudolfo C. Chávez. 1995. *The Leaning Ivory Tower: Latino Professors in American Universities*. Albany, NY: SUNY Press.

Pedraza, Pedro, and Melissa Rivera. 2005. *Latino Education: An Agenda for Community Action Research*. Mahwah, NJ: Lawrence Erlbaum Associates.

Prieto, Linda, and Sofia A. Villenas. "Pedagogies from 'Nepantla': 'Testimonio,' Chicana/Latina Feminisms and Teacher Education Classrooms." *Equity and Excellence in Education* 45, no. 3 (2012): 411–29.

Rosa, Jonathan. "Community as a Campus: From 'Problems' to Possibilities in Latinx Communities." In *Civic Engagement in Diverse Latinx Communities: Learning from Social Justice Partnerships in Action*, edited by Mari Castañeda and Joseph Krupczynski, 111–24. New York: Peter Lang Publishers, 2018.

Saavedra, Cinthya M., and Michelle S. Pérez. "An Introduction: (Re)envisioning Chicana/Latina Feminist Methodologies." *Journal of Latino/Latin American Studies* 6, no. 2 (2014): 78–80.

Stoecker, Randy. 2016. *Liberating Service Learning and the Rest of Higher Education Civic Engagement*. Philadelphia, PA: Temple University Press.

Torres, Carlos A. 2009. *Globalizations and Education: Collected Essays on Class, Race, Gender, and the State*. New York: Teachers College Press.

Torrez, J. Estrella, Santos Ramos, Laura Gonzales, Victor del Hierro, and Everardo Cuevas. "Nuestros Cuentos: Fostering a Comunidad de Cuentistas through Collaborative Storytelling with Latinx and Indigenous Youth." *Bilingual Review/La Revista Bilingüe* 33, no. 5 (2017): 91–106.

Villenas, Sofia A. "The Colonizer/Colonized Chicana Ethnographer: Identity, Marginalization, and Co-optation in the Field." *Harvard Educational Review* 66, no. 4 (1996): 711–31.

Yosso, Tara J. "Whose Culture has Capital? A Critical Race Theory Discussion of Community Cultural Wealth." *Race, Ethnicity and Education* 8, no. 1 (2005): 69–91.

Zambrana, Ruth E. 2018. *Toxic Ivory Towers: The Consequences of Work Stress on Underrepresented Minority Faculty*. New Brunswick, NJ: Rutgers University Press.

37

Bridging Activism and Teaching in Latinx Studies

LORGIA GARCIA PEÑA

We need mass-based political movements calling citizens of this nation to up-hold democracy and the rights of everyone to be educated, and to work on behalf of ending domination in all its forms—to work for justice, changing our educational system so that schooling is not the site where students are indoc-trinated to support imperialist white-supremacist capitalist patriarchy or any ideology, but rather where they learn to open their minds, to engage in rigorous study and to think critically.[1]
—bell hooks, Teaching Community: A Pedagogy of Hope

A few years ago, I was invited to give a keynote presentation for the Latino Stud-ies graduation at a small liberal arts college. The mandate of the presentation was to reflect on the significance of my activism with the undocumented community in my own teaching and research. The nature of the talk was very different from the typical academic intervention, as it was an incredibly personal ask (how has *your* work with undocumented people shaped *your* scholarship and teaching), yet it also demanded that I reflect on and articulate two parts of my public life that many—even myself—have often considered separate: my activism and my academic work. As I wrote the talk, I found myself going deeper into my personal academic journey from college to graduate school to tenure track. My reflection on the journey allowed me to articulate, in no uncertain terms, that the work that led me to obtaining a PhD in Latino/a Studies and eventually becoming a professor was grounded precisely on a commitment to social justice: to find-ing answers to questions that emerged from my experience as a Black Latina of immigrant background confronting everyday racism and sexism. It was activism that led me to academia, to teaching. Activism was both the method and the impetus for my journey through Latinx Studies.

Writing at the turn of the twentieth century, Black Puerto Rican scholar and bibliophile Arthur Schomburg advocated for the creation of departments of Black history and for Black people to become historians as a way to contrast the lies, silences, and outright violence produced about Black and Brown people in the university. His proposal was to reintroduce "that which slavery took away": the possibility of humanity and belonging.[2] Ethnic studies (Black, Latinx, Asian, Native, and Arab studies) is charged with the immeasurable task of returning to us what slavery took away, filling the gaps left by all the Eurocentric fields of knowledge that make up academic departments, and creating a learning environment that contrasts the supremacy of whiteness, inequality, racism, and exclusion that dominate our canons, libraries, and archives. Ethnic studies privileges those who have been left out of books or produced as less than human, less capable, less worthy of study. What could possibly be a clearer form of activism? Yet, over the years, and in particular as I entered the world of the tenure track, my activism—from the founding of Freedom University, an organization that provides college instructions to undocumented students in the state of Georgia, to the public disobedience actions that lead to my arrests, to my work with queer of color communities, to my commitment to Haitian rights in the Dominican Republic—has often been met with both caution and trepidation by colleagues and well-meaning advisors: "Should you wait until you have tenure to be so vocal about XYZ? Is it safe for you to be so open about your politics in the classroom?" While I would have loved to dismiss these questions, the increased violations of academic freedom that left some Ethnic Studies colleagues out of work or otherwise hindered their careers through tenure denials were simply too many to dismiss.[3]

The cautionary tales and well-meaning advice reflect the widely accepted idea that while professors are indeed expected to be politically engaged and informed, there needs to be a clear separation between said engagement and their research and teaching in order to retain academic integrity and a sense of objective knowledge. But how do we separate our teaching from our practices when the community we study and serve is under attack? How do we, as Latino/a/x Studies teachers, study the historical violence experienced by our communities while simultaneously staying silent as families are separated, as people are deported, as young people go to prison, as schools are defunded, as neighborhoods are gentrified, as people die. Don't we, as scholars and teachers, have a responsibility to "work *for justice*" as we are invited to do by bell hooks? To work toward returning a little of "what slavery took away," as Schomburg envisioned? Education, the arts, and the humanities have always been sites of sociopolitical engagement, in part due to the freedom of creativity and creation they afford us, and in part because the arts, education, and social justice programs are often the first institutional sites to feel the effects of neoliberal politics (budget cuts, personnel reduction, etc.). And yet, I also understand that commitment to social justice, whether it is in the classroom, in the community, or in grassroots organizing, has many faces. Commitment to social justice—or what some call activism—emerges from a deeply personal place that is not always named. Therefore, my intention here is less to invite teachers to be "activists" or to provide a method for engaging social justice in the classroom than to share some of the deeply personal lessons I have learned in my own crooked *vaivén* through teaching Latinx Studies in the multiple and very different institutions and classrooms I have inhabited over the years (from Freedom University to Harvard). My purpose is then to simply invite a dialogue about the possibilities that can emerge if we foreground social justice as a clear goal in our teaching.

Latinx Studies as *Acompañamiento*

One of the classes I teach regularly is "Performing Latinidad," a course I developed my first semester as an assistant professor of Latinx Studies at Harvard University in 2013, and that has become a sort of sanctuary for first-generation students of color. Harvard does not have a department, program, or center for Latinx/o/a Studies. It does not provide students of color with a meeting space for community events. For many students of color, the classroom—and in particularly, the Latinx Studies classroom—has become such space.[4] It is in these courses that students meet each other and build alliances and networks that allow them to confront the violence and racism of their environment.[5] The first of its kind at Harvard, "Performing Latinidad" examines the constructions, imaginings, and representations of Latinidad as performed in a variety of genres, including poetry, fiction, drama, music, slam, and film in conversation with various sociocultural movements that have helped define notions of US Latinx identities. By bringing Latinx/o/a Studies criticism, border theories, Chicana feminism, race, and ethnicity theory into conversation, we address issues of identity, notions of citizenship, language authenticity, representation, and belonging. But because the class has a hands-on performance and art-making component, it is also incredibly engaging for students of all levels (from first year to doctoral). Every semester, students enrolled in "Performing Latinidad" work with a visiting artist to develop an artistic intervention based on readings from the class. Students look forward to their final performances, as they are one of the very rare instances in which they become visible in a campus that seems to constantly invisibilize its students and faculty of color. They work in groups, meet outside class, make physical artistic structures, rehearse their intervention and, at the end of the semester, take over the entire Harvard Yard through artistic, visual, and sonic interventions.

In 2015, for example, students erected an altar to Saint JLo (see figure 37.1) that became a shrine for ethnic studies "prayers" and *ofrendas*. With letters and notes asking Saint JLo to intercede on behalf of Latinx students in asking Mr. Harvard to finally provide "a space for Latinx students, approval for a concentration and a department, and the hiring of professors in the field of Ethnic Studies," the shrine became a site of activism and representation for Latinx and other students of color on campus, who guarded the shrine and brought flowers, candles, and other offerings to demand the *milagro*. The shrine remained in place over a week due to the complicit relationship between Latinx students and the custodial staff charged with removing it.[6] A year later, amid the presidential election campaign,

Figure 37.1. Altar to Saint JLo, "Performing Latinidad," 2015.

the students enrolled in "Performing Latinidad" decided that their theme for the final performance was going to be "Taco Trucks on every corner of the Harvard Yard" (see Figure 37.2) challenging the then-popularized controversial statement by Marco Gutiérrez, cofounder of Latinos for Trump, that "if you don't do something about it, you're going to have taco trucks on every corner."[7] Over the fall semester, each of the six groups prepared, under the direction of performance artist Josefina Báez, an installation and a performative text based on class readings and that spoke to both the overarching topic of the class and to the specific intervention (taco trucks) they had chosen for the performance. For the visual installation, students built cardboard trucks that moved throughout the campus sharing "poetry tacos" with passersby (see Figure 37.2). Students wrote original texts, made installations on various trees, and even transformed the iconic John Harvard statue into a "bad hombre" sculpture that challenged the rhetoric of the Trump campaign as well as the language of Harvard administration that continued to refuse the creation of an ethnic studies department despite forty-seven years of student demand. The performative intervention thus bridged the larger national political climate with the local campus climate, exposing the hypocrisy of the university in its refusal to recognize Latinx Studies (and, by extension, ethnic studies) as a legitimate field of inquiry while simultaneously celebrating its strides in diversity. The energy these students brought to campus was contagious. In the final moments of the performance, students staged a procession

Figure 37.2. Students park a "poetry taco truck" in front of Widener Library on Harvard campus.

that was joined by students, faculty, and tourists.[8] It was a triumphant day, and everyone felt great about the work done. The morning of the next class meeting, in which we were supposed to unpack the performance and think critically about the work done, we woke up to the news that Donald Trump had been elected president.

That Wednesday morning, I struggled with the decision of whether or not cancel class as many of my colleagues had done. It was an overwhelming day: a day of mourning, a scary day for many of the mostly Black, Brown, queer, and undocumented students enrolled in "Performing Latinidad." I simply did not have any words of comfort or wisdom that could assuage their fears, even a little. As I searched for an answer in my syllabus as to what to do that day in class, I stumbled upon an essay by Barbara Tomlinson and George Lipsitz entitled "American Studies as Accompaniment." In it, the authors argue that scholars need to "know the work we want our work to do and how our scholarship can serve to accompany positive changes in our society"[9] if we want to actually dismantle the oppressive systems that persistently reproduce inequality and oppression in time of terror and repression:

> Centrally important to the success of our scholarly endeavors is *knowing the work we want our work to do* [emphasis added], taking responsibility for the world we

are creating through our endeavors, for the ways of being in the world that we are modeling and promoting. The work of American studies can be organized around the concept of *accompaniment*. Accompaniment is a disposition, a sensibility, and a pattern of behavior. It is both a commitment and a capacity that can be cultivated. Two metaphors of accompaniment are particularly relevant: (1) accompaniment as participating with and augmenting a community of travelers on a road; (2) accompaniment as participating with others to create music. Thinking about American studies in terms of these acts of accompaniment can promote new ways of knowing and new ways of being that can equip scholars.[10]

The work I wanted my teaching to do, the reason why I became a teacher, was to enact social change: to create the kind of classroom that had been denied to me, a first-generation Black Latina daughter of immigrants from Trenton, NJ. My commitment to my students was thus grounded in justice and on a hope for the impact that I wanted students to have in their communities, starting in the classroom and expanding beyond it. Instead of cancelling class, I opened my classroom to all students who needed a place to process what it meant for them to now be forced to live in a Trumpian world. I decided to accompany them, trusting that the community we had worked to cocreate the past several months would hold us. As I stood in front of that Harvard lecture hall that morning, I was reminded once again of the power of community. Students came in holding each other; many cried. And for the first forty minutes of class, we allowed ourselves to feel fear, express anger, and to simply listen.

I did my best to make sure students felt safe in the classroom by setting the tone for respectful processing. At the beginning of class I made the following announcement: "If you voted for Trump or sympathize with his narrative and politics, this is simply not your space today. You may leave or sit silently. This is a safe space for people who may not feel safe anywhere else today. Nothing we say here today leaves the classroom." There were many undocumented students enrolled in the course who woke up terrified that they would be deported or persecuted. My first priority that day was to make sure they felt safe to speak if they chose to, at least for the duration of the class. And they did speak, and we all listened. We listened to their fears, we listened to their stories, and we listened to their sobs. Then I asked: "What now? What do you do in the space we inhabit here at Harvard to support our most vulnerable in our community? How do we *hope* and how do we learn amid fear and terror? What is the work we need to do?" What followed will stay with me forever: one student spontaneously got up and went to the board and began writing as her peers shared their thoughts and ideas. I sat down and watched my students take the lead in identifying the most urgent needs they saw in their community: to protect undocumented students. They continued working after class, and within three hours they had drafted a document that would be adapted nationally calling for university campuses to

Figure 37.3. PUSH student demonstration on Widener Library steps, November 2016.

become "sanctuaries" to protect their undocumented peers from the violence that was to come. Their actions, their accompaniment, went beyond the class; it extended for several years as they continued to organize and think together through writing, discussions, teach-ins, and eventually through rallies, civil disobedience, and media interventions. Their actions lead to the founding of an organization in support of undocumented students, PUSH (Protecting Undocumented Students at Harvard), and to the creation of several university resources including the hiring of staff and the allocation of financial resources for DACA renewal and legal fees.

Recently, I reflected on those early postelection days with a student who has since graduated and become a union organizer about what the experience had been like for students like herself. She said to me, "The syllabus gave us the tools, and the class gave us the community. The method for organizing was always in the class."

Latinx Studies as a Method

Social engagement and community-grounded learning have always been at the center of Chicano/a, Puerto Rican, and Latino/a Studies since its early formation. The 1960s Chicano/a student walkouts in the West of the United States lead to the founding of the first Chicano/a Studies Program at California State (1969). In the 1970s, the sit-ins and demonstrations in the Northeast also lead to the Puerto Rican and Hispanic Caribbean Studies programs at Rutgers, CUNY, and Hunter. Most recently, the actions of students at Williams, Wellesley, and Yale in New England resulted in the hires of Latinx studies faculty, the creation of spaces, centers, and departments, and most importantly, in building alliances between faculty, students, and staff. Social justice is at the core of how we *do* Latinx/o/a Studies. Yet, while we know that history, how this commitment translates to the everyday life of our students in the classroom is less evident, though not less important.

The example of the postelection class, inspiring as it is, is also exceptional. The political circumstances, the campus environment in 2016 amid a dining hall worker strike and the national elections, and the performative nature of the class allowed for these expressive forms of activism that would have proven impossible, or at the very least less natural, in a more traditional classroom and in a different political climate. What I want to highlight as a lesson for thinking about Latinx teaching as a method of social justice is not the performative political interventions of my students (from the rallies to the taco trucks), nor the administrative responses to their activism (the funding and staff support), but rather the more tacit elements that lead to their accompaniment, to their working *together*, to what my student identified in her own reflection: the class as a method of social justice through *acompañamiento*. I want to reflect on how to move from individual faculty-lead initiatives to broader faculty collective and/or collaborative projects that can accompany structural and lasting changes in our learning communities and beyond. The concept of "accompaniment" as Lipsitz and Tomlison remind us, comes from Central American liberation theory and activism: "It relates to the idea that social change is a process that is not given to the people but that emerges from the people. Allies cannot create social change, but they can accompany it with patience and courage."[11] They can "walk" together and participate in the creation of social changes. Accompaniment opposes the "self-made" model of the capitalist market and NGO-driven development in which "progress" is brought to a community rather than emerging from within. This dominant model has failed us in moments of crisis, even when those implementing it are well intentioned (as seen in the failure to reconstruct Haiti after the earthquake or in the post-Katrina rebuilding in New Orleans). In this increasingly market-driven world, we are encouraged to think of ourselves as individual owners of our lives, identities, careers, our courses, our research, our syllabi. We are each, as such, responsible for our own successes and failures (from graduation to tenure track to tenure). The dominant reward structures in this society— and in academia—promote competitive practices rather than collectivity and *acompañamiento*. In the classroom this often manifests in students' desire to protect their work, their research, and their sense of authorship. For faculty it manifests in the secretive ways in which information about tenure processes, hiring practices, fellowships, publishing, and so on seem to never reach everyone equally, hindering opportunities for advancement and development, particularly for junior faculty of color and first-generation faculty. To contrast this toxic environment, Tomlinson and Lipsitz urge us, we must turn to accompaniment—to the collective, open sharing of knowledge and resources—to a way of doing our work that promotes the growth of the field and the well-being of all involved; we need to reject the neoliberal practices of individual success and embrace collectivity. There has never been an easier time to this with the wide access to information and online community. Accompaniment needs to be at the center of our Latinx Studies Organizations, our departments, centers, and classrooms.

We know that our work as scholars grows through collective conversations with our peers and audiences. The same is true of active learning in and out of the classroom. However, to learn together it is first necessary to trust one another, to feel comfortable and secure in the space we inhabit in the classroom, to know our ideas will never be dismissed as silly or stupid, and to appreciate the significance of every voice rejecting the dominance of a single voice. This is not an easy task as most students of color are survivors of deep classroom traumas. We have all been, at one point or another, the only or one of few of our ethnicity or race. We have had to learn our own histories as side projects, and we have been asked to speak for the collective due to our presumed expertise, which is based solely on occupying racialized bodies.

To develop a trusting community in the classroom, I begin by acknowledging these traumas as I experienced them while also inviting students to strive to create with me a different kind of learning environment. Together we create simple rules for respecting one another that go from not dominating the conversation to checking our own privileges and subject positions before posing questions. Additionally, there are three requirements that I include in all my courses: 1) Everyone must learn each other's names regardless of the size of the class. This is the first homework. We must study the roster and learn each name. We later add more information such as learning one fact about each person. These facts cannot be academic but rather something personal we feel comfortable sharing (is a dog lover, has a twin, hates onions). 2) We read together. We read together as a class, and we create reading groups that meet outside of class. The groups are randomly assigned and require short weekly commitments. As the semester advances, these reading groups are reconfigured so that by the end of the term everyone has read with a different group. 3) We do group projects. While there are individual reflections and papers, the majority of the assignments are done in groups of three to five. These are challenging at first as students have to let go of their ways of understanding grades and authorship, but prove rewarding as they learn to relay on each other's strengths, make each other accountable, and learn to make room for each other's mistakes. Throughout the semester, all assignments are peer reviewed, all writing begins with workshops, and students slowly learn to become invested in collective learning as the philosophy of the classroom demands we accompany each other and make it together to the end of the term. In a society that constantly urges people *to have more*, Tomlinson and Lipsitz remind us the real task is to learn *how to be more*.[12] Collective learning teaches us how to be more through accompanying others.

In Fall 2018, I taught a course entitled "Diaspora Archives." The entire course revolved around the collective construction of an alternative digital archive that was grounded on oral interviews. Students worked in groups of five, following thematic guidelines and using as a premise for their research a set of oral interviews that had been collected by myself and a group of students from a previous course. The idea was to continue the work that their peers had started. The class was composed of graduate students, advanced undergraduates, and two first-year students. The groups were balanced accordingly. In addition to reading theory on critical archival studies and learning about methodologies of research and oral histories, students worked on providing a historical framework and historical evidence about the person they focused on. One group, for instance, worked on a project they titled "Birthing Across Borders," which centered around the life of Doña Ofelia, a woman who crossed the US–Mexico border to birth her two daughters and found herself entangled in a long legal battle with the California medical system. The group created an archive that documented the practice of crossing borders to give birth, dismantling the narrative of the "anchor baby" through concrete comparative data, archival research, and historical mapping. Another group documented the work of La Peña Gallery, a small Latina artist collective in Austin, Texas, that has been under attack by the Marriott Corporation as its neighborhood becomes gentrified. The final projects have been curated and placed on an online digital library we call *Mind the Gap: Archives of Justice*. The projects and the class were particularly successful because students were able to tap into their own personal interests and experiences as they approached the topic. Each group had a research leader who had a personal connection to the archive they developed.

Students come into the classroom with a diversity of experiences and perspectives. Tapping into that rich diversity can be a powerful contradiction to the academic culture of individuality as well as an important way of bridging teaching and activism in and out of the university walls, of promoting a democratic form of learning that extends beyond the classroom. For me, this type of teaching and learning gives me hope—the kind of hope that philosopher Jonathan Lear qualifies as "radical" as it encompasses the possibility of change for the world we want to create rather than the one we inherited. Lear writes, "What makes this hope *radical* is that it is directed toward a future goodness that transcends the current ability to understand what it is."[13] Radical hope is not so much something you have "but something you practice."[14] It demands flexibility, openness, and what Lear describes as "imaginative excellence."[15] Radical hope is our best weapon against despair, as Junot Díaz reminds us, even when despair seems justifiable; it makes the survival of the end of your world possible: "Only radical hope could have imagined people like us into existence. And I believe that it will help us create a better, more loving future."[16] To hope radically thus means to act amid a logic of war and cultural devastation, enacting effective changes for the next generation.

Teaching practices that are progressive, that ask about the work we want our work to do, allows us to confront trauma, the feeling of loss, that "which slavery took away." It allows both teachers and students to connect and to understand what we do and why we do it. Latinx Studies as a field—as do other ethnic studies fields—exists within a framework of radical hoping, as an antidote to the white-supremacist, exclusionary teaching and learning many of us are still trying to recover from. Whether we are explicit about it or not in our teaching, what we teach demands that students think of themselves as actors and relate to the reading from a personal space, from what Latina feminist writer Cherríe Moraga called "the flesh." When teaching Latinx students and other students of color, it becomes even more urgent to make that relationship with the text explicit, to acknowledge the affective link that exists between subject of study and subject position. That acknowledgement does not distance us from a critical dialogue but rather opens the possibilities for a more sincere critique that leads to action in and out of the classroom. It allows us as teachers to create classroom environments that are free from violence and that guarantee the protection of the most vulnerable, a classroom where collective learning takes precedence over the individual success. The lessons I have learned in the fifteen years I have been teaching Latinx Studies transfer to both my research and my life praxis; they guide my actions and my thoughts both in and out of the classroom. In a path that often pulls us in different directions (from tenure, to faculty meetings, to national conferences) it is easy to lose sight of why we do what we do. Teaching in/for justice, asking ourselves what work we want our work to do, can serve as reminder that there is a goal that connects us all beyond our fields, departments, and individual responsibilities: justice and equality for all human beings.

NOTES

1   bell hooks, *Teaching Community: A Pedagogy of Hope* (New York: Psychology Press, 2003), xiii.

2   Arthur A. Schomburg, "The Negro Digs Up His Past," *The Survey*, March 1, 1925, 231–238, 233.

3   One example is the case of American Studies scholar Steven Salaita, whose tenured job offer from the University of Illinois at Urbana–Champaign was withdrawn due to a controversial tweet Salaita posted in support of Palestine.

4   I am appointed to teach Latinx Studies but there is no department, so I teach my courses within existing units (romance languages, American studies, etc).

5   Students enrolled in my Latinx studies classes have organized to create publications, form organizations, and build community beyond the classroom.

6 The Harvard student body has become more diverse over the last ten years, particularly as the administration has strengthened its commitment to admitting first-generation minority students. An unintended effect of this has been student activism in support of custodial and dining hall workers, who first-generation students of color often perceive as closer to them—or as one student put it: "They are my family."

7 Mathew Rodriguez, "Latino for Trump Supporter Warns of 'Taco Trucks in Every Corner' if Immigration Does Not Get Under Control," *Mic*, September 2, 2016, www.mic.com.

8 The Harvard University campus receives hundreds of tourists per week who visit the yard and line up to take pictures with the Harvard statue. During the performance, many of the tourists became part of the action—some with knowledge, others accidentally.

9 Barbara Tomlinson and George Lipsitz, "American Studies as Accompaniment," *American Quarterly* 65, no. 1 (2013): 1–30.

10 Tomlinson and Lipsitz, "American Studies," 9–10.

11 Barbara Tomlinson and George Lipsitz, "Insubordinate Spaces for Intemperate Times: Countering the Pedagogies of Neoliberalism," *Review of Education, Pedagogy, and Cultural Studies* 35, no. 1 (2013): 3–26, 7.

12 Tomlinson and Lipsitz, "American Studies," 11.

13 Jonathan Lear, *Radical Hope: Ethics in the Face of Cultural Devastation* (Cambridge: Harvard University Press, 2006), 12.

14 Junot Díaz, "Under President Trump, Radical Hope is Our Best Weapon," *The New Yorker*, November 14, 2016, 65.

15 Lear, *Radical Hope*, 117.

16 Díaz, "Under President Trump," 65.

38

On Being a White Person of Color

Using Autoethnography to Understand Puerto Ricans' Racialization

SALVADOR VIDAL-ORTIZ

This is an abridged reprint of a 2004 article, where I utilized my experience as a light skinned Puerto Rican, writing through the fusion of autobiography, theory, and social analyses, to produce a counternarrative to the dominant views on Puerto Ricans and race. It was also a talking back to traditional science making—which often presumes neutral data collection and analysis, that an actual reality can be apprehended through "data," and that findings produce valid, "objective" results (separating knowledge-making into real and fiction, possible and impossible, rational and emotional, logical and illogical, truth and perception or imagination). This autoethnography challenges the negation of experience as contributing to understanding the self and the social.

Reproduced in the *Community Engagement, Critical Methodologies, and Social Justice* section, this chapter—influenced by feminist formations and critical race studies—showcases Puerto Ricans and other Latinas/os in their relation to migration, assimilation, militarization, and linguistic hierarchies of power through a reflexive analysis of emergent themes. As a methodological innovation, it does not avoid the subjective lived experience, but uses pedagogical, activist, and academic lenses to make its claims. As a first generation academic, I found no other way to document the challenges of being unintelligible along the racial, ethnic, and national mechanisms (such as the U.S. Census) to explain militarized experiences that cut across pan-ethnic ethno-racial lines.

Since its publication, changes on Census data collection (e.g., reordering questions on race and ethnicity), and cultural debates (e.g., "White passing," and other categorizations that promote an either/or White/Black reading of Latinas/os) took place, which require more nuanced ways of addressing the complex relationship of militarized and colonized territories, and of showing the dual racial formation systems some populations operate under. For instance, the discussion you are about to read about Vieques in the 1990s/2000s referenced the mined U.S. military base on that Island that concluded in the death of a Puerto Rican guard—Puerto Ricans had been told the bullets utilized in military exercises were harmless. Even now, there are ongoing protests against the U.S. government demanding that environmental waste be cleaned.

Abridged reprint from: *Qualitative Sociology* 27, no. 2 (2004): 179–203.

Introduction

Latino populations in the United States are at a crossroads of race discussions and race making (Almaguer 2003). The experience of racialization is one that combines elements of both ethnic identification and racial difference. Puerto Ricans face a particular relationship to U.S. racial and ethnic categories. Their experience of mass migration for over a century, combined with compulsory U.S. citizenship (Berman Santana 1999), frames Puerto Ricans' participation in U.S. political, social, and economic systems. I explore the tension between racial formation systems from the U.S. and abroad, with a focus on Puerto Rican–identified (and, to a lesser degree, Latino-identified) people's experiences as racialized selves while living in the United States. By arguing an alternative racialization process, in which U.S. racial formations and other countries' racial formations inform each other, I complicate U.S. discussions on "race," ethnicity, and nationality.[1] Thus this chapter is concerned not with comparing racialization models. Instead, it studies the effect of more than one racialization system operating simultaneously in the context of U.S. ethno-racial politics and in the lives of Puerto Ricans and other Latinos.[2]

My use of autoethnography places biography in context, highlighting my sexual orientation, class, and skin color experiences without assuming generalization of such experiences to a whole group of people. While the title draws attention to the experiences of light-skinned Puerto Ricans, I am not implying that all Puerto Ricans think of themselves as white or "are" white. The term "white person of color" does not privilege "white" over "people of color": In English, the noun "person of color" is described/qualified by the adjective "white." As I will illustrate, racialization is a process that unifies Puerto Ricans' racial experiences in the United States, while skin color still operates as a distinct marker of access and treatment. Moreover, by focusing on all Puerto Ricans' racialization in the United States, I am not negating the long history of racism and discrimination toward dark-skinned Puerto Ricans in Puerto Rico: While racism is experienced by dark-skinned individuals in many parts of the world, I am discussing the difference in racial formation systems and how their presence on U.S. soil challenges current U.S. racial analyses. Autoethnography, I argue, is an untapped way of exploring the complexity of issues when studying "race" and ethnicity for Puerto Ricans (and other Latinos).[3]

My argument here emerges out of the explicit tension between structural forces and group responses in forming, maintaining, and reshaping identities. Group identification, when imposed by institutions as structures of domination, can be contested by its members. The U.S. Census is a pertinent example (U.S. Census Bureau 2001a) because it does not simply document, but creates, racial categories (Lee 1993; Nobles 2000; Rodríguez 2000). In U.S. Census 2000, 48 percent of the "Latino" respondents identified as white, but almost as many respondents

(42 percent) noted they were of "some other race" (U.S. Census Bureau 2001b). For those "*unable* to identify with any of these five race categories, the Office of Management and Budget approved including a sixth category—'some other race' . . ." (ibid., p. 3; emphasis added). In fact, most of the Census respondents who said they were of "some other race" were Hispanics. Given the impositions of the Census, it is remarkable that two out of five Latinos challenged U.S. racial *and* ethnic categories that classified them as, for example, "white, of Hispanic origin." By choosing to see themselves as "some other race," Latinos marked their experience in the U.S. differently from that imposed by Census mechanisms. Even before Census 2000, Latinos have contested the very premise of their ethnic label and have self-categorized as a racial group (Almaguer 2003).

My goal is to demonstrate the need for better tools to explain how racial and ethnic identity boundaries accommodate groups not typically associated with each other. In this case, the term "people of color" has become an umbrella for all groups that identify as racial/ethnic minorities. I, however, want to argue that the label "people of color" warrants a more systematic understanding of "race" and ethnic identity for Latinos in general, and for Puerto Ricans in particular. The term "people of color" encompasses experiences of discrimination at an individual, institutional, and structural level. It also allows for discussion of global matters as they relate to territoriality and militarization as colonial/post-colonial strategies of dominance. Therefore, "people of color" is useful in that it steps outside the U.S. territorial/Census boundaries, yet refers to the relationship the U.S. carries to its territories, the rest of the world, and on the mainland. The term refers to African Americans (often including Blacks and Caribbeans), Latinos, Asian/Pacific Islanders, and Native Americans—and only sometimes including Arabs (see, for example, *The Audre Lorde Project*: www.alp.org). Not simply meaning "nonwhite," the term has key uses ranging from political mobilization to coalition building, with much possibility of adding complexity to race/ethnic discussions.[4]

* * *

Autoethnography and "Racial"/Ethnic Analyses

My partner and I lay in bed one morning, at his house; I can hear the river right outside the bedroom window. His and my skin contrast each other—his, a dark brown tone that at times I know I envy; mine, a pale one that shines next to his body. We talk about a trip we are about to make together—in fact, to the (now defunct) National Task Force on AIDS Prevention Conference for Gay and Bisexual Men of Color, later on this year (it is the summer of 1997). I bring up the paleness of my skin, since it is almost inevitable to notice my skin color pressed at his. This skin color has often materialized for me body image issues, because at times it renders how I see myself in the world, invisible. Yet that is a struggle for me: to peacefully live within *my* skin. I wonder if he knows this. In a tone especially or-chestrated, and in a playful manner, he says to me: "Why do you think I like you so much?" I am afraid to ask . . . "Because . . . you are very light-skinned, yet you are a person of color. I get my way both ways." I still remember my reaction to his statement—it has little to do with me, my insecurities and self-image; at the same time, he has just shared with me a complicated desire. Then, a pause . . . and I just let myself run, once again, with the sound of the river . . .

This autoethnographic article, like other autoethnographies, locates indi-vidual experience as an important part of social relations, or "as a form of self-narrative that places the self within a social context" (Reed-Danahay 1997, p. 9). Autoethnographies "turn the eye of the sociological imagination back on the ethnographer" (Clough 2000, p. 179) as they critique the social sciences' sole focus on "subjects" other than ourselves. As feminists have demonstrated, auto-ethnography is creative because it "transform[s] the conditions of knowledge production" (Clough 2000, pp. 172–173, 174). Still, this kind of ethnography/ autobiography also claims an authoritative position instead of disrupting power altogether (Clough 2000; Seale 1999). Dramatic description, native/outsider structures, and a critique of realism and representation practices all are charac-teristics of autoethnographic work (Clough 2000; Reed-Danahay 1997). I write about a variety of experiences and emotions, providing a diversity of tone and reflexivity, in hopes that my work builds on that emergent body of literature.[5]

Specifically, I am using autoethnography to reconceptualize structurally imposed ethnic and racial categorizations (through illustrating everyday inter-action practices where the structural permeates)—activating different types of identities, where a mixture of dominant and subordinate ideas coexist. By using autoethnography, my claim of a distinctive identification—one that contests state and control apparatuses—is a claim for authenticity, for naming that complex identity. The endpoint of this task is to question current identities and to dislo-cate their foundations. My purpose is *not* to add another political category,[6] but to bring up inequality and stratification outside these rigid identity parameters. By using various layers of identification—national (Puerto Rican), pan-ethnic (Latino),[7] and a broader coalition term (people of color), and a physical/pheno-typical (light skin—often read as white)—I attempt to complicate racial binary systems and racialization processes, and to recognize how oppressor/oppressed and native/outsider can indeed be false dichotomies.

Puerto Ricans' Racialization: On Being a Person of Color in Relationship to the United States

August 1994: I moved to Washington, DC, and during my first week after moving permanently to the U.S., I receive a last check from work while a student in Puerto Rico. I come to a cashing place to redeem it. While trying to explain to the teller that I just moved to the U.S.—that being the reason for not having a local ID other than a Puerto Rican drivers' license (and the U.S. passport!)—she *struggles* with my English. With a straight face, she tells me: "Speak English!" That's what I've been doing all along. I revisit this feeling constantly—while in grad school, at work, when meeting a stranger—how my accent is measured, establishing some level of knowledge or capacities. Sometimes a word does not come up—and I swim in my mind, searching for the right way of saying it in English. This is what people in my life-world have learned to recognize as ESL (English as a second language) moments. I still freeze, just like that first week, when a professor, or an employer, or a stranger does not understand what I am saying. I still think twice when speaking publicly—at times lowering my tone, or speaking fast, so that my mistakes are not easily caught.

When a Puerto Rican is seen as part of a U.S. racial extreme—light-skinned or dark-skinned—he/she tends to fall into the racial dichotomy of the United States, although as many as 40 percent of Puerto Ricans identify instead with a "browning" of their identities in the United States, and not with white or Black (Montalvo and Codina 2001; Rodríguez 2000). The ongoing development of a U.S. racialized social order (with its impact on Puerto Rico in the nineteenth century), the occupation of Puerto Rico, and subsequent implementation of "Americanization" during the first half of the twentieth century have contributed to this racialization (Bigler 1999). Furthermore, attempts to impose English education in Puerto Rico early in the twentieth century, and their subsequent failure (Allen 1999), have significantly established a distinct cultural identity from that of the United States. But Puerto Ricans, like other immigrants, experience a challenge in identification when living in the United States—even those who are light-skinned.

* * *

The process of racializing and marking is initiated at various stages: If it is not skin color, or experiences with disempowerment, then it is the contradiction of privileged status as U.S. citizens. And there is always the accent, pronunciation, writing, or comprehension (Lippi-Green 1997; Urciuoli 1996; Zentella 1997). Light-skinned Puerto Ricans become "people of color" in the United States because the term means more than "race"; it now incorporates racialization and displacement as Puerto Ricans. Racial inequality and discrimination are still key elements of the people of color identity. But markers have expanded to include inequality in the context of globalization, colonial nexus, and citizenship contradictions.

Citizenship and Colonialism: *Las dos caras de la moneda*

It is the year 2000. The Treasury office has released the new one-dollar coin. On it, a Native American woman—remembered mostly because of her assistance to the colonizers—is celebrated.[8] I cannot understand, or move beyond the irony, that she is there, on that coin. While touching its curved borders for the first time, I think of Puerto Rico's coasts and beaches, affected by the military bases and daily practices of war—the foundation on which the U.S. stands. I look at her again, and in a similar way I think of the Native American reservations I have visited; the borders can be beautiful (as in mountains) and very imaginary (as borders often are). They are also strong; I see how the curved coin imprisons some in for the benefit of the rest—often demarcating borders is only useful for the one splitting the land . . .

For Puerto Ricans, there is a connection of migration and labor that binds the people in Puerto Rico with the people outside the Island. In addition, there is also the history and current experiences of colonization, first by Spain and, during a hundred-plus years, the United States (Allen 1999). Puerto Rico's sudden citizenship in 1917 with the Jones Law was a perfect venue for cheap labor and the supply of large numbers of "nonwhite" soldiers for World War I (Allen 1999; Berman Santana 1999). "Operation Bootstrap" was the United States' attempt to economically develop the Island. It drew many people to the United States, after the failure of previous attempts to transform the plantation economic system to an industrial one and, later on, from manufacturing to services.

Conferring U.S. citizenship does not compensate for the trade-off of Puerto Rico's exploitation, colonization, and invisibility. The role of citizenship imposition is to mask colonial relations, inverting the coin to make it seem as if Puerto Ricans choose their status. The imposition of military practices in Vieques is probably the most prominent example. Colonization and citizenship are for Puerto Ricans *las dos caras de la moneda* (two sides of the same coin). A subordinate population experiences the process of colonization to its very core. Ironically, economic dependency furthers the colonization, migration, and settlement experiences. Citizenship is indeed not a blessing (Flores 2000).

Cultural anthropologist Ellen Bigler (1999) has argued that Puerto Ricans have more in common with Chicanos, Native Americans, and African Americans than with other Latinos because of their experiences of colonization. Sociologist Juan Flores (2000) also denotes how some Puerto Ricans can find affinity with African Americans due to their dual experience of citizenship and economic displacement. Ramón Grosfoguel, Professor of Ethnic Studies, and Legal and Cultural studies scholar Chloé S. Georas (1996) illustrate the economic disparities that both African Americans and Puerto Ricans experienced, as forced migrations that offered cheaper labor affected the economic ladder in places like New York. And, while sociological discussions on the "immigrant analogy" and "colonized minorities" (Blauner 1972; Glazer and Moynihan 1963) permeated much of racial theorizing in the aftermath of the civil rights movement, African Americans *and* Puerto Ricans continued to be compared to white immigrants in hopes that the former would emulate the newcomers' attempts to achieve economic and social mobility. Such work has been rightfully critiqued on the grounds of not recognizing a distinctive cultural identity; moreover, by focusing on these groups' citizenship, this work obscures the relationship among structural forces, economic conditions, citizenship as limitation, and racial discrimination (Steinberg 1995, pp. 83–86; Grosfoguel and Georas 1996, pp. 193–195). While African Americans and Puerto Ricans share the history of colonial relations and a second-class citizenship experience within the United States, other groups in the United States experience a structural placement in a similar fashion to that of Puerto Ricans.

* * *

Sociologist Michael Pérez (2002) offers a similar picture of another site where the relationship to the United States is also full of contradictions. Specifically talking about the Chamorros—the name designating people from Guam—Perez describes the ambiguity that Chamorros experience in the United States, as their association with the category "Asian" makes them virtually invisible; this, as mainstream stereotypes of Asian people are far from associative to Chamorros. Chamorros were given congressional U.S. citizenship as residents of Guam in 1950. Due in part to this legislative decree, they currently make up the third-largest group of Pacific Islanders in the United States. With about half of the Island's land being utilized for U.S. military forces, Guam's population is entrenched in massive migration patterns with the United States, including military enrollment.

I suggest that Puerto Ricans share a similar experience of colonization, territorialization, and militarization with the people of much of the occupied Pacific jurisdictions, more so than with most Latin Americans. Take the case of Puerto Rico and Guam. Both experienced U.S. colonization in the late 1800s; both have had great areas of land occupied by the military; and both are U.S. territories—although with no permanent ties. Guam's government even explored, but was not granted, the same political designation of commonwealth that Puerto Rico has had for over fifty years (Pérez 2002). Both are economically dependent on the United States, although that was not always the case. Residents of both islands travel as U.S. citizens and experience rates of Americanization that are significantly higher than those of other immigrants. Similar relations have been documented between Puerto Rico and the Philippines, Guam, the U.S. Virgin Islands, American Samoa, the Northern Mariana Islands and/or Hawai'i (Berman Santana 1999; Morín 2000; Rivera Ortiz and Ramos 2001).

Thus, the "people of color" label, which is dependent on, but has the capability of transcending, pan-ethnic ideologies, offers us a malleable opportunity for renegotiation and rearticulation of racial/colonial relations. These malleable categories (African American, Latino, Asian/Pacific Islander, and Native American) within the "people of color" umbrella term, however problematic in representing the realities of its members, offer possibilities for alliances based on similarities other than culture or language. Moreover, these potential alliances give rise to a newer conceptualization of people of color, one that recognizes alliances within as well as between categories. I conclude with some remarks addressing these possibilities.

Conclusion: Re-writing Racial Systems and Exploring Coalitional Possibilities

Racialization processes need to be central to "race" discussions in the United States. Given the constant change in racialized dynamics, racialization offers multiple venues to connect issues of discrimination based on ethnic, racial, national, or religious affiliation or identity. Much of the basis of my arguments has been the racialization of "people of color." Yet whites are also a racialized group in the current U.S. racial order (Martinot 2003), although whiteness is not "racialized as subordinate" (Ahmad 2002). Returning to the U.S. Census, Middle Easterners are identified as "white," and are not covered under a minority status as are African Americans, Latinos, Asians, and Native Americans. The last twenty or so years have influenced the American imagery of Middle Easterners. The terrorist events of September 11, 2001, solidified the continuous marking of Arabs, Muslims, and South Asians as others—and with it, discrimination moved away from color as a main factor and toward issues like nationalism and religious beliefs. The backlash attacks on people of Middle Eastern descent concretized this sentiment. While the imagery had already settled, a large process taking place as a result of the 9/11 events reordered racial positions in the U.S. (Ahmad 2002).

* * *

In Closing: Autoethnography and the Study of "Race"

Autoethnography assists in illustrating how personal biographies are linked to larger structural and institutional constraints. Autoethnography helps uncover the complexities of racialization while contextualizing regional racial formations. It has helped me to link my own experiences to theoretical ideas that only partially explore U.S. racialization, and to connect globalization and militarization to the study of "race." I have shared many instances where I felt powerless around identification. There are other moments where I posit the challenges of recognizing that Puerto Rican-ness does not exclude the enactment of oppression while also recognizing that light-skinned Puerto Ricans are also recipients of discrimination. It is this complexity that merits attention, and autoethnographic scholarship will undoubtedly open the door for more of such discussions. With the idea of being a white person of color, I have explored both native and outsider, and oppressor and oppressed as incomplete pieces of the puzzle. Intense narrative, with challenges to representation and discomfort about uneasy topics, is one of the ways in which autoethnography achieves thought anew. Autoethnography will continue to be a tool to demystify the use of the "personal" to discuss and theorize on social relations, to teach race and ethnicity, and to address social inequalities.

NOTES

1 Using the term "race" in quotation marks reflects the problems with its multiple interpretations; others have considered a similar use . . . I focus on "race" because it figures heavily as a category of discussion in the U.S. Yet I am not attempting to solidify the term "race" as *the* defining category of a person . . . even though I aim at suspending the terms commonly used to refer to "race," at times I depend on them as necessary to my argument. Thus, while the terms "white" and "people of color" are actively contested, I use, for purposes of this analysis, seemingly homogeneous categories: "Puerto Ricans," "United Staters," and "Westerners," and do not destabilize them as they should be. (A particular problematic slippage is my use of "white" and "light-skinned" interchangeably—which I address throughout the article.)

2 Racial systems in the U.S. focus on a Black/white, one-drop rule framework. In Latin America, other elements are involved, including a stronger Indigenous background, socioeconomic status, familial social position and citizenship, as well as racial classifications between Black and white (Montalvo and Codina 2001; Rodríguez 2000—see also Wade 1997 and Graham 1990). Work focusing on Puerto Rican experiences of "race" can be found in that of Rodríguez, most notably her (2000) book; for historical discussions on racialization, refer to Grosfoguel and Georas (1996) and Santiago-Valles (1996).

3 *Autobiographical* work has already been utilized in describing Puerto Ricans' racial and racialized experiences in the past. For instance, academic writings, such as those of Grosfoguel and Georas (1996), Flores (2000), and Almaguer (2003) all cite the autobiographic work of Caribbean and other Latinos that identify their own racial experiences in relation to U.S. racialization. Another pertinent racial autobiographical writing can be found in Cherríe Moraga's "La Güera" (1983a).

4 For a critical engagement of the concept "women of color," refer to Anzaldúa and Moraga (1983). For a discussion of *Bridge*'s impact and its limitations, refer to Alarcón (1990) and Moraga (1983b). For a different exploration of the people of color possibilities through the idea of *latinidad*, affective excess, and a continuation of the work of radical women of color by gay men of color (a project Moraga herself [1983b] commented on, and seemed encouraged by), refer to Muñoz's (2000) "Feeling Brown" article.

5 For influential autoethnographies/autoethnographers, refer to Carolyn Ellis (1995, 1999) and Ellis and Bochner (1996), as well as the work by Norman K. Denzin, Laurel Richardson, and Mary Louise Pratt. For the relationship between autobiography, ethnography and

autoethnography, refer to Reed-Danahay (1997). . . . although not self-titled authoethno-graphic, the work of Lâm (1994)—especially her use of stories to generate a reflexive analysis of her relationship to (and her position within) feminism—highly influenced some of my writing. Note a similarity between Anzaldúa and Moraga's (1983) framework and Lâm's critiques of feminism as either an Anglo project or "Western"—and thus problematic in terms of the authority of a feminist project of liberation contrasting with priorities and situations faced by immigrants of color.

6 In the past ten years, multiracial people and organizations have challenged the idea of simplistic racial categorizations—and more importantly, the notion of a single obligatory choice from an array of racial identifications that apply to people (Root 1992). This challenge has taken many forms—among them, a proposal to add a "multiracial" category to the U.S. census was suggested, well received, and incorporated in the early 1990s. Although the addition of biracial/multiracial options on the census responds to individual identity choice and, by its mere existence, complicates U.S. racial discourses, we have yet to see the damages in utilizing these multiple options in census categorization (its operational-ization and economic redistribution) in the political and economic terrain. This point was well illustrated in the 2003 Lillie and Nathan Ackerman lecture on Justice and Equality in America, held by Baruch College's School of Public Affairs on April 30, 2003. There, former U.S. Census Bureau Director, Dr. Kenneth Prewitt, discussed the political charges behind the changes in the "race" categories (Prewitt [2005]).

7 The concept of pan-ethnicity has been discussed at length (Espiritu 1992; Flores 2000; López and Espiritu 1990), and its emergence has been noted as a consequence of the civil rights struggle (Omi 1996). Defined as the generalization of solidarity among ethnic subgroups, pan-ethnicity and ethnicity are different constructs (Espiritu 1992). The main criticism of pan-ethnicity is the homogenization of peoples from diverse religious, ethnic and language communities. For instance, Espiritu illustrates how pan-ethnicity incorporates colonized people, refugees, documented and undocumented immigrants, and second-, third- and fourth-generation U.S. citizens. Pan-ethnicity also ignores language differences, class statuses, and cultures. While Omi asserts that pan-ethnicity is "driven by a dynamic relationship between the specific group being racialized and the state" (1996, p. 180), labels such as "pan-Asian" and "pan-Latino" are created in part because of the political necessity of forming such coalitions. ("Pan-Latino" is a not-so-new term indicating cohesiveness among various culture- or language-sharing communities [Flores 2000]; we also know that the term did not originate in the North [Alcoff 2000]). Pan-ethnicity can, on the other hand, create turf between the four recognized minority groups in the United States (African American, Asian, Latino, and Native American), as the necessity to retain and police boundaries benefits both the leading groups within those factions and the state.

8 The inscription on the coin reads: "This is the Sacagawea dollar, commemorating the Shoshone Indian woman who served from 1804 to 1806 as guide and translator to the Lewis and Clark expedition as it trekked across the high Rockies and continental divide to the Pacific coast." (Visit www.findarticles.com/cf_dls/m1061/3_108/56744989/p1/article.jhtml for the article discussing the history of the U.S. government's use of American Indians on its currency.)

REFERENCES

Ahmad, M. (2002). Homeland insecurities: Racial violence the day after September 11. *Social Text, 72*, 101–115.

Alarcón, N. (1990). The theoretical subject(s) of *This bridge called my back* and Anglo-American feminism. In G. Anzaldúa (Ed.), *Making face, making soul—haciendo caras: Creative and critical perspectives by feminists of color* (pp. 356–369). San Francisco: Aunt Lute Foundation Books.

Alcoff, L. M. (2000). Is Latina/o identity a racial identity? In J. J. E. Gracia & P. De Greiff (Eds.), *Hispanics/Latinos in the United States: Ethnicity, race, and rights* (pp. 23–44). New York: Routledge.

Allen, T. W. (1999). "Race" and "ethnicity": History and the 2000 Census. *Cultural Logic: An Electronic Journal of Marxist Theory & Practice, 3*, (http://eserver.org/clogic/3-1&2/allen.html).

Almaguer, T. (2003). At the crossroads of race: Latino/a studies and race making in the United States. In J. Poblete (Ed.), *Critical Latin American and Latino Studies* (pp. 206–222). Minneapolis: University of Minnesota Press.

Anzaldúa, G., & Moraga, C. (Eds.) (1983). *This bridge called my back: Radical writings by women of color*. New York: Kitchen Table Press.

Berman Santana, D. (1999). *No somos únicos*: The status issue from Manila to San Juan. *CENTRO: Center for Puerto Rican Studies Journal, 11*, 127–140.

Bigler, E. (1999). *American conversations: Puerto Ricans, white ethnics, and multicultural education*. Philadelphia: Temple University Press.

Blauner, B. (1972). *Racial oppression in America*. New York: Harper & Row.

Clough, P. T. (2000). *Autoaffection: Unconscious thought in the age of teletechnology*. Minneapolis: University of Minnesota Press.

Ellis, C. (1995). *Final negotiations*. Philadelphia: Temple University Press.

Ellis, C. (1999). He(art)ful autoethnography. *Qualitative Health Research, 9*, 653–667.

Ellis, C., & Bochner, A. P. (Eds.) (1996). *Composing ethnography: Alternative forms of qualitative writing*. Walnut Creek, CA: Altamira Press.

Espiritu, Y. L. (1992). *Asian American pan-ethnicity: Bridging institutions and identities*. Philadelphia: Temple University Press.

Flores, J. (2000). *From bomba to hip-hop: Puerto Rican culture and Latino identity*. New York: Columbia University Press.

Glazer, N., & Moynihan, D. P. (1963). *Beyond the melting pot: The Negroes, Puerto Ricans, Jews, Italians, and Irish of New York City*. Cambridge: MIT Press.

Graham, R. (Ed.) (1990). *The idea of race in Latin America, 1870–1940*. Austin: University of Texas Press.

Grosfoguel, R., & Georas, C. (1996). The racialization of Latino Caribbean immigrants in the New York metropolitan area. *CENTRO: Journal of the Center for Puerto Rican Studies, 8*, 190–201.

Lâm, M. C. (1994). Feeling foreign in feminism. *SIGNS: Journal of Women in Culture and Society, 19*, 865–893.

Lee, S. M. (1993). Racial classifications in the U.S. Census: 1890–1990. *Ethnic and Racial Studies, 16*, 75–94.

Lippi-Green, R. (1997). *English with an accent: Language, ideology, and discrimination in the United States*. New York: Routledge.

López, D., & Espiritu, Y. (1990). Pan-ethnicity in the United States: A theoretical framework. *Ethnic and Racial Studies, 13*, 198–224.

Martinot, S. (2003). *The rule of racialization: Class, identity, governance*. Philadelphia: Temple University Press.

Montalvo, F. F., & Codina, G. E. (2001). Skin color and Latinos in the United States. *Ethnicities, 1*, 321–341.

Moraga, C. (1983a). La güera. In G. Anzaldúa & C. Moraga (Eds.), op cit. (pp. 27–34).

Moraga, C. (1983b). Refugees of a world on fire: Foreword to the second edition. In Anzaldúa & Moraga, op cit.

Morín, J. L. (2000). Indigenous Hawaiians under statehood: Lessons for Puerto Rico. *CENTRO: Journal of the Center for Puerto Rican Studies, 11*, 5–25.

Muñoz, J. (2000). Feeling brown: Ethnicity and affect in Ricardo Bracho's *The Sweetest Hangover (and Other STDs)*. *Theatre Journal, 52*, 67–79.

Nobles, M. (2000). *Shades of citizenship: Race and the census in modern politics*. Stanford: Stanford University Press.

Omi, W. (1996). Racialization in the post-civil rights era. In A. F. Gordon & C. Newfield (Eds.), *Mapping multiculturalism* (pp. 178–186). Minneapolis and London: University of Minnesota Press.

Pérez, M. (2002). Pacific Identities beyond US racial Formations: the Case of Chamorro Ambivalence and Flux. *Social Identities* 8, 3: 457–79.

Prewitt, K. [2005]. The Census counts, the Census classifies. In N. Foner & G. M. Fredrickson (Eds.), *Not just black and white: Historical and contemporary perspectives on immigration, race, and ethnicity in the United States*. New York: Russell Sage.

Reed-Danahay, D. E. (Ed.) (1997). *Auto/ethnography: Rewriting the self and the social*. New York: Oxford.

Rivera Ortiz, A. I., & Ramos, A. G. (2001). *Islands at the crossroads: Politics in the non-independent Caribbean*. Boulder: Lynne Pienner Publishers.

Rodríguez, C. E. (2000). *Changing race: Latinos, the census, and the history of ethnicity in the United States*. New York: New York University Press.

Root, M. P. P. (1992). *Racially mixed people in America*. Newbury Park, CA: Sage Publications.

Santiago-Valles, K. (1996). Policing the crisis in the whitest of all the Antilles. *CENTRO: Journal of the Center for Puerto Rican Studies, 8*, 42–55.

Seale, C. (1999). *The quality of qualitative research*. London: Sage Publications.

Steinberg, S. (1995). *Turning back: The retreat from racial justice in American thought and policy*. Boston: Beacon Press.

U.S. Census Bureau (2001a). *The Hispanic population* (B. Guzmán). U.S. Department of Commerce, Economics and Statistics Administration, May (www.census.gov.population/socdemo/Hispanic).

U.S. Census Bureau (2001b). *Overview of race and Hispanic origin* (E. M. Grieco & R. C. Cassidy). U.S. Department of Commerce, Economics and Statistics Administration, March.

Urciuoli, B. (1996). *Exposing prejudice: Puerto Rican experiences of language, race, and class*. Boulder: Westview Press, Inc.

Wade, P. (1997). *Race and ethnicity in Latin America*. London: Pluto Press.

Zentella, A. C. (1997). *Growing up bilingual: Puerto Rican children in New York*. Malden, MA: Blackwell Publishers, Inc.

39

Brujx

An Afro-Latinx Queer Gesture

AISHA M. BELISO-DE JESÚS

My dream, a gift from spirit, reminds me that I am indeed engaged in "curandera work," healing work. My tools are my words. The tools of neither the oppressed nor the oppressor "locked in mortal combat," but simultaneously of and beyond both in the creation of a third transformative space. Standing in rigid opposition is a strategy for survival, but this strategy has also killed us and will continue to sever our souls and assail our hearts.
—Irene Lara, *Healing Sueños for Academia* (2002, 2)

Hector La Woke,[1] a queer, Afro-Latinx gender-nonconforming priest of Afro-Cuban Santeria who lives between the Bronx, New York, and Bayamón, Puerto Rico, cut down the middle of a cow's tongue and placed a picture of Donald Trump in the center. Using scented oils made for spells to target enemies, Hector poured nine drops of "Overcome Bully" oil (*Amanza Guapo*), and "I Can More Than You" oil (*Yo Puedo Mas Que Tu*) on Trump's paper face. Stabbing the flesh with twenty-one pins, they sutured Trump's face inside. The tongue was placed on Hector's spiritual cauldron and covered with a red cloth. On the third day, Hector took the tongue to a graveyard and nailed it to a tree. Hector was one of nine people across the country performing this spiritual action after the election of Donald Trump to the US presidency. Hector is among a growing group of witches of color who identify as "brujx" (pronounced bru-hex), a gender-nonconforming mobilization that is taking shape in the age of social media activism and organizing. Similar to the move that reconfigures the gender-binary term Latino/a into Latinx,[2] "brujx" queers the Spanish word for witch/sorcerer, "bruja/o." Brujx has also become popular through social media hashtags.[3]

Drawing on research with a relatively new and loosely formed unnamed collective of brujx who live in the United States and the Caribbean, I explore the different ways they are mobilizing spiritual hexes or "brujxing" (bru-hexing) as a form of political activism. This collective has joined many others who are employing alternative forms of justice and activism. For example, they began to actively conjure against white supremacy in 2014, when they bru-hexed George Zimmerman, the racist half-Peruvian white Hispanic who was acquitted of the

February 26, 2012, killing of Black teenager Trayvon Martin, who he racially profiled, stalked, and then murdered in Florida. Some of my interlocutors then subsequently joined others to brujx high-profile white fascists, misogynists, and other xenophobic right-wing leaders such as Supreme Court Justice Brett Kavanaugh, who was accused of rape before ascending to the highest court in the country, and former Attorney General Jeff Sessions, whose cruel anti-immigrant policies brought a new level of fear and intimidation to Latino/a/x immigrant communities in the United States. Some of the brujx in this collective discussed their work with me as part of an Afro-Latinx spiritual activist component of the larger global movement for Black lives. Equally compelling is that brujx are not only activating Afro-Latinx and Indigenous ritual knowledges in their practices, they are also employing queer of color feminist scholarship in their collective rituals and spiritual philosophies.

This chapter examines the spiritual dialogues of brujx as a form of Afro-Latinx activist magic and warfare.[4] I show how brujx are in dialogue with schol- arly "sources" that is, the writings (and spirits) of academic scholars—dead and alive—who are activated and whose scholarship is animated in spiritual ways. It explores the brujx conjurings of Audre Lorde, Octavia Butler, Gloria Anzaldua, and other queer feminist scholars, not merely through metaphor, but also in ritual and practice. This essay is an opportunity to bring the scholarly writings of women of color feminists into critical dialogue with the spiritual inspirations that have emerged from our writings. These scholarly and spiritual intimacies can be thought of through what Gloria's Anzaldúa (1987) describes of as "spiritual activism," a frame of conjure that mobilizes cultural heritage, decolonial approaches, and queer feminist resources for survival and futurity. Brujx as spiritual activism similarly animates the queer feminist aesthetic and languaging power of the bioenergetic magic of words: intentionality, networking, and spirit forces in tandem. Through social media and spiritual magic, I show how *Blacktino/a/x* hexings (African American, Afro-Latinx, and other Black and Brown intimacies) are thus part of a long tradition of queer of color feminist scholarly/activist alchemy.[5]

Nourishment

Hector La Woke tells me that Audre Lorde, Gloria Anzaldúa, and James Baldwin are their "abuelx brujx," their witchy spiritual grandparents.[6] Hector has pictures of these dead scholars on the ancestor altar (*boveda*) and Hector reads their poems and essays during seances (*misas espirituales*), calling upon their spirits to assist Hector in fighting the battle against homophobia, sexism, anti-Blackness, xenophobia, and white supremacy. Like Hector, the brujx collective was made up of other Black, Latinx queer conjurers who also found the heterosexism and racism of Afro-Cuban and Afro-Haitian religions difficult to navigate. All of the brujx I have worked with were trained in different spiritual and religious techniques. As someone born and raised in African diasporic religions in the United States, I knew a few of the brujx from growing up. Others worked with me previously and were interlocutors who I conducted research with for many years in New York City, Miami, the San Francisco Bay Area, Los Angeles, as well as in Puerto Rico and Cuba. Some of the brujx knew each other for many years, while others only met each other through my research.

A number of the brujx I work with are initiated priests of Santeria and Vodou and have undergone extensive apprenticeships with elders in their spiritual fields; however, they have restructured their practices through queer of color feminist writings as a way to combat racism, sexism, homophobia, and heteronormativity in their traditions and in the world. Prior to taking on the gender-nonconforming term "brujx," many had already considered themselves "bruja feminists," which, since at least the 1960s, has drawn upon African, Asian, and Indigenous-inspired epistemologies, pagan spellcrafting, herbology, New Age Spiritism, and other spiritual healing techniques such as Reiki, Qi Gong, and hypnotism, with a Black womanist and Latina/Chicana feminist theological (*mujerista*) groundings. Four of the seven practitioners in the collective were introduced to feminist writings in college, majoring in Africana, Ethnic, and Latino/a Studies, as well as Women's Studies. Indeed, bruja feminism is a way of life for many women of color scholar-activists, artists, witches, and poets who are committed to what Chicana scholar Laura Pérez (2007, 21–22) has described as "spirit work." Recognizing women's writing as a form of spellcraft that wields powerful interventions through the practice of telling or *hexen*, brujx follows this tradition of "literary witchcraft" (Kitaiskaia 2017) enacted through on and offline incantations.

The loose collective of brujx that I follow here came together when a few people in the collective started reading the Black feminist self-help book by Adrian Maree Brown, *Emergent Strategies: Shaping Change, Changing Worlds* (2017). *Emergent Strategies* is a poetic radical manual that has turned into a networking and organizational strategy for activist groups. Inspired by the rhizomatic, electric philosophy and writings of Afro-futurist science fiction writer Octavia Butler, *Emergent Strategies* offers a radical vision of unity as a model for activism and organizing based in tracing nature, animals, and energy as inspiration and connectivity. Not beholden to standard punctuation nor sentence structure, *Emergent Strategies* defies definition, moving fluidly from topic, to metaphor, to strategy, to spell:

> This is a nonlinear spell. Cast it inside your heart, cast it between yourself and any devil. Cast it into the parts of you still living. Remember you are water. Of course you leave salt trails. Of course you are crying. Flow. (Brown 2017, Location No. 1659)

I followed up with Hector about how they incorporate queer feminists in their brujx. Hector then texted me a link to www.Blackpast.org website, which has an open source to self-described Black lesbian warrior poet Audre Lorde's powerful 1981 speech, "The Uses of Anger: Women Responding to Racism." "This is the Shit I'm talking about," Hector tells me, referencing how they draw on Lorde as spiritual guide to channel anger into warfare.[7] Hector identified with Lorde's critique of how white feminists expected her to teach them how to deal with their own rage in her seminal text. "When she [Lorde] says, 'I do not exist to feel her anger for her,' I was like, 'Yes, Queen! Preach Puta!'" Hector tells me.

In "The Uses of Anger," Lorde discusses how every woman of color has a "well-stocked arsenal of anger potentially useful against" personal and institutional oppression, "which brought that anger into being." Lorde continues, "Focused with precision it can become a powerful source of energy serving progress and change." Hector harnesses this rage in hexings by releasing the anger into the spell and calling on the elder feminists of color as spiritual guides to fight the oppression they are targeting. Before Hector had become gender nonconforming, they felt like they had to rein themself in—performing a form of gendered "respectability." Allowing out the rage has allowed for Hector to focus. Hector texts me, "As Lorde says, 'Anger is loaded with information and energy.'"

There is a number of brujx who sell charms, potions, and other magical items online. Hector disagrees with this practice, as Hector believe that brujx energy shouldn't be commercialized. Nevertheless, you can still buy candles that specialize in ridding someone of "toxic machismo" or herbal bath mixtures, rubs, and oils that bring out your "inner brujx."

Yamileth, a US-born practitioner of Afro-Latinx and Asian descent living in the Los Angeles area, sells potions, candles, baths, and soaps to calm the body, mind, and spirit and allow people to fight oppression through her online social media. She has been part of collective hexings and organizes around Black cis and trans women's rights globally. Yamileth combines a number of Indigenous healing practices and draws on protection from Afro-Caribbean healing copresences (ancestors, Orisha, lwa, and other energies) in her rituals. Yamileth describes how Octavia Butler was a big influence in her own brujx philosophy that came both from her family's Asian background and her Afro-Caribbean heritage: "The Xenogenesis books really impacted my thoughts on race and gender, and humanity," she tells me, about the trilogy also known as *Lilith's Brood*. Playing with topics of DNA, race, alien breeding, and colonization,[8] the series follows Lilith Iyapo, a Black woman salvaged by aliens because humans are an extinct species. When Lilith is awakened 250 years after earth is left uninhabitable from human violence and destruction, she must contend with the Oankali aliens' expectation to breed her because of her unique DNA. This series reveals how Butler envisions strategies for social change, where she shows how humans must not become comfortable with their earthly limitations, but instead be willing to always reexamine their propensity toward violence and constantly create new solutions (Stickgold-Sarah 2010, 428–9). Yamileth discusses how this principle of evolution and self-modification is something that she incorporates into her ritual healings. For example, she uses a tantric-style "healing souls" technique to cure past generations and ancestors, which she sees as similar to Butler's call for an "evolution" of humanity's limitations. For $121 sessions, Yamileth guides a person's spirit "out of their body" to "heal them and [their] ancestors," and then successfully returns them to the body to complete their "spiritual evolution" on Earth that she describes as similar to how the Oankali aliens "fixed" human DNA to not reproduce its propensity for violence.

Yamileth understands her work as part of a broader momentum of "Black girl magic," which is also a viral social media hashtag that promotes Black women and girls' strategies of survival as magical and miraculous. She tells me, "I mean, cis and trans Black women and girls, we got to develop our magic . . . it's the only way [to survive]. The planet is dying, we are dying. And by Black I mean diasporic Blacks, all Black people, everywhere." When I mentioned to her some Black feminist critiques of the social media hashtag #BlackGirlMagic, she had already read up on it, telling me that what is circulated online is mostly about the visual politics that relies too heavily upon beauty, glamor, and slender, able bodies. Yamileth, to my surprise, recommended I read the work of Black feminist literary scholar Jalondra Davis. She directed me that Davis had pointed out that we must be careful to not render Black Girl Magic in such a way that it reinscribes "a 'strong black woman' narrative that trivializes black women's pain and demands their labor rather than addressing the conditions that necessitate their allegedly super human strength" (2018, 13–14). Following Davis' guidance, Yamileth tells me that she sees the healing "gift" of Black Girl Magic as a "calling . . . but it shouldn't be a burden." She is careful to replenish herself when she does any healing work either on or offline, and any time she teaches other people of color, she cautions that it can't always be "taking, taking, taking" from us. "We need to nourish ourselves too." Indeed, brujx take up academic work in queer ways. As we explore more next, for feminist scholars of color in particular, it is important to recognize how our work is engaged and circulated philosophically and ontologically.

Reciprocity

Sarah, a light-skinned African American priestess, artist, and dancer who also teaches dance classes at various universities, said that while in college she was introduced to the writings of queer Chicana scholar Gloria Anzaldúa. Sarah disagrees with the social media aspects of brujx-ing and does not like the way in which magic is mobilized online "like a spectacle." Although she participates in collective ritual hexings, she feels strongly that social media technology is an "evil" Western/Christian imposition that colonizes how people interact with each other. She's concerned about the connective tissue of society, which is being harmed by the circulation of what she describes as the "hyper-visual energy movement" of the internet.

As a heterosexual woman of color, Sarah is inspired by the decolonial healing technologies in the work of Gloria Anzaldúa's *Borderlands* (1987, 103), what the author herself describes as a "morphogenesis" or an "inevitable unfolding." This transformative model for society uses Coatlicue, the feminine serpent goddesses' movement of transformation from Nahautl philosophies, as her understanding of spiritual *mestizaje* (mixing). Sarah was especially taken with Anzaldúa's acknowledgment that for women of color, spirituality was not some romantic excursion into Otherness but a radical politics of urgency and survival. "They [the ancestors; including the spirit of Anzaldúa] speak through . . . They guide me and speak through me," Sarah says of her artistic inspirations. Sarah has been visited by Gloria Anzaldúa's spirit, who has shown her how to draw inspiration for decolonial healing. Sarah adds:

> This really pushed me to get back to my ancestors and heal myself, generationally— and not just throw people away. How the white feminists do that. But like the Combahee [River Collective] elders taught us, we can't do that. We can't afford to do that. We need to heal all our people. We need to heal All Our Relations. And it's the spiritual mixing that she [Anzaldúa] talks about. For us to be able to go to those things that work and not bother with the stuff that doesn't [work].

Sarah honors the Black feminist critique launched by the Combahee River Collective (1977) statement, which decries how white liberal feminists urge women of color to purge themselves of patriarchy by ridding themselves of men.[9] This is what I describe of as a form of "disposability politics," where some liberal feminists urge (cisgendered) women that "they" don't "need" men.[10] Sarah pushes back on this type of disposability, by reclaiming the need to heal "all" her relations. As a cisgender woman married to a cisgender man who herself suffered through molestation as a child, she has had a difficult road to this philosophy. She describes how "we must even include abusers," those Black and Brown men who also suffer through the traumas of slavery, white supremacy and structural racism, and who are colonized by patriarchy. Specifically addressing the intimate sexual violence of patriarchy in families, Sarah tells me we have to heal people, "like my uncle Joe . . . who was molested as a boy and grew up to be an abuser."

Mateo, one of the few cisgender, heterosexual men who participated in the hexings against white supremacy, is of Central American background, lives in the greater Bay Area, and considers himself "queer friendly." As a formerly incarcerated man who became a priest of Santeria to help his luck before he went to prison for a year, he recognizes the importance of alternative forms of justice.

He believes that Afro-Latinx religions offer a way out of the "eye for an eye" mentality that we see in the current carceral system and in society more broadly. Although he did not mention the feminist scholars of color that he was drawing upon by name, many of the ideas that Mateo echoed sounded quite familiar to me. For instance, he described himself as a "male intersectional feminist" (using critical race scholar Kimberlé Crenshaw's term) who practiced Santeria in a "queer-friendly" way that did not "reproduce anti-Blackness, sexism or homophobia." When I asked him about where he learned this from, he discussed how these ideas were part of the activist circles he worked with as a prison abolitionist and priest and that he had taken some Women's Studies courses at San Francisco State University that really helped him clarify "patriarchy" and "the prison industrial complex." Mateo believes that the Orisha can assist in spiritual activism to combat structural racism. For example, he is part of another Bay Area group who have begun to use Santeria rituals to appease the spirits of young Black and Brown people killed by police violence. This group, of mostly elder African American Santeria priests, advocates for a noncarceral form of justice and African understandings of reciprocity. They draw on the all-seeing powers of the Àjé, mystical witch bird of Yoruba philosophies, to combat police brutality.[11] This "great mother warrior" energy beholds all, exacting judgement through electrocution, death, sickness, or misfortune (Washington 2014, 90).

As we see, there are many forms of energetic mobilization that are accomplished in spiritual activism. Through the honing of what Anzaldúa describes of as *la facultad*, that is, the exercising of our spiritual epistemologies as a resource of power to fight back, many brujx and brujx-adjacent activists expertly draw on ritual justice. Sasha, an African American queer brujx from Southern California, tells me that "writing is magic." A gender-fluid person, Sasha has an MFA and teaches creative writing courses in a high school as well as does poetry workshops for children as a side job. Sasha discusses how we sometimes forget the power of words—literature and poetry as part of spells and curses. By acknowledging writing and scholarship as itself a form of magic, Sasha mobilizes a queer Afro-Latinx sensibility to their (plural self) feminist praxis. In doing so, however, Sasha also critiques the presumed secularity of feminist writings, particularly those writings of Black and Latinx women of color. Sasha draws on how Anzaldúa identifies that writing can be used as an examination and a diagnosis of colonization as well as an embodied tool toward decolonization (Delgadillo 2011, 7–8). In this formula, decolonization is an existential futurity, a "site of Coatlique" (Delgadillo 2011, 7–8), where the feminine serpent goddess of death and rebirth transforms into new consciousness.

Healing herself from the alienating violence of academia, bruja-scholar Irene Lara describes how she has brought her spiritual practices into her scholarship. Lara offers the strategy of healing *sueños* (dreams) to suture the false mind/body divide that enacts a cosmic rupturing that impedes collective work. Academia itself, she rightly notes, is a disconcerting process of fragmentation—it disembodies the psychic and spiritual network of people, their bodies, and their communities, and if left within its Western paradigm, it can continue to colonize the spiritual strengths and wisdom of scholars of color. Lara asks what if her "scholarship has been a prayer all along?" and calls for a philosophical approach to scholarship that returns the alchemy of words to the site of prayer/magic. In her essay she provides healing *sueños*, or aspirational offerings that can be heard by the cosmos (Lara 2002, 437):

> May these words heal the de-spiritualization of the academy
> May these words heal the de-politicization of the spiritual
> May these words heal the de-eroticization of the body, mind, and spirit
> May these words heal our separation from ourselves, each other, and the visible and invisible world
> May these words "transfix us with love," so together we, will soar
> In Lak Ech

As bruja/x feminists have taught us, these healing techniques should not be a mortal combat but instead a fight for love that enables survival where there is genocide and debilitation. In academia we must recognize how our research is in spiritual conversations—being taken up in queer ways and applied in everyday failures, futures, and longings. Even as most of my interlocutors were introduced to feminism in academia and incorporated these teachings in their spirituality, it is not a singular experience but rather a movement of the energy that emerges from the writing itself. Across the country people are organizing read-ins of *Emergent Strategies* and the Octavia Butler books and circulating the work of Audre Lorde and Gloria Anzaldúa as ancestors. These practices can allow us to think of our scholarship as itself forms of alchemy, conjure, prayer, radical reciprocity, and enchanting incantations. Black feminist anthropologist and doula Dana-Ain Davis similarly calls for this type of recognition when she discusses how our citation practices are themselves forms of spiritual activism.[12] She discusses the importance of citing Black women's work in particular, and how we might understand the work of citational practice as a form of reciprocity and relationality. Taking up these inspirations, we can think of scholarship and citation as a form of spiritual work and incantation.

Conclusion: Momentum

Let us recall Sarah's assertion that women of color feminists cannot afford to reproduce a disposability politics that does not serve to actually heal the disease of colonialism. Rather than canceling people who are sick by toxic machismo and white supremacist patriarchy, brujx consider alternative forms of justice that are not modeled on carceral Christian logics of "eye for an eye." Sarah describes how brujx draw on this energy as a way to counter everyday hostilities from microaggressions, insults, and intimate partner abuse to outright physical attacks, police brutality, poverty, illness, and death. Through potions, spells, powders, ritual acts, writing, and incantations, these techniques of justice permeate and penetrate spaces and bodies, lives and institutions.

Brujx offers healing techniques that are acts of love and justice; they are strategies to deal with violence in a noncarceral and accountable way. Drawing from queer Cubana feminist scholar Juana María Rodríguez (2014), I see brujxing as *queer gestures* or "amorous gifts" that reach out and manipulate how matter and energy flow in the world. As a form of spiritual activism, brujx gestures intervene, push, block, and open social forces in the material world, but they are also ephemeral; they leave no trace. These queer gestures are what Rodriguez describes of as intimate politics for a futurity that is at the interstices of "utopian longings and everyday failures." They hold the offer of queer friendship and love and nondisposable justice with open cupped hands. Modeled after a radical politics of transformation, similar to that of trans activist Dean Spade's call for a "critical trans politics," brujx is a queer healing-centered warfare that dares to imagine a future "of a world without imprisonment, colonialism, immigration enforcement, sexual violence, or wealth disparity" (in Rodríguez 2014, 16). As a radical reciprocity by queer Afro-Latinx spiritual activists, brujx attempts to alleviate harm by harnessing all its resources. It is not afraid to fail, as spiritual temporality operates in different continuums. Brujx is thus a momentous bioenergetic striving—a queer embrace—a gesture of love and power.

NOTES

1   This pseudonym was selected by my interlocutor, who wanted to queer the famous Puerto Rican salsa singer Hector Lavoe, an iconic representation of Latinx masculinity and a favorite musical preference of my interlocutor. As an Afro-Latinx transman, Hector La Woke prefers the pronoun "they/them/theirs" rather than the more binary "he." I use the pluralized pronoun of "they/them/theirs" throughout the text when referring to gender-nonconforming research subjects as per their preference.

2   A number of scholars have looked at the embrace and rejection of the "X" as a nonbinary and nonwhite radical reformulation of Latino/a/x identity in the United States that also centers English language and questions of fluidity [see Milian (2017); Rodríguez (2017); Vidal-Ortiz and Martinez (2018)].

3   The queer relanguaging of brujeria into brujx also follows multiculturalist identity recuperations that challenge normative ethnic, gendered, and sexual assertions. Brujx draw on a variety of cosmologies, rituals, and media technologies to enact their spells. While some are practitioners of Afro-Cuban Santeria and Palo Monte, others are also initiated into Wicca and Haitian Vodun among other practices.

4   Rather than perpetuating violence, I use Irene Lara's notion of warrior and warfare, which is an invocation of the unification of bodies, spirits, and consciousness through healing battles as a vehicle for freedom. For her, the bruja epistemology of flying toward alternative humanities is a project of freedom-making (Lara 2002, 436).

5 Throughout this text, I understand brujx and Afro-Latinx through what E. Patrick Johnson and Ramon Rivera-Severa describe as "ethnoracial intimacies," that is, how *Blacktino* queer rituality is part of longer histories of Black and Brown intimacies. These intimacies are inclusive of a range of Black and Latinx interarticulations: "African American and Latino mixed heritage as well as Black Latinos or Afro-Latinos with Afro-diasporic ancestry outside the U.S. national boundaries . . . the historical legacy of Afro-descendant Latin American migrants to the United States as well as slightly more contemporaneous social and cultural exchanges between U.S. African American and U.S. Latina/o communities" and more.

6 Many of the brujx were millennials in their late twenties and midthirties, with two of the older women I spoke to in their fifties.

7 This is the link Hector sent me where Hector accessed Audre Lorde's speech about the uses of anger. Last accessed July 21, 2019, www.blackpast.org.

8 The three-volume series *Dawn* (1987), *Adulthood Rites* (1988), and *Imago* (1989) ultimately introduces us to the hybrid human-Oankali, who is able to unlock the unique potential of both species.

9 See the entire Combahee River Collective at Statement at Rise Up. Last accessed May 24, 2019, https://crabgrass.riseup.net.

10 An example of this troubling rhetoric comes from the feminist sociologist Suzanna Walters's *Washington Post* op-ed, "Why Can't We Hate Men?" Last accessed August 12, 2019, www.washingtonpost.com.

11 In *The Architects of Existence: Àjé in Yoruba Cosmology, Ontology, and Orature*, Teresa N. Washington describes the feminine energy of the Great Mother (*Eye Oro*) as a "force beyond definition" that can be likened to power, creation, and the combined energy of the Cosmos (2014, 19). The Cosmos is understood as the womb of the universe, a protective container, shield, and enveloping force that is mirrored in the spiritual craftings of an enclosed calabash or clay pot used in ritual initiations of Orisha practitioners. These are modeled in the symbolic roundness of the mother's belly, a shaved head, and mother earth. Washington tells us how the Spirit Bird or Àjé, which has been described of as "witches," is also the protective genitalia, the clitoris and labia majora and minora that safeguard the vaginal chamber and secure the uterus of the Great Mother (2014, 84).

12 "Citation as a Spiritual Practice" with Dana-Ain Davis. Found at the Cite Black Women podcast, Last Accessed March 31, 2019, https://soundcloud.com.

REFERENCES

Anzaldúa, Gloria. 1987. *Borderlands: La Frontera*. San Francisco: Aunt Lute.

Brown, Adrian Maree. 2017. *Emergent Strategies: Shaping Change, Changing Worlds*. Chico, CA: AK Press. Kindle Edition.

Davis, Jalondra A. "Power and Vulnerability: BlackGirlMagic in Black Women' s Science Fiction." *Journal of Science Fiction* 2, no. 2 (2018): 13–30.

Delgadillo, Theresa. 2011. *Spiritual Mestizaje: Religion, Gender, Race, and Nation in Contemporary Chicana Narrative*. Durham, NC: Duke University Press.

Johnson, E. Patrick, and Ramón H. Rivera-Servera, eds. 2016. *Blacktino Queer Performance*. Durham, NC: Duke University Press.

Kitaiskaia, Taisia. 2017. *Literary Witches: A Celebration of Magical Women Writer*. New York: Basic Books.

Lara, Irene. "Healing Sueños for Academia." In *This Bridge We Call Home*, 447–52. New York: Routledge, 2002.

———. "BRUJA POSITIONALITIES: Toward a Chicana / Latina Spiritual Activism." *Chicana/ Latina Studies* 4, no. 2 (2005): 10–45.

Lorde, Audre. "Scratching the Surface: Some Notes on Barriers to Women and Loving." *Black Scholar* 9, no. 7 (1978): 31–35.

Milian, Claudia. "Extremely Latin, XOXO: Notes on LatinX." *Cultural Dynamics* 29, no. 3 (2017): 121–40.

Pérez, Laura E. 2007. *Chicana Art: The Politics of Spiritual and Aesthetic Alterities*. Durham, NC: Duke University Press.

Rodríguez, Juana María. 2014. *Sexual Futures, Queer Gestures, and Other Latina Longings*. New York: NYU Press.

Rodríguez, Richard T. "X Marks the Spot." *Cultural Dynamics* 29, no. 3 (2017): 202–13.

Stickgold-Sarah, Jessie. "'Your Children Will Know Us, You Never Will': The Pessimistic Utopia of Octavia Butler's Xenogenesis Trilogy." *Extrapolation* 51, no. 3 (2010): 414–30.

Vidal-Ortiz, Salvador, and Juliana Martínez. "Latinx Thoughts: Latinidad with an X." *Latino Studies* 16, no. 3 (2018): 384–95.

Washington, Teresa N. 2014. *The Architects of Existence: Àjé in Yoruba Cosmology, Ontology, and Orature*. Oya's Tornado.

ABOUT THE CONTRIBUTORS

Leisy J. Abrego is Professor in the Department of Chicana/o and Central American Studies at UCLA. Her research and teaching interests are in Central American migration, Latina/o/x families, day-to-day experiences of US imperialism, and the production of "illegality" through US immigration laws. Her first book, *Sacrificing Families: Navigating Laws, Labor, and Love Across Borders* (Stanford University Press, 2014), examines the well-being of Salvadoran immigrants and their families—both in the United States and in El Salvador—as these are shaped by immigration policies and gendered expectations. Her second book, co-authored with Cecilia Menjívar and Leah Schmalzbauer, is *Immigrant Families* (Polity Press, 2016).

Frances R. Aparicio is Professor Emerita at Northwestern University, where she directed the Latina and Latino Studies Program and served as Professor in the Department of Spanish and Portuguese. She has previously taught at University of Michigan, University of Arizona, Stanford University, and University of Illinois at Chicago. Author of *Listening to Salsa: Gender, Latino Popular Music, and Puerto Rican Cultures* (Wesleyan University Press, 1998), she has published numerous articles and co-edited anthologies that examine Latinx popular music, gender, cultural studies, language, literature, and identity. Her most recent publication, entitled *Negotiating Latinidad: Intralatino/as in Chicago* (University of Illinois Press, 2019), interprets the experiences of twenty Latino/as with multiple Latin American nationalities as they negotiate their ethnic hybridities within their family and social lives.

Sara Awartani is a postdoctoral fellow in Global American Studies at Harvard University. A broadly trained social movement historian, she researches Latinx and Arab American radical politics, interracial solidarity, and US policing and empire. She has published in *Radical History Review*, *Middle East Report*, *La Respuesta*, and *Kaflou: A Journal of Comparative and Relational Ethnic Studies*.

Lloyd Barba is Assistant Professor in the Department of Religion and core faculty in Latinx and Latin American Studies at Amherst College. His teaching and research include topics such as Chicanx religious history, material culture, the Sanctuary Movement, and Latinx Pentecostalism. His book *Sowing the Sacred: Mexican Pentecostal Farmworkers in California* (under contract with

Oxford University Press) uses photographs and oral histories of midcentury Mexican Pentecostal farmworkers to render a counternarrative of their religious and cultural productions.

AISHA M. BELISO-DE JESÚS, PhD, is a cultural and social anthropologist who has conducted ethnographic research with Santería practitioners in Cuba and the United States and police officers and Black and Brown communities affected by police violence in the United States. Her research and teaching span the Caribbean, Latin America, Africa, and Afro-Latinx circulations. Dr. Beliso-De Jesús's work contributes to cultural and media studies, anthropology of religion, critical race studies, Black and Latinx transnational feminist and queer theory, African diaspora religions, and studies on police and militarization. Her first book, *Electric Santería: Racial and Sexual Assemblages of Transnational Religion* (Columbia University Press, 2015), won the 2015 Albert J. Raboteau Award for Best book in Africana Religions. It details the transnational experience of Santería in which racialized and gendered spirits, deities, priests, and religious travelers remake local, national, and political boundaries and actively reconfigure notions of technology and transnationalism. She is completing a book, *Zombie Patrol: Policing African Diaspora Religions*, which examines the criminalization and racialization of Black and Brown religions in the United States. Dr. Beliso-De Jesús is the cofounder of the Center for Transnational Policing (CTP) at Princeton University and associate editor of *Transforming Anthropology*, the flagship journal for the Association of Black Anthropologists. For over twenty years, she has worked with numerous grassroots, public policy, substance abuse, and other nonprofit organizations in the San Francisco Bay Area advocating social justice issues, teen-parent support, alternative healing approaches for Latinx communities, and empowerment strategies for youth of color.

ULLA D. BERG is Associate Professor at the Department of Latino and Caribbean Studies and the Department of Anthropology, and Director of the Center for Latin American Studies at Rutgers University. As a sociocultural and visual anthropologist specializing in Latin America and in Latino communities in the United States, Berg's research focuses on historical and contemporary processes and experiences of migration and mobility within Latin America and between this region and the United States. Her book, *Mobile Selves: Race, Migration, and Belonging in Peru and the U.S.* (translated to Spanish as *Sujetos Móviles*, IEP, Lima, 2016), examines how transnational communicative practices and forms of exchange produce new forms of kinship and sociality across multiple borders among racialized global labor migrants. Berg is also co-editor of *El Quinto Suyo: Transnacionalidad y formaciones Diaspóricas en la Migración Peruana* (IEP, 2005) and *Transnational Citizenship Across the Americas* (Routledge, 2014). Berg's current research and book manuscript, supported by the Wenner-Gren

Foundation, examines the effects of US immigrant detention and deportation on migrant communities in Ecuador and Peru.

PEDRO CABÁN is Professor of Latin American, Caribbean, and US Latino Studies at the University at Albany, SUNY, and served as the department's chairperson from 2014 to 2020. He is the founding Vice Provost for Diversity and Educational Equity, SUNY System Administration (2007–2011). He is the author of *Constructing a Colonial People: Puerto Rico and the United States, 1898–1932* (Westview Press, 1999) and has published journal articles, book chapters, and review essays and commentaries on Puerto Rico's political status, colonialism, the political economy of US–Puerto Rico relations, and the development of race and ethnic studies as academic disciplines. He has held tenured appointments at the University of Illinois–Urbana Champaign, Rutgers University, and Fordham University. A past president of the Puerto Rican Studies Association, he has also served as associate editor of the interdisciplinary journal *Latino Studies*, senior editor of the *Oxford Encyclopedia of Latinos and Latinas in the United States*, and consultant and author for *The Latino Experience in U.S. History*.

LISA MARIE CACHO is Associate Professor at the University of Virginia, Charlottesville in the Department of American Studies. Her book, *Social Death: Racialized Rightlessness and the Criminalization of the Unprotected* (NYU Press, 2012) won the John Hope Franklin award in 2013 for best book in American Studies. The book examines how illegality, criminality, and social death work interdependently to assign and deny human value and to render relations of inequality normative and natural in both dominant and oppositional discourses. She has also published in several journals and edited collections.

MARITZA CÁRDENAS is Associate Professor of English and faculty affiliate for Latin American Studies, the Program in Social Cultural, Critical Theory, and the Institute of LGBTQ studies at the University of Arizona. Her research and teaching interests focus on US Central Americans, Latinx cultural productions, marginalized identities and subjectivities, disability studies, and transnational community formations. She is the author of *Constituting Central American-Americans: Transnational Identities and the Politics of Dislocation* (Rutgers, 2018), which highlights the historical, sociopolitical processes that have facilitated the construction of a pan-ethnic transnational cultural identity (Central American) to emerge in the US diaspora. Her work has also been published in journals such as *Studies in 20th and 21st Century Literature, Journal of Commonwealth and Postcolonial Studies, Symbolism*, and *Oxford Encyclopedia of Latina/o Literature* and in the anthologies *Race and Contention in Twenty-First Century US Media* (2016) and *U.S. Central Americans: Reconstructing Memories, Struggles, and Communities of Resistance* (2017).

MARI CASTAÑEDA is Professor of Communication and Dean of the Commonwealth Honors College at the University of Massachusetts Amherst. She is also affiliated with the Center for Latin American, Caribbean, and Latina/o Studies and Women, Gender, Sexuality Studies. Her fields of study include Latinx/Chicana communication studies, academic cultures of care, digital media, and communications policy, and her engaged scholarship has appeared in various journals/monographs. She is the co-editor of *Mothers in Academia* (Columbia University Press, 2013), *Soap Operas and Telenovelas in the Digital Age: Global Industries and New Audiences* (Peter Lang, 2011), and *Civic Engagement in Diverse Latinx Communities: Learning from Social Justice Partnerships in Action* (Peter Lang, 2018).

MARÍA ELENA CEPEDA is Professor and Co-Chair of Latina/o Studies at Williams College. Her research focuses on the intersection of gender and ethno-racial identity in Latina/o/x media and popular culture. Cepeda is the author of *Musical ImagiNation: U.S.-Colombian Identity and the Latin Music Boom* (NYU Press, 2010) and co-editor of *The Routledge Companion to Latina/o Media* (Routledge, 2019). Her current projects include a co-edited special issue of *Latino Studies* on US Colombianidades and the book *Brand Colombia: Gender and Transnational Media Narratives of Global Colombianidad*. Cepeda has published in *Women's Studies Quarterly*, *Feminist Media Studies*, *Women and Performance*, and *Identities*, and her commentary has been featured by National Public Radio, the *New York Times*, and *Rolling Stone*, among other media outlets.

SUSAN COUTIN holds a PhD in anthropology from Stanford University and is Professor of Criminology, Law and Society, and Anthropology at the University of California, Irvine, where she also serves as Associate Dean for Academic Programs in the School of Social Ecology. Her research has examined legal and political advocacy by and on behalf of immigrants to the United States. She is the author of *Exiled Home: Salvadoran Transnational Youth in the Aftermath of Violence* (Duke, 2016), *Nations of Emigrants: Shifting Boundaries of Citizenship in El Salvador and the United States* (Cornell, 2007), *Legalizing Moves: Salvadoran Immigrants' Struggle for U.S. Residency* (Michigan, 2000), and *The Culture of Protest: Religious Activism within the U.S. Sanctuary Movement* (Westview Press, 1993).

REBIO DÍAZ-CARDONA is Associate Professor of Psychology at LaGuardia Community College-CUNY and affiliated faculty in the Critical Social/Personality and Environmental Psychology Doctoral Program at the CUNY-Graduate Center. Publications include "Ambient Text and the Becoming Space of Writing" (2016) in *Environment and Planning D: Society and Space* and "The Urban and the Written in Lefebvre's Urban Texts" (2019) in *The Routledge Handbook of Henri Lefebvre, the City, and Urban Society*. He is a regular contributor to the Puerto Rican publication *80Grados*.

ALICIA IVONNE ESTRADA is Professor in the Chicana/o Studies Department at California State University at Northridge. She has published on the Maya and Guatemalan diaspora in Los Angeles as well as on contemporary Maya literature, film, and radio. She is co-editor with Karina O. Alvarado and Ester E. Hernández of the critical anthology *U.S. Central Americans: Reconstructing Memories, Struggles and Communities of Resistance* (University of Arizona Press, 2017). Estrada's work has appeared in *Romance Notes*, *Latino Studies*, and *Revista Canadiense de Estudios Hispánicos*, among other journals and anthologies. Her current book project is on the Maya diaspora in Los Angeles. Since 2006, she has actively collaborated with the Maya radio collective *Contacto Ancestral*. The show has been on the airwaves for over a decade on the community radio station KPFK.

ANGELA GARCIA is Associate Professor of Anthropology at Stanford University and author of *The Pastoral Clinic: Addiction and Dispossession Along the Rio Grande* (UC Press, 2010). Garcia is an anthropologist working at the intersection of social and political theory, ethics, medicine, literature, postcolonial, and feminist thought. Her research in Mexico City examines discourses of recovery in the context of criminal and political violence. This work focuses on coercive drug rehabilitation centers that are run and utilized by the informal working poor. An outgrowth of this work is a binational research project that examines mutual aid for Latinos with addiction and mental illness.

LORENA GARCIA received her PhD in Sociology with doctoral emphasis in Women's Studies (now the Department of Feminist Studies) from the University of California at Santa Barbara. Her book *Respect Yourself, Protect Yourself: Latina Girls and Sexual Identity* (NYU Press, 2012) examines the meaning and practice of safe sex and sexuality in the lives of second-generation Mexican and Puerto Rican girls. Garcia's work has also been published in academic journals including *Gender & Society, Latino Studies, and Identities: Global Studies in Power & Culture*. She has also co-edited a special issue of the *National Women's Studies Association Journal* (NWSA) [now *Feminist Formations*] on Latina sexualities with Prof. Lourdes Torres.

LORGIA GARCIA PEÑA is the Roy Clouse Associate Professor of Latinx Studies at Harvard University and the co-founder of Freedom University. She specializes in Latinx studies and Hispanic Caribbean literary and cultural studies with a special focus on the Dominican Republic and its diaspora. Her research poses a dialogue among history, literature, and cultural studies, paying close attention to questions of marginality, migration, and racial and ethnic identity formation.

Dr. García-Peña's first book, *The Borders of Dominicanidad: Race, Nations and Archives of Contradictions* (Duke, 2016), examines the ways in which Dominican national identity has been imagined and constructed through literature and history since the nineteenth century to the present in relationship to Haiti and the United States. *The Borders of Dominicanidad* won the 2017 National Women's Studies Association Gloria E. Anzaldúa Book Prize, the 2016 LASA Latino/a Studies Book Award, and the 2016 Isis Duarte Book Prize in Haiti and Dominican Studies.

MICHELLE A. GONZÁLEZ (MICHELLE GONZÁLEZ MALDONADO) is Professor of Theology/Religious Studies and Dean of the College of Arts and Sciences at the University of Scranton. She received her PhD in Systematic and Philosophical Theology at the Graduate Theological Union in Berkeley, California in 2001. Her research and teaching interests include Latino/a, Latin American, and Feminist Theologies, as well as interdisciplinary work in Afro-Caribbean Studies. She is the author of *Sor Juana: Beauty and Justice in the Americas* (Orbis Books, 2003), *Afro-Cuban Theology: Religion, Race, Culture and Identity* (University Press of Florida, 2006), *Created in God's Image: An Introduction to Feminist Theological Anthropology* (Orbis Books, 2007), *Embracing Latina Spirituality: A Woman's Perspective* (St. Anthony Messenger Press, 2009), *Caribbean Religious History* (co-authored with Ennis Edmonds, NYU Press, 2010), *Shopping: Christian Explorations of Daily Living* (Fortress Press, 2010), and *A Critical Introduction to Religion in the Americas: Bridging the Liberation Theology and Religious Studies Divide* (NYU Press, 2014).

ESTER HERNÁNDEZ is Professor of Anthropology at Cal State LA. She is co-editor of *U.S. Central Americans: Reconstructing Struggles, Memories, and Communities of Resistance* (University of Arizona Press, 2017). Her work on Salvadoran migration and remittances appears in the *Journal of American Ethnic History* and *Economy & Society*. She was a Rockefeller Fellow (2003–2004) at Cal State LA on the theme of "Families and Belonging in the Multiethnic Metropolis." She serves on the Board of Directors of the Coalition for Humane Immigrant Rights of Los Angeles (CHIRLA). Her research interests are linked to immigrant rights, economic development, and cultures of memory among Central American and Mexican immigrants in greater Los Angeles.

JILLIAN HERNÁNDEZ is a scholar, community arts educator, curator, and creative. Her work is inspired by Black and Latinx life and imagination, and is invested in challenging how working-class bodies, sexualities, and cultural practices are policed through gendered tropes of deviancy and respectability. She studies Blackness and Latinidad as relational formations and attends to the political, cultural, and communal dynamics of aesthetic production. Hernández is Assistant Professor in the Center for Gender, Sexualities, and Women's Studies Research at the University of Florida. Her book, *Aesthetics of Excess: The Art and Politics of Black and Latina Embodiment*, is in production with Duke University Press for Fall 2020 publication. Her articles have appeared in venues such as *Signs: Journal of Women in Culture and Society*, *Women and Performance: A Journal of Feminist Theory*, and the *Journal of Popular Music Studies*, among others. She is also the founder of Women on the Rise!, an insurgent collective of women of color artists who work with Black and Latina girls in Miami, Florida.

TANYA KATERÍ HERNÁNDEZ is the Archibald R. Murray Professor of Law at Fordham University School of Law, where she co-directs its Center on Race, Law & Justice. She received her AB from Brown University and her JD from Yale Law School. Professor Hernández is a Fulbright Scholar who is a Fellow of the American Bar Foundation, the American Law Institute, and the Academia Puertorriqueña de Jurisprudencia y Legislación. Professor Hernández serves on the editorial boards of the Revista Brasileira de Direito e Justiça/Brazilian Journal of Law and Justice, and the Latino Studies Journal, along with the Advisory Board of Latinx Talk. Her books include *Racial Subordination in Latin America: The Role of the State, Customary Law and the New Civil Rights Response* (Cambridge University Press, 2013) (including Spanish and Portuguese translation editions), *Research Perspectives in Comparative Law: Racial Discrimination* (Brill, 2019), and *Multiracials and Civil Rights: Mixed-Race Stories of Discrimination* (NYU Press, 2018).

JENNIFER A. JONES is Assistant Professor of Sociology at the University of Illinois at Chicago where she specializes in race and ethnicity, immigration, political sociology, Latinx studies, Afro-Latinx studies, and Latin America and the Caribbean. Dr. Jones's recent work can be found in such journals as *Contexts*, *International Migration Review*, *Sociology of Race and Ethnicity*, *Ethnic and Racial Studies*, and *Latino Studies*. Her first book, *The Browning of the New South* (University of Chicago Press, 2019), examines a case study of shifting race relations and the experiences of Mexican immigrants who have settled in the Winston-Salem area of North Carolina to explore regional racial change.

JOSEPH KRUPCZYNSKI is Director of Civic Engagement and Service-Learning and Professor of Architecture at the University of Massachusetts Amherst. A designer, public artist, and educator, his creative work and scholarship promotes reciprocal community partnerships and creates participatory processes to explore equity and social justice within the built environment. Professor Krupczynski is a founding director of the design resource center, The Center for Design Engagement (CDE) in Holyoke, MA (www.designengagement.org). He co-edited (with Mari Castañeda) *Civic Engagement in Diverse Latinx Communities: Learning from Social Justice Partnerships in Action* (Peter Lang, 2018).

LAWRENCE LA FOUNTAIN-STOKES (AB, Harvard, 1991; PhD, Columbia, 1999) is Professor of American Culture, Romance Languages and Literatures, and Women's Studies at the University of Michigan, Ann Arbor, and the former director of the Latina/o Studies Program. He has published *Queer Ricans: Cultures and Sexualities in the Diaspora* (University of Minnesota Press, 2009), *Uñas pintadas de azul/Blue Fingernails* (Bilingual Review Press, 2009), *Abolición del pato* (Terranova Editores, 2013), *A Brief and Transformative Account of Queer History* (Dave Buchen, 2016), *Keywords for Latina/o Studies* (NYU Press, 2017), and *Escenas transcaribeñas: ensayos sobre teatro, performance y cultura* (Editorial Isla Negra, 2018). His book *Translocas: The Politics of Puerto Rican Drag and Trans Performance* will be published by the University of Michigan Press in 2021.

ALBERT SERGIO LAGUNA is Associate Professor of Ethnicity, Race & Migration and American Studies at Yale University. His research and teaching interests include transnational Latinx literatures and cultures, comparative ethnic studies, performance studies, and popular culture studies. His work has appeared or is forthcoming in *Latino Studies*, the *Journal of Latin American Cultural Studies*, *Latin American Research Review*, *Contemporary Literature*, *Cultural Critique*, *Diario de Cuba*, the *Miami Herald*, the *Washington Post*, and on CNN.com. Laguna's first book, *Diversión: Play and Popular Culture in Cuban America* (NYU Press, 2017), won the 2018 Robert K. Martin Prize for Best Book from the Canadian American Studies Association, the 2018 Peter C. Rollins Book Prize from the Northeast Popular/American Culture Association, and received "Honorable Mention" from the Latina/o Studies Section of the Latin American Studies Association in 2019.

JOHANA LONDOÑO is Assistant Professor in the Department of Latin American, Caribbean, and US Latina/o Studies at the University at Albany, State University of New York (SUNY). Her published work appears in several edited volumes, such as *Latino Urbanism* (NYU Press, 2012), and journals including *American Quarterly* and *Social Semiotics*. Her research has benefitted from fellowships at the Ford Foundation, the Princeton-Mellon Initiative in Architecture, Urbanism, and the Humanities, the Smithsonian Latino Museum Studies Program, NYU, and the Northeast Consortium for Faculty Diversity at Northeastern University. Londoño's book, *Abstract Barrios: The Crises of Latinx Visibility in Cities*, is forthcoming from Duke University Press.

PAUL JOSEPH LÓPEZ ORO is Assistant Professor of Africana Studies at Smith College. He's working on his first book manuscript, *Hemispheric Black Indigeneity: The Queer Politics of Self-Making Garifuna New York*, an ethnographic and archival study on how gender and sexuality inform the ways in which Garifuna New Yorkers of Central American descent negotiate, perform, and articulate their multiple subjectivities as Black, Indigenous, and Latinx. His work has been published by *Small Axe* salon, Oxford University's Press *Dictionary of Caribbean and Afro Latin American Biography*, Palgrave Macmillan's *Afro-Latin@s in Movement*, and the University of Arizona Press's *Indigenous Interfaces: Spaces, Technology, and Social Networks in Mexico and Central America*.

ELENA MACHADO SÁEZ is Professor of English at Bucknell University. Her recent publications include "Debt of Gratitude: Lin-Manuel Miranda and the Politics of US Latinx Twitter" in *sx archipegalos*, "Generation MFA: Neoliberalism and the Shifting Cultural Capital of U.S. Latinx Writers" in *Latino Studies*, and "Bodega Sold Dreams: Middle-Class Panic and the Crossover Aesthetics of *In the Heights*" in *Dialectical Imaginaries: Materialist Approaches to U.S. Latino/a Literature in the Age of Neoliberalism* (University of Michigan Press, 2018). Machado Sáez is also author of *Market Aesthetics: The Purchase of the Past in Caribbean Diasporic Fiction* (University of Virginia Press, 2015) and co-author of *The Latino/a Canon and the Emergence of Post-Sixties Literature* (Palgrave Macmillan, 2007).

CECILIA MENJÍVAR holds the Dorothy L. Meier Endowed Chair in Social Equities and is Professor of Sociology at UCLA. Her research focuses on understanding the multiple effects of the legal context on the lives of Central American immigrants in the United States, and on examining multisited violence, particularly gender violence in the lives of women in Central America. Her publications include *Fragmented Ties: Salvadoran Immigrant Networks in America* (University of California Press, 2000), *Enduring Violence: Ladina Women's Everyday Lives in Guatemala* (University of California Press, 2011), *Eterna Violencia: Vidas de mujeres ladinas en Guatemala* (FLACSO 2014—adapted from *Enduring Violence*), and *Immigrant Families*, co-authored with Leisy Abrego and Leah Schmalzbauer (Polity, 2016). She is the recipient of a John S. Guggenheim Fellowship and an Andrew Carnegie Fellowship, and she is past Vice President of the American Sociological Association.

BAHIA M. MUNEM received her PhD in Women's and Gender Studies from Rutgers University and is currently a Postdoctoral Fellow in the Department of Women, Gender, and Sexualities Studies at Washington University in Saint Louis. Her scholarship brings together the fields of Latinx & Latin American and Middle East Studies by examining, through ethnography, forced transnational migration, ME diasporas, and gendered and racialized modes of belonging in Brazil and the Americas.

SUZANNE OBOLER is Professor of Latin American and Latinx Studies at John Jay College of the City University of New York. Her research and teaching interests center on Human Rights in the Americas, focusing on race, immigration, citizenship, and national belonging. She is the author of *Ethnic Labels, Latino Lives: Identity and the Politics of (Re)Presentation in the United States* (University of Minnesota Press, 1995), as well as various articles and book chapters. She edited *Latinos and Citizenship: The Dilemma of Belonging* (Palgrave Macmillan, 2006), and *Behind Bars: Latino/as and Prison in the United States* (Palgrave Macmillan, 2009) and co-edited (with Anani Dzidzienyo), *Neither Enemies nor Friends: Latinos, Blacks, Afro-Latinos* (Palgrave Macmillan, 2005). She has also co-edited two encyclopedias on Latinxs in the US, most recently, *The Oxford Encyclopedia of Latinos and Latinas in Contemporary Politics, Law and Social Movements* (Oxford University Press, 2015). She is the founding editor of the journal *Latino Studies* (2002–2012). In 2011, she was named Fulbright Distinguished Chair in American Studies at PUC, in Rio de Janeiro, Brazil.

GINA PÉREZ is a cultural anthropologist in the Comparative American Studies Program at Oberlin College. She is the author of two award-winning books—*The Near Northwest Side Story: Gender, Migration and Puerto Rican Families* (2004, University of California Press) and *Citizen, Student, Soldier: Latina/o Youth, JROTC and the American Dream* (2015, New York University Press). She is also the coeditor of two anthologies: *Beyond el Barrio: Everyday Life in Latina/o America* (coedited with Frank Guridy and Adrian Burgos Jr., 2011, New York University Press) and *Ethnographic Refusals, Unruly Latinidades* (coedited with Alex Chávez, forthcoming, University of New Mexico Press). Her research interests include Latinas/os, youth, militarism, gender, migration, urban ethnography, and faith-based organizing. Her new project focuses on sanctuary movements and multiethnic faith-based organizing among Latina/o communities in Ohio.

SEBASTIÁN PÉREZ is Assistant Professor of English at Fairfield. He completed his dissertation entitled "Beyond Borinquen: Images and their Afterlives in the Puerto Rican Diaspora, 1970–Present" and received his PhD in American Studies from Yale University. His work archives and critically analyzes the material cultures of urban crisis and gentrification in Latinx diasporic communities, focusing on the photographic and image-making practices of Puerto Rican and Latinx communities in the South Bronx. In linking the processes of urban renewal and urban crisis in 1970s postindustrial New York City to the present-day contestations over urban space under gentrification, he centers the photograph as a site that makes visible the daily lives of Latinx diasporic subjects beyond and in addition to narratives of resistance.

LAURA PULIDO is the Collins Professor of Indigenous, Race, and Ethnic Studies and Geography at the University of Oregon where she studies critical ethnic studies, environmental justice, and human geography. She is the author of numerous books, including *Environmentalism and Economic Justice: Two Chicano Struggles in the Southwest* (University of Arizona, 1996), *Black, Brown, Yellow and Left: Radical Activism in Los Angeles* (University of California, 2006), and *A People's Guide to Los Angeles* (with Laura Barraclough and Wendy Cheng, University of California, 2012), a radical tour guide that explores power in urban landscapes. Together with Barraclough and Cheng, she edits a book series based on *A People's Guide.* Currently, she is working on an historical atlas of US white supremacy supported by a National Science Foundation grant. Pulido has received a variety of honors including a J.S. Guggenheim Fellowship, the Presidential Achievement Award from the Association of American Geographers, and the Carey McWilliams Award from the California Studies Association.

ANA Y. RAMOS-ZAYAS is Professor of American Studies, Ethnicity, Race & Migration, and Women's, Gender, and Sexuality Studies at Yale University. She is the author of *National Performances: Class, Race, and Space in Puerto Rican Chicago* (The University of Chicago Press, 2003; ASA Latino Studies Book Award, 2006), *Street Therapists: Affect, Race, and Neoliberal Personhood in Latino Newark* (The University of Chicago Press, 2012; Frank Bonilla Book Award 2010–12). She is also co-author of *Latino Crossings: Mexicans, Puerto Ricans, and the Politics of Race and Citizenship* (Routledge, 2003) and the author of *Sovereign Parenting: Class, Whiteness, and the Moral Economy of Privilege in Brazil and Puerto Rico* (under contract with Duke University Press). Ramos-Zayas's ethnographic work aims to understand and disentangle systems of power and privilege at a variety of scales, ranging from US imperial and white supremacist politics to how individuals and communities make sense of everyday forms of power and subordination in the Americas.

VANESSA ROSA is the Class of 1929 Virginia Apgar Assistant Professor of Latina/o/x Studies at Mount Holyoke College. Her research explores dynamic and deceptive relationships between state-level diversity management efforts, on the one hand, and community organizing in the context of structural inequality, on the other. Rosa has published about race and public housing in North America in the *Journal of Critical Race Inquiry*, *Meridians*, and the *Canadian Journal of Urban Research*. Rosa serves on the national steering committee for the Consortium for Faculty Diversity.

NELLY ROSARIO is the author of *Song of the Water Saints: A Novel* (Vintage, 2003). Her fiction and creative nonfiction have appeared in many journals and anthologies, including *Callaloo*, *Review*, and *Teaching Black: Pedagogy, Practice, and Perspectives on Writing*, forthcoming by University of Pittsburgh Press. She is the recipient of a Sherwood Anderson Award in Fiction and a Creative Capital

Artist Award in Literature for desveladas, a collaborative graphic-novel project about the Americas. Rosario holds an SB from MIT, an MFA from Columbia University, and is Associate Professor in the Latina/o Studies Program at Williams College.

MÉRIDA M. RÚA holds a PhD in American Culture from the University of Michigan and is a faculty member in the Latinx Studies Program at Northwestern University. She is editor of *Latino Urban Ethnography and the Work of Elena Padilla* (University of Illinois Press, 2011) and author of *A Grounded Identidad: Making New Lives in Chicago's Puerto Rican Neighborhoods* (Oxford University Press, 2012). Her current research examines issues and themes at the intersection of aging and urban life, with an emphasis on older adult Latinas and Latinos in Chicago.

ELENA SABOGAL is Associate Professor of Community and Social Justice Studies and Latin American and Latino Studies at William Paterson University in Wayne, New Jersey. She is the author of articles about Peruvian and Latin American migration to South Florida, co-author of *Making a Life in Multiethnic Miami: Immigration and the Rise of a Global City* (Lynne Rienner Publishers, 2014), and is currently working on her latest research about Peruvian immigrant women in New Jersey.

ODILKA S. SANTIAGO is Assistant Professor at the University of San Diego. Her research interests include urban sociology; critical criminology; surveillance studies; housing justice; ethnography; Caribbean, Black, and (Afro)Latinx studies; and world historical sociology. She co-published the "Central Park Five Syllabus: Towards Understanding the Historical and Contemporary Criminalization of Working-Class Youth of Color" in *Abolition Journal*.

SUJEY VEGA is Associate Professor of Women and Gender Studies and Interim Lead Faculty of American Studies at Arizona State University. Using ethnography, oral history, and archival analysis, her research includes race/ethnic studies, social networks, gendered experiences, and ethno-religious practices. Her book, *Latino Heartland: Of Borders and Belonging in the Midwest* (NYU Press, 2015), places in dialogue Mexican Hoosiers and non-Mexican (mostly White) Hoosiers of Indiana as they come to terms with living in the same communal space during a highly politicized moment. Vega's current project historically locates the growth of Latino Mormons, gendered social networks, and Latino millennials in the Church of Jesus Christ of Latter Day Saints.

SALVADOR VIDAL-ORTIZ's scholarship cuts across racialization, sexuality, gender, migration, and religion, and it is interdisciplinary. He co-edited two award-winning books, *The Sexuality of Migration* (NYU Press, 2009) and *Queer Brown Voices* (University of Texas Press, 2015); co-authored a book with two former students, Brandon Andrew Robinson and Cristina Khan, titled *Race and Sexuality* (Polity, 2018); and is completing a book manuscript about race, gender, and sexuality in Santería (an Afro-Cuban religion). An engaged American Sociological Association (ASA) member, he has served as convener (and first non-elected chair) of a section called Sociology of the Body and Embodiment, is past Chair of the Sexualities Section, and editorial board member for Sociology of Race and Ethnicity. He is also a tri-chair for ASA's Sexualities Section Pre-conference for 2018, titled Sexualities, Race, and Empire: Resistance in an Uncertain Time.

ANAHÍ VILADRICH, a native of Argentina, is an interdisciplinary social science scholar and public health specialist whose work focuses on international migration, Latinos in the United States, health disparities, gender, and culture. The author and co-author of more than sixty peer-reviewed publications, her book *More than Two to Tango: Argentine Tango Immigrants in New York City* (University of Arizona Press, 2013) received an Honorable Mention for the 2012–2014 ALLA Book Prize of the American Anthropological Association. Viladrich's research and teaching in the US, Spain, Argentina, and Cuba has resulted in several recent articles in journals such as *Latino Studies* (2020) *Ethnic and Racial Studies* (2019), *Latin American Research Review* (2019), *Qualitative Health Review* (2019), and *European Societies* (2019) among others. Viladrich is currently Full Professor in the Department of Sociology (with a courtesy appointment in Anthropology) at Queens College. She is also affiliated with the Graduate Center (Sociology) and the Graduate School of Public Health and Health Policy of the City University of New York (CUNY).

INDEX

1.5 generation, 37n1, 129, 387, 390

Abrego, Leisy, 171, 539; Central American family separations, 173–181; on axis of stratification, 71
abuse: in homeless shelters, 381; of children by Custom and Border Protection, 179
academia: activism in, 504–505; collective learning in, 512–513; engaging communities in, 492–493; institutionalization of Latinx studies in, 493; social justice and knowledge production in, 500; social movements and, 491, 493; spiritual healing in, 534–535. *See also* Latinx community-academic praxis; scholar-activists
accompaniment: Latinx studies as, 506–611; sanctuary movements and, 30, 35
acequia madre, 412
acompañamiento. See accompaniment
activism: Afro- Latinx spiritual, 529; immigrant rights movement, 33–35; in academia, 505; Latinx studies and, 492, 5,11; social media; 528; teaching and, 506–511; visual arts, 292–293. *See also* Afro-Latinx spiritual activisms; "Performing Latinidad" class
Acuña, Rodolfo, 76
Adult Family Intake Center, 377
African Americans, 96; Afro-Mexicans and linked fate with, 433–434; citizenship and labor of, 75; political coalitions with Latinx populations and, 431; Puerto Rican affinity with, 521–522; real blackness and, 368; reconstruction of New Orleans post Katrina and, 74
Afro-Cubans: definition, 99; religion and, 99–101; Latino anti-black discrimination of, 363; white Cubans and, 368
Afro-descendants: Afro-Latino and, 230; denial of, 435n3; Cuaji and, 436n5; Garifuna, 230; Latin American denial of, 426; Latin American migrants, 537n5; mestizaje and, 426, 436n6; Mexican census and, 430–432
Afro-Latinidad, 223–236; African American health and, 36; Afro-Latinx Studies and, 225- 227; all-encompassing term, 230; as

a contestation of ethnoracial nationalism, 228–229; as a political project, 227–229, 429; census data and 367–369; in the US, 364–365, 367–369; Latin American racism and, 363–364; Latinidad and, 228–229, 427; "triple consciousness" and, 428. *See also* Garifuna
Afro-Latinx spiritual activisms: alternative forms of justice in, 534–536; black girl magic and, 532; disposability politics and, 533; queer gestures in, 536; queer of color feminist scholarship and, 529–530; spiritual activists, 530. *See also* brujx
Afro-Mexicans: in North Carolina, 432; linked fate with African Americans, 433–435; migration and shifting perceptions of blackness for, 430; racialization as black in the US., 431
Afro-pessimism, 54
Afro-Puertorriqueñidad, 482
afterlife of slavery: migration and, 387, 395–396; US disciplining institutions and, 387–388, 393
"Aguanile," 477, 486n3; affective reconciliation and, 483, 485; Afro-Puerto Ricanness and, 482; belonging and, 478–479; collective mourning, 479, 483; critical listening and, 477, 481- 482; mourning as resistance, 480; power of music and, 482–483; Puertorriqueñidad and, 485; the *nieta* and, 478–479, 482–483
Aguilar, Laura, 301
Ahmed, Sara, 193
Àjé (bird witch), 534, 537n11
Albrecht, Maryanne, 204
Alcalde, M. Cristina, 348
Altamirano, Teofilo, 345
Alvarado, Leticia, 443
Alvarez Guedes, Guillermo, 267–276; centering of Spanish language in linguistic power relation in Miami and, 274–276; *choteo* (humor) and, 269–270, 273–275, 276n6; *momentos de diversión* and, 268; narrative of Cuban exile and, 268; naturalness and, 269; whiteness and anti-blackness and, 270–273